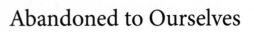

Abandoned to Ourselves

Abandoned to Ourselves,

being an essay on the *emergence* and
implications of SOCIOLOGY in
the writings of

MR. JEAN-JACQUES ROUSSEAU,

with *special attention* to his claims about
the moral significance of *dependence* in the
composition and self-transformation
of the *social bond,* & aimed to uncover the
tension between those two perspectives—

CREATIONISM &
SOCIAL EVOLUTION—

that remains embedded in our
common sense & which still impedes
the *human science* of *politics.* . . .

PETER ALEXANDER MEYERS

Yale
UNIVERSITY PRESS

New Haven and London

Published with assistance from the Annie Burr Lewis Fund.

Yale University Press books may be purchased in quantity for educational,
business, or promotional use. For information, please e-mail sales.press@yale.edu
(U.S. office) or sales@yaleup.co.uk (U.K. office).

Set in Electra and Trajan types by Tseng Information Systems, Inc.
Printed in the United States of America.

Library of Congress Cataloging-in-Publication Data
Meyers, Peter Alexander.
Abandoned to ourselves : being an essay on the emergence and implications of sociology
in the writings of Mr. Jean-Jacques Rousseau, with special attention to his claims about the
moral significance of dependence in the composition and self-transformation of the social
bond, & aimed to uncover the tension between those two perspectives — creationism
& social evolution — that remains embedded in our common sense & which still
impedes the human science of politics. . . . / Peter Alexander Meyers.
p. cm.
Includes bibliographical references and index.
ISBN 978-0-300-17205-8 (cloth : alk. paper)
1. Rousseau, Jean-Jacques, 1712–1778 — Political and social views.
2. Political sociology. I. Title.
JC179.R9M49 2012
306.2 — dc23
2011048887

A catalogue record for this book is available from the British Library.

This paper meets the requirements of ANSI/NISO Z39.48–1992 (Permanence of Paper).

10 9 8 7 6 5 4 3 2 1

Abandoned to Ourselves

*Nous disions qu'il n'est nullement probable, que le Créateur bon & sage, ait aban-
donné l'homme à lui-même, sans guide & sans direction pour sa conduite. . . .
Que seroit l'homme & la Société, si chacun étoit tellement le maître de ses actions, qu'il pût tout faire à son gré & n'avoir d'autre principe de conduite que son
caprice ou ses passions? Supposez que Dieu abandonnant l'homme à lui-même,
ne lui eut effectivement prescrit aucune Régle de vie, & ne l'eut assujetti à aucune
Loi.*

> *Principes du droit naturel* (1747, 163 & 158)
> Jean-Jacques Burlamaqui

*La plus utile et la moins avancée de toutes les connoissances humaines me paroît
être celle de l'homme, et j'ose dire que la seule inscription du Temple de Delphes
contenoit un Précepte plus important et plus difficile que tous les gros Livres des
Moralistes. . . . l'étude serieuse de l'homme, de ses facultés naturelles, et de leurs dé-
veloppemens successifs, ... les recherches Politiques et morales . . . consid[èrent]
ce que nous serions devenus, abandonnés à nous-mêmes.*

> *Discours sur l'origine et les fondemens de l'inégalité
> parmi les hommes* (1755, OC III.122, 127)
> Jean-Jacques Rousseau

*Hommes, soyez humains, c'est vôtre prémier devoir: soyez-le pour tous les états,
pour tous les âges, pour tout ce qui n'est pas étranger à l'homme. Quelle sagesse y
a-t-il pour vous hors de l'humanité?*

> *Émile* (1762, OC IV, 302)
> Jean-Jacques Rousseau

We would say that it is hardly probable that the Creator, good and wise, had abandoned Man to himself, without guide and without direction for his conduct . . . What would Man and society be, if everyone was so much the master of his actions that he could do everything according to his own designs and have no other principle of conduct than his caprice and his passions? Suppose that God, abandoning mankind to ourselves, had effectively prescribed no rule of life for us, and had subjected us to no law.

Principes du droit naturel (1747, 163 & 158)
Jean-Jacques Burlamaqui

The most useful and least advanced area of all human knowledge seems to me to be Man himself, and I dare say that the lone inscription at the Temple of Delphi contained a precept more important and more difficult than all the fat books of the Moralists. . . . The serious study of Man, of his natural faculties and their successive developments, ... research into political and moral life. . . . considers what we would have become, abandoned to ourselves.

Discours sur l'origine et les fondemens de l'inégalité parmi les hommes (1755, OC III.122, 127)
Jean-Jacques Rousseau

Men, be human, that is your primary duty: be human for every circumstance, for every age, for everything that is not foreign to mankind. What wisdom is there for you besides humanity?

Émile (1762, OC IV, 302)
Jean-Jacques Rousseau

GENERAL CONTENTS

Detailed Contents

ACKNOWLEDGMENTS

This book stands at the intersection of a number of larger projects and summarizes some lines of my inquiry into political theory. It seems fitting, therefore, to dedicate it to my best and continuing teacher and lifelong friend Kurt P. Tauber.

Over the long period of its gestation, many people have privileged me with their reflections on the ideas set forth here. I would like to thank especially Benjamin R. Barber, Rüdiger Bittner, Déborah Blocker, Peter Breiner, Éric Brian, Claudia Brodsky, Craig Calhoun, Michelle Chilcoat, Giovanna C. Cifoletti, Andrew Feffer, David Gauthier, Harvey S. Goldman, Anthony T. Grafton, John Gunnell, Marie-Hélène Huet, Jonathan Israel, George Kateb, Nannerl O. Keohane, Pierre Manent, Bernard Manin, Patchen Markell, Jim Miller, Bruce Miroff, Amélie O. Rorty, Alan Ryan, Morton Schoolman, Will Selinger, Nancy S. Struever, Laurent Thévenot, Mino Vianello, Maurizio Viroli, and Linda Zerilli. In addition, I have benefitted immeasurably from the support of the Institut du Monde Anglophone of the Université Sorbonne Nouvelle—Paris III, the French Ministère de l'Éducation nationale, the Centre National de la Recherche Scientifique, the Centre de Théorie du Droit, the École des Hautes Études en Sciences Sociales, the School of Historical Studies of the Institute for Advanced Studies in Princeton, the Department of Philosophy, the Department of History, the Department of Sociology, and the Department of French and Italian of Princeton University. Many ideas herein originally came to me around 1986, as I was making my initial attempts to write out a general theory of political power. However, it was the pressure of rich collegial dialogue and disagreement that subsequently led to their development, first around the Groupe de Sociologie Politique et Morale with Luc Boltanski and Laurent Thévenot, where I propounded these ideas several times to Bruno Latour, and then in sustained conversations, both real and imagined, with Mino Vianello and Craig Calhoun. I owe, too, a debt to many students; as we confronted Rousseau's texts together, they pushed me toward a clearer understanding of what remains vivid and useful in his writings. Again here, my every word, an act, is refracted by that miraculous lens, Effie Rentzou, and the uncanny patient delight of my son Alexi.

NOTE ON SOURCES AND USES OF WORDS

The vast majority of references in this book point to the definitive critical edition published in the *Bibliothèque de la Pléiade*:

Jean-Jacques Rousseau: Œuvres complètes (Paris: Éditions Gallimard, 1959–95)

All citations to this edition follow this formula—OC x.y—where "x" is the volume and "y" is the page. References to Rousseau's correspondence are cited by date of the letter and may be found in chronological order in the

Correspondance complète de Jean-Jacques Rousseau, édition critique, établie et annotée par R. A. Leigh (Geneva: Institut et Musée Voltaire, 1965–91)

All translations are my own. As my aim is to bring Rousseau's symbolic universe to light, and not to find an Anglophone equivalent, I have largely opted for literal flat-footedness in rendering his sentences in English. Please keep in mind that where it is Rousseau who speaks I use almost exclusively the eighteenth-century French orthography as reproduced in the *Pléiade*. Orthography is occasionally updated for single words or short phrases that would, in their original form, make the sentence into which they are inserted less clear.

Only partly due to this program of literalness does the phrase *contract social* appear persistently throughout the book. That is, I do not reduce it to *contrat social* because it is precisely in Rousseau's time that the orthography is shifting. Additional research—so extensive that I have decided not to include it in this book and which I will publish separately—has shown that this orthographic shift is companioned by a change in the weighting between different significations of the term "contract." Thus, when I write *contract social* I do not mean *contrat social*, largely because that is not what Rousseau himself meant.

In addition, it is a peculiarity of this type of study to disturb utterly the sense of many familiar terms and to introduce some new ones. Thus, while many commonplaces are qualified and detoured away from a typical reader's expectations, and this is done in an orderly fashion throughout the book, the new expectations imposed by each stage of this process cannot be made explicit at every subsequent iteration of the term, phrase, or concept. For example, when later in the book I make free and shorthand use of the phrase "state of nature" the reader will only grasp what is meant by letting the earlier qualifications sink in. This same need to collect results as the argument moves forward has also led me to introduce an unusual but functional schematic system of superscripts beginning in §49.

FOREWORD

Despite the many parts and diverse detours of the argument presented in this book, at least one of its lessons may be stated summarily at the outset. It concerns both a major figure in the history of political theory and his reader in the early twenty-first century, which is to say you.

Rousseau proposes a "theodicy," a view of how we human beings relate to God and thus relate to ourselves. The surprising effect of this theodicy is to bring to light a purely social space in which mankind is discovered as "abandoned to ourselves." Sociology emerges from the working out of that fact; political theory is transformed by it.

Although Rousseau is not the first to view mankind as a whole, or as a single object for theoretical inquiry, his way of seeing *société* as a richly articulated totality is both unprecedented and profoundly influential.

As Rousseau undertakes a detailed analysis of this social space, the figure of the Citizen is his guiding criterion. Thus, his "sociology" — the word had not yet been invented — both retains certain classical features of political theory and its relevance to politics is assured. The modern image of *society* and the ancient figure of the *citizen* come together precisely because the motive to analyze in detail the composition of social space is part and parcel of a concern with the specific and situated sort of action of which only the Citizen can be the agent. To this extent, there is nothing inherently irreligious about Rousseau's social theodicy. His could easily have been the views of a strong Providentialist.

Rousseau identifies *dépendance* as the primary fabric of social space. Dependence is a moral substance that arises not from the human relationship with God but from the complex and everyday fact that human beings must live together over long periods of time. He asserts a fundamental distinction between two sorts of dependence: one involves our relations with things, the other involves our relations with persons.

As Rousseau's inquiry deepens in this way, it courses through facts and reasonings central to the many heated discussions of the eighteenth century. On crucial points, he increasingly sides with and advances a view that today can only be called "evolutionary" (that term, common in English in his time, had not yet entered the French language). In other words Rousseau's strongest intuitions and analyses reveal in humankind and in our world a mutability, the phases of which are not pre-ordained by Creation or a Creator's design, and the development of which has no external motor. Moreover, at the level of the individual, at the level of society, and at the level of the species, the principle of motion driving this "evolution" is neither Nature nor Man.[1] It is rather an incessant dialectic of these two, in which habit becomes a "second nature" even as Nature emerges as "first custom."[2]

Rousseau recognizes that for certain crucial purposes of human understanding Man and Nature must be distinguished. He is a—perhaps *the*—modern master of this distinction. But he also knows full well that in fact Man and Nature are inseparable. What is the issue of the paradox? Only after another century of refinements in the modern antithesis between "the human" and "the natural" will the discursive conditions emerge within which the synthetic principle of evolution can don its definitive Darwinian garb. What we can see in retrospect is that Rousseau and some of his contemporaries were feeling their way in this direction.[3]

Do not be distracted by mention of Darwin. Like Rousseau himself, we are concerned here primarily with how the evolutionary dialectic of Man and Nature operates on society and social human beings, and not with its application to the organic transformation of the species, even if these two "levels" are ultimately interrelated.[4] Likewise, it is important to remember that in applying a preliminary version of this principle to *human nature*, and even in considering as absolutely fundamental the "concern with one's own preservation,"[5] Rousseau is utterly unlike the so-called "social Darwinists" of the next century who, with an unembarrassed brutality, will simply reduce human beings to animals of prey.[6]

It would be absurd to think of Rousseau as merely precursor to evolutionary thinking. I will argue no more, and no less, than that these emerging evolutionary perspectives turned out to have been of enormous significance for his ideas and for the subsequent use and development of them up to the present day.

Rousseau complements his social theodicy by working out several accounts of the relation between Man and Nature. As just mentioned, one approach identifies this relation as the dialectical evolution of society. Another approach derives it from the premise of the distinction between types of dependence. There are two sorts of dependence because persons and things are fundamentally different. Thus, we experience the relation between Man and Nature through the contradictions between two sorts of dependence. In the description of these contradictions—especially in answer to the basic question Why are persons and things fundamentally different?—a series of theistic commitments intervene in Rousseau's thinking.

It is a commonplace of, although not original to, the Christian eighteenth century to see Man in the light of God, and to personify God with human characteristics like "Will." Again, the social focus of Rousseau's theodicy does not require him to exclude theistic belief (although his political theory eventually tends that way). Thus, as he thinks through the consequences of mankind "abandoned to ourselves" he is confident in drawing major conceptual resources from many discourses that explicitly or implicitly convey theological interests. Whatever the biographical reasons for this turn, its consequences for Rousseau's social theory of politics are what will matter here. Particularly important is the way in which "Will" becomes one of his pivotal categories. By means of "Will" persons are distinguished from things.

"Will" orients Rousseau's thinking in ways that go far deeper than his famous appeal to a "general Will." Once consideration of the relation between Man and Nature—that is, the dialectical process of "evolution"—has been overlaid with the vocabulary of "Will" many related terms and patterns of reasoning seize hold of Rousseau's thought. The result is again contradictory. Why? Because this vocabulary, with its specific but often subterranean theistic prejudices, cannot easily accommodate a notion of "evolution" that is at least deistic and, on the key points concerning society and politics, entirely humanized.[7]

It seems that the contradiction itself is not apparent to Rousseau. Why? Perhaps because neither "evolution" nor the consequences of a commitment to that way of seeing the world have yet to be worked out. But—I think for just that reason—this contradiction nonetheless facilitates Rousseau's extraordinary creativity as a political theorist.

There would be no point in pretending that if Rousseau had been an atheist he would have made precisely the discoveries that Darwin made. It is, however, important in a more general way to see that Darwin's thought does not simply belong to Darwin. It is part of the development of a *mentalité* that had begun and was already taking new forms long before *The Origin of Species* was published in 1859. We remain deeply invested in some version of this view of life. As readers of Rousseau and as his inheritors, we would do well to make that investment more explicit and precise.

Although Rousseau relies on insights from deist naturalism, transposing them to his special topics of society and politics, he will not follow his more radical contemporaries in drawing atheistic conclusions.[8] This is the kernel of truth in Gustave Lanson's famous assertion that, despite all who attacked him, it was Rousseau who returned religion to an atheistic century.

Crudely put, even if deism is compatible with Rousseau's evolutionary outlook, his theism is not. The difficulty here is not just the one experienced by many thinkers in and after the eighteenth century: that he both clings to Christian beliefs and fails to find a balance between them and an evolutionary point of view. It is that specific and primary symbolic and logical forms of Christian theology permeate key areas of Rousseau's social inquiry. The result is that his arguments sometimes have to overreach to contain two largely incompatible views of the place of mankind in the world and in relation to ourselves.

Not surprisingly, the pivotal notion on the theistic side of this tension is Creation. The basic figuration given by Rousseau follows these familiar twists: God, the Creator, has the anthropomorphic attribute of Will, but, being God, has it more than any human being could, and thus God becomes the measure and paradigm for human Will, which, by a kind of mirroring, is magnified into a still-human but God-like creative capacity, writ small and ordinarily incomplete, but nonetheless miraculous. What matters is not just *that* God created Man and the world. Equally important are the answers to two additional questions: *How*, with what faculty and means, could God do that? and What does this tell us about our own capacities, about the means available to human beings who create and must correct our own edifice, society?

Because Rousseau is committed to a theism in which "creation" is an essential explanatory *topos*, he responds to both the divine question and the human one in terms of the Will. As a result, he cannot pursue beyond a certain point the larger implications of his evolutionary view of society (which I think would lead to an unexpected kind of ecological holism, but that is an issue beyond the scope of this book).

Between these two commitments, one emphatically theological and the other ellusively scientific, a defining tension arises in the way he puts his thoughts on page after page. In some ways it is extremely productive. On balance it leads his readers into a dead end.

The flaw in Rousseau's view—a flaw which still infects our contemporary beliefs about society and politics—derives from the fact that these two questions are answered in the same terms. Happiness, order, peace, and other human aspirations all come down to a peculiarly modern and untenable image of the Will. It would not be an exaggeration to call this flaw tragic because it occludes resources Rousseau himself provided for thinking another way, for an alternative approach to the basic beliefs which form our actions, and which could be fruitful even today were we not so paradoxically bound up with thinking like the theistic Rousseau, rather than like the scientific Rousseau who despite the omnipresence of a deity nevertheless sees the human world as evolving according to a logic of its own.

It is instructive to describe this fundamental tension in Rousseau's social theory of politics in a blatantly anachronistic way. He puts on display the conflict between a "creationism," guided by "intelligent design," and "evolution." Indeed, in some respects what is at stake in the contemporary and peculiarly American version of this debate may be clearer in Rousseau's context than in ours. For, reading Rousseau today brings to light several obvious points that typically escape our public discussion.

Foremost among these is this: any doctrine with the name "creationism" cannot be entirely theological. It must also present an anthropology, which is to say a theory of who and what human beings are, and the means we have for relating to one another. As oxymoronic as this may seem to today's readers, the fact is that there can be both sacred and secular, religious and irreligious, "creationists." And although we tend to ignore this secular side of "creationism," it is far more developed, pervasive, and consequential than its theological counterpart. It sustains a cultural imaginary in which the image of the "Will" has an almost unescapable gravitational pull.

This book is about how such tensions in Rousseau's way of writing his thoughts open unprecedented spaces and directions for social and political theory. It also aims to show how efforts to understand God and Man with the same terms and symbols can lead us profoundly and dangerously astray. In ways that I will not try to demonstrate in this book, I suspect that *secular* "creationists" facilitate and abet *religious* "creationists," even when they clearly and viscerally detest one another.

Some kind of evolutionary view—one that may have been hinted at in early American Pragmatism, but which has not yet been adequately developed—is the only alternative consistent with the essential fact that human beings need to form political relationships, and that this need is constantly changing over time in ways that are results of our actions but not subject to our control. Rousseau's contributions to such a project of understanding are many, but none so great as to have exposed clearly that the difference between our relations with persons and things is at the heart of our experience of society. His second contribution, once having staged the evolutionary story of mankind "abandoned to ourselves" in terms of dependence, is to have gotten it so wrong. The tensions and contradictions between persons and things, the inexorable motive power in the primary fact of human dependence, are always key generators of change in social, and thus in political, relationships. A social theory of politics like — in the last analysis — Rousseau's which attempts to skirt this issue, and sees the world as shaped and constrained primarily by Wills, entirely mistakes the nature of what it seeks to explain and advance: our civic existence.

Part I

"Society" as the Ethical Starting Point for Political Inquiry

"LE TOUT EST BIEN?"

From its origins in the Scottish Enlightenment through developments in France and Germany, the "classical" tradition of social theory adopted Jean-Jacques Rousseau as one of its figureheads.[1] It was, no doubt, a love-hate relationship. But Rousseau made apparent for many a new and general object for inquiry: *society*.[2]

The ideas Rousseau began to publish around the 1750s came as a sort of revelation and a prod for his own and then for successive generations of thinkers. It is exactly correct to say that "the Enlightenment invented society as symbolic representation of collective human existence and instituted it as the essential domain of human practice" as long as we add that the enduring "conceptual grid within which the discussion of the social" operated—along axes like needs/Will, contract/constraint, nature/artifice, religion/society—was primarily composed and animated by Rousseau.[3]

Over the subsequent two centuries, the sense that *society* is an autonomous force in our experience gained traction. The first reason for this was empirical. Practices—big and small, momentary and sustained, local and extensive— of which *society* is said to be composed expanded exponentially and reached deeper into everyday life. A growing number of effects that touch the lives of most human beings could no longer convincingly be traced back to specific persons, to nature, or to God. The sustained influence of Rousseau's writings derives from the way he attributed significance to such changes in our "life-world"[4] and the meaning they have for us.

Rousseau is known today primarily as a provocative theorist of two major topics of modern political thinking: liberty and equality.[5] Both of these topics, and Rousseau's contribution to them, have been debated in depth and at length. While it is not my central purpose here to enter these debates, it is worth recalling that Rousseau saw human freedom as *essentially* a collective, rather than an individual, problem. That is, he revived an ancient political conception of human being. However, he accomplished this revival within an emerging climate of modern individualism which—one has good reason to suppose—should have been fatal to the ancient view. This required substantial innovation, some of which we shall consider below.

The topic of human freedom frames many of Rousseau's most important innovations. I want to begin by focusing on one of these. It is, I believe, the point from which Rousseau's influence on subsequent social thought most clearly arises.

In a world intractably full of evil, Rousseau asked "Where does evil come from and how can we moderate its effects?" This question of *theodicy* had been owned almost exclusively by theologians since Plato.[6] In an especially striking manner, Rousseau brought it to the center of an ethically-charged inquiry into politics and attributed new significance to it. For, unlike the vast majority of his European predecessors who entered upon this terrain, Rousseau did not directly adopt the theological topography of Saint Augustine. The Biblical story of the "original sin," of the Fall and its consequences, shaped Rousseau's anthropological narrative in complex new ways. As he attempted to identify the source of evil and the resources for its resolution, the primary distinction that had structured much of Christian thought—distinguishing between a "city of God" and a "city of Man"—receded into the background.[7]

The word "evil"—which I will use to translate the less specifically charged French word *mal* or (plural) *maux*—tends to evoke a narrowly theological register. The discursive context in which Rousseau was entangled inevitably amplifies this effect. Yet, as we shall see, it is precisely in the zone of uncertainty between the theological and the secular, between the relation of a Protestant conscience to God and the social relationships entertained among persons, that Rousseau operates. This ambiguity is a vehicle for his innovations, and we should be acutely aware of it from the beginning.[8]

Rousseau's *Émile, ou De l'éducation* (1762) will be the primary terrain for exploration in what follows. Open its first pages and find this striking phrase:

> Everything is good leaving the hands of the author of things: everything degenerates in the hands of Man.

Translation here veils something important in the French, which goes this way:

> *Tout est bien, sortant des mains de l'auteur des choses: tout dégénére entre les mains de l'homme.* (OC IV.245)

This is without doubt a play on one of the most famous lines from one of the most famous poems of the generation of Rousseau's own youth. Challenging theological skepticism, Alexander Pope published in his *Essay on Man* (1733) the provocative claim that

> All nature is but art, unknown to thee
> All chance, direction, which thou canst not see;
> All discord, harmony, not understood;
> All partial evil, universal good:
> And, spite of pride, in erring reason's spite,
> One truth is clear, *Whatever is, is right.*[9]

This final line reappeared in French three years later in the widely read translation of Etienne Silhouette as "*Cette vérité est évidente: que* tout ce qui est, est bien."[10] In this eccentric formula a Panglossian vision of Providence was sustained in the French philosophical discourse of Rousseau's time.[11] It seems inevitable, therefore, that Pope's commonplace would suffer collateral damage when the author of the *Discours sur l'origine et les fondemens de l'inégalité parmi les hommes* (1755) laid literary siege to "everything that is [*tout ce qui est*]." Rousseau understood perfectly how the question of theodicy would resurface at the very center of his social critique.[12]

When Rousseau was attacked the next year in the *Mercure de France* by his fellow Genevan Charles Bonnet, he provided what may be the pithiest summary of the accomplishment of his prize-winning *Discours sur . . . l'inégalité* and he placed it in just this socio-theological perspective:[13] "Faced with the enumeration of the evils which befall mankind and which I claim to be the work of their very own hands, you assure me, Leibniz and you, that *everything is good* [*tout est bien*], and that therefore Providence is justified" (OC II.232).*

Barely months later the infamous earthquake of 1756 laid Lisbon low and shook the faith of believers across Europe. Voltaire shouted down the "the deluded philosophers who cry out 'all is well' [*tout est bien*]" in a *Poème sur le désastre de Lisbonne*. Rousseau took this as an opportunity to state again the view he opposed, but opposed in a manner distinct from Voltaire:[14] "Pope and Leibniz tell me 'Man, hold steady; the evils that strike you are a necessary effect of your nature, and of the constitution of this universe. If the eternal Being didn't do better, it's because he couldn't do better.'"† This paraphrase reflects Rousseau's reticence—more from authorial pride than from intellectual humility—to propose unadorned commonplaces to the greatest literary figure of his age. With

---

* "A l'énumération des maux dont les hommes sont accablés et que je soutiens être leur propre ouvrage, vous m'assurez Leibniz et vous que tout est bien, et qu'ainsi la providence est justifiée."

† "'Homme, prends patience,' me disent Pope et Leibnitz. 'Tes maux sont un effet nécessaire de ta nature, et de la constitution de cet univers. Si [l'Être éternel] n'a pas mieux fait, c'est qu'il ne pouvoit mieux faire.'"

Bonnet he had no such compunction, to whom he simply writes that "according to Leibniz and Pope, everything that is, is good [*tout ce qui est, est bien*]." Rousseau's eloquence is regrouped in the next phrase, where he adds that "it is neither to Leibniz nor to Pope that I have to respond . . ."[15] This is the gesture of a schoolmaster, at once exposing and exploiting *tout ce qui est, est bien* as a commonplace. All the while, of course, he continues the debate with Leibniz and Pope.

It is striking that Rousseau believed, or wanted his reader to believe, that these two authors spoke to him with a single voice. This was exactly the voice that Rousseau mocked as he set out to write the pointed beginning of the final version of *Émile.*[16] One must be careful, he chides Voltaire further, to distinguish between "*mal particulier*" and "*mal général.*"[17]

> . . . instead of "everything is good," it could perhaps be better to say: "the whole is good," or "everything is good for the whole."*

Just behind this metonymic reduction lie Rousseau's primary efforts to isolate the individual—he will evoke the metaphor of Nature for this—and identify the social—he will invoke the metaphors of *contractus* and *pactum* for this. Already the image Rousseau opposes to Pope and Voltaire has, like all topics of part-and-whole, a spatial quality. He extends this image by displaying the significance of the maxim *tout ce qui est, est bien* as a function of time as well. This conjunction of time and space is what will join a vision of order and society to the question of theodicy. Yes, Rousseau tells us, perhaps it can be said that up to the moment when things leave the hands of God "*tout est bien.*" At that decisive threshold, however, the condition of our existence, our world, begins to degenerate. It becomes utterly human.

---

*"... au lieu de Tout est bien, il vaudroit peut être mieux dire: le Tout est bien, ou Tout est bien pour le tout."

§2

"THE ISLAND OF THE HUMAN RACE"

This is where the study of the development of humanity begins. Across the portal of his book Rousseau, as if in emulation of Dante, plasters a declaration alerting readers that they enter here a new and uncharted domain where our human lives have "left the hands of the author of things" (OC IV.245). In this realm — *société* — evil is our "own creation." It is something we have made and we must own. It cannot be laid at the doorstep of God or Nature, or of the "Laws of Nature and of Nature's God."[18]

Nor, Rousseau insists, does evil arise in the individual as such. It is, rather, a product distinctively *social*, a quality that appears only in the *"homme social"* and his condition (*"état"*). "The island of the human race is the earth" (OC IV.429) and, like Robinson Crusoe on his island, we must collectively make our way with what is at hand.[19] We must become "sovereign of the world like Robinson on his island" (OC III.354).

What sense does it make to represent the study of society with the most famous trope of modern individualism?[20] I think Rousseau is both blunt and subtle on this point.

Later in *Émile*, Rousseau will tell us "I hate books,"[21] but that the first reading for the child in his educational program should be Daniel Defoe's fantastically famous book. It is, as Charles Dickens noted, a kind of science, and, as Harold Bloom suggests, "a book that cannot fail with children."[22] And, indeed, in Rousseau's scheme "the child's entire library will consist of *Robinson Crusoe* alone for quite some time."[23]

It is obvious that everyone who encounters the ink-and-paper Defoe will be unlike Crusoe, who is "on his island, alone, deprived of the assistance of his kind and of the instruments of all the arts or crafts, yet looking after his subsistence, his own preservation, and even obtaining a kind of well-being" (OC IV.455).* With

---

*"....dans son isle, seul, dépourvu de l'assistance de ses semblables et des instrumens de tous les arts, pourvoyant cependant à sa subsistance, à sa conservation, et se procurant même une sorte de bien-être..."

Defoe in hand, the reader brings before his or her own imagination "the desert island that serves first and foremost as comparison."[24] While this isolation is not the condition of human beings in society and, obviously, it must be nothing like the situation of the young Émile,

> . . . it is with respect to this condition that he must assess all others. The most certain manner to raise oneself above prejudices and to order one's judgements concerning the real relations amongst things is to put oneself in the place of an isolated man, and to judge everything as that man himself must judge, particularly attentive to his own utility.[25]*

Precisely because the "island" represents a condition having little or nothing to do with our real social existence, it can, placed conceptually within a framework of radical contrasts, provide a measure by which to evaluate life in society.

Establishing this distance between "island" and "society," and suggesting its analytic utility, Rousseau brings forward a second and extraordinarily subtle deployment of Defoe's figure.[26] To write that "the island of the human race is the earth [*la terre*]" is to locate as unitary and entire the object Rousseau proposes to study—mankind in society. This is "*le tout*" he recommends to Voltaire, with and against Pope. It is an object both figurative and, like an island, utterly material, for something literal in all metaphors must bring to life what is fantastic about them.

What is *la terre?* Notes Rousseau made for a "Course in Geography" propose "description of the earth" in ways both familiar and surprising: there is a "*cosmographique*" side to his description that deals with physical features, but also a "*historique*" side that considers "government, forces, religion, and mores [*le gouvernement, les forces, la réligion, et les moeurs*]."[27] The "terrestial globe" is distinct from the "celestial" but must be studied "in relation to the heavens" (OC V.535). The hint of old theodicy is present, but Rousseau also places mankind squarely on the island of the earth, and his approach, here through *géographie*, literally writing-the-world, is like a sailor to an uncharted place. He follows—in image and in text—the only unequivocal sign that heaven provides: the stars. Thus, the fragmentary "Course in Geography" is punctuated by "the names of the constellations and planets set in Latin verse."[28] Just after this moment of hesitation, an ephemeral chapter "*Of the Sphere*" ["*De la sphére*"] opens. Then the course trails off.

*"... c'est sur ce même état qu'il doit apprécier tous les autres. Le plus sur moyen de s'élever au dessus des préjugés et d'ordonner ses jugemens sur les vrais rapports des choses, est de se mettre à la place d'un homme isolé, et de juger de tout comme cet homme en doit juger lui-même eu égard à sa propre utilité."

Rousseau's caesura again echoes Dante, as "we come out to traverse apace the vast expanse of the heavens."[29] Even if the earth, in its celestial surroundings, "is only a point [*n'est qu'un point*],"[30] it is also a "theater of disputes, and of the ambition of mankind."[31]

Rousseau pushes on. He tries his hand at a *Traité de sphére* ["Treatise of the Sphere"], adopting an old theological genre primarily associated with Johannes de Sacrobosco, whose book *De Sphaera* from the year 1230 passed through 295 print editions before the end of the seventeenth century[32] and gave birth to a large number of imitations. One version by Nicolas Malezieulx (Paris, 1679) under the title *Nouveau Traite de la sphere* states on its first page the traditional purpose of such books: "Taken literally, the word Sphere means 'a ball,' but here we understand by 'Sphere' a figure composed of several circles, which serves to explain the movement of stars, the sun, the moon & other planets, and which represents the order and situation of the principal parts of the universe."* In Rousseau's hands, however, the *Sphére* is brought down to earth. His treatment is inflected in a way that resonates with another hugely successful contemporary work, Buffon's discourse on the *Histoire et théorie de la terre* from 1749, where "it is not a question of the figure of the earth, nor its movement, nor the exterior relations it can have with the other parts of the universe; it is its interior constitution, its form and matter, that we propose to investigate."[33]† In a clear rejection of the tradition of Sacrobosco, the earth alone becomes the object in Rousseau's *Traité de sphére*. However, his study of *la terre* is also radically different from his friend Buffon's.[34] It is configured, astonishingly, as a general method for learning to think and act, for the study of plural men in diverse times and places, and "in the contrasts," he adds, "we will learn to extricate man from his mask."[35]

This is how Rousseau makes the island of mankind reappear in a very different light. He interrupts our desire to interpret it as a sign of nature, a *topos* of the primitive or timeless. Nor is isolation, here, solitude, that unhappy life of constrained communication which Rousseau, however much he lived it, certainly did not want or recommend to the rest of humanity.[36] And if the island amplifies the image of a "state of nature" as contrasting critical hypothesis to our social

---

* "Le mot de Sphere pris a la Lettre signifie une Boule, mais icy on l'entend par Sphere une figure composée de plusieurs cercles, qui sert à expliquer le mouvement des Estoilles, du Soleil, de la Lune & des autres Planettes, & qui represente l'ordre & la scituation des principales parties de l'Univers."

† "Il n'est ici question ni de la figure de la terre, ni de son mouvement, ni des rapports qu'elle peut avoir à l'extérieur avec les autres parties de l'univers; c'est sa constitution intérieure, sa forme et sa matière que nous nous proposons d'examiner."

estate, it also pushes in the opposite direction. It depicts absolutely clear boundaries around the human enterprise; it envisions, in the language of *De Sphaera*, a "circle" with no beyond. And "Man is king of the earth."[37]

Within that sphere, distinct spatial possibilities and material conditions come into focus. Only the "island of the human race" can tell us all we must and all we can know about the composition of relations among ourselves, of *société*. As if to underscore the point, Rousseau suggests that it is "at least very plausible that society and languages were born on islands" (OC III.169). Such are the elements, the only elements, from which to conceive the *civitas terrena*,[38] the ancient *cité*, or the modern *république*.[39]

The human sciences in the mid-eighteenth century are in their infancy. No wonder Rousseau imagines himself as Émile without a tutor, in need of both the new form of education and "principles of political right [*droit politique*]"[40] he will invent. It is Rousseau who must begin from scratch because there are no worthy books on his subject.[41] He is, on the island of the earth, in the uncharted territory of *société*, just like Crusoe, a "*solitaire.*"[42] Were there a convenient treatise on navigation it would serve no purpose for a man without a boat.[43] A Bible may bring comfort to the "solitaire" but does not enlarge his limited communication, nor lift the "city of man" into holy communion and divine justice.[44] A person shipwrecked will not be interested in "systems of the world [*sistemes du monde*]."[45] Rousseau, like Crusoe, will have to read the "island" from top to bottom. The "solitaire" must look around at the "world"; he depends on sense and perception. The nature of the "island" and its inhabitants will instruct him. "The most certain manner," we may paraphrase here, for *mankind* "to raise itself above prejudices and to order its judgments concerning the real relations amongst things" is for the *student* to put himself in the place of a single and unitary *society* "and to judge everything as that [society] itself must judge, particularly attentive to its own utility."[46] Rousseau, preceptor of humanity,[47] finds himself writing in the first period of an education consistent with *nature*—the overture of an authentically human history?—during which, "in a word, we would have worked our way around the whole island [*en un mot, nous [aurions] parcouru l'isle entiere*]" and after which, by means of which, "we come back to ourselves [*nous revenons à nous*]."[48]

And thus Rousseau deploys a single figure to bring together two apparently antithetical tropes—Crusoe shows us at once an isolated individual and mankind as a whole, "abandoned to ourselves."[49]

AN INFLUENTIAL ERROR

Corresponding to this double view, Rousseau's passionately personal way of thinking is decisively inclusive of the life human beings lead with one another. Within the framework he constructs Rousseau succeeds in linking the problem of evil—or should one always say *evils?*—to the problem of freedom. We will return to this link shortly. Suffice it to say for now that Rousseau's combination of interests opened a whole new continent for sociological investigation, suggested a method with which to pursue that investigation, and, above all, gave it a purpose. That is why the classical theorists of Society could articulate both what they were doing and why they were doing it with a gesture toward Rousseau.

This point cannot be overstated. Rousseau's major works had immediate and astonishing success throughout the Atlantic world of Europe and North America. This fact alone was an invitation to other writers seeking a wide audience to adopt topics he set in place or definitively refigured. He was a catapult for the discourse of "the social." It rarely mattered whether or not those who adopted his terms agreed with his conclusions.[50] In France, most of Rousseau's contemporaries felt obliged to take his claims into account, all the more so once the revolution was under way.[51] For more than a century political debates were powered by repulsion from and attraction to Rousseau, as were the efforts of first-rank authors of French sociology like Robespierre, Comte, Fouillée, Tarde, Durkheim, and Halbwachs.[52] This effect extended far beyond French borders. Scots like David Hume and Adam Smith and Adam Ferguson, Thomas Jefferson and the anti-Federalists and (surprisingly) Alexander Hamilton in America,[53] as well as Immanuel Kant, G. W. F. Hegel, and Karl Marx in Germany,[54] were all profoundly influenced by Rousseau. Even Nietzsche, to some extent, would define his conception of politics explicitly against Rousseau.[55] In fact, practically every major subsequent development in social theory can be traced back to some engagement with Rousseau through these four traditions.[56]

Likewise, tracking the phenomenal persistence of Rousseau into the twentieth century would produce an extensive catalogue of those who explicitly embraced or rejected him.[56a] Although this would involve a kind of research outside the scope of this book, it is worth noting the diversity of this engaged reception, which in France alone includes figures as strikingly different as Lévi-Strauss (1958), Derrida (1967), and Bourdieu (1993).[57]

Something else is of greater interest here. It is the extraordinarily widespread and continuing agreement with Rousseau's way of thinking through certain questions about the moral foundations of politics.

Now, if it was possible to identify an original, unique, and ever-present author of Western European, and thus in its many ways global, common sense, Rousseau would certainly be a candidate. But we have no need to play this sort of game here.

Rather, I begin from an observation. There is much in a wide range of the moral and political thought on the table for discussion today that corresponds to what Rousseau had to say. Sometimes the correspondence is explicit. More often than not it is implicit. Here and there it sports his name. Typically his ideas appear anonymous.

As a consequence, it is clear that after more than two centuries the word *Rousseau* does not just refer us to an original and influential writer. It operates as a point of reference, a *topos*, by means of which a great deal of affirmation or contest is brought to a head. Rousseau, it may be fairly said, has become exemplar. And what I shall insist on, especially toward the end of this book, after we have considered much of the brilliant insight and erudite wisdom to be found in his pages, is that he exemplifies for us moderns, you reading and me writing, one of our greatest mistakes.

§4

ANXIETIES OF INFLUENCE

Dépendance as the Key to Société

To the fact that practically every modern social thinker of importance owes something to Rousseau must be added an acknowledgment that efforts to make his vision the vehicle for sociological theory have never been smooth or simple. Rousseau's little boat loaded with pointed conjectures tossed about in a sea of contradictions.

In 1932, the greatly underappreciated Ernst Cassirer adopted a familiar German academic genre intending to settle "the problem of Jean Jacques Rousseau."[58] As a writer, Rousseau had made political statements from which his readers—philosophers among them—found it convenient to extrapolate. Cassirer reversed this balance to treat Rousseau primarily as a philosopher, but one whose thought was rich in implications for politics. Cassirer distinguished himself by sorting out with unusual clarity a variety of muddled interpretations. As an attempt—I borrow, for reasons that will soon become clear, Rousseau's own terms here—"to resolve all the contradictions" of Rousseau's literary world, Cassirer's account was in certain respects definitive. It set the stage for subsequent luminous readings along rather different lines.[59]

Cassirer reiterated for an increasingly receptive audience that Rousseau's discoveries could still be of fundamental importance for the modern project of self-understanding. Despite the many eccentricities in Rousseau's oeuvre, Cassirer insisted, Rousseau had "advanced to treating problems of absolutely universal significance ... which even today have lost nothing of their force and intensity."[60]

Times change. Today it is no longer obvious which of the problems in his own milieu Cassirer had had in mind or exactly what hold those problems had on his historical moment. Certain conjoined social and intellectual transformations—one thinks of the new gravity amassed by the term *democracy* after the Second World War, or the related development of a richly articulated feminism since the 1970s—have reasserted the question of Rousseau's coherence and again unsettled his claim to universality.[61]

And it must be said that the "force and intensity" of the problems most prominently treated by Rousseau does not derive in any simple way from solutions he proposed to them. Lifting a series of conceptual Davids to the stature of Goliath, Rousseau was a promoter of Titanic but unresolved contests. It is well known that Rousseau has been used by those who aimed to advance the cause of revolution over tradition, of equality over liberty, of action over deference, of the secular over the religious, of the majority over the privileged few, and so forth.[62]

What Rousseau empowered most, however, was the cause of popular justice. In the field where "power decides between equal rights" there is and can be no preordained winner.[63] So, the appeal of Rousseau was not that he might serve as final arbiter. It was rather the way his words multiplied the powers of the weak. This is where he most famously touched the moral nerve of politics. Rousseau linked justice to history and action through claims about personal identity, dignity, and self-command.

If these seem like qualities of individuals, it is a false appearance. Rousseau demonstrates that identity, dignity, self-command, and the like are social facts manifest in persons. Nowhere is this clearer than in the way the central doc-trine of the "Will" is generalized from an attribute of the one—a god, a king, a person—to an attribute of the many.[64]

Moreover, these are not just social facts but also the sorts of things that are fought over in society. Society itself becomes thereby the object of politics. The fighting is intense. And Rousseau himself never won this kind of battle. What he did was to make them bigger. Earth-shattering.

Such topics are woven into a certain rhetorical *sensus communis*, which is to say the common ground of contest where literary antagonists from Robes-pierre and Benjamin Constant to François Furet and Louis Althusser have met, and where a vast range of everyday disputes rise up. However, even this fact of common ground does not constitute the most widely distributed of our own intu-itions exemplified by Rousseau.

Disputes must have a moral field of operation. It is a primary purpose of this book to explore that general field as it appeared in Rousseau's writings and as it is mirrored in our imagination, and thereby to both advance our understanding of it and to increase the theoretical instruments we have for inquiry into politics today.

To this point we have seen only that what makes up this field is the consti-tution of society, that single "island" where we are "abandoned to ourselves."[65] Indeed, it was Rousseau who first, and with vertiginous acumen, construed this moral field as *social*, and not as bodily habit, psychological attachment, or stal-wart facade of sacred or civic devotion.

In other words, what we shall consider below stands prior to the resolution or the rejection of the political problems and solutions branded as Rousseau's. Our concern is with a basic vision of how the world works, how—chicken-or-egg—that vision becomes part of the operation of the world, and how in that reflexive process problems and solutions are shaped by human belief and imagination.

Thus, if this inquiry is to bear fruit it must bring under the steady light of scrutiny one or another of the first and foremost conditions of possibility for poli-tics. This process of making something that is basic and normally invisible into a complex object of inquiry is of unremitting import not just for the scholar or the sciences of society, but for the citizen.

Another of Rousseau's methodological assertions bears on the framing of this inquiry. He writes that "it is necessary to study society by way of men, and men by way of society," adding caustically that "those who would like to investigate the political and the moral separately will never understand anything of either" (OC IV.524). Contemporary readers may hear in this the tones of Aristotle. Listen again. Rousseau's admonishment does not simply identify the political and the moral. It requires an additional step, in which society is shown to be the site of the moral, and the ongoing articulation of the moral the constitution of society. This step is specifically modern. It is a modernity that begins with Rousseau. It is a view of human life that gears things toward politics in a new way.

And this returns us to the fundamental conditions of possibility for politics. One is at the center of attention in this book. We shall refer to it as *dépendance*.[66]

It is through representations of the fundamental fact of human dependence that Rousseau figures the *moral* field of *society*. I will show in what follows that, for unexpected reasons and in unexpected ways, this image resonates most strongly and uniformly with contemporary common sense. I will argue, on the one hand, that in this way Rousseau located the proper terrain for inquiry into politics. At the same time, I will argue further that in some absolutely essential respect Rousseau mistook the significance of his discovery. Despite unparalleled insight he failed to understand how the constitution of society makes politics what it is. Neither the success nor the failure of Rousseau can relegate our conversation with him to the history books. For, *we*, too, today, continue to tend in the same — right and wrong — way.

When I say that Rousseau uses the *topos* of "dependence" to articulate and explain the moral field of society, I mean this in a strong sense that many readers may find surprising. It is widely assumed that for Rousseau, as for Hobbes, the basis of morality is "contract." If by that word is meant a juridical document, or even a simile of such a document, the supposition is false. Rousseau harbors no illusion that society — as characterized by morality and constituted by dependence — arises from or in a founding moment certified by a *"pacte social."*[67] Make or imagine all the contracts you want — says Rousseau — if this helps you in theory or in practice. This does not change the fact that society, with its *ordre* and its *loix*, rests ultimately on *"moeurs,* customs, and above all opinion [*des moeurs, des coutumes, et sur-tout de l'opinion]"* (OC III.394) and is a matter of *contrahere res*, of the contraction of things, the drawing together of persons, and not anything even resembling a juridical *pactum.*[68] Rousseau's real position, all things considered, it that *dépendance* is the basis of morality.

Understood in a general way, dependence is both the source of evil and a practical potential for its solution that is always already inherent in the social condition. Operating through the *topos* of "dependence" adds a specific sort of weight and direction to the theory of civil life. It forces the theorist to interpret needs and capacities in this essentially contingent and relational way. All sorts of associative facts or modes of *société* — such as "the people" [*le peuple*], "the public" [*le public*], or even "the world" [*le monde*] — are "systems of dependence."[69] And systems of dependence are themselves necessary for the operation of other primary conditions of possibility for politics, such as the human capacity to speak. In this perspective, communication and persuasion are not functions of beliefs *per se*, but complements of a particular system of dependence; within that system of dependence those beliefs that take symbolic form provide discursive "handles" by which the constraints and opportunities of action present in the system emerge and are realized.[70]

It is important to note the broad cultural context in which Rousseau articulates the fundamental fact of human dependence. In his time and after, dependence achieves extraordinary prominence by virtue of the ways in which it is denied and rejected.[71] "Independence"—that powerful and practical name for the human desire not to be pushed around, turned through bad philosophy to an almost infinite list of other purposes—is the master trope of this denial.

Rousseau's contemporary and primary interlocutor among the *philosophes*, Denis Diderot, provides, with typical and peerless disdain, a description of the hold this untenable position has over their contemporaries: "The philosopher's stone of human pride; the chimera chased blindly by *amour-propre*; the term which Men always offer to themselves & which impedes their efforts & their desires to ever have it, that is independence."[72]* Diderot is unerringly against such proud philosophical nonsense. His line is familiar. Only in one application can sense be made of this supposed ideal: "There is only one independent being in nature, that is its author. Everything else is a chain of which the links are mutually connected, each dependent upon the others."[73]† Here, in a familiar voice, Diderot takes a sort of "scientific"[74] angle toward a theological topic. He considers the "physical order" of nature as it was increasingly brought into focus by followers of Bacon, Descartes, and Newton.[75] Nonetheless, the older image of a "great chain of being" still seems apt to him, although now applied with Spinozistic intent.[76] "For a blade of grass to grow," Diderot proclaims, "all of nature must, so to speak, concur [*pour qu'un brin d'herbe croisse il faut pour ainsi dire, que la nature entiere y concoure*]." Likewise in the "moral and political order, to whatever rank we may cling, dependence is still our inheritance, and he that commands all others, the sovereign himself, sees over his head laws of which he is only the first subject."[77]§ Despite these obvious facts, Diderot goes on to ob-

---

* "... la pierre philosophale de l'orgueil humain; la chimere après laquelle l'amour-propre court en aveugle; le terme que les hommes se proposent toujours, & qui empêche leurs entreprises & leurs desirs d'en avoir jamais, c'est *l'indépendance* ..."

† "Il n'est qu'un seul être *indépendant* dans la nature; c'est son auteur. Le reste est une chaîne dont les anneaux se lient mutuellement, & dépendant les uns des autres. ..."

§ "... .quel que soit le rang que nous y tenions, la dépendance est toujours notre apanage, & celui qui commande à tous les autres, le souverain lui-même voit au-dessus de sa tête les lois dont il n'est que le premier sujet."

serve that "mankind consumes itself in continual efforts to arrive at that independence which exists nowhere . . ."[78]*

Now look squarely at Rousseau's position. To many readers it has seemed as if he aspires to what Diderot scorns. Famously in the *Discours sur . . . l'inégalité* human beings are painted as both "free and independent [*libre et indépendant*]" (OC III.174). And in *Émile* Rousseau stands ready to tell us what "renders men independent and free [*rend les hommes indépendans et libres*]" (OC IV.524). Yet, such statements are quite misleading. The phrase "independent and free" is not positively attached to political life; both words occur specifically as antonyms to slavery. Throughout *Émile* the word *indépendance* is understood as something relative, not absolute. It certainly does not describe an ontological condition. There is no natural or generalized independence. Thus, children, to take just one obvious example, must through education be brought to the qualified sort of independence necessary for moral agency.[79] If there is a subject of unqualified independence it is collective, as Rousseau makes clear in observing that peoples or nations can approximate liberty by remaining independent of other such groups. No important methodological implications follow from any of these positions.

In the final pages of *Émile* Rousseau hammers home his agreement with Diderot. To mark this definitive moment a now familiar image is again brought forward.[80] Émile himself has become the thoroughly experienced wanderer or inquirer (which is to say, *theoros*). He has *parcouru* the *univers* itself, the "island" of mankind, or, in this instance, simply "the states of Europe." The pupil recounts for the tutor what he has learned. He tells us that "the more I examine the work of men in their institutions, the more I see that pressed by the desire to be independent they make themselves slaves, and that they consume even their liberty in vain efforts to maintain it" (OC IV.855).†

The political significance of Émile's lesson is clarified by the companion book that Rousseau wrote at the same time, *Du Contract social*. Here the reversal is rigorous and complete although not explicit. Attentive readers will note that the word "independence" rarely appears without the qualifying adjective "natural."[81] This means that if "independence" is possible at all, it is limited to the so-called "state of nature." Moreover, the relation between freedom and independence is severed. Whereas Rousseau could once take these as synonyms[82] he writes that with the *contract social* citizens give up "natural independence in favor of

---

*". . . les hommes se consument en des efforts continuels pour arriver à cette indépendance, qui n'existe nulle part . . ."

†". . . plus j'éxamine l'ouvrage des hommes dans leurs institutions, plus je vois qu'à force de vouloir être indépendans ils se font esclaves, et qu'ils usent leur liberté-même en vains efforts pour l'assurer."

freedom [*de l'indépendance naturelle contre la liberté*]."[83] Once having entered the "civil estate, the sweet voice of nature is no longer an infallible guide for us, nor is the independence we have received from nature a desirable condition" (OC III.283).*

It is typical for Rousseau to imagine the development of things, including a condition like "independence," against a backdrop of historical time. (This is the evolutionary perspective that I will increasingly identify with one side of Rousseau's thinking as the argument goes forward.) So perhaps what he has in mind in this: once upon a time there was and someday there will be again a sort of *indépendance*; now, however, in the moment of any person reading Rousseau's words, there is *dépendance*, and although civilizing history begins with the perfection of nature and aims toward the perfection of humankind, in between we are consumed by degeneration and *dépendance* is the cause.

This way of reading Rousseau is wrong. It neglects too much his dialectic. For dependence is also the solution to the problems of which it is the cause. And Rousseau likewise speculates that "natural independence" must have always borne in it "an essential fault" that "undermines the development of our most excellent faculties." That fault is simply the presumptive absence of the *lien social* (OC III.283). Rousseau therefore concludes that real constitutions—such as the one he proposed for Corsica—had better acknowledge that even "natural independence" is a source of corruption in society; the purpose of a constitution is to construct between the citizen and the state further relations of dependence (OC III.916).

Thus, Rousseau, as usual, disagrees with his interlocutor until the other agrees that they disagree, and then he agrees. Diderot's description is not exactly denied by Rousseau, who rather takes it as a challenge and starting point for inquiry. If one key phrase could capture the idea they share it would be that *human order is composed of dependence.*

Pressed by the facts of *société* Rousseau identifies *dépendance* as constitutive. He is driven to develop a microscopic account of it. Why? So that dependence might be overcome, or, as dependence motivates a kind of social evolution, it might overcome itself.[84]

Rousseau's genius was to have isolated and analyzed the characteristically modern form of human relationship: *société*. Nearly everything else in his work serves this end: the image of nature, the recollection of Rome and other republics, the stages and staging of the "self," the vision of a civic life to come. There is nothing in Rousseau's way of thinking to stop him from seconding Diderot's ges-

---

* ". . . la douce voix de la nature n'est plus pour nous un guide infaillible, ni l'indépendance que nous avons receu [*sic*] d'elle un état desirable. . . ."

ture to "a chain of which the links are mutually connected, each dependent upon the others" and applying it specifically to the human world. Perhaps in a hypothetical first or utopian final phase of the human condition this image loses its sense, but Rousseau nonetheless makes clear that in human contacts with other human beings of a mankind abandoned to ourselves—now returning to Rousseau's own words—"the first link is forged in that long chain from which social order is formed [*se forge le premier anneau de cette longue chaîne dont l'ordre social est formé*]."[85]

What Rousseau ultimately shows is this: *dépendance*[86] is the quality and substance of the *lien social*, the amorphous and invisible "bond" or "cement" that makes society *something*. It is the topic to which all social thought, and thus all political thought,[87] must, with or without self-consciousness, return. Although Rousseau famously deployed the figure of a "*contract social*," and eminent interpreters of his work insist that such a purportedly juridical instrument is the origin of the *lien social*,[88] he, unlike Hobbes, uses it for purposes strictly at odds with individualism.

In fact, we find in Rousseau's writings an image of society that no "contract" can adequately represent.[89] On one side, society is presented as a thoroughly discrete totality, an "island" where mankind is "abandoned to ourselves"; on the other side, Rousseau's figuration of the complexity of human entanglements within these bounds is so rich as to escape all juridical simile. More like his once admired and then detested contemporary David Hume, almost everything in Rousseau's work but the words "*contract social*" is an argument against it.[90] If we had had a *Jean-Jacques juge de Rousseau*—completing the self-exposure and justification of the actual book *Rousseau juge de Jean-Jacques*—perhaps he would have added the "*contract social*" to the list of "*fausses notions du lien social* [false conceptions of the social bond]."[91] The notion he actually holds and develops is instead centered around "social relations [*les rapports sociaux*]" in general, and relations of dependence in particular,[92] through which "the true sense" of the word "*cité*" will be rewritten.

As the argument of this book moves forward, we will examine critically the most fundamental claims advanced by Rousseau concerning *dépendance*. In homage to Cassirer, but also to go beyond him, let us call this an inquiry into the *new problem of Jean-Jacques Rousseau*. What is the basis of these claims? What do they imply for experience? For our other beliefs? If, even today, we take something akin to Rousseau's notion of *dépendance* for granted, should we continue to do so? Is the account of the human condition that Rousseau develops around the notion of *dépendance* apt for the social context of political experience as we live it today?

"LE MAL" AND "LA SCIENCE DES MOEURS"

Mankind! Stop your search for the author of evil, that author is you. (OC IV.588)*

Leibniz coined the term *theodicy*—combining the Greek words θεός ("god") and δίκη ("justice")—to name as "a kind of science" an old puzzle: "the doctrine of the justice of God—that is, of his wisdom together with his goodness."[93] Rousseau takes theodicy to a humanistic extreme. As I suggested earlier, his argument may be understood as exculpating God altogether for the misery of the world. Such a view has sociological significance because, by contrast, it marks humanity as something cosmologically distinct and as the unique source of evil.[94] Evil without supernatural origin or supernatural powers appears in peculiarly human forms. In this view, the most terrible evils and sufferings of human beings must be held to our own account.

To be subject to evil is to suffer. Suffering is not one thing. For Rousseau, as in contemporary usage, there are at least two primary forms. One involves almost exclusively effects perceived by the senses, as when the newborn baby suffers his or her birth. Rousseau insists that *"naturellement,"* which is to say where there are no doctors, philosophers, or priests to tell us what awaits us, "man knows how to suffer."[95] But even without these alarmist proctors, suffering is a complex matter for people who are not in the "state of nature." In *Émile*, Rousseau tells us that even for the infant "to suffer is the first thing he must learn" (OC IV.300). The range of predicates that can attach to the verb *souffrir* proliferates with the growth of relationships with others, and it becomes possible, for example, to "make the imagination suffer [*faire souffrir l'imagination*]"[96] or even to "suffer injustice [*souffrir même l'injustice*]." We can call what is learned "social suffering" and take instruction from it here.[97]

Beyond this first assessment, however, suffering is clearly not basic. It is a composite of sense perceptions, emotions, imagination, material circumstances, and so forth. Within this complex, certain components suffuse *suffering* and tend to

---

*"Homme, ne cherche plus l'auteur du mal, cet auteur c'est toi-même."

mark it as a unitary experience. Of these, Rousseau emphasizes *unhappiness*, offering as a maxim that "happiest is he who suffers least" (OC IV.302).

Although the unhappiness component in suffering has this symbolic effect—it makes suffering seem like a single kind of fact—Rousseau's analysis does not stop there. For unhappiness (*malheur*), and reciprocally happiness (*bonheur*), are also composites. They are results of imbalance or balance between *besoins* ["needs"] and *forces* ["forces" or "capabilities"]. We shall consider this triadic relation (*besoins/forces/mal-* or *bonheur*) at length below.[98] For now, I only want to introduce my claim that the ratio *forces* greater than or equal to *besoins* equals *bonheur*, or

$$forces \geq besoins = bonheur[99]$$

is a central and characteristic feature of Rousseau's thinking.

This is not, however, a free-standing philosophical assertion. In addition, happiness also depends—in a very clear material sense—on being able to do what you want to do. In other words, happiness and liberty are also linked.

One may ask: what has this to do with evil (*le mal*)? An obvious connection appears in the opposition between the words *malheur* and *bonheur*. But the nexus of these topics is more intriguing, and in the next few pages I shall sketch it in a way that expands on my initial claim (made in the preceding sections) that Rousseau identifies *société* as a distinct site for inquiry, both demonstrating its unity and providing a complex account, centered by the *topos* of *dépendance*, of its internal composition, inherent forces, and pivotal mechanisms.[100] Rousseau is the first modern writer to capture with pen and ink what Alain Touraine called, two hundred years later, the "self-production of society" and that is what we are concerned with here.[101]

So, in Rousseau's view *bonheur* and liberty are linked. The type of liberty conjoined with happiness is a topic of morality. This is because both the *besoins* and *forces* of a person are not strictly speaking qualities of individuals. Both are ultimately constituted through *liens sociaux*, connections and relationships with others, and this *sociale vinculum* is characterized by dependence.[102] How one and the others move within and make use of such fields of dependence will be decisive for the balance a person achieves between *besoins* and *forces*.

These movements and fields are ethical in the oldest and literal sense of the word. From this we can see in what sense happiness is an ethical problem. Human unhappiness—as a component of suffering, and as opposed to sin—is the evil of the utterly human world, and with the advent of *société* it happens often that "all that remains to us are bad choices [*nous n'aurons plus que le choix de nos maux*]."[103] For this reason, the issue of freedom—which, however much it may appear as an individual need or desire or accomplishment, is in fact a social and political condition—is at the center of Rousseau's theodicy.[104]

Notice that the topic of liberty shifted us between the terms "moral" (a domain of precepts, commands, and reason) and "ethical" (a domain of social practice). I did this because, in my effort to explain Rousseau's theoretical project, I occasionally mimic the way he uses particular terms and thus sometimes where (in my effort to maintain continuity between Rousseau's text and my discussion) the word "moral" appears, what I really mean, more strictly speaking, is "ethical." While some things may be lost in this elision, I think that it allows for a clearer picture of the nexus of the inquiry into *société* with political theory. I digress briefly now to explain why.

Our topic is Rousseau's conception of the basic fabric of human relationships as they occur in the modern form of *société*. To describe this weave from various perspectives and with attention to its different modes and features, Rousseau mobilizes an impressive array of terms, including the encompassing "order" [*ordre*], "body" [*corps*], and "system" [*système*], the more formal "pact" [*pacte*], "contract" [*contract*],[105] "treaty" [*traité*], and "institution" [*institution*], the incisive "engagement" [*engagement*], "convention" [*convention*], and "relation" [*rapport*], the action-oriented *res publica* or "public thing" [*chose publique*], *polis* or "city" [*cité*], and "state" [*état*].[106] Even *religion*—because it can be "a purely civil profession of faith" with articles that are "sentiments of sociability" [*sentiments de sociabilité*] rather than dogma of a church[107]—belongs to the same loose group of corresponding terms for the social "knot" [*noeud*] or "bond" [*lien social*] which may signify a *union* or *unité* but which, crucially, points back to some kind of internal and complex structure.[108] It is the practical and effective intricacies of this structure that the *topos* of *dépendance* brings before us.[109]

This structure is, in turn, something that grows from within human relationships over time, and, manifest in habits of all sorts, becomes binding upon those relationships. On this point deference is due first to Aristotle,[110] who directs his interlocutor to a type of virtue [ἀρετή] that is specifically ethical [ἠθική] and which "emerges from habit [ἔθους], and has indeed derived its name, with a slight variation of form, from that word."[111] From this perspective, it is clear that the complex but identifiable weave of human relationships represented in Rousseau's writing as *le lien social* is inherently ethical in the literal sense of the word. This is something that G. W. F. Hegel—ardent philhellene and perspicacious follower of Rousseau—would later make explicit with his use of the pivotal notion of "ethical life" [*Sittlichkeit*], and who in turn and like Rousseau will join the topic of *moeurs* and "the ethical" to the issue of freedom. This forward-looking correspondence between Hegel and Rousseau also suggests a rethinking of Rousseau's retrospective relation to Spinoza. For despite his passing jibes at Spinoza, once the new theodicy directs our attention to the purely human space of *société*, to the home of mankind "abandoned to ourselves," tensions between Rousseau's theism and Spinoza's atheism become less urgent. What all three share is a central concern with "ethical freedom."[112]

Although the temptation to continue in this direction is strong, let us for now seek further precision by staying nearer to Rousseau. Louis de Jaucourt—who wrote more of the *Encyclopédie* than any other contributor and who better than its more famous authors reflects the common sense of his time and place[113]—comes to our assistance. Likewise Denis Diderot.

Jaucourt traces *moralité* to *moeurs* and identifies *"morale"* as *"la science des moeurs."*[114] His thread runs back from *morale* and *moeurs* to the Latin *mos*, a general term for custom, usage, practice, or habit. From *mos* Cicero coined the word *moralis* to find—as he often sought to do—an equivalent for a Greek concept that had not yet entered his language. The Greek here was again *ἤθη*.[115]

Jaucourt provides a genealogy of *la science des moeurs* that ranges from Socrates to Montesquieu. No surprise that Aristotle's *Nichomachean Ethics* appears prominently as the first "methodical system" and then as impetus for various schools of ethics after Boethius. The key, however, is Cicero, and how the Roman orator brings Greek conceptions into his own world, into the Latin language. Jaucourt implies that *De Officiis* is the source of his own writing. It is an "excellent book. . .that everyone is familiar with" and which is, as "everyone knows, . . .without any doubt the best treatise of moral life, the most regular, methodical, and exact that we have." Together these two outstanding authors exemplify the conjunction under consideration here: how *société* is articulated by *la morale* in Rousseau precisely because the latter is identical with, not distinct from, "the ethical."[116]

From another angle Jaucourt indicates the object of *la science des moeurs*. *"Moeurs* are free actions of human beings susceptible to rule [*règle*]." His thought here concurs with Diderot, who uses nearly the same formulation and adds that the "free actions of human beings" may be "natural or acquired, good or bad, susceptible to rule and direction [*naturelles ou acquises, bonnes ou mauvaises, susceptibles de regle & de direction*]."[117]

Are these statements underpinned by the contemporary view, in which action is centered around a conception of human Will that plays down choosing-capacity and emphasizes instead a peculiarly modern and secular creative power? By the nineteenth century this "new model Will" had become a primary and increasingly global cultural fact and is for that reason implicated in reiterations of the distinction between the *moral* and the *ethical*.[118] And indeed Jaucourt, Diderot, and ultimately Rousseau often appear to point towards a conception of *la morale* that is much narrower than the conjoined image of *mos* and *ἤθη* that I have identified above with "the ethical."

Be that as it may, closer inspection belies this appearance. Under the heading of *moeurs*, Diderot does *not* define action by intention. The pivotal topic for him is *not* the Will as it comes to be understood just half a century later. The view of action at mid-eighteenth century is more akin to earlier, complex, and composite humanist views with classical roots.[119]

Moreover, every type of *"action"*—as Diderot specifies, "natural or acquired, good or bad"—is to be taken into account in study of the moral field. The variety of such *"actions"* is large because action is inexorably contingent. Diderot states this, one might say, sociologically, like Montesquieu, by insisting that actions "depend on climate, religion, laws, government, needs, education, manners, and examples." Again in concurrence with Diderot, Jaucourt reformulates this principle theoretically. With *la morale*, we never discover "the real essence of substances." The investigation and pursuit of action in morale life instead involves precise identification of relationships and careful comparisons between them (*"Morale"* X.700).

Together, Jaucourt and Diderot (along with many others) set a common tone for Rousseau. They offer a perspective on action that encompasses a vast range of human experience. *All of this* is implicated in *moeurs* and in *la science morale* that investigates them.[120] Thus, under the term *morale* we find in fact the wide compass of Greek ἤθη and Latin *mos*, brought to us through Ciceronian *moralis* and *civitas*.[121]

Much is at stake in the treatment of these issues by writers in the eighteenth century. They tend not to draw the bright lines around and of secular morality that will become common after Kant. The whole vocabulary of *la science des moeurs* operates in a different way and serves a different purpose. It is not philosophically oriented. Rather, the interests and operations of this science are civic. It was understood by its practitioners as related to traditions of *rhetoric* and it is best understood by us in that way as well.

Admittedly, to introduce rhetoric here in this way is to broach a vast topic that extends far beyond the scope of this book.[121a] However, a connection between *la science des moeurs* and rhetoric lurks just below the surface in the eighteenth century that cannot pass without some comment. That connection bears directly on how we understand both the genealogy and the current practical affinities of inquiry into the social foundations of moral and political life. Jaucourt again helps us to glimpse this in the following passage:

Passage by Jaucourt	Commentary
"I declare that one cannot undertake the science of *moeurs* by way of demonstrative arguments, and I know two or three principal reasons for this.	■ Jaucourt's verb here (*avouer*) expresses a very high degree of confidence, emphasizing his vigorous rejection of "demonstration." One

1st the lack of signs. We do not have sensible traces which represent moral ideas to the eyes; we only have words to express them; now, however much these words remain the same when they are written down, nonetheless the ideas that they signify can vary with the same person, and it is exceedingly rare that they are not different for different persons.

2nd moral ideas are typically more complex or composite than the figures used in mathematics. It follows from that that the names of moral ideas have more uncertain meaning, and, moreover, that the mind cannot easily keep hold of precise combinations, in order to examine the relations and mismatches of things.[122]

3rd. Human interest, that tricky passion, stands in opposition to any demonstration of moral truths; for it is probable that if mankind wanted to apply itself to the search for these truths, following the same method and with the same indifference that

could say that this is aimed against Hobbes or Spinoza. At the same time, this formulation has in the back ground the first distinction of Aris totle's *Rhetoric:* it is a way of siding with rhetoric against "dialectic."[123]

■ The object for *la morale* is intangible (like Durkheim's *fait social*) and necessarily discursive (shades again of Aristotle). The polysemy of discourse expresses moral pluralism (today associated with John Rawls), epistemic pluralism (associated with John Stuart Mill), and the inherent plurality of human beings (associated with Hannah Arendt). These are familiar reasons why rhetoric has persistently focused on the "probable" rather than the "necessary."[124]

■ "Demonstration" also fails *la science des moeurs* because moral ideas are too complex for this kind of formalization (such complexity is another aspect of the polysemy mentioned above). This conceptual difficulty reflects again the living object of moral inquiry, which is neither *the "good" and the "bad,"* nor *the approbable and the shameful,* but rather *the way the human world fits together* (the relatedness and lack-of-fittingness of persons and things).

■ "Demonstration" does not leave room for the issue of "interests," which rhetoric, with its inherent pragmatism, embraces. This conditional statement about the possibility of a mathematical ethics is, I think, made in exactly the same ironic tone that it seeks mathematical truths, it would find them with the same ease." Rousseau brings to his pivotal proposition about the perfection of laws (see the "main passage" discussed below).

I gloss Jaucourt's article in this way to evoke the rhetorical inflection of his thinking and extend the framework he makes explicit elsewhere. In companion articles on *rhétorique* and rhetorical *invention* he tells us explicitly that the ethical system of mutual obligation[125] and adjustment,[126] of articulated dependence and the division of action,[127] is the object of rhetoric. And by the word *rhétorique* he intends precisely the sense that appears when Aristotle asserts that rhetoric is a mode of inquiry into the circumstances of human relationships that make persuasion possible in any given instance, which is to say it is *not* what most people take it to be—the sheer fact of persuasion or persuasive speech.[128] Anyone who thinks like Jaucourt will not recognize what is for many a well-guarded border, the wall supposed to separate rhetoric from morality and both of them from science. Although he would not have put it in exactly these synthetic terms, what Jaucourt convincingly shows is that *la science des moeurs* is rhetoric.

Could Rousseau align himself with such a capacious, informal, and rhetorically informed conception of *la morale?* The answer is an emphatic *yes.* Indeed, Rousseau is impelled further. He brings before us an extraordinarily detailed field for *la science des moeurs.* Once *société* becomes the distinct and primary object of Man's inquiry into mankind "abandoned to ourselves" every last nook and cranny, joint and muscle, must be accounted for. Paraphrasing Diderot's striking Spinozistic maxim,[129] one might say that *for a moral being to live all of society must, so to speak, concur.*

In this perspective *loi* (law) serves as a keyword and even a code for Rousseau. It is a binding principle that binds together the beginning and the end of history, uniting "all the advantages of the natural condition with those of the civil condition." With the right kind of *loi,* "one would join to the liberty which maintains Man exempt from vice the morality which raises him to virtue."[130]

In an almost Mosaic mood, Rousseau sees *loi* as a source of *moralité.* Thus, what is meant by *loi* suggests from another angle what is meant by *morale.* Although most readers have ignored the precise words Rousseau wrote, what he actually has in mind could not be clearer. We will consider this now in some detail.

Having catalogued the familiar divisions of modern law—public law, civil law, criminal law—Rousseau adds the following and, in my view, decisive passage:[131]

Translation	Rousseau on types of law	Commentary
"To these three types of law **a fourth** attaches itself, the most important of all,	"A ces trois sortes de lois il s'en joint une quatrieme, la plus importante de toutes;	■ Rousseau does not leave law to the lawyers; he both goes beyond their standard categories and points to a more fundamental type of law (that is emphatically *not* natural law).
which is engraved in neither marble nor bronze but in the hearts of citizens,	qui ne se grave ni sur le marbre, ni sur l'airain, mais dans les coeurs des citoyens;	■ As with the word "*cité*," Rousseau suggests that the "true sense" of law "has been almost entirely obscured among the Moderns," who believe (as Jaucourt also suggested above) too much in the authority and automaticity of the written word and the formalization of concepts by the advocates of "method."[132]
which is the **true constitution of the State**,	qui fait la véritable constitution de l'État;	■ "*L'État*" is what *la cité* "is called by its members . . . when it is passive," and thus the fourth kind of law constitutes political life but is not subject to direct command by the Will of the people (in which case Rousseau would call it the "*constitution du Souverain*").[133]
which every day gathers new forces, which,	qui prend tous les jours de nouvelles forces;[133a]	■ It is (again reading here with Jaucourt) more sure than formal or written law and gains force from the sheer fact of its dura-

when the other laws age or are extinguished, revivifies or supplements them, conserves a people in the spirit of its founding,

qui, lorsque les autres lois vieillissent ou s'éteignent, les ranime ou les supplée, conserve un peuple dans l'esprit de son institution,

bility; it would be suggestive but anachronistic and finally misleading to call this "tradition" . . .

■ . . . but it is correct to call this literally "conservative."

and imperceptibly substitutes the force of habit for that of authority.

et substitue insensiblement la force de l'habitude à celle de l'autorité.

■ Reiterated here is the difference between habit and Will, between *État* and *Souverain*, and between the force of "social facts" that cannot be dictated and those aspects of social life actually effected by commands; in fact, the former always win out over the latter.

I am speaking of *moeurs*, customs, and, above all, opinion;

Je parle des moeurs, des coutumes, et surtout de l'opinion;

■ The fourth type of law is identified in this striking way, in which *moeurs*—as the material of a science thoroughly implicated in rhetorical interests (see just above)—are further subsumed into the discursive fabric of society, which is *opinion*.

■ It is not just the lawyers, but also those concerned with politics, who have misunderstood the social/ethical substance of law.

it is the part unknown to our politicians, but from which depends the success of all the others;

partie inconnue à nos politiques, mais de laquelle dépend le succès de toutes les autres;

it is the part with which the great lawgiver concerns himself in secret,	*partie dont le grand législateur s'occupe en secret,*	■ Even the greatest lawgiver cannot simply command the direction of ethical life, the habits to which it corresponds, or the discursive forms in which it is conducted. Effect in this realm is indirect, not publicly declared, i.e., secret.
while he appears to limit himself to particular rules which are only the ring and ribs of the vaulted arch,	*tandis qu'il paroit se borner à des réglemens particuliers qui ne sont que le ceintre de la voûte,*	■ It will always seem as though formal positive law is the occupation of the lawgiver and the edifice that brings order to society . . .
of which *moeurs,* slower to grow, finally form the unshakable keystone." (OC III.394)	*dont les moeurs, plus lentes à naitre, forment enfin l'inébranlable Clef."*	■ . . . but in fact, in the process of time, *moeurs* are what hold everything together.

Even today, many people continue to cling to an image of "modernity" that derives from nineteenth-century sociology or philosophy of law; commonplaces like Henry Sumner Maine's status/contract (1861) or Ferdinand Tönnies's *Gemeinschaft/Gesellschaft* (1887), together with obtuse and artificial critiques of "contract theory" like John Austin (1834) or Otto von Gierke (1883/1934), continue to show their effect in more or less explicit ways. Readers of this sort confronted with the passage just examined should find Rousseau's performance remarkable, indeed, almost impossible for someone so thoroughly attached to the presumptively formalistic-juridical language of contract. Yet, the perspective expressed here underpins Rousseau's theory of *société* and the consequences for civic life that he draws from it. He clearly assimilates law to νομος and εθος, and, with the emphatic addition of that modern word "*opinion,*" perhaps even to δόξα, which is to say to a primary set of ancient categories that gesture toward the informal and habitual relationships that are, as we saw a few pages back, inherent in *la morale.*

Rousseau's pointed criticism supports this view of *loi* and *la morale.* He mocks the abstraction that increasingly dominates legal thinking in his time, asking "But what, finally, is a law?" His answer is blunt: "As long as one rests content to only attach metaphysical ideas to this word, one will continue to reason without understanding [*raisonner sans s'entendre*]" (OC III.378).* This is the classic objection rhetoricians held against philosophy and the distance from experience implicit in metaphysics; we can almost hear Callicles laughing at Socrates in the background.[134] In the instance of law, as in the instance of other cultural practices such as theater and *fêtes*, Rousseau argues against distancing-spectacle-formalism and for proximity-participation-praxis. In just the way he commands us to "present the spectators as spectacle, turn them into actors themselves [*donnez les Spectateurs en Spectacle, rendez-les acteurs eux-mêmes*],"[135] we might say *find the citizens in the* cité, *for they are themselves the agents of the law.*

Indeed, wherever the word *loi* appears in Rousseau's writings, do not imagine the *deus ex machina* (ἀπό μηχανῆς θεός) delivering from outside the significance of or remedy for our words or actions.[136] *Loi* is instead the marker for a highly structured vision of one of several phases of the *lien social* in the broadest, methodologically internalist, hermeneutic, and generally sociological sense.[137]

Likewise, when Rousseau proposes *loi* as the solution to the problems that arise from within the social field of *dépendance*,[138] he is at the same time suggesting that social relationships, too, are best understood as composed of this same matter: *moeurs, coutumes,* and *opinion*.[139] The traffic, so to speak, goes both ways. Insofar as the *corps politique* is a subset of the "general society of the human race [*société générale du genre humain*]," laws that issue from within the political system will also extend order into the totality of society through this uninterrupted weave of dependences.[140]

Reiterating a long list of overlapping terms—*moeurs, morale, coutume, opinion,* and now, as we have just seen, even *loi,* together with all the other relational terms I listed some pages back—Rousseau constitutes a complex but nonetheless singular and general field. This field is *société,* the *lien social* conceived as a fabric of dependences. It provides a consistent backdrop against which Rousseau plays on ambivalences inherent in his other major terms, terms with more familiar political weight. In this way, and with dizzying facility, Rousseau transports his reader back and forth between discourses that he himself insists are distinct. The effect is to neither affirm nor efface those distinctions, but to create—topically—new modes of speech and action.

One such double-faced keyword is *le mal.* In the texts we consider here, *le mal* becomes a passage between, on one side, the religiously charged topic of *evil* around which the question of theodicy circulates, and, on the other side, analysis of the social totality within which *bad* things happen to people living

---

* "Mais qu'est-ce donc enfin qu'une loi? Tant qu'on se contentera de n'attacher à ce mot que des idées métaphysiques, on continuera de raisonner sans s'entendre, . . ."

among others of their own kind. From the moment when we are "abandoned to ourselves" the *mal* well-known to the believer must become a social fact, an object of sociological inquiry, and the material of political endeavor. This is the realization that Rousseau attempts to articulate in an unprecedented way.

Within an analysis of society as a structure or order of dependence, the political problem of freedom appears in a particularly clear light. One line of Rousseau's thinking goes this way: man is the author of evil; evil is a kind of suffering; the unhappiness identified with suffering is a subjective side of social experience; that is why we can, even must, *learn* to suffer[141] and, in part thereby, learn to be happy. At the same time, because suffering is *social*—i.e., not natural, but also not providential or, as metaphysical, individual—it has a more clearly objective (or, perhaps more precisely, intersubjective) aspect as well. This aspect is oppression. The summary statement which begins *Du Contract social* goes to the heart of the matter: "Man is born free, and everywhere he is in chains [*l'homme est né libre, et par-tout il est dans les fers*]" (OC III.351). While conveying a complex implicit engagement with the common view of an interdependent world expressed by Diderot,[142] this bold statement is of course a direct challenge to any existing relations of power. It attributes an inalienable natural quality to individuals.[143] This challenge was the handle by which French and subsequent revolutionaries seized upon Rousseau's thought to make it into a sword.[144] In somewhat different terms, Rousseau supposed his concept of Society to have political value because it exposed the moral structure of, and thus, too, the possible moral constraints on, the problem of power (a theme developed with finer grain in §20 below). This is how the claim of *injustice* took first place in the arsenal of modern politics.[145] In turn, the sociology descendant from Rousseau treated the political problem of power within the frame of Rousseau's moral conception.

§6

MORAL DYNAMICS

The moral condition of a people is less the result of the absolute condition of each of its members than of the relations among them.* (OC III.511)

*"L'état moral d'un peuple résulte moins de l'état absolu de ses membres que de leurs rapports entre eux."

With the topic of Rousseau's moral conception we return to the main line to be considered here. It is not an easy line to draw. It is clear that the topic of morality occupied him in various ways.

Readers of Rousseau often give special attention to the theme of moral sentiments. One focuses easily on pity or compassion. It has been suggested that this is one central feature of his political thought.

To say this is not necessarily to say that Rousseau promotes an immediate application of fellow-feeling or love in one's relations with others. Nor is it to claim that it would be admirable to do so. Any cautious thinker is aware of the complex and often perverse stakes inherent in action. It is evident that "compassion and goodness may be related phenomena, but they are not the same," and plausible that "absolute goodness is hardly any less dangerous than absolute evil."[146] Indeed, Rousseau, with many other thinkers, has shown that it is best not to take the implication of compassion in politics *au premier degré*.[147]

Rousseau did prompt and remark upon the increasing gravity of compassion in social affairs. The potential for harm in this social fact appears when it is viewed within an analysis of the peculiarly modern belief that the human Will is a generative faculty and not simply a capacity for choosing. I shall have more to say about this later. Let it suffice for now to recall the way Hannah Arendt's inquiry into the idea of revolution highlights this problem. She makes clear how *avant-gardist* leaders like Robespierre justified supposedly selfless revolutionary acts of Will on the grounds of compassion, even as they produced terrible results.[148]

My point here is that although the theme of compassion may have consumed some of Rousseau's followers, it occupies only a corner of the moral domain explored in Rousseau's writings. There is an important sense in which compassion is simply left by the wayside of his major arguments. The capacity of some to imagine themselves as feeling the pain of fellow human beings, and thus to be, or to aspire to be, motivated not by self-interest but by identification with the suffering of others is only from a certain point of view a topic of morality. At times it may be a kind of narcissism.[149]

Considered from the perspective of the most fundamental conditions for the formation of political relationships, compassion may not be a topic of politics at all. At one extreme compassion is a mode of seeking agreement; it is intimately related to appeals to consensus. And no special perspicacity is required to see that where consensus is present politics becomes unnecessary. Rousseau was capable of extraordinary clear-sightedness on this point, notwithstanding the unitary image of both State and Society he often brings to mind. "If there were no difference at all between interests," he writes, "the common interest would never be faced with obstacles and one would hardly feel it: everything would run by itself, and politics would cease to be an art."[150]*

If compassion—understood here as a both capacity and disposition of an individual person—is not essential to the art of politics, which moral sentiments are?

This is a much more complicated question than it may seem. To answer it, one must at least provisionally set aside a whole discursive realm that is ultimately of high importance for Rousseau: *le contract social*.[151] This "social contract" brings before the mind a powerful image of radical rupture in historical time (either as a matter of fact or hypothesis). Such images ultimately impede our thinking with Rousseau. For, even a cursory reading of *any* of his texts will show that the most illuminating discussions do not focus on the "founding" of a polity, or, indeed, on ruptures of any kind.[152] This is obviously true for his first political "best-seller," the *Discours sur . . . l'inégalité*.[153] And even in *De la formation du corps politique* and *Du Contract social*[154] Rousseau is more concerned with what leads up to, and what develops after, that singular moment of discontinuity supposed to be implicit in the image of a "social contract." Unlike Hobbes, Rousseau never proposes that "man could be alive, and all the rest of the world annihilated."[155] Everything he has to say represents instead something implicated in processes of evolving *société*.

As Rousseau describes Man's historical developments of himself—which is to say, in the emergence of Society from the "state of nature," in the extended educational formation of a citizen like Émile, or in the maintenance of political order through enduring practices like "civil religion"[156]—the driving moral forces are typically *amour de soi-même* and *perfectibilité*.

These are key terms in Rousseau's vocabulary, and it would only muddy the waters to give single English equivalents here. Generally speaking, this emphasis on the human qualities of *amour de soi-même* and *perfectibilité* confirms what we have already seen: *la science des moeurs* does not study virtue *per se*, but rather it opens onto the indeterminate field of human relationships, where capacities and dispositions of persons play constitutive but not definitive roles.

Rousseau had in mind a distinction—that can be traced back to Augustine[157]—between approbable *amour de soi-même*, in which one cares for oneself, and destructive *amour-propre*, or pride. Of his near contemporaries, he seems in this respect to have followed Jacques Abbadie's popular *L'Art de se connoître soy-même, ou la Recherche des sources de la morale* (1694).[158] He appeals to this distinction in a famous and precisely stated footnote in the *Discours sur . . . l'iné-*

---

* ". . . s'il n'y avoit point d'intérêts différens, à peine sentiroit-on l'intérêt commun qui ne trouveroit jamais d'obstacle: tout iroit de lui-même, et la politique cesseroit d'être un art."

galité.[159] It will be relevant later in our argument that Rousseau confirms this view in *Émile*, writing that the quality of *amour de soi-même* is "essential to every sentient being [*essentiel à tout être qui se sent*]" (OC IV.589) and positive because it is "always good and always in conformance with order" (OC IV.491).

Figures of speech slip between the two books Rousseau wrote together, and a similar phrase in *Du Contract social* enlarges the significance of the claim just cited from *Émile*: "That which is good and in conformance with order is such by the nature of things and independently of human conventions. All justice comes from God, he alone is the source of it" (OC III.378).* The implication that only nature can be ordered is, of course, hyperbolic; we shall see that Rousseau's entire political project would be meaningless if this were literally true. Nonetheless, the application of this maxim to the topic of justice highlights what is at stake in Rousseau's distinction. The antithesis of *amour-propre* (which carries the sense that pride can be the servant of unregulated "self-interest") and *justice* was a widespread commonplace in the eighteenth century. To describe *amour de soi-même* in the same terms as *justice* is to solidify the wall between it and *amour-propre*. *Amour de soi-même* is shown to be a fact of human nature but nonetheless compatible with the highest of civic conventions.[160]

The second term—*perfectibilité*—refers to the fact that "we are born with the capacity to learn [*nous naissons capables d'apprendre*]";[161] it is nothing more and nothing less than the potential of human beings to apply experience to self-transformation.[162] How this potential fits into Rousseau's system will be considered at some length later in this book. A sort of sociological fate—in which, because intentions can only be realized through what I have elsewhere referred to as a "division of action," human qualities are actualized in *unintended* ways[163]—may wring perverse and corrupting effects from both *amour de soi-même* and *perfectibilité*.[164] Such effects are, as we have seen, entirely consistent with Rousseau's particular theodicy.

This brings us to another prominent point on Rousseau's moral compass. Its sign is the Will, or *volonté*.[165] It is on this point that many readers have facilely assimilated Rousseau to Immanuel Kant. At least in one important respect these two remarkable figures did see eye to eye, for Rousseau may fairly be thought to have advanced "the most categorical form of a pure ethics of obligation [*Gesetzes-Ethik*] that was established before Kant."[166] Kant himself might well have affirmed this; he viewed Rousseau as "the Newton of the moral world," and was influenced by him in many ways.[167] With this in mind, however, we should

---

* "Ce qui est bien et conforme à l'ordre est tel par la nature des choses et indépendamment des conventions humaines. Toute justice vient de Dieu, lui seul en est la source. . ."

also listen to those perspicacious critics who even while underscoring Rousseau's "rationalism" have objected to finding in him a Kantian *"avant la lettre."*[168] It is—in general and certainly for present purposes—a mistake, an all too common one at that, to conclude from Kant's attachment to Rousseau that Rousseau is best understood as a "precursor of Kant." These are the words of Alexis Philonenko, an important French-language translator and interpreter of Kant, whose monumental three-volume study of Rousseau has attained the status of required reading for French scholars. The historiographic problems with such a view are self-evident; the interpretive difficulties are as severe although less obvious. Readers like Philonenko take for granted that Rousseau was a philosopher, perhaps one of the sort we later find transforming all questions into metaphysics under the influence of professionalized German philosophy after Kant, Hegel, Husserl, and Heidegger. The by-product of such philosophical interests is unfortunate comments like "less human than Jean-Jacques, Kant was more rigorous," in which the stereotype of Rousseau is mirrored by one of Kant (in fact neither sustained a complete separation between passion and reason).[169] By contrast, I treat Rousseau as a social and political writer whose writings are, in many key respects, fruitfully antiphilosophical.[170]

Anyone familiar with contemporary philosophical ethics may perceive at this point a looming tension: is Rousseau's position a proto-Kantian deontology or some species of Aristotelian "virtue ethics"? I want to stress that here these classifications are beside the point. While virtue is a pivotal political notion for Rousseau, the themes under discussion here neither arise from nor culminate in considerations of virtue *per se*; his *science des moeurs* studies the field of human relationships, *le lien social*, and is thus closer to a type of sociology than to philosophy.[171] For this reason, and prompted by the comparison with Kant, we shall still need to consider how the Will enters into Rousseau's image of *la morale*. Thus extends before us a vast fabric of which only a few threads can be taken up here. Indeed, it will even be necessary to set aside for now another of Rousseau's most appealing and frustrating subjects, *la volonté générale*. We touch instead on the relationship between Will and the topics already introduced in this section.

Several pages back, I referred to *amour de soi-même* and *perfectibilité* variously as capacities or dispositions, or simply as human qualities. The Will is supposed to be something more precise: a primary faculty. Where the Will is by definition open-ended, *amour de soi-même* and *perfectibilité* are in certain respects highly structured or structuring. These qualities channel human action toward the good, amplifying and augmenting life alone and together. Nothing guarantees the same for the Will.

Although human Will may go its own way, it can, in Rousseau's view, sometimes be modulated by these other qualities. A *good* Will is typically guided by *amour de soi-même* and constantly refigured by *perfectibilité*.[172] If Will is a general motive force of change, *amour de soi-même* and *perfectibilité* have a more precise relation to human temporality: they are motors of social evolution.[173]

Of course, the modern image of the Will was to a large extent modeled on the Will of an omnipotent God.[174] The consequences of this fact for Rousseau's political theory of society will consume much of our attention in the following chapters. The basic pattern, however, is rather straightforward. In human Will, God re-created his own creative power, and made a gift of it to Man. No faculty could be greater: it is God's Will that has set the world in motion; without it the world would be nothing but dead matter. This is what the making of Man in God's own image requires: His abdication of responsibility for our actions and our world. And why should He not correct our mistakes? Because it would disallow His crowning achievement. Nature is the sign God leaves behind. The sign of human nature is Will. This sign must be as legible to reason and the heart as everything else in the order of nature. No one is born with this perspicacity. Thus, God gives another quality to human beings. This is the capacity to learn from experience, and especially from mistakes. We need *perfectibilité* in order to read ourselves, to discover the meaning of the Will. What is that meaning? It is our imperfection; it is that no matter how we are made in God's image, we are not gods, but fallen mortals who may see his heavenly city only at the end of time.

You may recognize all this. It is from another angle the theodicy by which Rousseau identifies mankind "abandoned to ourselves." What is striking about this is that *for just that reason* a thoroughly secularizing theodicy remains compatible with theological discourse. The very and entire humanness of our predicament exhibits the power of the Almighty. The island of the earth and its inhabitants manifest the memory of God. Theological language ceases to correspond to divine intervention. It becomes instead the sign-system — indeed, the most effective and persuasive sign-system — of an utterly human world.

God gives *volonté* to Man. Of God's gift Man makes something for himself. We make evil. *Volonté* is not sufficient to make good. Only from our second fundamental quality, *perfectibilité*, does Mankind obtain the possibility to rid ourselves of the evil we have ourselves wrought. We must apprehend the significance of our own Will. No additional tutelage from God can be expected.

Between *volonté* and *perfectibilité* a guiding force intervenes. That is *amour de soi-même*. In combination these three qualities become instrumental to the same end. That end is the human good, which is happiness. As we shall eventually come to see, movement toward this end is "intentional but not subjective";[175] it is neither the anticipation of nor the product of a Kantian deontology.

RUPTURE

The First Sign of the Will

Once having registered that Rousseau's primary analytical concern is with patterns by which *société* constantly undergoes transformations,[176] a more familiar facet of his engagement with politics may be admitted. Rousseau sometimes presents himself as interested in advancing the image of a radical break with the past. Indeed, it is not entirely by way of misunderstanding that he was taken as one of the "first authors of the French revolution" and became a motive for those who tried to extend it or who followed in its wake.[177]

This image of rupture may be seen to represent three things. The first is the topic that frames the inquiry of the book you are holding: it is a break with the divine, after which humanity is responsible for its own problems and solutions alike. The second is a boldly declarative assertion that became the central focus of readings of Rousseau offered by many subsequent political thinkers, but which will stay mainly in the background in this book: it is the radical break that occurs when *your*—the person who reads or hears Rousseau's words—situation is shown to be both bad and unjust. The third belief Rousseau hopes to inspire with the image of a radical break is that *we*—as individuals and as collectivities—have the potential for action, and thus to become something other than what we once were or are today.

This third belief involves a prophetic claim. No one has the potential for action the way an apple released from its branch has the potential to reach the ground. Human beings act, or they don't. But without this utopic moment, the symbol of the radical break would be crushing—figuring us as "abandoned to ourselves" in a terrible situation with no exit. Action is the way out.

Rousseau's oeuvre is bursting with representations of this type of rupture, displaying apparently uncrossable chasms of categorical difference. The "state of nature" stands for one, of course, but so does the simile of "the child," or the staging of the pedagogic relation between tutor and tutored.[178] Philosophers and followers of "systems" are likewise locked out from common sense. Even the drama of theological speculation sharpens our distance from the supreme being, and a *profession de foi*, unlike a demonstration of the existence of God, marks out one's unbreachable distance from Him.[179]

More prominently, however, and most famously, Rousseau also adopted the ripe terms of "contract theory" in this vein. While the present book will barely touch on this vastly complicated historical and theoretical *topos*, my purposes at this point are served by taking it, as most of Rousseau's followers and critics have, at face value. Consider the "social contract" in the following ways.

When Rousseau writes that "the social contract is the basis of all civil society" (OC IV.839) it appears as reference to a founding moment. Real or imaginary, that moment is necessary to justify the—one must again add, prophetic— assumption of perfect liberty. However, what comes into being from perfect liberty and its contraction is polity, not society, and especially not society in the distinctively modern sense that Rousseau himself invents.[180] For even if it were Rousseau's intention to situate the "social contract" within the broader group of human beings from which citizens emerge, he could not do it with a simple gesture to a concept—*société*—that is just taking its new and relevant form in his pages. When, then, Rousseau writes that "it is in the nature of that act that one must look for the nature of the society that it forms" (OC IV.839),* he points to the heuristic quality of the "social contract" itself. This leaves open whether any assembly actually voted or any document was signed. The radical break may be imaginary and still be a fact that bears fully—yesterday or tomorrow—on society. This much is well known.

Here I want to dwell for a moment on two additional of the various reasons for Rousseau's turn to this image. The first is that, in Rousseau's time, the *topos* of "contract" figured with increasing prominence in those discourses that sustained an emerging new conception of human Will.[181] This new way of understanding human beings' relation to their own acts and situations would soon become the brightest star in the conceptual constellation of modernity. The New Model Will—as I have called it elsewhere—was new because, instead of giving expression to the human capacity for judgment and choice, Will came to be seen as "a power of spontaneously beginning a series of successive things or states . . . a power of self-determination, independently of any coercion through sensuous impulses."[182] The structure and history of the New Model Will is the frame and staging of the "social contract" and it, too, is vastly beyond the scope of what we can consider in this book.[183] Nevertheless, we shall catch glimpses of its sig-

---

*"... c'est dans la nature de cet acte qu'il faut chercher celle de la societé qu'il forme. . . ."

nificance below. My point here is simply that, with an ideal of independent and even spontaneous action as its center of gravity, as the *informe* that constitutes the formative bond,[184] the "social contract" stood apart from other images of rupture. It prompted a rejection of nostalgia. This gave it a powerful political potential.[185]

The political potential Rousseau had in mind, however, was not the supposedly unmediated rupture associated with revolution. It is true, of course, that he often wrote inspiring sentences like "the passage from the state of nature to the civil state produces a very remarkable transformation in man" (OC III.364) or "by way of the social pact [*le pacte social*] we have given existence and life to the body politic [*corps politique*]."[186] But these are speculative facts, not historical ones.[187] The "social contract" is used here to figure the otherwise invisible human faculty of the Will, and to justify its application. One might even say that this represents the transmission, however distorted, of Will from God to Man. By contrast, the conceptual paradigm for applied human Will in society is not founding but legislation, for "the general Will . . . is the law [*la volonté générale . . . est la loi*]" (OC III.380, note). It is from this application that the historical facts will issue, not the other way around.[188]

A second reason for Rousseau's attachment to the image of "social contract" follows from the first one.[189] The Will was—as he himself clearly indicated— Rousseau's "first principle." Against, for example, Thomas Hobbes's mechanistic account of motion, and thus of life,[190] Rousseau adopts the voice of a *"Vicaire Savoyard"*[191] to insist that "the principle of every action is in the Will of a free being" (OC IV.586) and "one must always trace back to some Will [to find] the first cause. . . . In a word, all movement which is not produced by another [external source] can only come from a spontaneous, voluntary act. . . . there is absolutely no true action without Will. There you have my first principle" (OC IV.576).* To this he adds the compatible theological generalization: "I therefore believe that a Will moves the universe and animates nature. There you have my first dogma, or my first article of faith" (OC IV.576).†

In Rousseau's construction, the Will can also become the primary force in social affairs. It can be put to ameliorative work. It can take juridical form through a

---

*"... il faut toujours remonter à quelque volonté pour prémiére cause; ... En un mot, tout mouvement qui n'est pas produit par un autre, ne peut venir que d'un acte spontané, volontaire; ... il n'y a point de véritable action sans volonté. Voilà mon prémier principe."

†"Je crois donc qu'une volonté meut l'univers et anime la nature. Voilà mon prémier dogme, ou mon prémier article de foi."

system of civil laws. These laws must be as inflexible as the laws of nature. Everything—the very possibility of freedom and happiness—hinges on these absolute yet voluntary obligations. That is why it is not an exaggeration, contrary to the intuitions of most interpreters, to say that "Rousseau—in opposition to the predominant opinion of the century—eliminated feeling from the foundation of ethics."[192]

Does such a shift, as voiced by the *vicaire savoyard*, place Rousseau as a kind of neo-Cartesian?[193] It does not.[194] More plausibly, it seems to affirm Cassirer's assessment of him as proto-Kantian in at least two linked ways: first, the Will has become fundamental;[195] second, as the Will manifests a type of instability inherent in the human condition, it escapes identification with reason, and appears instead as always already entangled with judgment. Attending judgment are both passion and reason, together with other faculties traditionally associated with the rhetorical triumvirate of *ethos*, *pathos*, and *logos*, such as memory and imagination.[196]

§8

JUDGMENT

The Significance of the Will

Even though Rousseau asserts the Will as a "first principle" in the context of a "profession of faith," the problem that structures his thinking is not, as Paul DeMan astutely observed, "how to construe an interpretation of existence by means of a rule of inner assent, but to account, by a critical act of judgment, for the occurrence of such an assent and to establish its epistemological status." Thus, "the main informing concept of [the *"Profession de foi du vicaire savoyard"*] is that of *judgment*, not inner light or inner assent."[197] Nor is it, we may add, any of the other practices the Will is typically understood to represent.

Few commentators have seen so clearly this political pressure-point in Rousseau's writings. No matter how much theological vocabulary is marshaled, Rousseau is not, finally, on Augustinian terrain; no matter how much the affiliation of Will and reason rings familiar today, he was not in this respect a Kantian.[198] Rousseau, with extraordinary perspicacity, deploys terms like Will to advance a kind of rhetorical sociology.[199] With this in mind we can see that DeMan sets a rare and admirable example by bringing into question the exact status of the Will as invoked by Rousseau.

There is good reason to insist that Rousseau's Will is conceived within a pre-Kantian tradition. For, as DeMan points out, no matter how one construes the *"Profession de foi,"* in it "the principle of immanence is in fact being superseded by an act of judgment which does not necessarily claim to possess the constitutive or generative power of a *cogito."*[200]

This point can be restated in somewhat different terms. However Rousseau may have heralded and contributed to what I have called the New Model Will, he must not be read as presupposing it. In the earlier *Discours sur . . . l'inégalité* he identifies "the capacity to will [*la puissance de vouloir*]" with "the capacity to choose [*la puissance de choisir*]" (OC III.142). This identification is reasserted in the *"Profession de foi"* when Rousseau makes clear that the Will is tightly tied to one's capacity for judgment. He writes that: "if one really understands that Man is active in his judgments, that his understanding is only the power to compare and to judge, one will see that one's liberty is only a similar power, or derived from it" (OC IV.586).* *Volonté–choisir–liberté*, Will–choice–freedom: this idea is noteworthy for its classicism. *Volonté* gleans from προαίρεσις the cultivated capacity to discern alternatives and put one before the other; like Aristotle Rousseau is careful to distinguish this from how one follows passion, wish, some form of opinion, or mere desire (as the source verb *vouloir* might suggest).[201]

Rousseau presses to specify *volonté* further with an unflinching series of questions. He asks himself "what is thus the cause that determines one's Will?" and replies "it is one's judgment." Then he asks "and what is the cause that determines one's judgment?" (OC IV.586).

This will be the last step Rousseau takes. "Beyond that, I understand nothing further." The position Rousseau adopts is striking: one's judgment is determined by "one's faculty of intelligence" which is "one's capacity to judge." In this way, Will and the liberty it represents, together with the faculties of understanding and intelligence, are all traced back to judgment, of which "the determining cause is in judgment itself [*la cause déterminante est en lui-même*]" (OC IV.586),

Is this a kind of Cartesian reduction of "judgment" to a first principle? Does it contradict DeMan's assessment of the *"Profession?"* Earlier in the text Rousseau seems headed in this direction when he asks "But who am I? What right do I have

---

* ". . . si l'on comprend bien que l'homme est actif dans ses jugemens, que son entendement n'est que le pouvoir de comparer et de juger, on verra que sa liberté n'est qu'un pouvoir semblable, ou dérivé de celui-là . . ."

to judge things, and what determines my judgments?" (OC IV.570).* From this he draws the immediate consequence that "It is, thus, necessary that I first turn my attention to myself in order to acquaint myself with the instrument I will employ and to know to what extent I can rely on it" (OC IV.570).†

Of course, such an ontological question and its interrogative mood[202] scream "Descartes!" But something different and more intriguing occurs at the same time. Rousseau immediately draws his reader's energies in another direction. The topic is not "being" but "judgment." Judgment is elaborated in terms of "instruments." Instruments are those things that connect mental life to one's practical engagement with the world. Building on these elements, the next paragraph responds in perfect antithesis to a Cartesian reader's expectation. Rousseau asserts Descartes' conclusion as premise—"I exist [J'existe]"—and adds that the "the first truth which strikes me [la prémiére vérité qui me frape]" is that "I have senses by which I am affected [j'ai des sens par lesquels je suis affecté]" (OC IV.570).

Everything begins with "being affected." In other words, everything begins with the connection to the world. Thus, if judgment is the basis of Will, and judgment is a matter of one's relation to the world through the fact of being affected by the senses, then, as DeMan suggests, the "principle of immanence" supposed (by, for example, Kant) to characterize the Will is "in fact being superseded." Perhaps Rousseau leads us through a closed or even tautological circle of concepts, but he thereby circumscribes a practical or sociological fact, not an epistemological one.

Keep this in mind. Is it this sort of Will that operates most often in *Émile?* How deeply does it extend into his other writings? Does it provide a basis for critical insight into Rousseau's application of Will to politics?

All of these possibilities must be measured against the figure of the Will as substance exhibited in the preceding section (§7). The two accounts seem profoundly contradictory, and how tenaciously, and with what consequence, Rousseau holds to the notion of the Will as substance is something we shall only see in detail much later in this book.

For now, however, we may ask why these contradictions remain as literary facts in the *"Profession."* DeMan is again helpful on this point. He applies in a particularly incisive way Rousseau's own *topos* of judgment to the operation of Rousseau's writing: "Despite the apparent confusion of its point of departure, it is

---

* "Mais qui suis-je? Quel droit ai-je juger les choses, et qu'est-ce qui détermine mes jugemens?"

† "Il faut donc tourner d'abord mes regards sur moi pour connoitre l'instrument dont je veux me servir, et jusqu'à quel point je puis me fier à son usage."

not in fact confused by its own inconsistencies. It immediately draws the correct inferences from difficulties that could well have paralyzed the argument from the outset. . . . Rousseau acknowledges at once the indeterminacy of his own self-reflection by moving into a *critical* vocabulary."[203] It should be said that Rousseau pretends to segregate critical self-reflection into the second part of the "*Profession*," where the topic quite explicitly shifts from belief in God to established religion. DeMan shows that this move occurs already near the beginning of the text. From this, he develops a general claim. A cooperation of certitude and skepticism is exposed as the alternatives are presented by the Vicar, to himself, for his own judgment. The result is not simply an exhibition of different perspectives; the reader is led to an altogether different theme: "The argument of the *Profession de foi* serves to reveal the structure of judgment in Rousseau and to establish its relationship to other key concepts such as Will, freedom, reason, etc."[204]

Thus, in this additional sense the priority given to *jugement* is anti-Cartesian because it fails to assert and maintain a clear boundary between what is intelligible and what is sensible, the cognitive and the bodily. Likewise, this second conception of the Will undermines the image of rupture typically associated with it. The Will functions as a marker for practical, not metaphysical, liberty, a liberty whose essence is the exercise of judgment.[205] Extending this point to Rousseau's political theory would eventually require us to understand even the paradigms of rupture—the "general Will" and the "social contract" it sustains— as evolutionary, rather than revolutionary, forces. And just this dedication to evolution—so profoundly evident in the *Discours sur . . . l'inégalité*—would be sufficient to distinguish Rousseau from Kant.[206]

Such an approach to larger questions about the political significance of Rousseau's way of thinking—ignited in this section by skepticism about the Will— gives further support to something I wrote in the preceding section. It is difficult to agree with those who argue that compassion (*pitié*) is the key to Rousseau's vision of politics. While the triumphs and failures of this sentiment are flamboyantly displayed in Rousseau's fictions, and it does enter as symptom and motive in his political diagnostics, only across a distance of several levels of analysis is it fundamental to them.[207] Even if Rousseau writes that "it is quite certain that compassion is a natural sentiment" (OC III.156), it is equally important to recall that Rousseau in no way believes that all that is natural is good. This is especially true after the evolution of society is under way, and "good social institutions are those which know how best to take Man away from nature [*les bonnes institutions sociales sont celles qui savent le mieux dénaturer l'homme*]."[208] Compassion should be understood in almost every instance not with respect to a supposedly immediate nature but rather as mediated by a deeper commitment to the Will.[209]

The purpose of this section has been to underscore, albeit without extensive development, what this commitment may involve. Rousseau does not bring the modern conception of the Will to fruition. His thinking is planted in the space in which the New Model Will is still growing. Thus, as DeMan suggests, Rousseau's commitment to the Will does not bring him over to the side of *reason*, as readers after Kant might expect. It locates him instead—in multiple and often obscure ways—on the much broader and explicitly social terrain of *judgment*.

It may therefore be fair to suggest that a proper reading of Rousseau would be of great service to contemporary political theory. For it reveals the quintessentially modern development of the New Model Will in a more incisive and productive way than anything we may learn by lingering *ad infinitum* over the full-grown philosophical version tended by Kant. But that is a story for another time.

§9

Persons *Versus* Things

Rousseau was the first to recognize that there are many ways to read what he wrote.[210] Whichever way one takes him, however, it is not hard to understand how his thinking began to orbit around the idea of *société*. He tells us where it came from in a defense of the idea itself as he responds to the condemnation of *Émile* by Christophe de Beaumont, archbishop of Paris, immediately following its publication in 1762.[211] For it is his "ordinary method" in polemics, he tells the antagonistic Beaumont, to "give the history of my ideas," and by this means to repeat the process of reasoning that led to his beliefs.

From the earliest age, Rousseau recounts, he "watched what people did and listened to them speak." When he discovered that "their actions in no way resembled what they said" he "sought the further cause" of that fact. This cause he found in the "contradiction" between "our social order" and the way things naturally fit together. "Tracing out the consequences of that contradiction, I saw that it alone explained all the vices of men and all the evils of society. From this I concluded that it was not necessary to suppose that Man is bad by his very nature, since one can locate the origin and the progress of his badness." In other words, it was the process of grappling with the central question of theodicy that moved Rousseau to sharply distinguish *société* from everything else. With that line drawn, he felt compelled to pursue "new research into the human spirit [*esprit humain*] considered in its civil estate." This led him to two further facts. The first is that "changes in enlightenment and vice always occur for the same reasons [*le développement des lumieres et des vices se faisoit toujours en même raison*]." The second is that these developments occur "not in individuals, but in peoples [*non dans les individus, mais dans les peuples*]." Guided by these observations it becomes possible to see the earth as peopled by plural mankind rather than isolated individuals; humanity occupies the "island" of Men, not Man.[212]

Rousseau knows full well that this fundamental distinction is novel and will be unfamiliar for many of his readers. While it is one that he "always made with the greatest care" it is nevertheless, he brittlely asserts, something "that no one among those who have attacked me has ever been able to conceive."

It may seem that since the discovery of *société* was driven by "new research into *l'esprit humain*,"[213] the mechanisms that collect and motivate this plurality may be understood in psychological terms. But Rousseau's psychology is not mentalistic; it is entirely relational in the manner of Aristotle's *Rhetoric* and the tradition generated by it.[214] Each human faculty casts and retrieves a specific and embodied person into and from relations with others of his kind. There is no purely inner life; even Rousseau's logorrhoetic confessional posturing exhibits the relational character of the "self."[215] The combined operation of reason and passion and Will constitute a space among persons. The only cement sufficient to hold together all the topics that appear in Rousseau's writings is a conception of "Society."

Whatever "Society" may be, it is in common sense and learned belief—from Rousseau's time to ours—made up of subjects and not objects. It is a matter of what goes on "intersubjectively" among persons. It seems almost a *non sequitur* to say that it is not essentially about the circulation of things.

Such a sharp distinction between *persons* and *things* is exceedingly old and deep-seated. It falls into Rousseau's hands not only from the world he hates to love, but also from the books he loves to read, as when Plato begins to lead the "young Socrates" toward the idea of the Statesman by dividing the whole of "knowledge which commands" into "one part [which] may be set over the production of lifeless [objects], the other of living objects."[216] On the one hand, this could be read as a major premise in Rousseau's basic logic of "the social." On the other hand, no matter how much he admired and was influenced by Plato, adopting from him many topics and fields of inquiry, Rousseau was no kind of Platonist. It is therefore not credible that he would fall back on the transcendental apparatus that will again provide a refuge for some who follow him, like

Kant. The source and significance of his particular use of this distinction lie elsewhere.[217]

Exactly how fundamental is this distinction for Rousseau? The astute reader, taking in with care one line after another of what Rousseau actually wrote, will have difficulty keeping in view a clear division between *persons* and *things*. It seems that the study of mankind "abandoned to ourselves" is complex in ways that cannot be so neatly contained.

A view of what this complexity entails for inquiry is laid out with remarkable clarity, method, and theoretical implication in the *Traité de Sphére*.[218] I take Rousseau to be less guarded in this unfinished draft, allowing his intuitions freer rein, than in works he fine-tuned for the public. In any event, consider the way Rousseau introduces his bold program here: "To learn to know ourselves, we thus begin by studying what surrounds us."* The steps in this process follow the order of the human sciences and the principle of plurality: "To know oneself, one must know Man. To know Man, one must study Men; and to know Men, one must study them in various times, in various places. One must begin by seeing them in the great tableau of History."† In this important respect, then, it is illuminating to view this program retrospectively. The *Traité de Sphére* offers itself as an early— perhaps the first—textbook of a comprehensive sociology.

With this in mind, it is Rousseau's next step that I want to underscore. For, a few lines later he counts among our "surroundings" all the things of the earth: "Before seeking the origin of the human species, cast a glance over its dwelling."§ It is as if, we may say half in jest, Lyell must come before Darwin who must come before Marx. And certainly Buffon precedes them all, for when our eyes begin to open we can see, again with Rousseau, "this earth covered with so many trees and plants, so many mountains and valleys, so many cliffs and seas, this vast world without limit and without end."** For "our material eyes [*nos yeux matériels*]" the earth is huge; for "the eyes of our reason [*les yeux de nôtre raison*]" it is tiny.

Rousseau's magnificent imagery now moves on, recalling and amplifying the *topos* of the "island."[219]

---

* "Pour apprendre à nous connoître, commençons donc par étudier ce qui nous entoure."

† "Pour se connoître, il faut connoître l'homme. Pour connoître l'homme, il faut étudier les hommes; et pour connoître les hommes, il les faut étudier en divers tem, en divers lieux. Il faut commencer par les voir dans le grand tableau de l'Histoire. . . ."

§ "Avant de rechercher l'origine du genre humain, jettons un coup d'oeil sur sa demeure"

** ". . . cette terre couverte de tant d'arbres et de plantes, de tant de Montagnes et de Vallées, de tant de rochers et de mers; ce vaste monde sans borne et sans bout. . . ."

Passage by Rousseau

"Into the immense space of the skies [*des airs*], that terrifying expanse where even imagination drowns, by thought I transport myself to one of these enormous and luminous masses that roll majestically over our heads,

and I perceive from afar a grain of sand afloat in that airy sea.

Minuscule, it escapes my view, and I can only pick it out with glasses [*lunettes*].

With a laugh I ask, Are there bugs small enough to inhabit this grain of sand? Undoubtedly, a local philosopher tells me, it is covered with who knows what kind of tiny insects who call themselves 'Men'. . . ."*

Commentary

■ The word *air* sets the polysemic tones of this passage as it resonates here in several ways: with the Classical/Renaissance view that the world is composed of four elements; with the belief that we live in a sphere that exists below God, as in Nicot's (1606) identification of the phrase "*a l'air*" with the Latin *sub dio*; with "*une certaine maniere que l'on a dans . . . la façon d'agir,*" as *air* is defined by the *Académie françoise* (1694), which refers especially to the signs of a person's character that can be read off his or her face (recall the image of the *masque* at note 35 above). That an *air* is also a song could not have escaped Rousseau's attention.

■ Referring here, presumably, to the rather different utopias of clouds and stars.

■ In this way the planet Earth, floating in the heavens, is assimilated to the island of mankind, also Earth, which is marked as precisely delimited by virtue of being surrounded by the sea.

■ *Lunettes* are glasses that improve close vision, but also the type of sliding telescopes used by a ship's captain and thought to have been invented by Galileo (*Académie françoise*, 1694). Thus, with one word,

---

*"Dans l'immense espace des airs, dans cette Etenduë effrayante où l'imagination se noye, je me transporte par la pensée dans quelqu'une de ces masses énormes et lumineuses, qui roulent majesteusement sur nos têtes; et j'apperçois de loin un grain de sable, qui flotte dans cette mer aërienne. Il échappe à ma vuë par sa petitesse, il me faut des lunettes pour

Rousseau invokes images of the close inspection of the scholar (literally, θεωρέω), adventurous travel to satisfy curiosity with civic intent (common figurative sense of θεωρέω), in this case specifically to an "island," and the figure and sensibility of Galileo by metonymy with his invention; these are the two eyes–"material" and "rational"–mentioned just above. All this is in the service of essentially rhetorical θεωρια, or social scientific "discovery," as in Aristotle, *Rhetoric*, 1355b25–26. This gesture, together with Rousseau's powerful admiration for both Galileo and his father, supports my argument that Rousseau has Galileo's method in mind at the architectonic level of his social theory of politics (see §31).

Again the "island" is more than the *locus* of mankind "abandoned to ourselves." It is a horizon, the vanishing point for human experience in a material universe. It also constitutes a nexus of the human sciences with the sciences of nature.

No wonder, then, that as we embark with Rousseau on his new program of sociological inquiry it is difficult to maintain the distinction between *persons* and *things*.

Indeed, the distinction fades further from view as bodies fill Rousseau's pages and persons appear in their most object-like forms. Even our author's words seem to have "guts and tits," as Joubert insisted.[220] Rousseau's characters are, from birth, "affected in various ways by the objects that surround us" (OC IV.248). They squabble interminably over the slightest child's toy or *bibelot*—every act and interaction seems thoroughly bound to its objects.

Compelled by this ambivalence, it is easy to imagine how some of the most

———

l'appercevoir. Je demande en riant, s'il y a des cirons assés petits pour habiter sur ce grain de sable? Sans doute, me dit un Philosophe de lieu, il est couvert de je ne sais quels petits insectes qui s'appellent hommes. . . ."

perspicacious readers of Rousseau loosened their attachment to the fundamental priority that, as we shall see shortly, he gave to *persons* over *things*. Marx, for example, who was attracted by the sociological account of inequality and repelled by the *a priori* fiction of "the state of nature," evokes in the pages of the *German Ideology* a "sensuous world" that is hard to square, especially after Kant, with a radical distinction between persons and things. Hegel, Rousseau-steeped and the proximate forebearer of this sensibility in Marx, bluntly places Rousseau's problematic at the center of his theorization of society as a "system of needs." Yet, already in its earliest version, this was "conceived formally . . . as a system of universal physical dependence on one another" because "for the totality of his need no one is independent."[221] After several decades of further reflection, Hegel will be figuring the same "system of needs" in terms of the many-sided construction of dependence in *work* precisely because he wants to illustrate the necessary role played by objects in social relationships.[222]

But these are ambivalent voices of dissent against a strict logic of the social, a logic most famously represented by Durkheim's utopian admonition to "treat social facts as things [considérer les faits sociaux comme des choses]" precisely because — despite lingering positivist aspirations — that is what they never can be. Contrary to the observations I have just registered, Rousseau asserted this logic with the greatest clarity and vigor. From that historical moment forward it has been incorporated into common sense. It is the conviction of Rousseau's assertion and the power of our common sense that motivate the following pages, where for my critical purposes I will emphasize the categorical divide between persons and things. I take this course even while admitting that, as a matter of narrative facility and propitious description, the blending of persons and things in Rousseau's texts seems natural, almost inevitable.

Rousseau depends on this double discursive effect. It inheres in his capacious and enchanting dialectical style. It is important because Rousseau's elaborately structured theoretical approach to the distinction between persons and things is imprinted on the vast majority of subsequent representations of society. It undergirds our thinking when we think about it, and it underpins our beliefs when we don't think about it. Thus, my aim here is to make explicit the fundamental architecture of his thought before setting out to tear it down.

10

Consequences of Intersubjectivity

In Rousseau's view of Society, the experience of things — to be aided, stumped, or trumped by *les choses* — is important primarily for psychological reasons. Spatial, physical, or immediately practical effects are secondary.

This psychology is not a blunt, perception-based cognitivism. It is concerned instead with the relation between mind and object as that relation is mediated through one person's relations to others.[223] As much as they shape interaction, psychological functions and developments also derive from interaction.[224]

But, within this psychological perspective, things themselves remain merely instrumental. The main point — as we shall soon see — is that they are not supposed to be of *moral* consequence.

With things excluded in this way Society may be understood as pure intersubjectivity, and *needs* are taken to be the central social fact.

Although the most famous theoretical accounts of intersubjectivity pictured it in unabashedly transcendental terms (that is, in the Kantian mood of speculation about necessary conditions a priori) that conception cannot be applied to Rousseau.[225] For, in his writings the intersubjectivity of Society develops over time, and narrative representation of this development makes intersubjectivity appear as an issue of history.

This appearance, too, is somewhat misleading. Rousseau's history is famously speculative, not factual. It is an emplotment of idea and experience.[226] Thus, the representation of intersubjectivity in works like the *Discours sur . . . l'inégalité* or *Émile* might be more aptly called a phenomenology of the social than a historical account of intersubjectivity.[227] The logic is clearly dialectical: at each moment along time's arrow the seeds of the next moment are cultivated. The process continues until a qualitative threshold is passed. The multiplication of simple needs leads not just to manifold and rapacious desires, but to a system of relationships in which such desire is imposed on individuals from outside the Self as a function of everyday life with others. Crossing this line also changes the primary use of the Will, which must subsequently be applied not just to the satisfaction of need but to holding desire in check.[228] This is what Rousseau believed himself to have discovered by observing his own contemporaries.

Still, the key theoretical framework eschews the empirical.[229] Depending as it does on the figure of the "state of nature," and subject to an obsessive analytical and terminological rigor, Rousseau's logic of the social turns out to be profoundly antihistorical.[230] In the *Discours sur . . . l'inégalité*, he summarily describes the system of social evil as driven by invidious comparison—a process in which natural Man, consequent to his entrance into social relations, is corrupted by increasingly unsatisfiable desires. While corruption may be historical, the object of that corruption is not. For Rousseau comparison is a fundamental human mechanism and it exists, in a certain sense, out of time.[231]

Such comparisons may center around things, or they may not. This either/or is important. It shows clearly that, in Rousseau's formulation of the problem of political morality, the relation between persons and things is inessential.

This observation turns us back to Cassirer and the way he measures Rousseau's moral theory. On this point Rousseau decidedly *does* make a shift similar to what Kant will later propose. Indeed, he does so with a beautiful, earthy crudity. This continuity went unacknowledged by Kant the writer but was clearly seductive to Kant the reader.[232] Insofar as Rousseau reduced *things* to a mere auxiliary in social life, he prepares the ground for a "categorical form of a pure ethics of obligation."[233]

Readers typically adopt philosophical terminology to grapple with Rousseau's excision of things from ethical and political thinking. They categorize him as an "idealist" rather than a "materialist." He is widely known as "the great forerunner of German and English Idealism" and the precursor or quintessence of Romantic naturalism.[234] These approaches are not edifying and are certainly incomplete. At best they provide a point of departure.

To see the basis for my objection here I need to bring to the foreground the framework of analysis in the present book. Rather than stage an encounter with Rousseau *as if* he were a philosopher, or between Rousseau and philosophical traditions like "idealism" or "materialism," my project is to read the wide range of materials Rousseau places before us within the pragmatic and empirical perspective of social and political theory.[235] This of course puts us, writer and reader, at odds with the aspect of Rousseau's thinking underscored in this section. For here he is indeed a precursor to Kant. This is the type of Kantianism that monopolized the social sciences as much as the field of ethics at the crucial moment of the formation of the modern disciplines in the late nineteenth and early twentieth centuries.

My wariness here concerns the founding assumptions of the social sciences. Sociology in the broad sense of this book has historically been and is properly understood as being driven by interests closely tied to rhetorical traditions. The interests of philosophy are a distraction at best and often outright incompatible with the project to connect sociology to a theory of civic life. That modern philosophers themselves have sometimes understood this problem is incisively expressed by Gillian Rose in *Hegel Contra Sociology*. "The thought of Durkheim and Weber," she writes provocatively, "in spite of the divergences, rests on an identical framework: 'the neo-Kantian paradigm.'" Although this "transcendental structure of [their] thought has been persistently overlooked," in fact "the neo-Kantian paradigm is the source of both the strengths and weaknesses of Durkheim's and of Weber's sociology." Even critical approaches like "Phenomenology and the Marxism of the Frankfurt School . . . remain essentially within that paradigm" and "the very idea of a scientific sociology . . . is only possible as a form of neo-Kantianism."[236]

I will not say whether or not Rose exaggerates this conclusion. Her observation, however, is astute and important. The images and analyses of *société* developed by Rousseau both *are* and *are not* neo-Kantian. To collapse this complexity from the outset by appeal to a neat binary division between "idealist" and "materialist" would frustrate rather than advance our purpose.

Within the perspective of social and political theory, the neglect or dismissal of *things* does not belong to a philosophical school or tendency; it does not have a single clear name. It is a characteristic feature of many approaches to the overlapping objects of inquiry we refer to as "*le lien social*," the "social fact," "intersubjectivity," and so forth.

It is the possibility of discovering the opposite that motivates this book. Could there be a sociology, a social theory of politics, that takes seriously the implacable fact that everyday life with *others* is necessarily filled with *things*? If such a way of "thinking what we are doing" exists today, it has no name at all. If human relationships are essentially mediated by a world of things, it is time to make political theory adequate to that fact.

11

The Political Sociology
of the "Golden Rule"

In the Sermon on the Mount, Jesus set out an ethical doctrine in striking sentences and with persuasive authority. Circling around issues of human justice, gesturing to God, the speech attains a high point in a powerful maxim where he invites the auditor to place himself or herself at the center of moral life:

> Therefore all things whatsoever ye would that men should do to you, do ye even so to them: for this is the law and the prophets.[237]

Many intuitions and commitments are reflected here. They are not specific to Christianity. Versions of this "Golden Rule" can be found as broadly spread across history and various cultures as any form of human wisdom.[238]

The attraction of the "Golden Rule," I think, is that it is a law that is not handed down from above and that it locates the prophets squarely within humanity. No lifting eyes up to heaven or casting down to damnation is required. It proposes simply that you look your neighbor and yourself in the eye and pause for reflection. This is common sense wide and deep. The "Golden Rule" is an ancient maxim with continuing currency, popular in every sense of the word, and it provides Rousseau with a kind of ground for argument that serves him well.

Rousseau appeals to it in two ways at once. He abstracts its core concept, thus moving it away from common sense. And he relies on his reader's everyday adherence to it, thus reinforcing its status as common sense. On the one hand, Rousseau attacks as unnatural and unrealistic the proposition "do to others as you want one to do to you," calling it with some sarcasm a "sublime maxim of rational justice" (OC III.156). On the other hand, it is just such a concept of rationally calculated reciprocity that will shape the architecture for his reconstruction of the *système social* through law. What separates these two gestures? What brings them together?

Much of what is essential to the "Golden Rule" is not stated in it. Just under the surface of this hypothetical imperative (of the form *if* this, *then* that) are assumptions about both the dignity of human beings and the special status of the relationships we entertain among ourselves.

This maxim also stands on and is fortified by one of the oldest and most basic features of moral thought: the distinction between persons and things. For the "Golden Rule" requires reflection, which things cannot undertake; it requires reciprocity, which things cannot offer; reciprocity requires equality, for which things have no use.[239] Equality is only meaningful among persons, and the "Golden Rule" demands that morality be measured by it. Thus a clear line is drawn between the domain claimed by the "Golden Rule" and the realm of things.

It is this second level of significance in the "Golden Rule," its subtext, that is of interest here. It brings a discussion of Rousseau back around to Immanuel Kant, the follower of Rousseau most often said to give precise definition to his ideas.

Inattentive readers of Kant have often thought that he simply restated the "Golden Rule." Or that he applied to it a new philosophical rigor. Kant explicitly denies this. Like Rousseau he is skeptical of the "Golden Rule" but his objections are different. Rousseau declines the "Golden Rule" *because it is* a "sublime maxim of rational justice"; Kant dismisses it precisely *because it is not* the "sublime maxim of rational justice" that he seeks. Indeed, as Kant finds that the "Golden Rule" could provide an argument for a convicted criminal to dispute the rule of a judge, he insists that it offers a trivial and misleading approach to ethics. It is merely "hypothetical" and not "categorical," merely contingent and not necessary. Thus, it cannot rise to the level of a universal principle.[240]

Concerning ethical life, Rousseau believes the "human race would have ceased to exist long ago if its preservation depended only on the reasonings of those who compose it" (OC III.156–57). When it comes to civic life, however, he takes a different position. Ready as he is to "take Men as they are" it is the task of reason alone to discover "laws as they can be" (OC III.351). Should there be a "sublime maxim of rational justice" that could hold us to the measure of reciprocity, for Rousseau it would be a matter of practical experience not theoretical speculation. Only where law in fact comes into force, in a political constitution that sustains the rule of law, can there be a principle of this kind.

Kant disagrees on this key point. He is dissatisfied with the "Golden Rule" because it cannot raise reciprocity to the level of universality.[241] Unlike Rousseau, however, he proposes a way to make reciprocity a satisfactory ethical principle. He postulates that human beings exist in a *noumenal* realm. This realm is both transcendental and intelligible but distinct from experience. For just that reason it is universal. Law also exists in this realm, where it is obligatory without the force and institutions we normally associate with it. This law imposes itself with nothing more than the pure reason of an autonomous agent. With reciprocity relocated under the universal law of this transcendental and intelligible realm, it is possible, Kant tells us, to state a principle that is as binding for ethical life as anything we can imagine for politics. The ethics of the "Golden Rule" assumes a binary relationship between *I* and *Thou*. Kant augments this with a third element, universal law. The two parties identify with the law (that is the meaning of autonomy, or "giving the law to oneself") and are also mediated by it. This principle is a "categorical imperative," demanding that one "Act only on that maxim through which you can at the same time will that it should become a universal law."[242] Again, the condition of universality derives from the way the law is abstracted from any particular circumstances. It guarantees that the maxim applies to the moral agent who applies the maxim because the law, made by an autonomous lawmaker, applies to subject and legislator alike. Framed this way, the "categorical imperative" is said both to define what is right to do and to force one to do it. It is enough that it appears in one's conscience for it to become obligatory.

Kant assumes that no rational human being would desire to be treated as someone else's instrument or slave. Thus, to show that the universal form given to the maxim imposes on it a certain content as well, Kant restates the "categorical imperative" this way: "Act in such a way that you always treat humanity, whether in your own person or in the person of any other, never simply as a means, but always at the same time as an end."[243] Kant excels as he first locates the fault in the "Golden Rule," then discovers the general perspective of which the "Golden Rule" is merely one incomplete instance, and finally attempts to strengthen the ethical mechanism it represents.

Now consider the logic of this argument. Kant effectively adopts Rousseau's political formulation of the rule of law; he refigures it as an ethical doctrine; to make it binding he applies Rousseau's principle of autonomy to that doctrine; appealing to autonomy he invokes the further assumption that no rational human being would rule over himself or herself in such a way as to make him or her unhappy.[244]

What is the purpose of this brief excursion with Kant? For, I still hold to the claim that we cannot understand Rousseau, or understand the fundamental structures that social theory inherited from him, if we simply accept or dismiss him as a precursor of Kant.

My purpose here is to qualify this claim. As a general matter, Kant formulated the problem of ethical life, which is to say the problem of freedom, in a way that makes it vastly simpler than the problem of freedom in political life that Rousseau confronted.[245] Yet the structures of thought remain analogous. And the simpler provides an excellent gloss for the more complex. This holds especially for the point that concerns us here, which is the distinction between persons and things. For, despite the shift from politics to ethics, Kant brings clarity and precision to the constellation of topics in which this distinction takes shape and produces its effects. His image of an ethical principle that raises the common sense of the "Golden Rule" to a philosophically rigorous "categorical imperative" will shed light on this important feature of Rousseau's social theory of politics.

More specifically, my purpose in this section is to move the discussion toward a central line of inquiry in this book. The distinction between persons and things is a station to be visited several times along the way. What is essential to understanding the structures and flaws of Rousseau's social theory of politics is to see the way he builds on and upholds the significance of that difference.

The introduction here of this topic and its problems has been oriented so as to lead our investigation in a particular direction. Let us now head that way.

Leave aside the complex architecture of Kant's ethical theory.[246] Its core idea can be—and frequently has been—restated with extreme simplicity: "Don't treat people like things."[247] On its face, this seems like a very good rule for conducting relations with others. However, the obviousness of this motto hides a second implication. "Don't treat people like things" opens wide the possibility of *treating things any which way at all.*

With this reversal in mind consider the perverse power of the "categorical imperative" in Kant's time. However much nineteenth-century bourgeois readers of Kant were concerned to act ethically within the limits of reason and to have sure ways to hold one another responsible, they must have also been delighted to be authorized in taking unchecked advantage of the material world.[248] One could seize, transform, and return things from and to the world within a new constellation of values. What those things subsequently "did" to other persons, effects they produced beyond the immediate ken and control of the persons who produced or set them in motion, was excluded from ethical consideration.[249] So long as the agent showed respect for persons in the first instance—in the reciprocity of the handshake or a tip of the hat, in the formalism of a promise or contract—he could go about his business even in the face of depredations on a massive scale.

To paint the scene this way is to evoke contexts of judgment ignored or excluded by the "Golden Rule" or the "Categorical Imperative." These principles offer no ecological doctrine. Nor do they address our treatment of animals, or of anyone excluded by new racialist doctrines from the company of humankind. They allow that as long as the rights of persons are respected the intrusions into human relationships of material facts like wealth and resources and situation can be ruled out of bounds. Such ethical maxims famously justified at one and the same time social processes leading to the abolition of slavery and those that created a grueling industrial system of "free" labor behind the facade of formal contracts between equally willing parties.

In Rousseau's time, and with Rousseau's urging, human equality was coming to be taken for granted and emerged as the main vehicle for reciprocity, for the balanced give-and-take of everyday life. Under the wheels of that vehicle, however, *things* were losing their sacred quality. Detached from makers and owners *things* became little more than the objects of commerce and science, nothing but instruments for human well-being and knowledge.

Following strictly the Kantian formula this might be taken as an objection that *things*—having no Will, no autonomy, becoming merely means rather than ends—lost their *dignity.* I have no particular stake in a view of this sort. What I mean to suggest at this point is rather different. It is that insofar as an internal logic or necessity to the production of effects by *things* could be maintained, it was a logic of nature and something to be considered only in the domain of the natural sciences. That *things* could be essentially part of human history even while they imposed certain necessities on human beings against human Will was beyond the ken of this worldview.

In this short-sighted way of seeing our relation to *things* some key resources for social and political theory were lost. Problems like famine—when markets set prices for food higher than individual incomes—or global warming—when normal pollutants from individuals change overall climate thresholds—were drawn away from the agenda of politics. They became instead, where noticed at all, problems for philanthropy or technical control. We can see today that these approaches have failed. In fact such matters are tightly integrated into, even inextricable from, the fabric of human interaction and the internal logic of mankind "abandoned to ourselves" on the "island" of the earth.[250]

Over the century following Rousseau's invention of *société,* vast amounts of attention went into the definition and manipulation of objects as a revolution in science nurtured a revolution in industry. Under the weight of predominant scientific and technical discourses the distinction between persons and things was further sharpened. An ever more precisely delineated realm of the *nonhuman* required by antithesis increased and reconfigured precision in the definition of the *human.* The *person,* once viewed as a part, a high part, in the totality of creation, took on new shape. From a moral and political point of view, whatever a *person* was, he was not a member of the scrupulously catalogued set of *things*—he was not his body, not his property, not his circumstances.[251]

As Kant's transcendental ethics was buoyed upward by the revived fiction of persons as juridical subjects, as essentially bearers of rights and not wearers of flesh, the New Model Will was born and became the defining imaginary for the modern individual.

These developments had an additional effect. They provided opportunities and motives to work backward from the refigured distinction between persons and things. Where the self-evidence of human dignity once led to an account of things, now the self-evidence of that entire distinction led to new investigations of the two terms that compose it.

On the one hand, this set the stage for a precise, egalitarian, and extremely attractive concept of human dignity or worth.[252] On the other hand, it decreased the effective application of that very same concept. Ever more precise conceptual delineation of social fields unprotected by moral worth constituted a whole new set of possibilities for unfettered action. It became possible for some people to operate with impunity within crucial and newly emergent fields of human activity like the economy and, eventually, state-centered politics. It left others with their dignity and nothing else to protect them. That these historical developments eventually, by the end of the nineteenth century, produced titanic moral battles over the meaning and "ownership" of society itself[253] does not diminish the fact that no one before or after Kant cut with the same conceptual precision the line—at once explicitly philosophical and implicitly sociological—between a "phenomenal" and a "noumenal" realm, or that this line is of high importance in understanding the structure of Rousseau's social theory of politics.

There are other philosophical traditions within which the formulation and significance of the distinction between persons and things may be understood. The characteristically modern version of the "subject/object problem"[254] takes shape well before the eighteenth century. That is the *topos* Thomas Hobbes—the Dr. Frankenstein of political theory—brought to the center of attention when he denied the Aristotelian tradition of natural sociability[255] and, in the famous introduction to *Leviathan*, represented the "Commonwealth," the whole of intention-directed relationships among human beings, as the life of an "Artificial Man."[256] Consistent with this view, the sociologists of the nineteenth century, forming the investigation of man into method-structured scientific disciplines, looking back to Rousseau through the lens of Kant, constituted the object of their scientific inquiry into social relationships by excluding *things* from it. They did so just at the historical moment when—it seems odd but fair to say—*things* were gaining unprecedented importance in the affairs of humankind.[257]

Thus was affirmed a crucial process—here and there contested but nonetheless predominant—in the development of the social sciences. A conceptual and methodological wall was raised between, on one side, the human being as *exemplum* of "the social" and, on the other side, an independent "context" or contextualizing world of things.[258] Over time, the relative importance for social inquiry of one side or the other has varied, but until very recently this gap has been constitutive of sociological knowledge.[259] This, too, corresponds to the major flaw I will analyze below: the woefully belated recognition that it does not diminish mankind to say that things are not extrinsic but essential to human relationships. The two—persons and things—are unavoidably integrated within the world we are making for ourselves and political theory had better have a way to take this into account.

Perhaps this failing is sufficiently clear in traditions of sociology that are explicitly Kantian. That it also infected the major nineteenth-century alternative reflects the true extent of the problem. For, against both Kant and Hegel's critique of Kant, Marx analyzes society in a way that magnified the Kantian formula separating persons from things. In *Das Kapital*, Marx at first presents the problem of Society, the reason and instrumentation of its evil, through an account of commodities in circulation. Further along, however, we discover that this circulation is just a surface phenomenon. Relations between things stand for relations among persons. Marx urges us to see beyond mere appearances and to confront the reality hidden beneath them. The deeper problem is that things, the commodities which flood markets and seize hold of market societies, are in some strange but fundamental sense identical with the persons by whom they are made.[260] Sometimes this is viewed in a positive light—as "labor embodied in things"—and sometimes it is viewed in a negative one—as "alienation." The *secret* of what Marx calls "the fetishism of commodities" is that things are treated like people. The *social* and ultimately *political* problem, however, is that people are treated like things. Reaching the bedrock of Marx's sociology, we find Kant lurking there.[261] Behind him, there stands Rousseau.

§12

THE SCIENCE OF DEPENDENCE

For several centuries and until quite recently, the study of society and politics has been oriented around a complex but crisp separation of persons from things. For most people—thinking about these matters, learning about them, living through them—this is just self-evident.[262] It is a prejudice long expressed in and reinforced by a strong conceptual and institutional separation between "human" and "natural" sciences. This way of organizing and thus of creating knowledge is widely taken to be the nineteenth-century invention of John Stuart Mill (1843) and Wilhelm Dilthey (1883), or an offshoot of philosophical inquiry into the foundations of modern science.

In fact, assertions of the specificity of human sciences had a strong and enduring presence already in the eighteenth century. It was proposed by advocates of declining rhetorical traditions against the advancing claims of the new science. This image and conflict makes an astonishingly clear appearance in Vico's inaugural lecture from 1707 and it is a guiding force in Hume's writing already in 1739.[263]

But it is also a shadowy presence in Rousseau. Time and time again he upholds the purely human against the realm of the sacred, against the domain of science, or against the corrupting influence of things.

Nowhere is this distinction between persons and things more flagrantly in force than when Rousseau turns to consider the dynamics of freedom. For Rousseau, freedom occurs, or fails to occur, only within the bounds of human experience. Nothing like Kant's *noumenal* account of freedom will advance our knowledge of political life. Rather, the key variable in the experiential dynamics of freedom is *dépendance*.

Up to this point in this book, the topic of dependence has been displayed several times in a variety of ways. In the pages that follow dependence will move to center stage. We are beginning to see why. The *topos* of dependence is a crucial point at which the social and the political come vividly together. It is the moral-political nexus at which Rousseau analyzes the foundations of social life, the sort of suffering society produces, and the ways that politics might provide a resolution.

Already in the 1740s, as secretary to the French ambassador to Venice, and still apart from his active work as a musician, Rousseau began to imagine himself as a political theorist. Only around 1750, however, did he begin to work at notebooks intended for a *magnum opus* called *Institutions politiques*.[264] By 1760 this project had been "long abandoned."[265] Nonetheless, these efforts bore fruit that continues to nurture us today.

In these drafts Rousseau placed *dépendance* squarely at the center of his enterprise. "Man cannot suffice for himself," he wrote,

> ... his ever resurgent needs require that he seek outside himself for the means to meet them. He always depends from things and often from those of his own kind [*Il dépend toujours des choses et souvent de ses semblables*]. We feel this

dependence more or less according to the extent and nature of our needs, and it is in these very same needs, more or less large, more or less felt, that the principle of all human actions must be sought. (OC III.529)*

Many things in this passage attract attention. Without the larger context of Rousseau's later works it will be difficult to see how much hinges on the assertion that the human being "always depends from things and often from those of his own kind."

Why does the subsequent corpus of Rousseau's writing show this sentence to be so important? Because in it the introduction of dependence into the political problematic is organized around the distinction between persons and things. At first this may have been little more than a passing insight or intuition. Over the course of a decade it gathers its full weight. This is made precise in *Émile*.[266]

It is the second of the five books and the story of human development is well under way. Rousseau exhibits the architecture of his thinking:

There are two types of dependence: that from things, which is of nature; that from men, which is of Society. Dependence from things, having no morality, in no way undermines liberty or engenders vices. Dependence from men, being disordered, engenders them all, and it is through [this dependence] that the master and the slave are mutually depraved. (OC IV.311)†

Rousseau signals the fundamental political significance of this passage in *Émile*. He connects it directly to *Du Contract social* (which is itself extracted from *Institutions politiques*). Although the two books were written in tandem and published just months apart in 1762, there are only two express intertextual references to the political writings in the whole of *Émile*. One of these occurs near the end of the book: as the tutor's summary views on politics are presented to the student, a note points to Rousseau's "little treatise" as the source. The other reference is a note appended to the passage just cited. Here Rousseau gestures to the same treatise using its subtitle — *"Principes du droit politique"* — as though to en-

---

*"L'homme ne peut se suffire à lui-même; ses besoins toujours renaissants le mettent dans la nécessité de chercher hors de lui les moyens d'y pourvoir. Il dépend toujours des choses et souvent de ses semblables. Nous sentons plus ou moins cette dépendance selon l'étendue et la nature de nos besoins, et c'est dans ces mêmes besoins, plus ou moins grands, plus ou moins sentis, qu'il faut chercher le principe de toutes les actions humaines."

†"Il y a deux sortes de dépendance. Celle des choses qui est de la nature; celle des hommes qui est de la société. La dépendance des choses n'ayant aucune moralité ne nuit point à la liberté et n'engendre point de vices. La dépendance des hommes étant desordonnée les engendre tous, et c'est par elle que le maitre et l'esclave se dépravent mutuellement."

sure against mistaking the topic of *Du Contract social*, and thus to ensure against mistaking the true significance of dependence.

In the book you hold in your hands, we shall after several large steps arrive in the final part with a clear understanding of this significance. For, what appears in this note as a passing characterization of *Du Contract social* goes exactly to the heart of Rousseau's new social theory of politics. *Émile* points to its companion volume to say *there* "it is demonstrated that no particular Will can be ordered in the social system [*il est démontré que nulle volonté particuliére ne peut être ordonnée dans le sistême social*]" (OC IV.311, note). Thus, by indirection, Rousseau makes a clear and pithy declaration that this brief comment is a key to what is being asserted in this passage and that this passage is a key to his thinking as whole.

Before moving on, I had better explain an oddity of my translation of the pivotal phrases *la dépendance des choses* and *la dépendance des hommes*. The etymologically literal sense of the word dependence—*de-pendere* in Latin means to "hang from"—illustrates with the utmost clarity the meaning of this concept and its fit into an account of the social world.[267] While the French preposition *de*—as in the qualification of *dépendance* either as *des choses* or *des hommes*—is consistent with this sense, the English preposition commonly joined with the word "dependence" is not. We are accustomed to speak of *dependence on things* and *dependence on men*. By applying the very different spatial sensibilities of the preposition "on," however, the English language seems to shift the balance between the subject and object of dependence in a way that is bound to confuse the discussion here. Thus, I will consistently translate *dépendance de* as "dependence from." I ask, dear reader, that for the sake of precision you be patient with the unwieldy expressions "dependence-from-things" and "dependence-from-persons,"[268] for they remain closest to what Rousseau actually meant to convey and illuminate the interstices of his architectonic social theory of politics.

The distinction between dependence-from-things and dependence-from-persons derives from the simpler distinction between things and persons. The former recasts and valorizes the latter. The modulation is so thorough-going that Ernst Cassirer found in the way Rousseau laid out the difference between dependence-from-things and dependence-from-persons a kind of synopsis of the whole ethical-political program presented in Rousseau's treatise on the education of the citizen. "The fundamental idea of *Émile*," he writes, "consists in this":

> ... that no physical obstacles must be removed from the path of the pupil who is to be educated to independence of Will and character. He is to be spared no suffering, no effort, no privation, and he is to be anxiously protected only from

violent coercion by an outside Will, from a command whose necessity he does not understand. He is to become acquainted with the compulsion of things from his earliest childhood, and he is to learn to bow before it; but he is to be spared the tyranny of men.[269]

Cassirer's summary is somewhat misleading, for although it is true that the child must learn something of independence, it is of the qualified and relative sort discussed above (in §4) and it remains "distinct from freedom [*contre la liberté*]" (OC III.375). What Cassirer correctly emphasizes is that across the field of experience dependence unceasingly reasserts itself through external compulsion.

This field, beyond the mental and the bodily, is where the distinction comes into social effect. If the source of dependence is "things," the child should be acclimated to it from the very beginning; the development of moral character will not be impeded. If instead the source is "persons," the child should be shielded from it, for dependence from other persons erodes the very fiber of the moral world.

Cassirer's way of grappling with these issues leads his reader quite directly back to the social theodicy we discussed earlier. This is what he identifies as essential to the coherence of Rousseau's works; this is the justification he provides for their continuing relevance.

Today, however, it is clear that on exactly these points Cassirer faltered. He did not pause to ask Rousseau the most obvious question: Why? Why does it matter, not only for individual character but for society, what is the source of the experience of dependence?

I am not suggesting that Rousseau would have been stumped by this question. He could have responded in several ways. What matters is that *we* understand the answer that stands to justify his social theory of politics. This answer is quite complex and will take the rest of this book to work through. In this process I shall argue that what is at stake here is how the moral and political theory of modern society can take into account the proliferation of human relations to things.

The New Problem of
Jean-Jacques Rousseau

As far as I am concerned, Rousseau's system as a whole would be totally consistent
with the parts.

—*Julie von Bondeli to Johann Georg Zimmermann, August 21, 1762*

These questions constitute a whole new problem, not only for readers of Jean-
Jacques Rousseau but for those who, even without realizing it, see the world his
way. This new problem is not, as the old one was, simply parasitic on a literary or
philosophical assumption that an author's contribution to wider culture hinges
on the internal coherence of his *corpus*.[270]

How one's ideas hang together is nonetheless important in many other ways.
The critical inquirer cannot help but ask: as Rousseau's arguments form new
partnerships with the presuppositions of today, as they invest the space of our
lives, can they, will they, harmonize enough to carry the tune we need or want
to hear in order to live? How does the continuing common sense to which Rousseau gave an early and persistent formulation fit with the needs of social and
political theory as we, citizens of many sorts, attempt to practice these arts today?

This is a problem of relevance and it is extreme. Each generation that reads the
canon of political writers must ask afresh and in earnest: What is living and what
is dead in Rousseau's political theory of society?

I have gestured to Ernst Cassirer's little book, *The Problem of Jean-Jacques
Rousseau*, not only because it is a brilliant hermeneutic endeavor by one of the
great social-philosophical thinkers of the twentieth century, but because Cassirer is exemplary. Take him as standing for a long line of readers and writers convinced that Rousseau's tutorship remains essential for the advancement of a science of society. Cassirer recapitulated a great deal of common sense from inside
and from outside the academy.

The purpose of the book you are now reading is to replay the basic question:

what can Rousseau do for social and political theory today? The answer to the new problem of Jean-Jacques Rousseau is simple to state and difficult to explain.

The statement goes this way: the importance for everyday life of the relationship between persons and things is increasing almost daily; Rousseau's moral conception excludes a fundamental reconsideration of the relations between person and things; the heritage of Rousseau's conception is deeply entrenched not only in moral understanding and everyday common sense, but also in scientific discourse; as long as it continues to frame the scientific treatment of political problems, our understanding of the contemporary world will remain impeded by an occluded system of theological belief; while it is not my concern here to discern who still believes in this theology or in what way they so believe, it is imperative to set these beliefs aside so as to discover the kind of sociology that could interrogate the political significance of all social facts, including precisely those beliefs.

This is a whole world compressed into a tiny package. Now we will begin to unpack it, to set things in order, to see where we stand. The primary mode will be a close reading of what Rousseau wrote. His marvelous prose, in which everything seems so simple, presents a major obstacle to our approach. Rousseau's thinking will often have to be reduced to its logical structure and primary prejudices. The appearance of simplicity will have to be replaced by a view into the complex and dynamic structuring context that sustains its commonplaces.

I shall concentrate on the configuration stated in the preceding section, in which the practical fact of dependence is divided into two parts and a different moral significance is then attributed to each of these. This configuration is fundamental to Rousseau's path-breaking social theory of politics. It will at first seem to most contemporary readers trivial and obvious. It has become common sense and we need to break that down. For, it is this complex of ideas that has helped to make Rousseau so remarkably convincing and, today, so utterly misleading.

Appendix to Part One. The Text of Rousseau's "Main Passage"

> The desperate first discovered in quotation the power, not to preserve, but to purify, to tear from context, to destroy; this is the only thing in which the hope still resides that something from this time and place survives— precisely because one beat it out of it.
>
> —*Walter Benjamin*, Karl Kraus[271]

A far-reaching discussion will take up the remainder of this book. To maximize continuity across that terrain I have adopted a single precise object on which to focus our attention. It is a brief passage of astonishing exemplarity that appears near the beginning of chapter two in Rousseau's *Émile*. From here on I shall refer to this as the "main passage." The original reads as follows:

Avant que les préjugés et les institutions humaines aient altéré nos penchans naturels le bonheur des enfans ainsi que des hommes consiste dans l'usage de leur liberté; mais cette liberté dans les prémiers est bornée par leur foiblesse. Quiconque fait ce qu'il veut est heureux s'il se suffit à lui-même; c'est le cas de l'homme vivant dans l'état de nature. Quiconque fait ce qu'il veut n'est pas heureux, si ses besoins passent ses forces; c'est le cas de l'enfant dan le même état. Les enfans ne joüissent, même dans l'état de nature, que d'une liberté imparfaite, semblable à celle dont joüissent les hommes dan l'état civil. Chacun de nous ne pouvant plus se passer des autres redevient à cet égard foible et misérable. Nous étions faits pour être hommes, les loix et la sociéte nous ont replongés dans l'enfance. Les riches, les grands, les rois sont tous des enfans qui, voyant qu'on s'empresse à soulager leur misére, tirent de cela même une vanité puerile, et sont tout fiers des soins qu'on ne leur rendroit pas s'ils étoient hommes-faits.

Ces considérations sont importantes et servent à résoudre toutes les contradictions du sistème social. Il y a deux sortes de dépendance. Celle des choses qui est de la nature; celle des hommes qui est de la societé. La dépendance des choses n'ayant aucune moralité ne nuit point à la liberté et n'engendre point de vices. La dépendance des hommes étant desordonnée* les engendre tous, et c'est par elle que le maitre et l'esclave se dépravent mutuellement. S'il y a quelque moyen de remédier à ce mal dans la societé c'est de substituer la loi à l'homme, et d'armer les volontés générales d'une force réelle supérieure à l'action de toute volonté particuliére. Si les loix des nations pouvoient avoir comme celles de la nature une infléxibilité que jamais aucune force humaine ne put vaincre, la dépendance des hommes redeviendroit alors celle des choses, on réuniroit dans la République tous les avantages de l'état naturel à ceux de l'état civil, on joindroit à la liberté qui maintient l'homme exempt de vices la moralité qui l'élêve à la vertu. (OC IV.310–11)

*Dans mes *Principes du droit politique* il est démontré que nulle volonté particuliére ne peut être ordonnée dans le sistême social.

You will note that here, as elsewhere, I have not modernized the orthography. In this I take over the practice of the definitive *Pléiade* edition. Quite simply, I am convinced that the lines and dots of writing can be an integral part of the world in which a writer lives and the world he or she creates by writing.[272] It serves no good to suppose that the only thing in the world that does not change is language.

Moreover, as issues of translation are deeply involved in the following discussion, I shall not give the impression of having decided those issues beforehand by offering an English version of the "main passage" at this point.

When no reference accompanies a quotation from Rousseau below, it derives from this text.

Part II

THE MORAL RELEVANCE OF DEPENDENCE

A. Dependence and the "Formula for Happiness"

§14

SOCIAL THEORY AS METADIDACTIC

An Apostrophe

Rousseau makes an argument concerning the moral character of dependence.[1] It is synthetically stated in two paragraphs in the second book of *Émile*,
his magisterial treatise on education.[2] The argument occurs at a special kind of
apostrophic moment in the text. Rousseau turns to address himself directly to the
reader, rather than to the parent, the preceptor, or the child. The address is made
in a theoretical mood. This mood is enhanced by writing that is particularly terse
and forceful. Subsequently, Rousseau returns to his main task: the didactic plot-
ting out of Émile's development. Framed by the larger narrative, clearly different
from it, the theoretical point is thus additionally underlined by a change in the
experience of reading.

It is not surprising to find the problem of dependence raised in a discussion
about childhood and education. Indeed, Rousseau makes much of the commonsense notion that all children are dependent. Nor is it surprising to find Rousseau, who always seems ready to preach, taking the opportunity to elaborate his
claims about dependence in broad, theoretical terms.

§15

THE RULE OF "NOT SPEAKING
AGAINST YOURSELF"

At first, Rousseau is concerned in a very general way with the deleterious effects of dependence. How are these effects to be measured?

The proper measure is *bonheur* (happiness). In choosing this measure, Rousseau has clearly followed his own imperative to the student: "Read Plato's *Republic*."[3]

No one could hope to accommodate in a single gesture Plato's theory of the good life, or its catalytic element of happiness. This has been the subject of almost twenty-five centuries of remarkably continuous discussion.[4] Nonetheless, recall that Plato, figuring his views through Socrates, pursues with obsessive insistence dialogical inquiry into the proper ordering of the "soul [ψυχή]." Such inquiry makes prominent appearance in the *Republic*. It is unmistakably an account of happiness. And it rather directly corresponds to the starting point for Rousseau's thinking. So let us briefly bring forward this Socratic view of happiness. In this way we may also herald several of the topics that are fundamental for Rousseau. These include "order," "noncontradiction," and the "Will."

This germ of an idea of happiness as a proper ordering of the soul has grown differently in different times and places. As it is interrogated below, we will do well to remain attentive to how Rousseau recast this view in decisively modern terms.[5] Still, it is fair to begin with passages in his writings—and there are many—where Rousseau presents happiness in a way that is closely similar to Plato. The happy Man, for example, "will find himself well-ordered [*se trouvera bien ordonné*]" (OC IV.304). And how do we know when something is *bien ordonné*? Émile's tutor underscores Plato's familiar approach to this question. He impresses on his student, as Socrates did with his, that "to be something, to be oneself and always one, you must act as you speak."[6] Indeed, "by removing man's contradictions one would remove a large obstacle to his happiness" (OC IV.251).[*]

[*] "Pour être quelque chose, pour être soi-même et toujours un, il faut agir comme on parle; . . . . en ôtant les contradictions de l'homme on ôteroit un grand obstacle à son bonheur."

Both Plato and Rousseau believed that there is a relationship between political life on the one hand and this constellation of good order and individual happiness on the other. But how are they connected?

Plato is primarily concerned with how a life may best be lived. He asks us to consider this from the perspective of a single person whose existence will continue even after he leaves the human world and enters the land of the dead. His account of the proper ordering of the soul, and the happiness arising out of that order, must cover the entirety of this experience. For this reason, it may be said that Plato appears first as a mystic ascetic, then as a moralist, and only derivatively as a political thinker. One may fairly read the magisterial architectonics of the "city [πόλις]" that Plato provides in the *Republic* (*Το Πολιτεία*) as an extended metaphor for the order of the soul. Indeed, as Rousseau incisively remarks, Plato's work about the "city [πόλις]" is "not at all a work on politics [*n'est point un ouvrage de politique*]."[7]

Theology is not the only motive for Plato's circuitous approach. Again, Rousseau provides a clue. Research into private happiness is impeded by the nature of its object. *Bonheur,* in the strict and personal sense, consists "in a sentiment that is permanent and utterly interior, of which no one except the person who experiences it can be the judge; no one can decide with certainty that another is happy, nor, as a result, establish the exact signs of the happiness of individuals."[8]* The study of public questions is an altogether different matter because "the situation is not the same with political societies. All things good and evil for them are apparent and visible, their interior sentiment is a public sentiment."[9]† Thus, if Plato offers the image of the "city [πόλις]" to illustrate the "soul [ψυχή]," it is because no literal representation of it is possible. The use of this image reverses Protagoras' sophistic judgment that "Man is the measure of all things." Another measure is required for Man himself.[10]

This is not to say that a well-ordered soul [ψυχή] is inconsequential for political life. This fact, which is experienced as happiness, may also be a bridge that facilitates Plato's identification of the "good man" and the "good citizen." This is, of course, another *topos* Rousseau inherits more or less directly from Plato, although he will detour and retool it for his own purposes.[11]

The image of the "city [πόλις]" would not be the only way to bring the in-

---

* ". . . dans un sentiment permanent et tout intérieur dont nul ne peut juger que celui qui l'éprouve; nul ne peut donc decider avec certitude qu'un autre est heureux ni par consequent établir les signes certain du bonheur des individus."

† ". . . il n'en est pas de même des societés politiques. Leurs biens, leurs maux sont tous apparens et visibles, leur sentiment intérieur est un sentiment public."

visible soul to light.[12] Rousseau's choice of this particular Platonic metaphor locates personal happiness on the map of "society." This is a political method. Still, it works in two directions, creating a slippery passage between *micro* and *macro* aspects on the human condition.[13] The tutor makes this explicit when he tells Émile that "[i]t is necessary to study society by way of men, and men by way of society: those who would like to investigate the political and the moral separately will never understand anything of either" (OC IV.524).* This maxim helps Rousseau to develop a complex image of the active constitution of society.[14] In the process, he applies Plato's political method to an object unknown to the ancient philosopher: the monistic sense of "society" that is Rousseau's own invention. By shuttling back and forth between *homme* and *société, morale* and *politique,* Rousseau relates *bonheur* to several levels of strictly human *ordre.* In turn, the external discourses that define and apply the concept of *ordre* (e.g., theology, mathematics, music), pointing back through the question of happiness, provide a conceptual scheme with which to interpret the primary topic: *dépendance.*

As these various concerns are used to articulate the topic of *dépendance,* a range of ambivalences and tensions inherent in *bonheur,* and especially in the associated use of the concept of *ordre,* appear. Rousseau's engagement with these tensions leads him back to considerations of the Will. We have already seen that he does not rely on the superficial and deeply misleading identification of Will with independence that comes to the foreground in the nineteenth century. Rather, Rousseau moves toward an even more fundamental and abstract connection between *dépendance* and Will. Rousseau is unable to state this connection as such. Nonetheless, it is unmistakably the Will—its presence or absence, its unity or plurality—that divides the significance of *dépendance* in two, separating dependence-from-persons and dependence-from-things.

The implications of this division multiply as the same "political method" is again brought to bear. As before, the object is one unknown to Plato: it is the Will itself.[15] In this case, however, the transfer—literally, μεταφορος—is made in reverse, not from the "city" to the "person," but from the *microcosmos* to the *macrocosmos.* Whether God's Will models Man's or the other way 'round, this image of motive force in a single indivisible subject is carried over to the human totality. The name for this is, famously, the *"volonté générale,"* or the Will that realizes itself in the republic. Where singular, self-consistent, noncontradictory Will acts, there is order and a potential for happiness.

---

* "Il faut étudier la société par les hommes, et les hommes par la société: ceux qui voudront traiter séparément la politique et la morale, n'entendront jamais rien à aucune des deux"

At the same time, this pendular movement brings to light the opposite fact. Rousseau finds that any multiplication of individual Wills is a source of disorder and, thus, of unhappiness. This problem is serious. Referring the reader of the *Émile* to *Du Contract social,* Rousseau claims to have "demonstrated that no particular will can be well-ordered in the social system" (OC IV.311).* This fact has additional political consequences. For example, "each individual can, as Man, have a particular Will contrary to or dissimilar from the general Will that he has as Citizen" (OC III.363).† In other words, simply by virtue of his existence in society, there is a high potential for contradiction even within a single person. In a sense that bears heavily on political life, the potential for contradiction increases within complex social roles.

The role of "magistrate" provides an example of this. Assuming that government is an intermediate body between the people and the state, Rousseau refers to its members as magistrates.[16] Generally speaking, there may be many of them, and it is easy to imagine conflicts within the group. Yet, the problem of disorder arises even if there is only one. We find

> in the person of the magistrate three essentially different Wills. First of all, the Will that belongs to the individual, which tends only to his particular advantage; second, the common Will of magistrates, which relates solely to the advantage of the Prince, and which one may call the Will of the association [*corps*], which is general with respect to the Government and particular with respect to the State of which the Government is a part; in the third place, the Will of the people or the sovereign Will, which is general both with respect to the State considered as the totality and with respect to the Government considered as part of that totality. (OC III.400–401)§

Here the complex motives of a single human being are analyzed through the social structure that defines the possibilities for that person's action. The source of

---

* ". . . démontré que nulle volonté particuliére ne peut être ordonnée dans le sistême social."

† ". . . chaque individu peut comme homme avoir une volonté particuliere contraire ou dissemblable à la volonté générale qu'il a comme Citoyen."

§ ". . . dans la personne du magistrat trois volontés essenciellement différentes. Premierement la volonté propre de l'individu, qui ne tend qu'à son avantage particulier; secondement la volonté commune des magistrats, qui se rapporte uniquement à l'avantage du Prince, et qu'on peut appeler volonté du corps, laquelle est générale par rapport au Gouvernement, et particulier par rapport à l'Etat, dont le Gouvernement fait partie; en troisieme lieu, la volonté du peuple ou la volonté souveraine, laquelle est générale, tant par rapport à l'Etat considéré comme le tout, que par rapport au Gouvernement considéré comme partie du tout."

disorder is not the simple presence of multiple Wills.[17] It is that each represents a different set of interests. The practical combination of interest and Will—in the person who is in society—is almost guaranteed to lead to two kinds of disorder. The first is self-contradiction; the second is direct conflict with others. It seems reasonable to say—as, of course, other writers would later say—that a person whose action was constantly frustrated and uncertain in this way would be neurotic and unhappy.

At the beginning of this section *bonheur* was identified as the measure of *dépendance*. We have seen, at least in a preliminary way, how an ancient ideal of happiness provides a bridge between two problems: disorder and dependence. Reading an author centrally concerned with inequality, this linkage makes intuitive sense.

However, having now made this point in this way, and heralded some of the consequences we shall consider more carefully later in this book, it is time to take a step back. Our entrance into Rousseau's institutional reflections is premature. The gestures made in this section only hint at the meaning within Rousseau's system of the key analytic terms *bonheur* and *désordre*. The real significance of dependence—for one person, for society, and finally for politics—remains obscure.

§16

THE AMPLITUDE OF *BESOINS*

Where, then, shall we look for an expanded account of happiness? Much later, with Émile's education almost at an end, the tutor-Rousseau focuses in on this topic again. He sees his student's capacity for reason dulled by love. He decides to deploy Émile's own passion against him and thus "render [Émile] attentive to my lessons."[18] As a "terrible preamble" to his next discourse on happiness, Rousseau plays a shocking trick on his student. He suggests that Émile's beloved Sophie is dead. In an operatic aside to the reader Rousseau explains, "now I am quite sure he will hear me" (OC IV.814). He then turns back to Émile and says: "You must be happy, dear Émile; that is the goal of every sensate being; it is the first desire that nature prints upon us, and the only one which never leaves us. But where is happiness [*bonheur*]?"[19]* Rousseau prolongs his own question with another one—"Who knows?" He does not hold out much hope for an answer. "Everyone seeks happiness and no one finds it [*Chacun le cherche et nul le trouve*]."[20]

Certain negative statements about happiness can be made with assurance. "*Le bonheur* is not pleasure." Nor is it the diminution of our desires, nor the extension of our faculties.[21]

While many things may be excluded, we are not likely to find a general positive answer. Neat, ultimately Platonic or Christian maxims like "be just, and you will be happy" or "Oh, let us be good first, and then we will be happy" are acknowledged by Rousseau to lead nowhere (OC IV.589). Finally, the main thing that can be said is that "we do not know what *bonheur* or *malheur* are in the absolute."[22]

If happiness is to be defined at all, it must be—consistent with Rousseau's general method of comparison—in relative terms. Once one realizes that it is "in the disproportion of our desires and our faculties that our misery consists" (OC IV.303–4)† the largest of—Socratic—questions opens again: "What therefore makes up human wisdom, or the path to true *bonheur*? (OC IV.304).§ Rousseau's answer provides a provisional definition of *bonheur*.

> It is not exactly to diminish our desires. . . . Nor is it to extend our faculties . . .
> *but it is to diminish the excess of desires over faculties, and to arrive at a perfect equality between capacity and Will.* (OC IV.304)**

In this view, happiness is a kind of balance or proportion. This is not a simple Stoicism. Rousseau's assertion rejoins the Socratic ideal discussed above. It also provides additional content to that notion of *order*. Below, we shall take care to specify further the characteristics of this proportion. Once having brought to light other aspects of social relationship that affect its operation, and which constitute its impact on the question of dependence, we shall return to the notion of order with a much enlarged view of the whole conceptual scene. This will allow us to judge the compatibility of Rousseau's account of *le lien social* with other beliefs and values we may want to advance, even as we tacitly rely on that account.

---

* "Il faut être heureux, cher Émile: c'est la fin de tout être sensible; c'est le premier désir que nous imprima la nature, et le seul qui ne nous quitte jamais. Mais où est le bonheur?"

† ". . . dans la disproportion de nos desirs et de nos facultés que consiste nôtre miséré"

§ "En quoi donc consiste la sagesse humaine ou la route du vrai bonheur?"

** "Ce n'est pas précisément à diminüer nos desirs . . . Ce n'est pas non plus à étendre nos facultés . . . mais c'est à diminuer l'excés des desirs sur les facultés, et à mettre en égalité parfaite la puissance et la volonté."

Well-honed readers of Rousseau will not be surprised by this turn. He has many ways of expressing this same essential idea of happiness as proportionality. I will not spend pages here to sort out its various terms and subtle inflections. I will only say that this is a point on which a reductionist approach is warranted and will be useful for moving forward the argument of this book.

Which are the proper terms of this proportion? From this point on, I shall use the word *besoins* ("needs") to refer to whatever it is that must be brought within proportionate reach for a person to be happy.

This choice is appropriate for the double purpose of this book: to follow Rousseau's thinking and to reconfigure contemporary engagement with his ideas. Several other terms used regularly by Rousseau do present themselves, including "inclinations [*penchants*]," "tastes [*goûts*]," "appetites [*appetits*]," perhaps "dispositions [*dispositions*]," or derivatives of the verb "to want [*vouloir*]" which is the source of the word for "Will [*volonté*]." The most prevalent alternative has already been mentioned: "desires [*désirs*]."

In Rousseau's writings the relation between *besoins* and *désirs*—and the range of other associated terms—is exceedingly subtle and often obscure. A full elaboration of this topic will not advance the main argument here. A brief survey, however, will deepen the sense of what is at stake in the analysis of *bonheur* and why *besoins* is the best *topos* for that inquiry.

The page that opens Book III of *Émile* presents a kind of summary. It strongly suggests an equivalence between *besoins* and *désirs* (OC IV.426). Leafing forward and back, however, quickly indicates how misleading this may be. We find that "soon desire no longer emerges from need but from habit, or, rather, habit adds a new need to the one that comes from nature" (OC IV.282).* Here, another feature of human life—*habitude*—pushes *besoin* and *désir* apart; the former appears to be a primary condition from which, in certain circumstances, the latter emerges.[23] Moreover, the first phrase suggests that *désir* need not be linked to *besoin* at all; *habitude* and *besoin* are placed side by side as sources of subsequent *désir*. Why, then, in the next breath, step back to identify the new *désir* as a *besoin*?

Elsewhere, Rousseau amplifies the idea that *désirs* arise from *besoins*; this occurs when the additional faculty of *imagination* comes into play. "The source of all the passions is sensibility, imagination determines their pitch [*pente*]" (OC IV.501).† Is *besoin* thus a passion, a passive fact determined from outside itself?

---

* ". . . bientot le desir ne vient plus du besoin mais de l'habitude, ou plustôt, l'habitude ajoûte un nouveau besoin à celui de la nature."

† "La source de toutes les passions est la sensibilité, l'imagination détermine leur pente."

Or is it an "active principle [*principe actif*]?"[24] This thorny question need not be answered here because the modal effect of imagination is not restricted to the passions. It also holds sway in the relations among human faculties.[25] Some of these faculties are original—*attention, amour de soi-même, perfectibilité, pitié,* perhaps *volonté*[26]—and operate even in primary neonatal and "natural" states. While imagination is essential to human life it is not a faculty of this sort. "In the beginning of life . . . the imagination is still inactive."[27] This faculty is likewise inoperative at the outset of the life of society.[28]

Are *désirs*, therefore, social? Something driven only by the social fact of imagination? And are, by contrast, *besoins* motives that are purely natural?

This alignment is exceedingly familiar. It is bolstered—as habit is our "*seconde nature*"[29]—when Rousseau adds that "in every case habit kills imagination" (OC IV.384). But look again: we just saw that *habitude* can be a source of *désir*; and, since Rousseau is also clear that there is no going back to nature,[30] the mapping of *besoins* as "natural" and *désirs* as "social" certainly seems misleading.

Giving for a moment the impression of impeccable clarity Rousseau prompts this way: "We always distinguish the penchants that come from nature from those which come from opinion" (OC IV.429).* But which "inclinations" are which? Consider that with the transformation of *amour de soi-même* into *amour-propre* "fantasy takes the place of need . . . [and] prejudices and opinion take their first roots."[31]† On the one hand, one could say that when society ignites and amplifies imagination it drives *besoins* over the border into *désirs*; or that the related personal psychology of *fantaisie* locates them in a different domain altogether. However, to suppose that *désir* is simply *besoin* plus *fantaisie* just spins the wheel again, since Rousseau nearly defines *fantaisie* as "desire without reason [*desir sans raison*]."[32] Elsewhere, he says that by the word *fantaisie* he means "all the desires that are not real needs" (OC IV.309–10). The frustrated reader wants to ask: but what about the ones that are "real"?

If "man in the wild . . . only feels his real needs" it may be because "he suffices to himself [*il se suffit à lui même*]" (OC III.160). None of this, however, requires that *besoins* are strictly natural, and Rousseau says as much: "The Author of things does not merely provide for the needs he gives us but also for those that we give to ourselves" (OC IV.407).§ Thus, *besoins* may be artificial. They can

---

* "Distinguons toujours les penchans qui viennent de la nature de ceux qui viennent de l'opinion."

† ". . . ainsi succéde la fantaisie au besoin, ainsi prennent leurs prémiéres racines les préjugés et l'opinion."

§ "L'auteur des choses ne pourvoit pas seulement aux besoins qu'il nous donne mais encore à ceux que nous nous donnons nous-mêmes . . ."

even be *"imaginaires"* (OC IV.426). Again in a Platonic mood, Rousseau proposes a contrast that obscures the difference, gesturing toward "the innate desire for well-being [*le desir inné du bien-être*]."[33]

Even if Rousseau—like his readers then and now—envisions a spectrum of human "inclinations" stretching from the "natural" to the "social," it remains that there is no way to locate on this spectrum the point that divides *besoins* from *désirs*.[34]

More than simple semantic incoherence upsets efforts to map clearly the shift from "natural" to "social." Even if it is true that "the more we distance ourselves from the state of nature, the more we lose our natural tastes" (OC IV.407),* the same development soon goes so far that "habit makes a second nature that we substitute so much for the first one that no one among us any longer knows [nature proper]" (OC IV.407–8).†

Just as it is impossible to know with certainty what comes directly to us from the "Author of nature" and what is the result of our own doing, the question of what ultimately divides *désirs* from *besoins* is beyond the more modest purposes of this book. Suffice it to say that Rousseau could agree with our using the term *besoins* to encompass both what one seeks in the natural condition and the extravagant multiplication of that seeking in social life. I am confident that this reduction does not alter the results of the investigation that follows.

If Rousseau cannot hold in any neatly synthetic way the idea that *besoins* are of nature and *désirs* are of society, can he at least maintain a distinction between socially constructed *besoins* and socially constructed *désirs*?

This will not work either. This kind of distinction is exactly what is dissolved by Rousseau's evolutionary account of the growth of whatever it is that must be brought within proportionate reach for a person to be happy. Rousseau views society as totality and system; he has an authentically sociological perspective. Within this totality, personal circumstances are always understood in relation to other persons; understanding itself requires a method of comparison. If we see, for example, that some people develop "desires," and—for reasons which are extrinsic to the "desire" as such but arise as side effects or unintended consequences within the material or symbolic domain in which the "desire" is expressed—these people are able to impose that "desire" on others, the effect is to expand the "system of needs." Perhaps Smith would like to keep up with neighbor

---

* ". . . plus nous nous éloignons de l'état de nature, plus nous perdons de nos gouts naturels. . . ."

† ". . . l'habitude nous fait une seconde nature que nous substituons tellement à la prémiére que nul d'entre nous ne connoit plus celle-ci."

Jones, but when the boss and the spouse and the children's schoolmates and the Mowed Lawn Commission at town hall all begin to make their judgments of Smith by comparison with Jones, Smith's "desire" to be more like Jones becomes for Smith the material imposition we tend to call a "need." This and other indirect modes through which "desire" is transformed into "need" muddy the distinction and purported hierarchy between them.

With these complexities in the background, then, let us adopt the narrower vocabulary of *besoins* as we return to the "main passage" and try to shed clearer light on the defects of dependence.

§17

NATURE AS UNTRANSFORMED NEED
AND AS HYPOTHESIS OF *LIBERTÉ*

In the decisive passage of *Émile* that is the focal point of our investigation,[35] Rousseau sets the definition of *bonheur* (happiness) within a counterfactual framework. His reader—then as now—can recognize this framework from his other masterpieces, the *Discours sur . . . l'inégalité* and *Du Contract social*. It is, of course, "the state of nature [*l'état de nature*]."

The fact to which the "state of nature" is opposed is explicit from the very first pages of *Émile*. It is not simply that we, readers and author, teacher and pupil, live in society. It is, rather, that as we are "dragged[36] along contrary paths by nature and by men, forced to divide ourselves between these diverse impulses, we follow a composite that leads us to neither the one nor the other end" (OC IV.251).* Thus, the central task set before the reader is not to picture a contrary fact, one which may have been true in another time or place. Rousseau asks us to counterfactually imagine Man outside of Society. This image will become an instrument for theory. Rousseau will use it to disentangle the threads that com-

---

* "Entraînés par la nature et par les hommes dans des routes contraires, forcés de nous partager entre ces diverses impulsions, [et] nous en suivons une composée qui ne nous mêne ni à l'un ni à l'autre but."

pose our actual situation. In the "main passage," he proposes a scene "before prejudices and human institutions have altered our natural inclinations."* Let us for now take this as a reference to the "state of nature," whatever this may mean, and whoever have been or might be its denizens. This seems to be the situation in which the greatest human happiness is possible.[37]

There is a reason for working within this frame. It allows yet another approach to the definition of happiness: "The happiness of children as well as that of men consists in the exercise of their liberty."† From this angle, Rousseau will construct a relation between happiness and liberty. The "state of nature" is one bridge between them.

§18

"LA FEMME EST HOMME"

It is impossible not to notice that, despite a lexicon rich with words pointing in the singular or the plural to adult persons in general (*personne, individu, être,* etc.), Rousseau's texts are riddled with the word *homme* or *hommes* ("man" or "men").[38] I believe that in the pivotal passages considered in the present book, and in literally hundreds of other ones, Rousseau intends by the word *hommes* ("men") to gesture toward the plural members of the *genre humain* ("human race"). The prevalence of occasions in Rousseau's writings where the phrase *genre humain* is followed by the word *hommes* as *amplificatio* increases my confidence in this belief. Where a preceding passage leaves any doubt *l'homme* becomes *l'homme en général* to point back to the regular application of the word alone.[39]

The significance of what Rousseau has written may differ from his intentions to a greater or lesser degree. In any event, however, I am not prepared to say that each use of the word *hommes* inherently excludes *femmes* ("women"). Rather, the word *hommes* becomes in his texts, as it has almost always been in speculative

---

*". . . avant que les préjugés et les institutions humaines aient altéré nos penchans naturels. . . ."

†". . . le bonheur des enfans ainsi que des hommes consiste dans l'usage de leur liberté . . ."

writings about the human condition, a kind of passage, often a secret passage, between two worlds. In one world gender makes a difference; in another, it does not. The history of reading such texts tells the story of some who have exploited this ambiguity to advance the dominion of men over women and of others who have deployed it against gendered power.

I think that any reader of Rousseau who is attentive to this symbolic fact does well to register another feature of his writings. He is capable of direct speech, and in that mode often says things that clearly discriminate in a way that is unfavorable to women. In Rousseau's various "states of nature" women and men lead rather different lives. The last book of *Émile*—where the education of Émile's mate Sophie is undertaken (OC IV.692 ff.)—seems to presuppose that men and women inhabit two different natures and two different moral realms. Consider where he writes that "Sophie must be woman as Émile is man; that is, to have all that is appropriate to the constitution of her species and her sex so as to fulfill her position in the physical and moral order" (OC IV.692).* It is difficult to imagine a conviction of essential gender difference stronger than that. Nor is what we see here a doctrine of "separate but equal": "woman is made," says Rousseau blithely, "to be subjugated," to "suffer" and "endure man's injustice" (OC IV.693, 710, 750). If Sophie is a "student of nature . . . she will be the woman of the man" (OC IV.769). And, as if to allay any doubt about which side he is on, Rousseau adds that "we begin, therefore, by examining similarities and differences between her sex and" —I emphasize Rousseau's choice of pronoun here— "ours" (OC IV.692).

The first task of the reader of such lines is not to look for hidden meaning. However, the same rule should apply when Rousseau boldly exalts women, as when he writes that "all the great revolutions [in ancient Rome] came from women" and that "women would have been able to give us even greater examples of largeness of spirit and love of virtue than men ever have if our injustice had not robbed them, along with their liberty, of all occasions to show themselves to the eyes of the world."[40] In the same vein he asserts with high theoretical generality that before puberty the equality of boys and girls is properly referred to with a single term—"child."[41] These equalities are not specific to one age. For, when one compares men and women, "she has the same organs, the same needs, the same faculties."† And therefore, despite everything else he avers, "those who re-

---

*"Sophie doit être femme comme Émile est homme; c'est à dire, avoir tout ce qui convient à la constitution de son espéce et de son séxe pour remplir sa place dans l'ordre physique et moral."

†". . . elle a les mêmes organes, les mêmes besoins, les mêmes facultés."

gard woman as an imperfect man are undoubtedly wrong, even if the superficial analogy favors their view" (OC IV.489).* Given the pendulum of his perspectives, it cannot be simply a passing matter when Rousseau asserts that

with regard to everything but sex, *woman is man.*[42]†

This is, of course, a remarkable sentence. In it, I think, Rousseau signals his large intention that the word *hommes* should apply to the *genre humain* as a whole, in which *femmes* are included. This usage leaves open the possibility of bringing questions of sex and gender difference into a discussion of humanity "abandoned to ourselves."

And while that is not our project here, one does well to remember that with Rousseau as with life these are not simple matters. Rousseau's ambiguous positions concerning gender extend very far afield. Especially as they come closer to home. Consider that by late August of 1762, with *Émile* banned, his "most ardent Swiss fan,"[43] Julie von Bondeli, reports that the once again peripatetic thinker—"I am here today, I don't know where tomorrow, and it doesn't matter" (CC XII.237)—has told his latest visitors: "I thought as a man, I wrote as a man, they found this bad, I am going to turn myself into a woman" (CC XII.236). Several weeks later, still in Motiers where he had begun to dress in distinctively unmasculine garb and had taken up an ambitious program of lace-making,[44] Rousseau writes to the Marquise de Verdelin: "I attempt to lose every memory of the past. . . . you see that I am more than half woman; would that I had always been so! I tried not to dishonor my sex; I hope to not be rebuffed by yours" (CC XIII.10).

There is no way in this book to resolve Rousseau's position with respect to women to one side or the other. However limited the domain of application of the inclusive term *hommes* may ultimately be, it is fair to say that it can and often does correspond precisely to what we consider here. For, if not *les organes*, certainly the *besoins* and the *facultés* which for men and women are the same are the essential components in the proportion that is *bonheur*, the "formula for happiness" we shall consider in the next section.

For these reasons, and others that would carry us even farther off course, I believe it will bring more light to the topics treated in this book if from this point forward we read the word *hommes* as signifying all the human beings who make up society.[45]

---

* "Ceux qui regardent la femme comme un homme imparfait ont tort, sans doute; mais l'analogie extérieure est pour eux."

† ". . . en tout ce qui ne tient pas au séxe la femme est homme."

The "Formula for Happiness"

So, imagine *hommes* before our natural inclinations have been transformed, before we have allowed others and their anonymous institutions to colonize our fundamental human capacity for judgment. In that counterfactual case "the happiness of children as well as that of men consists in the exercise [*usage*] of their liberty."* This speculative frame brings forward an utterly practical fact. "Liberty" is not only a topic of philosophy. What matters for Rousseau is lived experience, even when our own experience is brought before us in fictional terms. Thus, everyone's happiness consists in actually making *use* of his liberty.[46]

Framing this claim in terms of the "state of nature" does not make it a fantasy. The word "exercise [*usage*]" shifts the discourse from philosophical speculations toward a sociological theory of practice. Indeed, Rousseau's passing comment in *Émile*—"we are uniquely concerned with practice here [*c'est uniquement de la pratique qu'il s'agit ici*]" (OC IV.305)—may well stand for his work as a whole.

Once this shift has been made, real differences in capabilities must be taken into account. Thus, talk of the "child" is a way to do this, and Rousseau makes clear that "this liberty is limited in children by their weakness."†

Nominally, the subject here is "children." This is *Émile* after all, one in a handful of the most influential Western educational texts of all time. But Rousseau is using "the child" as a theoretical *topos* at this point.[47] His reference to "the child" will establish a limiting condition on the definition of happiness. He thereby makes that definition more precise. Children, because weak, cannot make full use of their liberty. Therefore, they cannot be fully happy. This move allows him to add to the definition a sort of general formula concerning happiness:

---

* "... le bonheur des enfans ainsi que des hommes consiste dans l'usage de leur liberté ..."
† "... cette liberté dans les [enfans] est bornée par leur foiblesse."

Whoever does what he wants is happy, if he suffices to himself; this is the case of the man who lives in the state of nature. Whoever does what he wants is not happy if his needs surpass his forces.*

If we read this definition of happiness in a psychological mode, it joins again the first version considered above,[48] in which a limited notion of order—understood primarily as noncontradiction—was the decisive feature. In the imagined absence of social relation, the possibility for a balanced and unitary *psyche* [ψυχή] or soul is clarified. For, "natural man is everything for himself . . . he is the numerical unity, the absolute whole whose only relation is to himself."[49]† This is the famous image that, in a moment at once stoic and nostalgic, prompts Rousseau to tell the unhappy person "withdraw within the limits of yourself, and you will no longer be miserable" (OC IV.308).

This psychological way of reading misses the crucial thematic line of the "main passage."[50] If one takes Rousseau's aim to be the creation of a sociological theory of practice with political implications, something else attracts attention. What gives this definition of happiness specific weight is the way it constitutes the following practical maxim: happiness is doing what you want under the proviso that it satisfies you. If you only have the capacity to satisfy some of your needs, you will not be happy.

This helps us to understand why a man in the "state of nature" could be happy. First, his requirements are minimal. Second, he has not lost his natural *forces*, as he will when he enters society. For these reasons the latter will very likely be greater than the former.

Thus, we may take Rousseau as proposing a formula of the following sort:

$$forces \geq besoins = bonheur \qquad [\text{"forces"} \geq \text{"needs"} = \text{"happiness"}]$$

and its corollary

$$forces < besoins = malheur \qquad [\text{"forces"} < \text{"needs"} = \text{"unhappiness"}]$$

When your *forces* are equal to, or greater than,[51] your *besoins*, you will be happy.

While this proportion has psychological components, it is an utterly practical matter. It is telling that it appears in roughly the same way early in the first version of *Du Contract social*; that may well be the source from which it is drawn for

---

*"Quiconque fait ce qu'il veut est heureux, s'il se suffit à lui-même; c'est le cas de l'homme vivant dans l'état de nature. Quiconque fait ce qu'il veut n'est pas heureux, si ses besoins passent ses forces. . . ."

† ". . . l'homme naturel est tout pour lui . . . il est l'unité numérique, l'entier absolu qui n'a de rapport qu'à lui-même . . ."

Émile.[52] In any event, Rousseau does not hesitate to underscore that "real education consists not so much in precepts as in practice" (OC IV.252).

And this, too, is why, and how, the early stages of an education must move the human being from infancy to maturity by producing what, in respect of the formula discussed here, can only be called happiness. The task of learning, the practical fact of growing, the process of becoming both *homme* and *citoyen*, requires a kind of antinarcissistic ecstasy. For this, we must "have profited from the overflow of our capacities relative to our needs so as to carry us outside ourselves, launching ourselves into the heavens, measuring the earth, gathering up the laws of nature; in a word, we have worked our way around the entire island" to finally "come once again to ourselves" and are "drawn imperceptibly into harmony with our habitat," all "too happy to find there"* that we are the ones we've been seeking.[53]

With this formula, we arrive at the first major point of reference for the discussion of dependence and the *lien social* constituted by it.[54]

§20

FORCES

No elaborate experiment is necessary to feel the great pleasure of acting through the hands of others, and to have only to wag the tongue to move the universe. (OC IV.289)†

The word *forces* is one of the two variables in the "formula for happiness." It merits more detailed elaboration than I can give it here, but some comments are in order.[55] The breadth and complexity of the significance of *forces* suggest the range of applicability for the "formula for happiness."

---

*". . . nous avons profité de la surabondance de nos forces sur nos besoins, pour nous porter hors de nous: nous nous sommes élancés dans les cieux; nous avons mesuré la terre; nous avons recueilli les loix de la Nature; en un mot, nous avons parcouru l'isle entiere; maintenant nous revenons à nous; nous nous rapprochons insensiblement de notre habitation. Trop heureux, en y rentrant, ..."

†". . . il ne faut pas une longue expérience pour sentir combien il est agréable d'agir par les mains d'autrui, et de n'avoir besoin que de remuer la langue pour faire mouvoir l'univers."

As it appears across Rousseau's pages the word *forces* covers many different kinds and degrees of capacity, potential, motive, pressure, impulsion. Other terms are located within this same discursive field. Related and pivotal notions of *puissance* and *pouvoir* are, to an important extent, differentiated by the circumstances in which they apply. Thus, *forces* may be understood as the basic matrix of these applications. It is as basic and extensive for Rousseau as the Greek word δύναμις (pl. δυνάμεις, pronounced *dunamis*) is for Aristotle, and it is Aristotle's word that I shall use in the following discussion. I do not mean to imply an equivalence between these two profoundly different thinkers. Nonetheless, because I want to minimize the many prejudices we bring to the word *forces* I will refer to the undifferentiated semantic field as δυνάμεις.

We turn once again to mankind "abandoned to ourselves." This focus devalues much of the normal eighteenth-century speculation about God—the originator, collector, coordinator, or director—as paradigm for all sorts of δυνάμεις.[56] However, our topic encompasses almost everything else, from pure nature to the most intricate artifice. As Rousseau's δύναμις always emerges from a phase in some process and operates in relations that include human growth or degeneration, most everything of interest here resides between these two poles.

At one outer limit, δυνάμεις have the quality of necessity; the paradigm for this necessity is nature.[57] At the other limit, δυνάμεις are a complement of or vehicle for liberty; on this side we find even the idealized and virtuous liberty of the *république*, where citizens, in Rousseau's words, "will force" one another "to be free."[58] Every δύναμις considered by Rousseau is—at one point or another—related back to the political phases of human activity.

In the arc between the natural and the human, δυνάμεις can range from composite, passive, diffuse, and blind to unitary, active, pointed, and intentional. On its face, Rousseau's politics may seem to be guided by a large-scale movement from the former to the latter. And it is true that a rare δύναμις like *autorité* often aims at and occasionally achieves this movement. Overall, however, this image is misleading. In another phase, even *autorité* will revert back to a kind of indistinct necessity as it settles into habit and *"seconde nature."* Thus, within the fabric of human relationships, δυνάμεις are better understood not so much in polar terms but as circular processes.

This image, too, is insufficient. While Rousseau's δυνάμεις are relational facts (that is, they occur within relationships and not in isolation) their various names are also related to one another. If it is correct to see in Rousseau's texts a hierarchy of these names, it may also be appropriate to figure the whole of δυνάμεις as a pyramid rather than as a circle: resting upon the broad base of *nécessité* we find sometimes narrower sometimes coterminous *forces*, out of which develops *puissance* and, eventually, the constructions of *pouvoir* and *autorité*. The higher levels depend on the lower ones. *Pouvoir*, for example, cannot exist without some kind of *force*, but it is not entirely reducible to it.[59] And various social *forces* often occur and effect without congealing into any kind of identifiable *pouvoir*. This relative priority of *force* is not the supposed political *a priori* of violence. Rousseau is not Max Weber, and the persistence of *force* in politics is much more subtle and indirect than a logical reduction to violence allows.[60] "Forcing . . . whoever refuses to obey the general will. . . . to be free" (OC III.364) is a condition in which the maintenance of the state resolves into the totality of social relations. Although politics in what is often considered its highest sense is about *pouvoir*—which is to say about the unitary and decisive composition of δυνάμεις through collective Will and purpose, and thus an achievement of freedom—the actualization of freedom itself is essentially "*l'usage de . . . liberté.*" This pragmatic fact, as we have already seen in the "formula for happiness," implicates *forces* and is measured by *bonheur*. This is why it makes some sense to conceive of δυνάμεις in terms of levels of a pyramid rather than as stages of linear or even as cyclical development.

This geometry does little more than provide a suggestive background for a topical approach. It would not be inaccurate (but still only heuristically correct) to say that the three most important terms for δύναμις can be distinguished as follows: *force* is physical, *puissance* is protosocial, and *pouvoir* is political.

As if to sweep away the old adage *might makes right*, Rousseau muses near the beginning of *Du Contract social* about a prepolitical—and admittedly hypothetical—situation ruled by the supposed "right of the strongest [*droit du plus fort*]." He makes clear that what is in play are *forces*. "The strongest [*le plus fort*] is never forceful enough [*assez fort*] to always be the master if he does not transform his *force* into law and obedience into duty. . . . *force* is a physical *puissance*; I do not see any way that some sort of morality can issue from its effects. To give way to *force* is an act of *nécessité*, not of Will" (OC III.354).* Here it seems that *force* is something less than *puissance* because it is merely physical. Carrying further this impression, Rousseau offers, almost as a principle, that "men cannot engender new forces, but only unite and direct those which exist" (OC III.360).† As submission to *force* involves not choice but unmediated *nécessité*, there is nothing moral about it. Absent this moral element, it is fair to say that *force* cannot be the definitive factor in moral or political relationships of mastery or domination.

---

* "Le plus fort n'est jamais assez fort pour être toujours le maitre, s'il ne transforme sa force en droit, et l'obéïssance en devoir. . . . La force est une puissance phisique; je ne vois point quelle moralité peut résulter de ses effets. Céder à la force est un acte de nécessité, non de volonté. . . ."

† ". . . Les hommes ne peuvent engendrer de nouvelles forces, mais seulement unir et diriger celles qui existent. . . ."

Puissance is not like a falling rock or a smashing fist. Nor does it arise within the fabric of relations of fully constituted society. It is somewhere in-between or over-lapping. A person preparing to enter *le pacte social* has *puissance* (OC III.361). A state in the anarchy of international relations is a *puissance*.[61] While all such examples retain an element of *force*, the maxim "obey *puissances*" would be super-fluous if it meant nothing more than "give way to force [*cédez à la force*]." And Rousseau thinks it is not superfluous. Were a brigand to stop you in the woods, "one must by *force* give up one's purse," yet "in the last analysis the pistol he holds is also a *puissance*." The difference, somewhat perversely, seems to be that the pistol-thing is in the hands of a human being, while the person-brigand confronts you like a thing (OC III.355).

As we have seen, with certain qualifications *force* becomes *puissance*; likewise, with certain qualifications *puissance* becomes *pouvoir*. For example, a *puissance légitime* is *pouvoir*.[62] Where *force* and *puissance* are manifold capacities, *pouvoir* tends to name the use of such capacities for mastery or control. The primary name of this mastery is *souveraineté* and it is, ideally, singular. That does not mean, however, that it is in any sense simple or that it can be achieved through immediate *force*.[63] Indeed, to speak of *pouvoir*, and the related notion of *liberté*, is always to bring into play a complex social fact, rather than a physical one.[64]

Two major points need to be made here. The first is that in spite of its irre-ducible difference, *pouvoir* remains entangled in — or, to speak more precisely, constituted from — the very wide range and complex applications of the other sorts of δυνάμεις from which it is distinguished. That this hybridity is essential to all sorts of δυνάμεις is made clear by the most extreme case, in which *force* and *pouvoir* would become identical: the "moral person [*personne morale*]" of "the city [*la cité*]" requires for its conservation a *force* that is "universal and compul-sory" and this "entirely absolute, entirely sacred, entirely inviolable *pouvoir* bears the name of sovereignty."[65] But Rousseau's theodicy makes clear that as it con-cerns humanity even God's power is no longer self-identical and universal in this way. Similarly, the architectonic project mapped in the "main passage" makes clear that humanity itself remains incapable of such a pure and unitary godlike power. Each instance of δύναμις has its boundary, across which it faces another instance of δύναμις. Outside the "limits of sovereign *pouvoir*"[66] and containing it we find sometimes the mundane *forces* of each person's *biens*[67] and sometimes the sublime "*usage de . . . liberté.*"[68] In fact, *liberté* and *pouvoir* "extend only as far as one's forces."[69] This means nothing more and nothing less than that *force* is a necessary, but not a sufficient, condition for these other δυνάμεις.

The second major point greatly complicates the first. It is that everything in Rousseau's sociology relates back to *la cité*, to the implication of the citizen in political relationships. In this respect, the image of a pyramid is again misleading, unless, perhaps, we turn it upside-down. As opposed to a physical model, which would derive all δυνάμεις from some basic unit of energy, in Rousseau's thinking political and moral *pouvoir* is the fundamental criterion by which the other δυνάμεις are measured. This means, for example, that only insofar as it is illuminating to refer to a "natural condition" is it accurate to call *puissance*—as I did above—protosocial. But in reality there is no such *état*. To assert, then, that *puissance* is partly social and partly not is to gesture toward a commonly occurring type of δύναμις that presents itself when the *cité* is not so much in composition as in decomposition, a δύναμις that bridges between social pathologies and correctives of them, or that plays out in one-on-one relationships which do not take the fundamental triadic form of the political.[70]

I now want to underscore a point that modulates much of what appears in the preceding three pages. For reasons analogous to what I just wrote about *puissance*, it turns out that even *force* is not just physical; to refer to it that way is merely to symbolize its objective compulsory effect. In relation to political and moral life all *forces* are social. Moreover, they are not created and they are not singular; appearing within the "division of action" *forces* are always combinations.[71] The regularity of these facts is expressed by the exceptions to them: it is awe-inspiring or terrifying when many *forces* move as one. Nature can do it: Rousseau recalls Newton's gravity, or the earthquake and tsunami that devastated the great city of Lisbon. And if the powers of the Republic could be so inflexible as to resist every other human *force*—which is to say, if the totality of human *forces* were turned toward one united end—mankind would be exempt from vice and raised up to virtue—which is to say, we would become gods.[72] But there can be little hope for this. No *force* ever issues *sui generis* from a single agent. And no human relationship or situation is ever subject to just one *force* at a time. Recognition of these conditions enters Rousseau's texts through a subtle fact of language: the word *forces* almost always appears in the plural.

From the level of the individual to the *volonté générale* and the *système social*, composition of force and the combination of forces are at the center of Rousseau's sociology. One may see the "*pacte social*" as a mechanism of this combination.[73] But this shining metaphor obscures something more vast. Underpinning civil, criminal, and constitutional laws by which the *corps politique* holds itself in check, primary *forces* operate through the body of persons and formulate their *bonheur*. This most fundamental type of law "engraves itself in the hearts of citizens" (OC III.394). *Forces* arise as *habitudes* to become pervasive practical social facts which *ordonnent*[74] life with others. Rousseau names them clearly; they are "*moeurs*, customs, and above all opinion."[75] Through the processes of life these *habitudes* "every day take on new *forces*" and "make up the true constitution of the state" (OC III.394). The essence of this total process itself is complex but not mysterious; indeed, it famously appears in most ancient conceptions of politics. It is through the living experience of language that the specifically *political* emerges from the social web of relationships with others.[76] The "political fact" has two aspects: when it congeals it gives form to widely distributed *habitudes*; when it animates, this fact is *force*.[77]

Thus, Rousseau speaks with Cicero not with Caesar when he says that "it is only the *force* of the state that makes for the liberty of its members."[78] In that phrase "above all opinion" we discover the maximum engine of decisive *force publique*.[79] There is more at work than the deployment of armies or the police in giving "the best possible form to the 'public thing' [*res publicum*]" (OC III.393).

Of course, Rousseau occasionally seems to insist on *forces* over and against language. Nonetheless, the clear republican sensibility that guides him as a political thinker leads such statements astray. A telling example of this type of statement occurs in the *Essai sur l'origine des langues* when he finally comes to consider the "relation of languages to governments" (OC V.428). A sharp distinction is made between Moderns and Ancients. For the former "no changes occur anymore except with arms and money" (OC V.428). For any careful reader of Rousseau it is clear that this is a sign of corruption, for if you "give money" to rulers "soon you will have chains" (OC III.429). For the Ancients, "persuasion took the place of public force." Although this seems like a simple opposition between *persuasion* and *force*, it is not. For, with respect again to the Moderns, Rousseau goes on to insinuate that "soldiers in homes" are, as much as "posters on streetcorners," ways of "speaking" (OC V.428). What is meant by this qualification? Obviously, guns are not words. The underlying point is that physical force and violence have political significance only in the context of social relationships, relationships which are in turn constituted through language, and that this broader context is ultimately more determinative than the guns themselves.

The range of Rousseau's δυνάμεις divides into several categories—like *force*, *puissance*, *pouvoir* —and can be mapped with geometric metaphors. These δυνάμεις also present this following further complexity: they vary with phases of human activity.[80] That is, even a single category like *force* may appear one way at one moment and another way at another moment.

A human being has a material existence and, in this respect, the word *force* applies to us as it applies to all bodies, including inanimate ones. A human being is also an animal and is thus implicated in an additional type of *forces* that derive from the simple fact of organic process. With animation, *force* becomes passional, reflexive,[81] or habitual; that is, in a specific and peculiar sense, it is passive.

To see this is to turn a bright light on a further phase. The human being is also entangled in the activation of *force*. In the activation of *force* its material and animal aspects are centered on an object; *force* takes on a new form and a new potential. The more centered and focused *hic et nunc*, the more *force* becomes unitary in this phase; the more significant the object, the more the composition of *force* becomes complex in this phase. Indeed, the focused unity of *force* corresponds to heightened significance which, in itself, typically brings complexity to the foreground.[82] This ambivalent structure—at once, and unavoidably, both unitary and complex—emerges in the arc of action. It is not a process of simple generation, but primarily involves acts of composition and combination. This suggests why *pouvoir* and *liberté* can be distinguished from but not disassociated from *force*. The highest unity of political *force*—which Rousseau represents with the famous phrase *volonté générale*—is the complete and total combination of all *forces* in the *cité*, the totality of the δυνάμεις of all citizens.

While notoriously obscure, this image of *force* can be clarified if we identify it—as Rousseau does—with *opinion*, and if we amplify our contemporary understanding of *opinion* with reference to *moeurs* and *coutumes*. Putting the question of *force* this way reveals it, again, to be always a question of *forces* in the plural, even if only a single person or a single Will is involved. Thus, it is not sufficient to see that *forces* always come in bundles. *Forces* are always distributed in time and space, across persons and through the environments that constitute action as such.[83] Moreover, this means that the struggles to appropriate and assign one's own title to *forces* (which are always ongoing)[84] can only result in "ownership" of *forces* in a special and limited sense. Just as property exists as a function of the state, the meaning of the claim *this is my force* and the effectivity of the fact it names are a function of the web of human relationships within which the meaning and the effectivity emerge. Individual agents have *forces* only in this profoundly sociological sense. It is against this background that the "formula for happiness," even the formula for personal happiness, should ultimately be understood.

As a systematic thinker, Rousseau takes this point very far.[85] Although he relates the *forces* of an individual back to society, it is finally politics that serves as the crucial matrix for *forces*.[86] How this operates depends on the aspect under which politics itself is viewed. The "body politic . . . is called . . . State when it is passive, Sovereign when it is active" (OC III.362). The fact that most of the time the *corps politique* is passive does not disentangle it from the ongoing composition and decomposition of δυνάμεις. It means, again, that "*moeurs*, customs, and above all opinion" are absolutely decisive. With the capacity to perceive itself—to obtain a "*moi* [self]"—the *corps politique* has the added *forces* that derive from "a sensibility common to its members" (OC III.399).

In the considerations just offered we can begin to see the failure of a simple categorical view of Rousseau's δυνάμεις. One expects to find *pouvoir publique* or *puissance publique* in the studied and precise terms of *Du Contract social* and yet there is no such thing. There is only *"force publique."* Whereas *"pouvoir souverain"* is unitary and focused, like a laser projected by the Will, *"force publique"* is a sort of radioactive emanation from or a field running through society.[87] It corresponds to the factuality and thus "passivity" of *l'État* rather than the actuality and activity of *souveraineté*. It "has as its end the conservation of *l'État*" (OC III.399). Yet, the one cannot exist without the other. The phases of *force* itself explain, at least in part, this coexistence.

Recall that when Rousseau declares his objection to the maxim "might makes right" he adds that he cannot see "any way that some sort of morality can issue from the effects of *force*" (OC III.354). This makes some sense if, as we just saw, *forces* are distinct from what can be Willed. The common physical metaphor for *forces* supports this intuition, and does so in precisely the terms we shall analyze later in this book.[88] Moreover, if we accept Rousseau's view that socially constituted *habitudes* play into *forces* (also as sketched above) it again seems plausible to assert that *forces* and *moralité* are not related. In either case, *forces* do not rise to the level of *moralité* because, as long as Will remains tangential, no identifiable *personne* or *être morale* is responsible for the effects of *forces*.[89]

What I have just written may seem like a source of clarity, but in fact it introduces complications that will ultimately unseat Rousseau's fundamental claims about "things [*les choses*]." On the one hand, the thinglike quality of *forces* should exclude them from the considerations of moral and political life. On the other hand, exactly what gives to *forces* this thinglike quality is that they emerge within the fabric of *moeurs*, which is to say the substance of *moralité* itself.[90]

Thus, Rousseau's declaration that "I cannot see any way that some sort of morality can issue from the effects of *force*" (OC III.354) is deeply misleading and his attempt to mobilize a commonplace—"might does not make right" (OC III.355)—in favor of his claims about the legitimate uses of *pouvoir* ends by reducing *force* to its opposite. *Forces* are in fact thoroughly implicated in the moral existence of social beings.

We may now begin to turn back toward the "formula for happiness" by reentering our discussion of *Émile* through the topic of *forces*. As Rousseau makes clear that the individuation of persons is essential to moral existence, he also suggests that this process depends on the development of *forces*. By the opening pages of Book II this process has arrived at a decisive moment. "Another development," Rousseau writes, "renders children's whining less necessary: it is the development of their *forces*" (OC IV.301). This development bears directly on happiness because "being themselves more able, they need less frequently to recur to others" (OC IV.301). While these initial changes may be measured within the "formula for happiness," they also have significance that can only be captured in broader terms, terms which relate back to how the question of happiness is to be integrated into the analysis of society as a whole.

> With their force develops the knowledge that permits them to direct it. It is at this second stage that the life of the individual begins in earnest; it is then that he becomes self-conscious. Memory extends the feeling of identity across all the moments of his existence; he becomes truly one, the same, and as a result already capable of happiness or misery. It is therefore important to begin here to consider him a moral being. (OC IV.301)*

This suggests that a distinction brought forward in the preceding section is of only limited heuristic value. Rousseau's psychology is not philosophical but rhetorical; that is, he understands human motives and emotions as part of society, not prior to it, and as something that can only be understood in practice.[91] This, again, is why "it is necessary to study society by way of men, and men by way of society" (OC IV.524). The unity of the "self" makes Man a moral being, capable of experiencing happiness and misery.[92] As the relevant type of unity arises from individuation, and individuation is a consequence of the development of *forces*, the proper retort when Rousseau says—one last time here—"I do not see any way that some sort of morality can issue from the effects of *force*" (OC III.354) would be this: *Jean-Jacques! Read more carefully your own book!*

This ambiguity in the *topos* of *forces* may lead readers into deep confusion. For, while the tutor is proposing that education advances by way of personal individuation, Rousseau also believes that this is exactly what society prevents. Proper individuation, it would seem, is only possible in the "state of nature." This suggests a quandary that will enter our considerations again later: if successful individuation is necessary for moral life, why is moral life an aspect of society rather than of nature?

For now, however, let us only take further note of the extent to which *forces* play a clear part in moral life as society advances. Rousseau declares to his pupil: "My child, there can never be happiness without courage, nor virtue without

---

* "Avec leur force se dévelope la conoissance qui les met en état de la diriger. C'est à ce second dégré que commence proprement la vie de l'individu: c'est alors qu'il prend la conscience de lui-même. La mémoire étend le sentiment de l'identité sur tous les momens de son existence, il devient véritablement un, le même, et par conséquent déja capable de bonheur ou de misére. Il importe donc de commencer à le considérer ici comme un être moral."

struggle. The word 'virtue' comes from *'force'*; *force* is the foundation of all virtue. [Thus,] virtue belongs only to a being that is weak by nature and strong by his Will" (OC IV.817).* Likewise with *forces* in the formation of the political order. The circuitous highway of social evolution set forth in the *Discours sur . . . l'iné-galité* forms a massive conceptual crossroads with *Du Contract social* at the beginning of the chapter called *"Du pacte social."* Rousseau picks up the story just as the "state of nature" has fallen deep into its inexorable decline. The most important accelerator of that decline is the development of individuals and their particular *forces*, which are applied, naturally, to maintaining themselves in that condition—an *état* which, having become a "war of all against all," is obsolete as a human way of life. "Thus, this primitive condition can no longer subsist, and the human species would perish if it did not change its way of being" (OC III.360).

The gravity of this situation is characterized through another telling paraphrase of the "formula for happiness" in which a shift from individual to social *forces* proposes itself: "I assume Men arrived at that point where the obstacles that undermine their preservation in the state of nature win out by way of their resistance over the *forces* that each individual is able to employ to maintain himself in that state" (OC III.360).† The slight grammatical oddity of this sentence is tied to its function: it begins the chapter *"Du pacte social"* of the book *Du Contract social*, as if that pivotal convention will be the logical consequence of a particular condition that has already been stated. Thus, as in formal reasoning, Rousseau opens by saying "I assume *x*," where *x* is the condition {*obstacles* > *forces*}; this is a paraphrase of the formula {*forces* < *besoins*} because *obstacles* include the fact that one increasingly needs the *forces* of others to survive. The word *"resistance"* here maintains its older human sense in addition to conveying its newer physical sense. If the ratio of *forces/besoins* describes society, the ratio *obstacles/forces* is more like an intolerable Hobbesian condition of war.[93]

To ameliorate this unhappy disproportion of *besoins* over *forces*, this disorder, humankind must "change its way of being." That means that we should "substitute law for man" and back the law with a "real force that is superior to the action of every particular Will." These many and contradictory Wills are the cause of so-

---

* "Mon enfant, il n'y a point de bonheur sans courage, ni de vertu sans combat. Le mot de 'vertu' vient de 'force'; la force est la base de toute vertu. La vertu n'appartient qu'à un être foible par sa nature, et fort par sa volonté; . . ."

† "Je suppose les hommes parvenus à ce point où les obstacles qui nuisent à leur conservation dans l'état de nature, l'emportent par leur résistance sur les forces que chaque individu peut employer pour se maintenir dans cet état."

cial disorder, and constitute, at this general level, the *besoins-obstacles* that must be overcome in order to achieve social happiness.

At least, this is where Rousseau is leading us. Reiterating in various versions and at various levels the "formula for happiness" is one way he brings together his whole project, which in nearly every text he wrote up to 1762 is to educate the citizen. Thus, it may fairly be said, the "formula for happiness" becomes a showcase through which to glimpse the hybridity and social constitution of various δυνάμεις. This is what makes Rousseau's sociology so important for politics. This is the context in which the use of the word *forces* in the "formula for happiness" expresses—directly and by wide implication—something general about mankind "abandoned to ourselves."

Still, there is no escaping the contradictory elements in the notion of *forces*. On the one hand, there are times when Rousseau really wants the reader to believe that *force*—appearing as a quality in the world of nature with its things and animals, but even as capacities in human beings—has nothing to do with morality. On the other hand, *force* is an absolutely primary component of happiness, virtue, and power, all of which are, according to Rousseau, moral and political qualities. *Forces* are also a primary component of liberty, which may appear in nature but achieves its fundamental significance in the moral world.[94]

One could read this as incoherence. I propose instead that this ambiguity is the birthmark of a new discursive field, an emerging sense of the whole of society and its *liens sociaux* as networks of relations within a flexible but structured fabric of dependence. These are precisely the contradictory elements that converge in the "main passage" which is the focal point of the inquiry in this book and to which we now return.[95]

§21

SOMETIMES A CHILD IS NOT A CHILD— SYLLEPSIS AND THEORY

The "main passage" is apostrophic.[96] It is also continuous with Rousseau's didactic program. The theoretical content is tied into that longer thread. Having now made explicit the inherent complexity of one of the key terms—*forces*—of the "formula for happiness," we can return to the discussion initiated in §19, where a general statement of the "formula for happiness" was drawn from a few lines in the "main passage." Recall Rousseau's maxim that "whoever does what he wants is happy if he suffices to himself" and "whoever does what he wants is not happy if his *besoins* are greater than his *forces.*"

In the "main passage" Rousseau repeatedly, insistently presents the image of the child. While initially it seems that the major theme of the first paragraph is *liberté*, reference to the child is a way to underscore the "formula for happiness." For, unlike the adult, the liberty of children will always "be limited by their weakness" and the significance of this fact reaches us through the "formula for happiness."

The situation of the child also reveals another aspect of the "natural condition." Readers often suppose, given other things that Rousseau has written, that happiness is the rule in the "state of nature." Yet, because it will almost always be true that the child's undeveloped *forces* are less than his *besoins*, the "formula for happiness" requires that the child will not be happy even in the "state of nature" and that, therefore, the "state of nature" is neither essentially linked to the condition of *bonheur* nor can it function simply as a symbol of *bonheur*. Likewise, if the child is not happy in the "state of nature" then the image of the child or childhood cannot simply be a metonymy for lost happiness. Indeed, Rousseau will soon invoke that image in a critical, even derogatory way.

This is an effective if somewhat superficial way to understand how Rousseau actually moves against a common interpretation of his thinking. Additional vectors of his real intention appear with a closer and more literal reading of the text. For, when it says that the child's "*besoins* surpass his *forces*," we read this as "the child is unhappy" only once we have accepted the "formula for happiness."

But the formula may not be applicable here.[97] While Rousseau does not make clear at exactly what point children become capable of *bonheur*, he does provide some clues concerning initiation into unhappiness. "Suffering is the first thing [the child] must learn." This is why Rousseau lets his student bump his head (OC IV.300). The lesson seems to take some time—"at sixteen the adolescent knows what it is to suffer." So, even if suffering sometimes appears in the realm of immediate sense perception, it is in fact a social construction and the object of an extended learning project.[98]

However one views suffering, happiness and unhappiness are in a different class. A child becomes a "moral being [*être moral*]" who is "capable of *bonheur* or misery" only with the development of *forces* and Will (OC IV.301). These capacities develop, in part, as consequences of the experience of suffering.[99] Their development marks the beginning of the life of an individual with his own identity.

Well-defined individuals are capable of comparing themselves with others (a fact more widely consequential than the ill effects marked out in the *Discours sur . . . l'inégalité*).[100] They cease to be merely natural beings; they become morally developed beings. Only moral beings are capable of happiness. This is the condition within which unhappiness emerges as a component of suffering.

Whether or not this series of qualifications seems clear, the way Rousseau plays them out leads to confusion. In this first part of the "main passage" we are asked to consider the *"état naturel."* This is a pre-moral condition. *Bonheur* is a moral quality. How, then, can Rousseau propose to evaluate the child's happiness in the "state of nature"?

Let us consider this as a curiosity rather than dismiss it as a contradiction. It brings something important to our attention. What justifies this difficult constellation of topics and claims is, I think, Rousseau's adoption of a particular literary strategy. This strategy has broad implications for his argument at many levels; it plays a constitutive role in his social theory of politics.

To be sure, the word "child" refers to a person at a particular developmental stage. Indeed, the specificity of childhood may be another of Rousseau's "discoveries."[101] The text—a treatise on education—compels us to take it first in this way. But Rousseau will also use "the child" as a metonymy. As I have already suggested, "the child" and "children" do not stand for happiness in a golden age. Rather, these images bring to the foreground difficulties that are associated with dependence in particular and political life in general. Thus, beyond the chain of single words in the text, the theory brewing in those words demands that we bring this usage into account as well.[102]

The ambiguity—does the "formula for happiness" apply to children or not?—is fed by the double use of "the child" as the subject or object of didactic claims and as a *topos* of theoretical argument. Each function opens onto its own complex semantic field. The single word therefore operates as syllepsis to bring forces from both semantic fields into play.[103]

My point here is that it will impede rather than aid our inquiry to choose one or the other of these semantic fields so as to assert a single correct interpretation. Rousseau's astonishing theoretical insight often derives from the way he operates through such ambivalence to clarify underlying structures of symbolic interaction. Thus, in my effort to bring to light Rousseau's *way of theorizing* and thus the *content of his theory*, I shall mimic his literary strategy, turning syllepsis into an instrument of interpretation. This will help us, as readers and as thinkers, to play back and forth between different levels of meaning. Concern for consistency on a specific point is secondary.[104]

Although I shall not make much of them at this stage in the argument, there are additional levels of meaning latent in many occurrences of the word "child" in *Émile*. Rousseau's is self-consciously a theoretical enterprise and, as he tells us, it is therefore "necessary to generalize our views." How shall we do this? It requires that we "consider the abstract man in our pupil [*considérer dans nôtre élêve l'homme abstrait*]."[105] Rousseau goes further. At a certain point in the gloss and companion volume to *Émile*—that is, *Du Contract social*—he writes of the "first societies." Rehearsing a familiar *topos*, he hypothesizes that "the family is thus, as it were, the first model of political societies: the leader is the image of the father, the people is the image of the children" (OC III.352).* This tip of the hat to classical patriarchy is not, in my view, the key gesture here. Rousseau engages in an insidious multiplication of syllepsis and this promotes the generalizations of theory. *Au premier degré*, "the child" is an immature human being; once removed, "the child" is a metonymy for dependence; two steps removed, "the child" stands not only for mankind in general, but is an icon for what mankind, "well-ordered," could be, which is to say "a people," or the self-governing *être moral* of political society. To these three "children"—the novice individual, the person suffering dependence, the nascent political being—Rousseau offers himself as tutor, and under his tutelage the three "children" become one, passing in time from child to man to citizen, from nature to *société* to the *cité*. As we have seen, this is a "method" that ties Rousseau to Plato, and at the very end of this book it will be possible to review in a different light the experience of the child as the emergence of the body politic.

For now, however, we will stay closer to the text. The definition of happiness and the formula by which it is attained and measured come together when Rousseau writes that "the first of all goods is liberty": "A truly free Man only wants what he is capable of, and does what pleases him. There you have my fundamental maxim. What matters is only to apply it to childhood, and all the rules of education will flow from it" (OC IV.309).† The claim is this: together with the rules of education, you, the reader of *Émile*, will be exposed to the proper vision of the happy and free person who must never want more than his capacities permit and only do what pleases him, even though he lives together with other human beings entitled to do the same.

A moment ago I raised a question about the applicability of the "formula for

---

*"... la famille est donc si l'on veut le premier modéle des sociétés politiques: le chef est l'image du pere, le peuple est l'image des enfans...."

†"L'homme vraiment libre ne veut que ce qu'il peut et fait ce qu'il lui plait. Voila ma maxime fondamentale. Il ne s'agit que de l'appliquer à l'enfance, et toutes les régles de l'éducation vont en découler."

happiness" to the child. This question was further complicated by the location of the child: is he in the "state of nature" or not? I tentatively resolved part of this difficulty by pointing out that, in Rousseau's text, sometimes a child is not a child. Sometimes "child" is metonymy for dependence; sometimes "child" is syllepsis between the discourse of education and the discourse of politics.[106] Sometimes "child" is a way of seeing the world, a way of doing *theoria*.

Before moving to the next step, I pause here to state summarily what will soon become more precise and clear. The "formula for happiness" is a powerful reductive maxim that brings together many aspects of Rousseau's vision and connects his thinking to traditions deep and wide. Yet the "formula for happiness" can only carry the argument—Rousseau's, but also ours—to a certain point. Thus, further, sometimes the figure of "the child" stands for weakness, for the failure of some fundamental trope that, from another perspective, seems to be the linchpin of the whole theory. Perhaps this is what Kant sensed when he began the famous essay "What Is Enlightenment?" with the admonition "Enlightenment is man's emergence from his self-incurred immaturity."[107]

Moreover, as we dismantle some of the complexities of dependence away from nature and in the "civil state" we will see that the main source of *bonheur* is neither the unrestricted satisfaction of particular needs, nor even the pleasure one might gain from applying ample *forces* to *besoins*.[108] The final source of happiness will eventually appear as a person's capacity to assuage anxiety and disrupt uncertainty.

This may seem far from the "formula for happiness" under discussion here. For Rousseau, however, the relation is close if obscure. Once happiness is understood as relative to *forces* constituted outside the self, with individuation allowing for the management of those *forces*, the continuity of the self enters the equation. We would not have the problem of anxiety or uncertainty if we did not care to know the future. But living both as a coherent individual self *and* in commerce with other people makes *prévoyance* a pressing and insatiable need.[109] Thus, we shall see that even to this problem the "formula for happiness" provides an impressive means of access.

22

Dependence Articulates *Bonheur*

To this point I have presented the "formula for happiness" (*forces ≥ besoins =
bonheur*) as though it were primarily applicable to individuals. This approach
seems justified by the place Rousseau gives to individuation in the moral development of the capacity for happiness.[110]

Why, then, must the problem be restated in the relational terms of dependence? Why is it not sufficient to see the problem of happiness as simply a personal balance of *forces* and *besoins?*

There is an easy reply to this question. Look back to where we started. A major
theme of this book is the process by which dependence becomes or fails to
become a moral problem; how one accounts for this has fundamental consequences for social and political theory. Our inquiry has dwelt at length on *bonheur* because this is the first topic used by Rousseau to assess the problem of dependence. Thus, it is obviously consistent to return now to "dependence."

Nonetheless, we cannot advance far by simply closing this circle. Rousseau's
psychology suggests that individuation is an always incomplete social process
involving ongoing, ambivalent, and unpredictable interaction with others.[111]
The *topos* of dependence opens a door onto this scene. And just as *bonheur*
is not a fixed category, neither is dependence. Thus, until the inherent complexity of dependence is more carefully explored, the value—in theory or in
practice—of declaring whether or not dependence measures up to happiness
remains small.

This exploration will now be guided by the idea that dependence articulates
bonheur—gives it detail and substance and motive and flexibility—and that it is
exactly such imbrications that constitute the moral structure of dependence.

As we insist that *bonheur* is not simply a mental state, that it becomes a topic
of personal or theoretical inquiry within a practical setting, and that this setting
must be articulated in terms of dependence, an additional question arises. Who
partakes in the relationships to be measured by the "formula for happiness"? In
the preceding section, it appeared that in the "state of nature" the most important difference between the child and the adult is not represented in the "for-

mula for happiness." The decisive difference was that, in the "state of nature," the child is dependent and the adult is not.

Some crucial aspects of the complex structure of Rousseau's thought inherent in this idea cannot be made clear until much later in this book. Still, it will help at this point to look ahead. To do so, we must first step back. Recall the idea that Ernst Cassirer brought to our attention. Rousseau makes a pivotal distinction between dependence-from-things and dependence-from-persons.[112] Another precise set of beliefs underpins this claim. A range of additional topics remain to be considered before this set of beliefs will come into clear light. What we shall see below (and then further in §29 ff.) is that dependence *per se* is not a problem for human beings, whether they are young or old. Dependence in the abstract is an analytic fiction meant to clarify practical circumstances for action. What matters in experience is the peculiar nature of the "object" from which one depends. Different "objects" may lead to varying degrees of uncertainty in the dependent.

Characteristically, Rousseau holds constant in thought one element of this theoretical composition to see precisely how the other elements move. Attention to the "object" corresponds to a certain approach to the "subject" of dependence. What is relevant here is that Rousseau often assumes that the dependent "subject" is a perfectly formed person who would not be anxious under conditions of certainty. This person would learn to be anxious only as the evolution of society introduced uncertainties into everyday life. He might then, with the extraordinary consolidation of social order emerging from "*le contract social,*" lose the habit of anxiety as uncertainties decreased over time.[113] These interrelated themes are played out over and over again in Rousseau's writings. It is not by chance that the general statement with which *Émile* begins — "everything is good as it leaves the hands of the Author of things" (OC IV.245) — is rapidly followed up with a similar claim about the education of the pupil and the author of the book: "in leaving my hands . . . he will be above all a Man."[114] This is Rousseau's theory of the perfectly formed person.[115] The *Discours sur . . . l'inégalité* presents Rousseau's theory of the emergence of social uncertainty and anxiety from the experience of a perfectly formed person. *Du Contract social* offers his theory of how personal happiness could be built on civil order. Implicit in the architectonic of these three books and constantly reappearing in their pages is the image of an imperfect person whose insecurities would follow a different pattern and produce different results. That is exactly why a measuring paradigm is required. What makes the "subject" susceptible to measurement is not just that the perfect and imperfect are both human beings, but that they are human beings with the specific and fundamental faculty of *perfectibilité.*[116] This is what joins the beginning and the end of speculative history; it is the motor of social evolution.[117]

Even if we can agree without hesitation that Rousseau excludes dependence-from-persons from the "state of nature," his appeal to its complement, dependence-from-things, is more ambiguous. On its face, this second kind of dependence seems identical with the "state of nature." A suspicion is raised, however, when Rousseau insists both that no return to the "state of nature" is possible and that we had best aim to make the civil estate a copy of it.[118]

Considering this tension more carefully below, we shall see that Rousseau actually conceives of three sorts of dependence.[119] More precisely, there are two sorts of dependence-from-things: one concerns the things of nature and the other the things of Man. The former begins in the "state of nature" *and it persists*; the other begins later. This additional distinction is held high or obscured as suits the rhetorical occasion; overall, it gives a bias to Rousseau's theory of society.

In addition, as dependence-from-things rises or declines in significance in relation to the "state of nature" it will be important to understand how the latter *topos* functions at several levels, within both a conceptual architecture and within a historical or developmental narrative. Considered, for example, as a moment in a process of social evolution, the "state of nature" presents Man in one of his specific stages, in a certain form. Although interpreters haggle over the "real" or "fictive" status of the "state of nature," few have taken seriously the ways that Rousseau *does not* adhere strictly to a developmental narrative: although he says clearly that we cannot return to the "state of nature," it may be possible that the "state of nature" (whatever it is) comes around again and again (cf. OC III.393). This is not, as in Hobbes, a collapse into civil war, but rather, as in Vico, a complex mechanism for expressing the historical character of human experience at every given moment without lapsing into the literary conceit of "memory."[120]

Only in the last part of the present book, once the largely subterranean edifice of Rousseau's worldview has been made visible, will it be possible to sort out these matters in a more satisfying way. The question *"why* does Rousseau take the difference between types of dependence to be categorical?" will increasingly be the pivot point of our investigation. From there we shall see not only what is at stake in the distinction between dependence-from-things and dependence-from-persons, but the consequences that follow for the way we perceive, conceive, and live out political life in modern society.

23

Dependence Is Not Weakness

While we have seen that dependence can be qualified in various ways, it is important to keep in mind that even without qualification Rousseau's usage also varies grammatically. This produces semantic, and ultimately theoretical, effects. From the beginning of *Émile*, Rousseau uses the verb *dépendre* almost exclusively in its logical or causal sense.[121] The noun *dépendance* appears just once in Book I. The discourse at this stage is primarily psychological and the word refers to a *sentiment* rather than to a condition in the person's environment. In Book II, in and around the "main passage," dependence becomes a circumstantial condition. That is, psychology is framed by sociology. Rousseau only uses the word *dépendance* to refer to a condition in the "state of nature" after the contrast with the *état civil* has been established. Before this point in the text, where the reader might have expected to see the word *dépendance*, Rousseau is prone to expressions like "remain in the position that nature assigned to you in the chain of beings."[122] Finally, in Book V, the general image of *dépendance* developed throughout the book is brought to bear as Rousseau deals with the education of Sophie, Émile's companion-to-be. Where the pregnant concept of dependence plays a prominent role in his stark discussion of gender difference, Rousseau's usage—and the theoretical position it supports—is clearly distinct from the earlier analysis of young men, and of mankind in general. Simply, and very much against himself, Rousseau writes: "dependence is a natural state for women."[123] As I have already indicated (§18 above) this reversal does not change the main argument pursued in this book, which is aimed to bring into question Rousseau's fundamental claims about dependence and the common sense for which they are both a source and an example. On the contrary, anyone who aimed to salvage Rousseau's position would need to address this peculiar reversal.

For now, we shall continue to take dependence as unitary. This will help clarify exactly how this aspect of experience is introduced into Rousseau's account of happiness. This shift in terms is thorny and merits a cautious approach.

Consider first the following quandary: a person with less *force* than *besoins* is unhappy; if a dependent person is unhappy, does that mean that being weak and being dependent are the same condition?

It is not unusual to answer "yes" to this question. For example, Pierre Burgelin suggests as much when, commenting on *Émile,* he writes that "the little child does not even have the liberty of natural Man, since he is necessarily born into dependence" (OC IV.1347, note 4).

This claim is not convincing. It is inconsistent with Rousseau's thinking.

Now, it is true that "We are born weak, we have need of force" (OC IV.248).* However, dependence is not the cause but the consequence of this weakness and need. The "first state of Man is poverty and weakness" and "from [children's] own weakness.... comes first the feeling of their dependence" (OC IV.286, 287).

One might assume that these "steps" in fact occur all at once, or unfold inexorably and indistinguishably as the biological clock of a human life begins to tick. In addition to imposing an unwarranted naturalism (a topic we shall pursue especially in §§43–46 below), this assumption would be misleading in fact and in theory. To see why, we need to pick up again briefly the discussion from the previous section on why dependence is the category through which happiness should be further articulated.

Here Rousseau's occasional avoidance of the term *dépendance* is telling. He does not use it to name the extremely "weak" condition in which the child finds himself after birth. This can be seen in his description of infants who have begun to develop their own and quite unsatisfactory *forces,* and who stop their use of crying as a simple communicative function: "Another development renders children's whining less necessary: it is the development of their *forces.* Being themselves more able, they need [*ont un besoin*] less frequently to recur to others" (OC IV.301).† It is in the organization of pedagogy around this fact that the problem of dependence reappears. Rousseau suggests that once a child has learned to speak, it is better to wait for him to stop crying. One should not respond to a child "when it pleases him, but when it pleases me; otherwise he would make me the servant of his Will and put me in the most dangerous sort of dependence which a tutor [*gouverneur*]¹²⁴ can be in with his student."¹²⁵§ The child is weaker than the tutor;

---

* "Nous naissons foibles, nous avons besoin de force . . ."

† "Un autre progrès rend aux enfans la plainte moins nécessaire: c'est celui de leurs forces. Pouvant plus par eux-mêmes, ils ont un besoin moins fréquent de recourir à autrui."

§ ". . . quand il lui plaît, mais quand il me plaît; autrement ce seroit m'asservir à ses volontés et me mettre dans la plus dangereuse dépendance où un gouverneur puisse être de son éléve."

the tutor risks dependence on the child. Thus, being weak and being dependent are not the same.

The child in the "state of nature" is unhappy because weakness limits the use of natural liberty, not because he depends on others to facilitate the "use of his liberty."

Indeed, when Rousseau offers his "fundamental maxim" concerning education — of Man, but also, I think, of Citizen and of Polity — he describes a situation we are inclined to think of in terms of dependence. He does not use the word. The key terms — *besoins* and *volonté* — are drawn from or related to the "formula for happiness": "The only person who actually achieves his Will is the one who, to do so, doesn't need to put another person's arms at the end of his own" (OC IV.309).* But the conclusion he draws directly from this observation concerns liberty, which is the context in which happiness is possible and the condition that defines dependence, so to speak, from the other side, "from which it follows that the first of all 'goods' is not authority but liberty" (OC IV.309).†

No one can deny that other people often help the child to satisfy his desires. But the relation between the child and these others seems to be something other than dependence. Remember that Rousseau states emphatically in the "main passage" that "dependence from Men . . . is of society."

As we have seen, a growing person in the *état naturel* individuates himself and gains an important kind of independence. This is, we might say, his birthright. It is, of course, crucial to his happiness. The reason, however, is that this kind of independence limits the proliferation of needs, although we need to keep in mind that this is not a *good* reason, because, as we saw in §4, independence is more often than not destructive and is in any event, as Montesquieu (1748, XI, 2) had argued, the antithesis of proper liberty.

On the other side of the equation, a person's *forces* come from the transformation of capacities (development of the body, increase in self-consciousness, proper functioning of memory, etc.). Rousseau would have us believe that these are outcomes of a natural education, but, of course, Émile is always under the watchful and programmatic eye of his tutor. At a certain point, the emergence of capacities must be recognized for what it really is — the outcome of the child's engagement in social practices.[126]

Whatever is its origin, dependence in the *état civil* is itself a social practice.

---

* "Le seul qui fait sa volonté est celui qui n'a pas besoin pour la faire de mettre les bras d'un autre au bout des siens . . ."
† ". . . d'où il suit que le prémier de tous les biens n'est pas l'autorité mais la liberté."

And, paradoxically, dependence typically constitutes a development of *forces*; for example, a soldier is dependent and stronger thereby.

The problem is that the same practices of dependence that generate additional *forces sociales* also multiply *besoins* at an exponential rate.

We shall return to this multivariate equation below. For now, this much is clear: dependence and weakness are related, but they are not the same.

§24

PROBLEMATIZING DEPENDENCE
AS UNHAPPINESS
A Platonic Riff

However, it is fair to assume provisionally that dependence can be a form of unhappiness. This assumption will lead us closer to the connection between the "formula for happiness" and the role played by dependence in Rousseau's social theory of politics.

It is not clear yet whether or not the maxim {*forces* ≥ *besoins* = *bonheur*}—the "formula for happiness"—can provide important insight into the *état civil*. Before we consider expanding the "formula for happiness" in that way we need to explore somewhat further the conceptual space opened by it.

Is it possible for a person to be independent but nonetheless weak and unhappy? This combination is quickly put to rest in the "main passage."

> Even in the state of nature, children enjoy only an imperfect liberty, comparable to that which is enjoyed by Men in the civil state. Each of us, no longer able to get along without others [*ne pouvant plus se passer des autres*],[127] becomes again in this respect weak and miserable.*

The child's imperfect liberty, even in the "state of nature," is similar to the condition of a mature person in civil society. The problem, the imperfection of

---

*"Les enfans ne joüissent, même dans l'état de nature, que d'une liberté imparfaite, semblable à celle dont joüissent les hommes dans l'état civil. Chacun de nous, ne pouvant plus se passer des autres, redevient à cet égard foible et misérable."

Man's civil estate, is that even, indeed especially, adults cannot do without other people. In society Man is pushed and pulled within a spiraling practical dialectic of *forces* and *besoins*. This dynamic situation is properly denoted in terms of dependence. At any given moment it can be measured by the "formula for happiness."

What Rousseau intends seems clear when he writes that "society made man weaker, not only by impeding the right he had over his own forces, but primarily by rendering those forces insufficient for him" (OC IV.309).* Yet, the problem only lurks in the background; its deep structure is manifest in the "formula for happiness." At first—for the child, or for the childlike inhabitants of the "state of nature"—dependence is not the cause but the consequence of weakness and need. In society, by contrast, it is dependence that causes a person to become weak.

Rousseau affirms this in a particularly suggestive way in the *Discours sur . . . l'inégalité*. He writes that Man, "in becoming sociable and Slave, becomes weak . . ."[128]† Of course, in the eighteenth and then the nineteenth century the Slave (one feels the capitalized French word *Esclave* hover between adjective and noun) is what Vico might have called the *universale fantastico* for dependence—the encompassing abstract image covering and connecting all of its real instances and necessary for apt judgment.[129] Famously in Rousseau and precisely in the "main passage," *Esclave* is the term of execration with which Rousseau judges the effects of dependence-from-persons.[130] What is less evident but absolutely central to Rousseau's thinking is that this weakness is relative, not absolute. Indeed, Rousseau explicitly defines weakness in relational terms: "When one says that Man is weak, what does that mean? The word weakness indicates a relation. A relation of the being to which one applies the term."[131]§

The important conclusion to be drawn from this is that an increase in weakness that is corollary to increased sociability and dependence may occur even while dependence increases *forces*. This is because the impact of dependence is twofold. The effect that typically draws our attention occurs on the *besoins* side of the formula. Nonetheless, it is interesting to note that under some circumstances *besoins* can also decrease; "slaves lose everything in their chains, even including their desire to get out of them" (OC III.353).

---

* "La societé a fait l'homme plus foible, non seulement en lui ôtant le droit qu'il avoit sur ses propres forces, mais sur-tout en les lui rendant insuffisantes."

† "En devenant sociable et Esclave, il devient foible . . ."

§ "Quand on dit que l'homme est foible, que veut-on dire? Ce mot de foiblesse indique un rapport. Un rapport de l'être auquel on l'applique."

So, again, while weakness and dependence are not directly related, they are indirectly related through the problem of needs. That is how the dependent person becomes unhappy. Weakness and misery are relative to one's position within a developing social system of dependence.

As we shall see below when the argument is fully developed, Rousseau proposes a solution for this. The imposition of inflexible law will constitute an attempt—he thinks it is the best attempt—to mitigate the ills of civil society by guaranteeing that dependence in the specific form of the need-for-others never surpasses *forces*; if dependence—deriving, for instance, from cooperation—was greater than *forces*, this would prevent the *usage de liberté*, and people would be unhappy.

I bring this point to the foreground now because it bears on the "main passage." Rousseau is well aware of the fact that most efforts to use the law in this way do not succeed. They have, unfortunately, a perverse effect, which is that although "we were made to be Men; laws and society have thrown us back into childhood."* Rather than mitigating the ills of civil society, law can exacerbate them. Every which way he turns, civil Man is dependent on his fellows.

To underscore the difficulties into which this fact leads us, Rousseau insists that Man *becomes once again* what he was as a child: a being too weak to meet his own needs and thus unhappy.[132]

Rousseau is emphatic in linking the image of childhood to the idea of dependence. The emphasis marks his intention. For, as we have already seen, infants are *not* considered by Rousseau to be dependent by nature. They are in fact and in nature weak. Only within a specific practical context and theoretical framework, however, can it be said that this is a corollary of dependence. That is how the metonymy becomes effective. That is how Rousseau can use the word "*enfants*" to characterize all those who are dependent in society. No one today will be surprised by this usage.

What strikes us is how he pushes this metonymy to an extreme. Rousseau writes in a stinging passage that great men *are* infants because they depend from, and even relish in, the care they demand from others: "The rich, the great, kings are all children who, seeing how one hurries to relieve their misery, draw from that very fact a puerile vanity, and they are quite proud of the care that one would never accord them if they were grown men."[133]†

---

* "Nous étions faits pour être hommes; les lois et la societé nous ont replongés dans l'enfance."

† "Les riches, les grands, les rois sont tous des enfans qui, voyant qu'on s'empresse à soulager leur misére, tirent de cela même une vanité puérile, et sont tout fiers des soins qu'on ne leur rendroit pas s'ils étoient hommes-faits."

This characterization functions within the overall system of *Émile*. It provides an opportunity to enlarge further at this point the image we are developing of the wider framework of his thinking.

Rousseau's *Émile* is part of a complex intellectual project. It bears the subtitle "On Education." It was not, therefore, a trivial matter when Rousseau explicitly advised his readers to read Plato's *Republic*,[134] which he called "the most beautiful treatise on education ever written."[135] Obviously, he is inviting comparison.

On one level, the reason is obvious: any author would be flattered, or could flatter himself, by such comparison. At another level, this seems like a strange gesture. Rousseau claimed to be writing "on education"; Plato claimed to be writing about politics. As if to leave no doubt, however, Rousseau brashly adds that the *Republic* "is not at all a work on politics." In this way, Rousseau seems intent on bringing the master thinker onto his own turf.

What is at stake when Rousseau so brusquely denies Plato's view of his own work and, quite frankly, several thousand years of common sense? How should we understand this? After all, the *Republic* does not cease to be a work of politics because Rousseau says so.

Reading these two works substantially after both Plato and Rousseau, we can see that the comparison encouraged by Rousseau actually cuts two ways. While he declares that his book is "on education," no one today can miss that it is at least as much as Plato's work a treatise on politics. In *Émile*, the representation of individual development becomes an instrument for the critical analysis of political life. There can be no doubt that this was Rousseau's purpose.[136]

These moves expose an integral relation between theory and its literary expression. Two magnetic questions draw readers to and through Rousseau's book: How can we be happy? and How shall we raise our children?

It is obvious that different answers may be given to these questions. Rousseau chooses to set up the first problem along certain lines. But in the balance of *forces* and *besoins* he offers a transparent way to consider at once happiness and the principles of education. These ideas are developed in an unexpected direction, since the "formula for happiness" is, in turn, articulated within the figure of *dépendance*. The whole complex argument is then connected back to the image of the child. And "the child," as we observed above, is by another syllepsis "the people." In this way, education is interpreted as civic education and is affirmed as the motor of political life.[137]

This is how Rousseau gives to his initial construction of the problem of dependence a motivation drawn from a very different set of concerns. The rhetorical force of his argument derives from exquisite *inventio*, a particularly fitting selection and combination of *topoi*. At the same time, he makes the problem of de-

pendence—with its eventual and narrower implications for liberty and government—from the beginning amenable to the solution he will give to it in the end.

§25

DEPENDENCE JOINS WEAKNESS
AND UNHAPPINESS

I now want to illustrate in a slightly different way my claim that the "formula for
happiness" is articulated through the figure of dependence. Here is an example:
the idea of dependence makes precise the linkage between "weak [*faible*]" and
"miserable [*misérable*]."

Stated in Rousseau's now familiar summary way, dependence in a social context makes us weak relative to needs and thus unhappy.

Rousseau further offers many terms with which to articulate this connection
in approximately the following way:

- Very soon after people come together in society, one can no longer make do
without others ["*ne pouvant plus se passer des autres*"];[138]

- in other words, they depend "from" one another;[139]

- through this dependence, the others become part of one's *forces*;[140]

- these *forces* are now unequivocally social rather than natural;[141]

- the development and maintenance of these transformed (but not necessarily
increased) *forces* almost surely will constitute new *besoins*;

- thus, society may increase both *forces* and *besoins*;

- moreover, the proportion between *forces* and *besoins* may also change, and
keep changing;

- the fact that this new balance derives from the social constitution of *forces* (as
much as from the more famous Rousseauean social constitution of *besoins*) is
important because

  (i) maintaining these new *forces* involves the costly matter of constant adjustments to and with other people, and therefore the new *besoins* asso-

ciated with it are likely to proliferate quickly, perhaps even one step ahead of the *forces* which are the result of those same dealings;[142]

(ii) unlike personal *forces*, which can typically be directed by personal Will toward the satisfaction of personal needs,[143] the extent to which the new social *forces* will be directed to the satisfaction of one's personal needs depends, roughly speaking, on enforcement—which is to say, on yet another newly created group of *besoins*—;

(iii) because socially composed *forces* are in ever greater measure distributed outside one's body, ken, and control, the more one draws upon and becomes accustomed to them the greater the likelihood that increased *forces* will be accompanied by increased anxiety, which is itself a motive for the further proliferation of *besoins*.[144]

All these changing proportions are measured by the "formula for happiness." Rousseau clearly believes that when everything is tallied up—total *forces*, old and new, minus existing *besoins*, minus the new *besoins* involved in bringing together the new social *forces*—the result will be that *forces* are no longer greater than or equal to *besoins*. Thus, dependence in society tends to make each person at once *faible* and *misérable*.

§26

DEMISE AND REINCARNATION OF THE "FORMULA FOR HAPPINESS"

Imagine that at least one step in the reasoning above is made too quickly. Is Rousseau really correct in believing that the element of social *forces* gained from others will be a net loss rather than an overall gain? Even if this extra force does constitute additional needs, perhaps it is, so to speak, a good investment? Could it not, all things considered, increase happiness?[145]

The answer to this question is rather obvious, if unexpected: one does not know in advance how the balance will come out. The "formula for happiness" is a heuristic of interpretation and judgment, not of prediction or teleology.[146]

Thus, let me now acknowledge clearly something that was only implicit in the preceding sections. I have been proposing and at each step providing a gloss for a blunt kind of "cost-benefit analysis." This has been useful as a point of departure and for some preliminary development.

But political life is not a market. Real problems cannot be reduced in this way and Rousseau is not so ignorant as to think that they can be. Indeed, Rousseau seems to have resisted pushing too far with the "formula for happiness," which is to say, with the maxim {*forces* ≥ *besoins* = *bonheur*}. He was increasingly reticent about its relevance for evaluating the *état civil*.

This reticence becomes visible in changes made from the first draft to the final version of *Du Contract social*. In the late 1750s Rousseau conceives his book in a commonplace way. "We begin," he says, "with inquiry into what gives birth to the necessity for political institutions" (OC III.281). He will build an initial argument drawing from what he and others have already written in the *Encyclopédie*.[147] He extends this with criticism of a range of familiar hypotheses. Most telling, however, is the detailed definition of the problem. It is drawn in terms of the "formula for happiness": "Man's *force* is so precisely proportioned to his natural *besoins* and to his primitive condition that, with even the slightest change in that condition and the increase of his *besoins*, the assistance of others of his own kind becomes necessary for him" (OC III.281–82).* A few more pages lead to a chapter called "Of the fundamental pact." The title itself—referring to the solution for the previously stated problem that occurs among human beings without reference to God or Nature—marks out the central idea that humankind "abandoned to ourselves" is responsible for the evils we endure. It confronts the reader with a first version of what will be the most famous line Rousseau ever wrote: "Man is born free, and yet everywhere he is in chains" (OC III.289; cf. 351).† He proposes to investigate this terrible fact in a way tied to an additional trenchant deduction: "the social order is a sacred right that serves as the basis for all the others; nonetheless, in no way is nature the source of this right; it is therefore founded on a convention" (OC III.289).§ In other words, at this early stage Rousseau sees his task as to "discover what that convention is and how it was able to take shape" (OC III.289).

The substance of the *"convention"* is an exceedingly complicated matter beyond the scope of the present book.[148] Here we are concerned with "the fundamental problem to which the institution of the state provides the solution" (OC

---

* "La force de l'homme est tellement proportionné à ses besoins naturels et à son état primitif, que pour peu que cet état change et que ses besoins augmentent, l'assistance de ses semblables lui devient nécessaire, ..."

† "L'homme est né libre, et cependant partout il est dans les fers."

§ "... l'ordre social est un droit sacré qui sert de base à tous les autres; cependant ce droit n'a point sa source dans la nature; il est donc fondé sur une convention."

III.289–90). And what we find is a long paragraph where that problem is composed as a set of variations on the "formula for happiness" (OC III.289–90).

I set before you these elements from the first draft of *Du Contract social* because — and this is my main point here — these iterations of the "formula for happiness" are absent from the final version. This absence is especially striking because much of the surrounding text remains the same.

The "formula for happiness" diminishes in importance as attention is directed away from the situation of individuals and toward the problem of politics. This does not just occur at the level of the sentence. With politics on the horizon in *Du Contract social*, Rousseau is generally more concerned with the constitution of *forces* than with the construction of *besoins*. This fact can be measured by comparing the book in its entirety with the other two main texts we consider here. Counting occurrences of the two words in the *Discours sur . . . l'inégalité*, we find that *force* appears at approximately the same rate as *besoins* (the textual ratio *forces/besoins* is 0.965); in the first three books of *Émile* that ratio is nearly the same (1.083) and overall it is a close 1.497;[149] by contrast, in *Du Contract social* the question of needs nearly disappears from consideration as the "formula for happiness" ceases to serve as the relevant measure; the ratio of *forces/besoins* goes up to 4.093.

These textual facts lead us back to the concerns of political theory. I mentioned above that we cannot expect the "formula for happiness" to tell us how things will turn out. I want to stress now that the problem is not with *this* maxim in particular, but with any such reductionist formulation. Simply, there is no adequate way to place a value on uncertainty. There are, of course, other reasons to set aside the "formula for happiness." However, I think that this one is sufficient to bring to light a limit inherent in the approach taken thus far.

This impasse bears on two topics we will need to consider. The first concerns a specific uncertainty. In fact it is difficult, perhaps impossible, to know beforehand what will make one happy in the long run.[150] The second concerns *how* we might take seriously this fact. Before pursuing the first question, it will be helpful to digress briefly to address the second. My aim in the next few paragraphs, then, is to bring to light the manner in which Rousseau exploits for his theoretical purposes nonquantifiable information like "uncertainty."[151]

Rousseau's thinking depends on personal and cultural beliefs which — as we actually live with and experience them — are never quantified or relativized in the formalistic way suggested by the "formula for happiness." No sustained attempt to think like Rousseau could remain within such strict formulae.[152] More generally, those who insist too much on applying rigid principles often find themselves faced with unexpected and perverse consequences of their own action. Indeed, these consequences may include distortions of the system in which the rule operates that are produced by the rule-follower's own obsessive attachment to formal doctrines or rules.[153]

With this in mind, I want to make further note of the important role that beliefs play in Rousseau's social and political thought, now considering *what*, rather than *how*, he thought. Rousseau makes much of something that is true for most people in everyday life. And while I have just hinted at a distinction between beliefs and principles, I now want to draw your attention to the mixed example of belief *in* principles.

Although the word *principio* refers only to the act of beginning, it is common to think of principles as rules to be applied. This is misleading, for in everyday life we rarely make any kind of direct application. The process is rather like this: a principle rises up from reflection, tradition, or another presumptively authoritative source; we seize upon it in many different ways; as it enters discourse or becomes a vehicle for action, it undergoes mutation in relation to circumstances; it is mere conceit to suppose that an event has been regulated by the principle (neither events nor control are that simple); in the very phase of action where it seems most effective, the principle is typically recast in a new or unexpected light; assuredly it may later gravitate back to its earlier expression, but then even that expression has new meaning.

In other words, adjustment is made *through* the principle, not *to* it. There is no "subsuming the case under the rule." Interpretation is not application. A principle or a maxim is only effective when it becomes a coherent way of living rather than a rigid formula.[154] This much is recognized by every significant and successful practice of education.[155]

A reader of *Émile* has a comparable experience: the author makes a simple claim in a striking manner; it is repeated in something like the musical mode of theme and variations; each repetition enacts the basic claim within a description of conditions that are materially different, covering different stages of development, engaging different interlocutors, responding to different problems, and so forth. Thus, even though the book *Émile* is filled with "principles" and "maxims," the reader pursues these through generally stated but nonetheless empirically oriented modulations, and thus comes away from the text with a kind of understanding that cannot be reduced to a set of rules.

Let me put this another way. Rousseau does not provide a *method* for living.[156] Nor is the "formula for happiness" merely information that is transmitted to the reader.[157] Rather, we should understand it—or, more precisely, my reconstruction of it—as a rhetorical *topos*. Its function is to draw the reader into a particular relationship. This relation, at least in the texts that concern us here, is not voyeuristic.[158] Nor is it the one ordinarily ascribed to rhetoric. That is, it is not a matter of "persuasion" or "identification." The relationship is, rather, a style of thinking and of character-formation in which reader and text complete one another; this is an apprenticeship to practical reason. It is presented with astonishing self-consciousness by Rousseau, who makes clear that a treatise on education is not just important *for* politics, it is a way of doing politics, of becoming a citizen. At this level, one might go so far as to say that some of Rousseau's substantive theoretical claims are dialectically constituted in the process of the relationship between the reader and the text. Indeed, almost none of the static propositions that could be abstracted from the *reading* process and described with an air of thorough-going accuracy from outside are novel or of independent interest.[159] The dialectical effect[160] of the text—that is, its "meaning"—is invisible to anyone but the reader and the meaning evaporates if the process is interrupted.[161]

The preceding paragraphs restate, at what might commonly but with a mischievous perversity be called "a methodological level," an assertion I developed above (beginning in §22): the "formula for happiness" is articulated through the figure of dependence; it only has meaning in a living pragmatic relationship of one's connection to others. From any point of view, Rousseau's success with this kind of strategy is what makes his arguments more convincing than formalistic analogues which—at least superficially—seem to have the same content.[162]

§27

LOCATING THE PROBLEM OF DEPENDENCE
Uncertainty, Insecurity, Unhappiness

With the express purpose of answering a substantive question, I just digressed to consider a problem of "method." Let us now return to the substantive question of whether or not social *forces* gained from others will surpass the new *besoins* to which they also give rise. Rousseau seems convinced that they will not. I suggested that one reason for this does not appear directly in the equation between *forces* and *besoins*. It concerns rather the derivative fact that the outcome of this balancing act is uncertain for those who undertake it. One does not know in advance what the outcome of a turn to explicitly social *forces* will be.

Social *forces* promise much; they are enticing, exciting. Yet, they are fundamentally uncertain. For just this reason, they are likely to produce in those who come to depend on them a deep sense of insecurity.[163]

This psychological insecurity has a real basis in social experience. Again: the *forces* gained from others produce new *besoins* at an exponential rate and are themselves not guaranteed to be at our service when and where we need them. The words "not guaranteed" name a fact of experience: uncertainty in our dealings with others. The personal response to this fact is *insecurity*.

Now, remember that in considering the development of society Rousseau assumes that one can always rely on oneself. I have mentioned one justification for this assumption,[164] but perhaps it is simply derivative from Rousseau's Platonic mood. Perhaps it is simply narcissistic fantasy.[165] In any case, this assumption is represented in the omnipresent image of the "state of nature." Natural Man is supposed to be perfectly consistent with himself. So is the ideally virtuous citizen. What matters here is that the real world of social beings is interpreted in light of, and by contrast with, this assumption. Within this frame, the characteristic fact of life in society can be stated as follows: we cannot rely on others the way we rely on ourselves. The presence of others is a serious source of experiential uncertainty and psychological anxiety.

Other interpreters of Rousseau have addressed this complex of topics in terms of "authenticity" — of needs, of the self and its forces. Reading Rousseau in terms of "authenticity" allows one to analyze the way Man turns inward to turn outward, and turns outward to find himself. It is a clever and evocative trick of philosophical speculation rewritten in social-psychological language. It brings the Platonic and Augustinian topics of self-consistency and self-exposure into a distinctly modern setting. It is my judgment — perhaps made too hastily — that the questions raised in this book cannot be satisfactorily resolved in this way.[166] I will admit, nevertheless, that the language and experience of "authenticity" may be a complement to — or a derivative of — the basic structure of society as proposed by Rousseau.[167]

Although Rousseau and many of his readers thematize invidious comparison as the source of the exponentially increasing individual needs in society, I have tried to show that the more basic fact of social connectedness is another such source. Thus, we do not need additional notions like "authenticity" to see that uncertainty and anxiety *are in themselves multipliers of needs.* This adds further substance to Rousseau's belief that, with the advent of society, the ratio between *forces* and *besoins* will change unfavorably. We shall come to see the extensive import of this point shortly.

Now, however, it should be fully clear why the "formula for happiness" must be articulated through the figure of dependence. Those implicated in balancing *forces* and *besoins* within a social environment experience an unquantifiable sense of insecurity. In turn, this insecurity has practical consequences for how they try to achieve the balance. It bears heavily on their happiness. The fact of uncertainty, the psychological response of insecurity, and the consequences for happiness—all taken together—locate precisely the problems Rousseau identifies with dependence from other persons.[168]

§28

PRAGMATIC RECOURSE TO LIBERTY

As the matter stands before us at this point, it seems that there would be only one way to make the balance of *forces* and *besoins* tip in favor of one's happiness. This would be to use one's (natural or social) *forces* to guarantee that those people from whom one depends continue to work to satisfy one's needs. Given that total *forces* are limited,[169] one would therefore also cease to use some or all of one's *forces* to satisfy those needs directly.[170] Only full-time masters would have the possibility of *bonheur*.

Such a solution to the problem of happiness is incompatible with Rousseau's wider views. Here is why.

If the move to society is understood as a rational choice—an interpretation that seems to be required by any literal and most figurative readings of the "social contract"—it is hard to imagine why anyone would substitute his natural *forces* for social *forces* unless some efficiency gain was made.[171] And it seems that, all things considered, such an efficiency gain could only be guaranteed in two ways: either by exploiting others (taking more from them than is given back) or by increased discipline (making them "work" harder).[172]

We may be confident that Rousseau (and, perhaps more obviously, followers of Rousseau like Marx) would not accept such solutions to the problem of happiness in society. There is a straightforward reason for this. Throughout his writings, a tight connection is maintained between happiness and liberty.[173] This connection is persistent and fundamental, although complicated in ways that I will discuss at length below.

Rousseau has often been said to offer an idealist vision of liberty; he has been called a "dreamer of democracy."[174] Aside from later, memorable uses of the word *rêveries* and the cultivation of his reputation as a *promeneur solitaire*, I think that the primary source for this image is the preface to the *Discours sur . . . l'inégalité*, where the model of perfect natural liberty seems to derive from "a condition [*Etat*] that no longer exists, that perhaps never existed at all, that will probably never exist," yet "about which it is nonetheless necessary to have some satisfactory notions in order to fairly evaluate our present condition" (OC III.123).*

Many have taken this to mean that liberty should not be understood as a real condition and that when Rousseau refers to liberty he is proposing a kind of "regulative ideal."[175] By such a "yardstick," presumably, one may judge one's actual circumstances and decipher the next move.

I do not believe that this is what Rousseau is up to. To see his conception of liberty this way limits too much the extraordinary complexity and corresponding interest of his thinking; it limits too much our understanding of how liberty occurs in society and the bearing of this occurrence on political life.

This hesitation before Rousseau's purported idealism should be reiterated when we come to the opposite end of the philosophical spectrum. For, at times, Rousseau offers a very narrowly materialist conception of liberty. In *Du Contract social* everything seems to come down to this: "What Man loses with the social contract is his natural liberty and an unlimited right to anything that tempts him and which he can lay his hands on; what he gains is civil liberty and property in anything he possesses" (OC III.364–65).†

With the book in hand, however, what the reader notices is that even Rousseau seems surprised by his own assertion that civil liberty amounts, essentially, to the security of property. In the very next sentence he launches us back toward a discussion of the moral dimensions of liberty. While these broad issues are addressed throughout *Émile*,[176] Rousseau recognizes that this kind of speculation has limited value for a social theory of the political. In *Du Contract social* he makes perfectly clear that "the philosophical sense of the word *liberté* is not part of my subject here."[177]

We do well, therefore, to consider his conception of liberty in a different light. I have already stated and I repeat now my conviction that it is most instructive to take Rousseau's aim to be a sociological theory of practice with political implications. If we are to read Rousseau this way, we must, first and foremost, imagine real people living under the conditions set forth in his arguments. We may

---

* ". . . et dont il est pourtant necessaire d'avoir des Notions justes pour bien juger de nôtre état présent."

† "Ce que l'homme perd par le contract social, c'est sa liberté naturelle et un droit illimité à tout ce qui le tente et qu'il peut atteindre; ce qu'il gagne, c'est la liberté civile et la propriété de tout ce qu'il possede."

admit that many of these conditions are extremely reductive, and sometimes seem incredibly thin, even ridiculous. Nonetheless, lack of verisimilitude is not a sufficient objection. These are not ideals, proposals for an imaginary end-state. Rather, Rousseau's simple maxims or principles function in a pragmatic perspective as points of departure for thinking what we are doing, where the thinking is, as is natural to humankind, an integral part of the doing. In this perspective, to begin the project of *Du Contract social* with the image of "Men as they are, and laws as they might be" (OC III.351)* is not to propose an *a priori* shift from the real to the ideal, or from nature to culture. It is rather to construct a problematic that includes constraints beyond our control and to which our own political engagement is the requisite mode of address. Pragmatic—which is to say, action-guiding—political theory always involves a combination of speculative and "positive" inquiry.[178] . . . even when it requires us to "set aside all the facts, for they do not in the least bear on the question" (OC III.132).†

Can these really be features of a pragmatic perspective? Only a false equation of pragmatism with "pure facts" could suggest that they are not. One need not be a shoemaker to think about making shoes; one need not talk about shoes in the language of a shoemaker to say something that touches on the experience of wearing them. With some exaggeration it might be said that proposed here is a difference between the Kantian operation of measuring experience by a "regulative ideal" and a living process in which ideas are constantly transformed by the measure of experience. While Rousseau engages in both sorts of metrics, I am emphasizing the latter. What may be difficult to grasp is that Rousseau understood— and I affirm—that *any* kind or level of idea can be treated in this pragmatic way.[179]

In this respect, Rousseau's reductive statements are not trivial but propitious. Their simplicity demands comparison with common sense; their clarity allows for evaluation. They practically beg to be taken out of context and juggled mathematically. Rousseau makes perfectly clear that he is a self-conscious master of this kind of abstract operation, as when in *Du Contract social* he punctuates an argument by writing "we reduce all of [what was just said] to terms that are easy to compare" (OC III.364).

Rousseau, it may therefore be said, helps the reader to think politically *through* his writing by avoiding verisimilitude. He makes transparent complex ideas by building from simple blocks. The theory brims with imaginable implications. The capacity to do this made Rousseau a great writer and thinker, and made his works an origin and paradigm of enduring *sensus communis*.

---

* " . . . les hommes tels qu'ils sont, et les loix telles qu'elles peuvent être."
† " . . . écarter tous les faits, car ils ne touchent point à la question."

Let me be clear. I praise Rousseau in this way even though I will ultimately argue that the foundations on which he built his edifice have since been swept away. But to cease to follow his obsolete conception of *le lien social*, to excise it from the vocabulary of political theory, we must first understand it better. That is the formidable task we are in engaged in here.

As for the topic of *liberté*, we have already examined some aspects of its connection to the problem of happiness. When—at the juncture of the theme of happiness and the variations of dependence—Rousseau brings liberty fully into consideration, the framework is clearly pragmatic. In that decisive phrase *"le bonheur . . . consiste dans l'usage de la liberté"* the accent unmistakably falls on the word *usage*.[180]

I will try below to clarify the full importance of this pragmatic emphasis. Here, it is enough to insist that the connection between *bonheur* and *liberté* is very strong. Provisionally, we may take Rousseau to be saying that in practice, in life as it is lived, *bonheur* and *liberté* amount to the same thing.

This is consistent with Rousseau's thinking in general. It suggests why the use of others to satisfy one's own needs is incompatible with the vision of the world he projects. Rousseau is a political modernist in the world-transforming sense that slavery and slavery-like arrangements are excluded from his conception of politics. For Rousseau, if for no one, the opposite of slavery is liberty. Happiness depends on the avoidance of slavery. Take this literally, but also take it metaphorically. It stands for the more general idea that to maintain happiness is to avoid situations in which *l'usage de liberté* is constrained by someone or several others.

In the light of another of Rousseau's major categories, the connection between *bonheur* and *liberté* becomes even stronger. This category is *égalité* ("equality"). Rousseau's aim is to show how all Men, and not just masters, might be happy. Thus, a society in which some prevent the *usage de liberté* by the others in order to have it for themselves cannot be counted among Rousseau's possible solutions to the problem of disorders in the social fabric of dependence. That was the point I wanted to show in the preceding sections.

Beyond this, Rousseau has no illusions: "They make me laugh, these people . . . who . . . dare to speak of liberty without having the least idea of it and, their heart full of all the vices of slaves, imagine that to be free it is enough to be a rebel" (OC III.974).* But that, too, is a topic for another time.

---

* "Je ris de ces peuples . . . qui . . . osent parler de liberté sans même en avoir l'idée et, le coeur plein de tous les vices des esclaves, s'imaginent que, pour être libres il suffit d'être des mutins."

B. *"Il y a Deux Sortes de Dépendance"*

§29

RECONFIGURING THE PROBLEM
From Happiness Back to Dependence

We are still far from solving "the new problem of Jean-Jacques Rousseau."[181] What remains valuable in the way Rousseau constitutes *society* as an object of inquiry? Does this conception of *society* allow us to grasp characteristic human relations of our own time? Does it provide insight into the political implications of those relations? Can it help us to illuminate the increasingly important and increasingly confusing relationship of human beings to things? I propose that the answer to these questions, and the best way to approach answering them, will be clearer if we can get to the bottom of Rousseau's thinking about dependence.

A kind of recapitulation will help here. Up to this point we have considered dependence indirectly. Having started from Rousseau's theodicy—which is to say, the position characteristic of secular modernity[182]—it seemed reasonable to focus on *bonheur*, indeed to take happiness as *the* ethical problem at the center of political life.[183] Dependence is the typical structure of that ethical problem. With this in mind, it is fair to say that the measure of dependence is happiness.

In approaching dependence, we have, so to speak, worked backward. That is, at first we tried to understand the problem of happiness on its own terms. Paradoxically, this focused approach widened our view. It required that some of Rousseau's other major categories be brought into the analysis. These ranged from individual psychological considerations like "insecurity" to broad context-shaping conditions like the "state of nature" and the "civil state" to fundamental moral-political topics like "liberty." However, an approach focused in this way on happiness could only take us so far.

As we excluded from consideration solipsistic accounts of happiness, it became clear that happiness not only can be considered in relative terms, it must be. This is true in two senses: happiness is a balance of personal qualities (e.g., *forces* and *besoins*) that arise from the fabric of society; and even as these qualities are set in a personal frame (e.g., in questions about "happiness") happiness is constituted in the relationship or proportion between the relative terms and in social constellations that the terms represent. This second kind of relativity confirms what was proposed at the beginning: that happiness is an ethical problem.

The "management" of the ethical problem of happiness from a first-personal perspective—that is, in the form "*I* could be happy if . . ."—becomes plausible, and perhaps even possible, only with personal individuation. Individuation occurs when a person locates, affirms, and operates from within certain boundaries that allow him or her to act as a coherent "self." This "self" is not the individualistic "ego and his own," but rather a person sufficiently balanced to pursue, develop, and enjoy relationships, as he or she must, with other human beings.

Here many of the threads in Rousseau's argument again come together, but with a twist. What impedes proper individuation in society is dependence, yet individuation itself is what specifies dependence as a particular set of problems. That is, before the process of individuation has advanced to the point at which, for any given purpose, one can distinguish oneself from the environment, it is not possible to conceive of one's relation to that environment in terms of "*my*" dependence from "*it*."[184]

It is easy enough to see that in *Émile* Rousseau represents the education of Man by tracing the course of a properly ordered childhood. Less obvious but again clear enough in this picture is the development of the Citizen. What I want to add to these familiar observations is that *Émile* also represents the process of individuation that straddles both the education of Man and the development of the Citizen.

Rousseau seems to believe that individuation is a simple matter for Man in the "state of nature." He clearly believes that it is extremely difficult for Man in society. The image of the child is meant to represent this complexity. Indeed, when Rousseau offers the contradictory judgment that dependent adults are "children" it is just this complexity that moves to the foreground. This is of course a metaphorical strategy. It is partly effective and partly counterproductive. That children are both dependent and unhappy is plausible, but dependent children are sometimes happy as well. It is implausible that grown men are children, whether they are happy or dependent or not. By identifying some adults in this way Rousseau moves us to inquire about certain features of their condition. And by raising the specific question "What makes *hommes faits* unhappy?" he reiterates the general issue we have now seen from several different angles: What makes *hommes* unhappy? How should we understand the composition of this unhappiness so as to relieve it?

We have persistently (since §12) turned to the category of dependence as a way to enlarge and give more detail to the problem of happiness. I now want to reverse this procedure. Against the background of the discussion centered on happiness, we will focus on dependence. For, it is within this framework that the various topics considered thus far shape a conception of society.

§30

WHERE DEPENDENCE DIVIDES
The Absent Πόλις

Thus far, two major themes in Rousseau's social theory of politics have occupied much of our attention. The first is the composition of the *lien social*, the fabric of society. The second is the problem of *bonheur*, or happiness.

In addition, Rousseau draws attention to the fact of dependence. He would have us believe that dependence has two categorically different forms. This distinction very much complicates the ways that the *lien social* and the problem of *bonheur* fit into his theory. Yet, large as this tension is, from Rousseau's perspective it is unavoidable. His whole project hinges on giving a more precise and differentiated account of *dépendance*.

Why are the stakes so high? The best way to answer this question is to consult once again the "main passage," where the significance of categorizing dependence is declared: "These considerations are important, and serve to resolve all the contradictions of the social system."*

Implicit in this wildly comprehensive claim are the following assertions. Mankind "abandoned to ourselves" lives in a "social system." Once human beings leave the "state of nature"—God's creation—and enter the human artifact of *société*, the warp and weft of the human condition is best understood in terms

---

* "Ces considérations sont importantes, et servent à resoudre toutes les contradictions du système social."

of *dépendance*. From the perspective of social theory, *dépendance* becomes the most basic marker for classifying problems within this "system." Generally speaking, these problems are "contradictions" in which one set of *forces*, possibilities, or constraints impedes or detours another such set. These contradictions may be brought to light by the "formula for happiness" but they are not explained by it.

Here again we can see the spirit of Plato. It lurks behind the word "contradiction."[185] One paragraph before Rousseau explicitly names the source of the idea, he declares that "to be something, to be oneself and always one, you must act as you speak" (OC IV.250). In other words, he raises old Socrates' flag: don't contradict yourself.

This is the beginning of *Émile*. The purpose of Rousseau's book is to create citizens, not hermits. While the problem of contradiction arises for each person, it is also an essential tension in how we live together with others. Since *forces*, possibilities, and constraints do not in any immediate sense "speak," no less "speak against" (*contra-dico*), the word contradiction is used here as metaphor. It is by way of this transfer ($\mu\epsilon\tau\alpha\phi\circ\rho\alpha$) that the problem of contradiction becomes at once ethical and political.

With this in mind, notice that a particularly disturbing contradiction appears when one pretends to live in isolation. This pretense is, in fact, a common, even characteristic, practice of modernity. It is a source of both constructive and destructive social disorder, and is, therefore, a conflict-constituting strategy that generates opportunities for some agents and a corollary shifting of burdens onto others.[186]

At this point, however, our attention needs to be directed another way. Consider the personal experience of this sort of contradiction as it occurs for someone in the position of the citizen. Although the citizen lives in the "civil order" of "society," what if he persistently clings to "the primacy of natural sentiments"? Such a person cannot be happy according to the "formula for happiness." Why? Because "he doesn't know what he wants." For this reason alone no amount of *forces* will suffice to meet his *besoins* (OC IV.250).[187]

In Rousseau's view, even when this sort of inconsistency is centered in the person it has much broader significance: "Always in contradiction with himself, always floating between his inclinations and his obligations, he will never be Man or Citizen; he will be of no good for himself or for others" (OC IV.250).*

---

* "Toujours en contradictions avec lui-même, toujours flottant entre ses penchants et ses devoirs, il ne sera jamais ni homme ni citoyen; il ne sera bon ni pour lui ni pour les autres. . . ."

Between Plato and the eighteenth century, it would be difficult to find a more vociferous and persistent secular advocate than Rousseau of the idea that a dis-ordered *psyche* produces personal unhappiness.[188] What draws our attention here, however, is that Rousseau takes an additional sociological step beyond psychology. Disorders of the *psyche* are at the same time functional (or dys-functional) forces within the suprapersonal structure or system Rousseau calls "*société*."[189]

We may put this in a slightly different way. Rousseau's account of the *psyche* refers explicitly to modern human beings living in *société*. Anyone who hopes to gain insight into politics from Rousseau must at this point keep two things in mind. The first is that this term *société* specifically names the *place* where "the moderns" live. The second is that the name of this place—*société*—is charged with a distinctively modern sense. It is Rousseau who lights that charge.

This, in turn, poses further difficulties for understanding Rousseau's contri-bution to the social theory of politics. For you, dear reader, will probably find that your common sense fits comfortably with a Rousseau-like orientation to the concept of *société*. This is a problem because my purpose is to carry us outside common sense; I am arguing that we need to see the *lien social* in a new light. This problem concerns not only how one sees the *lien social*, but the fact that we can identify it at all. For Rousseau and his contemporaries *société* was an in-choate concept-in-formation, garnering new significance from its appearance at the edges and intersections of various discursive fields. Not long after Rousseau these affiliations and affinities would sharply decrease. This heightens the con-trast between what Rousseau invented and our capacity to understand it.

With just such complexity in mind, we have approached Rousseau's con-cept of *société* from various directions. Now we make an additional attempt, ap-proaching through something the new word *société* fails to name.

Rousseau adopts familiar images in an effort to articulate the new concept of *société*. Any observant reader will have noted the mechanical, organic, and moral metaphors that abound in his works and express one or another aspect of his vision of the *système social*. However, one traditional figure is remarkably absent.

Where, Jean-Jacques, is the πόλις, the *cité*, the "city"? Rousseau's beloved Plato, author of Πολιτεια, and centuries of writers after him, would have without a second thought turned to this representation of the *lien social*. But by the eigh-teenth century, the tectonic plates of polity and society have drifted apart.[190] The πόλις/*cité*/city has lost its transparency as a symbol. Its signification is obscure.

Now, it is true that in the hundreds of pages of *Émile* Rousseau frequently exhorts the *citoyen* and appeals to *civil* relationships. His motive in this, how-ever, is hardly affirmative. He is moved by a signal anxiety and sense of loss. This vast tract on civic education is necessary precisely because the πόλις/*cité*/city no longer exists; nowhere but in an imagined future will the *citoyen* be bred. The moderns have been left with only a simulacrum of the political.[191]

Rousseau does not ordinarily hesitate to name the lost, the unrecoverable, or the utopian. Yet in *Émile*—Rousseau's great homage to Plato's Πολιτεια, with all its pronounced ambivalence between the topics of education and politics— the word *cité* appears only twice. The first time is a sarcastic aside—"as if there were Citizens who were not members of the City . . . !" (OC IV.667, note)— suggesting the impossibility of citizenship in the current absence of true cities.[192] The second time is within a brief lexicon meant to support *Émile*'s lesson on the *"contract social"* and again it refers to an imagined future not just for the pupil but for the reader as well. The didactic vocabulary tells us that those who belong to the *"personne publique"* or *"corps politique"* are to be identified collectively as the "people [*peuple*]" and "in particular as members of the *cité* or participants in sovereign authority they are called *citizens*" (OC IV.840).

Émile and *Du Contract social* were published back-to-back in 1762. These passages in the former book are a sort of advertisement, a teaser, for the latter. The pupil and the reader are prompted to *Du Contract social* for instruction in politics. And opening Book 1, Chapter VI, "Du pacte social," we find these lines repeated almost verbatim. But now the key word's general absence from Rousseau's text and from the contemporary world is explained.

> Once upon a time, the *personne publique* formed by the union of all the other persons took the name *cité* . . . [but] . . . the true sense of this word is almost entirely effaced among the moderns; most take a *ville* [geographical and administrative term] for a City and a *bourgeois* [someone who dwells in a *ville*] for a Citizen. They do not know that the houses make the *ville* but the Citizens make the City. (OC III.361, note)[193]*

In the streamlined exhortatory mood of *Du Contract social* Rousseau more frequently allows himself the image he wishes had not died.[194] However, insofar as his contemporaries can even imagine the πόλις/*cité*/city, Rousseau tells us precisely that the *"personne publique* . . . now goes under the name *République* or *corps politique"* (OC III.361–62).

For the reader of *Émile* this is a kind of provocation. The word *"république"* appears almost as infrequently as *"cité."* When it appears it refers only to the his-

---

* "Le vrai sens de ce mot s'est presque entierement effacé chez les modernes; la plupart prennent une ville pour une Cité et un bourgeois pour un Citoyen. Ils ne savent pas que les maisons font la ville mais que les Citoyens font la Cité."

torical past.[195] There is one exception. And this exception brings us to the point I want to underscore here.

The single significant reference to the *"république"* —and thus to the *"cité"* and thus to the πόλις—occurs in the "main passage." It bears enormous theoretical weight. While isolating other versions of politics, this gesture will identify, by mutual exclusion, what is distinctively modern about both *société* and about the political solution to the problems that arise within it. It will also reconcile society with the nature from which, ultimately, it springs and from which, finally, it cannot escape.[196]

This brings us back yet again to the similarity with Plato. Or, rather, to the difference. For, whatever Platonic elements are appropriated into Rousseau's thinking, the "contradictions" he aims to "resolve" are specifically modern as well.[197]

§31

RÉSOUDRE

The Art of Breaking Things Down and Putting Them Back Together

A general point may now be presented. I repeat in slightly different terms something brought to the foreground much earlier in this book. Rousseau is profoundly oriented by the following question: how can social Man approximate the liberty he would have had in the "state of nature"?

In the "state of nature," liberty derives from a particular unity of the self, a self with access to a coherent set of *forces* clearly greater than the limited *besoins* one has or could have developed in the natural condition. In *Du Contract social*, Rousseau projects this idea in a somewhat narrower frame: "one surely must distinguish between natural liberty, which is only limited by the forces of the individual, and civil liberty, which is limited by the general Will" (OC III.364–65).* To put it this way is consistent with the equivalence I proposed some pages back,

---

* "... il faut bien distinguer la liberté naturelle qui n'a pour bornes que les forces de l'individu, de la liberté civile qui est limité par la volonté générale."

at the end of Part Two A (§28): in practice, in life as it is lived, *bonheur* and *liberté* amount to the same thing. This proposition, as I said then, was only meant to be provisional. Now I want to further limit its application to the "state of nature." This narrower view will serve at least until we can establish a more precise sense of the sort of liberty that is specific to *société*.

We have now seen (§30) that for Rousseau this social liberty is not strictly political, which is to say it is not, as the Ancients might have construed it, of the πόλις, not *civitas*.[198] It is instead a matter of "system." Exactly what this means and why it is the case cannot be explained quite yet. We must first investigate some underlying elements of this particular "system."

This much is clear: whatever the *"système social"* turns out to be, "to resolve all the contradictions of the social system" cannot be a small task. It will be impossible if "one is too closed-minded" and Rousseau underscores the difficulty—consistent with his symbolic assignments to age and gender—by adding that "to resolve these questions cannot be left to a little girl."[199]

So, linger over this verb *résoudre*. It reveals Rousseau's aspirations in a number of ways. *Résoudre* first appears in the "main passage." The only other instance of the word in this sense in the first two books of *Émile* is also associated with a problem of *dépendance*. Moreover, Rousseau's use of it confirms what I said above about the special didactic tone and placement of the "main passage" itself (§14 above). By the third book of *Émile*, *résoudre* repeatedly becomes a kind of pressure point in the process of instruction. To educate his pupil, the tutor should, for example, "put the questions within his reach and let him resolve them," perhaps offering from time to time "some laconic question that puts him on the path toward resolving the problem" (OC IV.430, 432).

Résoudre is something one does in the process of learning. It is a matter of untying the knot, loosening the weave of things to find their warp and weft. One "resolves" a question or a puzzle by working it through; one draws it toward a conclusion; one makes a judgment (*"haec est mea sententia"*) and "resolves" to stick to it, with "resolve."[200]

Add to this the fact that Rousseau's student "learns by doing." It then becomes clear that *résoudre* is a point of intersection between theoretical and practical knowledge. *Résoudre* may therefore be understood as, at once, an invocation of *perfectibilité*—that most primitive learning faculty of single persons and humankind as a whole—and an injunction to the reader, indicating what we should expect to accomplish by reading Rousseau's book.

By following the word *résoudre* in these preliminary ways, some of the discursive resources that underpin Rousseau's proposition—"to resolve all the contradictions of the social system"—come into view. This remains entirely inadequate.

Thus, I will now show how that word carries the writer and the reader into several other domains. Each and all of them are essential to Rousseau's theoretical activity. *Résoudre* stands for the methodological interests of expanding scientific inquiry, for the practical civic interests of declining rhetoric, and for the conceptual architectonic interests of Baroque polyphonic music. In addition, by standing simultaneously for each of these interests the single term *résoudre* performs something easily within the ken of Rousseau's contemporaries: science, rhetoric, and music are reasserted as complementary ways of approaching the world. Let us now consider each of these in some detail.

Rousseau's use of the word *résoudre* is a shining invocation of the pivotal discourse of modern science, which is to say the idea and practice of Method. Under that term the intersecting interests of theoretical and practical knowledge gave rise to a long tradition of reflection and debate that we find still bubbling in Rousseau's books.

The distinctive modern doctrine of Method stems from Aristotelian seeds sown in the pages of Robert Grosseteste (born 1168—died 1263).[201] The subsequent history of discourse concerning Method is complicated and most of its details are not relevant here. Suffice it to say that by the time Rousseau set ink to paper, key contributions had been made by the likes of Petrus Ramus (born 1515—died 1572) and Jacopo Zabarella (born 1533—died 1589) in the sixteenth century, opening the way for decisive developments by Galileo Galilei (born 1564—died 1642), René Descartes (born 1596—died 1650), and Isaac Newton (born 1643—died 1727) in the seventeenth century.

Familiar categories often fail in the ebbs and flows of intellectual history. The issues taken up by these authors cut across many lines that today we take for granted. A brief sketch of that confluence will help to further situate Rousseau.

In the centuries before the publication of *Émile*, much of the thinking about Method took place inside mathematics. In this context *résoudre* was a synonym for the older and more familiar term "analysis"[202] and that is why Rousseau could conflate them. Even within this most theoretical of disciplines, the Method of resolution/analysis was not just a theoretical matter but also a mode of demonstration or a technical means. In other words, again, Method joins theoretical and practical interests. Constituting a bridge from mathematics into other realms of inquiry, resolution/analysis was then pursued in the empirical sciences.[203] With the epistemological success of constructivism[204] and the practical achievements of the empirical sciences, Method was adopted to meet the needs of the emerging human sciences.[205]

Here another element enters the mix. Rhetoric, which originated and persisted "inside politics," had long been the primary vehicle for concerns about civic life. As these concerns reappeared within the human sciences rhetorical interests emerged within them as well.[206] The result was encounters between rhetoric and Method. Many antagonisms arose and, indeed, continue to work themselves out to this day.[207] But there were also key partnerships between rhetoric and Method, one of which returns us to mathematics.

In the late sixteenth and early seventeenth centuries common rhetorical training and orientations provided crucial symbolic forms for the invention of algebra and analytic geometry.[208] Widening our view, we see that even key terms of Method, *resolutio* and *compositio,* entered this whole field of discourse from the rhetorical writings of Cicero and Boethius.[209] Seeking insight beyond such technical innovations, we see a larger transformation of *mentalité* in the West. A well-placed reconstruction of logic and pedagogy, especially as inspired by Ramus, has this double effect: it shifted the center of gravity of rhetoric from inquiry to eloquence and undermined rhetoric's utility; it propagated a version of Method, grounded in intuition rather than erudition and aggressively offering its own universal utility, that was to become not just a process of scientific discovery but, so to speak, a way of life.[210]

This all-too-thin gloss is sufficient for my purposes here. It gestures to several of the discourses—mathematics, physics (properly speaking, "natural philosophy"), the human sciences, rhetoric—that are implicated when, in 1762, the word *résoudre* appears on Rousseau's page. It suggests how those discourses are interrelated.

Now to touch base again with *Émile.* Rousseau knew perfectly well that the word *résoudre* was pregnant with the concerns of Method; he was aware of the synonymy of the key terms *analyser* and *résoudre* and acquainted with the traditions behind those terms.[211] And while "there are disputes," he tells us, "about whether to choose analysis or synthesis to study the sciences, it is not always necessary to choose. Sometimes one can *résoudre* and *composer* in the same research" (OC IV.434).* It is possible that the proximate source of these lines is, as Burgelin proposes, Condillac's critique of Descartes in the *Traité des sistêmes* (1749).[212] To see it that way, however, circumscribes a much larger scene from which Rousseau's intentions are invigorated. Descartes, as much as Condillac, advanced versions of "analysis"[213] in the context of an ongoing transnational dialogue. It is from within a different and decidedly non-Cartesian part of that discussion that the complementary pair *résoudre/composer* are construed as parallel

---

* "On dispute sur le choix de l'analyse ou de la synthése pour étudier les sciences. Il n'est pas toujours besoin de choisir. Quelquefois on peut résoudre et composer dans les mêmes recherches, ..."

to analysis/synthesis. "Resolution," and with it *résoudre*, derives from a tradition that extends, most famously, back to Galileo, but then through him back to Zabarella and the school of Paduan Aristotelians.[214] Outside that small sphere, it is unquestionably linked into the wider discursive fields of the Renaissance.[215]

In this wider discursive sphere, and well before Descartes, the terms "analysis" and "resolution" were often conflated, especially when they referred to mathematical operations. Zabarella, however, goes beyond this. Important for our purposes here is that he proposes to extend the term "resolution" into the study of experience. From the "theory of proof . . . set forth in [Aristotle's] *Analytics*" he works out "a logic of investigation and inquiry" and "makes the Avveroistic distinction between the resolutive method suitable for natural science and the 'analytic' method of mathematics."[216] His approach is adopted and refigured by Galileo. Parallel to and in part preceding Zabarella these topics are alive in England, too. Everard Digby (born 1550 — died 1592) attacks Ramus's claims in favor of a single universally applicable Method in a book entitled *De duplici methodo* (1580). As an instructor of Bacon he advances the English branch of the general discussion of Method, although before long Zabarella's voice is heard there as well.[217] Thus, when Newton appears on this scene he can draw from several wells. As his fame for establishing Method in the field of experience overshadows even Galileo's, he eventually reverses the terminology we discuss here to establish the language of "analysis" we know today. Nonetheless, it may be relevant here — where we are concerned specifically with Rousseau's use of the word *résoudre* — to note that as Newton arrives at his "twofold method"[218] of analysis and synthesis he prominently continues to apply the term "resolution" to describe the activities of both the mathematicians and the "experimental philosophers," and does so more or less interchangeably.[219]

Certainly it was Newton, along with Locke, that Condillac took as a paradigm. Likewise Newton was held in high esteem by d'Alembert and the collaborators of the *Encyclopédie*, where mention of his name (786 times) is surpassed only by references to Aristotle (1,044) and Jesus (1,786). Rousseau no doubt read his much-admired friend Condillac as he voraciously read everything he could, but, like Hume, one must say that he aspired to be the Newton of the social world. This is the title Kant pinned on him.[220]

For the moment, however, the issue is still Method, and the question is this: having explicitly set out the synonymy of analysis/resolution, why does Rousseau adopt for the central purpose of his social theory of politics — "to resolve all the contradictions of the social system" — the term "resolution"?

I will now engage a little trick of exposition. In the wide variety of the discourses of Method the term "resolution" is most firmly associated with Galileo.

As I want to make clear the background significance of Method in the "main passage," let us suppose provisionally that when Rousseau writes the verb *résoudre* the voice that speaks is one that belonged also to Galileo.

Stated simply, the astronomer's *metodo risolutivo e compositivo* is a way to learn about a complex object by investigating it along two related lines, first by "resolving" what is already known into its more basic components, and then "composing" it again into a comprehensible whole. The appearance of the object in question will be very different at the beginning and at the end (e.g., a twinkling star vs. the solar system). The process, and the new perspective, will only be valuable if one identifies the correct components.

With this—both historical and conceptual—background in mind, we can extrapolate Rousseau's purpose in using the word *résoudre* in the "main passage." It is not simply to solve a problem in an authoritative way. Rather, it is an invitation to address the problem through methodical analysis, consistent with Rousseau's deep dedication to science (notwithstanding the common view that he despises it).[221] It is at the same time an indication that Method itself is not settled *a priori* and must be both made thematic and performed in ways that reveal the inherent complexities of civic and (now with Rousseau) social inquiry.[222]

The vast majority of readers today will have a narrow and misleading view of what is entailed by the identification of *résoudre* as an utterance of Method. This is because at mid-eighteenth century the relentlessly reductionist ideal of Method to which we have since grown accustomed had not yet so thoroughly captured and reoriented the human sciences, no less the Western imagination.[223] For Rousseau, *résoudre* still refers to a very broad and capacious process of inquiry.

The question is, how broad, and how heterogenous? Keep in mind that the *metodo risolutivo*, or simply the topic of "resolution," had wide publicity and multiple forms. I have already said that it linked to rhetorical concerns and now I want to exhibit that connection in some more detail.

An especially well-placed and suggestive illustration appears in the famous Port-Royal logic published by Jansenists Antoine Arnauld and Pierre Nicole in 1662. They are Cartesians only by their program of theology, and of course cannot yet be Newtonians.[224] They are, with their collaborator Pascal, fully involved in widespread debates about logic and mathematics. They also express a range of other interests and that is where the persistent resonance of Method in the verb *résoudre* shows itself to be especially encompassing. *La logique, ou l'art de penser* distinguishes "two sorts of methods." Of these, "one, for discovering the truth, is called analysis, or method of resolution, and can also be called method of invention, and the other, for making it heard by others when one has found it, which is called synthesis, or method of composition, and which one can also call method of doctrine."[225]* They intend to state the commonplace distinction between a logic of inquiry and a logic of presentation. I want to emphasize what happens along the way. First, the identity of analysis and resolution is reasserted. Then Arnauld and Nicole go further to add a third synonymous term, writing that "one can also call" this the "method of invention."

Invention had, of course, been a foundational operation in rhetoric before Ramus—Cicero had made sure of that—and continued so for some in a diminished capacity after him. Arnauld and Nicole are in tune with this rhetorical fact and thematize it elsewhere in the *Logique:* "That which the Rhetoricians and the Logicians call 'places,' *loci argumentorum,* are certain general headings to which one can refer all the proofs employed in the diverse matters treated: and the part of Logic that they call invention is nothing but what they teach of these 'places.'"[226]† This means that, within the very notion of Method that is attached to analysis/resolution, and in some respects against their own intentions, they keep alive an element of precisely that form of humanistic inquiry that Method is everywhere eroding.[227] Thus, the word "resolution" works with two discursive vectors, one in science and one in rhetoric, that cannot simply be reduced to one side or the other.

With this ambivalence in mind, we can glean another significant feature of the distinction between *resolutio* and *compositio* (both of which are originally rhetorical terms). When Arnauld and Nicole maintain that the first is for inquiry and the second is for teaching ("*doctrine*" is the word in the *Logique*) they preserve the essentially rhetorical interest in joining inquiry and pedagogy. By contrast, to see, as Newton will see, the two methods as a single dialectic of inquiry applicable specifically to experimentation and not simply to experience is to once again diminish rhetorical interests. A residual of this shift highlights its import: when Newton retains the word *invention* he does not use it in its rhetorical sense.[228]

I want to suggest that these facts help us to understand what is happening in

---

*"... ainsi il y a deux sortes de methodes; l'une pour découvrir la verité, qu'on appelle *analyse,* ou *methode de resolution,* & qu'on peut aussi appeller *methode d'invention:* & l'autre pour la faire entendre aux autres quand on l'a trouvée, qu'on appelle *synthese,* ou *methode de composition,* & qu'on peut aussi appeller *methode de doctrine.*" [emphasis in original]

†"Ce que les Rhetoriciens & les Logiciens appellent Lieux, *loci argumentorum,* sont certains chefs generaux, aufquels on peut rapporter toutes les preuves dont on se sert dans les diverses matieres que l'on traite: & la partie de la Logique qu'ils appellent *invention,* n'est autre chose que ce qu'ils enseignent de ces lieux."

Rousseau's text. The claim that "one can 'resolve' and 'compose' in the same re-search" (OC IV.434) resonates with the twofold versions of Method offered by Newton, Galileo, or Zabarella. It is clear that Rousseau is drawing on their authority and he wants the reader to follow him in entering a scientific perspective. At the same time, however, Rousseau's dialectic of *resolution* and *composition* is importantly different. His version is less formal and more complex, even though the divide between discovery and presentation of what is discovered is maintained.

In the "twofold method" it is the sequence—first *resolution*, then *composition*—that articulates the parts in a specific ways. Rousseau sets this aside. The rejection of sequence would seem to erase the line between those parts. Oddly enough, I think the opposite is true. It is the absence of this preestablished (i.e., methodical) scaffolding that forces a reconfiguration of the distinction between *resolution* and *composition*. This approach is at once more precise and more flexible, as it emerges in the context of production and reception, in the practices of writing and reading.

Émile is not an experiment. It is the *mise-en-scène* of an apprenticeship. As a treatise on education it exhibits an ongoing experiential dialogue between the subject positions of the teacher and the pupil. This relationship is inherently circular or, more exactly, spiral. It is enacted in the process of reading. As a result, resolution-as-*inventio* and composition-as-*dispositio* can easily and fruitfully coexist within the pages of the book; they are, as Vico might have said, microscopic instances of *corso* and *ricorso*.

What we see here, in wholly other garb, reiterates the historical deployment of rhetoric as an educational path alternative to the instruction of philosophy. Apprenticeship to rhetorical, and thus civic, culture does not choose to be of one type or another (e.g., epideictic, deliberative, forensic); it is rather all of rhetoric all at once. This rhetorical/educational impetus models the overlapping appeal to science, and this is what allows for a coexistence of several methods. All this forms another of the contexts within which Rousseau proposes "to resolve all the contradictions of the social system."

How would one proceed? A *metodo risolutivo* sets out to explain something already known from experience. Rousseau's theodicy demarcates the object of inquiry: it is humankind "abandoned to ourselves." The totality of the world of human relationships—*société*—is conceived as a *système*. This *système* confronts us as the fact of everyday life. We experience it both as a whole and as riddled with contradictions. What are the components into which it can be "resolved" and its riddles thereby "resolved"?

Rousseau could not be more clear: such an inquiry commands no resources outside its object; one cannot step off or outside the "island of the earth."[229] We must proceed—as Hans-Georg Gadamer's great challenge to the hegemony of Method will demonstrate two hundred years after Rousseau[230]—from within the fabric of experience.

On the question of what constitutes the foundation of this experience, Rousseau's equivocation between *société* and language takes on new meaning. In the *Discours sur . . . l'inégalité* he famously declines to reduce the relationship between them to one or the other:

> For my part, put off by proliferating difficulties, and convinced by the nearly demonstrated impossibility that languages could have been born and established themselves by purely human means, I leave to whomever would like to tackle it the discussion of this difficult problem: which was most necessary, society already formed [*liée*, constituted as a *lien social*] for the institution of languages, or languages already invented for the establishment of society.[231]*

The coexistence of language and *société*, within and constitutive of the fabric of experience, humanizing our relationships with others, is another foundational fact for rhetoric. It is at this nexus that we find the primary elements into which *société* is to be "resolved." These elements are facts but not merely that; they are representations but more charged with and entangled in experience than the flashing of light and sound; each such element is the sort of complex object that is brought to the foreground when we use the word "topics" (i.e., *topoi*).

The active process through which topics appear within discursive frameworks and situations is *inventio*. The distinguishing feature of topics is that they are both widely distributed and widely effective representations *and* experience-shaping social facts. With topics we conduct inquiry *and* we get on with the communicative process of living.

My contextualizing appeal to Arnauld and Nicole was intended to provide a bridge to this next theoretical point. In the convergence of the sociological and the semiotic, handled with extraordinary *finesse* by Rousseau, *resolution* and *invention* become synonyms and these processes of inquiry reveal themselves to be as much experiential as they are cognitive.

This point needs emphasis. It is difficult for us, living at arm's length from the norms and habits of rhetorical culture,[232] to fully appreciate the sense in which topics of invention are not merely "arbitrary signs" or "social constructions" but

---

*"Quant à moi, effrayé des difficultés qui se multiplient, et convaincu de l'impossibilité presque démontrée que les Langues ayent pû naître et s'établir par des moyens purement humains, je laisse à qui voudra l'entreprendre, la discussion de ce difficile Problème, lequel a été le plus nécessaire, de la Société déjà liée, à l'institution des Langues, ou dês Langues déjà inventées, à l'établissement de la Société."

social facts in the richest possible sense. It is difficult for even the greatest thinkers among us to see how the "web of human relationships," the fabricated "world," and the language-constituted field of *"sensus communis"* are in experience three aspects of the same social totality.[233]

There are also different orders of resolution. Some of these topics are primary and reflect *contradictions* inherent in *société*. Rousseau's famous appeals in terms of "inequality [*inégalité*]" are excellent examples. Rousseau further "resolves" *inégalité* without "solving" the problem it presents. It and other such topics are investigated in terms of the fabric of *dépendances* that they presuppose. This move provides the basis—as we shall see, the unsteady basis—for his social theory of politics.

The word *résoudre* appears at strategic points in many of Rousseau's texts in conformance with the patterns I have described so far. Now we consider again *Émile*. In the whole book the word is rare. Still, *résoudre* appears repeatedly in the extraordinary treatise-within-the-book that Rousseau called *"Profession de foi du vicaire savoyard."*[234] Here the reader is hammered and taunted with the idea that, unlike questions in the natural and human sciences, theological and metaphysical doubts cannot be "resolved." The *"vicaire"*—which is to say Rousseau himself[235]—has learned that "far from delivering me from my useless doubts, the philosophers only multiplied the ones that tormented me and resolved none."[236]

All this changes when sociology takes the place of theology. In other words, when we adopt Rousseau's theodicy as the basis for our self-understanding, fundamental questions can indeed be "resolved."

This last point could be taken as indicating the powerful link between secularism and enlightenment. Rousseau *is* a shining figure of the Enlightenment, but he is not Spinoza, no less Diderot.[237] Something much more subtle, complex, interesting, and important is occurring when he writes. It has to do with the combination of Method and rhetorical interests described in this section,[238] something that again suggests a creative convergence between Rousseau and his contemporary Giambattista Vico.[239]

But here the conversation is with Rousseau, and we must ask: in applying such a rhetorically oriented *metodo risolutivo*, why begin with the decomposition of *"système"* and *"contradictions"*? From what we have already seen, in this choice of object is Rousseau simply moved, like so many before and so many after him, by Plato? Perhaps. But I believe another much more proximate force drives Rousseau's inquiry in this direction. It is an invisible presence from the beginning to the end.

To see this, recall for a moment now the question I asked above. Why did Rousseau choose the language of "resolution" rather than the language of "analysis"?

The first part of the answer was that he wanted to invoke issues of Method and align himself in some way with the projects of the new science. We then saw how Rousseau linked through the word *résoudre* to rhetorical traditions. This makes an almost inherent sense if one is prepared to accept my view that rhetoric is the original social science, the theory of practice for πόλις and *civitas*.

Now recall, too, the very first step in Rousseau's theodicy. He nearly screams to us, "Mankind! Stop your search for the author of evil, that author is you" (OC IV.588). As this accusation unfolds, a paraphrase of Rousseau's general intention is brought forward. He writes that a "shocking dissonance in the universal harmony would make me seek to resolve it" (OC IV.589–90).* There can be no question that the terms here are not loosely literary, methodically scientific, or strictly rhetorical. This is the discourse of music. And just as *langage* and *société* can neither be reduced one to the other nor remain for long pulled apart,[240] Rousseau believed that *langage* and *musique* are related in a fundamental dialectic that is constitutive of specifically human existence.[241]

Thus, *résoudre* has a third dimension. The discursive and conceptual resources of music triangulate the interests of science and rhetoric. It is this musical moment that requires the choice of "resolution" over "analysis" (we shall see why just below). *Résoudre* makes possible a corresponding amplification of the imaginary landscape in which the heterogeneity and dynamic evolutionary processes that compose society and join it to politics are brilliantly illuminated.

Nothing could have been more predictable than Rousseau's recourse to music for thinking. As he said of himself, "Jean-Jacques was born for music" (OC I.872). He reinvented musical notation, composed a wildly popular opera, and by himself wrote a complete dictionary of music. These are not, however, the facts that count most. What is decisive is that every day Rousseau sat at his desk, the same desk where he wrote his words, copying out music one note at a time.

I venture to say, therefore, that it is impossible that the mental processes and terminology, the impulses and structures of musical discourse were not thoroughly imprinted in some way in everything else Rousseau thought and wrote.[242] Nor should one be surprised to discover that he was more intimately acquainted with Vincenzo Galilei than he was with that sixteenth-century music theorist's famous son.[243]

Key terms of Rousseau's musical mode of understanding are clearly stated in his dictionary.

---

*". . . une choquante dissonance dans l'harmonie universelle me feroit chercher à la resoudre. . . ."

System . . . is the assemblage of the rules of harmony, drawn from some common principles which hold them together, which form their relationship, from which they flow, and by which one makes sense of them.[244]*

A characteristic feature of polyphonic music is the rational relation of each element to every other one.[245] It is deep insight into these *liaisons* among pitches in musical time and space that suggests to Rousseau symbolic forms with which he conceives and represents the *liens sociaux* that constitute the order of the *système social*.

For inquiry into *systèmes*, Rousseau insists, "I suppose that the necessity of dissonance is recognized."[246] This itself is a discovery of Modern music, for what the Renaissance took as inessential or expressive pathos the Baroque made into an internal principle of harmonic motion.[247] Rousseau adds to this conceptualization of dissonance in this way: "It is not sufficient to make dissonance heard; it is necessary to resolve [*résoudre*] it. You only shock the ear at first so as to then please it more agreeably" (OC V.772).†

What we are reading in lines like this is an infiltration of musical into scientific and rhetorical discourse. This gives to the key word *résoudre* an additional sense beyond those I catalogued above. What must be "resolved"—the dissonance—is integral to the *système*, as is the resolution itself. Dissonance is at once a constitutive element and a kind of "distrust of categories" that occurs as an "intermediate moment of deconstruction between description and redescription"[248] in the process through which the *système* itself is reproduced. The way in which "to resolve . . . dissonances arises from the same principle as their preparation: for just as each dissonance is prepared by an antecedent relation within the harmonic system, it is likewise redeemed by consequent relation within the same system."[249]§

This musical sensibility, more than even the perpetual overreaching of "methodized" science, is what permits Rousseau to conceive of his project in such totalizing terms.

Today such an assertion may seem odd because intellectual tastes concerning

---

* "Système . . . est l'assemblage des regles de l'Harmonie, tirées de quelques principes communs qui les rassemblent, qui forment leur liaison, desquels elles découlent, et par lesquels on en rend raison."

† "Il ne suffit pas de faire entendre la Dissonnance, il faut la résoudre; vous ne choquez d'abord l'oreille que pour la flatter ensuite plus agréablement."

§ ". . . à résoudre . . . les Dissonnances naît du même principe que leur préparation: car comme chaque Dissonnance est préparée par le rapport antécédent du Système harmonique, de même elle est sauvée par le rapport conséquent du même Système."

conceptualization of "parts" and "wholes" have changed radically, and because almost no one continues to think in conceptual terms about anything but the poetic element in music, if they get even that far. But as a matter of historical and largely transcultural fact music has often located and provoked some kind of inspiration about totality small (the fusional, experiential microcosm) or large (the universal macrocosm).[250]

With this in mind, we may now return to two key phrases in *Émile*. Let us read them side by side as they are articulated by the discourse of music. One, from the *"Profession de foi,"* is theological; the other, from the "main passage," is sociological.

"Profession de foi . . ."	*"main passage"*
"Une [] choquante dissonance dans l'harmonie universelle me feroit chercher à la resoudre"	*"à resoudre toutes les contradictions du système social"*
["a [] shocking dissonance in the universal harmony would make me seek to resolve it."]	["to resolve all the contradictions of the social system"]

A *système*, like the *univers*, is, by definition, in some powerful sense "well-ordered [*bien-ordonné*]."[251] It is characterized by *harmonie*. To perceive it as totality—that is, not as a function of Plato's divine, or of a Christian divinity, or of anything outside itself—is a singular human achievement.[252] Rousseau's theodicy does this for the *système* of *société*. Once achieved, however, the sublime and thus inexplicable glimpse of totality demands "resolution" into its parts.[253] Living, timeliness, effect, and all their attendant failures, demand such "resolution." When one part of the "harmonized" *système* "speaks" against another, there is *contradiction* or, in the purely abstract language of music, *dissonnance*, where voices collide. The system that "prepares" the dissonance—that makes one pitch "sound" against the others—pushes—like the note stepped out of its place, that place constituted by the "harmony" of all notes, urges forward—toward "resolution." Jean-Jacques—"born for music," successful music-maker, insistent theorist—feels in himself the power to give form to music—the very fact of it, the whole language of it—and to give order to the *système social*. In the way of the *metodo risolutivo e compositivo*, in an operatic way, Rousseau is a "composer." In the composition the moment of inquiry ceases. It is a moment of presentation, a time to speak, the *elocutio*,[254] the *educatio* of things to come: *Discours sur . . . l'inégalité—Émile—Du Contract social . . . .*

The "*contradictions du système social*" resolve into the sociological language of *dépendance*; the resolution of the "*contradictions du système social*"—the *finalité* of *dépendance*—is the *contract social* toward which the evolution of society can only be drawn by a perfectly general human Will. This *compositio* is at once an *ordre*, a *système social*, and the representation of a dream. There is Rousseau, as the title of his smash hit opera would have it, "the village soothsayer [*le devin du village*]," the one who foretells the community of mankind.

Why this discourse layered with science, rhetoric, and music?[255] It is worth noting here that however much Rousseau strives to salvage rhetoric, the historic decline in the status of philosophy is spurred on by him. He does not merely reiterate the rhetorical critique,[256] or other common tropes. Philosophy is represented in the same terms as "society," which is to say as a mass of activities by which one aims to satisfy oneself or another but instead multiplies the problems at hand. It is by contrast to such professionalizing *philosophes*—despite his occasional identification with them—that Rousseau provides a manifesto for the coming sociological revolution. He does so in the—scientific, rhetorical, musical— terms he has at hand.

What music adds to the mix of Method and rhetoric, then, is an unparalleled way of *seeing* the world. Resolution is not a fix. It is a *modus vivendi* with the inevitable, with contradictions of a social system that, like the musical totality, is a system of interdependence where dissonances are not errors to be expunged but facts for which we must prepare and resolve and still, and again, wake up tomorrow to face afresh. Resolution is inquiry by analysis which here and there leads to synthesis, here and there leads to composition, but which, unlike in mathematics or physics or even rhetoric as it was practiced as aestheticized eloquence in the eighteenth century, will always be done from inside life: "sometimes one," and now I underscore the modality, "*must résoudre and composer in the same research.*" But these facts, like contradictions rampant in a heterogenous human world, are essential; they do not go away; rather, the process of human adjustment to them is ongoing, and that going-on with human energy is the motor of the self-transformation of the system itself, the world system, the *système social*. With music preparing the field for theory the primary forces of social evolution become visible, tangible. The substance of that process—which is to say, what one sees when it is "resolved" into its primary elements, before the synthetic machinery of Method or the composer's hand or the speaker's living words bring it back to the level of civic life and to the experience of the citizen as such—is *dépendance*. Dependence constitutes the elements of harmony, the dynamics of the polyphonic narrative; it is the key motive force, a gravitational force, that through dissonance and contradiction make music and society move. These things must all be understood in terms of dependence if they are to be understood at all. And this understanding is a necessary prerequisite to political insight, and for the artificial, institutional, postnatural creation of what we allow ourselves to call *liberté*.

The magnitude of Rousseau's ambition may cause his reader to pause. Rousseau often pictures himself as tormented by doubts.[257] It is therefore particularly noteworthy that, at certain points in *Émile*, he is fully confident about his own capacity in a field he can only see at the horizon. Toward the end of Book V, again dropping the pretense of dialogue with the student Émile and apostrophically addressing himself directly to the reader (as in the "main passage"), Rousseau does not hesitate to call the giants of political thought Grotius and Hobbes "children with bad faith" and, with a tip of his hat to the "illustrious" Montesquieu, proclaim that "political right has yet to be born [*le droit politique est encore à naître*]" (OC IV.836).[258] *Principes du droit politique* is, of course, the subtitle of *Du Contract social*.[259] In this transparent and uninhibited way he proclaims himself the father of modern political theory.[260]

This heroic dimension of Rousseau's social and political theory is likewise affirmed when *résoudre* appears at the beginning of the first book of *Du Contract social*. There, Rousseau declines to consider *how* it came to pass that "Man is born free, and everywhere he is in chains."[261] He writes, however, "I believe I am able to resolve the question. . . . What can render it legitimate?"[262] And if the point of departure in *Du Contract social* is Rousseau's singular capacity (OC III.351), the point of arrival is just the problem before us here: "I will finish this chapter and this book with a remark that should serve as the basis for the whole social system" (OC III.367).

§ 32

––––––⬤–◆–⬤––––––

SYSTÈME

Whatever Rousseau's dreams of the πόλις or *civitas* amount to, the insistent topic of his inquiry is *what really exists*, what is in motion here and now in the life of humankind. He was quite clear regarding this orientation.[263] What exists for us, aspiring citizens, is *société*. This *société* is something composed in an entirely modern way. It requires a specifically new, if complex and incomplete, mode of *resolution*. The purpose of the new science, the new rhetoric, the new art, will be to bring oneself and others along toward a politics fit for this *système social*. That is where Rousseau is aiming when he writes down the one "remark that should serve as the basis for the whole social system" (OC III.367).

We will get back to that remark soon enough. First, we do well to collect some further thoughts about what it means to add the word *système* to the word *société*.

Système is not a new topic. It has appeared repeatedly since the beginning of this book, and the sense Rousseau attributes to and draws from that word may already seem clear. Nonetheless, I want to make it explicit now.

For a word of ancient Greek vintage the modern history of "system" is relatively simple. It emerges from obscurity at the end of the sixteenth century.[264] At first the word is "used by Reform theologians for ordered compilations of Christian teachings."[265] Then it springs to life within the debate—we encountered this in the preceding section (§ 31)—between single-method Ramists and Aristotelians. Twofold methodists, like Zabarella, start to reach beyond the impasse. At once borrowing from Ramus and Aristotle and leaving them behind, the German Bartolomaus Keckermann and his circle are "apparently the first to be convinced that the notion of 'system' could be fruitfully applied on a major scale to philosophical and other knowledge." Tellingly, their group becomes known as the "Systematics."[266] By the end of Keckermann's life in 1609 he has produced more than a dozen "systems"—of logic, Hebrew, theology, ethics, politics, law, rhetoric, metaphysics, astronomy, geography, physics. This copiousness seems to have lit the fire of the fad. The use of the word "system" then grows exponentially during the century from the English Civil War to the *Encyclopédie*; "systems" are published in an astonishing variety of areas, to wit: acoustics, agriculture, algebra, anatomy, the apocalypse, apothecary, astrology, astronomy, divinity, the earth, the elements, finances, geography, government, grace and free will, grammar, the heavens, law, logic, love and sex, mathematics, medicine, metaphysics, morality, music, natural law, navigation, "new inhabited worlds," "Popism or anti-Christianism," philosophy, physics, physick (i.e., medicine), the planets, politics, regulations, religion, the soul, stock-jobbing, the "symptoms of . . . spiritual falling," the *"circulation du sang par le trou ovale dans le foetus humain,"*[267] tabular musical notation, theology, trade, the universe, the world, world trade, and the list goes on![268]

Now it is 1762, the extraordinary year in which both *Émile* and *Du Contract social* come off the press. The Académie française issues a fourth edition of its authoritative *Dictionnaire* that includes a revision of the entry for "*Système*." Lagging behind the general use of the term by almost a century, the academicians have added this brief qualification to their definition: "One also calls System an assemblage of bodies. The planetary system." What the Académie acknowledges here for the first time is the material reality of relationship among the parts that form a whole. By contrast, the main definition they have upheld since the inception of their *Dictionnaire* allows only for *système* as an "assemblage of several propositions." *Système* stands indifferent to its own "truth or falsity" and requires only that on its principles "one may establish an opinion, a doctrine, a dogma." With this, a final sentence—"He imagined, he had created a new system [*Il a imaginé, il a fait un nouveau système*]"—functions as both example and judgment, and insinuates not just the pretensions involved in creating a *système* but the fantastic character of the whole enterprise.

Any scribbler in the eighteenth century could have provided a broader view of *système*. It points three ways. *Système names* a cognitive organization for thinking or teaching *about* something that is distinct from its object. *Système is* identical with the real constitution of parts into a whole, a complex object that may be artificial (like a clock) or natural (like the planets) or conceptual (like analytic geometry). Finally, *système performs* an epithet or an accusation, one that typically arises when a cognitive *système* fails to convincingly map an objective *système*. The question of this success or failure of correspondence seems to inhere in the modern topos of *système*, a consequence of its birth in the middle ground between idea and experience in debates about Method.[269]

These three senses of *système* were well known and widely used even as, in 1694, the Académie built its first edition on a dictionary by Furetière (1690) where all these perspectives were exhibited. Nonetheless, they stuck to the pejorative sense of *système* while suppressing the objective sense that they would only with reluctance admit seventy years later.[270]

By mid-century all of this was clearly on the table. In Rousseau's circle all three *systèmes* were well represented. Condillac—whom Rousseau met in 1741 and with whom he remained in close and positive contact during the formative next decade and after—aspired to system of the cognitive sort.[271] From the materialist side of the *Encyclopédistes*, d'Holbach—perpetually in conflict with Rousseau, who acerbically referred to the *"coterie holbachique"*—proposed objective systems with great *succès de scandale* in *Système de la nature* (1770) and *Système social* (1773). To create or discover a real system, d'Holbach declaimed, "you need a Newton [*il faut un Newton*]."[272]

Unabashed in building systems, many such writers felt an almost perverse obligation to defend their own enterprise by issuing a general attack on *système* itself. Condillac's *Traité des systèmes* (1749, chapters 2 and 3 *et passim*) is an extended critique of the "uselessness" and "abuse" of "abstract systems." A similar view is succinctly asserted in the first line of the *Système de la nature*, although d'Holbach had something rather different in mind than the editors of the *Dictionnaire de l'Académie* as he declared like them that "Men will always fool themselves when they abandon experience in favor of systems hatched by imagination."[273]

More than a century after Keckermann it was not difficult to propose a definition. Condillac took for granted that a *système* must form some convenient conjunction between the world of things and the world of ideas, and wrote that it "is nothing other than the disposition of the different parts of an art or a science in an order in which those parts are entirely mutually sustaining, and where the last is applied according to the first. Those which explain the others are called *principles*."[274]* In the same spirit, d'Holbach could easily have written, borrowing these words for his own purposes, that an objective *système* is nothing other than the disposition of different parts that are entirely mutually sustaining, where every last element is under the influence of its primary forces.

We have already found in Rousseau a master of ambivalence, of polysemy and syllepsis, of comparison and the play of differences. Through variations on a theme he constantly brings something new to light. The careful reader will notice that this is exactly what he does with *système*. While Rousseau attacks "men of system" he also admires great system builders, the "Bacons, the Descartes, the Newtons."[275] In the same tones that Goethe will ring Rousseau demurs to accept that he has a *système*, and yet his responses to critics, fierce in logic and exhaustively complete, display a way of seeing the world in which, somehow, every "part is entirely mutually sustaining."

This ambivalence is not terminal. With the multiple facets of *système* in mind, with all these literary tools under his belt, Rousseau finally decides to join that word to his most encompassing term, *société*. He does not simply settle on this terminology. He places the *système social* at the pivot point of his entire project: "to resolve all the contradictions of the social system."

For Rousseau, as friend and study partner of, as advocate and social connection for his drinking buddy Condillac, this choice seems almost inevitable. Although by 1749 Rousseau had long been cogitating his *Institutions politiques*, he was just on the point of having the revelation that, he would latter say, set him on his true path of discovery.[276] It must have been during that time that he read Condillac's *Traité des sistêmes*, a book that proposes to "disentangle" the "inconveniences and advantages" of systems. I think, therefore, we must imagine, at this formative moment, Rousseau's eye laddering down the pages of Chapter XV, "On the necessity of systems in politics."[277]

---

* "Un sistême n'est autre chose que la disposition des différentes parties d'un art ou d'une science dans un ordre où elles se soutiennent toutes mutuellement, & où les dernieres s'expliquent par les premieres. Celles qui rendent raison des autres s'appellent *Principes*, ..."

Condillac begins that chapter with his typical caution: "If there is a domain in which one should be warned against systems, it is politics [*la politique*]."[278] The danger is not error *per se*. Condillac is on guard against practical mistakes *vis-à-vis* a public realm of citizens. Two pertinent facts appear. First, he observes that "the public never judges except according to each event." This is a striking and tantalizingly republican and essentially rhetorical way to say that contingency is at the heart of politics. Second, experience shows that having been burned by harmful projects the public shies away from any type of planning, any type of "system."

The warning is there to preempt criticism. For, Condillac goes on to ask, "is it possible to govern a State, if one does not bring all the parties under a general point of view, and if one does not bind them one to the other in such a way as to make them move in concert, and by one and the same spring?"

This is a powerful expression of a fundamental dilemma of political thought and action.

Indeed, Condillac's purpose is not to expunge systematic thinking about politics but to *get it right*. The problem has in fact been the debility of those who make or implement bad systems.

So, now imagine, too, Rousseau perking up as the advice comes down. What constitutes a good system? A coherent and thorough-going program must be "preceded by a mature examination of all that competes with domestic and foreign government," for politics is a complex play of forces and "one unforeseen circumstance will suffice to bring about failure." However, comprehensive study does not result in a fixed and timeless set of principles. Revealed again and again is the essential fluidity and contingency of political life. Thus, "one must be ever-ready to change one's principles on each occasion, and a system of politics must in a certain sense undergo the same revolutions as the state for which it was made."

Condillac's is not a recipe for chaos. Things do not change all at once or in any which way. Contingency operates within a totality constituted by "the reciprocal action of the parts." Over and over again the political body passes through states of "equilibrium" (this is Condillac's word). With each part "as happy as it can be" the "State has its most robust constitution." Government can only "maintain perfect equilibrium" when it is "possible to find each citizen's interest within the interest of society. It must be that, in acting in accordance with different perspectives, and with each one making his own more or less local program, citizens necessarily conform to the perspective of a general system." State action is constrained by the practical requirements of what allows citizens "to get along, one with the other."

Likewise with foreign policy. What counts is not the natural resources of neighbors, but rather the type of government they have: that is what "determines the force or weakness of a people." Leaders at home must therefore "know the perspectives of those who govern" abroad, "know their systems if they have such; and sometimes even the smallest intrigues of court." Politics again depends on the details.

> It is evident that a system formed according to these rules is absolutely relative to the particulars of the situation. As this situation comes to change, it must be, too, that the system changes in the same proportion, which is to say, that the changes introduced must be so well combined with the things preserved that the equilibrium among all the parts of society continues to maintain itself. This is something that can only be successfully executed by someone who has imagined, or at least perfectly studied, the system.*

It is not unfair to say, at least loosely, that this is the methodological program Rousseau established for himself when he set out to "resolve all the contradictions of the social system."[279]

Concerning the improvement of humankind, Condillac does not deign to offer pictures from the "state of nature." Yet he, too, is searching for a way to understand social evolution. His approach bears comparison with Rousseau's:

> At their beginnings, societies were only composed of a small number of equal citizens. The magistrates and the generals were superior only during the exercise of their functions: with the moment passed, they returned to the ranks of the others. The citizen thus had no superior other than the law. Subsequently, as societies grew, the citizens multiplied and the situation of equality altered. In time one witnessed the gradual birth of different orders; that of the warriors, the magistrates, the shopkeepers, etc., and each of these orders took its place according to the authority that they had obtained. In the times of equality, the citizens had only the same interest, and a small number of quite simple laws sufficed to govern them. With equality destroyed, interests varied in proportion with the growth of the orders, and the original laws were no longer sufficient. We need only this reflection to feel that one cannot govern with the same

---

* "Il est évident qu'un sistême formé suivant ces regles, est absolument relatif à la situation des choses. Cette situation venant à changer, il faudra donc que le sistême change dans la même proportion; c'est-à-dire, que les changemens introduits doivent être si biens combinés avec les choses conservées, que l'équilibre continue à se maintenir entre toutes les parties de la société. C'est ce qui ne peut être éxecuté avec succès, que par celui qui a imaginé, ou du moins parfaitement étudié le sistême."

system a society at its origin and then along the steps of growth or decadence by which it passes.*

Contingency within historically changing circumstances is an essential feature of the political; civic programs, practices, and institutions must change as political bodies develop. Any political leader who does not systematically investigate the social-historical facts of growth and decadence is bound both to fail and to drive the people away, or into the arms of traditionalist, unenlightened rulers.

At the beginning of this section I promised to come around to the "remark that should serve as the basis for the whole social system." I admit some sleight-of-hand here. For what concerns us more than the substance of this remark is the possibility, heralded by Condillac and advanced by Rousseau, that *such an open-ended and generative system could have a basis.* So, here is what Rousseau declares: the "fundamental pact"—which, as we have seen, is not the origin of society but rather a way that society takes charge of itself[280]—"does not destroy natural equality, but, to the contrary, substitutes a moral and legitimate equality for whatever physical inequality may by nature occur among men." In this way, "despite inequality of force and intelligence, everyone becomes equal by convention and right" (OC III.367).

Someone who understood system with Condillac would have to ask himself not merely, In what does such natural equality consist?—Hobbes and his contemporaries had an answer for that[281]—but What is the evolving form and substance of relationships among human beings such that such a substitution might occur?

That evolving form and substance is *société.* And how shall we understand *société?* The modes of "resolution" and "composition" open to Rousseau in the eighteenth century—philosophy, science, rhetoric, music, not to mention other

---

* "Dans leur origine les sociétés n'étoient formées que d'un petit nombre de Citoyens égaux. Les Magistrats & les Généraux n'avoient de supériorité que pendant l'exercice de leurs fonctions: ce tems passé, ils rentroient dans la classe des autres. Le Citoyen n'avoit donc de supérieur que la Loi. Par la suite, les sociétés s'aggrandirent, les Citoyens se multiplierent, & l'égalité s'altéra. Alors on vit naître peu-à-peu différens ordres; celui des Gens de Guerre, celui des Magistrats, celui des Négocians, &c. & chacun de ces ordres prit son rang, d'après l'autorité qu'il avoit obtenue. Dans le tems d'égalité, les Citoyens n'avoient tous qu'un même intérêt, & un petit nombre de Loix fort simples suffisoient pour les gouverner. L'égalité détruite, les intérêts ont varié à proportion que les ordres se sont multipliés, & les premiers Loix n'ont plus étés suffisantes. Il ne faut que cette considération pour sentir qu'avec le même sistème on ne peut pas gouverner une société dans son origine, & dans les dégrés d'accroissement ou de décadence par où elle passe."

conceptual/symbolic frameworks important to him, deriving from the epistolary novel or the game of chess or the study of botany—indirectly suggest what that object might be and how it could be investigated. This much becomes visible to the informed eye with the word *résoudre*.

Something different happens when Rousseau adopts the word *système* and joins it to *société*. He turns to the most powerful broadcasting term of his contemporaries. With that term he names directly the object of the most modern of the human sciences. Then, by syllepsis, each and every facet of *système*—as idea, as reality, displaying its implication with Method or within debate—is brought into play before the mind of the reader. That is how Rousseau burrows so deep into his subject; that is how he writes so lucidly about it.

But finally Rousseau is not Condillac. Something else resonates in the word *système* to make it not merely necessary to his purpose but desirable as well. For Rousseau is a codemaker,[282] and something hidden in the word *système* pulses with the primary inspiration of his enterprise. It will not, ultimately, suffice to merely "*résoudre* all the contradictions of the social system." What writer and reader together must ultimately do is to turn the social into the political. Rousseau is here to devise not just a better equality but to advise would-be citizens on the metamorphosis of ancient liberty into something modern. Something beyond.

Clues scattered everywhere in Rousseau's pages press on us this question: What is the latent sense of this ancient Greek word, σύστημα/system? The answer is strikingly close to home. System/σύστημα is association, human association in various forms. Look at Aristotle, who writes of the πόλις/city as an instance of σύστημα/system. Turn to Polybius, who seems to use the words as synonyms.[283]

Let us suppose, then, that traces of original meanings cling somehow to words despite metaphorical transformations. Imagine that those traces survive the death of metaphor and the resurrection of the literal in common sense. Then, Rousseau's combination of *société* and *système* would be at least in part redundant, a magnificent pleonasm. For shouldn't it be enough to call, as he does, the peculiar way the Moderns form entire associations *société*? Is that phrase *système social* more than the creaking of popular science a century after Keckermann? Can it be, perhaps, Rousseau's way to secure the πόλις, *civitas*, for Modernity? Or his way to excavate the absent πόλις from under the conditions of Modern life?

These questions cannot but take us back to Rousseau's line and we must now follow it. What we will see is that the locus of social man's liberty, the social system, must be—paradoxically, you will say—interpreted as a system of dependence. Only then shall we understand how its contradictions are to be resolved and with what results. Only then can we determine whether or not Rousseau successfully accomplishes his task.[284]

$$\mathint{\int} 33$$

<hr>

THE SIGNIFICANCE OF DEPENDENCE-FROM-THINGS AND DEPENDENCE-FROM-PERSONS

In the "main passage" Rousseau moves the whole theory of society to another level when he makes explicit a division between types of dependence. It refines his position in an important way and it brings us to the nub of the argument here.

> There are two types of dependence: that from things, which is of nature; that from persons, which is of society.*

At this pivotal juncture, I reiterate a point of translation mentioned earlier (§12). To reduce somewhat the prejudice of interpretation, I render "*dépendance de*" in English as "dependence *from.*" The purpose of this unpleasantly literal translation is to revivify the "dead metaphor" inherent in the word *dépendance*, which derives from the Latin *dependere*, from *pendere*, or "to hang." This way we maintain in the word "dependence" the clear sense that something important is at stake in the fact.

Another aspect of translation tends away from the literal. I have already explained why it has been correct and consistent to translate the word "*hommes*" as "Men."[285] This conforms both to the English usage of Rousseau's time and to the particular construction of gender in the relevant parts of Rousseau's theoretical *oeuvre*. However, from now on, where appropriate, I shall freely translate the word "*hommes*" as "persons." Why? Because we have reached the topic that bridges between precisely what Rousseau has said and the much more general argument I want to make through this engagement with Rousseau. This shift to the word "persons" is intended to underscore emphatically that my own argument—at least on this point—is neutral with respect to gender.

<hr>

* "Il y a deux sortes de dépendance: celle des choses, qui est de la nature; celle des hommes, qui est de la société."

What Rousseau claims in these few lines is that there is a categorical difference between dependence-from-things and dependence-from-persons. The first is natural, the second social. The ambiguity in the phrase *de la nature*—does it mean "as in the state of nature" or something else?—will be addressed before too long. Rousseau goes on:

> Dependence-from-things, not having any morality, does not undermine liberty at all, nor does it in any way engender vices.*

By contrast,

> dependence-from-persons, being disordered, engenders them all, and by way of it master and slave mutually deprave themselves.[286]†

In short, the first sort of dependence stands outside the moral world and thus—because "liberty" and "vice" are moral facts—cannot have a negative impact on liberty or make one vicious. The second sort of dependence cultivates vice and slavery.[287]

This matrix becomes the frame for Rousseau's social theory of politics, and for his project "to resolve all the contradictions of the social system."

§34

---❖---

MORALITY AND DISORDER

Dependence-from-persons has everything to do with morality. Rousseau does not state this directly; it is implied by the juxtaposition between the two sorts of dependence and the way in which they are qualified.

This indirect transfer and, in a sense, quarantine of moral significance is in itself worth noting. It exemplifies Rousseau's construction and deployment of categorical oppositions. Two types of "liberty" are distinguished in just the same way; likewise two types of "equality."[288] This categorical mode of thinking is ex-

---

* "La dépendance des choses, n'ayant aucune moralité, ne nuit point à la liberté, et n'engendre point de vices. . . ."

† ". . . la dépendance des hommes étant désordonnée les engendre tous, et c'est par elle que le maître et l'esclave se dépravent mutuellement."

pressed figuratively in the bridge made by that master trope — *"le pacte social"* — between a "natural" and a "civil" condition.

Return for a moment to the lines from the "main passage" cited in the preceding section. Notice how the terms change at this decisive moment. Dependence-from-things is considered with respect to properties (*ayant*, having), whereas when it comes to relations within a group of people Rousseau shifts his reader's focus to an ontological domain (*étant*, being).[289]

What matters most at this point, however, is the new category that comes to the foreground as Rousseau lays out the architectonic of dependence. This innovation appears within a familiar parallel structure and will greatly complicate the overall picture. We see that, on the one hand,

dependence-from-things = a-morality

while, on the other hand,

dependence-from-persons = disorder

Literally the new word here is "disorder." The important, indeed fundamental, term is its opposite: "order."

Let me be clear. This is not the first time the word "order" appears in *Émile*. It is rather common. It has in French, as it has in English, a variety of senses, including "command," "sequence," "arrangement," and so forth. It is also closely related to "system."[290]

One sense of the word, however, is less frequent and especially apposite. Throughout *Émile*, the phrases *état de nature* and *état civil* or *état de société* are used interchangeably with *ordre de nature* and *ordre civil* or *ordre de la société*. Thus, the word "order" may be understood as a synonym for "condition" or "state."[291]

Nonetheless, the relation between *"état"* and *"ordre"* is not symmetrical. To say that an *ordre* is an *état* adds no further information. To think of an *état* or "condition" as an *ordre* is clarifying. Thus, when, in the "main passage," Rousseau enters a theoretical mode and adopts the language of "order," we should take note. He aims thereby to add to our understanding of the two primary *états* of Man: natural and moral.

Indeed, Rousseau will ultimately use images of order to define both the natural and the moral world. It is important to emphasize this very large scope of Rousseau's thinking. It will, in turn, provide the frame within which "order" becomes the key to the distinction between types of dependence.

The limits of this assertion need to be clearly stated. I am not saying that "order" is the deepest foundation of Rousseau's argument.[292] We shall soon see that beneath all of this elaborate edifice lies the Will, which Rousseau calls his "first principle . . . first dogma . . . first article of faith" (OC IV.576). It is Rousseau's—ultimately unwarranted—assumption that order derives from Will. This is, from where we stand today, his most profound, enduring, and influential error. Indeed, at the end of this book, I shall propose that we cannot today justify continued allegiance to Rousseau's distinction between two types of dependence, nor to the conception of society that derives from it.[293] But that is a conclusion; we have quite a few steps in the argument before we reach it.

For now, observe closely that Rousseau uses the phrase "being disordered [*étant désordonnée*]" to describe the situation of morality. Disorder is why the moral world engenders vices and slavery. It is this disorder that we must try to understand.[294]

Part III

NATURE AND THE MORAL FRAME OF SOCIETY

Another View on *Société* and *Moeurs* in the Eighteenth Century

For mankind "abandoned to ourselves," society is the inherent structuring framework for morality.[1] Society is constituted by dependence and it is a source of disorder; this has an impact on moral life, and therefore on politics.[2]

Viewing *société* through the optic of *système* has permitted us to see it as concept, as fact, and as rhetorical *topos* all at once.[3]

Ways of resolving and composing *société* — as much in practice as in theory — hinge on one preliminary fact that derives from the common sense and commonplaces of the communities of speech that use the word. This conditioning fact appears in response to the following question: what, as a fact of speech, does society exclude and what does it include?

Spinoza's famous point — *omnis determinatio est negatio* — is *à propos* here. In drawing boundaries something must be excluded. But this cuts the other way as well: any gesture of negation posits something.[4] Whichever way one sees things here, the mixed tide of natural philosophy and theology leading up to Rousseau and the theodicy advanced by him require some kind of link between the advent of society and strong secular commitments. Whether it is God out then Man in, or Man in then God out, this is the price of human responsibility for human life. The day-to-day negotiation of this transformation may not always have been so black and white, but the long-term result was. As Europeans underwent this change of heart and mind and developed new types of extended relationships, society came into its full-blown and comprehensive modern form in the eighteenth century. The result was that neither society nor religion "could be thought without reference to the other: the institution of society as the conceptual frame of human collective existence required (indeed, it found its ultimate logic in) the displacement and reworking of the prior claims of the divine."[5]

This line is from a brilliant, allusive essay by Keith Michael Baker. In it, he identified *société* as a keyword of the eighteenth century. In his terse formulation, "'Society' and 'Enlightenment' belong together." It was, he asserts, the Enlightenment that "invented society as the symbolic representation of collective human existence and instituted it as the essential domain of human practice."[6]

No one can doubt the assimilation of these two terms, of these two facts. And no serious historian or political theorist could imagine that gradual historical-cultural processes are not at work when new terms, practices, *mentalités* become dominant. Yet, unlike Baker, or the likewise remarkable Daniel Gordon who develops this perspective further, I find within the century's arc, within and at odds with the Enlightenment as a complex movement, that one extraordinary and extraordinarily influential writer became an exemplar, an inspiration, a provocateur. Rousseau, as an author and an icon, constituted the unmistakable cultural face of this phenomenon, a "tipping point" into a new way of experiencing collective life. So much does Rousseau function in these ways for the transnational republic of letters and the growing literary public sphere that I am prepared to call him the inventor of society, even if we know that literally no one is that.

I do not want to quibble with my colleagues around small details. I agree on the big picture. Gordon is certainly correct to say that "as late as 1694, . . . it was possible to define *société* without invoking in any way the concept of a general field of human existence."[7] But it was possible after that, too; indeed, this continued to be true even after Rousseau; parallel usage accompanied the new meaning he invested in the word. It is likewise plausible, as Gordon also suggests, that *société* was first generalized in Furetière's (1690) dictionary.[8] But it is equally possible that the entry there for *société* refers to general qualities of limited groups and thus does not attain the extension reached by Rousseau. Indeed, Furetière's hint that *société* really is shorthand for *société civile* means that his reference is to some version of polity and not to society in Rousseau's sense at all.[9] Most important, however, is this: even if Furetière hit on the new sense, or, in that same moment, as Baker says, Pierre Nicole "first analyzed the logic of society as a merely (and irremediably) human order,"[10] these flashing facts passed more or less unnoticed. What imprinted them indelibly in the languages of Europe and the self-conception of much of the world was—as I make clear in this book—Rousseau. It was Rousseau who developed the significance of the generalization and the secular logic of *société*, and his writings became the main means of its dissemination. That, as Baker points out, the *Encyclopédie* carried a comparable banner settles nothing, since those avid and revolted readers of Rousseau did not publish their entry until 1765.

Some statistical data compiled by Gordon offers especially telling evidence for the Enlightenment invention and promulgation of *société*. Within a corpus of about eight hundred texts published between 1600 and 1800, the word appears 620 times before 1700 and then 7,168 times after 1701. Closer analysis shows that a kind of explosion in the use of *société* and its cognates took place between 1751 and 1760 (to 1,102 occurrences from 357 the decade before); then use jumped again (to 1,746) in the decade after.[11] This convincingly shows that the dissemination of the word *société* corresponds almost exactly (how exactly we cannot know) with the publication of Rousseau's two *Discours, Du Contract social,* and *Émile.*[12]

Twenty years after Gordon's research it has become possible to undertake carefully delimited searches of a vastly larger corpus through Google Books. This shows that already in the sixteenth century some older versions of *société* circulated more widely than we once thought. It confirms, however, the basic fact that *société* gains traction initially in the second quarter of the eighteenth century and then "goes viral" after tentative use by Montesquieu and aggressive use by Rousseau.[13]

We now need to refine our interpretive repertoire for the key term of *société*. To this end, the following observations:

—Rousseau writes at the cusp between different senses of the word *société*. Sometimes he uses it in a way long traditional by his time. A particular group or association is a "society."[14] Conforming to this usage, he qualifies the most inclusive form of association as *société générale, société humaine,* or *société civile*. Elsewhere, he neglects to qualify the term. He lets it stand alone for the seamless web of human relationships. One might compare this shift with a similar movement at the end of the nineteenth century, during which time the qualifier "political" was detached from the word "economy,"[15] and the "economy" came to be conceived as an autonomous system.[16] Be that as it may, Rousseau understood clearly that his new way of thinking was beyond the ken of his contemporaries. "Not one," he wrote, "among those who attacked [him] was ever able to conceive" the "distinction that [he] always scrupulously made" between individuals and social groups (OC IV.967). This usage is the innovation we consider here.[17] It is decisively sociological, and it redefines *les lieux* in which, and the audience for which, thinking about politics will henceforth operate.

—Leave open here the important question of whether *société* as an inclusive form of association is coextensive with, overlapping, or larger than "the political."[18] The main issue for Rousseau is, so to speak, the density and complexity of the fabric of human relationships. *Société* is a totality but it is not therefore limitless. Overextension of the concept may not be compatible with his central concern with the *Citoyen*. This appears, for example, as *Du Contract social* ends with a kind of false modesty. Rousseau seems to apologize for the shortness of his vision; he excuses his failure to treat all sorts of "external re-lations" that his reader could expect to find in subsequent sections of the book. His conclusion—"I should always have fixed my view closer to myself [*j'aurais dû la fixer toujours plus près de moi*]"—must, however, be ironic. "After having posited the true principles of political right and undertaken to found the State on this basis," his job is done. He writes to suggest, without blame or provoca-tion, that if readers expect him to go beyond the experience of the Citizen they have missed the point of his book.[19]

—This boundary around his enterprise is more clearly affirmed by contrast to the universalism of Christianity and the cosmopolitanism we now associate with "human rights." While "the articles . . . of a purely civil profession of faith" should be seen "as sentiments of sociability,"[20] inherent in the "*pur Evangile*" is a reaching beyond the "co-citizenship [*concitoyennité*]" of the State[21] that may be

> "too sociable, embracing too much the entire human race for law-making that must be exclusive, inspiring humanity rather than patriotism, and tending to give shape to Men rather than Citizens."[22]*

In fact, Rousseau seems to recognize that giving too much theoretical weight to "the great society, human society in general, founded on humanity and uni-versal good deeds [*la grande société, la société humaine en général, . . . fondée sur l'humanité, sur la bienfaisance universelle*]," could undermine exactly the theodicy that makes his sociology possible. He insists that "particular societies, political and civil societies have an entirely different principle. These are purely human establishments from which, consequently, true Christianity detaches us as it does from everything that is only 'of this world.'"[23]† Indeed, the ease with which Rousseau swings between the old senses of the word *société* and his new one can mislead his reader. For example, immediately after writing that "*l'ordre social*" is fundamental and conventional, Rousseau does not hesitate to add that "the most ancient of all societies and the only natural one is that of the family." I underscore this because it represents a qualitative shift between two conceptual domains, even though they are linked by a single term.[24]

---

*" . . . trop sociable, embrassant trop tout le genre humain pour une Législation qui doit être exclusive, inspirant l'humanité plutôt que le patriotisme, et tendant à former des hommes plutôt que des Citoyens."

†"... les Sociétés particulières, les Sociétés politiques et civiles ont un tout autre principe. Ce sont des établissements purement humains dont, par conséquent, le vrai Christianisme nous détache comme de tout ce qui n'est que terrestre."

—The aspect of Rousseau's innovation that will later be associated with Durkheim and then grow into modern common sense is captured neatly in a fragment from Rousseau's notebooks for the grand treatise he never completed, *Institutions politiques*. There he writes: "The moral condition of a people follows less from the absolute condition of its members than from the relationships among them" (OC III.511). In other words, the social foundation that determines the quality of a body politic is the type of relationships the members form with each other and not their individual well-being.[25]

—By way of comparison, consider Thomas Hobbes's *Leviathan*, published one century earlier in 1651. The word "society" is used there in the traditional sense just mentioned. It is a particular association. Fearful Man seeks the company of his kind (chapter XI);[26] economic Man forms corporations (XXII). These facts are simply noted as "society." Man in Nature lacks many things, he has "no arts, no letters, no society" (XIII), which is to say no refined "fellowship." For the *general* fact of association, Hobbes mainly uses other terms—e.g., "body," "*civitas*," "Commonwealth"—in the process of emphasizing the artificiality of that overarching type of relationship, which is held together by law.[27] Subgroup associations are called "systems."[28] When Hobbes points to a general fact with the word *society*, he qualifies it as "civil." In a time "before civil society" (XIV) life lacks steady patterned practices of association (i.e., societies) *and* an attendant tranquility (i.e., civility or civicness). This may be, despite Hobbes's withering comments against Aristotle, the remnant of the latter's *koinonia politike*.[29] One suspects that "political community" for Hobbes meant something more concrete than it does for us, since "moral philosophy is nothing but the science of what is good and evil in the conversation and society of mankind" (XV). That criminal intentions are destructive of "human society" suggests the latter is equivalent to "civil society" insofar as it is regulated by law (XXVII). While the "laws of nature" are "a means of the conservation of men in multitudes" for both thinkers, for Rousseau they establish aspects of the human condition in general—*society* as a stage of the natural evolution of mankind "abandoned to ourselves"[30]—whereas for Hobbes they "only concern the doctrine of civil society" (XV).[31] Thus, after Rousseau, and under the typical conditions of urbanized industrial life in the nineteenth century, crime and criminality become (e.g. for Durkheim) social and sociological facts, not their antitheses. Only when Hobbes says that those who "destroy all laws . . . reduce all order, government, and society to the first chaos of violence and civil war" (XXXVI) does the word "society" seem to rise to the level of inclusiveness and precision it will have in Rousseau. But even this may be exceptional; or it may simply be misleading if, for example, the list is meant to indicate decreasing generality rather than an emphatic synonymy. Hobbes tells of a person of bad faith who joins with others for the central purpose of the "social contract"—peace—but has other intentions. Such a person who has been "received into any society that unite themselves for peace and defence" can be "cast out of society" once he is discovered (XV). The phrase "any society" requires the existence of *plural societies*, the plural phrase "unite themselves" (implying "they") shows that *society* is not an encompassing group noun, and the phrase "cast out of society" implies that the malefactor has someplace else to go. However, between *this* society and *that* one, there is in Hobbes's view a kind of relational void. Every failure of specific membership, every moment of disorder, is a return to nature and civil war.

—For Rousseau, a person ejected from, let's say, the Rotary Club would not return to the "state of nature." He remains within "civil society"—or, at this point, simply *société*—as a social type called "outcast."[32] Part of the generality of *société* in Rousseau's usage is that one cannot be expelled from it the way one, and mankind, has been expelled from Paradise. Hell is, perhaps, merely having no other home to which to return. If Rousseau, the solitaire, is persistently anxious, this may be why: he is constantly striving to escape to nowhere, and, whatever woods he may wander, he continues to write for the denizens of the Parisian salons that he detests.[33] To trace Rousseau's restlessness to a nostalgia for the "state of nature" absurdly understates the problem. There is no going home, not just because the past is irredeemably past, or all of earth's hiding places have been uncovered and despoiled, but because with the advent of *société* human endeavor is itself a transformation of nature. And as all of humanity is the island on which each person lives, there is no *other* place where that home could be.[34]

—This is *société* in Rousseau's innovative sense and it simply does not exist for Hobbes.[35] The conceptual break here does not derive from the difference between English and French. In an important early dictionary bridging between Latin and French—Nicot's *Thresor de la langue française* (1606)—*société* is clearly presented in the traditional Ciceronian sense I mentioned above. When association extends to "society among people of the same country, and among citizens [*societé entre gens d'un mesme païs, et entre citoyens*]" it is qualified as *societas interior et propior* ["internal and proximate society"]. Likewise Richelet's *Dictionnaire francois* (1680), where *société* is only described as a "a good faith contract by which one shares something so as to profit honestly from it."[36] A comparison with Furetière (1690), the last great dictionary before the Academy's, is also telling. The primary definition of *société* is "assembly of several men in a place for the mutual and joint satisfaction of their needs [*Affemblée de plufieurs hommes en un lieu pour s'entrefecourir dans les befoins*]."

Here limits concerning number, specific persons, and space still apply that will be pushed aside by Rousseau. The authoritative *Dictionnaire de l'Académie française* (first edition, 1694) does not even contain a separate entry for *société*. The primary word is *sociable*. Thus, priority is given to a human quality and an Aristotelian or Ciceronian example: *sociable* is "he who is naturally capable of company, who is born to live in company." The examples under the sublisting, where *"societé"* appears as a substantive, may seem like modernized versions of ancient political understanding—"society is something natural for Men"—but the definition strongly suggests the pre-Rousseauean tradition in emphasizing acts like "getting together [*frequentation*]" and "exchange [*commerce*]." One century later, after two generations of Rousseau's enormous success—and, admittedly, after the Enlightenment and the Revolution—the 1798 edition of the same *Dictionnaire de l'Académie française* had thoroughly absorbed the new vocabulary. *Société* merits its own entry. It is no longer a particular kind of act by a particular kind of person, but rather "an assemblage of Men who are unified by nature or by laws."[37] In other words, it is consistent with the idea of particular association, but allows that such groups may be entirely inclusive. It is striking that the particularity which, earlier, was felt to be self-evident is in 1798 made explicit by contrast to the general and inclusive usage: a *société* can *also* be a "company, union of several persons joined together for some interest, or some business, and under certain conditions."

—Whatever the language, it bears repeating that Rousseau did not accomplish by himself the shift to the modern sense of "society." This was a broad historical-cultural development channeled by some very effective and successful writers. Rousseau was eventually foremost among these, but Montesquieu may still be viewed as his predecessor. Simply opening the pages of *De l'esprit des lois* (1748) one finds a similar double-edged use of the word. In some respects, Montesquieu is even more consistent than Rousseau in applying the term in a modern sense. Rousseau read Montesquieu's book carefully, first as a researcher for his patrons, the Dupins, around the time it was published. It is telling that he avoided critical conversations about Montesquieu.[38] Rousseau compared his contemporary to Plato and, on hearing of Montesquieu's death, he wrote that "he had no need of so long a life to become immortal; but he ought to have lived forever to teach people their rights and duties."[39] Although Rousseau claims to have developed his idea for a fundamental work on politics before *De l'esprit des lois* was published, the shape of Rousseau's inquiry and the direction of his subsequent thinking were certainly influenced by that book.[40] Notwithstanding all of this, and despite whatever ambition or admiration lay in the background, Rousseau was still right to distinguish his own project from that of Montesquieu. The illustrious Montesquieu, wrote Rousseau,

> was cautious about treating principles of political right; he limited himself to positive right of established governments, and nothing in the world is more different than these two types of study.[41]*

Rousseau, as always, chooses his words with care. Recall that the phrase "principles of political right" is the subtitle of *Du Contract social*. Moreover, these lines appear in *Émile* just before several pages summarizing aspects of that other work. Thus, what Rousseau is saying here is that he and Montesquieu do not study the same thing. The basis of the distinction is, we may say anachronistically, that while positivism purports to stand alone, "principles of political right" join *what exists* to *what could be*. This requires mediation, a "third" to which both can be referred. The most important feature distinguishing Rousseau's work from Montesquieu's—at least for the purposes of the present book—is that Rousseau identifies *société* as that mediating "third" and intertwines considerations of it with an inquiry into dependence.

—It must be acknowledged that Rousseau sometimes hesitates in the development of his innovation. The opening pages of his initial draft of *Du Contract social* treats "first notions of the social body." As he sets the largest frame of the inquiry, Rousseau takes care to qualify his object as "the general society of the human race [*la société générale du genre humain*]." Nonetheless, this is what, when revved up, he will refer to simply as *société*.[42]

—When Rousseau enlarges the term *société* to cover the general fact of human association, he paves the way for another important aspect of his thinking. *Société* is characterized by morality and not, for example, by particular institutions (of family, government, corporation, sect, purposeful association, etc.).[43] This is no doubt consistent with so-called "social contract" thinking in general; consider Hobbes's claim that "justice and injustice . . . are qualities that relate to men in society, not in solitude."[44] Nonetheless, that correlation is misleading. The connections between *société* and morality take on new significance in light of Rousseau's theodicy, his detailed account of the "self," and, especially, the *topoi* through which his analysis of *société* is conducted.

—As we have already seen in some detail (§§4 and 5 above), the basis of that morality is not "contract." It is the ceaseless experience of dependence. Not-

---

* "... eut garde de traitter des principes du droit politique; il se contenta de traiter du droit positif des gouvernemens établis, et rien au monde n'est plus différent que ces deux études."

withstanding the (heuristic, provocative, ironic) title of his most famous book, Rousseau harbors no illusion that society—as characterized by morality and constituted by dependence—arises from or in a supposed founding moment certified by a *"pacte social."*[45] Rather, society, with its *ordre* and its *lois*, is ultimately constituted by and operates on itself through *"moeurs*, customs, and above all opinion."[46]

—And the claim that dependence, not "contract," is the basis of the moral substance of society does not require the distinction Rousseau makes between the two types of dependence. I underscore this again here because it is, in a sense, one of the fundamental points of this book. To grasp, and to pursue, Rousseau's enormous insight into the social conditions of political life it is sufficient to see in a general way that dependence is both the source of evil and the practical potential for its solution, a potential that is inherent in the social condition itself.

—However, for reasons that will be laid out in detail in the remainder of this book, Rousseau's fully considered view does require the distinction between two types of dependence. Once this distinction becomes entangled in Rousseau's thinking his image of the social conditions of political life changes significantly. As he puts it: because dependence-from-persons is disordered, the moral world is disordered; in Rousseau's way of thinking dependence must be qualified in terms of order and Will before it can become a primary element of politics. This is a powerful and persuasive and largely misleading approach.

—When the single word "social" is used to qualify the dependence-riddled and disorderly moral world, another equivalence comes to the foreground. We can now see the content of the "social system" that is full of "contradictions" in need of "resolution."[47]

$$\frac{\text{moral world}}{\text{society}} \ = \ \frac{\text{disorder}}{\text{contradiction}}$$

but also

$$\frac{\text{moral world}}{\text{disorder}} \ = \ \frac{\text{society}}{\text{contradiction}}$$

—In other words, it seems to me that Rousseau is speaking of the same set of problems when he refers to contradictions and to disorder. I shall have quite a bit more to say about this later on. For now, this much is clear: if Rousseau is to live up to the promise I have made so prominent here—"to resolve all the contradictions of the social system" — he will have to show how the moral world can be ordered. And he will have to show in what way this order is related to the problem of dependence.

$$§36$$

RESOLVING THE PROBLEM OF *DÉPENDANCE*
The Harmony of Equality Before the Law

To have stated that evil for Man is resident in society is at best a first step toward resolving — in any sense of that word — the problem. Rousseau moves on in this way: "If there is some means to remedy this evil in society, it is to substitute law for Man, and to arm the general Wills [*les volontés générales*] with a real force, superior to the action of any particular Will" (OC IV.311).*

We have already mentioned — concerning the scope of Rousseau's ambition (§§17 and 22 above) — that although this statement is found in *Émile* it expresses the program of *Du Contract social*. It is with such resolution and remedy in mind that Rousseau ends the first part of that treatise by offering "a remark that should serve as the basis for the whole social system."

This "remark" has already drawn our attention several times. In §32 above it was considered in a heuristic way so as to elicit the structure of Rousseau's thinking and to show how he proceeds. As a result we have barely touched on the substantive concerns it advances.

Here we are at the nexus of inquiry and theoretical program for action. The substance of the "remark" can no longer be evaded and we need to see it in a relevant way. Rousseau goes beyond the assertion that the fabric of human relationships *can have a basis*. His interest is to identify and engage that basis, to strike at the root of the problem.

This is why it is important to see that the summary statement contained in the "remark" reasserts, from another angle, the proposition set forth in the "main pas-

---

* "S'il y a quelque moyen de remédier à ce mal dans la societé, c'est de substituer la loi à l'homme, et d'armer les volontés générales d'une force réelle, supérieure à l'action de toute volonté particuliére."

sage." In other words, the "remark" also states a way "to resolve all the contradictions of the social system."[48] Here again from *Du Contract social* is that proposition:

> the fundamental pact[49] does not destroy natural equality, but, to the contrary,
> substitutes a moral and legitimate equality for whatever physical inequality
> may by nature occur among men, and as such everyone becomes equal by con-
> vention and right, despite inequality of force and intelligence. (OC III.367)*

The explicit subject here is the "fundamental pact." In Rousseau's literary universe, however, a "pact" is not a program or even a concept; it is an icon or image
that stands for a wide range of interrelated concerns. On its face, it may seem that
here the foremost concern is equality or the absence thereof; indeed, that word
enters five times in a single sentence. However, this appearance, too, is mistaken.

Rousseau's purpose at this point is to thematize the program for resolution
and remedy. In that respect, the real issue, the essential political consideration, is
barely made explicit. It is the rule of law.

Stated here in a general way, the problem to be confronted is *les maux sociaux*,
the evils of society. The fix for that problem, insofar as the continuing presence
of natural inequalities will permit a fix, insofar as informed and intentional civic
practice can be the vehicle for that fix, is the imposition of "convention and
right." This imposition involves "the moral" and "the legitimate/lawful." The
question this raises, the question that has burned in the minds of readers ever
since, is who is the subject, the agent, of this imposition?

Any satisfactory answer to this question—as a matter of textual criticism, as a
matter of theory, and as a matter of fact—demands that we keep in mind something made explicit in §5 above. Law for Rousseau includes the imperatives of
the State but is in no way coterminous with them. The most fundamental law,
the foundation of positive law, is the field of "*moeurs*, customs, and opinion."
This field extends through the State and far beyond it. Furthermore, this field
is the moral substance of society itself (§§31 and 32 above). This is how law and
society are joined, through *le lien social* and its inflections. This is how law can
provide a resolution and remedy for the evils of society.

If the resolution is clear, the remedy is imperfect. "Abandoned to ourselves"
we had better, Rousseau imagines, make what we can of our estate, check and

---

* "... c'est qu'au lieu de détruire l'égalité naturelle, le pacte fondamental substitue au
contraire une égalité morale et légitime à ce que la nature avoit pu mettre d'inégalité
physique entre les hommes, et que, pouvant être inégaux en force ou en génie, ils devien-
nent tous égaux par convention et de droit."

transcend the evils our social nature and habits have brought and will always bring upon us by replacing the rule of Man—of the one, the few, or the many— with the rule of law.

That "general Will," what the law wants, must be armed "with a real force, superior to the action of any particular Will [*d'une force réelle, supérieure à l'action de toute volonté particulière*]" (OC IV.311). It has escaped no one's attention that this apparent concession to *force* opens a path for the return of men to power, if not as despots then as police or jailers.

I will say only one thing about this here. Rousseau does not finally fall into this trap. For, as we have seen in §20 above, that *force*, too, is part and parcel of the society it controls. Everything comes back to *société*. And everything comes down to the "stuff" from which *société* is composed, which is *dépendance*.

§37

THE "FORMULA FOR HAPPINESS" RETURNS, WRIT LARGE, BETWEEN *NATURE* AND *SOCIÉTÉ*

As Rousseau points us toward a *force* that is both *réelle* and *supérieure*, you will notice that space opens for a return of the "formula for happiness" (cf. §19 above). It now seems possible to extend it across a broader terrain. This is, of course, not coincidental.

In the opening pages of the first draft of *Du Contract social*, the "formula for happiness" is integrated into an account of social evolution as the precondition for politics.[50] Rousseau situates his reader at a primordial moment in which the boundary between *l'état de nature* and *société* is indistinct and fluid. Nowhere is the complex constellation of the primary ideas that compose Rousseau's political sociology more synthetically presented.

Prefaced the way a determined author will often tell himself what he is about to write—"we begin by seeking what gives birth to the necessity of political institutions"[51]—Rousseau's chapter entitled "*De la société générale du genre humain*"[52] sets the stage this way:

Man's force is so thoroughly proportioned to his natural needs and his primitive condition that, however slightly this condition changes and his needs increase, the assistance of others of his own kind becomes necessary for him, and when finally his desires embrace the entirety of nature, the cooperation of the entire human race is hardly sufficient to satisfy them.[53]*

Writ large into the figure of *société générale*, the "formula for happiness" brings into more detailed focus the evil that grows among us when mankind is "abandoned to ourselves." It also highlights the forms that evil takes that may be susceptible only to political resolution, as we find "in art-perfected the reparation of these evils that art-begun had wreaked upon nature [*dans l'art perfectionné la réparation des maux que l'art commencé fit à la nature*]" (OC III.288).

The central theme from the *Discours sur . . . l'inégalité* is imported into the mix this way:

> Thus, such general society as can emerge from our mutual *besoins* offers not a whit of effective assistance to man become miserable, or at least it only gives new *forces* to those who already have too much *force*, while the weak, the lost, the suffocated, the crushed in the crowd finds no asylum where to take refuge, no support for his weakness, and in the end perishes, victim of that treacherous union from which he expected his happiness.[54]†

As we have already seen (§20 above), in the evolution of society *forces* available to human beings will multiply. Nonetheless, these new *forces* will likely be overwhelmed by the simultaneous multiplication of needs. At this point, in the incomplete development of society and prior to the political constitution, Rousseau adds that inequality—itself another consequence of social evolution—will determine the distribution of these additional *forces*. It will surprise no one that "them that's got, gets more, while the weak ones fade" as morality and politics become entangled in the most general formation of society:[55] "exactly that which renders us wicked [*méchans*] makes us again slaves [*esclaves*], and subjugates us by depraving us."§ In this process, the motivating experience of weakness loses

---

* "La force de l'homme est tellement proportionnée à ses besoins naturels et à son état primitif, que pour peu que cet état change et que ses besoins augmentent, l'assistance de ses semblables lui devient nécessaire, et, quand enfin ses desires embrassent toute la nature, le concours de tout le genre humain suffit à peine pour les assouvir."

† "La société générale telle que nos besoins mutuels peuvent l'engendrer n'offre donc point une assistance efficace à l'homme devenu misérable, ou du moins elle ne donne de nouvelles forces qu'à celui qui en a déjà trop, tandis que le foible, perdu, étouffé, écrasé dans la multitude, ne trouve nul azile où se refugier, nul support à sa foiblesse, et périt enfin victime de cette union trompeuse dont il attendoit son bonheur."

§ ". . . les mêmes causes qui nous rendent méchans nous rendent encore esclaves, et nous asservissent en nous dépravant . . ."

its direct relation to our natural endowments. For, "*méchans*" and "*esclaves*" are terms of society. Weakness becomes—as so vividly imaged in the *Discours sur . . . l'inégalité*—a form of social relationship and "the sentiment of our weakness comes less from our nature than from our cupidity."* The structure of this sentence obviously repeats what everyone knows: cupidity is an imbalance within social relationships.

As these relationships grow, "our *besoins* bring us together to the extent that our passions divide us, and the more we become enemies of our own kind the less we can do without them."† The full and fundamental perversity of society radiates here from the page. And this last phrase, of course, duplicates the definition of dependence given in the "main passage," where Rousseau writes that "each of us, no longer able to get along without others [*ne pouvant plus se passer des autres*], becomes again in this respect weak and miserable" (OC IV.310).

Observing the way in which the effects of the "formula for happiness" are transformed by social evolution, we can see how these peculiar sorts of dependence are explicitly recognized by Rousseau as "the initial bonds of general society."⁵⁶ Prior to that, *dépendance* itself is practically ruled out: "In the state of nature there is a *de facto* equality that is real and indestructible because in that condition it is impossible that the mere difference between man and man would be sufficiently large to render one dependent on the other" (OC IV.524).§ *Dépendance* and *société* come into existence together; because the former is constitutive of the latter, it is of fundamental importance for moral life on one side and political life on the other.

Viewed one way, the account of social evolution presented in the draft of *Du Contract social* shows that *dépendance* issues from a hybrid state, where mankind has one foot in nature and one foot in society. This image of origins displays the most basic sociological fact, *le lien social*, as articulated by *dépendance*.

Viewed another way, the account of social evolution indicates something rather different. While society does evolve it does not have a beginning. This fact is represented with great dramatic effect in the *Discours sur . . . l'inégalité* when, as he considers whether society is necessary for the origin of language or language is necessary for the origin of society, Rousseau throws up his hands and abandons the search for origins (OC III.151).

The two views work together. As we have seen repeatedly, the *topos* of *l'état*

---

* ". . . .le sentiment de nôtre foiblesse vient moins de nôtre nature, que de nôtre cupidité."

† ". . . nos besoins nous rapprochent à mesure que nos passions nous divisent, et plus nous devenons ennemis de nos semblables moins nous pouvons nous passer d'eux."

§ "Il y a dans l'état de Nature une égalité de fait réelle et indestructible, parce qu'il est impossible dans cet état que la seule difference d'homme à homme soit assez grande, pour rendre l'un dépendant de l'autre."

naturel is heuristic for inquiry into politics. Society is always already this hybrid; the relation between *nature* and *société* is, so to speak, vertical rather than horizontal, synchronic rather than diachronic. What we have here, then, is less a genealogy than a justification for undertaking the diagnostic of mankind "abandoned to ourselves" in terms of *dépendance*.

The web formed by *dépendance* is at once intricate and tight and unstable and disconcerting: "From this new order of things [*nouvel ordre de choses*] are born a plethora of relationships without measure, rule, or reliability that men continually alter and change, a hundred working to destroy them for every one who works to make them stable" (OC III.282).*

The word *ordre* here indicates Rousseau's provocative mood. And while for another author an *ordre de choses* might be merely a "state of affairs," we know—because "*dependence . . . des choses . . . est de la nature*"—that this is a gesture to the thematic or symbolic dimension of *nature*.

But it also signals a new star in Rousseau's constellation, one that he has not clearly observed: this is a potential difference between dependence-from-nature and dependence-from-things in the form of a nonnatural-dependence-from-things. This intermediate category will take a clearer shape when we consider, some pages hence, the sources of education; it will come to the center of the argument toward the end of this book.

At this point, Rousseau is prompting the reader in a slightly different way. This "order of things" is "new" because it gives "birth" to the most characteristic feature of society, an unmeasured and unruly multitude of relationships, and is therefore, from the perspective of the increasingly social human being, a proliferation of disorder. In other words, this (strictly speaking) nascent society is not an order at all.[57] But it is something susceptible to order.

The intermediate and contradictory category posited here, between the *état de nature* and the *état civil*, is given another appellation. Rousseau writes of the "relative existence of a man in the natural condition." This condition "depends on a thousand other relations which are in continual flux" and thus "he can never rest assured of being the same during two instants of his life; peace and happiness are only a flash for him; nothing is permanent but the misery [*misère*] that results from these vicissitudes" (OC III.282).† Unhappiness is, famously, the essential feature in Rousseau's account of society. Readers well-schooled in the

---

* "De ce nouvel ordre de choses naissent des multitudes de rapports sans mesure, sans régle, sans consistence, que les hommes altérent et changent continuellement, cent travaillant à les détruire pour un qui travaille à les fixer . . ."

† ". . . il ne peut jamais s'assurer d'être le même durant deux instants de sa vie; la paix et le bonheur ne sont pour lui qu'un éclair; rien n'est permanent que la misére qui resulte de toutes ces vicissitudes . . ."

Discours sur . . . l'inégalité should therefore be surprised to find him insisting here that *"la misère"* is a feature of *"l'état de nature."*[58] The blatant peculiarity of this combination highlights the importance of the formulation Rousseau apparently had in mind when he first sat down to write *Du Contract social*. Unhappiness already characterizes the protean social mix of evolving entanglements with dependence, disorder, and insecurity.[59]

A moment ago I insisted on the hybrid or synchronic conjunction of *nature* and *société*. Rousseau's sarcastic play with the word *ordre* serves to reopen the space between them. It permits the processes of social evolution inherent in that space to, so to speak, reveal themselves to theoretical inquiry.[60] The result brings us back around to the fundamental political problem.

Rousseau wants to state an aspiration toward a resolution and remedy for this problem. To make this statement he reasserts the language of order. This time he is serious. Speaking again as if the hybrid of *homme* and *citoyen* were, now as always, in the act of transition from *homme* to *citoyen*,[61] Rousseau confides that even "when his sentiments and his ideas could be elevated to the love of order and to sublime notions of virtue, it would remain impossible for him to make a sure application of his principles in a situation [*état de choses*] that would allow him to discern neither the good nor the bad, neither the honest man nor the evil one" (OC III.282).*

I think that Rousseau is tracking here a subtle conceptual shift that he himself cannot quite manage. He realizes, perhaps just in the course of drafting this passage, that the "new order of things [*nouvel ordre de choses*]" is in fact less than it seems. It is merely an *"état de choses."*[62] This inflection gestures in two familiar ways. The most basic form of society—"the general society of the human race [*la société générale du genre humain*]"—does not rise to the level of an "order." Moreover, because social evolution does not have an eschatology, it may tend to slip back into the natural world of "things."

I want to put this more precisely and underscore its remarkable implication: the process of social evolution may at some moments be decisively inflected by *nature* and derive its character therefrom.

Nevertheless, with the spontaneous formation of the primitive *lien social*, "the sweet voice of nature is no longer our infallible guide, nor is the independence we have received from her a desirable condition" (OC III.283).†

---

* ". . . quand ses sentimens et ses idées pourroient s'élever jusqu'à l'amour de l'ordre et aux notions sublimes de la vertu, il lui seroit impossible de faire jamais une application sure de ses principes dans un état de choses qui ne lui laisseroit discerner ni le bien ni le mal, ni l'honnête homme ni le méchant."

† ". . . la douce voix de la nature n'est plus pour nous un guide infaillible, ni l'indépendance que nous avons receu [*sic*] d'elle un état desirable . . ."

Rousseau's literary strategy is both leading and misleading, a fact I have persistently tried to illustrate with reference to the strange figure of the *état de nature*; I will engage this full on in §42–§45 below. What Rousseau aims to capture, however, even with that figure, is the essentially hybrid character of mankind between *nature* and *société*, or as the centuries after him have put it, between nature and culture. To achieve this, Rousseau needs a theory that unabashedly presents precisely this ambiguity, attributing to it a structure but without reducing one side to the other. That is why the shifting back and forth between vertical/synchronic and horizontal/diachronic views of relations between *nature* and *société* is an essential aspect of his exposition.

With the shift between the synchronic and the diachronic, there is a turning back the hands of the clock. But it has nothing to do with "the happy life of the golden age" which "was always a condition foreign to the human race."[63] True happiness for mankind "abandoned to ourselves" comes only with the "love of order"—which itself grows with society—and can only be realized through something inescapably social: the law.[64]

§38

THE CHARACTER OF LAW AS A PROBLEM

Now, one may easily associate the idea of law with the idea of order. But the precise relation between them is not self-evident. It requires some careful unpacking, especially if we are to understand this relation in terms of *dépendance*. Rousseau provides an important clue when he proceeds this way in the "main passage": "If the laws of nations could have, like those of nature, an inflexibility that no human force could ever be able to overcome, dependence-from-persons would thus become again dependence-from-things."* Let us underscore this extraordinary point. Rousseau is saying that if human law was as overwhelmingly and unshakably consistent as natural law, dependence-from-persons would *become once again* an instance of dependence-from-things. We know well from the "main passage" itself that the implications of this possibility run deep.

---

* "Si les lois des nations pouvoient avoir, comme celles de la nature, une inflexibilité que jamais aucune force humaine ne pût vaincre, la dépendance des hommes redeviendroit alors celle des choses."

A transformation of this sort is what *Du Contract social* was meant to inform. Now recall that Rousseau begins that book by claiming two grounds for political inquiry. He will take "men as they are and laws as they might be" (OC III.351). The first has been well established by 1762; no reader of the Dijon-prize essay, the *Discours sur . . . l'inégalité, Julie,* and eventually *Émile* could have missed seeing what Rousseau thought "men . . . are." As for what the "laws . . . might be," Rousseau lays this out in the "main passage."

It is worth focusing on this possibility. To arrive at the equivalence of the pairs political law/natural law and men/things proposed by Rousseau and for this equivalence to produce the desired effect, laws would have to achieve a certain kind of perfection. That is, they would have to be perfectly unitary, perfectly transparent, forming an order perfectly free of contradictions. We shall soon see that the model for this perfection is the Will of God. Whether or not human law could attain this perfection, or is even constitutively compatible with such a model, the theoretical import of Rousseau's sentence is clear enough, as is the way it fits into his program for the social theory of politics.

Nonetheless, the peculiarity of this program stands out. How can Rousseau, of all people, propose such an equivalence? How can relations with persons become relations with things? How can this make any sense? And even if its sense can be made clear, why would it solve the problem of social evil?

§39

LEARNING FROM EXPERIENCE
COMPLICATES *DÉPENDANCE*

When Rousseau wrote in the "main passage" that "dependence-from-things . . . is of nature [*dépendances-des-choses . . . est de la nature*]," he glossed over a subtle and important additional distinction that he admits elsewhere. I will now bring this to the foreground and then show why it bears on our central problem.

We return to the beginning, the first pages of *Émile*, where the entire project to be developed in the book is being set forth: "we are born weak, we have need of forces," and everything that one lacks at birth and which one needs as an adult "is given to us by education." And where does one acquire this essential education? It comes "from nature, or from persons, or from things [*de la nature, ou des hommes, ou des choses*]." Three "sorts of masters," he says, provide three different educations: "The internal development of our faculties and our organs is the education of nature; the use we are taught to make of this development is the education of persons; and the mastery, deriving from our own experience, over the objects that affect us is the education of things" (OC IV.247).* The major point that I want to draw from this passage is that *la nature*/nature and *les choses*/things—at least when they are considered as sources of education—are clearly distinguishable here, whereas at many other key points they are synonymous and stand together in contrast to *les hommes*/persons. Moreover, we know that this is not simply a loose use of language. After having applied his more familiar perspective in the first version of *Émile*—writing that there are "two educations, that of nature and that of society [*deux éducations, celle de la nature et celle de la société*]" (OC IV.58)—Rousseau opted instead to publish the book with the tripartite distinction of nature/persons/things.

This raises a question: Why isn't this tripartite distinction at odds with the assimilation of "things" to "nature" in the "main passage"? This is worth considering in more detail.

Rousseau distinguishes three entities by which one is educated. He indicates how the student is related to each of the three entities. He uses the concept of *dépendance* to explain these relations. However, by contrast to the "main passage," his approach at this point allows us to see *dépendance* from exactly the opposite side.[65]

> Now, of these three different educations, the one from nature does not depend
> at all on us; the one from things only depends on us in certain respects. We are
> really the masters of only the one from persons. (OC IV.247)†

The reader is urged by this passage to shift ground. The word *éducation* is already being used with such literalness that it becomes metaphorical[66]—that is how human organs can be said to do what teachers do. When Rousseau speaks of how an *éducation* does or does not depend on us, the use is metonymic: the education we get from Nature does not depend on us because Nature does not depend on us, and it is the latter that the reader is meant to take to heart. Statements

---

* "Le developement interne de nos facultés et de nos organes est l'éducation de la nature; l'usage qu'on nous apprend à faire de ce developement est l'éducation des hommes; et l'acquis de nôtre propre experience sur les objets qui nous affectent est l'éducation des choses."

† "Or de ces trois éducations différentes, celle de la nature ne dépend point de nous; celle des choses n'en dépend qu'à certains égards. Celle des hommes est la seule dont nous soyons vraiment les maîtres. . . ."

about the "three educations" are at once made in two discursive systems—they are about pathways of learning, and they are about types of entities by which one is educated. The word *éducation* becomes a syllepsis within this framework.[67]

What I mean when I say that Rousseau comes at the problem of *dépendance* from the opposite side is as follows. In the "main passage," he writes of the dependence of a human being from either things or from other human beings. In these additional passages, he is concerned to show how nature, things, or people depend "from" a human subject. The purpose of this reversal is, of course, to show that each of these objects "educates" us in "its own" manner. But to arrive at his point the two-directional character of our relations to the world must be presupposed. In other words, we need to make explicit the sense in which *dépendance* is a relation.

The two directions of *dépendance* are, of course, themselves related to each other. *La nature* does not depend from me at all.[68] When I depend from nature, it remains unchanged, unaffected. No matter how active or vital the relationship, nature will not, for example, reflect my ambivalence, reticence, or uncertainty. Nature—its order perfect—will not "learn" such disorders from me and, therefore, neither will it educate me to them. Perhaps its intransigence will invoke such feelings in me? Then I am a bad student. If, instead, I accept stoically its lessons, nature will have a calming influence.

When it comes to *les choses*, the relationship is different. *Les choses* listen to me; I can to some extent determine their shape by making them. A relationship to things, by comparison with the relationship to nature, offers me increased mastery. But the relationship is still two-sided and this partial mastery is my undoing. Whatever I put into things I shall have to live with when I depend from them; something about me, now become a quality of things, may come back to haunt me. The closer things are to nature, and thus the more resistant to my present touch, the less anxiety they will produce in me. The closer things are to human activity, made objects given form by a maker's Will, the more they will shine with "the madness and contradiction in human institutions."[69] In the meddling with nature from which things are made, I may make a mess of the things, and then have to live with *my* mess in *them*—even while they "teach" me with spiraling ambiguity.

Finally, only in the education gained from other persons could one take the formation of the "self" fully in hand. The inherent qualities of the entity from which I learn, which is to say *a person*, open fully a possibility not present with nature, and only partially present with things. I may become the "master" of my own education. But how? Does the student become the master? Or master the master? To what avail? What use is an education in which what I learn from others depends entirely from me? If the student's Will becomes manifest in the master, the presence of two Wills in the person from which I depend makes this sort of dependence utterly contradictory and futile. What is presented as best is instead the worst of all. Indeed, as Rousseau exclaims elsewhere, whatever the pupil wants the tutor must resist—the way natural stones resist? the way man-made books resist?—otherwise pupil subjects master to his Will and puts him "in the most dangerous sort of dependence which a tutor can be in with his student" (OC IV.339).

Notice that here relationship between tutor and pupil—the one articulated and promoted by Rousseau in *Émile*—threatens to become exactly what Rousseau's social and political theory seeks to avoid, which is the relationship between master and slave. In this setting, to ask "who can hope to control completely the words and actions of everyone?"[70] is part *interrogatio* and part interrogation, partly a decisive assertion and partly a question that can be answered.[71] The risk in the dependence of one person from another is precisely *that* hope and the acts which follow from it; the result is, in the words of the "main passage," that "master and slave deprave themselves mutually."

Thus, while *dépendance* is shown to be two-directional, it is not a two-way street, it does not have two parallel lanes. It is complex and misleading terrain, a moral topography within which the multiplication of Wills may lead to destructive disorder.

Reading these two passages from Rousseau together, we arrive at this remarkable result: what looks like a hierarchy of three types of education—rising from nature to things to persons as the degree of the student's control increases—brings more clearly to light at the same time its opposite—a hierarchy of dependence, rising from the incertitude of human relations through a relatively durable human world up to the comforting inflexibility of nature. The best in one case is the worst in the other. Is this not the nub, and the rub, of dependence?

§40

TENSION IN THE CLASSIFICATIONS OF *DÉPENDANCE* INTERSECTS WITH THE CONCEPTION OF LAW

Rousseau offers two ways of resolving relations that involve *dépendance*. The first classification occurs in the "main passage," where two possibilities are presented. Either

1) I depend from things, or
2) I depend from persons.

The second classification is given in the passage on types of education discussed in the preceding section. In this version three alternatives are present:

1) nature does not depend from me at all, or
2) things depend only somewhat from me, or
3) persons depend from me altogether.

Although the prospect of a contradiction between these two classifications was raised earlier, this is no reason to ignore them. It is precisely the difference between these two perspectives that is informative. This difference provides one key to understanding the structure and implications of Rousseau's thinking concerning *dépendance* as the moral substance of *société*. And this offers an approach to the broader question: how does the conception of *dépendance* bear on the solution to the problem of social evil?

Any attempt to answer this question brings many other factors into play. The one I want to emphasize here is law.

Generally, as Rousseau seeks the resolution and remedy for social evil he recommends civil laws. More precisely, he recommends what is now commonly referred to as "the rule of law." In the present instance he is not concerned with the content of the law. Rather he points our attention to the quality he calls "flexibility." Law can be more or less "flexible." What Rousseau proposes is that civil law should be completely inflexible. There is a paradigm for this perfect

178

inflexibility. It is the laws of nature. In sum, we are asked to imagine that "the laws of nations could have, like those of nature, an inflexibility that no human force could ever be able to overcome . . ."* This is a powerful analogy. Is it as self-evident as Rousseau would have us believe? I do not think so. For as soon as one asks how it could be more than a literary gesture, how it could be accomplished in fact, it shows itself to be disturbingly vague.

The modeling of one domain on the other presupposes answers to some very difficult questions. What exactly are laws of nature? What precisely is the property of "inflexibility" and can it be the same from one domain to another? For readers who want simple answers to such questions, Rousseau himself provides no solace. Many other things that Rousseau tells us introduce further complications. Suppose, for example, we admit the existence of "laws of nature." Or we admit that "laws of nature" derive from the "state of nature." What knowledge of the latter would be sufficient to correctly identify the former? And is the "state of nature" the best, the only, or the unalloyed source of knowledge about "laws of nature?" For, remember that Rousseau insists that the "laws of nature" continue their applicability under all conditions, i.e., outside as well as inside the "state of nature." If so, even thorough knowledge of the "state of nature" might be insufficient to warrant a conception of the "laws of nature."[72]

In other words, Rousseau's analogy is obscure. Although it has theoretical force and is methodologically suggestive, it also brings into play many complications that make it difficult to see exactly what is fruitful and what is misguided in the construction of the central problematic for Rousseau's social theory of politics.

It is in this context that the difference between the two classifications of *dépendance* brings something important to light.

Keep in mind first that the proposal concerning law does not stand by itself. It is part of a larger conditional assertion. Rousseau writes that *if* it were possible to make the metaphorical transfer of "inflexibility" from natural to civil law, *then* "dependence-from-persons would thus become again dependence-from-things [*la dépendance des hommes redeviendroit alors celle des choses*]."

This conclusion seems to contain a tacit proposal to return to the "state of nature." This will hardly come as a surprise. Both admirers and detractors—think of d'Holbach's advice that readers should "not for a minute listen to a cowering philosophy that invites us to flee society"[73]—have often taken Rousseau to be an advocate of just that.

---

* "Si les lois des nations pouvoient avoir, comme celles de la nature, une inflexibilité que jamais aucune force humaine ne pût vaincre, ..."

In fact Rousseau advocates nothing of the kind. To the contrary, he states pointedly his conviction that "the happy life of the golden age was always a condition foreign to the human race" (OC III.283). There are many reasons to take this statement as definitive. Thus Rousseau is not proposing the utterly perverse idea that the imposition of civil law would somehow return people to the "state of nature."

Yet Rousseau has no qualms in telling us things like this: "dependence-from-things . . . is of nature [*dépendances des choses . . . est de la nature*]." Thus the question remains: What does he have in mind?

This is where the gesture we have been discussing from the "main passage" gains in salience. It represents an intersection of the appeal to law with the resolution of the evils of society in terms of *dépendance*. The two classifications of *dépendance* suggest different ways of seeing the significance of law.

On the one hand, the simple distinction between persons and things presents just two alternatives. Start with dependence-from-persons, change from flexible to inflexible the quality of the law that gives order to that relationship, and arrive at dependence-from-things. This either/or proposition allows only one step. Nevertheless, *nature* lurks just behind the encompassing term "things." Thus the step to dependence-from-things may or may not also be a step to dependence-from-nature. This is why Rousseau's pivotal theoretical claim seems compatible with some kind of "return to nature," and why both an Enlightenment eye and a Romantic one will see in what he proposes a return to the primitive way of life that Rousseau himself said is impossible.

On the other hand, Rousseau sets persons apart and then draws a clear line between things and nature. This brings into view another perspective on the structure and implications of the rule of law for the self-mastery of society through politics. That is, the tripartite classification of *dépendance* adds another step in the image of macro-structural transformation, where, as Rousseau is careful to say, dependence-from-persons *becomes again* dependence-from-things. In this intermediate space inflexibility need not imitate the law of gravity. It can be modeled on human capabilities and designs rather than on their antithesis, nature. Of course, this, too, hinges on what is meant by *nature*; we shall soon see to what effect.

For now, the point is just this. The significance of law as a solution to the problem of evil is partly clarified and partly obscured by the two different classifications of *dépendence*. Here it is important to bring again to the foreground (as in §§4, 5, 20, 36 above) the active, practical, and energizing foundation of law in "*moeurs*, customs, and opinion." To understand what Rousseau is actually proposing we need to keep in mind that both the constitution of law and its field of application is *société*. For this reason the two classifications of *dépendance* point not only toward two different ways of seeing the substance and problem of dependence itself but also toward two different ways of seeing the moral substance of society. In one view, the assimilation of nature and human things leaves only a sort of pure intersubjectivity to the realm of the nonnatural, which is to say *société*. In the other view, the nonnatural may include things and the vision of *société* encompass human beings and our world together. This second view, by a kind of transitivity from persons to things and from things to nature, is also susceptible to an evolutionary, even ecological, interpretation. In each case we are led to a very different approach to a social theory of politics.

Rousseau exposes two alternatives when it comes to regulating dependence-from-persons. We may try to transform human relationships into the type of relationship we have with nature, or we may try to transform human relationships into the type of relationship we have with things. Perhaps Rousseau is saying that we aspire to the former and we end up with the latter. Or perhaps he is simply not clear on this point. In any case, this exposition uncovers a tectonic fault in Rousseau's theory of politics that remains to be explained.

Let us assume—with or without Rousseau—that it is correct to distinguish between dependence-from-nature and dependence-from-things. That distinction sharpens the complementary question: What exactly is the relationship between these two forms of dependence? As both the distinction and the relationship are clarified below a new perspective on how Rousseau establishes the whole social field will come into view.

§41

THE ISSUE OF "THINGS" AND "NATURE"

Rousseau classifies *dépendance* in a way that distinguishes "things" and "nature" from "persons." In the preceding section we saw that this way of organizing the problem of *société* intersects with the conception of law. This is one way that it bears on the resolution and remedy of that problem.

The issue of "things" and "nature" is complicated in another way already from the very first page of *Émile*. A kind of semantic latitude brings this before the reader. Rousseau writes both of "the author of things [*l'auteur des choses*]" and of "the author of nature [*l'auteur de la nature*]." What he has in mind is clear enough.[74] These are meant as synonyms for one thing, for a single "author." God is the one maker of the one universe.

This unity prompts us further. We—especially the reading "we" of the eighteenth century, captivated as "we" are by increasingly tense claims between natural philosophy and theology—incline to take *"les choses"* and *"la nature"* as identical.[75] The qualities or predicates of each of these terms attach easily to the other.

This slippage—not the equation, but the slippage—is supported in Rousseau's time by several pervasive and opposed ways of understanding the relation between *nature* and *grace*.

One perspective maintains the theistic identification of *nature* with all of Creation while holding it distinct from God the Creator and Provider. This is exemplified by Abbé Morin, who in 1735 writes that

> For us, we do honor to ourselves by very soberly restricting use of the word nature [. . .] The law, the order, the mechanism that the Will of the Almighty laid down and established in everything that it created and that it preserves is what one must properly understand by the word nature.[76]*

Another perspective also involves a radical break between *nature* and God. This disjunction does not favor Providence, however. Instead it supports an antitheistic or atheistic conception of *nature*. This perspective is what the author of the entry "Naturaliste" in the *Encyclopédie* tries to capture when he writes:

> One also gives the name naturalists to those who do not in any way acknowledge God, but who believe that there is only one material substance, . . . [and that] everything is necessarily self-executing in nature as it appears to us; 'naturalist' in this sense is synonymous with atheist, spinozist, materialist, etc.[77]†

Lurking behind these lines is yet another perspective. While clearly in tension with established theistic beliefs, and perhaps also with most forms of monotheism, naturalism can be compatible with deism. This possibility is hidden here

---

* "Pour nous, nous nous ferons gloire de n'user que très sobrement du mot Nature [. . .] Les lois, l'ordre, le Mécanisme que la volonté de Tout-Puissant a posé et établi en tout ce qu'elle a créé et qu'elle conserve, est proprement ce que l'on doit entendre par le mot Nature."

† "On donne encore le nom de naturalistes à ceux qui n'admettent point de Dieu, mais qui croyent qu'il n'y a qu'une substance matérielle, . . . [et que] tout s'exécute nécessairement dans la nature comme nous le voyons; naturaliste en ce sens est synonyme à athée, spinosiste, matérialiste, &c."

as the name Spinoza is squeezed between twin epithets and thus becomes one itself. Indeed, the equation of an atheistic "naturalism" with Spinoza was a commonplace of the Enlightenment.[78]

However, it is fair to say that Spinoza was despised by many theists not because he challenged God—no committed theist would suppose God in need of defense against the unilluminated—but because he radically altered the terms of debate about God and about the relationship between nature and grace. By the time Rousseau appeared on the supercharged literary scene of the mid-eighteenth century the word "Spinoza" was an emblem for atheism. But so, too, had Spinoza's equation of God and nature become a commonplace for all sorts of debates about theology and its relation to natural philosophy or metaphysics. No matter what Spinoza intended by *"deus sive natura,"*[79] the beautifully off-hand phrase inserted several times into his *Ethica* (1677), those words posed for readers, interlocutors, and a wider republic of letters two very simple questions: are God and nature one or two? And if one, is God nature or nature God?

It is stunning and *bouleversant* interrogatives like these, rather than an atheistic naturalism, that are in the background when Rousseau, a believer, struggles with and slides between the category of "things" and the category of "nature."

By framing these questions this way I intend to expand the discussion both into and beyond Rousseau. I mean to suggest that the issues joining and separating "things" and "nature" are inflected by how one sees the relation between God and nature. How one goes forward from the most general propositions defended in this book may ultimately depend on the views one holds on this topic.

However, my point for now is that the interaction between these two domains or symbolic registers is an essential feature of the historical and theoretical background for the argument of the present book: questions of God and nature structure Rousseau's thinking and writing, they set terms for the reception and influence of his social theory of politics, and they ultimately shape the domain of possible understanding for most major traditions of political sociology.[80]

Having restated the broad field that will occupy much of the remainder of this book, I now want to draw your attention back to another detail in *Émile*. By the closing pages of that work, a fabric of claims around the notion of *dépendance* has been gathered into a tight and incessantly recursive weave. The protagonist is at the end of his *parcours*, at the end of the journey Rousseau has imagined and figured before the eyes of his readers. Now Rousseau himself adopts the voice of Émile to provide precisely the assessment that, just a few lines before, Rousseau has demanded. The ventriloquist wants his fully educated and *expérimenté* subject to see this—that he must "not willingly add any other chain to the one with which nature and the laws have burdened [him]" (OC IV.855). In these figures—*nature* and *loi*, which is to say the terms proposed in the "main passage" to triangulate the political solution to the problem of *société*—the Stoic theme resurfaces one last time as Rousseau-in-the-guise-of-Émile praises Jean-Jacques, declaring "it's you, oh my master, who made me free by teaching me to give way to necessity" (OC IV.856). Firm but flustered, the Émile-voice adds: "I would only know how to withdraw from dependence-from-persons by coming again under that from nature" (OC IV.856).* Rousseau's intervention in his own narrative and theory at this point is crisp and telling. Émile has learned his lesson; thus is affirmed the lesson Rousseau most wants us, the readers, to learn. Here Rousseau's monument to Plato and exposé of the evolving political culture of the (imagined, dreamed) republic hits precisely the target set hundreds of pages earlier in the "main passage" (OC IV.310–11).

There are two ways to read Émile's declaration. First take it to be informed by the distinction between dependence-from-persons and dependence-from-things set out in the "main passage." In this light this statement seems obviously to confirm the identity of *la nature* and *les choses*.

Now look again. This identity, and all it implies, is thrown into doubt if instead we gloss Émile's declaration with the three-way distinction that appears in the educational scheme of *Émile* (cf. §§39 and 40 above). There, you will recall, he differentiates types of *dépendances* by reference to persons, things, and nature.

Again we are struck by the image of a compulsion, and "inflexibility," that may not simply derive from the objective world but which is effected when we "come again under dependence from nature."

Again we are forced to ask what could this mean? For recall that Rousseau clearly excludes return to a pre-social condition; this is, he writes in the revelatory *Rousseau juge de Jean-Jacques*, "one of the principles on which [Rousseau] most insisted" (OC IV.935). From there the complications only multiply. Indeed, it is difficult to even imagine *dépendance* in a "state of nature" where "the natural person is all for himself—he is the numerical unity, the absolute whole."[81]

In the preceding section and this one, two topics were shown to modulate Rousseau's conception of *dépendance* and instantiate its significance. Here, closing *Émile*, *la nature* and *les lois* are explicitly joined again in a clear echo of the "main passage," reiterating the suggestion that human law should mimic natural law.

But this prospect remains obscure. In what respect? The distinction itself be-

* "Je ne saurais de me tirer de la dépendance des hommes qu'en rentrant sous celle de la nature."

tween human law and natural law resists identification. It is simply tautological to insist that because each is called "law" some shared quality, a kind of necessity, compulsion, or "inflexibility" joins them together.

In the final part of this book (e.g., §§68 ff.) we shall uncover what Rousseau declines to explain here. It is the answer to this question: why is "inflexibility" so important and what provides the paradigm for it? Finally, Rousseau's focus on this aspect of law, or this aspiration for law, and the consequences supposed to follow from it for moral and political life, derives from the role he attributes to certainty in human relationships. We will see that Rousseau further believes that the relevant sort of certainty is itself only made possible by those types of "order" that derive from a single Will; he believes further that this certainty is undermined by anxieties that arise in correspondence with practical effects deriving from the multiplication of Wills in society itself.

To say this here is to go well beyond the present stage of the argument. The immediate point is that both the beginning and the end of *Émile* are misleading. The difference between *les choses* and *la nature* cannot pass without further specification. Two lines of approach are possible. One is to ask What is a *thing?* This is the question we shall come to later (i.e., §68). Here, with a more refined eye, we reenter the other topic: What is *nature?*

§42

───────────•─────────────

NATURE

Seeing every particular thing in the world, an eye that discerns just one thing may be said to be seeing *nature*. A daunting prospect. One feels easily the frustration that could drive a Voltaire to write, "Nature, you are only a word [*Nature, tu n'es que un mot*]."[82] The alternative seems, literally, unimaginable. Yet, *nature* performs; it contains and encompasses. Thus, it constrains, and, in the event, it generates.

If this is a pagan view it is not against theology. Nature is the common dwelling of many gods. The monotheistic eye still sees one thing but may call it by another name: Creation. The *nature* explored by modern secular science remains a theological *topos*.[83] *Nature* is either inside *grâce*—as God "is not playing at dice"[84]—

or it is the outer limit of God's present action, for which God is either origin or an ever-present *a priori*. A singular image of the θεος amplifies the coherence and unity of *nature* as part, continuation, or antithesis of Creation.

Whether *nature* is just one encompassing word or the single substance, or both, it promoted in the early Modern period a powerful and decisive prejudice:[85] the constant impulse of *nature* was, as Jean Ehrard has written, to "unite unreconcilables."[86] During the century before Rousseau, thinkers often remarked and were driven by a presumed correspondence between "the unity of the universe" and "the unity of science."[87] More than staid science, however, the expansive appeal to *nature* in the first half of the eighteenth century has aptly been called "euphoric."[88] "The majority of cultivated minds inclined to accord to nature an unconditional confidence." It was everywhere, "invading everything, morality, medicine, religion, science, art and politics." The *topos* of *nature* served to bring the world's panoply of things into a single discursive field. *Nature* thrived in constant and supple encounter with a long list of other key terms: *loi, raison, sentiment, vertu, bonheur, innocence, société, nécessité, providence, ordre, liberté.*[89]

Nature bears, in this period, and notwithstanding the ancient pedigree of this very trait, an unparalleled presumption of unity . . . comparable, perhaps, to the word *human* in our time. And like the great plurality we have discovered in ourselves since the nineteenth century, for Rousseau and his contemporaries the spectacular "fortune of the idea of *nature* derived from its aptitude to unite contraries." "Whether it concerns the definition of the world, of mankind, or the fallen place of the latter in the former, the idea of nature responds to all. It is the place where the contradictions of the age, its aspirations and fears, its strengths and weaknesses, intersect."

This assessment is drawn from the concluding chapter of Jean Ehrard's magisterial reconstruction of "the idea of nature in France in the first half of the eighteenth century."[90] Anyone hoping to understand the context in which Rousseau wrote does well to rely heavily on Ehrard's scholarship. Nonetheless, I will not undertake here to weave Rousseau's thought back into the complex contextual fabric represented by Ehrard.[91] Nor shall I rehearse in any detail Ehrard's many arguments and plentiful examples. I propose simply to lay before the reader certain considerations generally known but made particularly clear by this extraordinary historian. Some of these are introduced here, others in §54 and generally below.

First of all, "nature" in the eighteenth century identifies the "*système du monde.*" It does so from several perspectives. At its margins, *nature* is distinguished from the "marvelous" and the supernatural.[92] As itself some single and motile thing, *nature* had appeared to many thinkers of the seventeenth century like a universal mechanism. It increasingly seemed to them that this mechanism could be described in mathematical terms and imagined in the figure of the clock.[93]

This image pointedly implied questions—Who made this clock? Who set it in motion?—that, in turn, led to further inquiry into what forces might be inherent in *nature* and how it could be possible for *nature* to transform, even transform itself, over time.[94] Newton's arguments about gravity came to the center of the former; early notions of evolution, as suggested for example by Buffon and Diderot, but somehow implicit already in Spinoza, were key to the latter.[95]

It is important to remember that all such questioning about the *"système du monde"* touched on theology and provoked both the hardening of its dogmas and their revision. Any claim about *nature* was at the same time a claim about *grâce*. This was in part because both types of discourse shared certain primary objects—the world, the human being, and the relation between them—and in part because during this period partisans from both sides came to hold many of the same beliefs about these objects. Thus, tensions between *nature* and *grâce* persistently produced attempts at reconciliation.[96] Theologians found it increasingly impossible to ignore the self-regulating mechanisms discovered by the "natural philosophers"; preceptors of the "new science" like Descartes and Newton wholeheartedly embraced theistic interpretations of what they discovered. As transitional thinkers like Malebranche devoted themselves to showing, this *nature* seemed compatible with a sovereign God.

On the one hand, the notion of "natural law" facilitated this kind of balancing act. "Situated at the hinge between the plane of science and that of theology . . . natural law . . . allowed for a reconciliation between the traditional cult of a God whose omnipresence fills the universe and the modern idea of a mechanical universe whose wheels turn by themselves."[97] At the same time, a pivotal thinker of wide influence like Pierre Bayle could insist that since "a *law* is the imperative order of a superior to his subordinates" it was far from clear that "the word still made sense when applied to matter"—"to speak of *physical laws* is only conceivable in a system of continuous creation."[98] This might be taken in several different ways. Rousseau's contemporary Maupertuis argued that *nature* in itself has none of the active power that is reserved entirely to God and thus the world has "a continual need for the power of the Creator."[99] One might also conclude, with Newton's follower Clark, that even regular and frequent natural forces manifest God's "Will."[100] Or with Leibniz reply that the idea that "God needs to rewind his watch from time to time" was sacrilegious, and insist directly on the distinction denied by the Newtonians: "When God makes miracles, it is not to meet the needs of nature, but of grace."[101]

Despite common discursive fields and *topoi*, the various attempts at reconciliation between *nature* and *grâce* became more and more difficult to maintain.
A formula like Spinoza's *"deus sive natura"*—which "remained at the center of
all the polemics of this period"[102]—might save the naturalist from atheism by
proposing *nature* as the substance of God. But how could one say that the "fi-
nite world"[103] of *nature* was a sufficient identity for God? That equation seemed
inherently to diminish Him. This urged some toward a "natural religion" and
eventually toward a "religion of nature" incompatible with Christian doctrine.
Others, as predicted by those who bandied about Spinoza's name, moved toward
atheism.[104]

The pious and scientific Newton himself was at the center of this paradox. If
the "mechanization of the world picture"[105] appeared at first to founder on the
science he developed, it would soon achieve a more complete form.[106] Thanks to
Newton's account of the force inherent in *nature* itself, it seemed that "nature
might supplant God altogether."[107] It was one thing to ask who had made the
"clock" of nature, or who had wound it. It was quite something else to consider
who rewinds it each time it runs down. If *nature* has its own force, it has no need
of "rewinding." If it has no need of "rewinding," it has no need of God. Gravity
obviates the need for divine Will and the Grace it bestows. Again Ehrard neatly
summarizes this point:

> If we only know matter by its sensible properties, how can one establish a hier-
> archy amongst those properties other than the one suggested by experience?
> The prudent positivist would say we should limit ourselves to the study of phe-
> nomena. But other audacious spirits inverted this reasoning: everything hap-
> pens, they said, *as if* attraction, that universal phenomenon, was an essential
> quality of matter; everything happens as if *nature* puts itself in motion; what,
> therefore, is the use of any other hypothesis?[108]

Here is a breeding ground for skepticism. It is a dynamic mode of thought. The
mechanistic worldview produced, with remarkable continuity, an apparently
antithetical image. Whatever animates itself is not so much a "clock" as a living
being. Thus, mid-century saw "the revenge of nature-as-animal on nature-as-
clock."[109] No one should have been surprised as more and more theistic qualities
were attributed to that "animal," or as "the intuition of the inexhaustible character of nature tended to eclipse again the very idea of natural law."[110]

With such equivocal *topoi* one could advance both a particular claim and
a general framework, and thereby navigate in many different ways the highly
charged intellectual scene. To express theological apprehension about "the necessary connection that disciples of Descartes seemed to institute between God

and Nature, to the detriment of divine liberty and the very idea of creation," could also serve to mark "the independence of the scientific spirit with respect to all religious metaphysics."[111] Once a certain circularity was established, who could say if the necessity and eternity of mathematical truths made them natural, or if they gained those attributes because they derived from *nature*? And if "around 1740 Newtonianism had won the contest" against Cartesian mechanism, and the "cultivated public had become *'attractionnaire,'*" the idea had broken free from its author.[112] Radicals like Rousseau's friend Diderot contended beyond "the sublime Newton" himself, in *Pensées sur l'interpretation de la nature* (1754), that all motion, including gravitation, is inherent in matter.[113] In this way, *nature* could become for the "naturalist" something more than an *ordre*; it appears as a *puissance*, and thus, no longer subject to the command of God, "has in itself its *raison d'être.*"[114]

Note now that these terms will feature in Rousseau's conceptual constellation—we shall come back to all this below—in ways refracted through his peculiar concerns. He will make a theoretical gesture that is formally similar but with significantly different results. The difference derives in good measure from the premise we have already brought to light. Rousseau is not a monist with respect to theology or natural philosophy. It is specifically in consideration of *société* that Rousseau adopts a theoretical premise analogous to the principle of a "single substance."

Whether or not *nature* "is just a word," the active pursuit of a perfect fit between *signifiant* and *signifié* drove debates in the century from 1650 to 1750 through several "paradigms," from a mechanism to a vitalism, from a mathematical idealism to an observational empiricism. The latter allowed a sort of compromise. It became possible, in the time of Linnaeus (1735 on) and Buffon (1749 on), to bracket certain theological dilemmas and operate from the principle that *nature* "is nothing other than the ensemble of phenomena discovered by scientific observation."[115]

A distinction between observer and observed seems consistent with the familiar perspective that *nature* is everything mankind is not. Yet, again, syllepsis between natural philosophy and theology complicated the picture. If *nature* is, at one extreme, independent from God, or at the other extreme, identical with God, either way the antithesis with mankind may hold. If, by contrast, *nature* is intermediate, and just another name for God's Creation and Providence, then, as scripture dictates and common sense makes clear, mankind must be included within it. Then, perhaps, we should say, adopting the terms through which this debate would be played out in the next century, that all the *Geisteswissenschaften* are *Naturwissenschaften*.[116] This ambiguity, however, was more Humanist persistence in 1750 than Positivist premonition. It allowed, and perhaps required, observation and insight from natural philosophy, drawn from rocks and insects, plants and the stars, to be carried by analogy over into the study of human beings.

Even if theological questioning initiated this movement, it was sustained by new enthusiasm for observation in many fields. All sorts of notetakers and Methodics—travelers, merchants, doctors, lawyers, historians, linguists, and the like—set their sights on the human world, pretending to the authority of this or that "new science." For a wakening anthropological eye, natural Man could be found outside society. For medicine, outside culture. For law, outside justice. For *la morale*, away from the vice of the Court and salon. And so it went as Man was again included in *nature*. I write *again* here because this movement mimicked, often explicitly, ancient pagan conceptions, from Heraclitus to the Epicureans and the Stoics.[117] However, what counted most was the forward-looking view. Once there was a Galileo, a Descartes, a Newton, everyone wanted to be the Galileo, Descartes, or Newton of the study of mankind, as Vico, Hume, and others would imagine themselves to be.

How all this at first gives shape to and then upsets the seemingly simple matrices of Rousseau's social theory of politics is a topic for later portions of this book. Let me now only raise these leading ensigns again: when it comes to *dépendance*, Rousseau distinguishes *les choses* from *les hommes* (§32 above); "dependence . . . from things . . . is of nature; that from persons . . . is of society" (from the "main passage"); if this is because *les choses* are, as the issue of God's hands, synonymous with *la nature* (§41 above), then *les hommes* predicated of *dépendence* are not *de la nature*; but Rousseau is ambiguous on just this point, as he also suggests the tripartite division of *dépendance* among "nature," "things," and "persons" (§§39 and 40 above); then, it seems, *les hommes* may be both in and out of *nature*—with *la nature* against *les choses*, or with *les choses* against *la nature*; while in tension with the literary *topos* that cleaves *"état naturel"*/*"état civil,"* this ambivalence is perfectly consistent with Rousseau's theoretical claims in particular and in general (§37 above); but, returning to the central topic of the present inquiry, it also blurs the crucial boundary between *les choses* and *les hommes*; to understand the significance of this fuzziness, we will have to treat more seriously the pivotal intermediate category of a nonnatural-dependence-from-things introduced briefly above (§37). This, however, we shall postpone until §68 below. For now we will conclude this survey of *nature* as a background to Rousseau's own thinking.

As the investigation of *nature* reaches into the human domain, two types of animating force, deemed to be inherent in the substance of human beings themselves the way *"attraction"* or gravity is inherent in dead matter, will be of particular importance for Rousseau. The first is *la volonté* or Will. What counts here is the particular version I have referred to elsewhere as the New Model Will,[118] which is to say the peculiarly modern twist given to the *voluntas* of Cicero[119] and Augustine as it begins, in Rousseau's time, to mutate from a faculty for choosing between options given, including notably the possibilities of being damned or saved, into the inexhaustibly generative faculty that the nineteenth century attributed to Man across all fields of human endeavor.

It is well known that many *lumières* and their critical interlocutors identified faculties other than *la volonté*—for example reason and the passions—as natural impulsions inherent in the human being and thus as sometimes contradictory and sometimes complementary but always primary motors of human existence. Were it necessary to explain further our avoidance in this book of the interminable debates about *raison et sentiment* in Rousseau and to justify our appeal to the instance of *la volonté* here, it would almost suffice to gesture to the obsessive attention Rousseau gives to it in his social theory of politics; we have seen already that in the theology threading through all his views *la volonté* is his "first principle . . . first dogma . . . first article of faith" (OC IV.576). However, there is no need to go further in this direction. According to Rousseau, reason and the passions are themselves formed by, not the origins of, individual human development and social evolution.[120] Thus, this debate may be avoided here altogether.[121]

We have already seen that Rousseau identifies as similarly fundamental other forces operative in human life.[122] Recall *perfectibilité*. Rousseau also believes "it is quite certain that compassion [*la pitié*] is a natural sentiment" (OC III.156) and is "the only natural virtue."[123] Two parallel modes of another motive—"the desire to preserve oneself" and *amour de soi-même*—are the primary material from which the social application of reason cultivates pride and arrogance (*amour-propre*) in the individual (OC III.156). But, while these were of interest earlier in the argument of this book, they are not our main concerns at this stage, nor will they be in the next.

After Will, the second great motive force for Rousseau is what we generally call "evolution," or the inherent capacity of Mankind as a whole to generate, without recourse to God's design or creation, its own history and future, to emerge through variation and transform itself as a species, at once within and against *nature*.[124]

It should not be difficult to see why a thinker whose aim is to understand mankind "abandoned to ourselves" and to "resolve all the contradictions of the social system" would be primarily intrigued by the imbrication of *nature* within humanity. Likewise, when Rousseau considers, in a famously prominent but (I insist) secondary way, the imbrication of humanity within *nature*, the effect is to invoke the latter as limit of and constraint on the former. For the whole eighteenth century, *nature* is both *idée-force* and *idée-frein:* both motor and brake. In other words, *nature* is understood as a function of what it offers us, or what it does for or against us. Where scores of Enlightenment scribblers engaged in purportedly "pure" philosophical or theological speculation, Rousseau makes no such pretense; all considerations for him serve the inquiry into Man, and, ultimately, practical civic intent.[125]

Once transposed to inquiry into the *genre humain,* the unifying euphoria of appeals to *nature* mentioned at the beginning of this section is fully manifest. Concerning beauty, morality, religion, society, happiness, and a panoply of other aspects of the human condition, *nature* came to be asserted as limit, framework, motive, criterion, and order.[126] That it was also increasingly denied to play just these roles alters the scene not one bit. It was the inescapable *topos*—or, as Kenneth Burke might have said with pointed irony, the "God-term"—of the eighteenth century.

§43

Rousseau's Modalities of Nature

How did this "god," *nature,* serve Rousseau? Turn back to the opening pages of *Émile.* The author roundly admits that "perhaps the word nature has too vague a sense" and declares that his task is to nail it down (OC IV.247). Now turn page after page to see that in this endeavor Rousseau seems to fail utterly. The book sets off on its kaleidoscopic gallop, as if to say "Do you want to know what *nature* is? Then read me, then live, for '*il faut que tout homme vive,*' but don't expect a definition." Rousseau manifests in every way and then some the encompassing and contradictory euphoric embrace of *nature* characteristic of his time (cf. §42 above). All the forces of *nature*—the physical effects of the substance and discursive effects of the word—are woven into his extraordinary rhetorical web. Tacitly, so to speak, Rousseau proposes a whole grammatical constitution, which we will now attempt to survey.[127]

Rousseau's use of the word *nature* is copious. By a series of antitheses, readers are quickly reminded of the commonplaces that *nature* is not *société,* not *opinion,*[128] not *convention,* not *art,*[129] and so on. The *nature* to which we are most accustomed (as in §42 above) is certainly present—as universal substance or active principle of everything but Man, and of Man-as-Animal, as the deep symbolic ambiguity between self and other, purity and menace. But, as we shall see in a moment, the transparency of such beliefs is constantly being problematized by other attributions of *nature* as source, paradigm, path, constraint, or condition.

In the "*éducation de la nature*" of the "three educations" that converge in the program for *Émile* (see §§39–40 above), we find a clear instance of *nature* as source. This exemplifies a more general pattern. A common modality of *nature*-as-source is *nature*-as-voice: there is the "voice of nature," even "the blessed voice," and thus a "language," a "book" of nature, through which the measured "teachings" of nature are meted out as it "prescribes laws," "writes" on our hearts, produces "spectacles," or tells one to love God. Nature as a source that all humans have within ourselves is, first after organic animation, an *amour de soi*, the passion that generates all the other passions.[130] It is again the "voice of nature" that speaks within us, but not "that of reason," which here, surprisingly for the eighteenth century but perhaps not for Rousseau, has a different status, and only becomes natural in society.[131] *Nature* is an original to be imitated—freely, as in the arts, or by necessity, where "it" sanctions those who drift or run from it. Thus, with right and active engagement by the human subject, *nature* becomes a paradigm, generally a paradigm for living, and takes one as its "disciple." In the ambivalence between the active and the passive subject, *nature* is described as a "path," "steps," or "route" that one had better follow but from which one might stray. The reader of *Émile*, the person who would best educate a child or himself as Man or Citizen,[132] is directed by Rousseau into "the true footsteps of nature."

Everywhere one looks—perhaps this is due to our especially strong contemporary attachment to this usage—*nature* spells out imposition and constraint. The *nature-frein* (as brake) seems to overwhelm the *nature-force* (as motor). This is nowhere more evident than in more than one hundred iterations of difference between the sexes in the final book of *Émile*. We need not thematize the structure of gender in Rousseau's thinking to state the obverse obvious: all of the harping on sexual difference makes Book Five a metonymy for the quality of constraint in *nature*.

Rousseau persistently ties *nature* to the word *état*, which is elsewhere attached to terms antithetical to *nature* like *société* or *civil*. It is certainly true and thus deeply misleading that *l'état de nature* [state of nature] occasionally points us toward the woods, to what is *sauvage* or wild. This again should be understood within Rousseau's discursive economy as metonymy. The sylvan makes present for readers the distinctive and surrounding feeling characteristic of an *état* as much as, perhaps more than, it identifies the specifically *naturel*. Occurrences in the murky forests beyond the frontiers of *la cité* have no real bearing on Rousseau's social theory of politics. Likewise his occasional prompting that *nature* is *origine*; little of significance under the sign of *nature* happens at the headwaters of the river of time, "before" *société*.

Many of these semantic patterns may be gathered together under the heading of *nature*-as-*ordre*. The basic sense of the word *ordre* will occupy much of our attention in coming sections of this book. A brief statement introducing the three most important ones will suffice here. *Ordre* may refer to command, to sequence, or to systemic harmony. *Nature*-as-command overlaps to a large extent with *nature*-as-source, especially in the modality of voice. *Nature* "orders" us to do or not to do with greater or lesser degrees of reward or sanction. The typically sequential character of what *nature* offers us is captured in the sense of *ordre*-as-sequence, familiar from the synonymous classical rhetorical notions of *ordo* and *dispositio* or the abstract notion of ordinal numbers. This is made explicit when Rousseau is ready to apply the principles of the "main passage" directly to educational practice, and he first commends the tutor this way: "maintain the child uniquely in dependence from things [and] you will have followed the order of nature in the progress of his education" (OC IV.311). We shall see below (§§51–58) that when additional steps are taken to apply the notion of *ordre* to society, the gesture to sequence becomes significantly more complicated.

The third connotation of *ordre* is the harmony of system. The discussions of music and system (§§31 and 32 above) may be taken to inform this image. With this *ordre* in mind Rousseau declares that a profound chasm stands between the *naturel* and the *humain*. While the ultimate significance of this divide is far from obvious, and will soon occupy our attention, it appears this way *prima facie*: "The scene [*tableau*] of nature offers me only harmony and proportions, that of mankind offers me only confusion, disorder! Amongst the elements [of nature] concert reigns, and Men are in chaos!"[133]*

Occasional statements qualify *nature* in terms of *ordre*—as when Rousseau gestures to "well-ordered nature" (OC IV.552)—and thus suggest that the two are not always identical. Indeed, Rousseau's entire civic and educational project may be said to depend on the assumption that *nature* can be preserved or destroyed, "cultivated" or "depraved" (OC IV.549), and that the natural features of human beings can be "choked." The message is clear that not all *ordres* are good. Likewise, by *nature* we are all "subject to the miseries of life, anxieties, evils,

---

* "Le tableau de la nature ne m'offroit qu'harmonie et proportions, celui du genre humain ne m'offre que confusion, désordre! Le concert régne entre les élemens, et les hommes sont dans le cahos!..."

needs, and pains of every type, and, in the end, condemned to die" (OC IV.504). But leave all this aside for the moment.

Where Rousseau's theism surfaces the picture is somewhat different. The *"ordre de la nature"* is conceived as "unalterable," which fact "best displays the supreme being."[134] The problem with this turn—which we shall underscore at the end of this book—is that it leads diametrically away from the answer Rousseau gives to the "theodicy question" (§§1, 2, and 5 above): if Providence, then evil derives from it. Nevertheless, it is from this starting point that the tropes of *ordre* and *désordre* are presumed to articulate the various types of *état* each human being confronts in the world.

The general significance of *l'état de nature* cannot be brought to light in the usual historical ("once upon a time"), anthropological ("in a land far away"), or even hypothetical ("imagine a world without . . .") terms. To understand what Rousseau's constant harping on *nature* is about, it is necessary, although not sufficient, to add a conception of *nature-as-ordre* and of *ordre*-as-the-harmony-of-system, or κοσμος.[135]

Thus we are brought back to the starting point of the preceding section. To speak of *nature* is a way to state metonymically the abstract *ordre* of any or all particular experience. Although this abstraction may appear in a Platonic vocabulary, or in the symbolic registers of mathematics, system, and harmony, each component has for Rousseau additional modern referents and meanings.

Who makes such statements? They may issue in the "blessed voice" of "the author of nature" (OC IV.245) or from the "preceptors of the human race [like] the Bacons, the Descartes, the Newtons" (OC III.29).

However, we should never forget that the primary voice here is Rousseau's. What he shows so richly is that *nature*—in all its reach and compass—is ultimately a human endeavor involving *inventio* and artifice. There may *be* something—light and energy, bubbling magma and microscopic amoebæ—but all that cannot be counted as extrahuman or intrahuman *nature*, as if magically reduced to *"degré zéro."*[136] Nature, without Man, and even for Man, is nothing if it is not realized as substance and made transmissible in its narrativization[137] or its "emplotment" as *mythos*.[138] The sheer range of its applicability requires multiple plots for *nature* that the term itself joins together by syllepsis. This is how Rousseau contributes as much as, or perhaps more than, the scientists and the theologians to the *mythos* of *nature*, the most profound myth of Western modernity. As an epistemology, this could be a kind of constructive nominalism.[139] It is, as we shall see, much more than that. Man's linguistic engagement with *nature* is a moment in the process of social evolution.

Over and over again, Rousseau writes as if one can be, or step, outside *nature*, or be "close" to it, as the "Ancients" were and the "Hurons" in his time are, although for entirely different reasons; *nature*, he pretends, can be in one's heart, a source of passion, or a place from which to contract, or a thing to contract with; he proposes that animals are closer to nature than Man, but that Man is an animal, whose place in the "chain of beings" is assigned by *nature*, the *maître* of Man.

Within the *mythos* of *nature* in general, the image of a "state of nature" is a consistently focused and persuasive synecdoche. The gesture made by this phrase is fruitfully, topically obscure, as it points to no clear position in space or time, makes no decisive categorical break, and is never an exclusive predicate of the human condition. And—we shall see later that this is a crucial point—it is subject to change over time. Even with urgent suggestions in the *Discours sur . . . l'inégalité* that Man in *nature* has "need and occasions to leave it" (OC III.199), Rousseau could not be clearer about the bottom line than he is in *Émile*: "One will say that I leave nature; I believe nothing of the kind" (OC IV.483).* *Nature*, rather, "chooses its instruments, and adjusts them, not according to opinion, but according to need [*besoin*]." However, "needs [*besoins*] change according to the situation of human beings," which means that *nature* will be transformed accordingly over time. The conclusion underscored by Rousseau is that "there is a great difference between natural Man living in the 'state of nature [*l'état de nature*],' and natural Man living in the 'state of society [*l'état de société*].'"[140]† Either way, one can distinguish "the man of man [*l'homme de l'homme*]" from "the man of nature [*l'homme de la nature*]" (OC IV.549). To *create* the latter—a prospect that in itself complicates the issue—has nothing to do with "making a savage and relegating him to the depths of the woods." It is something one can do even "trapped within the social whirlwind." "It is enough that he does not let himself be apprenticed to the passions or opinions of others [*hommes*]; that he sees with his eyes, feels with his heart; that no authority governs him, beyond that of his own reason."[141]§

We see here that the *état de nature* is not meant to stand alone as a regulative ideal or figure of origin. It is an *image* or a *representative anecdote*,[142] the function of which is to motivate a panoply of claims, diagnoses, and suggestions while

---

* "On me dira que je sors de la nature; je n'en crois rien."

† "Il y a bien de la différence entre l'homme naturel vivant dans l'état de nature, et l'homme naturel vivant dans l'état de société."

§ ". . . il suffit qu'il ne s'y laisse entraîner ni par les passions ni par les opinions des hommes; qu'il voye par ses yeux, qu'il sente par son coeur; qu'aucune autorité ne le gouverne, hors celle de sa propre raison."

giving to them a kind of unity and driving necessity. It is a gesture to, and gains its rhetorical force from, the *mythos* of *nature* as a whole.

Although Rousseau is not the origin of this myth—indeed, myths have no origin, but are a genre of discourse for representing origins that can never be known—his is a canonical expression of it: especially after the seventeenth century, every antithesis of which *nature* is a part is refigured by it. This is the mirror of the effect remarked by Ehrard as characteristic of the eighteenth century: while *nature* tends to "unite unreconcilables"[143] it also forces them further and further apart. Thus, it sometimes pushes toward the monism of a Spinoza or the Positivism of the nineteenth century, and sometimes toward a reinvigorated dualism, as in Rousseau. This does not reduce the ambivalence inherent in theism in an age of science (or in science in an age of fundamentalism): if *nature* and God are torn asunder, Man must choose between them, and any such choice is an eccentric acceptance of both.[144] The question—the pivotal question for readers of Rousseau—is where this ambivalence will reemerge within his thinking and what will be its consequences for our own.

§44

THE IMMUTABILITY OF NATURE
Priority, Necessity, and Inflexibility

At the beginning of the preceding section, I asserted that Rousseau fails in the task he takes on: he does not fix precisely the sense of the vague word *nature*. Perhaps this assessment was too glib; have we overlooked some principle?

The first hypothesis Rousseau offers himself for analysis is that "nature, they tell us, is only habit" (OC IV.247). While the treatment of this paradigm in the opening pages of *Émile* is mildly derisive, it immediately focuses attention on what *nature* is *for* human beings, the topic Rousseau takes most seriously.[145] Referring first to plants and then to people, he suggests that habits are alterations of dispositions. By antithesis, dispositions "before that alteration . . . are what I call in us 'nature' [*avant cette alteration . . . sont ce que j'appelle en nous la nature*]" (OC IV.248).

I want to emphasize two things here. The first is the phrase *avant altération*—

before alteration—which I will be repeating frequently in the following discussion. The second is that these are just the terms in which the "main passage" opens the whole program of mankind's political redemption, where Rousseau locates us "before prejudices and human institutions have altered our natural inclinations [*avant que les préjugés et les institutions humaines aient altéré nos penchans naturels*]."

Is this *avant altération* or "before-ness" the key to a general definition? Indeed, many attributes that circle around the word *nature* have been characterized by the *a priori* or the *immer noch* ["always already"] of the philosophers. But we need not follow them to this extreme. *Avant*/before is neither "in the beginning" nor "eternity." It is just a step back from some, any, "now" of *altération*. Understood this way, *nature* is prior in time, somehow less mediated, less complex in substance, purer and more impulsive than its issue.

For the *avant*/before to be taken as a principle of *nature*, the status of the *altération* it precedes must be discerned. How does Rousseau go about this? While generous with historical examples and anecdotes, he does not rely on this empirical discourse to distinguish between the *avant*/before and its *altération*; what precedes and follows in history is more history.[146] Rather, his inquiry into *nature* is a kind of speculation, which, as you will recall (§7 above), begins by "setting aside all the facts" (OC III.132). Although the *altération* in the "passage from the state of nature to the civil state [*passage de l'état de nature à l'état civil*]" is described as "very remarkable" (OC III.364), only a hypothetical exercise can distinguish between these two conditions. The "*contract social*" seems to be a hypothesis of this sort. Thus, the characteristic feature of this and innumerable analogous procedures is that they can be enacted at any time, in any place, and with any object. One leaves the "*état de nature*" every day, so to speak. The *nature* thus derived is an idea, an image. In the specific instance of *société*, the antithetical *nature* is just a speculative proposition and not a prior *état*. We can be sure of this because, unlike "the life of the body politic" which can "degenerate" and "die,"[147] *société* in general, with its continuous overlapping of generations, is nearly immortal.

However, the *avant*/before of *nature*, the "something" that precedes *altération*, becomes material and perceptible in another way. It is manifest in the birth of a child. The experience of a child, before instruction, *avant altération*, gives real gravity to the edenic or pastoral idyll of a "state of nature" where human beings might reside unburdened by and without suspicion of the tribulations of "today."[148] It should thus be no surprise that *Émile* is five times longer than *Du Contract social*, and that the latter is literally contained within the former (OC IV.836 ff.). There is a lot more to work with, as *Émile*'s narrative of individual development builds on detailed experience with which every reader is intimately familiar.

The strictly literary task Rousseau assumes gives a performative force to his political vision. Starting from the generation of human life, *Émile* at every turn sets out to sustain this miraculous fact and extend its significance, even as, inexorably, the child grows into himself and into his life with others. Can the reader and his or her fellow human beings really, from what we are today, every today, at every age, reiterate natality and become something new? Whatever the answer, this is the question Rousseau poses to the imagination.[149]

His choice of genre declares just this theoretical intention. He does not offer, in the popular manner of other publications by himself and his contemporaries, a *traité*, a *système*, a *discours*, a *roman*, a *dictionnaire*, and the like, all of which genres have their own logics of closure. Instead, the first line of *Émile* describes the succeeding six hundred pages as a "collection of reflections and observations without order [*recueil de réflections et d'observations, sans ordre*]." That is, Rousseau does not "order," but assumes, takes on himself, the ordering principle of *nature*, which is to say a dialectics of "before-ness" and *altération*. To best illustrate the *nature* it cannot define, the book must avoid any pretense to mastery. Even as the ink flows from Rousseau's pen, he renounces any personal claim to authority (OC IV.242). No authority but *nature* itself may command the proceedings.[150] It is a deeply stoic program in full epicurean proliferation. If planned too precisely, executed too methodically, and thus tipping the cards to allow the reader to witness the fall of *nature* under the siege of the author-as-instructor (instructor-as-author?), the balance would shift entirely away from the topic that hundreds of alternations of *altération* and "before-ness"—which are the warp and weft of the book—are meant to expose: *nature* itself as the right path to civilization.[151]

This *nature*, which comes to us like a child untouched by human hands, stages an unexpected "before-ness" for the political scenario of *Du Contract social*. It is the quality of our experience specifically absent the artifice of instruction. In this story, *nature* should also be read as a symbol for the person in need of instruction and for the type of instruction required. In reality and in Rousseau's own terms, instruction is a social fact. It only exists in the "*état civil.*" On its face, then, the divide between "Man" and "Citizen"[152] should appear as a distinction between the "state of nature" and a situation in which people are properly instructed. The triumphant recapitulation of *Du Contract social* in its penultimate chapter— "*De la religion civile*"—is only a synoptic version of, a sort of maintenance plan for, the informal formation of character that emerges from everyday life as portrayed in the pages of *Émile*, a book aptly subtitled with a recently popular word: *de l'éducation*.[153] Having so enlarged the field of "proper" instruction, it can be seen as a backdrop against which the metaphor "state of nature" often becomes a metonymy for "the untutored" or "uncivilized" person.

The astute reader of Rousseau will then not rest having simply identified as useful and exciting fictional representations of "savage" persons and places (whether in Paris or the Americas). From, by contrast to, in rhetorical tandem with the "state" of the not-yet-instructed, readers must make the *cité* emerge in a form that corresponds to what it was not. Nothing mysterious here: when you become no-longer-a-child, you become an adult, not a butterfly; there is a continuity of opposites. *Du Contract social* is not *Metamorphoses.* Let us imagine then that the initial "state of nature" of Rousseau's great treatise of politics is not *avant*/before every *altération*, but specifically "before" the transformative experiences and instruction that in fact give shape to citizens and rise to republics. Bad laws and the evils of society are improper instruction because, as the "main passage" tells us, they "have plunged us again into childhood."

One conclusion to draw here in passing is that we will not perceive the full significance of Rousseau's political program unless we refigure the meaning of the *contract social* in parallel with a correct image of what it rejects or overcomes, the "state of nature."[154] Developing Rousseau's theme of the centrality of education to civilization, this metonymic infancy is what the latecomer Kant—in his *Was ist Aufklärung?*—will propose to overcome.

Before all this, however, some further effort is required to map the characteristic features of *nature.* Recall now that it was within the sort of unsteady identification of *"enfans"* and *"hommes"* just mentioned that the "formula for happiness"—that shorthand proportion of {*forces* ≥ *besoins*}—first entered the discussion (cf. §19 above). This is also how Rousseau introduced *liberté* into the considerations of the "main passage" (cf. §19 above). He emphasized at that point the way *liberté* in itself can fail to make us happy because the *"usage de la liberté"* must always reckon with obstacles. Such obstacles, in general and *in extremis*, are called *nécessité.*

These considerations connect directly with what we have said in the last few pages. Of all that is *avant*/before *altération* in the child, the most urgent dispositions are the ones we call *besoins*, or needs. The newborn's needs are paradigmatic, iconic. They leave no doubt as to what *avant*/before means and they represent clearly a key sense in which "necessity" may be taken as another definitive feature of *nature.*

Common sense tells us that "necessity" is a feature of the physical realm, with its gravity and orbits and cycles of birth and death. In this discursive setting—nourished by natural philosophy from the ancient materialists to quantum mechanics—the opposite of "necessity" is "chance." This common sense, however, takes shape as human concerns unfold within the physical realm and in the course of our inquiry (in every possible sense) into that realm.

As a result, the *topos* of "necessity" derives a significant part of its semantic content from moral discourse. In moral discourse the opposite of "necessity" is not "chance" but Will.[155] This triad itself—Will/necessity/chance—becomes a way of triangulating the meaning of *nature*.[156]

When Rousseau distinguishes between the two types of *dépendance*, and identifies dependence-from-things with *nature*, he clearly aims to invoke "the law of necessity, always renascent" (OC IV.444). His purpose, so powerfully invoked in the "main passage," is to provide a model for "an inflexibility that no human force could ever overcome."[157] A "thing [*chose*]," a "physical being [*être physique*]," unlike a "moral being [*être moral*]," is "bound by the chains of necessity."[158]

This group of ideas forms an important pillar for Rousseau's thinking; we saw an example of how he builds on such ideas when we examined the topic of *forces* in §20 above. However, we now need to step back from these ideas for a moment. Granted that it is a commonplace to find "necessity in things" or to accede *"ex necessitate rei."* The question now is Why? What is the source of this belief?

Diderot's entry in the *Encyclopédie* provides a clue by exhibiting the common sense of the eighteenth century:

> Thing, n.f. (Grammar) With this word one designates without distinction every inanimate being, whether real or modal; "being" is more general than "thing," insofar as it speaks of everything that is, without distinction, whereas there are some "beings" for which "thing" is not said. One does not say of God "that is a thing," one does not say this of Man.[159]*

This is precisely the sense that guides Rousseau's hand when he writes that one should "see this necessity in things, never in the caprice of men" and that "it is in the nature of man to endure patiently the necessity of things, but not the bad Will of others" (OC IV.320). The consequence is that the citizen who wants to "live happy and wise," whose character will be both consequence of and guardian for the civic resolution of "all the contradictions of the social system," should follow the "formula for happiness," making sure that "his condition limits his desires" and that, as the program of the "main passage" suggests, he "extends the law of necessity to morality [*aux choses morales*]" (OC IV.820).

---

* "chose, s. f. (Gramm.) On désigne indistinctement par ce mot tout être inanimé, soit réel, soit modal; être est plus général que chose, en ce qu'il se dit indistinctement de tout ce qui est, au lieu qu'il y a des êtres dont chose ne se dit pas. On ne dit pas de Dieu, que c'est une chose; on ne le dit pas de l'homme. . . ."

The point seems exceedingly clear: as Diderot asserts, and Rousseau concurs, *les choses*, things, are bearers of necessity because they are not "Willed."[160] By this definition, things are whatever does not have this common trait of God and Man: *la volonté*.

Nonetheless, these statements are in key respects entirely misleading. Look first at the obvious: simply by pointing to a common trait in God and Man—however exalted or distorted in one or the other—the reader is drawn back onto theological terrain. This suggests that where *nécessité* forms a bridge in the eighteenth century between the physical discourse of nature and the moral discourse of Will, various theological positions will always be lurking, if in unexpected forms.

The issues at stake here are clearly represented early in the century in the antithetical positions of Jesuits and Jansenists. The former aimed to maintain a theology of human "free Will" while the latter insisted on "divine omnipotence." This debate first gave terms to and then, in some circles, gave way to deism. As "natural religion tended to become the religion of nature," the *nécessité* of *nature* easily took the place of the *nécessité* of Grace.[161] But *nature* is the memory of God, and it is difficult to imagine how it would not always, in due course, acquire God-like attributes in the absence of explicit efforts to develop an alternative that could satisfy the other human desires that lead toward anthropomorphic religious beliefs.[162]

The more fundamental point here, however, is, if I may put it this way, that a lapse in the logic of deism allowed one to hold to Creation, to Grace, to Providence. In correspondence with any such belief, the origin of *nécessité* must simply be, as it was for Rousseau, divine Will.[163]

This is an important twist. It means that while the obstacle to the freedom of the human Will appears to be *nécessité*, it is in fact God. I can write "in fact" here because, even if the existence of God is denied, whatever "God" is as a human experience or creation, as a social and symbolic effect, "it" remains nevertheless either the name for or—in certain respects too complicated to spell out here—the source of necessity.

Were it possible in a book to have a crowd of thousands chanting in the street before Rousseau's door, I would usher them into my text here. For, as this additional swing of the pendulum takes us back to theology from natural philosophy it imposes upon us the inescapability of God, and this situation seems entirely incompatible with the other major premise of Rousseau's social theory of politics, the one derived from his theodicy, the declaration of mankind "abandoned to ourselves."

As we have seen repeatedly in this book, Rousseau nowhere directly renounces and everywhere hammers on this idea and image of mankind "abandoned to our-selves." Indeed, it is what leads to and shapes the analysis of society and politics that concerns us here. As we shall see, however, the collateral theistic underpin-nings I have just introduced impeded the sociology Rousseau inaugurated. This theism—although perhaps not *every* theism—still stunts the growth of political theory today.

Now, the issue of whether a "thing" gains its qualities from a Will or not, and how this does or does not change one's relation to that "thing" and to other per-sons, is ground we shall have to cover more carefully in the final parts of this book. What we can see already here is that the implication of the Will in the question of *nécessité* casts doubt on whether *nécessité* can be the primary feature of *nature* that Rousseau has in mind. For, his theoretical purpose in identifying *les choses* with *la nature* was to justify the proposition that dependence-from-things has nothing to do with moral life.[164] Regardless of whose Will is involved, it is not plausible—for us or for Rousseau—that something that has Will as its source has nothing to do with moral life; thus, oddly enough, *nature* seems inher-ently moral in the way Rousseau presents it here. One way around this would be to insist that divine and human Will are categorically different, and their single name is just an effect of metaphor. Rousseau does not take this path. And, in any event, another obstacle stands in his way.

One may wish to state as axiom that whatever issues from God's Will is *avant/* before *altération*, and thus by fiat make it natural in a sense discussed above. But this can never be the case for *les choses* in general. Human action on the "things" of the world is, by definition, *altération*, at the very least because we always take things up after the divine Will has already done its work. And how many "things" come to us untouched by human hands?

Exposed here is the difficulty of conceiving something as necessary *in itself.* Such efforts seem inexorably to point back to a metaphysics, and if not strictly to God then at least to attributes of *nature* that we can only understand by way of "God-terms."[165]

Necessity in symbolic constructions—like a geometrical proof or a law[166]—is something that is made. It reflects the constitutive rule that the whole of which x is a part would be something else if x were not present. In an analogous fashion, human interactions with the nonhuman world are constantly interweaving it with constitutive elements through language. For example, when the empiricist says "every time I drop the apple it falls down" the key to understanding the predicate "it falls down" as necessary is the subject phrase "*every* time I drop the apple." Physical necessities, like symbolic ones, are made within relationships. Necessity involves some movement against the grain of "things."

This brings us back to the two lines that opened our consideration of *nécessité* as a feature of *nature*. As a paradigm for human institutions, Rousseau seeks in what he calls the "the law of necessity, always renascent" (OC IV.444) "an inflexibility that no human force could ever overcome." Like so many of his contemporaries, Rousseau often invokes this image of physical *nécessité*.

But perhaps even the image of physical *nécessité* is misleading. Suppose that the language of physics is not the source of, but simply metonymy for, a set of claims that already had meaning within the discourses of social and political theory.[167]

From this point of view, Rousseau's many and various allusions to *nécessité* may be considered as supports for a somewhat different concern. The hypothesis of the "main passage," after all, is "if laws . . . could have . . . inflexibility . . . dependence-from-persons would become again that from things." In other words, he wants to draw our attention not so much to *nécessité* as to *inflexibilité*, and specifically to the inflexibility characteristic of certain kinds of law.

Does Rousseau therefore mean by the identification of *les choses* and *la nature* that the distinguishing property of "things" is that they are governed by "laws of nature?" His writings provide strong support for an affirmative answer to this question. It is worth pursuing this idea again briefly here. This way, too, we shall for the moment delay further consideration of what will in the final chapter come to the very center of our attention: the foundational role of the Will in Rousseau's sociological approach to politics.

One thing is immediately puzzling. Could a "law of nature" govern the *état naturel* the way human laws govern the *état civil?* "Natural law" generates conditions for order, or describes those conditions, or both. But can it be said to *govern?* Rather than answer this question directly, we should bring again to mind when and where the "law of nature" is supposed to apply. We already know that it operates in both the *état naturel* and the *état civil*.[168] Thus, regarding "things," Rousseau's main concern must not be whether some "thing" came to us *avant*/before *altération* or was made by Man. He may care only if the "thing" obeys "natural laws." This focuses attention on an overall "order." Rousseau persistently suggests that within this "order" *les choses* and *la nature* are in some sense one and the same. As we find ourselves related to the world through dependence, the "order" of what we depend on is crucial. The more inflexible this "order," the less the ill effects of dependence. Again, this *inflexibilité* is the point. Rousseau's belief that *les choses* constitute an inflexible order is sustained by his belief that "things" obey "laws of nature" and thus conform to its "order."

Let us suppose, for now at least, that this way of thinking reflects something important about *nature*. That still leaves unanswered a key question. Why should we believe that human laws, laws that we make and apply ourselves, could stand before us with this same majestic inflexibility? And exactly what impact would such laws have on our experience of dependence?

The problem here is to understand how "laws of nature" enter Rousseau's social theory of politics. One such passage is quite direct. Rousseau tells us that wherever human beings confront the inflexibility of *nature* they have force and courage, just as "all the animals abandoned to the care of nature . . . have almost everywhere a larger size, a more robust constitution, more vigor and force, and more courage in the forest than in our homes" (OC III.139). Perhaps this holds, too, for the human animal "abandoned to ourselves." Perhaps these qualities are good for politics.

But if Rousseau's presumption is that *nature* is always operative, why wouldn't human beings in the *état civil* share in *nature*'s benefits? First, because the simple fact of "becoming sociable" is a counterforce to those benefits. This, in the most reductionist perspective, is the whole problem of the exponential increase of *besoins* over *forces* that we traced out in the first part of this book. The second reason is that endowments derived from our interaction with *nature* are not the only positive human capacities; we are also improved by social development. This complicates the claim that *nature* is inflexible in ways we will consider in a moment.

Still, the principle of natural *inflexibilité* suggests that some kind of return or adherence to *nature* constitutes one potential for mankind "abandoned to ourselves," as it would serve to discipline or instruct us for the task of making a political order without recourse to God or, eventually, without a king.

Given literally centuries of misreading Rousseau, the following declaration should be for us a kind of mantra: "the happy life of the golden age was always a condition foreign to the human race" (OC III.283). Rousseau explains this abrupt assertion by insisting that "either we did not recognize it when it was possible for us to enjoy it, or we had already lost it when we would have been able to recognize it." Thus, no sort of "return" will bring *nature* and its *inflexibilité* to bear.

To this Rousseau adds another decisive conclusion: "the sweet voice of nature is no longer our infallible guide, nor the independence we received from her a desirable condition" (OC III.283).*

The lesson here is obvious: if *nature* is to become effective in the social theory of politics, it must be in another way. From the principle of *inflexibilité* Rousseau

---

* ". . . la douce voix de la nature n'est plus pour nous un guide infaillible, ni l'indépendance que nous avons receu d'elle un état desirable . . ."

turns to the inflexibility of principle. The "laws of nature" are taken to constitute a paradigm for total *inflexibilité*, and thus to be emulated (completely? perhaps not) by human laws.

Rousseau is particularly emphatic on this point. His appeal to *inflexibilité* here must be understood with reference to a structure of human relationships: there is a background that conditions events; this is the context in which dependence becomes a foreground object of concern; the more "ordered" the background, the more contentiousness and insecurity will be dissipated in the foreground. We know this because, for example, people do not fight about who will jump over mountains or swallow up the seas. The conclusion is that human laws would improve if modeled on, for example, the law of gravity or the principles of thermodynamics.

Neither in theory nor in practice is this as simple as it may at first seem. Such a gesture to inflexible natural forces brings a totalitarian image easily to mind. Is Rousseau simply promoting a strong state, one which could regularly overwhelm individuals with well-armed police or jailers?

Only in the most remote sense do questions like this shed light on what Rousseau imagines. This becomes clear as several qualifications cut into the striking analogy between "natural law" and human law. First, Rousseau says unequivocally that human beings should not pretend to be like the "Author of nature": "If we want to create a durable establishment, let us not in any way dream of rendering it eternal. To succeed, one must not attempt the impossible, nor flatter oneself by pretending to give to the work of Men a solidity that does not belong to human things."[169]* This plea against political hubris bears unexpectedly on the fundamental commitment under scrutiny here. Appealing to the commonplace that "human things are not eternal," Rousseau seems to tacitly admit in this passage what he elsewhere denies: *les choses* are not identical with *la nature*.[170]

Of course, Rousseau would hesitate—elevating human "things" to the majesty of *nature*—to take a position insulting to God. But there are other considerations in play here as well. Even while he obsessively extols *inflexibilité*, Rousseau also acknowledges that it is not always beneficial. For example, the ancient institution of dictatorship is applauded in *Du Contract social* because it allows law to "bend to events" and this *flexibilité* is useful *for social order*.[171] Here pragmatism seems to triumph over deontology. It suggests, against much of what we have

---

* "Si nous voulons former un établissement durable, ne songeons donc point à le rendre éternel. Pour réussir il ne faut pas tenter l'impossible, ni se flatter de donner à l'ouvrage des hommes une solidité que les choses humaines ne comportent pas."

seen, a balance to principle, as if legal constraints are to be valued for indirect effects, not so much for imposing conformance as for dragging the problem of dependence out from the "disordered" space of everyday social interaction and resituating it in contexts where harm and remedy can be measured, albeit in some allusive way, against *nature* and her laws.

In other words, what inspires Rousseau may simply a version of "the rule of law." In this condition, inflexibility derives, first, from an uncoupling of rules from the personal circumstances of the lawgiver and, second, from the establishment of clear and consistent and public links between those rules and the subjects of the law.

How inflexible "the rule of law" can be in practice is one of the great unresolved dilemmas of modernity. Rousseau is no positivist; he states explicitly that informal, practical, and historical features of culture are what make human laws what they are. We discussed this point in some detail in §5 and §20 above. Thus, even though the aspiration to make human law as inflexible as "natural law" would seem to require it, Rousseau cannot be proposing that human law constitutes a perfectly closed and autonomous system. Those who believed they were carefully following his position to its consequences—I am thinking of Kant here in particular—have seen that even when law is supposed to be sequestered in a transcendental realm, its effectiveness resides not in some vast mechanism but in the terrible unsteady character of human beings. Law is and can be nothing without a specific kind of sacred awe that we (can, but do not always) experience before its majesty.[172] This sentiment permeates the tone and terms of the pivotal chapter *"Du législateur"* in *Du Contract social* (OC III.381–84). One may say with great pomp that the virtue of the citizen is to experience this awe, and that the institutions of a well-ordered republic inculcate this virtue,[173] but it can also become in more modest ways an everyday fact of life: people in many times and places do, in fact, obey the law.[174] This fact is typically maintained by rather mundane practices. The law's inflexibility can be reinforced by those charged with making and executing laws, from a policeman who reads a criminal suspect his "Miranda rights" to the government official who feels "obligated to look to legal points of reference to describe and justify official behavior . . . even if, because law and political interest may coincide, it is sometimes superfluous. . . . It is the habitual commitment to this interpretive regime that perhaps most pervasively differentiates a government of laws from a government of unadorned power."[175]

At the beginning of this section, I wrote that Rousseau's inquiry into nature in *Émile* begins with what seems like a derisive dismissal of a commonplace of his contemporaries—"nature, they tell us, is only habit" (OC IV.247). We did not ask why, exactly, he would begin with this point. It is not just that this common-place derives from Aristotle.[176] We can now see something unexpected: this view is not so far as he would have us believe from his own. *Nature* does not only press on law from outside. It becomes a force *within* law through the organic emergence of habits, which in turn give shape to the "*moeurs*, customs, and opinion" that are the essence of the law (OC III.394).

It should surprise no one that Rousseau expresses little interest in the chance formation of personal habits. These are disorderly eccentricities. By contrast, he is often absorbed by how the steady mechanism of habit-formation acts in general and predictable ways on both the individual and the species. No single person, no *Émile*, could be educated as man or citizen if *nature* did not produce in the infant and then the child a predictable developmental sequence of habits. These habits are not *avant*/before *altération*: it is our *nature* to be altered, by other human beings and by our experience, in consistent and patterned ways. Likewise, groups of people develop habits that are the same among themselves but different from other groups of people. Whether or not we understand it, this natural ongoing *altération* surely conforms to the environment in which it occurs.

Rousseau has what may aptly be called an ecological vision in this regard. He reiterates tropes from a wider debate about the impact of climate on character and culture[177] when he tells us that to render "the constitution of a State truly solid and durable," "the relationships born from the local situation and the character of the inhabitants" must always be "in concert on the same points with the laws." Now, this could be just a way of saying that when one serves two masters it is best to make sure they agree. But, as he develops his explanation, a contrast case emerges in which we see that a much larger and different point is being made. If legislation "follows a principle different from the one to which the nature of things gives rise" then the "State will not cease to be agitated, up to the point that it is either destroyed or changed" (OC III.393, 392).

Look closely: an equation is made here between relationships grounded in locality and character on the one hand and the "principle . . . to which the nature of things gives rise" on the other. Together, these describe the paradigm to be followed by the legislator. While the ultimate meaning of this directive depends, once again, on whether or not *les choses* and *la nature* are the same, Rousseau seems to be saying that something immutable and general is at the same time mutable and local.

This same contradictory impulse is taken to an extreme when Rousseau issues a challenge to the legislator:

Whoever dares undertake to found a people [*instituer un peuple*] must feel himself capable, so to speak, of changing human nature. (OC III.381)*

Thus, there at times seem to be two Rousseaus. One rails against "vain" and "ridiculous" efforts to "control nature . . . to improve on the handiwork of God" (OC IV.491). The other advises that *nature* had better be the paradigm for law, even while understanding law as a kind of cultural system.

What, finally, does all this suggest? That *to be inflexible* the law must be a living thing, something adaptive to the fluidity of human circumstances even while it channels them in consistent directions.

§45

THE MUTABILITY OF NATURE
The Dialectic of Social Evolution

Rousseau believes that human laws must be adaptive and fluid at the same time that they are inflexible. Does this make a mockery of his program to model our laws on *nature?*

The answer depends again on what is involved in that irrepressible word *nature*. We have tracked our way through various representations of *nature* that were important for Rousseau and for his contemporaries (cf. §§42–44 above). What is decisive, finally, is the modal force of that word, that is, how it inflects everything it touches.

This observation, however, does not settle some very basic questions: Is *nature* a static thing or a process? Does it stand apart, or over, or under us? Or is it utterly integrated with human life?

These questions take us back to the preceding section, in particular to where we saw that Rousseau's efforts to establish the immutability of nature met resistance from other quarters of his own thinking. After all, Rousseau makes some rather striking claims for human action. He extols the State as "celestial and inde-

---

* "Celui qui ose entreprendre d'instituer un peuple doit se sentir en état de changer pour ainsi dire la nature humaine . . ."

structible" (OC III.318). He writes that "the great soul of the legislator is the true miracle" (OC III.384) and that "one would need Gods to give laws to Men."[178] If "the legislator is in every respect an extraordinary man" it must be because he can, in some sense, "change . . . human nature" (OC III.381, cf. also 313). What could *nature* be in the face of such facts?

The presumption of *inflexibilité* may be unwarranted for another reason as well. For, Rousseau demonstrates time and time again that *la nature humaine* is changing all the time. The agency of this change is to be found neither in the forces of an external entity nor internal to any individual from the class of mankind. The agency identified by Rousseau is *société* and—this is the point—*société* in turn is shot through with, inextricably entangled with, *nature*. In other words, the transformation of human nature is an effect of ecologically integrated social processes.

Thus we open wide the door to Rousseau's conception of social evolution, a topic that has surfaced sporadically throughout this book so far. I now want to bring it to the foreground. This evolutionary perspective is, I think, the greatest motive force in Rousseau's social theory of politics. Moreover, it suggests an approach to "the resolution of all the contradictions of the social system" that few, and especially few of Rousseau's avowed followers, have been able to effectively pursue.

One impediment to this pursuit is worth mentioning before we attempt to enter this perspective. It is an aspect of Rousseau's position in common understandings of intellectual history that stands in the way. Recall that many of his contemporaries used "Spinoza"—the hottest name of the early eighteenth century—to brand real or imagined atheists. Rousseau himself used the word that way. This defensive measure was meant to illuminate his profoundly held religious faith. However, a collateral effect of this gesture was to hide two important things. One is that Rousseau's and Spinoza's contributions to political theory had something important in common; they shared a deep substantive concern with "ethical freedom."[179]

The second thing hidden under the brand "Spinoza" bears more directly on the topic of this section. As Rousseau declared his distance from the iconic "Spinoza" he obscured the structure of discourse within which his most extraordinary innovation occurs. I do not mean that he actually was a Spinozist (whatever that means). Nor am I suggesting that he was in fact a purely secular thinker. What I am saying has several twists, so please bear with me.

First, Spinoza—in fact and as figure—constituted a new and decisive space of conceptual engagement and debate in and around theology. This space served as rich resource for all sorts of inquiry. Rousseau's thinking and polyvalent position took shape within this space. Indeed, it is only because of his engagement—at once committed and critical—with the transformations of theology that Rousseau could conceive of civic life within an integrated self-generating view of *société*.

But then there is a second half to the story, and in this instance genealogy and analysis do not concur. Rousseau's view of *société*, emerging from his theodicy, creates certain cognitive potentials. From these new possibilities for thinking about and speaking within civic life, specifically political insights may be drawn. What I want to suggest here is that these insights only come fully to light when the concerns of theology are pushed to the background or drop out of consideration altogether. It is not my task here to decide if these insights are ultimately compatible with religious belief but, as a matter of political *theory*, at some point theology stands in the way. This is what is disguised by "Spinoza."

Rousseau's presumption is that—"abandoned to ourselves"—the links between *grâce* and *société* have been severed; nonetheless, considerations of *nature* and *grâce* continue to structure the conception of *nature*; as a result it becomes increasingly difficult to see any relationship between *nature* and *société*. This wall of separation is sustained by the persistent reference to the "state of nature" that—I think it is fair to say—Rousseau makes for other purposes and in many places repudiates (cf. §37 ff. above). The difficulty is manifest in the complementary equations of Spinoza with atheism and Rousseau with deism (of one sort or another). How could any kind of naturalistic view be attributed to Rousseau once we accept that "Spinoza" is just another name for "naturalist"? (See again that entry in the *Encyclopédie* mentioned at §41 above, note 77.)

This cautionary background brings into high relief the topic of this section. I propose to set aside markers like these that show a Rousseau dedicated to the immutability of *nature* and to a *société* distinct from it. This will allow us to consider instead the extent to which Rousseau's account of *société* may constitute a theory of social evolution, and specifically a theory that can be understood both as naturalistic and as grounded in a modern monism.[180]

Any careful reader will see that Rousseau's recourse to evolutionary explanations has almost nothing in common with appeals to "progress"—a word that for Rousseau just means "forward steps" and will only assume its current meaning after him[181]—or any other form of teleology. Nor should we imagine, as many readers incorrectly have, that the evolution of society is simply a matter of unmitigated corruption or degeneration. Rousseau observes, follows, and extrapolates from a capacity inherent in Mankind as a whole to generate our own history and future, to emerge through variation and transform ourselves as a species. This line of reasoning is sometimes difficult both for his readers to comprehend and for Rousseau to sustain because social evolution occurs at once within and against *nature*. Indeed, social evolution *is identical with this paradox*, a dialectic of Man and Nature that constitutes both. Let us now consider how this paradoxical process comes to light.

Nothing is more striking than the way *nature* and *habitude*—commonly understood as antitheses —become interchangeable within the processes Rousseau describes. The transformation of needs over time illustrates this:[182]

> The author of things did not only provide for the needs that he gives us, but also for those that we give to ourselves, and so as to always put desires side-by-side with need he makes sure that our tastes change and alter [themselves] according to our ways of living. (OC IV.407–8)*

It is the mechanism of habit that configures the significance of our needs and thus their effect:

> The more we distance ourselves from the natural condition, the more we lose our natural tastes, or rather, habit makes for us a second nature that we so much substitute for the first that no one amongst us any longer knows the original. (OC IV.407–8)†

Rousseau is not just saying that human beings in society become confused. This process is Providential; God, in giving us our Nature, in giving us to Nature, provided a process in which the driving forces of humanity—*besoins*—are adapted by and to changing circumstances.

One may be inclined to group together the first two uses of the word *nature* here—"*état de nature*" and "*goûts naturels*"—and thus distinguish them from the third use—"*seconde nature*." This is a misreading. The continuity is between "*goûts naturels*" and "*seconde nature*." It is, as we have seen repeatedly, the "*état de nature*" that has a wholly different status. Indeed, the correct implication here is that we never actually, fully, and definitively leave the "*état de nature*," but are rather constantly thrown back into it as generative *nature* is refreshed by the very

---

* "L'auteur des choses ne pourvoit pas seulement aux besoins qu'il nous donne, mais encore à ceux que nous nous donnons nous-mêmes, et c'est pour mettre toujours le désir à côté du besoin qu'il fait que nos gouts changent et s'altèrent avec nos maniéres de vivre."

† "Plus nous nous éloignons de l'état de nature, plus nous perdons de nos gouts naturels; ou plustot l'habitude nous fait une seconde nature que nous substituons tellement à la prémiére que nul d'entre nous ne connoit plus celle-ci."

fact that *we live it.* The mutability of *nature* appears in the human being and in *everything* — making, thinking, dreaming — that we do.[183] Thus, it is not merely a metaphor to say that *habitude* is our *"seconde nature."* Whatever its source or moment, it is *nature* nonetheless.

Besoins are only the most obvious manifestations of social evolution because they are clearly defined by changing circumstances and constitute an animating pressure on everyday life.[184] This process also operates with respect to other fundamental dispositions and capacities of the human being. If passions like *pitié* are something pure, *a priori*, why can they only be seen through the lens of a speculative enterprise like the *Discours sur . . . l'inégalité?* In fact, compassion, every time we meet it, is thoroughly and indistinguishably blended into *"seconde nature."* Does that make it less motoric? Less decisive? Of course not. The same is true for *la raison*, which, as Rousseau does not hesitate to point out, can barely be said to exist without development through social interaction.[185] If it were primary in the most extreme sense, it would always already be operative in the "first men," children, women, or the occasional king . . . but it is not. Throughout Rousseau's writings we find basic motive forces persistently described as natural *and* as developing over time.

Nothing represents more clearly the way *nature* is both timeless and time-full than the weight Rousseau gives to education. Just a decade before Rousseau gave the title *Émile, ou de l'éducation* to his masterpiece, the French word had had only a relatively technical sense and had been understood as an antonym for *nature.* After Turgot expanded *éducation* to include all of human experience[186] it become possible for Rousseau to take the further step of conceiving an *éducation naturel.* As a patterned and apt intervention in processes independent of human control, as synthesis of *nature* and *coutume*, education becomes a perfectly evolutionary idea, "rival to *nature* among the divinities of the epoch," at once an account and a practice of dialectical development in which the "transcendental reality" persists even as the historical process of civilization unfolds.[187] Imagining that, by contrast, "there was neither education nor steps forward," Rousseau pictures Mankind without evolution:

> . . . generations multiplied fruitlessly, and with each always starting from the same point, the centuries flowed on with all the imbecility of the first times, the species was already old, and Man remained always child. (OC III.160)*

* ". . . les générations se multiplioient inutilement; et chacune partant toujours du même point, les Siécles s'écouloient dans toute la grossiéreté des premiers âges, l'espéce étoit déjà vieille, et l'homme restoit toujours enfant."

Pascal, a century before, had expressed a "great fear" that whatever one could identify as truly natural, *avant*/before *altération*, might itself be only a "first custom."[188] "First custom" or "second nature"—who could say? The point is it that Rousseau played mightily on such hesitations and, in just that way, went far beyond them. The real question, to which Rousseau's theory of social evolution is the answer, is What does it mean that no clear distinction can be made?[189]

Education is where evolution appears at the level of the individual. It is a process of human development. *Émile* stands—again, reversing Plato (cf. §15 above)—not just as the story of one or even many pupils coming to maturity, but as the allegory of the human species coming into its own.[190] This allegory re-writes the narrative Rousseau presented several years earlier in the *Discours sur . . . l'inégalité*. Summarizing the first half of the essay, he tells us what he has accomplished. He claims to have

> shown that *perfectibilité*, the social virtues, and the other faculties that Natural Man had received in plenty, could never develop of themselves, that for that they needed the fortuitous concurrence of several foreign causes that might never have emerged, and without which he would have remained eternally in his primitive constitution. (OC III.162)*

Here the picture of human faculties developing over time is enlarged. Rousseau adds two specifications. The first is that the motive force of the evolutionary process is not inherent to the human being, at least not as an individual body. Development of what is most basic depends on interaction with the environment, "foreign causes" of all sorts. The second specification is that this interaction involves chance and that various pathways were and are possible.[191]

It is, therefore, particularly striking that just where the pastoral of *"l'homme Sauvage"* in an *"état de nature"* seems most vividly in swing, creating an imaginary center of gravity, the full force of Rousseau's narrative presses blatantly and unequivocally toward the concept of social evolution. This is confirmed as the *Discours* arrives at its dramatic conclusion. After "discovering and following the forgotten and lost paths which must have led Man from the natural condition to the civil one," Rousseau drives home a didactic point: "every attentive reader can only have been struck by the immense space which separates these two condi-

---

*". . . .montré que la *perfectibilité*, les vertus sociales, et les autres facultés que l'homme Naturel avoit reçues en puissance, ne pouvoient jamais se developper d'elles mêmes, qu'elles avoient besoin pour cela du concours fortuit de plusieurs causes étrangeres qui pouvoient ne jamais naître, et sans lesquelles il fût demeuré éternellement dans sa constitution primitive . . ."

tions," and have noticed that this "space" is filled with "intermediate positions" and a "slow succession of things." Quite simply, "the human race of one age is not the human race of another age."[192] In precisely these—evolutionary—facts the reader "will see the solution to an infinity of moral and political problems that philosophers cannot resolve."[193]

A series of evocations are embedded in this last sentence. We should understand that moral and political life is not a closed system, just as its "opposite," *nature*, does not exist "in itself"; that the problems of moral and political life are infinite, which signifies not just a large quantity but the idea that life with other people is generative; that problems are generated by interaction between Man and Nature, and not just Man and Man (which in any case is part of Nature); that this inevitably involves chance and unpredictability; that solutions emerge slowly over time, a fact which all but excludes "acts of will"—including that supposedly quintessential act of Will, the *contract*—as solutions in themselves; that the philosophers are inept, as they see in *nature* only a mythic origin or a transcendental idea, and not the empirical fact of evolution that makes *nature* at once mutable and immutable, always both present and absent for human beings; that what the philosophers cannot do, unlike Rousseau himself, is *résoudre*; that the solution made apparent by the *Discours* is the "resolution" Rousseau offers here, elsewhere, and in the "main passage"; and that to *résoudre* is not only to analyze but also to "harmonize," or to restore order after inevitable dissonance, where dissonance is constitutive of movement, or development, or evolution. (I am of course recalling §31 above.)

In this long lyric passage, the penultimate of the *Discours sur . . . l'inégalité*, two great themes converge to invigorate Rousseau's powerful political passion.

That passion is the brutally lucid testament that, no matter how the "law of nature" is defined, "it is unquestionably contrary to the Law of Nature . . . that a child commands the aged, an imbecile leads the wise, and a handful of people stuff themselves with extravagance while the starving multitude lacks the bare necessities of life" (OC III.194).

Against this outrage is posed one of the two great themes just mentioned. It is, of course, social evolution. Having made the general case for Man's ongoing transformation of *nature*, and thereby his transformation of himself, Rousseau begins to shift ground back toward the other theme. As he prompts the reader to understand "how the human soul and passions, altering themselves insensibly, change, so to speak, their nature"* and to see "why our needs and our pleasures

---

* ". . . comment l'ame et les passions humaines, s'altérant insensiblement, changent pour ainsi dire de Nature; . . ."

change their objects in the long run,"* he insinuates, in an altogether different voice, that this is

> why the original Man disappears by degrees, why society no longer offers to the eyes of the wise anything but a bunch of artificial men and fake passions which are the product of these new relations and have no real foundation in Nature.[194]†

You will recognize, from the first part of the book you hold in your hands, that this other theme is Rousseau's version of theodicy. Social evolution is a process of interaction between Man and Nature. It produces some bad things. How could this subject be broached without asking, Why doesn't God intervene? Even, we are informed, from Edenic origins mankind "abandoned to ourselves" can go astray. Thus, described in this last paragraph is the particular instance of the general rule: it is social evolution gone wrong.

At the intersection of these two themes, evolution and theodicy, we are thrown again on the rocks of the question raised over the preceding three sections: which *nature* is it that *société* does not stand on? For, Rousseau does not say here that society *cannot* offer anything but artifice and fakery—indeed, he says the opposite in many places—but only that it *does not*, or has not so far. It all could have gone another way.[195] And it still might. And exactly what might take us that way is Man's changing *nature*.

So, we repeat another question: What does the anecdote of "the state of nature" represent? It is easy to forget as we read Rousseau, even in the *Discours sur . . . l'inégalité*, but surely in *Émile* and *Du Contract social*, that just as things are constantly becoming—sometimes for good, sometimes for ill—*dénaturé*, they are constantly being naturalized as well. It is not just that yesterday's actions turn into the habits of tomorrow. Every thing slips gradually into the indistinguishable sediment of the world. Every day what was fresh before becomes invisible, its origins forgotten. Measured now, some "thing" is *avant*/before *altération*, as if prior in time, without mediation, simple in substance, pure and impulsive. "If only you knew . . ." one will say—but we don't.

Why this drift toward stasis, immobility, obscurity? It is precisely because human beings are active but not omnipotent. To do, right now, is to accommodate present conditions, not to change them. It is to operate within the fabric of

---

* ". . . pourquoi nos besoins et nos plaisirs changent d'objets à la longue; . . ."
† ". . . pourquoi l'homme originel s'évanouissant par degrés, la Société n'offre plus aux yeux du sage qu'un assemblage d'hommes artificiels et de passions factices qui sont l'ouvrage de toutes ces nouvelles rélations, et n'ont aucun vrai fondement dans la Nature."

dependence. This means that however long it has taken to arrive *hic et nunc*—an hour or a millennium or the age of the earth—the *avant*/before *altération* of *nature*, its necessity, is just whatever stands before us, making or breaking, making and breaking, the act.

If *nature* is *avant*/before *altération*, in the dialectic of social evolution each *altération* becomes, sooner or later, a "before." I doubt there are narrow predictive rules for this process and I can only conceive of it in circular terms: as long as "before-ness" can maintain itself, elude *altération*, it is within its own frame "necessary;" when "before-ness" succumbs to *altération*, it loses, insofar as it is altered, it quality as natural. This implication in human action is what makes *nature* a moral fact.

Rousseau's allusive conception of social evolution suggests the error of his contemporaries and ours who suppose they can dominate *nature*, escape from it, or to it, or in any other way treat it as an object that stands apart from the human subject. Whether we "cultivate" or "deprave" it,[196] we never "leave" *nature* but only inflect it from within, weaving ourselves back into it, and thus changing our place within it. Even this little bit is an evolution.

In the dialectic of *avant*/before *altération* that constitutes the necessity of *nature*, the trick, so to speak, is to discover, understand, and perhaps even pick, the sort of necessity to which one will give oneself. The "choice" involved in "necessity" is possible because not everything is relevant at once, because one can make mistakes and be unhappy or not, and because things are naturalized and denaturalized all the time.[197]

This possibility of intervention—we should call it more accurately "participation"—in *nature* fills out something of Rousseau's antiphilosophical posture and performance. On its face, his suggestion that *nature* be the paradigm for law and for politics seems absurd for precisely the reason it is offered as such: it seems like a demand for certainty, for a guarantee. What we glimpsed earlier, however, is now confirmed: the real issue for politics is not the *certain* but the *probable*;[198] what politics should emulate is not the philosopher's vision of an inherent necessity in *nature*, but the fact that it is, with respect to circumstances, relatively, or relativistically, inflexible.

Rousseau partly realized and often obscured his own conception of *société* as an evolving totality. It is not anachronistic to say this. We see him struggling, juggling. This part of his project is interrupted when he identifies *les choses* and *la nature*. He fails—willfully, one might say—to be consistent with what the evolutionary view entails for the definition of *nature* because it would upset completely his use of that word for various other rhetorical purposes. He is totally convinced that his social theory of politics needs theology, just as, he thinks, the Republic needs religion.

In spite of these many complications, we may say in complete accord with Rousseau that society is the realization of *nature*. What should astonish us is that he finds new meaning for what appears to be an old Aristotelian trope. One day,

> the true moment of nature finally arrives, as it must. Since Man must die, he must reproduce himself, so that the species endures and the order of the world is preserved . . . at that instant cease forever your old tone. Still your disciple, but no longer your student, there stands your friend, there stands a man, treat him henceforth as such. (OC IV.639)*

This is unmistakably a depiction of puberty. But, within the web of metaphors we have attempted to reconstruct in the preceding pages, where child and adult, individual and society, are continually transposed, a larger image emerges. Should it someday arrive, as, we hope, it must, the moment when *nature* truly reveals itself would be the realization of Man, of humanity. This is not just for Man, but for *nature* as well. Without specifically human regeneration the world itself would fall into ruin. On that day, we will speak differently, just as friends, as equals, as citizens. This is a natural theology of mankind "abandoned to ourselves."

Mankind "abandoned to ourselves" — even that pregnant phrase is theological sleight of hand in the service of sociology. "*Mortels*," writes Jean-Jacques, "you are not abandoned, nature lives still." Yet, it is not the Divine voice that speaks this way. It is the first violet in the spring woods. There is consolation. It just isn't God; it's nature. And it is just this same voice that speaks every time we meet one of our own kind.

---

* "Le vrai moment de la nature arrive enfin, il faut qu'il arrive. Puisqu'il faut que l'homme meure, il faut qu'il se reproduise, afin que l'espéce dure et que l'ordre du monde soit conservé . . . . à l'instant quittez avec lui pour jamais vôtre ancien ton. C'est vôtre disciple encore, mais ce n'est plus vôtre élève. C'est vôtre ami, c'est un homme, traitez-le désormais comme tel." Is this the source for "O Freunde, nicht diese Töne!"?

§46

A PROVISIONAL CONCLUSION IN
TERMS OF CIVIC HAPPINESS

What drives the interaction between Man and Nature? The emphasis given just above to circumstance and chance should not allow us to lose sight of the most powerful motor of social evolution. What keeps the pressure on are *besoins*. Here, as before, *besoins* will be construed broadly to include many senses of the word "needs."[199]

Besoins do not stand alone. They are woven into each person's relationships with the surrounding world. These two primary facts—need and relationship—cross paths.

Dépendance is this convergence. *Dépendance* points directly to the strongest pressure all human beings feel to go outside themselves. Although *dépendance* is usually experienced in specifiable ways, it is not the sort of *lien* that can be represented by a diagram for the simple reason that it is a living dynamic connection. That is why—even while appealing to many significations of the word—Rousseau develops his account of the social totality around the key term of *dépendance*. It is consistent with his thinking to distinguish *besoins* as moments in the process of *dépendance*.

It is a constitutive feature of *besoins* that they will not go unheeded, nor be ignored for long. *Besoins* evoke a vast variety of responses. Whether or not these responses are carried out, the fact that they are necessarily evoked by *besoins* brings into being and gives shape to a variety of *forces*. I use the word "evoke" because even though the *forces* called out may in some respects conform to particular *besoins*, the latter are not the whole origin of the former, and a map of the one will not guide us through the terrain of the other. Precisely because there are many modalities of *forces*, Rousseau develops a fairly substantial lexicon to show their different sources and composition (see §20 above).

I want to ignore this variety for the moment in order to reiterate a general point. As understood within the framework of human needs and actions, what all *forces* have in common is the deployment of human energies. This is true even when nonhuman energies are triggered, channeled, or leveraged in the process. Earlier, I used the ancient Greek word δυνάμεις to underscore this common denominator in the diversity of *forces*. My point is that what needs call for are δυνάμεις, and in this sense *besoins* always imply *forces*.[200] By contrast, one can imagine surplus *forces* that are not consumed by needs but which find other outlets or expire.

The evocation of *forces* by *besoins* has an impact on *besoins*. Over time, both are transformed. We saw something of this in the preceding section. I add now that this transformation is often, but not always, a multiplication. Moreover, there is no reason to expect that the multiplication of *besoins* and *forces* will occur evenly. In fact, it rarely does. This is important insofar as we consider this call-and-response process between *besoins* and *forces* as something that propels the ongoing interaction between Man and Nature. From this perspective, it is irrelevant whether *besoins* and *forces* develop and produce effects in equal proportion. This is true even though they typically operate in relation to one another.

Let me now make the obvious explicit: *besoins* and *forces* were the terms of the "formula for happiness" discussed at length in the first part of this book. There, we traced several steps. Rousseau first delimited a social totality by answering the "theodicy question" in way that, at least for establishing a theoretical groundwork, "bracketed out" theological issues. He then embarked upon an analysis of social relationships in two tightly overlapping ways. One was through the category of *dépendance*. This brought to the foreground the issue of what instigates *dépendance* and how to measure its effects. On this ground the category of *bonheur*, or happiness, opened a second way for analyzing social relationships. Crucial variables in both instances are the same: *besoins* and *forces*.

The point I want to make now is that the issue of whether one's *forces* are greater than, or at least equal to, one's *besoins*—that is, whatever one concludes in this or that case from the "formula for happiness," or {*forces* ≥ *besoins* = *bonheur*}—is largely independent of how things go in the evolution of society.

This repeats what I said at the end of the last section. We may add now that even when assessment of one's happiness, as an individual or as a group, motivates efforts to change one's actions or leads to interventions in ongoing developments, such reflection or judgment concerning happiness will not stop or restart the evolutionary process. Do not construe this to mean that individual action does not make a difference: as an issue, that, too, is separate, and, as a conclusion, would be absurd.

We also considered at some length who is capable of happiness. As usual Émile provides an example. Rousseau says clearly that at a certain point in the development of his character—when "memory extends the sentiment of identity over all the moments of his existence"—he is "capable of happiness and misery." This assertion ties into a complex system of metaphor and metonymy that I shall not repeat here. We need only recall for the moment that this applies to society as well as to the individual. As Rousseau insists, "it is important therefore to begin to consider" the one and the other "as a moral being" (OC IV.301).

The *être moral* is not born. "It" emerges well into the course of social evolution. "It" is beyond *nature*, yet, at the same time, natural. This means that the question of happiness, which applies only to the *être moral*, hinges not just on *nature*, and not just on *société*, but on the dialectic of the two. In other words, the "formula for happiness" seems somehow to be implicated in the processes which are, as I argued above, at the core of Rousseau's social theory of politics. Is it therefore worth asking again if the "formula for happiness" bears on the resolution of "all the contradictions of the social system"? And if it does, how so?

Much of what I have written in this chapter raises a difficulty of a somewhat different sort. From what perspective should these questions be answered? On the one hand, I have shown that Rousseau is deeply attached to the claim that *nature* is mutable. Many of his most perspicuous insights into social and political life stem from this commitment. However, this powerful evolutionary perspective cannot be taken for granted, in part because it is not his only deep theoretical commitment and in part because this key feature of his thinking has often been ignored by those who presumed, in the following centuries, to shape social theory in his image. Indeed, it must be admitted that my attempt to piece together the puzzle of Rousseau's view of the mutability of *nature* is to some extent speculative, and the sketch I offered in §45 is certainly incomplete. The real obstacle, however, is the story told in §§43–44 above. No matter how intriguing and fruitful the evolutionary themes Rousseau pursued, he also, avidly, with striking language and effect, sought immutability in *nature*. This other region of his thought is equally important if we are to understand what he intended to say, to sort out what it means, and to discover what follows from his analysis of society.

These two conceptions of *nature* seem clearly distinguishable. In fact they are not. The border is permeable and Rousseau, unwittingly or with wit, often slides across it. We can see this from the side of "immutability." On its own terms, his theory is richer in implications if we take *inflexibilité* rather than strict *nécessité* as the primary quality of *nature*. Whereas *nécessité* points to *nature* as if it exists "in itself," the quality of *inflexibilité* urges us to conceive of *nature* in terms of its relation to someone or something that tries, so to speak, to "flex" it. Thinking this second way helps to clarify and advance the consequences that are supposed to flow from Rousseau's bold claims. At the same time, it represents a retreat from some of his punctuating and memorable statements on the very same topic.

Likewise for Rousseau's other conception of *nature*. As we saw in §45, the word "mutable" offers only a partial description. It is clear that ongoing inter-actions of Man and Nature transform both to such an extent that one cannot, once and for all, say which is which. This can be considered statically as hybridity (i.e., a "mix" of two elements, "Man" and "Nature"), or dynamically as a single fact. The latter is what we have referred to as "social evolution." The dynamic process will, however, here and there be experienced as static. That is, at any given point, key aspects of this mutation remain impervious to particular or collective interventions.[201] This is the case even though these aspects are constituted from human actions and energies. This imperviousness—a kind of *inflexibilité* and overlap with Rousseau's other view of *nature*—is manifest in bodily habits ("*se-conde nature*"), material objects (*les choses* that Rousseau claims are *de la na-ture*), language (as Saussurean *langue* or Vician *sensus communis*), and so on.[202] All together, and in the ongoing process of social evolution, we may refer to emergences of this "imperviousness" or *inflexibilité* as the instance of naturaliza-tion. I mean by "naturalization" either that the word *nature*—pointing to the sort of qualities discussed above—comes to be an apt name or description, or that the instance of imperviousness loses its name altogether, and falls into silence or in-visibility.[203] This process is, so to speak, the obverse side of what Rousseau means when he says that things can be *dénaturé*.[204] The point is that at any given mo-ment within an evolutionary process some important things are immutable; not only do they not change, but they cannot be changed then and there.

The deep complexity of the two views of *nature* (§§44 and 45) appears here: only if *nature* itself is understood as mutable, which is to say in evolutionary terms, can these temporarily immutable "things" be said to be "natural"; if *na-ture* itself is immutable, such "things" must be of a categorically different sort. In other words, the basic question concerning the identity or difference of "nature" and "things" hangs on which way one understands *nature* itself.

We have seen that Rousseau's approach to society takes an evolutionary turn. In the final Part of this book we will emphasize exactly the opposite. That is, we will shift focus to again consider those theoretical commitments that seem in-compatible with his theory of social evolution. The most obvious example is the conception of *nature* as immutable. This example continues to be important be-cause, as we have seen, it is the basis on which he proposes to solve the problems that emerge in the evolution of society. The *rapprochements* I have just sketched between these two perspectives already suggest that there will be many difficul-ties in pursuing a social theory of politics in this way.

Moreover, by placing the conception of *nature* as immutable at the center of our inquiry we may reenter the problem of *dépendance* and finally conclude our assessment of how it fits into the social theory of politics. The route we will follow has already been suggested. The conception of *nature* as immutable emerges from and is sustained by Rousseau's theistic convictions. It is figured through an image of the Will. Rousseau believes that he can "resolve" the contradictions of society by transferring qualities from God to Man through the *topos* of the Will. This sequence of ideas will be unfolded with greater precision in the next part of this book. It will then be possible to measure this way of thinking about Man and Nature against Rousseau's own evolutionary conception of society and his analysis of social dynamics in terms of dependence. I will argue that, in this light, the double application of the doctrine of the Will—an elaborate sort of "creationism"—appears to be profoundly contradictory and theoretically sterile. It has misled our thinking about society and the political relationships that emerge from it.

As we move back to consider again Rousseau's program from the perspective of natural "immutability," the questions raised earlier in this section can now be entertained. Does the "formula for happiness" continue to be important in Rousseau's overall theoretical program?

Now, recall that Rousseau's strongest representation of the immutability of *nature* was made in terms of "natural law." He proposed that we should try to make dependence-from-persons into dependence-from-things by modeling human law on "natural law." Can an *être moral* faced with such dependence be happy?

It seems obvious that *no* amount or kind of human *forces* are sufficient to satisfy a need that runs counter to the total *inflexibilité* of a "natural law." If *bonheur*, the "*usage de liberté*," is having an equilibrium[205] between one's forces and one's desires, then simply to be dependent-from-things—however "things" are understood, as "natural," as legal simulacra, as the fabricated environment, etc.—should not be sufficient for happiness. Force and weakness may be relative (e.g., OC IV.305), but one's force will always be wanting in the face of Nature, natural laws, or naturelike human laws.

This leads to something of a contradiction between Rousseau's paradigm for the republic and the "formula for happiness." What if our needs require us to go against such laws? There is a greater chance of success, which is to say a chance of moving the balance between *forces* and *besoins* in favor of *bonheur*, when we confront human, as opposed to natural, laws. If a falling person needs to fly, there is not much hope; the condemned may at least appeal his sentence. At least, more possibilities remain open. So, as long as the two sorts of laws are different, the "formula for happiness" could lead us to believe that human law is preferable to "natural law." Rousseau, of course, recommends exactly the opposite. Yet, the closer we come to conforming human to "natural law," the less *bonheur* seems possible.

I do not think that Rousseau believes *bonheur*—individual or, in some sense, collective happiness—is or should be absent from the society he envisions. Yet the "formula for happiness" seems relevant only in certain situations. Or, at best, if it is to be used to assess civil happiness, other factors must be taken into account. The equilibrium between *forces* and *besoins* is not enough.

While it is not my task here to find a comprehensive maxim for civil happiness, this impasse is instructive. The obstacle appeared when Rousseau called for human laws to be modeled on "natural laws." The justification for this proposal was a presumed difference between dependence-from-things and dependence-from-persons. This formulation has two dimensions. The first, *dépendance* in general, directs us into Rousseau's analysis of the composition of the *le lien social*, an illuminating account of dynamic social relationships, and the evolutionary transformation of the social totality. The second underlays the distinction between persons and things. At the conjunction of these two dimensions we might find, if not the answer, then at least an approach to answering the question, Can human beings be happy in society? For, what is at issue here is the structure of the moral world. This should provide criteria, beyond the initial formula, for the achievement of *bonheur*.

The first of these two dimensions is governed by an evolutionary logic. The second is grounded in theistic commitments. They conflict in important respects. Thus, despite the way *dépendance* is used to analyze mankind "abandoned to ourselves," the distinction between two sorts of *dépendance* becomes a point of access through which theology passes into sociology. A potential for contradiction is thus diffused into many specific points in the theory.

One major contradiction has surfaced often in this book. It occurs precisely where the distinction between the two sorts of *dépendance* breaks down because *les choses* and *la nature* are not identical. I have proposed to refer to this intermediate space as nonnatural dependence-from-things. This category is clearly implicit in the arguments made by Rousseau, for example when he refers to the "three educations" (cf. §39 above) or has recourse to perfectly inflexible human laws. We have also seen that for the most part he pays little attention to this third essential sort of *dépendance*.

This is a big and influential mistake. Nonnatural dependence-from-things is the category on which Rousseau's edifice comes to rest. It is of high importance for a social theory of politics of just the sort he otherwise advances. This is why we now turn to show that nonnatural dependence-from-things is as fundamental as the dependence-from-persons underscored by Rousseau.

Part IV

MORALITY IN THE ORDER OF THE WILL

A. *Ordre* Comes to the Foreground

§47

WHY CAN'T WE BE HAPPY?

Rousseau tells us that to be happy, one's *forces* must be at least equal to one's *besoins. Besoins,* or needs, are forms of relationship that are constantly reconstituted as the individual and society evolve. The structure of each and every *besoin* is *dépendance,* of which there are two kinds, from-things and from-persons. In either case, one's *forces* may be sufficient; but faced with dependence-from-persons the quantity of *forces* required for happiness is likely to be incompatible with liberty or with virtue. And, in this dynamic scene, needs always involve expectations; there is always a looking-ahead, not just reaction and response. Amplified by uncertainty, even anxiety becomes a *besoin,* an open-ended form of relationship projected in time that pulls this way or that. That is why, in the ongoing life of a person or a society, *ordre* is as necessary as *forces* for happiness, for *bonheur.*[1]

This summary brings us all the way back around to *dépendance,* where *ordre* is decisive. In the coming sections we will see that the difference between the two sorts of dependence comes down to a difference in the order that characterizes the object from which one is dependent. Things are ordered; persons are not ordered. In this way *ordre* presents itself as the major criterion for assessing the problem of *bonheur.* Indeed, the "formula for happiness" turns out to be just one version of the more general problem of *ordre.*

Why exactly does *ordre* matter so much? A consideration of Rousseau's answer to this question will occupy most of this final part. Here it is in brief. Insofar as one is dependent-from-things one can be happy because one will not have false, mistaken, or unsatisfiable expectations. The perfect rigidity presented to us by things controls the formation of our needs before the "formula for happiness" comes to be applied. By contrast, when we are dependent from other people we will almost always be unhappy. This is because human beings are not perfectly rigid and there is no way to rest assured that today's expectation will not be tomorrow's disappointment. Exactly that indeterminacy, restlessness, and spontaneity which makes others *persons* and not *things*, together with the correspondent fact of human *plurality*,[2] is what also ensures that our experience of other people will constantly generate new needs *in us*, needs that may be satisfied only with great difficulty if at all.

Since happiness is determined in largest part by what happens on the *besoins* side of the formula, these qualitatively new needs (in us) will often tip the scales away from our happiness. In other words, it is one thing to count up the amount of *forces* one has and set them off against needs. But this does not take into account at all the application or misapplication of those *forces*. "It's the abuse of our faculties that makes us unhappy" (OC IV.587). Misapplication in any given moment is possible, and itself becomes manifest as a new need, a new problem to be solved, and one that is often especially difficult to recognize as such. This will not only happen to congenital misappliers of their own *forces* because, just as needs stretch out over time, so does the application of *forces*. Thus, you may begin in the right place with skill and good will only to have the ground shift from under you.

Now remember that the structure of each and every need is dependence. Recall, too, that according to Rousseau the moral, and therefore political, relevance of *dépendance* is demarcated by the distinction between persons and things ("main passage," initially discussed at §12 above). The foundation of this distinction is *ordre*.

What we observed from the beginning and the point I underscore again now is that a whole tradition of social and political theory follows Rousseau in seeing things this way. Common sense with this same content has solidified in the two centuries after him. This concerns a way of perceiving and imagining society that is deeply ingrained in our thinking about politics.

Upon the convergence of many complex issues in this book, the largest question I ask is rather simple: should we continue to accept Rousseau's or a Rousseauean sociology that excludes things from the moral fabric? Should we continue to acquiesce as our theory and practice of politics is shaped by a sociology of this sort?

Believing the stakes here to be high, I have set out to identify Rousseau's claim, to articulate it in a manner resonant with common current beliefs, to elaborate in a general way certain implications of those beliefs, and consequently to propose that we turn another way, that we stretch our understanding of society as a fabric of interdependence toward something more adequate to the specific facts and difficulties of civic existence.

Throughout this book I have invited you to rethink with me many key topics of social theory. Rousseau is the vehicle for this undertaking. Why? In part because he is copious and lucid and profound, in part because he is to a great extent the original of what in us needs to be rethought.

In the process of examining Rousseau's engagement with *société* I bring to light many internal inconsistencies and contradictions. Do not suppose for a moment that this familiar logical operation is my main mode or purpose. Contradiction must not be the first, or even the final, ground for rejecting, as I propose we should, a major feature of the view of society Rousseau advances. To the contrary, we have already seen that his complex and internally tense positions can be extraordinarily productive (explicit at §21 above *et passim*). This is something worth holding on to.

Of course, inconsistency can be a most annoying problem. Yet—and this is the point—sometimes denial or rejection of contradiction heightens its negative consequences. Sometimes the more important question is how to live with contradiction rather than how to make it go away. This is, as I stressed earlier (§31 above), the spirit in which Rousseau proposes to "*résoudre* all the contradictions of the social system."

Thus, what matters is not the sheer fact of contradiction but rather its significance and effect. A philosopher may pretend that that significance is self-evident. A citizen may not. In politics we must seek to understand how the significance of a contradiction derives from the additional or larger frames within which it occurs.

It is with reference to such frames that this book is an attempt to take measure and stock of Rousseau's categorical invention and the worldview it sustains. In other words, the social theory of politics must *both* respect canons of thinking and respond to practical reason and the pragmatic commitments of life.

So why can't we be happy? Whatever our *forces*, whatever our *besoins*, happiness is a function of ordered practice. The order of practice implicates *forces* and *besoins*, but that order also stands apart. It arises within the frameworks of human beliefs. That is why so much of the discursive setting of Rousseau's words has been spelled out in this book: this variety of beliefs is important not only for him, but for us.

Let me add at this point, then, the foremost belief framing our civic happiness. We are "dreamers of democracy." Whether or not Rousseau was one too is not essential.

But make no mistake. This mighty aspiration becomes a fool's errand if we allow the science of ourselves to be colored by it in any simple or direct way. Dreaming and the interpretation of dreams had better not be the same thing.

We, readers and citizens, are engaged, as Rousseau would have expected, in an argument about society with political implications dressed as an analysis of concepts. Now we call, just as Rousseau did, on the term *ordre* to bridge these various interests. And in this final part we will see, first *with* and then *against* Rousseau, how the social theory of politics hinges on it.

What we undertake here is not just a description of words thrust forward by an eighteenth-century writer. The task is to lay groundwork for a special kind of choice. And there again is that pesky question: should we extend, or should we turn away from, Rousseau's account of *le lien social*, framed as it is by a categorical distinction between two types of dependence? This view, coterminous with much contemporary common sense, is full of implications for our practice and belief, for how we situate human relationships in the world, and what we make of them through politics.

§48

DIGRESSION ON THE "CONTEXT"
OF ROUSSEAU'S WORDS

Since I have been in New York it has been easier for me to understand the mentality of that rich American who had bought a Gothic window so as to have the privilege of looking from his house in Paris at Notre Dame through a setting of the Thirteenth century. Only someone accustomed to living in a city of skyscrapers could develop such a perverse sense of windows.

— *Nicolas Calas*, Confound the Wise (1942, 260–61)

The terrain we are about to enter overlaps some of the main and most widely diffused theological and philosophical debates of the eighteenth century. Before crossing the threshold, some further comments are warranted concerning an aspect of the approach that I take in this book.

Throughout this book I have made many digressions to contextualize our engagement with Rousseau. These forays offer ways to imagine his texts as patterns woven within the larger fabric of eighteenth-century ideas and beliefs. One could pursue this strategy much more rigorously than I have; one could make it the main purpose of this or, indeed, several books. That would not however suit my purposes and I have declined to take this approach.

One reason for this choice is simple. To fully identify and reconstruct the relevant "background," if that is what it is, would be a monumental task. This would be especially difficult with respect to a writer like Rousseau who, as we have seen, operated upon a great diversity and range of interests. Since no one can do everything my choice has been to balance among a strategic reconstruction of period concepts, an untangling of the extraordinarily intricate literary artifacts produced by Rousseau, and the living concerns that constitute social and political theory.

Within that balance, when faced with elements of context that are unwieldy but nonetheless essential implements for grasping the argument, I have augmented my own research with a kind of virtual collaboration. A major instance of this has been my reliance on Jean Ehrard's (1994) extraordinary *thèse d'état* from 1963, *The Idea of Nature in France in the First Half of the Eighteenth Century*. My inquiry into the topic of *nature* in §§41–46 would have been much poorer without this compendious and insightful resource. Also illustrated in my use of Ehrard is one fruitful way for political theory to build on the work of historians without simply becoming the history of political thought. While the theorist must take responsibility for his or her own research, attunement with fine scholarship in the disciplines is a necessary complement and can provide important buffers against contextual ignorance or historical absurdity without sidetracking the main task.[3]

The lines of such collaboration are not easy to draw. It seems that one could bring many things to bear. For example, one might ask why I do not make more use of recent attempts to redescribe "Enlightenment," such as the impressive project of Jonathan Israel (2002, 2006a, 2011) or the massive collaboration led by Kors (2003).[4] In this instance my reason can be expressed by pointing to a significant difference between works like these and works like Ehrard's. Whereas the latter helped us to follow a single term that flowed repeatedly from every eighteenth-century pen, studies of "Enlightenment" are organized around a middle-level interpretive frame, one that was introduced retrospectively. "Enlightenment" is itself composed by and the object of a wide range of conflicting claims and interests. From at latest the 1750s it has not been clear where Rousseau fits or does not fit within this complex scene. I could give reasons like this for hundreds of exclusions, but it is not directly relevant in this book to decide this or comparable questions, or even to get caught up in them.

Still, one might ask for greater contextualization within the narrower frame provided by the topics at the core of my argument, such as *dépendance*, *ordre*, and especially *société*. While here the arguments favoring this kind of contextualizing work are stronger, the simple fact is that I have not found studies comparable to Ehrard's work on *nature*. Indeed, the lack of such research has been lamented elsewhere (cf. §35 above). A few excellent books like Robert Mauzi's (1960) study of *bonheur* have been useful in passing but are not generally pertinent. Other far-reaching efforts— like Taylor (1989) or Seigel (2005)—barely touch on my topics here.

To these considerations I want to add something of particular interest to professional political theorists: my theoretical reasons for avoiding a thoroughly "contextualist" approach. By "contextualist" I mean the models and methodological assertions deriving from research programs associated with Quentin Skinner (e.g., 1978 and 2002), J. G. A. Pocock (e.g., 1957, 1972, 1975), and, in a somewhat different way, Reinhart Koselleck (e.g., Brunner et al. 1972).

Let me be clear on this point. I know full well that the extensive debates around "contextualism" are in some sense relevant to what I have undertaken in this book. The same is true for the complementary criticisms of so-called "conceptual analysis" or other "internalist" approaches to the study of texts. These and similar methodological questions could bear heavily on the kind of intellectual or imaginary experience I intend to create for the reader. However, even with all this in mind, I remain convinced that a proper discussion of these matters would lead too far afield. Therefore, I will limit myself to two brief comments meant to indicate my position.

Contextualism offers itself as a capacious frame of acceptance. Anyone attracted by the vitality of ideas is likely to find the pull of context inexorable. A specific interest in politics amplifies that pull. The first point I want to make here is that this attraction is itself paradoxical. The difficulty in this instance is not the desire to draw close to some synthetic core concept or to the structure of an idea,[5] but to draw close to the context in which words were written. This desire necessarily pulls us as inquirers, as living subjects, away from ourselves. That is, the contextualist *per se* must to some extent lose sight of, and cast off intellectual and emotional attachment to, the motivating source of his or her interest. Insofar as signs, symbols, gestures—that is, what we call "ideas"—follow the logic of "context" they slip the bonds of the present. Anything perfectly contextualized would fade off over the horizons of time and motive, and thus a project to increase comprehensibility would make comprehension impossible, and the attempt to bring a past "concept" back to life would kill it.

The full effects of this paradox are rarely felt because perfect "contextualism" is, obviously, illusory. Purportedly authentic return to a past passed is always and always must be a simulation and nothing more. It is, in other words, the opposite of what it seeks. The oddity here is that this simulation implies not just self-denial but a denial that the self exists in history, an abdication of history itself.

The paradox of contextualism is just one feature of the motive to pursue context and of the highly developed pursuit of it. There is a more general and complex problem in, so to speak, the context of contextualism itself. I can only allude to this here in the most simplistic terms.

"Contextualism" in political theory is just one instance of a very widespread and accelerating obsession with "context." This need to fill in all gaps in experience has appeared in many other modes of research (e.g., anthropology, ethnography, social history) but also, and I think more strikingly and with greater consequence, in other domains of cultural production (e.g., museums, theme parks, textbooks). Over the course of the twentieth century, many different uses of thinking, writing, teaching, displaying, and so on have become more and more inflected by an explicit articulation of "context."

I am not referring here to the impulse to total control that is characteristic of "virtual reality" and descendant from the aspiration to *Gesamtkunstwerk*, or "total work of art." That enterprise is also quite important, but its poetic thrust has been to displace context, not to represent it.

An apt exemplar for generalized "contextualism" is rather the museum docent, that informed and companionable instructor. Visitors to nineteenth-century galleries largely carried within themselves the knowledge and practical aptitude necessary to engage its works of art, or at least to teach themselves how to do so. The visit to a gallery was an integrated part of an education; personal cultural formation, what the Germans call *Bildung*, was presupposed. Processes in the later nineteenth century typically (although misleadingly) referred to as the democratization of civil society and of its cultural institutions created not only new demand for a wide range of symbolically mediated experience but also new expectations about who could have such experience and what use they could make of it. Around the turn of the century some progressive reformers undertook to respond to this demand and to fulfill these expectations by enhancing the educational function of the museum through the person of the docent.[6] In effect, this was an attempt to externalize and thus make *Bildung* more easily and spontaneously transmissible. From the early twentieth century forward a fairly direct line may be drawn from this human docent to the so-called "self-guided" tour of today; I say "so-called" because the "self" does little more than physically carry an electronic headset, while the "guiding" is in fact done by the vast team of experts that created a script representing along several dimensions the "context" of, say, the *Mona Lisa* or Mickey Mouse.

The docent mentality—that is, the increasing desire for context and the practical satisfaction of that desire—comes in the course of the twentieth century to apply not just to works of art but to commodities more generally. A bag of rice in 1900 would have been labeled "rice," if that; a bag of rice today is inscribed with several varieties of cooking instructions and recipes, and it may even inform you of its hazards and provenance. And while no screwdriver ever came with an instruction sheet, no computer ever came without one.

The purpose of this digression has been to underscore within the general cultural phenomenon of "contextualism" a common element—the sophistication of artifacts relative to the humans who use them—and an unstated point of agreement—the presumptive need to complete experience by making context explicit. Against this background I assert without further argument that "contextualism" as a mode in intellectual disciplines like political theory, in the university-based production and reproduction of knowledge, cannot be unrelated to these much broader trends.

Let us now again move closer to Rousseau and the social theory of politics. My *avoidance of too much "context"* is still the topic. To bring this section to an end I want to add that my varied and partial appeal to "context" also derives from the kind of thinking this book aims to advance. This may be seen in some of the observations from which it begins: that contemporary sociological sensibility is oriented in a way that sets limits on possibilities for conceiving the prospects and problems of politics; that for several centuries this orientation has pervaded common sense not just in regions around the North Atlantic but across the globe; that this way of seeing the social world was mapped out in an extraordinarily influential and representative manner by Jean-Jacques Rousseau. You will have already understood that I take these observations as premises from which to rethink aspects of social and political theory, and that it is my intention to facilitate assessment of our own orientations *indirectly* through an engagement with Rousseau's. Although, of course, I make extensive use of contextual information in trying to understand what Rousseau wrote, I see no reason to disguise my broader approach behind the pretense of "contextualism." To the contrary, there is every reason to open this balanced approach to critical inspection.

Insofar as this book is at once about *them* and about *us*, it maps a classic problematic of the "human sciences," or *Geisteswissenschaften*, more or less as spelled out by Giambattista Vico, Wilhelm Dilthey, Hans-Georg Gadamer, and others. Simply, *we*—which means literally *I* as the author and *you* as its reader—do not escape the object studied in this book. *Abandoned to Ourselves* is not about Rousseau; it is about us reading Rousseau, which is to say about a specifiable and living relationship (which, by the way, entails dependence-from-things). This fact adds complexity to a problem I have already mentioned: how should we determine which or how much reconstructed "context" is appropriate to this enterprise? For, once we engage the hermeneutic relationship between subject and object, even the aspiration to completeness is undermined every time a new reader picks up the book.

In this sense the "context" of the arguments considered in this book is our thinking, today, about basic questions of society and politics. To admit this fact does not require us to be overwhelmed by it. Indeed, any kind of crude "presentism" is also self-defeating. The crucial fact that readers live and think in their own world cannot be license to ignore the past and its other worlds, or the continuities and ruptures that join or sunder them all. Just as history is an essential characteristic of all present action and an essential characteristic of all present meaning, it is also a vortex into which action and meaning disappear.

For these reasons, one could loosely call my position a variety of "historicism" that self-consciously takes every present moment as part of history.[7] That is why in this book I neither ignore entirely the "world of ideas" of the eighteenth century nor do I stick assiduously to it.

§49

THE ARCHITECTONICS OF METAPHOR

In what follows we will be in the odd position of setting aside theology to consider Rousseau's theism. Another perspective is required. What matters here is how this theism operates as a formative element in the structure of Rousseau's social theory of politics. Moving this way, I mean to awaken a point I will emphasize shortly: theology and natural philosophy are sources of belief for Rousseau or they are propositions for him, but they are also much more than that. Separately, but especially in what they share, these two discourses provide Rousseau with elementary structures which, through a series of metaphorical transpositions, shape the way he articulates a problem, the way he shifts the problem from one level of inquiry to another, and the way he conceives of its solution.

The starting point is a theological position that is only partly explicit; the end is, he claims, the resolution of all the "contradictions of the social system" through politics.[8]

This process of theorizing is motivated by a tension that has surfaced several times in the course of this book. One thing that makes Rousseau's *Émile* startling is that, for every profuse profession of faith and religious sentiment, another step toward the absolute divorce of the problem of evil from the concerns of God is taken. Remember how emphatic Rousseau is—"Mankind! Stop your search for the author of evil, that author is you" (OC IV.588).

This—which is Rousseau's answer to the theodicy question—plays in another key exactly the separation of God and *nature* that appears in the pressuring but not yet entirely successful discursive distinction between theology and natural philosophy in eighteenth-century Europe. I shall now sketch this modulation and suggest what Rousseau hopes to accomplish thereby.

The procedure followed in this section is unlike anything else in this book. I reduce an extremely complex set of arguments to schema; to do otherwise would lead very far afield. Indeed, the following representations are not meant to encompass or explain all the debates and positions common in the eighteenth century and which flow into Rousseau's thinking. Nor are they, strictly speaking, meant to outline all of what Rousseau has to say on these questions.

Taken as whole Rousseau's writings contradict one another with some regularity. This bears repeating not as an excuse but because it is, in a sense, the passage to the main point of this book. As a logical fact, it would be misleading both to ignore these contradictions and to insist too much on them. But as a mechanism for theorizing, the variety of positions he holds should be understood as a response to the variety of problems he confronts. Viewed this way, it is clear that incompatibilities are not impossibilities, but may—and I do mean *may* here, not *must*—be adjustments to circumstance in the spirit of theoretical pragmatism mentioned in §47 above. What the contradictions do show is that certain solutions are not carried over from one problem to another, while others are. The question becomes, Why does he adjust in this, and not another, way? or, Why does he lever the reader to adjust in this, and not another, way?

My aim in this section is to speculate about the procedure Rousseau follows in organizing the large frameworks of his social theory of politics. To do so we must consider how Rousseau conceives the problems he sets for himself and how the formation of problems shapes his solutions to them. I shall now spell these out in terms of abstract relationships represented schematically in a series of diagrams and explanatory notes.

1. The primary categories at this point are Grace, Nature, and Mankind. Of the six distinct relationships among them, we will be directly concerned with four: the relationship between Nature and Grace, between Mankind and Grace, between Mankind and Nature, and between Mankind and Mankind. I shall refer to these by name and shorthand as follows: the Fundamental Question ($Q^{fundamental}$), the Theodicy Question ($Q^{theodicy}$), the Ecological Question ($Q^{ecological}$), and the Political Question ($Q^{political}$). The relation between Nature and itself, or the Evolution Question ($Q^{evolution}$), will be mentioned only in passing; the relation between Grace and itself, or the Metaphysical Question is not relevant here. The following table summarizes these guiding questions as functions of the relationships just mentioned:

	GRACE	NATURE	MANKIND
GRACE	METAPHYSICAL QUESTION	FUNDAMENTAL QUESTION	THEODICY QUESTION
NATURE	FUNDAMENTAL QUESTION	EVOLUTION QUESTION	ECOLOGICAL QUESTION
MANKIND	THEODICY QUESTION	ECOLOGICAL QUESTION	POLITICAL QUESTION

Diagram 1. Primary Relationships

2. Now we can be more precise. Begin with the Fundamental Question ($Q^{fundamental}$): Is Nature inside or outside Grace?

3. There is a corollary to the Fundamental Question ($Q^{fundamental}C$): What principle of motion is inherent and necessary in Nature and in Grace?

4. In $Q^{fundamental}$, the relational term "inside" can mean several things:

a. one part is less important than or encompassed by the other (as in "God created the Garden of Eden and rules over it"), or

b. the two parts are identical (as in Spinoza's "*deus sive natura*"), or

c. the parts are dialectically related such that they could not exist one without the other and form something distinct together.

We leave open which of these senses of the word "inside" applies here.

5. Here is the first answer to ($Q^{\text{fundamental}}$), or ($Q^{\text{fundamental}}A^{\text{nature} \in \text{grace}}$):* Nature is inside Grace, and the moving principle of both is God's Will.

6. The second answer to ($Q^{\text{fundamental}}$), ($Q^{\text{fundamental}}A^{\text{nature} \notin \text{grace}}$): Nature is outside Grace; each has its own moving principle. The principle of Grace is still God's Will, the principle of Nature is exemplified by gravity, but may not be limited to that.[9] See diagram #2.

7. Comment on Rousseau and ($Q^{\text{fundamental}}A^{\text{nature} \in \text{grace}}$): Rousseau is emphatic in rejecting monism and materialism; he is in this respect a dualist;[10] his dualism—which distinguishes in a typical way between matter and motion—is clearly hierarchical, that is, one part is more basic than the other; his primary principle is the one that concerns motion; that primary principle is Will; in other words, Rousseau is not a "naturalist"[11] who believes that motion is inherent in matter (the increasingly important view after Newton); thus, Rousseau holds to ($Q^{\text{fundamental}}A^{\text{nature} \in \text{grace}}$). This in itself does not commit him to any particular version of "natural religion."

8. Comment on Rousseau and ($Q^{\text{fundamental}}A^{\text{nature} \notin \text{grace}}$): Rousseau argues extensively that human nature transforms itself; this transformation does not only occur in *société*, but also before society is formed, which is to say in "nature" (cf. §§41–45); it is sufficient to observe its occurrence through human interaction over time, or what I referred to earlier as "social evolution"; however, we must not ignore that human nature also transforms itself in the living process of satisfying needs, and this is visible in the impact that that process has on fundamental human capacities like reason; for different (if parallel) thematic purposes Rousseau emphasizes social evolution in the *Discours sur . . . l'inégalité*

---

*I use here standard symbols from naive set theory, so that "nature ∈ grace" signifies "nature is inside of grace." The general rule that X is a member of or belongs to A is expressed as $X \in A$, and X is not a member of or does not belong to A is expressed as $X \notin A$; cf. Halmos (1974). $X = A$ expresses identity, as qualified in the text; $X \neq A$ expresses disjunction or exclusivity, again as qualified in the text. This approach will allow us an overview and comparison of alternative hypotheses in response to the questions that structure Rousseau's theory, following this pattern: $Q^{\text{fundamental}} A^{\text{nature} \in \text{grace}}$ registers the claim that "nature is inside grace" specifically as an answer to the "fundamental question."

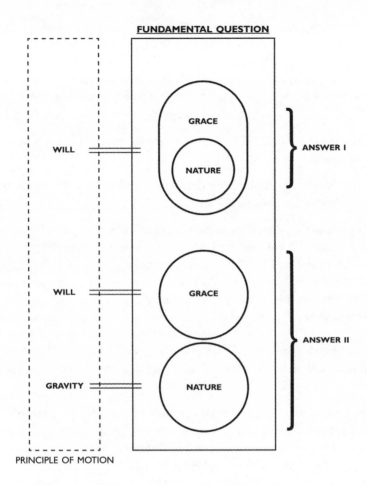

FUNDAMENTAL QUESTION

GRACE

NATURE

WILL

ANSWER I

WILL

GRACE

ANSWER II

GRAVITY

NATURE

PRINCIPLE OF MOTION

Diagram 2. Fundamental Question, Rousseau's Two Answers

and an evolution that reshapes single human beings in *Émile*; more generally, in both books, but especially in *Émile*, social evolution appears (at least *in potentia*) as an instance of or model for a general account of the evolution of Nature, where Nature includes human beings; this whole line of development suggests that Rousseau holds to ($Q^{\text{fundamental}}A^{\text{nature} \notin \text{grace}}$).[12]

9. Initial conclusion concerning $Q^{\text{fundamental}}$: Rousseau sometimes holds ($Q^{\text{fundamental}}A^{\text{nature} \in \text{grace}}$) and other times holds ($Q^{\text{fundamental}}A^{\text{nature} \notin \text{grace}}$).

10. Now we turn to the Theodicy Question (Q^{theodicy}): against the background just described, the Theodicy Question asks "Where does mankind stand in all

this?"—are we "abandoned to ourselves" or not (symbolized below as ~~abandoned~~)? To ask this question is to introduce a third element, mankind, into the equation; while (Q^{theodicy}) thematizes the relation between mankind and God, we already know that Rousseau raises that question in order to count God out of the sociological picture; thus, only after (Q^{theodicy}) is taken as settled will it make sense to ask further about the relation between mankind and Nature.

11. Rousseau's answer to (Q^{theodicy}) will create the need to answer a corollary question, which we might as well introduce now.

12. The Corollary to the Theodicy Question ($Q^{\text{theodicy}}C^{\text{motion}}$): What is the principle of motion for mankind?

13. To speak of a "principle of motion" for mankind may seem odd. Nonetheless, it is entirely consistent with Rousseau's vocabulary and thinking. As we will soon see in detail, the conjunctive term joining the discourses of theology and natural philosophy is *ordre*. On its face, the word *ordre* is a gesture to a condition; however, in practically every instance that the word *ordre* appears in Rousseau's texts, there is lurking just under the surface the invocation of a past or present act. This implicit transformation between *condition* and *act* opens another door to the concept of *volonté*, or Will. Viewed one way (I underscore that there will be other ways), Will is the principle of motion for mankind: ($Q^{\text{theodicy}}C^{\text{motion}}$) = *volonté*.

14. Rousseau capitalizes time and time again on *ordre* as syllepsis between *condition* and *act*. It becomes a structural feature of his social theory of politics even while it continues to be informed by theology and natural philosophy. As Rousseau builds on the concept of *ordre*, because of the slippage between order[as action] and order[as condition], *volonté* is constantly invoked under another name. The alternative name for *volonté* is *ordre*. In this way—and in other ways as well—*volonté* also becomes a structural feature of his social theory.

15. Now we can visit the first answer to the Theodicy Question, or ($Q^{\text{theodicy}}A^{\text{~~abandoned~~}}$): God intervenes constantly in human affairs and character, through Revelation, Election, Destiny, Providence, etc., and the principle of motion is God's Will.

16. The second answer to the Theodicy Question, or ($Q^{\text{theodicy}}A^{\text{abandoned}}$) is the affirmation of what the first answer negated: God has left mankind "abandoned to ourselves," and the principle of motion is something other than God's Will.

17. Comment on Rousseau and ($Q^{\text{theodicy}}A^{\text{~~abandoned~~}}$): While in some respects Rousseau's assertion of *volonté* as his "first principle" seems compatible with ($Q^{\text{theodicy}}A^{\text{~~abandoned~~}}$), practically everything else he wrote speaks against it; having

this in mind, we should note that Rousseau only says that his "first principle" is *volonté,* and not that the Will to which he refers is only or necessarily God's Will. In *L'Économie politique,* for example, Rousseau lays down "the general Will as first principle of public economy and fundamental rule of government [*la volonté générale pour premier principe de l'économie publique et règle fondamentale du gouvernement*]" (OC III.247).

18. Comment on Rousseau and ($Q^{\text{theodicy}}A^{\text{abandoned}}$): As just suggested, we conclude that Rousseau maintains ($Q^{\text{theodicy}}A^{\text{abandoned}}$); we may assume therefore that theology will not provide an answer for ($Q^{\text{theodicy}}C^{\text{motion}}$); this assumption is only partially correct, since the symbolic form he adopts and adapts to ($Q^{\text{theodicy}}A^{\text{abandoned}}$) is profoundly rooted in theology; that symbolic form is *volonté;* thus, as just mentioned (#13 above) one principle of motion for mankind "abandoned to ourselves" is Will; unlike ($Q^{\text{fundamental}}A^{\text{nature}\in\text{grace}}$), however, the operative Will here is human rather than divine; I say *one* principle of motion because we know that

a. Rousseau does not say that single human beings (HB^{singles})* are bad or evil, but that the internal consequences of forces inherent in the totality of human beings (HB^{totality}) constitute badness or evil,

b. Rousseau therefore distinguishes between the social totality (HB^{totality}) and individuals (HB^{singles}), and

c. (HB^{totality}) develops in large measure simply through the living process of the satisfaction of needs of (HB^{singles}).[13]

This suggests another principle of motion which I will only consider much later but can allude to now; consistent with Rousseau's evolutionary account of society, the inherent principle of motion for mankind becomes the primary and undivided fact of *dépendance;* this second perspective contradicts the importance just attributed to Will.

19. First general note: the problem of social evil and political life is conceived in terms of the difference and contradiction between two modalities of Will as a principle of motion; the first is the cumulative (and destructive) effect of the many Wills of (HB^{singles}); the second is the cumulative (and constructive) effect

---

*At this schematic level of abstraction, I adopt relatively neutral terms to differentiate a number (1+N) of single human beings in a group (HB^{singles}) from the totality of human beings as such (HB^{totality}); my purpose for this ugly usage is to evade the common bias of terms like "individual" and "society," which is to say just that term the genesis of which we are tracking here. A further benefit is to erase the residual implications of gender in terms like "Man" and "Men."

of the single Will of ($HB^{totality}$), or the *volonté générale*; the analogy is, of course, to the perfect *ordre* created by divine Will as understood by the monotheist.

20. Second general note: within this schematic view, it appears that the *volonté générale* can be understood in functional rather than substantive or literal terms; whatever the principle of motion of the social totality is, Rousseau wants to call that *la volonté générale*. This is consistent with Rousseau's abstract and capacious way of theorizing and with his literary sensibility.

21. First qualification concerning ($Q^{theodicy}A^{abandoned}$): Before moving to the next question, we will now assume that Rousseau is unequivocal in holding ($Q^{theodicy}A^{abandoned}$); this is not entirely accurate, but on the whole it is correct. It represents, obviously, the line of inquiry developed in this book.

22. Second qualification concerning ($Q^{theodicy}A^{abandoned}$): We will also hypothesize that Rousseau conceives the next problem—which I will call loosely the Ecological Question ($Q^{ecological}$)—by metaphorical transposition from the first one. That is, the relationship between Grace and Nature becomes the map for the relationship between Nature and the totality of human beings, or Grace : Nature :: Nature : $HB^{totality}$.

23. This transposition occurs at a high level of abstraction; it does not mean that the two relationships are the same; it means that the problems posed in each case have analogous structures, such that one may answer the question about mankind's relation to Nature in the same ways that one answers ($Q^{fundamental}$).

24. Thus, we now come to the Ecological Question, or ($Q^{ecological}$): is ($HB^{totality}$) inside or outside Nature?

25. As this question is approached through the first two, it is complex rather than simple; specifically, the answer to ($Q^{theodicy}$) has an impact on ($Q^{ecological}$); Rousseau takes the position ($Q^{theodicy}A^{abandoned}$); the significance of this position depends in important respects on whether one holds ($Q^{fundamental}A^{nature \in grace}$) or ($Q^{fundamental}A^{nature \notin grace}$); we saw a moment ago that Rousseau has grounds for holding either one or the other; we will ask later if he can hold both.

26. Thus, we first approach an answer to ($Q^{ecological}$) under the assumption $\{(Q^{fundamental}A^{nature \in grace}) + (Q^{theodicy}A^{abandoned})\}$, and we will refer to this answer as ($Q^{ecological}A^{mankind \notin nature}$): if one believes that Nature is inside Grace ($Q^{fundamental}A^{nature \in grace}$), then Rousseau's answer to the Theodicy Question ($Q^{theodicy}A^{abandoned}$) requires a split between Nature and ($HB^{totality}$); that is, if God is active in Nature, ($HB^{totality}$) must be (in some sense) outside Nature; that is the only way it makes sense to say that mankind is "abandoned to ourselves"; this means, as we will see in just a moment, that $\{(Q^{fundamental}A^{nature \in grace}) + (Q^{theodicy}A^{abandoned})\}$ is incompatible with ($Q^{ecological}A^{mankind \in nature}$). See diagram #3.

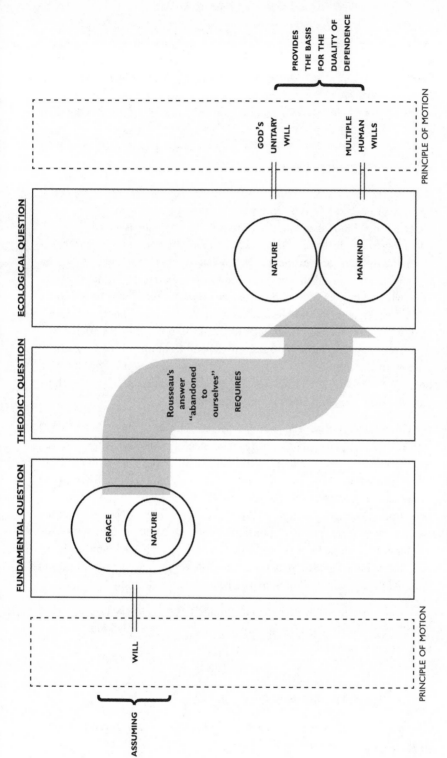

Diagram 3. Rousseau's First Answer to the Ecological Question

27. The second answer to ($Q^{ecological}$) approaches the question under the alternative assumption $\{(Q^{fundamental}A^{nature \notin grace}) + (Q^{theodicy}A^{abandoned})\}$, and we will refer to this answer as ($Q^{ecological}A^{mankind \in nature}$): if one believes that Nature is outside Grace ($Q^{fundamental}A^{nature \notin grace}$), then Rousseau's answer to the theodicy question ($Q^{theodicy}A^{abandoned}$) allows for the conjunction of Nature and ($HB^{totality}$); this does not mean that $\{(Q^{fundamental}A^{nature \notin grace}) + (Q^{theodicy}A^{abandoned})\}$ is necessarily incompatible with ($Q^{ecological}A^{mankind \notin nature}$), but many aspects of Rousseau's writing militate against taking it this way.

28. Comment on Rousseau and the first answer ($Q^{ecological}A^{mankind \notin nature}$) [#26]: the crucial outcome of this sequence of positions, that is, {Nature is inside Grace} ⇒ {mankind "abandoned to ourselves"} ⇒ {mankind is outside Nature}, is that it provides the basis for the fundamental distinction Rousseau makes between the two sorts of *dépendance*; Nature has its inherent and necessary principle, which is God's Will, and mankind has its inherent and necessary principle, which is human Will; when Rousseau says that dependence-from-Nature is "ordered,"[14] he means that to depend-from-Nature is to depend-from-God's Will; when Rousseau says that dependence-from-persons is "disordered," he means that to depend-from-persons is to depend-from-human Will; Rousseau is perfectly consistent in deriving this structure of *dépendance* from his position ($Q^{fundamental}A^{nature \in grace}$); that is, from a kind of monism at a prior level, he derives a kind of dualism at a subsequent level.

29. Comment on Rousseau and the second answer ($Q^{ecological}A^{mankind \in nature}$) [#27]: the intriguing outcome of this sequence of positions, that is, {Nature is outside Grace} ⇒ {mankind "abandoned to ourselves"} ⇒ {mankind is inside Nature}, is that it provides the basis for what we have referred to in passing as Rousseau's ecological sociology; where ($Q^{ecological}A^{mankind \in nature}$) holds, the inherent and necessary principle of the identity of Mankind/Nature is neither God's Will (Nature "alone")[15] nor human Will(s) (Mankind alone), but the machinery/organism/force of social evolution, or simply evolution; as I suggested a moment ago, this may be understood as powered by and in terms of the single and general fact of human *dépendance*. See diagram #4.

30. What does it mean to say that mankind is "inside" Nature? As with ($Q^{fundamental}$), [see #4 above], with respect to ($Q^{ecological}$) the relational term "inside" can mean several things:

a. mankind is subsumed by, or a subset of, Nature, or

b. mankind is identical with Nature, or

c. mankind and Nature are dialectically related such that, even though we can from one moment to the next make distinctions between them, they are ultimately so entangled as to be indistinguishable.

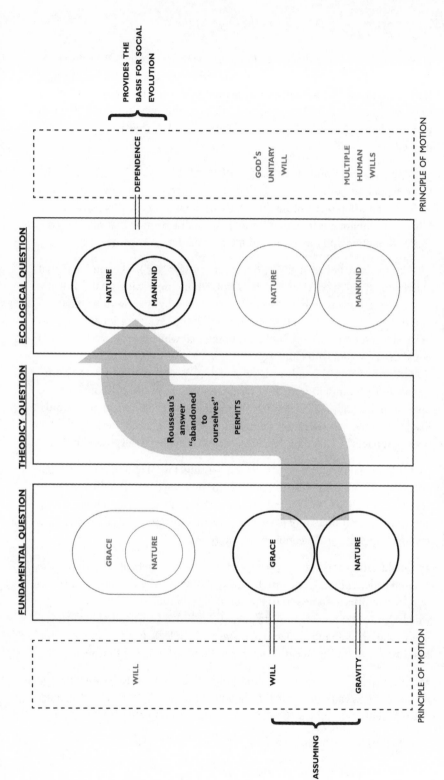

Diagram 4. Rousseau's Second Answer to the Ecological Question

31. We have seen in this book that Rousseau typically means ($Q^{\text{ecological}}A^{\text{mankind} \in \text{nature}}$) in the third sense (30c); this is often the case both when he refers to (HB^{totality}) or (HB^{singles}) in the "state of nature" and when he refers to (HB^{totality}) or (HB^{singles}) out of the "state of nature;" this paradox, which has largely to do with the literary status of the phrase "state of nature," has already been addressed.

32. At some points Rousseau holds ($Q^{\text{ecological}}A^{\text{mankind} \notin \text{nature}}$). This is clear and relatively explicit in both the basic distinction between types of *dépendance* and in Rousseau's statement of his (theological) "first principle" for natural philosophy. He maintains in both instances the dualist position that *volonté* is the source of motion and motion is distinct from matter.

33. Comparison between the two answers to ($Q^{\text{ecological}}$). The situation that characterizes ($Q^{\text{ecological}}A^{\text{mankind} \in \text{nature}}$) is not symmetrical with what I just described [#32], precisely because it is contradicted by the assertions that sustain ($Q^{\text{ecological}}A^{\text{mankind} \notin \text{nature}}$); thus, from the plentiful evidence for and analysis of social evolution, we work backward to see that while ($Q^{\text{ecological}}A^{\text{mankind} \notin \text{nature}}$) could be consistent with either ($Q^{\text{fundamental}}A^{\text{nature} \in \text{grace}}$) or ($Q^{\text{fundamental}}A^{\text{nature} \notin \text{grace}}$), ($Q^{\text{ecological}}A^{\text{mankind} \in \text{nature}}$) is only consistent with ($Q^{\text{fundamental}}A^{\text{nature} \notin \text{grace}}$); this corresponds to the common sense that characterized 150 years of debate—that is, only naturalism or a radical deism is compatible with evolution; in other words, insofar as Rousseau pursues his account of social evolution, he defeats what may reasonably be called his "creationist" first principle (as expressed in #32).

34. General qualification: here, at least in passing, I want to underscore the applicability of the word "creationist" both to the issue of God's Will and to the adoption of Will as a "God-term" (in Kenneth Burke's sense) for human affairs; any and all claims that say of *la volonté* (as Rousseau does) that "there you have my first principle" are "creationist" in this sense.

35. Qualification concerning ($Q^{\text{ecological}}$): there is a hypothetical exception to the ante-precedent point; if one asserts reflexively that God is the master of evolution, one returns to some sort of Providentialist position ($Q^{\text{fundamental}}A^{\text{nature} \in \text{grace}}$), which (probably) renders unsustainable ($Q^{\text{theodicy}}A^{\text{abandoned}}$), and effectively denies evolution as an inherent and necessary principle. I am not aware of a position like this in the eighteenth century, and it is certainly not Rousseau's.

36. Summary of the argument to this point: thus far, we have considered the impact of Rousseau's answer to the Theodicy Question ($Q^{\text{theodicy}}A^{\text{abandoned}}$) under two different assumptions, ($Q^{\text{fundamental}}A^{\text{nature} \in \text{grace}}$) and ($Q^{\text{fundamental}}A^{\text{nature} \notin \text{grace}}$);

    a. the first led to the conclusion ($Q^{\text{ecological}}A^{\text{mankind} \notin \text{nature}}$) and

    b. the second led to the conclusion ($Q^{\text{ecological}}A^{\text{mankind} \in \text{nature}}$);

 c. we also found that

  i. both conform to views that Rousseau holds, and

  ii. they are incompatible.

37. Now we can turn to the last of the four questions Rousseau confronts. This Political Question ($Q^{political}$) is in fact the guiding thread of his entire inquiry and the center of his social theory of politics.

38. Structural premise for ($Q^{political}$): we will assume, once again at this point, that Rousseau conceives this third and final level of his multidimensional problematic by way of metaphorical transposition from the first and second levels. That is, just as the relationship {Grace : Nature} became the map for the relationship {Nature : ($HB^{totality}$)}, this same structure becomes a map for the relationship of one modality of mankind to another, or {($HB^{totality}$) : ($HB^{singles}$)}.

39. Qualification of the structural premise for ($Q^{political}$): I reiterate that this further transposition also occurs at a high level of abstraction; it does not mean that the two relationships are the same; it means only that the problems posed in each instance have analogous structures, such that one may approach questions about the relationship between the individual and society, single persons and political bodies, or ($HB^{singles}$) and ($HB^{totality}$), in the same ways that one approached the Fundamental Question ($Q^{fundamental}$) and the Ecological Question ($Q^{ecological}$).

40. Return to the argument: assume, now, a new starting point for political inquiry after Rousseau's answer to the Theodicy Question, *viz.* after ($Q^{theodicy}A^{abandoned}$). Against this background, Rousseau asks a fourth question.

41. This last question is the Political Question, or ($Q^{political}$): What is the *contract social?*

42. Limiting qualification: posed this way, there are many answers to ($Q^{political}$). Our attention here goes to the one that illustrates the structure of Rousseau's social theory of politics.

43. Structural precision: in the response to ($Q^{political}$), the structure of the problem remains the same but is moved metaphorically to another level. Just as the answer to ($Q^{fundamental}$) had an impact on ($Q^{ecological}$), the difference between ($Q^{ecological}A^{mankind \notin nature}$) and ($Q^{ecological}A^{mankind \in nature}$) has an impact on one's response to ($Q^{political}$).

44. Premise reasserted: we still take as given that Rousseau holds the position ($Q^{theodicy}A^{abandoned}$); because we are "abandoned to ourselves," the *contract social* concerns the relation human beings maintain with themselves, for example, {($HB^{totality}$) : ($HB^{singles}$)}, rather than with God and with Nature.

45. Exclusion: for the moment we leave out of consideration the answer to ($Q^{fundamental}$), as it is nearly implied in the answer to ($Q^{ecological}$)—that is, as we have seen, while ($Q^{ecological}A^{mankind \notin nature}$) could be consistent with either ($Q^{fundamental}A^{nature \in grace}$) or ($Q^{fundamental}A^{nature \notin grace}$), Rousseau joins it regularly and explicitly with ($Q^{fundamental}A^{nature \in grace}$); under the proviso ($Q^{theodicy}A^{abandoned}$), ($Q^{ecological}A^{mankind \in nature}$) is only consistent with ($Q^{fundamental}A^{nature \notin grace}$).

46. Additional premise: following Rousseau, we also assume that whatever the *contract social* is, it is in some key respect a departure from the "state of nature."

47. Direction of the argument: Rousseau holds both ($Q^{ecological}A^{mankind \notin nature}$) and ($Q^{ecological}A^{mankind \in nature}$) and we need to consider

　　a. the consequence that follows in each instance for ($Q^{political}$), and

　　b. if the results in the two instances are compatible with one another.

48. Now we can answer ($Q^{political}$), at least in a limited way, in light of ($Q^{ecological}A^{mankind \notin nature}$), and we will refer to this answer as ($Q^{political}A^{individuals\,=\,society}$): if one believes that mankind is outside of nature ($Q^{ecological}A^{mankind \notin nature}$) then the motive for and result of the *contract social* depend in important respects on the inherent and necessary principle of motion assumed by that belief; Rousseau claims that the principle of motion for both Nature and ($HB^{totality}$) is Will; what drives Nature is the singular Will of God, and what normally drives ($HB^{totality}$) are the multiple Wills of ($HB^{singles}$); singular Will is ordered, multiple Wills are not ordered; as ($HB^{totality}$) is already distinct from Nature, the goal of the *contract social* cannot primarily be to remove ($HB^{totality}$) from Nature; rather, the goal of the *contract social* is to use the principle of motion to create *ordre* and gain its positive effects; here, the problem of *ordre* is the problem of what relationship human beings will have to themselves; all things considered, ($Q^{political}A^{individuals\,=\,society}$) allows for a conjunction of ($HB^{totality}$) and ($HB^{singles}$), specifically by subsuming the latter under the former; that the tendency to create *ordre* by subsuming many Wills into one Will is a metaphorical transposition from ($Q^{ecological}A^{mankind \notin nature}$) is clear from the "main passage," where Rousseau writes that "if the laws of nations could have, like those of nature, an inflexibility that no human force could ever be able to overcome, dependence-from-persons would thus become again dependence-from-things [and] one would reunite in the Republic all the advantages of the state of nature with those of the civil condition [*si les lois des nations pouvoient avoir comme celles de la nature une inflexibilité que jamais aucune force humaine ne put vaincre, la dépendance des hommes redeviendroit alors celle des choses, on réuniroit dans la République tous les avantages de l'état naturel à ceux de l'état civil*]." See diagram #5.

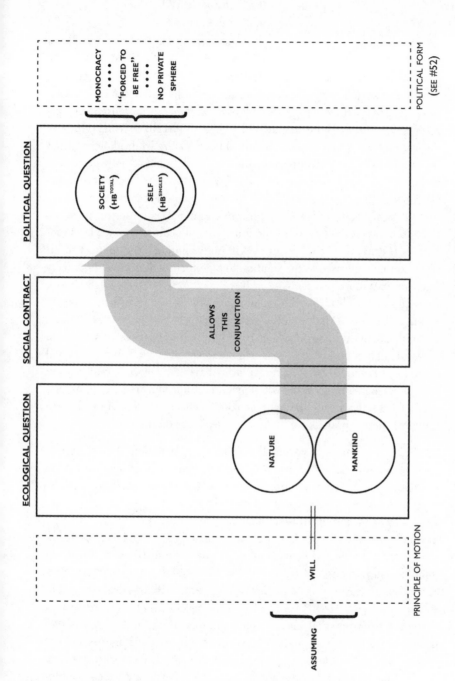

Diagram 5: Rousseau's First Answer to the Political Question

49. The next step is to answer ($Q^{political}$), at least in a limited way, in light of ($Q^{ecological}A^{mankind \in nature}$), and we will refer to this answer as ($Q^{political}A^{society \neq individuals}$): if one believes that mankind is inside Nature ($Q^{ecological}A^{mankind \in nature}$) then, in at least one sense (following Rousseau's insistence on the distinction between *nature* and *société*), the motive and result of the *contract social* must be to separate mankind from Nature; as mankind includes both ($HB^{totality}$) and ($HB^{singles}$), the *contract social* may separate mankind from Nature by dividing one from the other and thus constituting a situation in which human beings are both in and out of nature at the same time; ($Q^{political}A^{society \neq individuals}$) does not so much assert that ($HB^{totality}$) is outside ($HB^{singles}$)—an implausible claim that sustains a metaphysical reading of *la volonté générale*—as it makes a strong practical distinction between the two; since the inherent and necessary principle of motion for ($Q^{ecological}A^{mankind \in nature}$) is not Will but evolution,[16] the *contract social* needs not be conceived as the solution to a problem that is posed essentially in terms of Will (as was the case in ($Q^{political}A^{individuals = society}$)—see #48 above); Rousseau makes clear that the evolutionary process is a feature of ($HB^{totality}$) and not a feature of ($HB^{singles}$); the dualism of ($Q^{political}A^{society \neq individuals}$) transfers the principle of evolution into society ($HB^{totality}$) and thus preserves a feature of Nature in politics while not reducing human existence to natural or animal existence; because *la loi* is identified at its base with "*moeurs*, custom, and *opinion*," which is to say with evolutionary transindividual features of human existence, it is the manifestation of mankind's collective Nature; this allows to ($HB^{singles}$) another principle of motion, (see #51). See diagram #6.

50. What does it mean to say that the "principle of evolution," as a "feature of Nature," is transferred into society? In one view, which is consistent with much of what Rousseau writes, and from many different angles, this "feature of Nature" might be construed as "natural law." However, to put it that way is to reassert a categorical split between mankind and Nature ($Q^{ecological}A^{mankind \notin nature}$) in which mankind and our laws are one thing and nature and its laws are another, even if the latter agency somehow governs the former object; this would imply a transformation of ($Q^{political}A^{society \neq individuals}$) back into ($Q^{political}A^{individuals = society}$). Thus, the feature of Nature that is preserved in ($HB^{totality}$) needs to be consistent with ($Q^{political}A^{society \neq individuals}$). In this perspective—which is the second of the two major lines of Rousseau's thought that appear in this book—*la loi* is understood in evolutionary terms as an outcome of social process and not as the "Will of the legislator" (as in, e.g., the so-called "command theory of law").[17] This is consistent with, and in some sense explains, Rousseau's astonishing comments about the "fourth sort of law," which includes "*moeurs*, customs, and above all opinion" and "which is the true constitution of the State" (OC III.394).

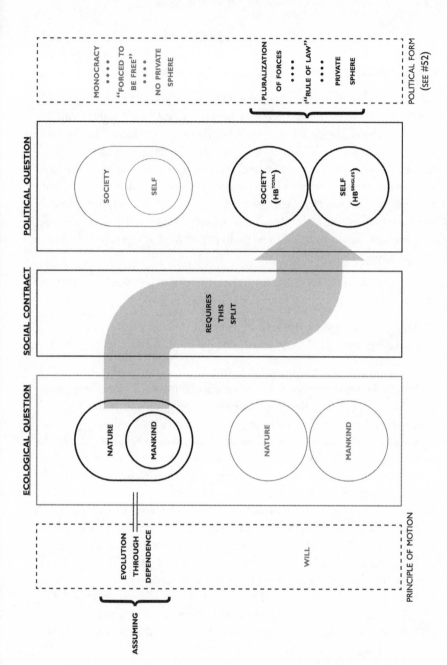

Diagram 6. Rousseau's Second Answer to the Political Question

51. What is the other principle of motion for ($HB^{singles}$) mentioned in #49 above? It could be "Will," or "*pitié*," or "reason," and so on. In fact, I am tempted to call this "freedom," although in some sense that we have yet to understand.

52. Let us describe the difference between ($Q^{political}A^{individuals = society}$) and ($Q^{political}A^{society \neq individuals}$) as the difference between monocracy[18] and the rule of law, where the characteristic mode of the former is a single identifiable agency as expressed in Rousseau's infamous phrase about "forcing . . . whoever refuses to obey the general will . . . to be free" (OC III.364) while the latter entails a multiplication and distribution of contending powers, maintains a distinction between (in the terms Hegel later gave to the nineteenth century) the state and civil society, allows for a "private sphere," upholds the political body as artificial (the principle of "we must act"), and exalts personal integrity as a fact of nature (the principle of human dignity).[19]

53. Is it inconsistent to say that ($HB^{totality}$) is artificial *and* is driven by a principle of Nature? I do not think so (for reasons discussed in §45).

54. Is it inconsistent to say that ($HB^{singles}$) rests on a "fact of nature" *but* is driven by something human (all too human)? I do not think so (again for reasons discussed in §45).

55. Finally, I want to propose a conclusion concerning the logic of these metaphorical transpositions: Rousseau replays and refigures the problematic of inside/outside—a common *topos* of theology and natural philosophy of his time—at several levels; we have followed it from Grace to Nature to Mankind, examining in each instance the relations between the terms; our purpose has been to provide a rough and tentative map of the interrelations among these domains; the intense debates of the eighteenth century show full well that they fit uneasily together; we know, too, that Rousseau traverses the terrain along two different paths, one primarily creationist (where, sacred or secular, everything reduces to Will) and one strongly evolutionist (where a kind of ecological sociology appears in which human action is constantly turned back on and integrated into a larger, more comprehensive, and changing world); let us call monist a position that sees one of the two terms of a relation as "inside" the other term, and let us call dualist a position that sees the two terms of a relation as "outside" each other; in the series of positions defined by Rousseau's many claims and arguments, a monist theology at the outset ($Q^{fundamental}A^{nature \in grace}$) leads to a dualist anthropology ($Q^{ecological}A^{mankind \notin nature}$) which leads to a monist theory of politics ($Q^{political}A^{individuals = society}$); conversely, a dualist theology at the outset ($Q^{fundamental}A^{nature \notin grace}$) leads to a monist anthropology ($Q^{ecological}A^{mankind \in nature}$) which leads to a dualist theory of politics ($Q^{political}A^{society \neq individuals}$). See diagram #7.

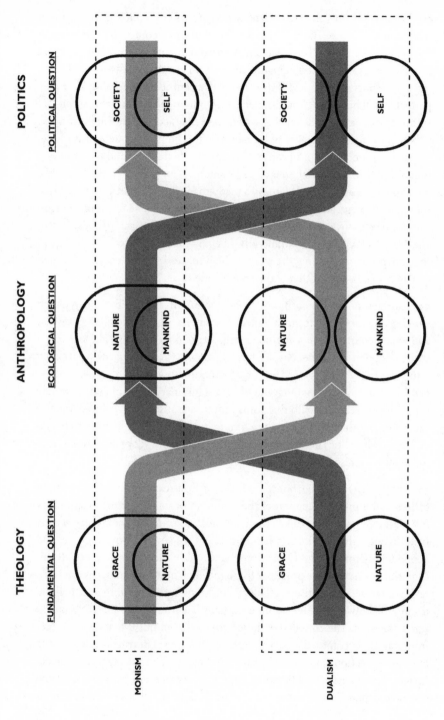

Diagram 7. Basic Structural Transpositions of Rousseau's Theory/Dialectic of Monist and Dualist Claims

56. We can put this in other terms which are more familiar and consistent with common sense. The theist, and particularly, in a context like Rousseau's, the person we might today call a Christian fundamentalist, cannot accept that human beings and the rest of Nature are parts of one integral whole, and tends toward monocratic political institutions.[20] By contrast, a naturalist, who may perfectly well be a deist, is positioned to see human beings and the rest of Nature as one dynamic and evolving system, and may accept political institutions which allow for the plurality of human beings. The paradox here, if it is one, is that monist conceptions promote inquiry into difference and the proliferation of finely tuned distinctions as negotiations in an ongoing process. That is, if you do not come to a problem with ready-made distinctions, you must make them up as you go along, and do so in a manner convenable to circumstances. The contrast is obvious: dualist conceptions have no such strong motivation to allow for, and thus foster, plurality; they begin—like Manichees—with a great machinery for cataloguing the world, which makes it all too easy to toss each case to one side or the other of the great divide.

57. Rousseau holds two positions; despite enormous insight into the dynamic workings of society that grows out of his answer to the Theodicy Question and which constitutes an evolutionary response to the Ecological Question, a structural point in his theory leads him to respond to the Political Question by returning to $(Q^{\text{fundamental}} A^{\text{nature} \in \text{grace}})$; that structural point is the problem of *dépendance* and is itself an outcome of his evolutionary view; of course, it may simply be his religious faith that turns him to this answer to the Fundamental Question, but that does not require him to apply that symbolic form to his social theory of politics in the way that he does; it certainly does not require us to follow him in this regard.

58. Another key point becomes a vehicle for Rousseau's evasion of the implications of his own conception of the evolution of society, or the evolution of Nature more generally. This is the identification of *la nature* and *les choses*, Nature and "things," from which he elides dependence-from-nature and dependence-from-things. On the one hand, this elision is consistent with his evolutionary view, as the processes through which human beings, day after day, satisfy their needs constitute a dialectic of Mankind and Nature in which the distinction between the two terms eventually becomes impossible to sustain as a *general* point. The correct conclusion to draw from this is that dependence-from-nature becomes like dependence-from-things. Rousseau goes in the opposite direction and, so to speak, winding back the evolutionary clock, images dependence-from-things as dependence-from-nature. Because of the ongoing implication of things in human action, the first conclusion tends

toward commensurability between dependence-from-things and dependence-from-persons; Rousseau's conclusion by contrast tends the other way—as he observes correctly from inside his own perspective—toward an incommensurability between dependence-from-nature and dependence-from-persons.

§50

The "Main Passage" as Atlas

When Rousseau asks the question, Why can't we be happy? he considers the human subject as always already entangled with life in three ways. First, the subject has a relationship with God, which, using a typical eighteenth-century shorthand, we have referred to as Grace. Second, the subject has a relationship with the totality of experience, which we have referred to as Nature. Finally, the subject has relationships with other human beings, a fact we have noted in the plurality of humankind. These three types of entanglements may or may not amount to the same thing; on this point Rousseau holds several positions, some of which are fruitful for his thinking, some of which are contradictory, some of which are both.

Images of Grace, Nature, and Mankind serve Rousseau's social theory of politics two ways. They are axes around which the theory takes shape. At the same time they are passages through which the topics and common sense of other discourses enter into Rousseau's diagnoses and proposals.

On the one hand, the considerations of the preceding section form a hermeneutic context for the assertions assembled in the "main passage." Without this context, what Rousseau writes could not make sense for us, at least not in a way that approximates the way the "main passage" made sense to Rousseau. On the other hand, these considerations exceed by far the more pointed proposal for civic happiness that appears in those few heraldic lines from *Émile*. Now is the moment to return to just those lines. This will focus our investigation back through its starting point, and down into the substrata of the question of *dépendance*.

Introducing the "main passage" (in the appendix to Part One) I resisted direct translation into English. With some feigned naiveté, I did not want to prejudice the reading of it. Now we have many cards open on the table and a straightforward translation seems appropriate. The translation itself should serve as reminder of the many lines of investigation we have already pursued. The focus here will be on the second paragraph, where Rousseau shifts from description to diagnosis. He writes:

> Ces considérations sont importantes et servent à résoudre toutes les contradictions du sistême social. Il y a deux sortes de dépendance. Celle des choses qui est de la nature; celle des hommes qui est de la societé. La dépendance des choses n'ayant aucune moralité ne nuit point à la liberté et n'engendre point de vices. La dépendance des hommes étant desordonnée les engendre tous, et c'est par elle que le maitre et l'esclave se dépravent mutuellement. S'il y a quelque moyen de remédier à ce mal dans la société c'est de substituer la loi à l'homme, et d'armer les volontés générales d'une force réelle supérieure à l'action de toute volonté particuliére. Si les loix des nations pouvoient avoir comme celles de la nature une infléxibilité que jamais aucune force humaine ne put vaincre, la dépendance des hommes redeviendroit alors celle des choses, on réuniroit dans la République tous les avantages de l'état naturel à ceux de l'état civil, on joindroit à la liberté qui maintient l'homme exempt de vices la moralité qui l'élêve à la virtue.*

Let's now take this as saying:

> These considerations are important and serve to resolve all the contradictions of the social system. There are two sorts of dependence. Dependence-from-things, which is from nature; dependence-from-persons which is from society. Dependence-from-things having not the slightest morality does not harm liberty in any way and engenders no vices. Dependence-from-persons, being disordered, engenders them all, and it is with this dependence that the master and the slave mutually deprave one another. If there is some way to remedy this evil in society it is to substitute law for human beings, and to arm the general Wills with a real force superior to the action of every particular Will. If the laws of nations could have, like those of nature, an inflexibility that no human force could ever be able to overcome, dependence-from-persons would thus become again dependence-from-things, one would reunite in the Republic all the advantages of the state of nature with those of the civil condition, one would join to the liberty that maintains mankind exempt from vice the morality that raises it to virtue.

The flourish Rousseau allows himself at the end is somewhat misleading. This paragraph is a sequence of synthetic, nearly axiomatic propositions. Following

---

*OC IV.311. I recall for the reader my steadfast use of eighteenth-century orthography.

again, and for the last time, a schematic procedure like that of the preceding section, I now want to survey this whole equation, stating briefly how each proposition functions in the text and the effect it produces within the theory. This is at once a gesture backward to many of the detailed discussions undertaken earlier in this book and a look forward to the conclusion. It will focus attention on pivotal questions that remain unanswered or whose answers merit emphasis now. "These conditions are important and serve. . . ."

	Proposition	*Function*	*Effect*
I	*à résoudre toutes les contradictions du sistême social.* [to resolve all the contradictions of the social system.]	Indicates goal in abstract terms	Makes sociology the starting point for political theory, asserting a high degree of certainty at this abstract level
II	*Il y a deux sortes de dépendance.* [There are two sorts of dependence]	Structures the problem and its solution	Asserts dualism as a theoretical approach, carrying concerns from one level of analysis to another
III	*Celle des choses qui est de la nature; celle des hommes qui est de la societé.* [Dependence-from-things, which is from nature; dependence-from-persons, which is from society.]	Establishes a basic distinction and matrix of terms	Distinguishes *choses* from *hommes* and *nature* from *societé*; equates (a) *choses* with *nature* and (b) *hommes* with *societé*
IV	*La dépendance des choses n'ayant aucune moralité* [Dependence-from-things having not the slightest morality]	Assigns a value to III.a	Makes *dépendance* a bridging term between sociology and *la science des moeurs* (and thus also a bridge to *la loi*)
V	*ne nuit point à la liberté et n'engendre point de vices.* [does not harm liberty in any way and engenders no vices.]	Provides criteria of moral value related to persons	Underscores the moral quality of sociological categories, linking them to politics; tacitly affirms link between *choses* and *nature* (via the parallels extended in XVI and XVII below)

	Proposition	Function	Effect
VI	*La dépendance des hommes étant desordonnée les engendre tous,* [Dependence-from-persons, being disordered, engenders them all,]	Assigns a value to III.b and introduces the topic of *ordre*	Provides a justification for the valuation of both parts of the distinction in terms of *ordre*, making *ordre* a key term for the constellation of *société-morale-loi-politique*; this also opens this constellation to thinking through other discourses which hinge on the word *ordre*
VII	*et c'est par elle que le maitre et l'esclave se dépravent mutuellement.* [and it is with this dependence that the master and the slave mutually deprave one another.]	Provides criterion of moral value related to politics	Reasserts with more force the political significance of sociological categories
VIII	*S'il y a quelque moyen* [If there is some way]	Shift to hypothetical mode	Affirms a difference between sociological analysis (about which a high degree of descriptive certainty and logical precision is possible) and politics (where the probable reigns)
IX	*de remédier à ce mal dans la societé* [to remedy this evil in society]	Redefines the abstract goal stated in (I) in political terms	By restating *les contradictions du sistême social* as *ce mal dans la societé*, the social theory of politics is linked to theodicy, and *ordre* becomes the pivotal term at all levels of analysis

	Proposition	Function	Effect
<u>X</u>	*c'est de substituer la loi à l'homme,* [it is to substitute law for human beings,]	Differentiates *la loi* and *l'homme*, proposes a solution through metaphorical transposition	*La loi* is associated with *les choses* by contrast to *homme*, making the problem of *loi/homme*, like the problem of *choses/hommes*, a matter of *ordre*; at the same time, a logical problem is transformed into a political one
<u>XI</u>	*et d'armer les volontés générales* [and to arm the general Wills]	First qualification of the solution in terms of Will	Exposes the problem of *ordre* as a problem of Will
<u>XII</u>	*d'une force réelle supérieure à l'action de toute volonté particuliére.* [with a real force superior to the action of every particular Will.]	Establishes hierarchy of general Will over individual Will	Proposes a distinction between two sorts of Will, and, by sequence within the argument, associates this distinction with the basic distinction between types of dependence asserted in (III)
<u>XIII</u>	*Si les loix des nations pouvoient avoir comme celles de la nature* [If the laws of nations could have, like those of nature,]	Second qualification of the solution in terms of "natural law"	Associates the distinction between two sorts of Will with two sorts of law, making this a metonymy for two sorts of dependence
<u>XIV</u>	*une infléxibilité que jamais aucune force humaine ne put vaincre,* [an inflexibility that no human force could ever be able to overcome,]	Proposes the difference between natural and human laws	Suggests why Will, as the basis for the difference between types of law, because it is the source of *ordre*, can solve the problem of dependence

	Proposition	Function	Effect
<u>XV</u>	*la dépendance des hommes redeviendroit alors celle des choses,* [dependence-from-persons would thus become again dependence-from-things,]	Makes explicit the link back to dependence and proposes the solution as transformation of one type into the other	Denies the dualism and its consequent *"sortes de dépendance"* asserted categorically at the beginning by proposing (hypothetically) a kind of monist reduction
<u>XVI</u>	*on réuniroit dans la République tous les avantages de l'état naturel à ceux de l'état civil,* [one would reunite in the Republic all the advantages of the state of nature with those of the civil condition,]	Joins the two conditions which elsewhere are asserted (with great vigor) as distinct	A reduction analogous to the one proposed in XV is applied to *nature* and *societé*.
<u>XVII</u>	*on joindroit à la liberté qui maintient l'homme exempt de vices la moralité qui l'élève à la vertu.* [one would join to the liberty that maintains mankind exempt from vice the morality that raises it to virtue.]	Associates *liberté* with *nature*; asserts not just an antithesis but also an asymmetry between *vices* and *virtue*.	Brings into question the major premises IV and V; if dependence-from-things "has no morality" why would remaking dependence-from-persons as dependence-from-things through law introduce morality into the Republic?

The following notes relate to each proposition advanced in the "main passage" and enumerated above. They raise questions which remain for us to consider and, where possible, provide concise answers to them. As the questions that cannot be treated in this summary way are brought to the foreground, these notes also serve to introduce the subsequent parts of this final chapter.

I

We have considered in some detail the four keywords that appear here: *ré-soudre* (§31), *contradictions* (§§15, 30, 31), *sistême* (§32), *social* (§35, Part One *passim*). A certain ambivalence is preserved in both the words *résoudre* and *contradiction*. It concerns what one should expect from Rousseau's diagnoses and solution. Is the difficulty inherent in these *contradictions* the impossible coexistence of something and its opposite? or is it the obtrusive but manageable fact that differences are spoken? Is the proposal to *résoudre* a way of "squaring the circle," of making unitary the plural? or is it a process of adjustment that produces harmony from what is at hand, in a particular time and place? Rousseau wants, in both cases, to have it both ways.

II

The existence of two sorts of *dépendance* does not mean that something prior to *dépendance* generates two similar but essentially different conditions; it is indicative that the word *dépendance* is singular, not plural. As shown in the development of this topic (in Part Two.A above, §§14–28), where Rousseau's sociological insight is most powerful he suggests that nothing underlies *dépendance*; it is the inherent and necessary principle of mankind "abandoned to ourselves," through which basic faculties like *amour de soi-même* and *perfectibilité*, in the circulation of *forces* and *besoins*, constitute social evolution. Each of the two sorts is a particular inflection or modality of the same basic fact of *dépendance*. Whether or not Rousseau himself always adheres to his clearest vision is another sort of question.

III

The matrix of terms put forward here—*choses, nature, hommes, societé*—constitutes a core of Rousseau's thought. From one side, divisions are made. The first of these is easy to follow; it is the claim that things and persons are not the same. We should further observe a subtle methodological implication in the way this distinction appears. When *hommes* and *choses* are offered as types of *dépendance*, they are both presented in the plural. This is important because it makes connectedness (the characteristic feature of *dépendance*) among plural entities the issue; Rousseau does not linger over metaphysical questions about what, *per se*, *a* thing or *a* person is. The second distinction is perhaps Rousseau's most familiar theme. It is the line he draws between *nature* and *societé*. We have seen at some length that this distinction is certainly not meant to be literal; but neither is it simply metaphorical (see §§42–45). Rather, it activates a range of far more complicated theoretical gestures as it is constantly modulated through the fundamental concerns we made explicit in the preceding section, which is to say ($Q^{fundamental}$), ($Q^{theodicy}$), and ($Q^{ecological}$). For Rousseau, these modulations set up the possibility of responding to ($Q^{political}$) in a way that "dependence-from-persons would thus become again dependence-from-things" and "one would reunite in the Republic all the advantages of the state of nature with those of the civil condition." What is remarkable in these last two sentences is that, in crucial respects, *nature* and *societé* are not divided by the *contract social* but brought together within it. That is the opposite of the way most readers of the *contract social* have understood it.[21]

So much for the divisions. From the other side, two equivalences are drawn in this proposition. The first one very nearly identifies *société* and *hommes* in the sense of (HB[totality]). Under the conditions discussed above (primarily §35, but also §18), this seems consistent with Rousseau's other views and is generally plausible. However, the second equivalence made in this proposition remains open. Are *choses* and *nature* the same? If the metaphorical solution to (Q[political]) is to, as Rousseau insists it will, "resolve all the contradictions of the social system," the attributes of *nature* will have to characterize *choses* as well. This is a topic we have persistently delayed addressing and it will be considered fully in the following sections.

IV

It is worth asking at this point a question that, in a sense, Hegel would answer half a century later: is Rousseau's word *moralité*, which seems to indicate the presence of a "moral charge" of good or bad, the same as *la morale*, which, as we have seen, may be understand as the conditions of human relationship that make possible such a "charge"? (§5) This bears on whether or not *dépendance* is, as suggested above, the "inherent and necessary" principle of living human beings in the world. We know—because the distinction between two sorts of *dépendance* itself tells us—that *dépendance* is the underlying fact and common term that joins together *la morale, société,* and *loi* with the material world of *nature.* So, to make this statement—"Dependence-from-things having not the slightest morality"—might mean that something has completely and utterly neutralized this "moral charge." Is it possible that *les choses* never had or never could have again the capacity to be so invested?

We also know that despite his emphasis here on the nuisance created by dependence-from-persons, this sort of *dépendance* does not only produce vices; for example, Rousseau shows very clearly that ongoing interactions within society at its earliest stages are the developmental sources of human reason. Since he also claims that without reason *moralité* is impossible, it is at best incomplete to say that dependence-from-persons is destructive of *moralité* and *ordre.*

As is often the case, Rousseau has two views that fit uncomfortably together: he certainly identifies *dépendance* as something bad in human affairs; but this very fact seems to focus his curiosity, and the inquiry turns to consider what *dépendance* actually is. The effect is analogous to the circle drawn around the "island" of mankind in response to (Q^{theodicy}), something that moved Rousseau toward a comprehensive account of the life of the "island" itself (beginning in §2).

V

Notice that here Rousseau brings in the political topic of *liberté* by paradoxically associating it with *nature* (by way of *choses*). More on this in the note to propositions XVI–XVII.

VI

The key term that appears here is *ordre*, and it becomes the measure of *dépendance*. If unmodulated *dépendance* is the substance of human experience, it is neither virtuous nor vicious, neither ordered nor disordered. Thus, it may be somewhat misleading for Rousseau to suggest that "being disordered" it "engenders" vices: on the one hand, it is often accurate to say that situations of "disorder" will make the people who participate in them more vicious;[22] on the other hand, *ordre* and *désordre* are manifestations of "moral charge," which is to say that what is ordered is both virtuous and free, what is disordered is vicious and slave; thus, what Rousseau means might be restated as simply "disorder engenders disorder." And indeed, "all the contradictions of the social system" eventually converge around the topic of *ordre*. Part Four.B below ("The Rhetorical Structure of Order") examines what is involved when Rousseau speaks through that word.

VII

Why are master and slave mutually depraved (i.e., vicious or immoral)? The answer to this question again shows clearly the constitution of the problem Rousseau aims to *résoudre*. Vice, as we just saw, is not a substance inherent in an individual; it is, rather, "disorder," which is something that inheres in the relation between parts and whole. It is this composition of a social/moral/legal fact—exemplified here by its worst instance, slavery—that needs to be "resolved." This view, certainly compatible with deism, probably compatible with some theistic versions of *la religion naturelle*, denies the doctrine of original sin and thus appears to be (whatever Rousseau says elsewhere to defend his own position) profoundly anti-Christian.

VIII

No further questions.

IX

Introducing the word *mal*, Rousseau transposes multiple instances of vice into one general syndrome of "evil." While "evil" is not an inherent quality of individuals, it is an inherent quality of society. This needs to be understood against the background of two other claims: the first is the image of mankind "abandoned to ourselves," as figured vividly by the "island"; the second is Rousseau's insistence that *société*, properly configured as *la cité*, is an *"être moral."* Against this background, another question emerges: Is *société* therefore a simple unity or an individual? I want to insist again on the negative answer to this question (cf. §49.52 above and diagrams 5 and 6). Rather, society is a *sistême*, and a *sistême* is an *ordre* (see §32 above). *Le mal*, which is to say "evil" in general, is the disruption of *ordre*, or *désordre*. We will not pursue at this point why *contradiction* is the functional equivalent of *désordre* (see §35 above and §61).

X

Another keyword enters the mix: *la loi*. While we, after the nineteenth and twentieth centuries, can easily appreciate a desire to adhere to the "rule of law" instead of the rule of one person or one party, how does Rousseau understand this? An essential element here is the way *la loi* is characterized by association with dependence-from-things, which makes it appear like a "thing." How plausible is this? The answer to this question emerges within Rousseau's complex sequence of overlapping *topoi*, where the distinction between *la loi* and *homme* borrows qualities from the distinction between *les choses* and *hommes*, and both turn us back to the question of *ordre*. At this point, we have no reason to expect what the next few lines will reveal: that *la loi* is something more than what is discussed in most of the pages of *Du Contract social* (that is, a complex human fact; cf. §5 together with §49.49–50).

XI

Rousseau has laid out a constellation of topics and problems that gravitates around the term *ordre*. Part Four.C below ("*Ordre* as the Deployment of Ambivalence") is devoted to making explicit some of the stakes in understanding the ($Q^{political}$) from this perspective. Here another fundamental shift occurs, as it is supposed that Will is, in turn, the pivotal term for the solution of a problem of *ordre*. The significance of this additional move is taken up in Part Four.D below ("Variation on the Will").

XII

In what sense does one Will overcome many? It would be perverse to suggest that a difference of number is being invoked here, even though in response to ($Q^{political}$) Rousseau imagines the energies of many persons collected through a single Will. The clinching topic of Rousseau's claim here is not Will but *unity*.

And why does unity matter? Unity matters because *one* is always, by definition, ordered, whereas *several* or *many* may or may not be ordered. Multiple Wills have a strong tendency toward disorder, which means *contradiction*, which means *le mal*, or "evil" in Rousseau's newly sociological sense. In any event, as Rousseau lays these matters out, Will becomes a more fundamental category than *ordre*. Why? Because Will is the source of good and bad *ordre*. The imposition of good *ordre* over bad is a matter of getting Will rightly organized, which means directed, or all focused in one direction, rather than allowing multiple tendencies to pull against one another.

XIII

Now the notion of *loi* is elaborated in another way familiar in the eighteenth century: "natural laws [*les lois naturelles*]" are distinguished from "the laws of nations [*les loix des nations*]."[23] Rousseau's turn to this distinction, however, is not (as many have thought) primarily a portal to traditions of "natural law." It serves a somewhat different purpose. Through this distinction in types of law, by analogy, Rousseau reasserts the whole constellation of terms around the primary distinction between *les choses* and *les hommes* and the different possibilities for *ordre* which derive when one depends from the one or the other. It would therefore not be fruitful to consider here whether the word "law" is being used in the same way in these two expressions; even if they are different, Rousseau proposes a metaphorical shift that might still be effective. Given the frames of reference Rousseau provides, two other questions are more important within the scope of our inquiry. The first is Are "laws of nature" also "laws of things?" In other words, we are pointed back to the idea that *la nature* and *les choses* are the same in the sense that they have the same kind of *ordre*. The second question is Can the type of *ordre* characteristic of *la nature* and/or *les choses* be reproduced in relationships human beings hold with one another?

Since, for Rousseau, questions of *ordre* are underpinned by considerations of the Will, it is important to push the interrogation further. When Rousseau distinguishes between *les lois naturelles* and *les lois des nations*, is he also asserting a distinction between Willed and not-Willed? The answer to this question is again negative; rather, what appears here is the opposite, a reduction of everything to Will, and a closing off of the possibility that *ordre* has some other source(s). (Cf. the Foreword and §§ 60, 61, 65, 69 below)

XIV

Rousseau indicates why *les lois naturelles* should be the model for well-ordered human law. The reason is their *inflexibilité*. And why are *les lois naturelles* inflexible? Because they derive from a single omnipotent Will that is always consistent with itself (that is, noncontradictory). We need to be clear

that there are two "tricks" here. One is the way Rousseau transforms something, the characteristic feature of which is its freedom, into its opposite, which
is perfect *inflexibilité*. This is how the "laws of nature" can be at once the issue
of Will and the model for the certain and unassailable human laws Rousseau
seeks. This "trick" is accomplished under cover of the morally ambivalent concept of *ordre*. The other "trick" is the equivalence made earlier between *la nature* and *les choses*. This prepares—by softening or mediating with a middle
term—the metaphorical shift of *les lois des nations* from the image of the
human to the image of the natural and back. This sequence of relationships—
in which *volonté* becomes the source of *ordre* that characterizes *les choses* and
gives to *dépendance* its moral significance—is what we will have to explore in
more detail in the remainder of this final part of the book.

I doubt that we should be convinced by Rousseau's account of key features of these relationships. But even if we take them as given, other questions
emerge that have bearing on Rousseau's political conclusions. Are "laws of nature" really so inflexible? Don't "human forces," day after day, win out over
the supposed *inflexibilité* of *nature*? Whatever the answer to these questions,
doesn't it remain that in many respects *les choses* are not at all like *nature*? And,
even when the two seem equivalent, isn't it often because, so to speak, *nature* is
more like things already touched and transformed by human hands than those
things are like "pure" *nature*?

Underlying these additional questions is a very fundamental point. I shall
insist on the fact—darkly visible to Rousseau, clear today but often ignored—
that *volonté* is not the only source of *ordre*. I suggested above that there are
"two Rousseaus" (see, e.g., end of §§44 and 45) and this will pit the one against
the other. The one is a founder of modern sociology and the great theorist of
social evolution, the other is a purveyor of "intelligent design" and the master
authority of a generalized "creationism." The latter is the enemy of the former;
the former idolizes the latter.

XV

Is Rousseau saying that society could become a "thing?" Remembering
that this is not metaphysics, I am convinced that Rousseau is not proposing
a "thing"-like political system. He is not dreaming of democracy. A common
misreading of *Du Contract social* takes it to be a totalitarian declaration; this is
absurd. With admittedly exaggerated restraint, one could say that finally Rousseau is saying no more than that the type of relationship we have with things,
that is, a relatively ordered relationship, is possible with persons, if the source
of *ordre*, which in all cases (for Rousseau) is Will, is unified (as this is the condi-

tion for the production of good order), where "unified" means just that no one will be allowed to bend or break the law simply because he or she "wants" to.

<u>XVI–XVII</u>

This picture is thrown into some confusion by the declaration that the metaphorical return to *l'état naturel*, which is by metonymy the realm of *les choses* and whose characteristic feature is *inflexibilité*, provides us with *liberté*. As in proposition V, the positions of *liberté* and *nécessité* thus seem to be switched. The background that justifies this is Rousseau's theistic response to ($Q^{fundamental}$).

Our inventory here suggests which important topics remain open and need to be examined before we finally arrive, as we will toward the end of this part ("The Gravity of *Dépendance*"), at an assessment of the distinction between the two sorts of *dépendance*.

Above all, we will need to make explicit the way that distinction is organized around the *topos* of *ordre*, and how *ordre* is understood as a function of Will. This will allow a closer look at the exact relationship between *nature* and *les choses*, the equivalence of which is the hinge of Rousseau's proposal to "resolve all the contradictions of the social system." Then it will be possible to see not only under what conditions the distinction between two sorts of *dépendance* does or does not make sense, but also to consider the status of *dépendance* itself as the foundation for a social theory of politics.

What we have undertaken in this section—which is to say, breaking down Rousseau's argument into a series of component propositions—does not countermand the fact that all these parts form one whole way of thinking. Several times in this book I have raised and delayed direct address to the question, Are *les choses* and *la nature* the same? As Rousseau himself puts it, "these considerations are important [*ces considérations sont importantes*]," since, for Rousseau's social theory of politics to accomplish its task through the series of metaphorical parallels described above (§49), certain attributes of *nature* have to hold for *les choses*. Earlier we approached this from the side of *la nature* (see end of §41 and following) but put off asking the mirror-question, What is a "thing?" or What are the attributes of "things" that make them, in the way Rousseau asserts they are, equivalent to *la nature*? Of the many, many ways this can be answered—some of which were hinted at in §§42–45—we shall frame it here more precisely with respect to the claim that elicited the question in the first place: "there are two sorts of dependence [*il y a deux sortes de dépendance*]." What makes that difference seems simple enough: "things" are not like persons, and *nature* is not like society.

The modulating factor of this difference in *dépendance* is *ordre*: Rousseau is perfectly clear that human beings, in the single and in the plural, are disordered, and that *nature* and "things" are ordered; this is the conceptual source of the equivalence between "things" and nature.

This excludes at least one line of approach. There would not be much point in defining the regulative distinction between order and disorder by insisting that it derives from the difference between things and persons; this would be to presuppose exactly what is in question.

The alternative is to pose the question another way: what is the source of *ordre?* And here Rousseau's answer stands out clearly: in all cases, Will is the source of *ordre*. The problem of *dépendance* is a function of the problem of *ordre* which is a function of Will. The relationships amongst these three topics sets the agenda for inquiry, specifying what we need to know about "things" to evaluate different sorts of *dépendance*:

For each of the following,

. . . natural "things"

. . . nonnatural "things"

. . . persons

. . . human laws

. . . laws of nature

we need to know if they are

. . . ordered by Will?

. . . ordered another way?

. . . disordered?

. . . interchangeable?

B. The Rhetorical Structure of *Ordre*

§51

THE COMMONPLACE OF *ORDRE* AND THE COMMON SENSE OF DEPENDENCE

Where is the order that I had observed? The whole scene of nature offers me only harmony and proportions, that of the human type offers me only confusion, disorder! (OC IV.583)*

Rousseau's use of the word *ordre* stands, in its context, at the crossroad of theology and natural philosophy. Between them there is a tug-of-war, but both sides are pulling on the same rope. In Part Three of this book we saw something of debates that animated the European intellectual scene throughout the century before Rousseau began his literary career. While theology and natural philosophy each had special ways of mobilizing the notion of *ordre*, they were profoundly interrelated. This fact provides Rousseau with commonplaces to mark out in several ways at once the conceptual terrain where he will go to work. From this polysemic ground he will elaborate moral and political conclusions at once uncannily familiar and utterly original.

To join theology and natural philosophy to his social theory of politics, Rousseau appeals—in the passage at the head of this section, and in dozens of analogous turns of phrase—to a commonplace concerning *ordre*. His imagined reader would have been entirely familiar with the equality of two ratios

nature : ordre :: moral : désordre

---

* "Où est l'ordre que j'avois observé? Le tableau de la nature ne m'offroit qu'harmonie et proportions, celui du genre humain ne m'offre que confusion, désordre!"

269

Indeed, Rousseau is tracking a common topic of his day. A clear example of this appears in works published around 1750 by the Genevan jurist J.-J. Burlamaqui, studied by a wide public over the next century. Burlamaqui is the first modern authority cited in the opening pages of Rousseau's *Discours sur . . . l'inégalité* (OC III.125), where paraphrases from *Principes du droit naturel* would have been recognized as such by Rousseau's first wave of readers.[24] In another part of that book Burlamaqui states clearly the common sense that will become a vehicle for Rousseau:

> In considering the beautiful order that supreme Wisdom established in the physical world, one can only be persuaded that [God] abandoned the spiritual and moral world to chance and lawlessness.[25]*

Burlamaqui states this to deny it. "Reason," he adds, "tells us the opposite." Because God endowed human beings with the capacity for choice, the moral world is an opportunity to express God's Will by exercising our own. Law is the source of moral order and human Will is the source of law. These are of course topics and themes familiar to any reader of Rousseau's.[26]

Great writer that he was, but also like anyone who speaks to others with effect, Rousseau expands the commonplace into an image of a better future.[27] As this purpose courses through the word *ordre* it is at some moments propelled by theology and at other moments by the philosophy of nature. We will touch on both.

Dieu is omnipresent in Rousseau's pages. Opening *Émile*, nothing is more obvious than the way theological terms become pivot points in his thinking. This vocabulary gains weight and detail in dozens of his texts. However, it is most precise, and, if one can say this, indirectly explicit in the part of *Émile* entitled *"Profession de foi du Vicaire savoyard."*[28] The *"Profession"* is a long and almost freestanding mixed-genre tract that takes up more than one third of Book IV (OC IV.558–635). Rousseau presents it as a "transcription," as if our music-copyist had recorded note for note the Vicar's unflinching sermon and subsequent skeptical self-critical commentary.[29] It is fair to take the *"Profession"* as the primary statement of Rousseau's own religious beliefs because he tells us that "the result of my painful researches was just about what I have since consigned to the 'Profession of Faith of the Savoyard Vicar',"[30] because he argues that this text "must be studied first" (OC III.694) and because he writes to the Archevêque de Paris, Christophe de Beaumont, in vociferous defense of *Émile*, as follows:

---

* "En considérant le bel ordre que la Sagesse suprême a établi dans le Monde Physique, on ne saurait se persuader qu'elle ait abandonné au hasard et au dérèglement le Monde spirituel ou moral . . ."

I will tell you, moreover, why I published the Vicar's profession of faith, and why, despite much clamor, I will always hold it up as the best and most useful writing of the century in which I published it. . . . I will pronounce my religion, because I have one, and I will pronounce it for all to hear, because I have the courage to do so, and because it would be desirable for the good of mankind that this was the religion of all the human race.[31]*

While Rousseau's particular theistic commitments are interesting for many reasons, I direct your attention to the consequences of these commitments for his way of theorizing the social circumstances of politics.[32] Simply, we must be attentive to the direct and pervasive influence of his particular Christian world-view even when the topics he presents appear to be entirely secular.[33] When—constantly—Rousseau decries theologians it is not because they are theistic but because they say nonsensical things. Moreover, the eighteenth-century vocabulary of religion is slippery and the ways Rousseau's social and political claims are inflected by theological terms and *motifs* are often obscure even when he presents them as if self-evident.

The difficulty of seeing exactly how theology serves political theory in Rousseau is exacerbated for today's reader. Many terms and concepts that seem to us to stand quite apart from matters of religious faith were in the eighteenth century still growing out from or being transformed by theological discourse. In the last sections of the preceding part of this book we considered in some detail how these entanglements operated through the concept of *nature*. That discussion was the background for this one: it would be all but impossible to make sense of the conception of *ordre* in the discourse of natural philosophy without reference to theology. Although with the passage through the seventeenth into the eighteenth century the influence of theology in conceptions of *nature* becomes increasingly indirect and subject, in some quarters, to ever more vociferous denials, the connections remain strong. This complicates the task of untangling the various threads within Rousseau's concept of *ordre*.

At the same time, the impression that theology is the key to everything—an impression that theologues in this period typically convey of it—would also be misleading. Early modern science, or natural philosophy, had by Rousseau's time become an exceedingly complex amalgam of contradictory elements—Aristote-

---

* "Je vous dirai, de plus, pourquoi j'ai publié la profession de foi du Vicaire, et pourquoi, malgré tant de clameurs, je la tiendrai toujours pour l'Ecrit le meilleur et le plus utile dans le siécle où je l'ai publié. . . Je dirai ma Religion, parce j'en ai une, et je la dirai hautement, parce que j'ai le courage de la dire, et qu'il seroit à désirer pour le bien des hommes que ce fût celle du genre humain."

lian, Humanist, Ramist, Baconian, Cartesian, Newtonian, and so on—with its own specific contents and limitations; it often stood more or less well by itself.[34] It must be allowed, too, that what was learned from experiment, mathematics, and rational speculation had, in its turn, profound impact on theological inquiry.

It is necessary, therefore, to set the stage for a consideration of Rousseau's notion of *ordre* in several overlapping ways. From one point of view, the topics of natural philosophy can be considered as relatively autonomous. At the same time, Rousseau's texts over and over again link the theme of *nature* to considerations of God. Thus, examining the concept of *ordre*, which will provide the next critical instrument with which to assess Rousseau's fundamental distinction between two types of *dépendance*, I emphasize points of contact between these two deeply related discourses.

Another possible source for the concept of *ordre* calls upon our attention here. It may be said that strands of distinctively "republican" political thought developed a conception of order clearly distinct from the versions of that concept operative within either natural philosophy or theology. However, it is certainly not the case that "republican" thinkers make no reference to *nature* or God. Thus, if this additional approach to *ordre* is to be considered as important in its own right, the *nature* to which it appeals would have to correspond in only insignificant ways with the *nature* of concern to the natural philosophers. Likewise, it would require a distinguishable conception of God, or an argument showing that the *ordre* considered by theologians is of no formal, material, or conceptual import for the "well-ordered republic."[35]

With this in mind, it is certainly worth remarking that familiar tropes of civic republicanism show themselves with vigor in many of Rousseau's writings and in works by his contemporaries.[36] However, even this apparently simple observation requires yet another qualification. This republican theme is not always so distinct from the other discourses of order. Indeed, it is easy and common to underestimate how analogous ideas and ideals, often drawn from the same classical sources as "civic republicanism," were already imbricated in the discourses of natural philosophy. Cicero is lurking, more or less in the wings, even where rhetoric organizes some of the most technical modern ventures in mathematics;[37] he is joined by the Stoics wherever versions of "natural law" appear;[38] a step further finds him likewise in justifications for "naturalism" and thus for "natural religion";[39] the whole enterprise of the "new science" is driven by a skepticism that evokes his name.[40] Nor is it by accident that Bayle's philosophical journal is called *Nouvelles de la République des Lettres*. Or that English experimentalism, after Bacon, after Boyle, after Newton, runs on a circumscribed ethic of trust and civility.[41] One could go on at some length. My purpose here is only to underscore my strong hesitation about bringing into consideration, as if out of nowhere, this third source for the concept of *ordre*. For, in addition to the ways that the "republican" version might have been touched by natural philosophy, there is the obverse but little recognized fact that natural philosophy was already in crucial ways threaded through with "republicanism."[42] And did not an analogous process bring various "republics" into church doctrines? Think of Augustine—reader of Plato, rhetorician, Roman provincial—who "drains the glory from the Roman past to project it far beyond the reach of men, into the 'most glorious City of God'" and insists that "it is only within the walls of the Heavenly Jerusalem that Cicero's noble definition of the essence of the Roman Republic could be achieved."[43]

I might feel compelled to work through these relationships, and thus make clearer the distinctive contribution of "republican" thought, if the primary purpose of this book was to examine Rousseau's construction of political institutions or a complementary notion of "civic virtue." You will have long since understood that these are not my goals. It may be said, rather, that my aim has been to draw you, dear reader, into the sociological zone that precedes politics, or, more precisely, from which politics emerges and into which it recedes. This social space is boldly asserted by Rousseau but remains amorphous in his pages because an initial image of it is just taking shape there. He knows that most people who turn his pages will fail to see the distinct social fact he is trying to represent, for it is something that "no one among those who attacked me was ever able to conceive" (OC IV.967). One might add—and it is a purpose of this book to show—that in our time the situation is not much improved: mostly ignored by moral philosophy on one side and political theory on the other, it has remained to an incomplete sociology, attentive to its own concerns but sometimes incautious with respect to politics, to decipher the significance of the social space prerequisite to political relationships.

What occupies this sociological zone is *le lien social*, which is to say the most general and dynamic structure of the unavoidable fact that human beings must live together every day. Rousseau's pivotal representations of *le lien social* are in images of *dépendance*. His turn to the language of *dépendance* provides a way to analyze the "cement of society" where that "cement" is a living, desiring, and suffering fact.[44] From another angle, Rousseau shows that it is misleading—even plainly false—to think of *dépendance* as only a problem of moral philosophy, as if it concerned only the (self-)management of individuals through the (self-)imposition of general rules.[45]

In retrospect, too, we can see this concern with *dépendance* as perhaps his most durable contribution to political thought. Rousseau's deployment of other terms, such as the vocabulary of master and slave, or the constellation of citizen, subject, and sovereign, exhibits a political language reaching its peak. For the next century, that language drives definitive enterprises of modernity like the denaturalization and abolition of slavery and the rise of the democratic state. Just as this language has come to ring increasingly hollow since the middle of the twentieth century, the discourses of fundamental *dépendance* have finally begun to find their purchase in the revived attractions of community, identity, and culture, and in the increasingly global demands of ecology, economy, and technology.

Rousseau avoids none of these topics; he owns them. It is precisely his virtuosity within discourses of moral philosophy and political theory that brings to light—and in some sense brings into being—what is absent from their insights but necessitated by their interrogations of the modern world. This is the distinctively social field. *Le lien social* holds together both society and inquiry into the human condition.

I will have two purposes as I carry you into these interstices of Rousseau's way of thinking through *dépendance*. The first is to articulate something that, it seems to me, weighs heavily but in silence on common sense. Every day we keep alive Rousseau's distinction between types of dependence because we have confidence—in crucial moments of action—in the moral and political significance he attributed to that distinction. My second purpose is to bring all this into question: should we follow Rousseau? or, more precisely, Should we follow the part of our contemporary common sense that Rousseau represents with such agility?

Should, of course, is a big word. It hinges on what one wants to accomplish. Many of Rousseau's other concerns remain inspiring in this respect: his hatred of inequality and injustice; his vision of a democratic republic ruled by law.[46] Whether or not they derive from Rousseau, these are exactly the type of concerns that may be called upon to measure whether we *should* follow him with respect to how we conceive *le lien social*.

Anyone can see that politics, or the "political option," is not present in all times and places. It arises here and there, from one moment or one century to the next, under specifiable conditions. The effort of political thinking would be more profitable if it were turned to analyze this variable potential in its context. While the historians and ethnographers aim to reconstruct many contexts, political theorists, like Rousseau, must work in partnership with them to seek a general statement of context, one which shows the conditions that, given the facts of life and lives together, *make politics an option*.[47]

As we shall see below, it is precisely in this respect that Rousseau's approach to the supremely apt topic of dependence becomes suspect. This suspicion will require us to consider with greater care the background that defines the varieties of this fundamental social fact. Features of the human condition that are "non-political" must be brought to the foreground first. Only then will it be possible to understand how dependence constitutes the field within which politics emerges. The coherence of this complex field Rousseau characterized with the concept of *ordre*. But even those two concepts—*dépendance* and *ordre*—joined together do not make clear what Rousseau is getting at. The conceptions of order that ultimately sustain his political theory are themselves elaborations of his attachments to beliefs about *nature*, and, finally, conceptions of God.

This brings us back to the distinctively "republican" notion of order. Let us admit that this might be one way to delineate important features of Rousseau's thought. However, to thematize it here would prejudice inquiry into *le lien social*. The roots of politics will not be found in its branches. A "republican" concept of order offers itself as inherently political; it must therefore take many things about politics for granted. It can only sustain a limited account of the "pre-political" conditions from which politics emerges.

Finally, let us take one more step back before leaping forward. To speak of the "pre-political" at this point is not to gesture to a "state of nature"; you will have seen that this theoretical strategy is vastly more complicated than the immediate discursive effect it creates. It is rather to accept the simple fact that not everything is political, and the corresponding need to identify exactly what it is—the *differentia specifica*—that permutes or inflects other sorts of relationships into political ones.

With this in mind, we turn to crucial tensions that, with the help of the conceptual maps drawn earlier in this book, may be found lurking in Rousseau's uses of the term *ordre*. This term, again, is the great crossroads at which the natural, the theological, and the moral converge and give significance to the political. This is the site we must now revisit.

SYMBOLIC FORMS OF *ORDRE*

I had often dressed up religion according to my fashion but I had never been entirely without religion. (OC I.228)*

Some would have us believe that Rousseau's relation to Christianity was, at best, instrumental. Judith Shklar seems to imply that this "fact" is well-known.[48] But this resonates with the kind of convenient smear antagonists make to avoid argument. It is implausible that Rousseau was not a "believer."[49] As they issue from a person who spent the majority of his life in solitude and primarily concerned with "his own true and complete self,"[50] Rousseau's massive and repeated defenses of his own Christianity cannot be convincingly attributed to political ambition. Isn't theology always, first or last, an instrument for understanding oneself?[51]

Cranston plainly states the obvious: Rousseau "loved and needed God."[52] It should be clear to readers of the present book that key features of his social theory of politics are shaped by this love and need. This is more important than any causality that might flow in the opposite direction. "Unless it was his passion for music," Robert Wokler correctly observes, "no other subject stirred Rousseau so deeply as his love of God."[53]

In the last year of his life (1777–78) Rousseau himself declared that "I never adopted the sorrowful doctrine" of the "missionaries of atheism" (OC I.1016). The intensity with which he rejected atheism led some perspicacious readers, once they were no longer directly caught up in the hot debates of the eighteenth century, to realize that Rousseau actually returned religion to an atheistic time.[54] *How* he believed and what uses he made of that belief are altogether different and more complicated matters.[55] What weight, for example, would charges of opportunism have in a context where a theologian gains renown with a book entitled *De l'utilité d'une révélation?*[56]

* "J'avois souvent travesti la religion à ma mode mais je n'avois jamais été tout à fait sans religion."

Indeed, anyone ready to assume that the issue has been settled will be disturbed by the briefest review of a vast literature that started to grow even as Jean-Jacques was just beginning to win his fame, in which his religious attachments and the theological significance of what he wrote are debated from every conceivable angle.[57] This alone should lead us to doubt that Rousseau was any clear-cut sort of theological opportunist.[58]

Of course, he sometimes appears that way. At the age of sixteen, arriving in Turin in 1728, Rousseau converted from Calvinism.[59] More than two decades later, in 1754, he sought and achieved readmission into the church of Geneva.[60] Perhaps his allegiance to Rome was one of outward observance and inward nonconformity? He did not think so, recalling that "as far as I can recall my ideas, at the time sincerely catholic, I was in good faith" (OC I.121). One may fairly imagine that he had something to gain with each conversion—a new life away from home in Turin, the return of his citizenship in Geneva—but that says nothing of how these goals were modulated by or integrated into "authentic" religious beliefs.[61] As Gouhier succinctly says, "Rousseau was able to change church twice," but "it seems that he never changed his credo."[62] The fact is that he was never coerced; would it not be odd that someone *entirely* false in his piety should bother to convert in Rousseau's situations? Indeed, a person who changes religious practices, or even someone who after careful reflection gives them up, may have an understanding, and even an attachment, to theological claims that is far more intense than the typical believer. The critical mind never simply lets the boat sail away.

For Rousseau this seems doubly true. Here is the theorist of *société*, plain and simple, "abandoned to ourselves." To locate the exact perimeter dividing *us* from the Divinity seems almost to require a prior critical theology. This would certainly have been the expectation of readers and their writers in eighteenth-century France. The counterpart of such a thoroughly humanized vision of the world would have to be a religious faith. Perhaps one without miraculous or supernatural signs; perhaps a "natural religion," even a "religion of nature," or eventually a "civil religion." But only God could say whether or not it was "authentic."

I do not wish to judge or even interpret Rousseau's religious conviction. My purpose here is to provide a sufficient basis for the following point: it would have been impossible for Rousseau to reason without faith. His thought is both implicitly and explicitly organized around reference to God and a number of theological categories.

This is true even as we leave the *promeneur solitaire* to the woods and reenter the civic realm. For, if Rousseau gave up Calvinism, first as convert then as expatriate, he did not, so to speak, give up Calvin.[63] Opening any of Rousseau's most important texts one sees easily that his childhood in Geneva left him deeply impressed not only with the republican idyll instilled by his father but with the overlapping marks of the sacred in the secular. In the most obviously political of his writings—*Du Contract social*—Rousseau insists that

> Those who consider Calvin as only a theologian misunderstand the extent of his genius. (OC III.382, note)*

This double admiration for Calvin sets the tone for Rousseau's civic refashionings of religious dogmas into "sentiments of sociability" (OC III.460 ff.). Rousseau has no compunction about calling the result of this *la religion civile*. It may be said that Rousseau took it to heart when Voltaire wrote in his *Lettre sur Mr. Locke* that

> Philosophers will never create a religious sect. Why? It is that in no way do they write for the people.[64]†

But Rousseau tacitly adopted a corollary of this maxim that Voltaire would have despised: to write *for the people* is to make *the law into a religion*.[65] The *rapprochement* from both sides—that of law and that of religion—is evident in the idea of "*la religion civile*," which acknowledges, with Machiavelli, that no "extraordinary laws . . . would be accepted . . . without recourse to God [*legge straordinarie . . . sarebbero accettate . . . senza ricorso a Dio*]" (OC III.348, note), that "the one sometimes serves as the instrument of the other" (OC III.318, repeated III.384), that it is "useful to be able to give to the moral bond an interior force which penetrates all the way to the soul" (OC III.318) because "there will never be a good and solid constitution except where the law reigns over the hearts of citizens,"[66] and that, admitting "the existence of the powerful, intelligent, good, foreseeing, and providing divinity" one must also admit "the sanctity . . . of the laws" (OC III.468). Moreover, if law requires a "civil religion," religion properly understood requires civility, for

> if Man is made for society, the truest religion is also the most social and the most human. (OC IV.969)§

The final pronouncement the Vicaire-Rousseau/Catholic-Protestant comes to in the "*Profession de foi*" has the tone not of an opportunist or flatterer but of a

---

*"Ceux qui ne considerent Calvin que comme théologien connoissent mal l'étendue de son génie."

†"Jamais les philosophes ne feront une secte de religion: pourquoi? c'est qu'ils n'écrivent point pour le peuple, et qu'ils sont sans enthousiasme."

§". . . si l'homme est fait pour la société, la Religion la plus vraye est aussi la plus sociale et la plus humaine; . . . ."

hard-nosed mediator with a deep-seated credo, ready to ignore doctrinal differences in favor of a universal theism; he commends his acolytes this way: "dare to confess your faith in God among the philosophers; dare to preach humanity to the intolerants."[67]

While what appears in the *"Profession de foi"* is not the doctrine Rousseau inherits from the earlier great Genevan, it includes theocratic symbolic forms that translate into a concept of *ordre* for a secular political setting. It serves well Rousseau's theoretical purposes.

Indeed, on just this point readers of Rousseau can turn back to Calvin with hermeneutic profit. We find for example Calvin's famous distinction between the "church invisible" and the "church visible" is made in terms of order. The former is perfectly ordered; the latter is disordered but striving for perfection in new political institutions. The unity characteristic of the order of the "church invisible" follows from "election," which is to say from a decisive application of God's Will.[68] The formal similarities between this argument and Rousseau's analysis of *dépendance* are striking. Even when Rousseau's conclusions diverge from Calvin's — as they did, for example, on the key question of power[69] — the difference between their views involves the same ambiguity in the notion of order that will carry enormous theoretical weight within the architecture of Rousseau's own representation of *le lien social.* This is the tension between an active, verbal sense of order (*ordonner*) and a substantive sense (*les lois de l'ordre*) which I shall make explicit shortly.[70]

I have suggested that a sylleptic mirroring process brings symbolic forms from theological doctrine into Rousseau's social theory of politics. An analogous process characterizes Rousseau's reliance on the categories and concepts of natural philosophy. Note that, as with theology, this reliance need not, and often did not, denote agreement. In 1740, for example, Rousseau with no compunction scoffed at the pretensions of natural philosophy:

> the Cartesians, who by their conjectures want to explain all natural effects, seem to me ridiculous, and the Newtonians, who would have us take their conjectures for facts, even more so.[71]*

But over the next ten years he changed his tune. In the closing pages of the first *Discours* of 1750, after having excoriated *"des Sciences et des Arts,"* Rousseau nonetheless finds a way to present Descartes and Newton as "preceptors of the human race," great men among just a handful to whom falls the task "of raising

---

* ". . . les Cartésiens me paroissent ridicules de vouloir rendre raison de tous les effets naturels par leurs suppositions, et les Neutoniens encore plus ridicules de donner leurs suppositions pour des faits. . . ."

monuments to the glory of the human spirit."[72]* Here the comments posted just above concerning Rousseau's relation to Christianity may be redirected to the topic of natural philosophy. Both theology and natural philosophy serve Rousseau's purposes as "instruments" in a way that is perfectly banal: all concepts and beliefs are, in some sense, instrumental; this is *a fortiori* true of major *topoi* that operate within systematic religious or scientific doctrines and, therefore, must be fit to accommodate a large plurality of perspectives.[73]

We should therefore not look exclusively for Rousseau's dedication to or rejection of the principles espoused by the "preceptors of the human race." It is more important to recall what these two thinkers—or, even more precisely, their *names*—represented in Rousseau's time and how references to them could be used by an author to establish a particular relationship with his readers. These are rhetorical facts, and there are many things one could say on this score.

The first of two points relevant here is that Descartes was explicitly and centrally concerned with *ordo*.[74] The exact significance of this concern may be obscure, but its probable origin is suggestive: from the heart of Descartes's mathematical and methodological writings it can be traced backward to the Ciceronianism of the later sixteenth century.[75] I do not think that it is merely coincidental— although neither are the reasons entirely self-evident—that Cicero, under the eponym *"le Prince de l'Eloquence,"* is counted by Rousseau on this same page among the few "preceptors of the human race."[76]

The second relevant fact is that the names Descartes and Newton stood, in the most rarified way, for an extraordinary balancing act between two conceptions of order. These conceptions are what I shall call—in the next section (53)—the verbal sense, or order[as act], and the substantive sense, or order[as condition]. Descartes was identified with the image of a perfectly deductive system, one in which a few simple and self-evident truths allowed for the willful production of an order through a methodical logic; his name thus symbolized the ideals of the project of "constructivism" that David Lachterman, with great perspicacity, has shown to be an essential feature in the "genealogy of modernity."[77] Likewise, no matter how many thinkers contributed to the long development of the modern "mechanistic world view," it was the summary of it in a few simple axioms that brought Newton's name to symbolize the ideal of the project of empiricism and the representation of the "order of things [*l'ordre des choses*]." Of course, neither of these paradigmatic "scientists" was entirely successful in stating the laws governing the "order of things" in the intelligible or the sensible realm. Nonetheless, it was in-

---

* "C'est à ce petit nombre qu'il appartient d'élever des monumens à la gloire de l'esprit humain."

creasingly accepted in the eighteenth century that such laws could in principle be known.[78] My point here is that the names "Descartes" and "Newton" were among the key symbols of this belief. Displayed and exchanged in conversation and in writing, these names were forms generative of discourse that connected Rousseau and many of his readers.

§53

THE PERFORMATIVE OF ORDRE

I almost never hear talk of government without finding that one comes back to principles which appear to me false or fishy. The Republic of Poland, one has often said and repeated, is composed of three orders: the Order of knights, the Senate, and the King. I would rather say that the Polish nation is composed of three orders: the nobles, who are everything, the bourgeois, who are nothing, and the peasants, who are less than nothing. (OC III.972)*

The sort of *ordre* here ridiculed by Jean-Jacques is of long standing. Its categories represent a pre-sociological and profoundly anti-egalitarian way of conceiving *le lien social*. No one should be surprised that he wants to leave it behind. Yet, embedded within it are ways of organizing the theory of society that Rousseau appropriates; they, again, feed the uses of the word *ordre* that he approves.

It is worth noting here that since it left the Greek word τάξις behind to be reborn in the Latin of Cicero and Vitruvius as *ordo*, one form or another of the word "order" has occupied the attention and the tongues of a large part of humankind.[79] It enters French before there was French, English before there was English. By the seventeenth century it occupies disproportionately large space in every dictionary, whatever the language. I propose therefore to engage it not frontally, but by tangent.

---

* "Je n'entends guere parler de gouvernement sans trouver qu'on remonte à des principes qui me paroissent faux ou loûches. La République de Pologne, a-t-on souvent dit et répété, est composée de trois ordres: l'Ordre équestre, le Senat et le Roi. J'aimerois mieux dire que la nation polonoise est composée de trois ordres: les nobles, qui sont tout, les bourgeois, qui ne sont rien, et les paysans, qui sont moins que rien."

In *The Three Orders: Feudal Society Imagined*, the great historian Georges Duby studied neither the ancient nor the modern world. That is, his object was unusually uninflected by the truths and mythologies of our present experience (for we are ancient-moderns and modern-ancients), and, for that, perhaps more susceptible to unbiased generalization. He points to a key ambivalence in the word "order," which has at least two senses. "Originally, . . . ordination was an inscription."[80] It organized and entitled a particular body of persons. To *inscribe* is an action; whatever relationships are initiated and sustained by the act are its effects, the *inscription*.[81] This *verbal* use of the word is similar to the sense of "order" as a command. It is a very old way of using the word and remains familiar today. From this point on, I shall refer to this verbal sense as order[as action].

There was also a second meaning of the term "order." "*Ordo*," Duby further instructs us by turning to the Latin, "referred to the just and proper organization of the universe."[82] In this sense, "order" denoted not an action but a thing, a status, a condition. This *substantive* use of the word is equally ancient, and continues similar to the contemporary sense of "order" as a state of affairs. From this point on I shall refer to this substantive sense as order[as condition].

The double sense, the *doubleness* itself, of order[as action] and order[as condition] is almost as old as the word itself. In moving the argument along, I want to stress the tension inherent in using one and the same term to point to very different aspects of experience. Simply, "order" hovers between act and condition. This ambivalence is performed by each iteration of the word and syllepsis again becomes a motor for Rousseau's innovative thinking.

It will come as no surprise that this mode of innovation, too, is vastly older than Rousseau; indeed, it is older than the French or English languages in which it now comes before us. It was the classical rhetoricians, with their particularly self-conscious political interest in using speech to connect acts with circumstances, who saw and exploited the tensions contained in this term. A good and proper order, fixed in practice and in the expectations of the auditor, open in its application to the subject at hand by the skilled orator, allowed a dialectic of an especially effective sort to be played out. That dialectic was, as sociologists today might put it, between *agent* and *structure*. Speech is what mediates between the two.[83]

More than the single sign in common binds together these two conceptions. The politician or the rhetorician uses "order" to denote the action of placing

> words—or men—in appropriate position relative to one another, and to arrange the composition of the parts in an appropriate whole.[84]

At the same, however, this "appropriate whole" *had an order*, in other words it was a substantial structure which was in some way predetermined:

for in ordination of this kind, a prior, immanent, immutable plan existed, and it was advisable to discover this plan by reflection before proceeding, so that it might be followed closely.[85]

In other words, there is a common passage joining order[as action] and order[as condition]. Both gravitate around the theme of relating parts to a whole. It requires the Augustinian assumption, however, to suppose that that whole is the Will of God. In the Ciceronian view that totality and its *ordre* are resident in the process of human self-creation.[86]

Here rhetorical understanding is more precise than sociology or the political thought it sustains. Every concept of "order" is about neither the parts nor the whole. It is about a third thing that appears only in performance. When Aristotle, toward the end of the *Rhetoric* (1414a), says "it only remains to speak of order [λοιπὸν δὲ περὶ τάξεως εἰπεῖν]," he is not referring to the whole of the "speech [λόγου]" itself. Nor is the "order [τάξις]" one of the elemental building-blocks from which the speech is assembled. "Order" is a characteristic of action—of the speaking—and it is a characteristic of the result—of the words spoken. It is akin to "word/style [λέξις]."[87] It must be understood as separate from both the parts and whole, but it cannot be understood without them.

This rhetorical perspective also suggests that a third sense of order—as *sequence*—typically intervenes between and sews together order[as action] and order[as condition]. We mentioned this tripartite division earlier, §43, and it is not difficult to see how order[as sequence] serves a crucial intermediary function. Speaking, even before— long before—it is grammatical, is sequential; speaking unfolds, unfurls, one word at a time, one word after another. *Act* becomes *condition* in this process, even if the eventual and static relation between the parts and the whole bears little recognizable resemblance to the *sequence(s)* from which it emerged.[88] At least in this general sense, the shift from ordered speech to ordered experience seems rather simple. Observe *out from the middle term*, the primal sequence, and it appears that *speaking* came from somewhere—an *actor-speaker*—and achieves some result—a new state of affairs, or *condition*. This kind of shift is reflected already in the vocabulary of the *Rhetoric*, where, for example, "order [τάξις]" is a differentia for types of political bodies.[89] The convergence of words and things implied here is elaborated by Cicero in a way that diminishes, as I have already suggested, the emphasis on predetermination—a later Christian theme—and assumes no immutability; he translates εὐταξία (literally: "good order") both as *modestia* and as *ordinis conservatio*, and defines it with the Stoics as "'moderation is the science of disposing aright everything that is done or said' . . . so the essence of orderliness and of right-placing, it seems, will be the same; for orderliness they define also as 'the arrangement of things in their suitable and appropriate places.'"[90]

As these considerations are meant only to ready the instrument with which we will analyze *dépendance*, I shall not carry them further at this point. For the main purposes of this chapter, it will be enough to consider just the extremes—*act* and *condition*—and allow the middle term—*sequence*—to return to the background.

It is important here, too, to say clearly that these ways of thinking about order were in no way foreign to Rousseau. Although he often disdains "eloquence," he was incomparably a master of it and was steeped in its classical texts. Where Rousseau relies on the word *ordre* he provides important clues about the reading and thinking that gave shape to his conception of *société*.

Let me insist on the phrase *gave shape to*, for inherent in the notion of *ordre* are certain limitations on the application of the term itself. As some kind of relation between parts and a whole is constitutive of the concept of *ordre*, a monad cannot be considered "ordered" because monads have only one "part." This means, for example, that *ordre* cannot be a predicate of God: all the One can do is to be consistent with Himself and command the universe. But He cannot be *ordonné* in any proper sense of the word.[91]

As *ordre* is ascribed to *société*—and remember that society in the innovative sense Rousseau concocts is conceived as some kind of "whole"—it must be understood as the development of complexity within the apparently simple entity it qualifies. Thus, *société ordonnée* cannot be monolithic; that would *eo ipso* deny the applicability of the notion of *ordre* to it. This is consistent with something we have already seen from several other angles. In Rousseau's view *société* is unitary as seen from the outside, where a single perimeter contains the whole "island," but, seen from the inside, is composed of manifold *dépendances*. Thus, the very language of *ordre* privileges the complex perspective sketched in the first part of this book.

Something important follows directly from this complexity. For Rousseau, to think of *société* in terms of *ordre* is always already to approach two rather different sets of problems. The first involves the relationships that constitute the social totality, from which and through which politics emerges.

The second set of problems points us back toward theodicy and the image of society as what remains when mankind is "abandoned to ourselves." This, in turn, is a proposition to understand *société* on its own terms, and reasserts, with great vigor, the need to examine in detail the composition of the social fabric. Indeed, Rousseau is perfectly clear that he is being carried toward a type of sociological inquiry in which theological questions need not arise at all.

> I judge the order of the world, even though I know nothing of its end, because
> to judge that order it is sufficient to make comparisons among the parts, to

study their convergence, their relations, and to take note of their concert. Why the universe exists is beyond me. (OC IV.578)*

This inclines with the contingent Ciceronian *ordinis conservatio* to which I alluded just above. But in Rousseau theological questions do arise. Indeed, they flood the pages of *Émile*. What is this mix of the secular and the theological? To what conception of society and politics does it ultimately lead?

As we have seen, the significance of dependence-from-things is, for Rousseau, grounded in the "order" that characterizes those things. It is this "order" that gives a special shape to our relation with them. I underscore this point. It means that the choice to analyze the structure of dependence, *le lien social,* in terms of "order" is fundamental to Rousseau's project as a whole. That is why, before we can draw conclusions concerning Rousseau's distinction between two sorts of dependence, we shall have to clarify still further his concept of "order." In particular, we must discover how he deals with and makes use of the fundamental ambiguity of the term. This is where, yet again, the secular and the theological cross paths.

§54

THE MODALITIES OF ORDRE

I would not want anything to do with an atheist prince . . . or, if I was sovereign, with atheist courtiers. . . . It is therefore absolutely necessary, both for princes and for peoples, that the idea of a Supreme Being, creator, governor, meter of reward and vengeance, be etched deep in their spirits.[†]

—*Voltaire,* "Athéisme," Dictionnaire philosophique

*"Je juge de l'ordre du monde, quoique j'en ignore la fin, parce que pour juger de cet ordre il me suffit de comparer les parties entre elles, d'étudier leur concours, leurs raports, d'en remarquer le concert. J'ignore pourquoi l'univers existe. . . ."

†"Je ne voudrais pas avoir affaire à un prince athée, qui trouverait son intérêt à me faire piler dans un mortier: je suis bien sûr que je serais pilé. Je ne voudrais pas, si j'étais souverain, avoir affaire à des courtisans athées, dont l'intérêt serait de m'empoisonner: il me faudrait prendre au hasard du contre-poison tous les jours. Il est donc absolument nécessaire pour les princes et pour les peuples, que l'idée d'un Etre suprême, créateur, gouverneur, rémunérateur et vengeur, soit profondément gravée dans les esprits."

The fundamental ambivalence that features in the concept of order is what generates, as we saw in the preceding section, its performative effects in political discourse. Before moving on to consider this force (Part Four.C below) I want to develop a somewhat different view of this ambivalence.

Even when deployed specifically for politics, the term *ordre* opens onto and invites images from other domains. In this course of events those other domains become vehicles for politics and serve political ends. This is not to say that *ordre* has several definitions; whatever its various meanings are, they are not distinct. What I am saying rather is that each operation and effect of the word *ordre* feeds off of the others. This is how it garners and redirects commitments and energies of various readers toward a capacious but singular new end. A single word has several modalities.

How shall we understand the modalities of *ordre* as sources of Rousseau's creativity and success? For the kind of analysis we pursue here it is important to identify abstract terms. As we shall see, the key to Rousseau's social theory of politics is the difference between, and conjunction of, order[as action] and order[as condition] [92]

These abstractions shape and transform Rousseau's social theory of politics. They are not sufficient basis for identification with it. Readers are implicated in the structuring elements of order[as action] and order[as condition] by engagements with other discursive fields. Theology and science overlap with the modalities of *ordre*. They invest it with living meaning.

This, too, is important. The various realms invoked by the word "order" exist both as discursive facts and as facts of experience. Of course, this simplifies matters greatly at the expense of accuracy; as the use of language is a central aspect of human experience, and essential for politics, these are ultimately facts of the same type.[93] Indeed, we have seen several ways in which the imbrication of speech in *le lien social* features in Rousseau's social theory of politics; this is, for example, what makes syllepsis such a powerful gesture in his writing and in bringing his ideas into the world. Nonetheless, for heuristic reasons, we will follow common sense here in distinguishing these two kinds of facts.

The two modalities of order can be represented in various ways. These diverse representations show—indeed, in some important sense make effective—the possible operations of the term. They are how it, a gesture at once single and several, produces effects. Before turning to map this ambivalence of order we shall now follow Rousseau back into the two main discourses he deploys. This will bring further into the foreground the machinery of his appeal to *dépendance* as a basic social fact.

Here, the vast terrain glimpsed briefly at the end of Part Three comes again into view. One might with profit proceed from this point through more details of the intellectual universe of the mid-eighteenth century, linking with greater precision the various sources, aspects, and conclusions of Rousseau's argument to the proliferating context of debates in his time.

I will not do this. Such a procedure would require the addition of not just several paragraphs, but of an entire book of an entirely different sort. Nonetheless, it will help to recall in passing the broad background against which Rousseau appeals to *ordre*, and to highlight two of the familiar bridging strategies he employs to bring together a version of *ordre* fed from various sources. The first is *la religion naturelle*; the second is a kind of philosophical dualism.

As it is played out in Rousseau's writings, the tension constituted within the concept of *ordre* parallels a tendency common in the first half of the eighteenth century. Many different writers in many different ways attempted to separate God and *nature* while trying to remain committed, so to speak, to both. The former came more easily than the latter. This division was increasingly pressed forward by the internal developments of natural philosophy.[94] Contradictions continued to grow between the new systematic accounts of the workings of *nature* and belief in a Christian God. And although many proponents of natural philosophy found these contradictions difficult to acknowledge, the wedge being driven between God and *nature* stretched all the more tightly the tension between order$^{as\ act}$ and order$^{as\ condition}$.

When Rousseau appeals to *ordre*, his gesture is delimited both by a more general attempt to reconcile these two, diverging, lines of thought and by the desire to muster at once the rhetorical force of two increasingly incompatible sets of beliefs.

In the eyes of many well-placed readers Rousseau could not always have it both ways. Charges of atheism are leveled against him. Rousseau defends his *"Profession de foi"* as "intended to combat modern materialism, to establish the existence of God and *la religion naturelle* with all the force the author can bring to bear" (OC IV.996).

With the rubric *la religion naturelle* Rousseau keeps his options open. He disguises himself—actually, his several selves—by entering into this very broad and diffuse movement. *La religion naturelle* aimed to reconcile the contradictory claims of theology and natural philosophy, making peace with the Faith, Grace, Scripture, and Divine Will of the former while developing attachments to the Reason, Nature, the "Book of Nature," and Natural Law of the latter.

La religion naturelle is not, of course, Rousseau's invention. In the representative and synthetic view that theologian Jean-Pierre de Crousaz advanced for students in his popular manual *La Logique* (1720, I, 249) it is composed in its ancient "majestic simplicity" from the following tenets:

... to study the great book of nature, to cultivate one's reason, to develop one's mind, to recognize a Creator of the universe, to respect his Providence, to admire him in his works, to perceive the difference between virtue, which God loves, and vice, which he condemns, and to go through this life, in his presence, with moderation and justice, in the expectation of a better destiny after death.[*]

While dedicated to a Creator and mindful of his Providence, the follower of *la religion naturelle* gives priority to human experience of the physical over the metaphysical realm. His first text is nature, not scripture.[95] The Messiah is not mentioned. The progress of this religious self is through reason, not sentiment, nor immediate faith. This is sufficient for morality, and morality is sufficient for the hereafter, whatever it may be. In this way, *la religion naturelle* may be said to encompass "our obligations toward God, toward ourselves, and toward others of our own kind."[96]

La religion naturelle is offered as a bridging strategy in Rousseau's social theory of politics. As such it is self-defeating and cannot carry us to Rousseau's conclusion. Its comprehensiveness is in itself a problem. It threatens all the prevalent European religious doctrines of the time. Much eighteenth-century speculation led to the nineteenth-century fact that "natural religion" could develop into the "religion of nature." In the minds of Spinoza's critics, and those who embraced the critics' view, this *naturalisme* was no religion at all.[97]

What, already in the world- and other-worldly-view described by Crousaz and like-minded thinkers, is the use of revelation and scripture? This is certainly not a new theological problem in the eighteenth century. Yet, in the period of Rousseau's own education this question appeared increasingly urgent. "To recognize that natural religion gives happiness to man and society, isn't that to neglect the mystery of the Fall and the Redemption, and to discount the value of Grace?"[98] This discount is taking its toll. It leads Voltaire, addressing himself directly to God in the *Ode sur le fanatisme* of 1732, to issue this hubristic challenge: "I am not Christian, but that's so as to better love you."[99]

It is commonplace and convenient to oppose Voltaire's God to Rousseau's.[100] But, as Jean Ehrard has made crystal clear, after "the first half of the eighteenth century the reality became much more complex than this summary dichotomy."[101] It is a complexity arising from implications for the belief in God in

---

[*] "... à étudier le grand livre de la nature, à cultiver sa raison, à perfectionner son esprit, à reconnaître un Créateur de l'univers, à respecter sa Providence, à l'admirer dans ses ouvrages, à sentir la différence de la vertu, que Dieu aime, d'avec le vice, qu'il condamme, et à passer cette vie, en sa présense, dans la modération et dans la justice, dans l'attente enfin d'une meilleure destinée après la mort."

the age of science that follow from new beliefs both in "physics" and the emergent "anthropology." This is a source of the inherent plurality in *la religion naturelle* that even while it tends against Christianity is a powerful instrument for
Rousseau's political thinking.

What is the plurality of *la religion naturelle?* Its compass can be roughly distinguished by its degrees. Diderot writes pointedly that

> The deist . . . is the one who believes in God, but who denies all revelation; the
> theist, by contrast, is the one who is ready to admit the revelation, and who
> already admits the existence of a God.[102]*

But even this divide is not so clear. For, who can say what is involved in "admitting the revelation?" To Jean-Jacques Lefranc de Pompignan, Diderot's deism
would look theistic:

> One has given the name "theists" to those who not only believe in the exis-
> tence of God, but also in the obligation to form a cult to him, the natural law
> of which he is the source, the free will of man, the immortality of the soul, the
> punishments and rewards of an afterlife.[103]†

Such fluid boundaries allowed for frequent fluctuations across this spectrum;
Voltaire, for example, desists from deism in 1751 and begins to consider himself
a theist.[104] This fluidity of *la religion naturelle*, like the plurality on which it is
based, is fruitful for Rousseau, the theorist of society.

Turning again to the *"Profession de foi"* will carry us back to the modalities of
ordre — order[as act] and order[as condition] — and allow us to complete this preface to our
analysis of the use of them.

This is not a free-standing tract. The *"Profession de foi"* is a functional part of
Émile. Émile in turn is a functional complement of *Du Contract social*. Rousseau aims, as he writes to Beaumont and others, to have the advantages of both
God and *nature*, dividing them or holding them together as it suits his analysis
of the fundamental conditions of political life.[105] *La religion naturelle* is a capacious topos that facilitates this purpose.

Nowhere is Rousseau's double game clearer than in the way he, champion of
la religion naturelle, clings to a philosophical dualism. Even within the camp
of natural religion this distinguishes him from many of his Enlightenment con-

---

* "Le déiste . . . est celui qui croit en Dieu, mais qui nie toute révélation, le théiste, au
contraire, est celui qui est près d'admettre la révélation, et qui admet déjà l'existence d'un
Dieu."

† "On a donné le nom de Théistes à ceux qui croient non seulement à l'existence de Dieu,
mais encore l'obligation de lui rendre un culte, la loi naturelle dont il est la source, le libre
arbitre de l'homme, l'immortalité de l'âme, les peines et les récompenses d'une autre vie."

temporaries. They, following or exceeding the counsels of Spinoza and Leibniz, tended toward monism in general and materialism in particular.

We have clearly seen Rousseau's vehemence against materialism. On certain occasions he also takes explicit and decisive objection to monism. This is important here because it joins the two modalities of the abstract concept of *ordre*—which is to say, order^as act^ and order^as condition^—with the integrative and rhetorically effective topics of religion and science. Thus, he writes of

> . . . the opinion I have always had concerning the eternal coexistence of two principles, one active, which is God, and the other passive, which is matter.[106]*

This dualism has clear correspondences in Rousseau's conception of human beings—"man is not a simple being, but is composed of two substances"—and it grounds a deep philosophical anthropology as well, in which "there are two forms of human sensibility—physical (or organic) and moral (or active)."[107]

When Rousseau gives a reason for seeing things this way, he further confirms the monotheism at the heart of his creationism:

> . . . the coexistence of these two principles seems to better explain the constitution of the universe. . . . but to suppose two principles of things. . . . is not to suppose two gods.† (OC IV.956)

A dualism of this sort appears everywhere in *Émile*. While Rousseau was already battered with charges of atheism, this also set him against materialists from La Mettrie (*L'Homme machine*, 1748) to d'Holbach (*Système de la Nature*, 1770) and Delisle de Sales (*Philosophie de la Nature*, 1770).

Why? Why assume this complex and apparently incoherent set of positions? The question is especially intriguing because Rousseau knew full well that his particular dualism would contribute to the rejection of his broader political views: "this opinion made the philosophers to whom I told it laugh in my face; they found it absurd and contradictory."[108]

That was fine with him. His breakpoint with the atheistic tendencies of *la religion naturelle* comes against those who have "established in the name of nature an authority no less absolute than that of their enemies" (OC I.967).

What we see here reiterates the parting words of the *Vicaire*-Rousseau: "dare to confess your faith in God among the philosophers; dare to preach humanity

---

*"... l'opinion que j'ai toujours eue de la coexistence éternelle de deux principes, l'un actif qui est Dieu, l'autre passif, qui est la matière. . . ,"

†"... .la coexistence des deux Principes semble expliquer mieux la constitution de l'univers . . . mais supposer deux principes des choses . . . . ce n'est pas pour cela supposer deux Dieux. . . ."

to the intolerants" (OC IV.634). At this point, however, his moderation is stated from the perspective of the *philosophe* rather than the priest. In like tone he vaunts the philosophy of nature against fundamentalists, for "the study of nature makes new discoveries every day" (OC III.739).

The final point I want to make here is that the different associations that emerge from the two modalities of *ordre* — order[as action] and order[as condition] — follow the lines of Rousseau's complex conjunctive *religion naturelle* and his philosophical-theological dualism. We shall see several consequences of this in the next section, where another facet of these problems confronts us. It concerns the complex relation Rousseau maintains to theism in the face of his extensive commitments to what is nothing less than an evolutionary perspective.

But this is how things stand as Rousseau picks up the term *ordre*. By mid-eighteenth century, after a period of relatively peaceful coexistence the conflict between the partisans of God and the advocates of *nature* is raging again.[109] We arrive with Rousseau on this field of battle. He contests from both sides. As theologue, Rousseau proposes that we take God's Will (again, measured by its effects) as the model for order[as action].[110] At the same time, joining the philosophers, Rousseau offers *nature* as the model for order[as condition]. Adopting these two very broad representations — as Rousseau does — one can articulate the ambivalence that features in the concept of *ordre*. We can do this in terms of Rousseau's account of the relation between God and *nature*. This provides a paradigm for how the concept of order functions in his political sociology.[111]

Linger for a moment on these last sentences. I want to underscore this point. In a fiercely partisan debate — which is to say, the struggle between religion and science that is the crucible of modernity — it is not Rousseau's final purpose to take sides. Asserting positions on both sides, Rousseau articulates the complex discursive field of the debate itself, with its tensions and contradictions and conflicts, to invest a political *topos* with new content. When Rousseau places the word *ordre* before his readers, he captures the energy of other people's motivating habits and beliefs from religion and from science (and from other domains, like music, as we saw in §14). And he redirects that living energy into specifically political symbolic forms. It is no longer *ordre* that defines religion and science but, conversely, religion and science that, through the *topos* of *ordre*, give shape to a new way of representing, and thus a new way of enacting, political relationships. This is one of the sources of Rousseau's unsurpassed creativity and the enduring magnetism of his writings. It is also why, as I have indicated in the title of this book, key and unresolvable tensions between religion and science, specifically between creationism and social evolution, remain embedded in our common sense and continue to impede our understanding of the political.

C. *Ordre* as the Deployment of Ambivalence

§55

NATURE INSIDE GRACE
The Original Will

We return to Rousseau's philosophical dualism. The principle that distinguishes between matter and motion is Will/*volonté*. Although it resonates more with seventeenth than with eighteenth-century common sense, Rousseau's belief is clear:

> The first causes of motion are not at all in matter; matter receives motion and communicates it, but does not produce it. The more I observe the action and reaction of the forces of nature acting upon one another, the more I find that . . . one must always come back to some Will for the first cause. . . . In a word, every motion that is not produced by another one can only come from a spontaneous, voluntary act; inanimate bodies only act by way of motion, and there is no real action without Will. There you have my first principle. Thus, I believe that a Will moves the universe and animates nature. There you have my first dogma, or my first article of faith.[112]*

The argument here is bold and clear: there is no movement without action, all movement comes from a spontaneous and voluntary act, and "there is no real action without Will."

---

*"Les prémiéres causes du mouvement ne sont point dans la matiére; elle reçoit le mouvement et le communique, mais elle ne le produit pas. Plus j'observe l'action et réaction des forces de la nature agissant les unes sur les autres, plus je trouve que. . . .il faut toujours remonter à quelque volonté pour prémiére cause; . . . . En un mot, tout mouvement qui n'est pas produit par un autre ne peut venir que d'un acte spontané, volontaire; les corps inanimés n'agissent que par le mouvement, et il n'y a point de véritable action sans volonté. Voila mon prémier principe. Je crois donc qu'une volonté meut l'univers et anime la nature. Voila mon prémier dogme, ou mon prémier article de foi."

This constellation of ideas, centered around Will/*volonté*, is of fundamental importance. It is linked to—or, more precisely, it is definitive of—the concept of order[as action].

Another feature of order appears in this perspective. Precisely insofar as Rousseau plays with *ordre* as syllepsis, Will comes to define order[as condition] as well. In other words, what seems to be antithetical to the Will turns out to be defined by it.[113] I will emphasize the way Rousseau operates through this surprising conceptual linkage.

Of course, it is not just any *volonté* that serves as the paradigm for Rousseau's principle-dogma-article-of-faith; it is God's supreme *volonté*.[114] In the case of God, the connection between Will and *ordre* can be made quite explicit. The universe is an "infinity of relations, from among which not one is conflated or lost in the crowd [*la foule*]. . . . [The beings] are all ordered, in such a way that they are all reciprocally ends and means, the one relative to the others."[115]*

The language, if not the intent, rings familiar. In the first version of that companion volume to *Émile*—*Du Contract social*—Rousseau had written in almost identical terms of "the first ties of general society [*les prémiers liens de la société générale*]." These are the initial relationships that will give to dependence its form. It is a hybrid condition, and "from this new order of things are born a plethora of relationships without measure, rule, or reliability" (OC III.282).†️ Where in the first passage Rousseau gestures to the order of *nature*, in this additional passage he uses analogous terms and images to show the disorder of *societé*. We shall soon see why this is so. What is clear now is that he marks out again exactly the problem that arises between the two types of dependence.

The order of the universe cannot but have a source, and Rousseau concludes that "the world is governed by a Will that is powerful and wise" (OC IV.580).§ Now, from this claim one need not move to the next step. But Rousseau goes on to insist that this Will is singular, and that this fact does not vitiate his dualistic view (OC IV.956). Scorn is brought down upon any other possibility:

> Those who deny the unity of intention manifest in the relations among all the parts of this great whole have a nice trick to cover their nonsense with abstractions, schemes, general principles, emblematic terms; whatever they do, for

---

* ". . . infinité de raports, dont pas un n'est confondu ni perdu dans la foule. . . .[les êtres] sont tous ordonés, en sorte qu'ils sont tous réciproquement fins et moyens les uns relativement aux autres."

†️ ". . . de ce nouvel ordre de choses naissent des multitudes de rapports sans mesure, sans régle, sans consistence . . ."

§ ". . . le monde est gouverné par une volonté puissante et sage . . ."

me it is impossible to conceive of a system of beings so unflinchingly ordered without conceiving of an intelligence that orders it.[116]*

Not only is *volonté* necessary for action, but in God's case, Will and action are immediately identical. With everything in constant flux, there can be no "means" or time lag separating the *volonté* from the *acte*: "God *can* because he *wants*; his Will *does*[117] his power" (OC IV.593).†

Nor should the reader be surprised when, sarcastically imitating a prophetic voice, Rousseau uses order[as action] in reference to what one is bound to think of as order[as condition] circumstances. "That a man comes to hold before us this claim: Mortals, I announce to you the Will from On High; recognize the voice of the one who sent me in mine; I order[118] the sun to change its course, the stars to form another arrangement, the mountains to lie flat, the waves to rise up, the earth to take on another aspect" (OC IV.612).§

The absurdity Rousseau finds here is not just that a Pope or a Priest or a Prophet pretends to have God's powers. It resides as well in the way that exceptions to rules are represented.

Even if *volonté* and *acte* are identical, Grace, which, in this perspective, is order[as action], and Nature, which is order[as condition], are not. Something intervenes between them that, from one side, is not simply God's Will and, from the other side, is not identical with Nature itself. Whatever name one gives to this mediation ("Providence," for example), Rousseau seems to think of it as a kind of plan. God works out and follows this plan in the act of ordering. Order[as action] is, so to speak, Willed but not willful. The specific representation of this plan that concerns us here is the one that appears in the "main passage": *les lois naturelles*, or natural law.

I refer to natural law as representation because Rousseau clearly states that "natural laws" are not "real beings, substances [*des êtres réels, des substances*]" (OC IV.575). Moreover, as Rousseau makes devastatingly clear in the preface

---

* "Ceux qui nient l'unité d'intention qui se manifeste dans les raports de toutes les parties de ce grand tout ont beau couvrir leur galimathias d'abstraction, de coordinations, de principes généraux, de termes emblématiques, quoi qu'ils fassent, il m'est impossible de concevoir un sistême d'êtres si constamment ordonés, que je ne conçoive une intelligence qui l'ordonne."

† "Dieu peut parce qu'il veut; sa volonté fait son pouvoir."

§ "Qu'un homme vienne nous tenir ce langage: Mortels, je vous annonce la volonté du Très-Haut; reconnaissez à ma voix celui qui m'envoye. J'ordonne au soleil de changer sa course, aux étoiles de former un autre arrangement, aux montagnes de s'aplanir, aux flots de s'elever, à la terre de prendre un autre aspect."

to the *Discours sur . . . l'inégalité*, we have no real idea what natural law is: "knowing so little Nature, and with barely any accord on the sense of the word 'law,' it would be quite difficult to agree on a good definition of natural law"* (OC III.125, and generally OC III.122–27).

Even with these sharp qualifications in mind, natural law is the closest we come to a disclosure of pure order[as condition]. The universe "is in motion, and in its rule-governed and uniform movements, subject to laws that are constant, there is nothing of that liberty which appears in the spontaneous motions of Man and animals" (OC IV.575).[†] Thus, he sees "in the system of the world an order that never bends."[119][§]

Rousseau does not stop with these putatively deist observations. He verges to the border of theism by adding that God is not merely invested in Nature; Nature is entirely within His compass, and He is the author of it. Rousseau extrapolates from this that God is able to order[as action] exactly following the plan he has made for Nature. It is because, and as long as, God acts that everything is in order[as condition]. That is why, as we recall from the very first lines of the *Émile*, "all is good leaving the hands of the Author of things [*tout est bien sortant des mains de l'Auteur des choses*]" (cf. §1 above).

And this seems like a satisfactory way to manage the ambivalence inherent in the concept of *ordre*. As long as God has his way, Nature remains inside Grace, and order[as action] and order[as condition] are identical. In brief, the ambivalence of *ordre* has no operational effect.[120]

You will not be surprised to learn that the question is not so easily smoothed over. Elsewhere in *Émile* Rousseau suggests that the laws of Nature and God's ordination of the *système du monde* are not identical.[121] As a consequence, the gap between order[as action] and order[as condition] may persist. And in this gap, the ambivalence between the two modalities of *ordre* does have some operational effect. What happens when Rousseau turns in this other direction?

---

* ". . . connoissant si peu la Nature et s'accordant si mal sur le sens du mot Loi, il seroit bien difficile de convenir d'une bonne définition de la Loi naturelle."

† ". . . est en mouvement, et dans ses mouvemens réglés, uniformes, assujettis à des lois constantes, il n'a rien de cette liberté qui paroit dans les mouvemens spontanés de l'homme et des animaux."

§ ". . . dans le sistême du monde un ordre qui ne se dément point."

NATURE OUTSIDE GRACE

The order of the Universe, as thoroughly admirable as it is, does not strike all eyes in the same way. (OC IV.951)[*]

How does Rousseau imagine a persistent gap between the laws of Nature and God's ordination of the *système du monde*?

The point from which to approach this question was discussed in §49 above. It is the answer to what I called the Fundamental Question that sees Nature as inside of Grace ($Q^{fundamental}A^{nature \in grace}$) and thus takes both to have the same principle of motion (cf. Diagram 2 at page 239). That principle is the *volonté* of God; God as the paradigm of *volonté*. In this version, God must continue to act (that is, order[as action]) so as to maintain what exists. That is what indicates the goodness of God:[122]

> the goodness of God is the love of order; for, it is by way of order [*ordre*] that he maintains what exists, and binds each part with the whole. (OC IV.593)[†]

Notice that the noun *ordre* in this sentence—in the first but especially in the second instance—is not used unambiguously in the sense of order[as action]. At this stage this is not important. Why? Because by connecting *ordre* to the verbs *maintenir* and *lier*, Rousseau makes evident that God is, and must be, *doing* something. The noun *ordre* is by discursive implication the verb *ordonner*, or order[as action].

What happens when God is so present in Nature? Where does God's *ordination* stand with respect to natural law? In the discussion of the immutability of *nature* (§44 above), we spent several pages taking seriously the claim that *nécessité* is the primary characteristic of natural law. As it is difficult to conceive of

---

[*] "L'ordre de l'Univers, tout admirable qu'il est, ne frappe pas également tous les yeux."
[†] "... la bonté de Dieu est l'amour de l'ordre; car c'est par l'ordre qu'il maintient ce qui existe, et lie chaque partie avec le tout. ..."

anything as necessary *in itself,* it appeared that the best sense can be made of this if we take it as a metaphysical claim. Otherwise, and of more interest here, the word *nécessité* seemed to mark a concern with relative *inflexibilité.* Some implications of this shift were spelled out in the subsequent discussion of the mutability of *nature* (§45 above), the purpose of which was to make explicit and develop a very different side of Rousseau's thinking. That alternative perspective will come again to the foreground in the conclusion of this book. Nonetheless, our attention here is focused on the primary line of Rousseau's thinking. Taking him at his literal word will show most precisely the difficulties involved at this point.

Thus—listen as Rousseau again suggests that natural law is not just relatively but perfectly inflexible:

> [Nature] was not satisfied to establish order, it [*elle*] took unshakable measures so that nothing could disturb it. (OC IV.580)*

An example of this is the fact that different species of animals cannot cross-breed; this is not so much the consequence of attachment to the form of the horse, the ape, or the butterfly (or of God's handiwork in them) as it is Nature's means of protecting the order that constitutes Nature itself.[123]

Does Nature then protect itself against God? The *"mesures certaines"* it takes are manifest in the single word we tried earlier to evade: necessity/*nécessité.* Indeed, in the course of the hundreds of pages of *Émile*'s education, four recurrent phrases, reinforcing one another, close this circle tight: there is "the law of nature [*la loi de la nature*]" which imposes on us "the law of necessity [*la loi de la nécessité*]" because of "the necessity of things [*la nécessité des choses*]," which are "of nature [*de la nature*]."

Obviously, Rousseau is not alone in finding necessity in Nature. But as the specification of Nature serves his primary purpose and becomes an approach to law, the stronger idea of necessity replaces the weaker idea of relative inflexibility. Rousseau intends to transpose metaphysics into politics and this intention itself shapes, so to speak, retroactively Rousseau's conception of natural law.[124] Thus, while Nature is ultimately the product of God's Will, in Rousseau's dualist view (as is the case for many other writers) its primary quality is the mirror-opposite of this spontaneous animating power:

---

* "[La nature] ne s'est pas contentée d'établir l'ordre; elle a pris des mesures certaines pour que rien ne pût le troubler."

... this visible universe is matter, matter scattered and dead, of which the whole has nothing of the union, the organization, the common sentiment of the parts of an animate body.[125]*

This is, of course, a way to reopen the gap between Grace and Nature. Rousseau hammers in the wedge: "The world is therefore not a big animal that moves on its own; of these movements there is therefore a cause that is alien to it."† The most important feature of that "alien cause [*cause étrangère*]," which is Will/ *volonté*, is its liberty. By antithesis, as we saw in the preceding section, Nature has none of that.

This same universe is in motion, and in its rule-governed and uniform movements, subject to laws that are constant, there is nothing of that liberty which appears in the spontaneous motions of Man and animals. (OC IV.575)§

Thus, viewed one way, it seems that what begins as an identity of Nature and Grace ($Q^{\text{fundamental}}A^{\text{nature}\in\text{grace}}$) is transformed into a conception of Nature outside Grace ($Q^{\text{fundamental}}A^{\text{nature}\notin\text{grace}}$). This is at once odd and, as Jean Ehrard astutely observed, a characteristic tendency of culture, and even theology, in the century that prepares Rousseau and readers for their encounter. As we know already that Rousseau holds, at turns, both positions, this should come as no surprise. Two consequences follow from this "contradiction."

The first is this: Rousseau considers a complex and sometimes contradictory set of theological and natural discourses; for the most part, these remain in the background, even as they sustain what he has to say about society and politics; the nexus of these elements is the concept of *ordre*; exactly by evading commitment on the question I referred to earlier as ($Q^{\text{fundamental}}$)—Is Nature outside or inside Grace?—Rousseau effectively reenergizes the ambivalence in the key term *ordre*; this allows him to advance his inquiry into mankind "abandoned to ourselves" and to speculate about how to "resolve the contradictions of the social system" by deploying the term as syllepsis between order[as action] and order[as condition].

The second consequence of this ambivalence is this: Rousseau offers a figuration of the law, which is inherently the outcome of Will, as something that

---

* "... cet univers visible est matiére, matiére éparse et morte qui n'a rien dans son tout de l'union, de l'organisation, du sentiment commun des parties d'un corps animé; ..."

† "Le monde n'est donc pas un grand animal qui se meuve de lui-même; il y a donc de ses mouvemens quelque cause étrangére à lui, ..."

§ "Ce même univers est en mouvement, et dans ses mouvemens réglés, uniformes, assujettis à des loix constantes, il n'a rien de cette liberté qui paroit dans les mouvemens spontanés de l'homme et des animaux."

sets an inflexible frame around liberty. As a feature of his social theory of politics, rather than as a metaphysical posture, this should be understood more precisely as an image of the "rule of law." Thus, whether or not the ambivalence that emerges within the theological/naturalist account of *ordre* has operational effects for theology or science, what Rousseau does with it makes it productive for, or within, his social theory of politics.

This dialectic of liberty and necessity appears on both sides of the analogy in the "main passage" between natural law and human law. Natural law is, so to speak, the liberty of God and, at the same time, necessary precisely by contrast to the many human Wills that must submit to it. Thus, we should not be misled when Rousseau exclaims "it is not the word liberty that means nothing, it is the word necessity" (OC IV.586).* What he means is that all things necessary can be traced back to a Will, and "there is definitely no real Will without liberty" (OC IV.586).† Only in this way can natural law provide a model for human law that is sufficient to the task of correcting the ills of moral life.

As we look past the quality of *nécessité*,[126] we see that this model has two features: its inflexibility, and its origin in a Will. This peculiar combination is what Rousseau foresees in the transformation of dependence-from-persons into dependence-from-things. It suggests—together with many passages in Rousseau's texts—that the corresponding *political necessity*, which he refers to as "a real force [*une force réelle*]," is not primarily manifest in institutions like the police or the courts. The *force réelle* is the totality of a way of living together, or the *cité* and its *citoyens* as a whole. Thus, the sentence cited above—"[Nature] was not satisfied to establish order, it [*elle*] took unshakable measures so that nothing could disturb it [[*La nature*] *ne s'est pas contentée d'établir l'ordre, elle a pris des mesures certaines pour que rien ne pût le troubler*]"—might as well have the subject "*les hommes*" instead of "*la nature*."[127] Yet, just so that "*les hommes*" could accomplish this for themselves, it was Nature that "took certain measures [*a pris des mesures certaines*]"[128] and thus made possible and effective this mutually reenforcing structural equivalence.

It seems from this that the law of Nature cannot be identical with an order that can only be maintained through constant and active intervention. The obvious alternative does not help matters: even if we construe God's intervention as the occasional reconstruction of natural law, that would mean that natural law is not perfectly inflexible; in that case natural law would represent a type of order

---

* "... ce n'est pas le mot de liberté que ne signifie rien, c'est celui de nécessité. . . ."
† "... il n'y a point de véritable volonté sans liberté. . . ."

much more flexible, much less substantial and free-standing, than order[as condition] would have to be to sustain Rousseau's political and moral claims. Again, Rousseau cannot allow this possibility, and he does not.

What this shows is that the laws of Nature and the order of the *système du monde* are not identical. This idea is exactly the opposite of what we saw in §55 above. We must conclude that Rousseau has not resolved for himself, or strategically refuses to resolve, the tension in the concept of order, a tension which comes to the foreground through syllepsis in its diverse applications.

§57

MIRACLES

Between Nature and Grace?

Is it God's Will that constitutes the total inflexibility of Nature, or is the *ordre* of Nature necessary because God has ceased to intervene? We have seen that Rousseau wants to have it both ways. Testing the depth of Rousseau's dedication to naturalist principles against scripture, sounding for atheism, interlocutors of dogmatic faith inevitably brought before him the question of miracles. Indeed, in the second of the *Lettres écrites de la montagne* (at OC III.722) Rousseau identifies the topic of miracles as the one around which his critics "made the most noise [*ont fait le plus de bruit*]."

In one respect Rousseau's reaction is unequivocal. He makes clear that religion does not depend on the existence of miracles. The proper understanding of Christianity points this way, and "Scripture itself attests that in the mission of Jesus Christ miracles are not at all a sign so necessary for faith that one could not have it without admitting them" (OC III.735).* Moreover, "far from having made miracles Jesus very positively declared that he would never make them" (OC

---

* "Vous voyez, Monsieur, qu'il est attesté par l'Ecriture même que dans la mission de Jésus-Christ les miracles ne sont point un signe tellement nécessaire à la foi qu'on n'en puisse avoir sans les admettre. . . ."

IV.1147).* Faith grows surely from reason, sometimes from introspection, and perhaps from revelation (OC IV.606–17; OC IV.736–39).

As to whether or not miracles actually *exist*, his position is less clear. This much he admits vociferously: the reader is defied to find "one single place in all my writings where I am affirmative against miracles" (OC III.747). Critics, he says, fail to see that "there is a great difference between denying a thing and not affirming it" (OC III.747). And if "the author of the '*Profession de foi*' makes objections as much concerning the utility as the reality of miracles . . . these objections are not at all denials" (OC III.750).

Indeed, even to consider the possibility that God does not have the capacity to make miracles would be "impious if it wasn't absurd" (OC III.737). Indeed, "what man has ever denied that God can make miracles?"[129] We may ask instead, Does God *want* to make them? But human beings have no direct knowledge of what God wants and put this way the question is impossible to answer.

None of this impedes speculation about whether or not miracles exist. Here and there Rousseau writes as if their existence was self-evident. Elsewhere he ridicules that very claim. It is precisely this fluctuation that interests us here. His expressions of both views reveal again the ambivalent relation between God's Will (order$^{as\ action}$) and Nature (order$^{as\ condition}$).

It is possible to see Rousseau's fluctuation between these two positions in several ways. Perhaps, as he sometimes says, he really has not made up his mind; perhaps he is trolling for wider readership; perhaps he fears persecution and seeks to disguise his real views. Whatever role these motives may play, the fact remains that this ambivalence is functional within Rousseau's social theory of politics. It sustains his larger purposes. This is what concerns us here.

Consider first Rousseau's affirmations of miracles. They are not unqualified. He will only admit miracles if they conform to certain basic conditions. In notes for the *Lettre à Beaumont* Rousseau proposes that a miracle can be neither "absurd nor contradictory in itself" and insists that "one will never make me believe an absurdity by way of a miracle."[130]

One passage—again from the *Lettres écrites de la montagne*—stands out as a kind of definition of miracles. Adding gravity to what he is about to say with a prefatory comment—"I take up again my reasoning [*je reprends mon raisonnement*]"—Rousseau writes: "A miracle is, within a particular fact, an immediate

---

* ". . . loin que Jesus ait fait des miracles il a déclaré très positivement qu'il n'en feroit point. . . ."

act of the divine force, a perceptible change in the order of nature, a real and visible exception to its laws."[131]* In this one sentence, three different claims are made that relate miracles to major topics of concern to us here: God, Nature, and law. The first assertion is that a miracle is an unmediated act by God. The presupposition here is, of course, that a miracle is not a meaningless, random, or chaotic event; indeed, for believers miracles prove that there are no such events. Thus, we may take this first claim as a particularly clear representation of order$^{\text{as action}}$. The second assertion is that a miracle changes the *ordre* of Nature, and specifically does so in a way that is perceptible for human beings. As perception here means sense perception, the change is understood to occur in the realm of matter, and in this way we are referred back to the paradigm instance of order$^{\text{as condition}}$. Finally, we learn that a miracle goes outside of and is an exception to natural law. These three claims do not sit easily together. One fact—the miracle—pushes open as wide as possible the gap between order$^{\text{as action}}$ and order$^{\text{as condition}}$. Whereas in consideration of ($Q^{\text{fundamental}}A^{\text{nature} \in \text{grace}}$) natural law stood as just a short passageway between Nature's order$^{\text{as condition}}$ and God's order$^{\text{as action}}$ (we saw this in §55), here the distance separating all three is sharply increased. As a result, the single fact of the miracle which collects them together is, so to speak, miraculous; when Rousseau writes that "a miracle is surely a supernatural thing" he seems to point with some irony to both the "fact" and its expression.

How does this fit into Rousseau's thinking? What he tells us here is that a miracle *changes the order of nature*, but it is *an exception to the laws of nature*. A *change* and an *exception* are not the same. The exception reaffirms an existing condition, whereas a change constitutes a new condition. The implication here is that even when the order of nature changes, the laws of nature, which represent God's Will as a plan for ordering nature, do not change. This ensures that natural law will provide a paradigm for inflexibility. However, it also seems to assert inflexibility against the source of *ordre* itself (God's Will) and against the facts that are changed by God's Will and which constitute the new *ordre de la nature*.

In this perspective, it seems that the laws of nature and the order of the *système du monde* are not identical. This is once again (as in §56) contrary to what I said earlier (in §55), that as long as God has his way, order$^{\text{as action}}$ and order$^{\text{as condition}}$ are identical. Thus, even in the case that serves as paradigm for Rousseau's social theory of politics, order$^{\text{as action}}$ and order$^{\text{as conditon}}$ may fail to coincide. God has, so to speak, the right to change His mind.

This, of course, should create a huge problem for Rousseau. What he wants

---

*"Un miracle est, dans un fait particulier, un acte immédiat de la puissance divine, un changement sensible dans l'ordre de la nature, une exception réelle et visible à ses lois."

from natural law is a model of perfect inflexibility. This inflexibility is understood in terms of *ordre*. The source of *ordre* is God's Will. If God can simply change his mind "at will" the paradigm offered in the "main passage" for *les lois des nations* becomes unstable, even suspect. This is why Rousseau needs natural law to remain inflexible no matter what happens; it must also be why he simply declares that even a miracle cannot change natural law; gravity is intact *and* pigs are flying.

In making this move, however, Rousseau's argument leads him diametrically away from where he wants to go. Where does it point?

One possibility is that natural law is constantly bypassed because all order^{as} ^{condition} reduces—in a kind of radical anti-Spinozism—to order$^{as\ action}$.[132] However, nothing written by Rousseau supports the idea that natural law is ever simply irrelevant; as we have seen, he goes very strongly in the opposite direction.

The other possibility is that the world is governed by two inherent principles of motion: God's Will and the laws of Nature. This is tantamount to accepting $(Q^{fundamental}A^{nature\ \notin\ grace})$.

Thus far we have considered only one side of Rousseau's complex position on miracles. In *Émile* a somewhat different tack is taken. With the initial affirmative claims of the *"Profession de foi"* established, Rousseau begins to deploy its conclusions dialectically. He subjects all purported instances of miracles to rigorous reasoning. While he does not, as he reminds us, deny the existence of miracles, the argument is now set to show that it is highly unlikely that a miracle has ever in fact occurred.

His tone is testy and sarcastic. If God really wanted to show himself through miracles, He would have the sense to perform them in public and on the grandest scale.

> With these marvels, who would not recognize in an instant the master of nature! [Nature] never obeys imposters; their miracles are done at the crossroads, in the deserts, behind closed doors ... If your miracles, made to prove your doctrine, must themselves be proved, what good are they? (OC IV.612)*

The problem is crisply stated. Miracles are not just acts. They are a form of evidence. If they can only be established by way of a vast and largely unmanageable quantity of esoteric knowledge, they defeat their own purpose. Who could sort out the real ones from the fake ones?

---

* "A ces merveilles, qui ne reconnaîtra pas à l'instant le maître de la nature! Elle n'obéit point aux imposteurs; leurs miracles se font dans des carrefours, dans des déserts, dans des chambres; . . . . Si vos miracles, faits pour prouver votre doctrine, ont eux-même besoin d'être prouvés, de quoi servent-ils?"

This perversity of those who claim miracles as sure and necessary signs for religion recalls something Rousseau wrote in *Du Contract social*: theologians and metaphysicians are ridiculous both because they constantly disagree and because they nevertheless expect everyone else to be able to sort out their profound question. This is exactly the situation concerning miracles. However, Rousseau points out that it just does not make sense that God would demand this from us. He proposes, therefore, that the ground God prepares for the faithful must lie elsewhere.

A moment ago it was the *exception* that made the rule, the *exception* that protected natural law against the whims of God and mutations in the *ordre de la nature*. Now the shoe is on the other foot. "If many exceptions occurred I would no longer know what to think of it, and for my part I believe in God too much to believe in so many miracles so little worthy of him" (OC IV.612).* Thus, Rousseau sees again that a gap between God's Will (order[as action]) and Nature (order[as condition]) belittles God. Miracles are supposed to be signs, but "it is the inalterable order of nature that best shows the supreme being."[133]† In other words, it is the norm, not the exception, that is productive of faith. The suggestion here may even be that there are no exceptions. Natural law is inflexible (and, thus, as if by definition, subject only to exceptions rather than corrections) precisely because it is a representation of God's Will as manifest in Nature as *ordre*. The *"être suprême"* has nothing more to do. This effectively closes the gap between order[as action] and order[as condition] by reducing everything to order[as condition]. Nature is immutable (§44) and inside Grace (§55). It is easy to see how this position would have led critics to charge Rousseau with a sort of "naturalism."

The depth of Rousseau's attachment to the ambivalence in the concept of *ordre* is exhibited at the most microscopic levels of writing. The sentence quoted just above appears in several of the existing manuscript copies of *Émile*. In one case, the words *"être suprême"* are crossed out; Rousseau instead writes that what is shown to us by the "inalterable order of nature" is the "wise hand that guides it [*sage main qui la régit*]." In other words, there seems to have been a hesitation between thematizing order[as condition] [*être*] and order[as action] [*régir*]; in the version he sent to press it is the former that wins out.[134]

Which of these two perspectives on miracles finally belongs to Rousseau? The answer, as already suggested by the two preceding sections, is both. Holding both views is yet another way to maintain the fluidity inherent in the twofold sense of

---

* "S'il arrivoit beaucoup d'exceptions je ne saurois plus qu'en penser, et pour moi je crois trop en Dieu pour croire à tant de miracles si peu dignes de lui."

† "... c'est l'ordre inaltérable de la nature qui montre le mieux l'être suprême."

ordre; in this way the term *ordre*—at once neutral and doubly charged—is deployed as a kind of screen behind which concerns of theology and natural philosophy are restaged in the form of a theory of politics.

Rousseau is self-conscious and confident in taking this path. By contrast, his reader must hesitate, if only to review the argument as a whole. Even Christophe de Beaumont, addressed with astonishing bluntness by Rousseau, would have been hard-pressed to see exactly what he had in mind in writing that "the co-existence of two principles seems to better explain the constitution of the universe and to remove difficulties that one is at pains to remove without it, such as, among others, the origin of evil" (OC IV.957).* For, Rousseau's theodicy is not based on familiar philosophical dualisms; it does not trace *le mal* to matter-in-motion, but to a process of social evolution, where we, human beings "abandoned to ourselves," are part of Nature, and Nature is distinct from Grace.

Why, then, does the "main passage" carry us in the opposite direction, finding in humanity and Nature two distinct (if analogous) principles of motion, an "ecological" perspective underpinned by a fundamental belief in the identity of Nature and Grace?

And which of these two views holds sway?

§58

TWO TYPES OF *ORDRE*
Living with Contradiction?

Dare to confess God among the philosophers; dare to preach humanity to the intolerants. (OC IV.634)[†]

Such words may be after moderation, but Rousseau is not Aristotle. He also seeks to provoke and would, it seems, press interlocutors with what they deny. Is

---

* ". . . . la coexistence des deux Principes semble expliquer mieux la constitution de l'univers et lever des difficultés qu'on a peine à resoudre sans elle, comme entre autres celle de l'origine du mal."
† ". . . osez confesser Dieu chez les philosophes; osez prêcher l'humanité aux intolerans."

there a breach between what Rousseau demands from others and what he asks of himself? Can he have it both ways? Specifically, can his appeal to the two types of order—order$^{\text{as action}}$ and order$^{\text{as condition}}$—be both consistent and contradictory?[135]

A trivial answer to this question is "yes." It is possible that Rousseau has written nonsense, and in nonsense there is often enough sense to make it stick. A more interesting answer—one suggested, for example, by Paul DeMan (see §8 above)—would also arrive at "yes." Rousseau illustrates a double relationship, some aspects of which are stable and other aspects of which are unstable. By representing this duality he forces a dialogical reading of what he has written. A peculiar vivacity thereby appears in the text. It is productive of theoretical insight and (one might add "therefore") true to its object.

This vivacity features in lines and dots of ink, the ink's pages, the here trembling there collected *mise-en-récit* lovingly cultivated by the author and adored by his readers. It is this and more. The text carries itself into the world. It is a procession.

How, then, do textual processes—perhaps as simple as dissemination from writer to reader and circulation among readers—become, if not part of the story, then part of the theory that writing has set out to advance? A foray into this question will take us back to why Rousseau could live with contradictory *ordres* and forward to why we, in crucial respects thanks to Rousseau, cannot.

As we have seen throughout this book, Rousseau's problematic of order, dependence, and *le lien social* draws on several overlapping but not always consistent discursive settings. Each has its own common sense and commonplaces. On the one hand, these are essential operators within Rousseau's system. Their co-presence in his writing produces a structural instability that is, in itself, a theme and ultimately a proposition in his social theory of politics. On the other hand, these very same elements are and have long been mutating over time. This is a second important reason why the problematic he defines—no less his "resolution" of it—has the highly unstable character I have been discussing. I have said a great deal about the first and want now to focus briefly on the second. This is not a contingent consideration: the historical mutation of language transforms the structural effects it produces.[136]

Given this double regime, readers then or now do not uniquely determine the meaning of what Rousseau wrote. Nor are readers in control of what their reading does determine. Nonetheless, the significance of the theory varies with how it is catalyzed by active living readers, in each case situated differently within the symbolic realm it maps and proposes. In a process that occurs over decades and centuries, what Rousseau wrote must lead *us* elsewhere, to a way of understanding that Rousseau himself, for all his magnificent insight, could not have grasped.

Let me underscore just one part of this process here. The movement — inherent in the text as a historical object of reception — that drives us beyond the historical Rousseau derives from a shift in the position of the reader that, in what might be thought of as a literary equivalent of the Heisenberg principle, reconstitutes the text as a symbolic object.

In this section, I want to amplify the significance of this historical-transformative process. One could say many things about this but I will focus on the particular part of Rousseau's theory under discussion here. This will take two steps. First, I will cast the topics in Rousseau's own terms, focused once again around the ambivalence of *ordre*.

With the second step, I will bluntly adopt some of our contemporary terms to measure Rousseau. The warrant for this is not simply the fact that we read his texts today. It is also warranted because, at least in part, retrospectively, we may recognize that Rousseau helped to create the bifurcated space of common sense within which this shift of the reader's position has occurred.

An inescapable motive lies behind the allegiances that shape Rousseau's writing and generate our readings. To highlight this motive, let me briefly recapitulate the dilemma of the present part of the book you are reading. This dilemma stems from questions raised in §40 and §47, where what had initially been offered (in the "main passage") as a twofold distinction between dependence-from-persons and dependence-from-things appeared under a different light. At that moment the key proposition of Rousseau's social theory of politics was represented as a threefold distinction between dependence-from-persons, dependence-from-things, and dependence-from-nature. This new representation was brought into the discussion as a way to raise questions about the status of dependence, and to consider with a more meticulous eye the relationship between the world of things and nature. Against that background, another set of concerns came forward. As framed here, these issues now have to do with a gap between the order of things, moved by the divine Will, and the laws of Nature. This gap maps directly over the ambivalence of *ordre* — that is, the difference between order$^{\text{as action}}$ and order$^{\text{as condition}}$. It is the particular way that the tension in the figure of *ordre* emerges through Rousseau's argument about the sources and consequences of morally relevant dependence.

When only God and Nature are taken into consideration — what I referred to above as the Fundamental Question or $Q^{\text{fundamental}}$ — this theoretical gap is of no consequence for Rousseau. In practice, if we may say this about God, it has no functional effect. God is always by definition self-consistent (*"Dieu constant à lui-même"* OC IV.591) and the *système du monde* that He commands (order[as action]) follows by definition the contour of the natural law (order[as condition]) which He has made. It all amounts to the same thing.

Why, then, is the gap present at all in this paradigmatic case? The gap is conceptually necessary for an altogether different reason. It constructs an interpretive space within which God's Will, registering on the laws of nature and then ordering, can operate. This interpretive space does not do anything for God, who is, by definition, presumed to be independent of how we see Him. But it provides human beings with something absolutely essential for Christian believers: a structure for the proof of the freedom of God's Will. In a sense, what applies to both natural and civil man—that he cannot go against the laws of nature—is also true for God. Thus, God's Will could not be said to be free if order and law were identical, that is, if God's Will was nothing but a law of Nature that is utterly inflexible. Nature, as a system of laws, and especially with the emergence of a mechanistic world view, must be understood as *dead* until and only if God's Will winds its great spring.[137]

This animation is encompassing. By nature, human beings die; by God's Will we are born and would be born again. With a footnote for his act of faith, Rousseau, the Geneva psalter in mind, turns the *vicaire savoyard* to Psalm 115:

> Not for us, not for us, Lord,
> But for your name, but for your own honor,
> Oh God! Make us live again!

> *Non pas pour nous, non pas pour nous, Seigneur,*
> *Mais pour ton nom, mais pour ton propre honneur,*
> *O Dieu ! fais-nous revivre !*[138]

Rousseau certainly argues that the consistency of nature, which one may suppose is manifest in law, should suffice to establish the existence of God and invoke faith. But as we have seen (§57) that does not stop him from allowing that God *could* make miracles if He wanted to; indeed, it would be ridiculous to assert otherwise. So, some room for God to display His Will is allowed, even though God has no need for such display. His Will operates without time intervals or means; it is identical with His divine force (OC IV.593).

Once again, in this way the ambiguity in the figure of order *in the paradigm case of God* is reconciled. The complex array of semantic forces brought together within that term coheres, even where tensions between order[as action] and order[as condition] press against that coherence. Rousseau, and so many of his readers, can live with this precisely because the tensions themselves remain generative of faith.

In other words, the contradiction is functional; this is a first and powerful motive to live with it. I now turn to consider the status of a somewhat different contradiction at the heart of Rousseau's project. In this turn, what is at stake for the social theory of politics will come into higher relief if we adopt more contemporary terms, ones that readers will have already seen here and there throughout this book.

The contradictory background that inflects Rousseau's social theory of politics has two snarled features. There is a conception of *evolution*—of nature, of society, of society within nature, and, therefore, of each and every member of the species. This *evolution*, rife with its own motivating internal contradictions, is entangled in, held up and brought down by, a devotion to the principle of *intelligent design*, a creationism that is supposed to somehow frame or, more precisely, capture and domesticate the evolving whole.

From where we stand today, the reader must—and I do mean must—reflect not only on Rousseau's creative, systematic, and intentional use of this tension between *evolution* and *intelligent design* but also on the practical historical development of this tension. This development is an unavoidable part of what Rousseau's social theory of politics means today; it is a major channel guiding our affinities with it.

What I am about to say will be supported in greater detail in the very last sections of this book. I think that the history of reading Rousseau, which is important both as a historical fact and for how it pointedly instantiates broader developments in the political culture of modern democracy, shows us this: attachments to *evolutionary understanding* and a thorough-going devotion to *creationism* are deeply incompatible; failure to recognize the resulting contradiction is destructive of the civic republican aims and purposes that Rousseau himself championed. Evangelicals are not deists; Stoics are not Augustinians.[139] The laws of scripture cannot stand as the *volonté générale*. Thus, already on Rousseau's own terms, and then even more so with respect to the conditions of contemporary democratic citizenship, a society "abandoned to ourselves" needs to grow beyond this contradiction. We cannot simply live with it, even if it has been exceedingly generative, productive for Rousseau in his time and after.

This is an extremely strong claim and some further grounds for it will appear in what follows. What we can see now, however, is that Rousseau's balancing act is out of kilter, lopsided, tenuous. When it stands straight, it is because God is the only agency in the narrative of *ordre*, because God's is the sole operative Will. Even if that balance may hold for the paradigm case, it inexorably fails when shifted elsewhere, to the plural human world. In other words, in God's Will Rousseau sought a model with which to "resolve all the contradictions of the social system." It is exactly this *creationist* model that fails. It must fail for a thoroughly secularized self-image of society "abandoned to ourselves." The attempt to disguise this blatant theoretical fact—that is, *the failure*—appears in Rousseau's conclusion as the inscrutable and obscure *volonté générale.*

It is, however, as fruitless to mock the *volonté générale* as it is to adore it. Rousseau's prejudice for *creationism* over *evolution*—I am tempted to say, for the Augustinian over the Stoic—is manifest within his analysis of society. It constitutes the way the problem is formulated, and thus also constitutes the possibilities for an approach to politics that aspires to resolve that problem. This observation is more important than any quibbling about the *volonté générale,* as what I observe here impedes the invention of alternatives to it, the discovery of other ways to "resolve all the contradictions of the social system."

This is the step that carries forward all the kaleidoscopically diverse considerations in this book. With this step I would have you concentrate all that diverse theorizing into one final end point, one new beginning for the social theory of politics. The contradiction in Rousseau demonstrates something that Rousseau glimpsed but could not grasp. It is that we must make the fundamental fact of *dépendance* into the first topic of inquiry.[140]

Where confronted with the human condition we also find the courage to face our position within it, a reflexive mood arises. This desire for turning over and back, for revisiting, for mirroring, for letting-go time-lost, relinquishing the mire of habit, is reason. Those for whom the admonition to *look closely and understand* is a vocation here give the final full measure of significance to the title of the book you hold in your hands. It is only fair now to permit Rousseau his full say on this score.[141]

Look at us! Where the whole picture is not gruesome—

> In considering human society from a calm and disinterested perspective, at first it seems to show only the violence of the strong and the oppression of the weak; the mind is revolted by the harshness of the former and one is brought to deplore the blindness of the latter. . . .*

—our situation seems absurd—

> And since nothing is less stable among men than the external relations produced more often by chance than wisdom, and one which calls weakness or

---

* "En considérant la société humaine d'un regard tranquile et desintéressé, elle ne semble montrer d'abord que la violence des hommes puissans et l'oppression des foibles; l'esprit se révolte contre la dureté des uns; on est porté à déplorer l'aveuglement des autres; . . . ."

strength, wealth or poverty, human establishments seem at first glance founded
on heaps of moving sand.*

And yet hope with the persistence of reason may be repaid, for—

Only on closer examination, only after having pushed aside the dust and sand
surrounding the edifice, does one perceive the unshakeable base on which it is
built and learn to respect its foundations.†

What Rousseau calls for, and what we are about here, is

the serious study of man, of his natural faculties and their successive developments.§

The stakes are high, for without this

one will never arrive at the point of . . . .separating in the present constitution
of things what the divine Will has accomplished from what human art has pretended to do.**

So, even though Rousseau offers an answer to just a single question in his magnificent essay—What is the origin of inequality?—his enterprise extends dra-
matically far beyond it

giving rise to political and moral research that is in every way important, and
the hypothetical history of governments is in every respect an important lesson
for Man.‡

---

*" . . . et comme rien n'est moins stable parmi les hommes que ces relations extérieures
que le hazard produit plus souvent que la sagesse, et qu'on appelle foiblesse ou puissance,
richesse ou pauvreté, les établissements humains paroissent au premier coup d'oeuil fondés
sur des monceaux de Sable mouvant; . . . ."

†" . . . ce n'est qu'en les éxaminant de près, ce n'est qu'après avoir écarté la poussiére et le
sable qui environnent l'Edifice, qu'on apperçoit la base inébranlable sur laquelle il est élevé,
et qu'on apprend à en respecter les fondemens."

. §"Or sans l'étude sérieuse de l'homme, de ses facultés naturelles, et de leurs développe-
mens successifs, ..."

**" . . . on ne viendra jamais à bout de faire ces distinctions, et de séparer dans l'actuelle
constitution des choses ce qu'a fait la volonté divine d'avec ce que l'art humain a prétendu
faire."

‡"Les recherches Politiques et morales auxquelles donne lieu l'importante question que
j'examine, sont donc utiles de toutes maniéres, et l'histoire hypotétique des gouvernemens,
est pour l'homme une leçon instructive à tous égards."

This is the frame within which the complete *tableau* of mankind becomes an object in the vocation of political theory. Human knowledge of our own civic existence and possibilities hinges on the

> consideration of what we would have become, abandoned to ourselves.

Abandoned to ourselves; in these three words, in the brutal, even traumatic, realization of humanism, we find the very possibility of a modern self-knowledge, a new way of seeing our place in the world, in nature, in the cosmos, and perhaps in relation to the divine.

Should we be therefore perplexed to find *abandoned to ourselves* stated not as existential fact but as cognitive precondition? For, Rousseau continues,

> in considering what we would have become, abandoned to ourselves, we must learn to bless Him whose beneficent hand, correcting our institutions and giving to them an unshakeable foundation, prevented the disorders they could well have produced, and gave birth to our happiness from means that seemed certain to complete our misery.[142]*

One can imagine a dozen good reasons for Rousseau to present *abandoned to ourselves* as a hypothesis for believers. And clearly the lines that preface the *Discours sur . . . l'inégalité* are intended to curry favor with Genevans.

Be that as it may, the book itself is not so intended, and its author not so inclined. What Rousseau offers in the year 1754 is a new scientific study of politics, the primary audience for which is *les lumières*, his fellow reasoners. Prone to excess and restless in his genius, Rousseau may be said to explain himself perfectly in the declaration "Dare to confess God among the philosophers" precisely because that command never overrides the complementary commitment—when urged to "believe an absurdity by way of a miracle" (OC IV.1027–28) or pressured by "authority . . . to reason poorly" (OC III.743)—to "dare to preach humanity to the intolerant" (OC IV.634).

These are frustrating nonanswers to the question that for many reigns supreme: are we *abandoned to ourselves* or not?

There simply is no sure answer. And ultimately Rousseau is not so stupid as to commit himself one way or the other.

Why can he live with this ambivalence, this contradiction? Because posing the

---

* "En considérant ce que nous serions devenus, abandonnés à nous-mêmes, nous devons apprendre à bénir celui dont la main bienfaisante, corrigeant nos institutions et leur donnant une assiéte inébranlable, a prévenu les désordres qui devroient en résulter, et fait naître nôtre bonheur des moyens qui sembloient devoir combler nôtre misère."

question and even evading the answer creates an opportunity. The contradiction is productive not only of faith, but of reason as well. The production of faith is part of the production of reason.

Rousseau's real dare, then, is not aimed at the confessor or the counselor. It is a challenge to those who follow today the Delphic admonition, "know thyself." *Whatever we believe,* we had better engage in the "serious study of mankind." The question remains *where it will take us.*

D. Variations on the Will

If Man is active and free, he acts on his own account; everything that he does freely is utterly outside the ordered system of Providence, and cannot be attributed to it. (OC IV.587)*

$§59$

WILL AS FINAL CAUSE

Rousseau's account of the relation between God and Nature is not only a claim about *the way things really are*, if it is that at all. Nor is it simply a didactic move in the game of educating Émile. His answer to the Fundamental Question (that is, $Q^{fundamental}$, introduced at $§49$ above) is also a major feature of a theoretical argument about society and politics. However, while that theory is underpinned by the claims of theology and natural philosophy, it is not limited to them.

Here we need to consider a somewhat narrower implication. The themes discussed in the present part of this book form a crucial line of development within what Rousseau believed was possible — and, I suggest, what is commonly believed among our own contemporaries to be possible — in moral life given that the *état civil* is an *état de dépendance*. The political and social significance of these possibilities appear with each use of the term *ordre*. That is why it is difficult to understand either Rousseau or the problem he represents by sticking too close to the complex but relatively self-contained theological version of the sources and composition of order. When it comes to inquiry into mankind "abandoned to ourselves," theology can open a perspective on society and politics but it cannot show us their inner workings.

Rousseau is not sufficiently clear on this point. For, despite his deeply humanist response to the theodicy question, he allows theology to infiltrate far into his so-

* "Si l'homme est actif et libre, il agit de lui-même; tout ce qu'il fait librement n'entre point dans le sistême ordonné de la providence, et ne peut lui être imputé."

cial theory of politics. When Kant identified as Rousseau's central insight the belief that human Will is a "first principle," he would have been more precise to call his mentor not just *the Newton of the moral world* but also *the Augustine of the modern world*. The two encompassing intellectual projects thus identified converge when Rousseau points to the analogy between *ordre* as constituted by God and *ordre* as constituted by human beings. For, in each instance he finds the inherent and necessary principle of motion for two otherwise distinct domains to be a sort of Will.

As we have seen, the structure of this analogy is as follows (see diagram #8 on page 316).

When Rousseau tends—the tendency we saw in the preceding section—to see Nature as inside Grace, he is pushed by his answer to the Theodicy Question (Q^{theodicy}) toward a sharp distinction between Nature and Mankind; this, in turn, requires a principle of motion for each. Then the metaphor drawn in the "main passage" between Nature and society cuts two ways. They can be seen as similar because both are motivated by Will. At the same time, the assumption that things and persons are categorically different is a powerful motive to likewise differentiate the principles of motion associated with each of them. Rousseau thus distinguishes—at the nexus of quantity and quality—between a Will that is unitary and plural Wills that are not.

Here the shift from theology to the social theory of politics weighs heavily. In moral matters, what counts is not just God's Will, nor the Will of single persons who stand alone before their Maker. Multiple Wills are always part of the scene. Once these *plural human Wills*, Wills which cannot operate outside the exigencies of time and the need for means, are introduced into the story—in any way—contradictions between the act of ordering and the order of system resurface in a powerful, expansive, and often overwhelming way.

We considered a theological version of these contradictions in §58. Concluding this section I want to set those issues aside for a moment. Under the sign of the New Model Will[143]—with its expectations and modes of framing, calibration, and judgment—the tension between act and condition produces a whole new field of instability and struggle. This social field will later in the history of sociology be understood as the site of the problem of *structure* and *agency*.[144] The tension itself is a primary characteristic of modernity. And it is Rousseau who first provided a clearly sociological framework within which to understand it.

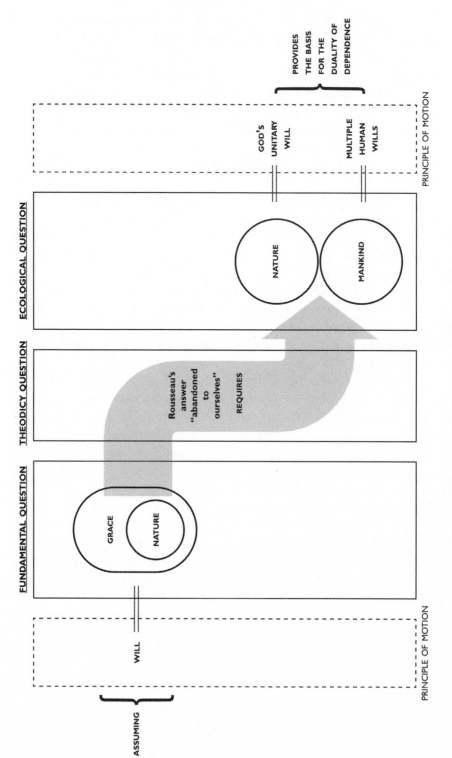

Diagram 8. Rousseau's First Answer to the Ecological Question

The Ambivalence of Will

In turning from the paradigm case of God's Will to the moral tribulations of social life, the ambiguity in the concept of order becomes more, not less, striking. In Rousseau's account of dependence in society, the complex of theological and naturalistic notions he has developed exerts an often unstated influence from the background. Now we consider more carefully how this story unfolds in a context that includes relations among human beings, in addition to the relation between Grace and Nature.

Rousseau proceeds by analogy. His solution to the social problem of dependence ($Q^{political}$) takes the same form as his solution to the contradictions inherent in the relationship between Grace and Nature ($Q^{fundamental}$). To "resolve all the contradictions of the social system," he proposes to close the gap between order and law, just as he closed the gap between the Willed order of the *système du monde* (order$^{as\ action}$) and the Will-free order of the laws of nature (order$^{as\ condition}$).[145] To see how he does this we will need to consider again in this section a certain ambivalence with respect to Will and then, in the next section, to consider how that ambivalence is glossed over by an appeal to the attribute of unity.

The paradigm case held that there is a distinct entity, Nature. Nature manifests certain regularities. These regularities constitute an *ordre*. The language of law may be used to express this fact. The source of *ordre* in the paradigm case is the distinct act of setting the parts of the world in proper relation to one another. Nature cannot do this for itself, although we imagine that this is accomplished in accordance with "laws of nature." In this sense, order$^{as\ action}$ runs together with order$^{as\ condition}$.

Here it becomes relevant to repeat something that Rousseau says about Will/ *volonté*: it "is known to me by its acts, not by its nature" (OC IV.576). This statement does not refer to the mechanism or metaphysics of the Will. Rousseau is quite blunt in this respect, for when he poses the question "How does a Will/ *volonté* produce physical, bodily action?" the reply he gives is "I know nothing about that." This is undeniably true in the paradigm case of God's Will. We should also understand that this is an accurate statement concerning human Will, which is a simulacrum of God's.[146] Thus, it is fair to take the assertion that Will is an empirical/behavioral matter in a straightforward way.

This means that in at least three senses of the word *nature*—as original condition, as habit, as law-governed system (§42 ff.)—Will cannot have a nature. And if *nature* is meant as a synonym for "essence," then of course *volonté* cannot be known by its nature because the essence of Will is to be absolutely free.

In this way the fact of *ordre* is separated from the *nature* in which it is manifest. It becomes—perhaps immediately—a sign of God's Will. As such, however, the ambiguity in *ordre* is further amplified. For, as soon as one takes *ordre* as a representation of Will it becomes yet more important that it *not* be identical with nature in any sense, with nature's law, or with any other type of law. The essence of law is visible and literal: it is what it says, and we know it with high degrees of predictability. Indeed, we only know it in that way.[147] By contrast, again, Will/ *volonté* "cannot be known by its nature" because the essence of Will is to be absolutely free, and for it, if for anything, *determinatio est negatio* ["determination is negation"].[148]

Thus, Rousseau is effectively obliged to become a critical nominalist on the key point here. He suggests that *ordre* in Nature has no properties called "laws." Recall his mordant comment in the *Discours surs . . . l'inégalité*: "Knowing so little Nature and agreeing with such difficulty about the sense of the word 'law,' it would certainly be difficult to bring together a good definition of 'natural law'" (OC III.125).*

This is not just pessimism; it is a literary preface for the radical position to which he is led by his theological-philosophical dualism. Faced with the provocation to admit an inherent principle of motion in Nature—"to admit that general laws have essential relationships with matter"—he vigorously and explicitly denies it: "These laws, not being in any way real beings or substances, have therefore some other foundation that is unknown to me" (OC IV.575).† What exists and is substantial, and is the inherent principle of motion in Nature, is God's Will. This Will, again, can only be known by its effects. The effect of Will is the empirical fact of *ordre*. *Ordre* is the perfect signature of the Will, while *désordre* is its weakness, its failure and anonymity. Only if Nature is inside Grace

---

*". . . connoissant si peu la Nature et s'accordant si mal sur le sens du mot Loi, il seroit bien difficile de convenir d'une bonne définition de la Loi naturelle"

† "Ces loix n'étant point des êtres réels, des substances, ont donc quelqu'autre fondement qui m'est inconnu"

($Q^{\text{fundamental}}A^{\text{nature}\in\text{grace}}$) does this indicate at the same time God's Will as an inherent principle of motion for Nature. Yet, to call this inherent principle of Will by the name "law" would be to deny what is for Rousseau its essential quality.

The problem is this: once the analogy between natural and human laws is in place—this is a hinge proposition in the "main passage"—what other name can this inherent principle of Will have? To call it, for example, "Providence" would be, with a single gesture, to return Nature inside Grace and ignore the invocation of the name "law."

This is the ambiguity in the discourse of *ordre* just mentioned, and it disguises two very different theological-philosophical conclusions. As long as Will remains the primary feature of Grace, only by holding to the view that Nature is outside Grace ($Q^{\text{fundamental}}A^{\text{nature}\notin\text{grace}}$) can one see "law" as the primary feature of Nature. The ambivalence in *ordre* allows it to cover this ambivalence with respect to Will.

The eventual issue here is the analogy between the way Rousseau grapples with contradictions inherent in the relationship between Grace and Nature ($Q^{\text{fundamental}}$) and his solution to the social problem of dependence ($Q^{\text{political}}$). It is Rousseau's ambivalence that impedes our arrival on just that point. For recall that in the paradigm case, the distinction between order and law was the basis on which to demonstrate the reality of God's Will (cf. end of §58 above).

Indeed, even within the analogy { ($Q^{\text{fundamental}}$) : ($Q^{\text{political}}$) } the proof of the reality of God's Will plays a part. Consider, for example, that this reality is not simple but rather composite. God's Will shows His omnipotence, and thus His goodness, and thus His justice: "The Being that is sovereignly good because he is sovereignly powerful must also be sovereignly just, otherwise he would contradict himself."[149]* Shifting across the threshold to Rousseau's social theory of politics, these qualities take on new and important functions. They are linked to the set of topics under consideration here through the *topos* of *ordre*. As a matter of theology Rousseau takes *justice* and *bonté* to be identical with order, "for the love of order that produces it is called *goodness*, and the love of order that conserves it is called *justice*" (OC IV.589).†

As Rousseau carries over the theological model to the analysis of society these same concerns continue to resonate. However, his purpose is no longer to prove or glorify the attributes of God. His purpose is to show society as a total system, and to color that picture with the hues of civic republicanism. The agency of this

---

*". . . l'Etre souverainement bon parce qu'il est souverainement puissant, doit être aussi souverainement juste, autrement il se contredirait lui-même . . ."

†". . . car l'amour de l'ordre qui le produit s'appelle *bonté*, et l'amour de l'ordre qui le conserve s'appelle *justice*."

system is represented as mankind "abandoned to ourselves." It is autonomous not just from Nature but from Grace as well. In this new secular context, order and law become identical.

We may admit that Rousseau's invention operates through theological topics. Yet, consistent with the thesis of "abandoned to ourselves," the source attributes of God are increasingly anomalous within the target image of the social system. The motive to maintain a gap between order and law is no longer present, and in correspondence to this secularizing movement that gap ceases to be an essential part of the theory.

Once the distinction between order and law has been dropped, Rousseau can shift without inhibition between order[as action] to order[as condition]. Indeed, the polysemy of *ordre* (and not the ethical ideal of "virtue") is the mainspring of the Rousseauean civic republican ideal of the rule of law because it seems to give sense to the image of a *volonté générale*.

For one moment, the reader may feel relieved. A major contradiction brought into Rousseau's social theory of politics by a theological-philosophical distinction seems to evaporate.

However, no one should be surprised to discover that a new problem has taken its place.[150]

§61

THE UNITY OF WILL

I suggested earlier (§§35, 54, 56) that Rousseau refers to the same set of problems when he uses the words "contradictions" and "disorder." That is, to "resolve all the contradictions of the social system" involves not only theoretical "resolution" (§31) but is also, as a practical matter, to repair the ills of disorder. To cash this out in political and moral terms Rousseau must still show how social life can be ordered, and to show in what way this order is related to the problem of dependence. These topics take up the remainder of this book. In this section we are still occupied with bringing into focus the way that Will/*volonté* haunts the structure of Rousseau's social theory of politics.

We saw in §56 and §58 that from one perspective—it is much too rough to simply call this perspective "theological"—Rousseau maintains a gap between *loi* and *ordre*. We also saw, especially in §60, that his attempt to map the *société* of mankind "abandoned to ourselves" diminished the value of that gap.

Is the increasing identification of *loi* and *ordre* a detour or the new line of march? How far in this direction will Rousseau go?

I have laid out the terms of this balancing act in great detail. With Rousseau, however, the unexpected always lurks nearby, and it is his art to make the surprising commonplace. We need to recover its surprise.

What I want to underscore now is that at a certain point Rousseau begins to speak in a hybrid of his own language. *Loi* and *ordre* come together, seeming to merge from antithesis, in the novel phrase "the laws of order [*les loix de l'ordre*]." By contrast to so much else that he has told us, with this phrase it seems that there could be a fixed and self-generating system that consists of properties called "laws" (OC IV.591).

Rousseau is not entirely alone in using this phrase. Indeed, by the nineteenth century the phrase "the laws of order [*les loix de l'ordre*]" will become almost a commonplace. And before Rousseau it also had some currency. It is plausible to suppose that he picked it up from Alexander Pope, who, as we saw at the very beginning of this book (§1), served Rousseau as a kind of literary foil against which to develop his theodicy and the image of mankind "abandoned to ourselves."

My point is that this phrase is made odd by Rousseau's own arguments, by way of the discursive fields reconstructed in this book. I can show this by touching again briefly on Pope's *Essay on Man* in the translation by Étienne Silhouette that Rousseau read.[151] For, the passage containing this phrase is a kind of sarcastic critique of pride; not just small puffiness or mundane *amour-propre*, but hubristic self-assertion against God. Rousseau is therefore again and famously on common ground with Pope — the marginal note attests "pride is the cause of Man's errors and his misery [*l'orgueil est la cause des erreurs de l'Homme et de sa misère*]." Yet, from that common ground Rousseau effectively reverses Pope's conclusion — for what is mankind "abandoned to ourselves" but the assumption of a God-like responsibility to command our own fate? This unsettling literary combination of similarity and distance is just what we saw in §1 above.

The trick here is that with precisely the collapse of the distinction between *loi* and *ordre* expressed in the phrase "the laws of order [*les loix de l'ordre*]" Rousseau again turns us toward an evolutionary view of society that is antithetical to Pope and most of his contemporaries. At the same time Rousseau contradicts the side of his own thinking so fiercely dedicated to the Will of the Creator.

Although we have seen this movement in Rousseau's writing before, after all his efforts to maintain and build upon the pivotal assertion that order is not identical with law the explicit projection of the identity of *loi* and *ordre* comes as something of a shock.

The differentiation of *loi* and *ordre* cannot but play a part in the analogy $\{\ (Q^{\text{fundamental}}) : (Q^{\text{political}})\ \}$. Now the identification of *loi* and *ordre* raises the question, How much of a part? Rousseau seems inclined to cast that differentiation aside; to understand what is actually happening here we need to see from another angle what is at stake.

The difficulty here is familiar enough. It is once again that the Will/*volonté* haunts the structure of Rousseau's social theory of politics. Ultimately Rousseau makes this explicit as the *volonté générale*. However, long before that banner is raised, Will/*volonté* has done a great deal in producing the structure, direction, and tone of the theory.

At issue here again is the New Model Will (see §§7–8, and contrasting at §42). This is the version of human Will that Kant later finds (and actually was in some key respects)[152] emerging in Rousseau's pages in an accelerating moment of a larger historical development. A Will conceived in this way—unmediated, generative, foundational, noumenalistic, which is to say, proto-Kantian in its humanistic emulation of the God of advanced monotheism—is what ultimately determines the relevance of dependence for moral life.

Applying the New Model Will to a comprehensive social theory of politics, Rousseau effectively presupposes a *generalized creationism*: Man is literally remade in the synthesizing anthropomorphic image of God as the definitive fundamental quality of both is taken to be the capacity for pure and perfect creation *ex nihilo*.

The "main passage" once again opens a door onto this scene: "all the contradictions of the social system" may be resolved where noncontradiction, or order, is defined not by direct reference to *volonté*, but to *"les loix de l'ordre."*

However, we have already seen that *ordre* itself is both a marker for *volonté* and a way of disguising it. By a hidden association through *ordre* to law, Will/*volonté* actually moves back to the center of the argument about ($Q^{\text{political}}$) as it had been in the analogous ($Q^{\text{fundamental}}$).

Hinging on the term *ordre* the Will/*volonté* gains wider application, exploiting the ambivalence between order[as action] and order[as condition]. It is from this constellation that Rousseau will eventually constitute the relationship between law and the *volonté générale*.

The path is circuitous but the consequence is clear: the gesture toward "the laws of order [*les loix de l'ordre*]" is to once again carry the ambivalence between order[as action] and order[as condition] to the foreground. The Will/*volonté* is extended from the former to the latter; *willed-ness* becomes a status; status is determined by the Will.

When, in these final sections, we at last come to assess and to reject Rousseau's claim that *dépendance-des-choses* is not relevant for moral life, it is just this increased insistence on order[as condition], advancing an image of the Will/*volonté* under the cover of "the laws of order [*les loix de l'ordre*]," that will focus the central argument of this book and amplify the skepticism I propose about the moral foundations of Rousseau's social theory of politics. For even as Rousseau's attention turns toward the social world, he does not disavow allegiance to Will as a "first principle." This allegiance was the primary feature of the paradigm case; it figures with greater and greater prominence in the social-political analogy. In short, a movement—to *loi* and *ordre* in the framework of the "rule of law"—that should, and indeed is thought to, undermine the centrality of Will has the perverse effect of reinforcing it.

The high degree of complexity in Rousseau's theory hides most of this. Indeed, even Rousseau, for reasons internal to his dialectical vision of society, casts doubt on the effectiveness of his own pivotal metaphor. In a footnote to the "main passage" Rousseau could not be more emphatic in telling us that the state of affairs in society, by contrast to Nature and Grace, is altogether different: "In my *Principles of Political Right*, it is demonstrated that no particular Will can be ordered in the social system."[153]* I have said that Rousseau is committed to a kind of *generalized creationism* concerning the inherent and necessary principle of motion in mankind "abandoned to ourselves."[154] In this footnote Rousseau seems to turn away from this commitment by limiting the relevance of Will/*volonté*.

What I want to underscore here is that this appearance is misleading. In fact, far-reaching adherence to Will/*volonté* as the source of order in society is modulated so as to reaffirm it. As Rousseau takes measure here of the "order in the social system," the emphasis is not on the word *volonté* but on *particulière*, which means in this case *separate* or *partial* or *private*, not *singular*; this is opposed to what is *general*.[155] For, exactly what a singular Will/*volonté* is is *ordonnée*.

This emphasis allows Rousseau to maintain that even within the plural and heterogenous scene of society there remains one pivotal sense in which Will/*volonté* can be ordered: when it is general. This, he is convinced, justifies the representation of God's Will as an apt paradigm for the social theory of politics. What Rousseau imagined is that citizens, plural persons and bodies living in the *cité*, can have a *volonté générale*. From the 1750s forward this "general Will" became a key term in the equation of the "*contract social*." It is expressly avowed as "the first principle of public economy and fundamental rule of government [*premier principe de l'*économie *publique et regle fondamentale du gou-*

* "Dans mes *Principes du Droit politique* il est démontré que nulle volonté particuliere ne peut être ordonnée dans le sistême social."

vernement]" (OC III.247). One could say that this phrase "conveys everything he most wanted to say,"[156] or one could finally realize that this phrase is emblematic of Rousseau's world historical failure. The single point to be underscored here is that the image of the *volonté générale* stands for unity despite plurality but does not supplant or overwhelm that plurality; indeed, this is its primary effect.

Rousseau is very careful to distinguish the *volonté générale* from the *particulières* and contradictory plural Wills of individual human beings found in groups. It is just the *absence* of this plurality that is the source of order. This claim holds for mankind as it does for God; the image of God authorizes it. Thus, by analogy, human Will can be ordered if it is one. That is the assumption on which the paradigm case is supposed to show how Will could give order to the social system.

There are obvious problems with this. The circumstances of the social system — and especially the circumstances of the phases of *ergon*, *logon*, and *poeisis* in society through which order[as action] becomes order[as condition] — are not at all like those that (one can only imagine) obtain in the paradigm case. The many contradictions in the paradigm case that we have reviewed above are multiplied rather than relieved as it is metaphorically transferred to the social theory of politics.

§62

DOES THE ATTRIBUTE OF "UNITY" TEND AWAY FROM WILL?

Although the phrase "the laws of order [*les loix de l'ordre*]" appears fleetingly, it reveals a strong underlying bias. In *Émile*, and in Rousseau's writings more generally, the discourse of natural philosophy often takes precedence. It does not exclude but channels a theology that eventually overflows its bounds.[157] This is evident in many ways, but perhaps nowhere more striking than when the reflexivity of reason turns theological inquiry back on itself.

How so? Open again the *"Profession de foi."* No sooner has the *Vicaire Savoyard* sealed his sermon than the Tutor jumps in to disavow it. The Author's voice insists that this "transcript" is included in his book not as a "rule to follow" but only to exemplify the type of reasoning about religion that would be consistent with his "method" (OC IV.635). Since a pupil-citizen like Émile should, for liberty's sake, escape the stamp of authority and prejudice, "the lights of reason alone, within the natural education, cannot lead us farther than natural religion, and I limit myself to that with my *Émile*" (OC IV.635–36).* As usual Rousseau here produces a double effect. Just as theology enters a dialogue with nature, the Vicar's reasoning, which is in fact Rousseau's, tends to show natural religion as theistic, not atheistic as others claim (OC IV.606–9, 614, 635–36; cf. §54 above). Indeed, the argument is aimed to "establish the existence of God and natural Religion with all the force the Author can muster."[158] What the Vicar-Rousseau finds in natural religion are just "the elements of all religion" (OC IV.609). If it is insufficient, "it is so by the obscurity that it leaves in the great truths that it teaches us."[159] For the rest, says Émile's tutor, "it's for him alone to choose it" (OC IV.636). Instructed by Nature, Émile has no need for priests; perhaps he has no need for God . . . at least not right now.

Rousseau sees it this way. We stand before Nature. For something to be natural, "it must speak immediately with the voice of nature" (OC III.125). That voice is its own; God is no miraculous ventriloquist. Perhaps God has already "said everything to our eyes, to our conscience, to our judgment" (OC IV.607). But when you "see the spectacle of nature, listen to the interior voice" (OC IV.607).† That is, listen to your own voice and this will connect you to the world.

It is not that Rousseau unequivocally admits the independence of Nature from God. Of course he does not. He tells us that "preceptors of the human race" (OC III.29) like Descartes and Newton can formulate "general laws" that describe the order of nature; but they do not explain it (OC IV.576). That metaphysical explanation must invoke God, the mover. However, the fact that Nature is increasingly being understood as immediately accessible to human beings facilitates the collapse of order[as action] into order[as condition], as the *why*, the act, ceases to be important.[160] Thus, within the narrower limits of mankind "abandoned to ourselves" even fundamental problems need not, and should not, bring God into account. Indeed, Rousseau is capable of great clarity on this "methodological" point:

> I judge the order of the world, even though I know nothing of its end, because to judge that order it is sufficient to make comparisons among the parts, to study their convergence [*concours*],[161] their relations, and to take note of their concert. I do not know why the universe exists. (OC IV.578)§

---

* ". . . les seules lumiéres de la raison ne peuvent dans l'institution de la nature nous mener plus loin que la religion naturelle, et c'est á quoi je me borne avec mon *Émile*."

† "Voyez le spectacle de la nature, écoutez la voix intérieure"

§ "Je juge de l'ordre du monde, quoique j'en ignore la fin, parce que pour juger de cet

Several implications seem to follow from this "methodological" commitment. To see these, we need first to recall the common theme in the two versions of order (cf. §53, and tangentially §32). It was the relation of "parts" to "whole." In the passage just quoted, Rousseau comes close to saying that no "whole" is required. At least, the "whole" entity accreted from "parts" in this way does not unequivocally call for explanation in terms of a plan, a design, or a Will.

However, as we have seen (Part Four.D, especially §61, and §§7–8), *unity* is the primary characteristic of the modern (but still theistic-creationist) conception of the Will that is coming to prominence in and around Rousseau's thinking. If objects and systems gain their unity from Will, in the absence of such Will, what sort of unity takes its place and what is its source?

While Rousseau's answer to this question is obscure, I want to underscore here its importance. In a crucial respect his insistence on unity tends away from the Will. This tendency obviously contradicts a predominant feature of his social theory of politics, which is organized around the belief that Will is the key *topos* of unity and therefore of order. This tendency manifests, once again, the tension between what I have anachronistically called the "creationist" and the "evolutionary" strands in Rousseau (cf. again §58).

The first thing to notice is that the neat heuristic dichotomy between order[as action] and order[as condition] breaks down at a certain point. Even the simple fact of emphasizing the active sense of order[as action] presupposes that the actor has time to move from one "part" to the next and thus form a "whole." This temporal theme was implicit in many older conceptions of order; both the Greek $\tau\alpha\xi\iota\varsigma$ and the Latin *ordo* at first referred to things placed in a sequence.[162] This is the intermediate sense of order[as sequence] mentioned earlier in passing (§53). The notion of unity applies to it in only an indirect way. Nonetheless, as long as the ambivalence of order — between act and condition — is strong, even the substantive sense of order[as condition] seems to offer a dynamic impression for which "harmony" would better substitute the static impression of "unity."[163]

But when Rousseau excises the action of ordering from the concept of order — as he effectively does with the phrase "the laws of order [*les loix de l'ordre*]" — he seems to assert thereby an alternative understanding of order as the unity of "parts" and "whole."[164] This alternative hinges on the conflation of Nature and order, a move that could easily have turned back to the Will-centered theological view were it not for the bias of natural philosophy. After all, Newton had shown

ordre il me suffit de comparer les parties entre elles, d'étudier leur concours, leurs raports, d'en remarquer le concert. J'ignore pourquoi l'univers existe. . . ."

"with a dazzling synthesis" which bound together "the stars in their courses and the fall of an apple"[165] that Nature has just one inherent and necessary principle of motion. The order of Nature is therefore unified. The source of this unity was not Will but gravity.[166] The noncontradictory character of the system no longer needed to be proved; it could simply be assumed.[167]

Viewed this way, Rousseau's adoption of *ordre* as a primary category of analysis turns out to be perfectly compatible with his theodicy. The totality of the social system no longer requires an explanation in terms of external forces. To study it is just to study structures as they evolve over time. However, the structures are, in turn, made by human beings from the handful of capacities God may or may not have given to us. Thus, when we turn to the tribulations of moral life, the problems of judgment and action are already central features of social structure.[168] As this dialectic of human agency and social structure advances, the breach between God and the world widens but also ceases to be an urgent concern. With "disenchantment" or "secularization" it recedes further and further into the background. Thus, at least in this limited context, Rousseau's thinking sheds the garb of creationist metaphysics. It assumes instead the mantle of that modern humanism expressed — with similar degrees of theological hesitation — by Rousseau's contemporary Giambattista Vico. The motto for the social theory of politics becomes *verum factum convertuntur,* or "we know what we make and we can make what we know."[169]

§63

————————◆————————

IS WILL THE GRAVITY OR
THE ENTROPY OF SOCIETY?

We have just followed a tendency in Rousseau's social theory of politics that moves away from Will. Still, there is at least one case in which the action of ordering cannot be excised from the concept of order. That is where God commands. Then order must be understood as having a clear and indisputable source. It is created by Will, one Will.

Although it starts from this straightforward image of divine Will, the creationist way of thinking produces a strange paradox as it is shifted metaphorically to society and as multiple human beings with their heterogenous Wills enter the picture. With more than one Will in play, that which defined order now destroys it. The Will—reiterated with each and every agent moving toward his or her interest, amplifying collisions among them—becomes the source of disorder. As conceived within Rousseau's architectonic, this is the most fundamental problem in the civil estate.

What is the *differentia specifica* of this problem? Consider what Rousseau says about a moment of extreme political crisis: "One is more likely to endure in absolute disorder than in a moment of unrest when everyone concerns himself with his position and not with the danger" (OC III.390).* This is a striking way to restate the rules of the game. Typically Rousseau insists that disorder is the fundamental problem of the *système social*. Here he is pointing to something different and apparently deeper. A people may survive moments of "absolute disorder" but not the proliferation and fragmentation of Wills, the play of contradictory interests, which is the cause of disorder itself.

This is remarkable. In its independence from God *société* becomes a system; multiple human Wills constitute its disorder; human law is the source of its order. In identifying this function for law, Rousseau conceives of it as the expression of a single Will. With a term borrowed from God, a God-term[170] standing for the attribute of God required by the theory, unity, the God that Rousseau otherwise worked so effectively to expel is brought back into the scene. One may fairly say that the *volonté générale* is the Will of God transposed to a social key.[171]

This result seems incoherent both on its face and measured by Rousseau's own aspirations. It only makes sense when his entire project is understood not as the expression of a single Grand Idea but as a series of phases through which one reasonably coherent problematic keeps shifting ground and is, in response, tracked in different ways by Rousseau. I proposed one very schematic (and thus admittedly insufficient) way to conceive of these phases in §49 above, where the combination of key topics yielded this series of leading questions concerning several binary relationships (see diagram #9, opposite).

In one phase, the *ordre du monde* represents (God's) Will, whereas Nature gives us something fixed and deterministic in "the law of necessity [*la loi de la nécessité*]." In another phase, as society becomes the object of analysis, law is no longer the marker for necessity, but for freedom. To make freedom compatible with order, law must come under the sign of one Will. The social world, however, is locus of many contradictory Wills. Society can be well ordered only if

---

* "On résisteroit mieux dans un désordre absolu que dans un moment de fermentation, où chacun s'occupe de son rang et non du péril."

	GRACE	NATURE	MANKIND
GRACE	METAPHYSICAL QUESTION	FUNDAMENTAL QUESTION	THEODICY QUESTION
NATURE	FUNDAMENTAL QUESTION	EVOLUTION QUESTION	ECOLOGICAL QUESTION
MANKIND	THEODICY QUESTION	ECOLOGICAL QUESTION	POLITICAL QUESTION

Diagram 9. Primary Relationships

the single Will expressed by law rules over the chaotic world of multiple Wills. Faced with the "political question" of how mankind will relate to itself, how we will relate to ourselves, this reversal seems essential to Rousseau. And although this position derives from consideration of the "fundamental question" it is an innovation, since no believer may allow that the universe would be well ordered if Nature ruled over God.

We now have a basis for understanding more clearly the association I made above between "disorder" and "contradiction" (§§35, 54, 56, 61). The *système du monde* is willed, commanded, ordered by God, who has but one Will and is "self-consistent [*constant à lui-même*]." Thus, the *système du monde* is noncontradictory, which is to say it cannot speak against itself. It is a system unified because mapped out according to a unitary Nature expressible as law *and* because motivated by the singular Will of God. I underscore the word "and" in the preceding sentence. In the *système du monde*, order (in both senses) and noncontradiction are functionally the same thing. By contrast, the *système social* arises from— although it certainly is not identical with—the commands and orders of human beings, who have many Wills. And, as we just saw, the negative effects of this plurality may even operate through the Wills of individual actors ("no particular Will can be ordered in the social system).["]172 These Wills are always speaking against one another and, by virtue of social circumstances, against themselves; as they are contradictory, so social life is disordered.

Does this provide sufficient impulse to move Rousseau's theory toward the image of a *volonté générale*, a faculty by which the social body could speak with just one voice, thus avoiding contradiction and disorder? I want to suggest that the issue of this proposition, and the mystique of inevitability that surrounds it in Rousseau's text and in the minds of his readers, is primarily a function of the way the problem has been framed by the latter.

Moreover: since in fact Rousseau frames the problem in two overlapping ways—one creationist, with Will as its inherent principle of motion, and the other evolutionary-ecological, which fails to nominate an alternative principle of motion for mankind "abandoned to ourselves"—the issue is structured and presented in his actual writings so as to remain unresolved (both in the everyday and in Rousseau's methodological sense of the word; cf. §31). This does not stop us, however, from asking what in Rousseau's writings might advance an alternative but still humanist principle of social motion.

On this point civic republican themes in Rousseau's thought seem to offer insight. Maurizio Viroli's work offers a suggestive example here, as it aims to situate Rousseau within a long republican tradition.[173] This tradition is centered around a specifically civic conception of virtue. While I do not think this approach will solve the problems we investigate here, it is worth considering whether or not it adds to our inquiry.

Expressions of civic republicanism urge one to ask why would citizens seek virtue, and what political consequences might derive from this motive. "Disorder" is, in this way of thinking, a name for the social fact that virtue is posed to overcome. One is focused, therefore, on the way disorder issues from misplaced pride or (roughly speaking) self-orientation when the *civitas* is at stake.[174] Everything then hinges on how virtue is conceived in opposition to these particular vices so as to relate it to order. Within these parameters, Viroli responds by arguing that specifically *civic* virtue "is always defined" by Rousseau "as it is in St. Augustine, as 'the love of order.'"[175]

While one may ask whether this is really the definition of virtue Augustine had in mind,[176] it fits with French Augustinians in the generations before Rousseau. We may suppose a proximate source for Rousseau's idea in, for example, Malebranche, who writes in the *Traité de morale*: "The love of order is not only the principal moral virtue, it is the only one."[177]* How overwhelming is this motive within the *système social*? On the one hand, the "love of order" could be understood as a motive to act through the *volonté générale*. Or, one might say that the "love of order" is the motive to act as if there were a *volonté générale* and thus,

---

* "L'Amour de l'ordre n'est pas seulement la principale des vertus morales, c'est l'unique vertu . . ."

speaking with one voice, to constitute the very thing the action itself presupposes. This would resonate strongly with the motivating function of reverence/ *Achtung* for the law in Kant's ethics;[178] indeed, no one has made this application of passion to law more philosophically appealing.

In any event, the Augustinian admonition to love is utterly entangled with explanatory recourse to the Will.[179] And it is important to remember that especially in the modern context in which Rousseau picks up these ancient threads the Will is taken to impose ever greater constraint on the other faculties. It is therefore implausible to suppose that Rousseau's references to the "love of order" indicate a belief that society is more deeply moved by love than by Will. In fact, Viroli gives no good reason why the former should supplant the latter as the inherent principle of motion, or for insisting that Rousseau takes the "love of order" as a first principle for civic virtue and thus for politics. Rousseau is not Malebranche and he does not, despite what Viroli avers, *always* define *vertu* in this way.

Moreover, the "love of order" is not in itself a sufficient motive. It requires a powerful correlate to carry the subject to virtue: we move "not only for the love of order, to which everyone always prefers self-love, but for the love of the Author of one's being" (OC IV.636).* Where others urge the Augustinian position— "Virtue, they say, is the love of order" (OC IV.602)[†] — even the Vicar resists, asking himself, "this love, can it and must it therefore always take precedence in me over my own well-being? What clear and sufficient reason do they give me to prefer it?" (OC IV.602).[§] In an amazingly perspectivist mood, he adds that "at its core their supposed principle is nothing but a word game; for I, too, say that vice is, from a different perspective, the love of order" (OC IV.602).**

If any doubt remains concerning the identification of virtue with Will, consider this heated passage from *Émile*. In a moment of instruction charged with the passion of love—Émile has been shocked by the false belief that his beloved Sophie is dead—Rousseau's tutorial voice leads us to a definition of virtue far from the "love of order":

> My child, there can never be happiness without courage, nor virtue without struggle. The word "virtue" comes from "force"; force is the foundation of all

---

* "... non seulement pour l'amour de l'ordre, auquel chacun préfère toujours l'amour de soi, mais pour l'amour de l'auteur de son être ..."

[†] "La vertu, disent-ils, est l'amour de l'ordre ..."

[§] "... cet amour peut-il donc et doit-il l'emporter en moi sur celui de mon bien-être? Qu'ils me donnent une raison claire et suffisante pour le préférer ..."

** "... Dans le fond leur prétendu principe est un pur jeu de mots; car je dis aussi, moi, que le vice est l'amour de l'ordre, pris dans un sens différent."

virtue. Virtue belongs only to a being that is weak by nature and strong by his Will. (OC IV.817)*

To conclude this etymological twist—which again with Augustine links virtue to Will—Rousseau points out that it follows that virtue cannot be an attribute of God. Indeed, "as much as we call God good, we don't call him virtuous, because he needs no effort to do good" (OC IV.817).† This fact should be understood together with what Rousseau says is the key feature of God's goodness/ *bonté*: "the goodness of God is the love of order" (OC IV.593).§ This is by contrast to the goodness of Man, which "in Man is the love of his own kind" (OC IV.593).** What appears clearly in this specific difference between Man and God is that virtue is not simply identical with the "love of order." Indeed, the "love of order"—as any observer of history knows full well—cuts two ways: "the good person orders himself in relation to the whole and the bad orders the whole in relation to himself" (OC IV.602).‡ Thus, not only is any relationship between virtue and the "love of order" more complex than a republican reduction might suggest, but it turns us back to the conceptual terrain of the *volonté générale* from which it seemed to offer an escape.

We see two things here. On the one hand, that *vertu* can be linked to *volonté* without passing through love makes clear that the "love of order" is not a plausible substitute for Will/*volonté* as the principle of motion for society. On the other hand, the implication of Will in virtue—as with the implication of Will in *ordre* (§49 ff.)—highlights again its ambivalence as social motive and force; Will may be a coherence-inducing analogue of gravity, but it may also, like entropy, wear society down, or even pull it apart.

This does not mean that virtue fails as any sort of principle. Starting from the individual, virtue may be understood as a feature of civic happiness. As described by Rousseau's tutor-figure in *Émile*, this would follow closely the general formula for *bonheur*, which in Stoic rather than Augustinian fashion prompts us to not overreach our *forces* (cf. §§19, 37).

---

* "Mon enfant, il n'y a point de bonheur sans courage ni de vertu sans combat. Le mot de *vertu* vient de *force*; la force est la base de toute vertu. La vertu n'appartient qu'à un être foible par sa nature, et fort par sa volonté; . . ."

† ". . . quoique nous appellions Dieu bon nous ne l'appellons pas vertueux, parce qu'il n'a pas besoin d'effort pour bien faire. . . ."

§ ". . . la bonté de Dieu est l'amour de l'ordre . . ."

** ". . . dans l'homme est l'amour de ses semblables, . . ."

‡ ". . . le bon s'ordonne par raport au tout et . . . le méchant ordonne le tout par raport à lui."

But then other signs of warning must be raised as well. Despite republican and therefore secular intentions, to define virtue directly as the "love of order" may have the collateral effect of assimilating Man too closely to God. Despite his brilliance, Rousseau is insufficiently attentive to the perils of modeling human law on the Divine. For, even if all human beings were virtuous, the law could only be the shadow of such a supreme order. Even the good will always be weak, and our law could never have, in the precise sense sought by Rousseau (and later by Rousseau-ian Durkheim), the inflexibility required to make human relations a part of a perfect world of things. Flexibility is not merely a social fact, it is a primary one.

If there is a republican vision in Rousseau that remains viable, it appears in a form that seems, in the terms of today's political theorists, entirely paradoxical. As I mentioned a moment ago, it is resonant with Kant. However, it does not require from us the "love of order" *per se*—the twentieth century showed the horrors of that. Rather, reverence/*Achtung* would have to be directed at law in its largest sense, as the expression of an evolving democratic people. Politics admires law not only for its relative inflexibility, but precisely in the knowledge that it is and must remain an unfinished project. This, I have to believe, is why Rousseau ultimately identifies law, even modernizing law, as νομος and *mos* rather than *lex* (cf. §5 *et passim* above). Only in this way, with this principle of motion, does social order have a chance to grow.

The distinction between order and law holds for Rousseau's theology, is absent from his sociology, and reappears again in his utopian political vision. The temporary eclipse of this distinction may be what makes his admiration for the law in the final phase appear to some as the "love of order." What we ignore at our risk is that the model for this love is not Stoic but Augustinian in a sense not yet mentioned: what is absent in the lessons of nature, what lacks in natural religion, is the heartwarming message of the Gospels. It is indicative of his contradictory stance that Rousseau both adored Christ and saw more clearly than anyone how the cosmopolitan teachings of Jesus could undercut the conditions of civic life.

§64

WILL

A *Tenacious Symbolic Form for Man and God*[180]

How could Rousseau authorize his reader to stop seeing the disorder of social life through the optics of theology? His secular perspective is nearly consistent with his metaphysics; time and time again the former turns back to or relies on the latter.

While God's Will, believers must believe, never fails to bring order and the good, the plural Wills of human beings typically fail in both. Divine Providence

> in no way wills the evil done by Man as he abuses the liberty it gives him . . . [but Providence] does not impede this, either because in her eyes evil done by such a weak being is insignificant, or because she cannot impede it without disturbing [Man's] liberty and degrading his nature, which would be even worse. (OC IV.587)*

And so God lets human Will generate disorder. He does this to prove what we pretend is His greatest achievement: the making of Man in His own image. Man has a Will and it is free. But, obviously, this does not make men into gods. God's Will applies itself to the world; Man's Will applies itself to himself—as one and as many.

The first modality of Man's application of his Will to himself is *amour de soi-même*. This "care for the self" is neither unabated self-love/*amour-propre* nor the community-forming impulses of *compassion* or *pitié*. These other modes arise with the development of the self and the evolution of society.[180a]

And from almost every perspective care for the self/*amour de soi-même* is antithetical to love of order/*l'amour de l'ordre*. Rather, from *amour de soi-même* there follows an inexorable tendency to disorder.

---

* " . . . ne veut point le mal que fait l'homme en abusant de la liberté qu'elle lui donne. . . elle ne l'empêche pas de le faire; soit que de la part d'un être si foible ce mal soit nul à ses yeux; soit qu'elle ne pût l'empêcher sans gêner sa liberté, et faire un mal plus grand en dégradant sa nature."

To counteract this tendency, God gives to man a second fundamental quality, a second mode for the application of Man's Will to himself. Rousseau identifies this as *perfectibilité*, or the capacity to learn from experience. As Man is made in the image of God, if he is to actualize this gift (which is his nature), he must *act* (*"il n'y a point de véritable action sans volonté"* OC IV.586) toward that image, toward perfection. This is why the capacity to learn from experience is called *perfectibilité*. However, *perfectibilité* is not identical with reason. It is, among other things, the evolutionary mechanism through which reason develops.[181] More generally, and because it does not (oddly enough) imply teleology, it is one of the proper names for evolutionary adaptation where Man exists inside Nature.

It cannot be denied that Rousseau's account of the capacity to learn from experience is, in key respects, metaphysical. This is not simply a function of its name, *perfectibilité*. For the same thing is in some sense true for all evolutionists. Simply, no one can identify the positive "reason" for variation or chance.[182]

For Rousseau, both *amour de soi-même* and *perfectibilité* are instrumental to an end: they aim at a good, which is happiness. Since they are not themselves ends, but means, they can be used for good or for evil. Likewise, when God gives Will to Man, he does not give him evil. Man takes his Will and makes evil for himself. Thus, although it is contingent, the eventual association of order with virtue, and of disorder with vice, should surprise no one. God's gift of *perfectibilité* opens the possibility that Men will rid themselves of evil. They can only do this by themselves; we can only do this by ourselves. This is the complementary result of Rousseau's theodicy. Corruption *and* virtue become entirely human problems.

One striking thing, then, about Rousseau's secular account of social disorder and unhappiness is that he is entirely convinced that it is compatible with deep religious conviction. He is half right.

Beyond that, the very humanness of the problem of and the solution to social disorder and unhappiness may be said to show at once the power of God and the fact that we—humankind—are abandoned to ourselves.

In what way can the human and the divine coexist? On this score, I think we do well to reconsider what Rousseau meant by one of his most famous maxims. In Cranston's well-known translation it appears this way:

Gods would be needed to give men laws. (OC III.381)*

It is quick and easy to read this as reiteration of a common trope: human beings are weak, God is strong; law-making is difficult and human beings are not up to the task; only if humans became a higher sort of being could we accomplish what

---

* "Il faudroit des Dieux pour donner des loix aux hommes."

our situation requires. In other words, we should become gods to get out of the mess of mankind "abandoned to ourselves."

This may indeed be what Rousseau had in mind when he penned the first version of *Du Contract social*. After enumeration of extraordinary qualities necessary for the "discovery of the best rules of society appropriate to nations," Rousseau draws the perhaps utopian perhaps fantastic conclusion:

> In a word, one should have a God to give good laws to the human race. (OC III.313)*

However, by the time *Du Contract social* is ready for the press, Rousseau's expression and, it seems, his thinking have been greatly refined. In this new version of the first paragraph of the chapter "*Du Legislateur*," the organization is similar but the sense has been significantly altered. As the phrase "in a word" drops out, the key sentence ceases to be summary and becomes instead some kind of gloss or comment; the one God is displaced by many, signifying not simply paganism or plural religions but the logical category of *gods* as complement to the human; instead of the distancing nomination of the "human race" Rousseau points to conditions of plural men/*hommes*, including himself and his readers as subjects of law; where the concern had been to *make laws good* now at issue is the category of *law* itself.

In other words, the register and tenor and insight are thoroughly transformed.

It is still possible that all this does not exclude the exasperating prospect that we are being called upon to become gods. However, Rousseau quickly adds that "the lawgiver is in every respect an extraordinary man in the state." I repeat: the lawgiver is a man, not a god.

Rousseau's famous line, therefore, may not be taken as a kind of hubristic if perhaps Platonic perfectionism. He is not saying that human beings, or at least our legislators, would have *to be gods* to achieve the well-ordered republic.

Indeed, didn't Aristotle tell us that politics happens in the human zone between beasts and gods? And who more than Rousseau has known that human beings are not and never will be gods? Are we really ready to write off one of the most precise reasoners of the eighteenth century for utopian, even monstrous dreaming?[183]

I do not recommend it. Rereading, we can see that Rousseau's words say just this and no more: *Il faudroit des Dieux pour donner des loix aux hommes*. "There should be gods." And why? Because if gods existed it would be possible "to give laws to men." Rousseau does not provide a grammatical subject; the verb is emphatically infinitive. The existence of gods is merely a generalized condition for

---

*"... en un mot, il faudroit un Dieu pour donner de bonnes loix au genre humain."

the giving of laws; the statement provides no information about the relation between the action and those gods; it does not identify who does the giving.

The title of the chapter—"*Du Legislateur*"—does identify the giver. And we know that the lawgiver for man is man.

So, what does Rousseau have in mind? It soon enough becomes clear to the attentive reader. Just a few pages later the name of Machiavelli is invoked. Whatever Machiavelli really believed, every person reading an early pressing of *Du Contract social* would have known that name as a preeminent icon of political atheism.

Machiavelli, the atheist, is made to convey this message to Rousseau's own readers: no "extraordinary laws . . . would be accepted . . . without recourse to God [*legge straordinarie . . . sarebbero accettate . . . [senza] ricor[so] a Dio*]."[184] Two points are driven home in this way. The first is that transformation of law— the task of the lawgiver—depends on something called "God." The second point—now emphatic because even "atheists" can see the first point—is that the figure or concept of "God," the sheer category of *gods*, is sufficient, whether or not God really exists.

Thus, Rousseau asserts the sociological or anthropological point that only if the human category of gods exists can we, ourselves, make human law. Why? Because, it seems that the symbolic form of God, which is to say a certain conception of *ordre*, one which, as far as the majority of Rousseau's readers are concerned, hinges on a perfect Will, a Will that only a God could have, must be in place before one can even imagine law, no less enact good instances of it.

Those familiar with this famous passage may still be inclined to see the "extraordinary man" as an aspiring angel. For the image with which Rousseau begins the chapter seems to be of just this sort:

> To discover the best rules of society appropriate to nations, a superior intelligence would be needed, one who could live men's passions without undergoing any of them, who had no relation to our nature and yet knew it to the core, whose happiness was independent from us and nonetheless really wanted to occupy himself with ours, and, ultimately, who in the march of time preparing himself a distant glory could work in one century and reap the fruits of his labor in another.*

---

* "Pour découvrir les meilleures regles de société qui conviennent aux Nations, il faudroit une intelligence supérieure, qui vit toutes les passions des hommes et qui n'en éprouvât aucune, qui n'eut aucun rapport avec notre nature et qui la connût à fond, dont le bonheur fût indépendant de nous et qui pourtant voulut bien s'occuper du notre; enfin qui, dans le progrès des tems se ménageant une gloire éloignée, put travailler dans un siecle et jouir dans un autre."

The sentence *il faudroit des Dieux pour donner des loix aux hommes* punctuates this remarkable description. One wants to know if this is truly a *god* or merely an *extraordinary man*.

I do not think it is either. Indeed, the subject here is not even the lawgiver. The *intelligence supérieure* is not a quality but a person. It is this person who discovers the rules of society, the conditions from which the modern *cité*, the nation, will be given order, although he will not give it the law. It is this person who lives men's passions in imagination rather than in fact, although he stands outside the society that gives them force and effect. It is this person who knows everything of nature, although he is in no way a natural man. It is this person who can never be happy in the company of others, although he has sacrificed everything for their happiness.

The subject of this preface is, of course, the sociologist, the political scientist, the novelist, the solitaire, the anthropologist, Jean-Jacques Rousseau himself.

As Rousseau's acuity increased from first to final draft he saw—and often stated outright (e.g., OC IV.967)—that his contemporaries could never grasp what he declared over and over again in the boldest terms. This, I propose, was the motive for the single addition to his description of this "superior intelligence" when the time came for publication. For Rousseau had nothing if not convictions; he saw himself "in the march of time preparing . . . a distant glory," working "in one century" but resigned "to reap the fruits of his labor in another."[185]

E. The Gravity of Dependence

§65

THE PRIMARY ANALYTICS OF *DÉPENDANCE*

What are the sources of order and how are they related to *dépendance?* Rousseau has pressed us to accept Will as a "first principle"; reasons to resist this—including Rousseau's own reasons—have been advanced. To this point, this resistance has not been against Rousseau, but in favor of one side of his thinking against the other. From now on we shall be less accommodating.

Earlier in this book (e.g., §§42, 49, 50) I alluded to the possibility that the inherent principle of motion in society is *dépendance* itself. That would be by metonymy to God's Will and Nature's gravity. What I mean is that sometimes Rousseau's analysis of *dépendance* suggests that nothing underlies it, that it is the primary and undivided field of experience, and those features of human nature that seem "deeper" are in fact not. Even basic faculties that modulate the Will—*amour de soi-même* and *perfectibilité*—are shown to be constituted in the circulation of *forces* and *besoins* that are the warp and weft of *dépendance*. This process is social evolution, and it gives rise to *la morale*, again an expression of *dépendance* as the inherent and necessary principle of living human beings in the world.

The distinction between two sorts of *dépendance* also urges us this way. The common term and its underlying social facts join together *la morale, société*, and *loi* with the material world of *nature*. Nature, writes Rousseau,

> chooses its instruments, and adjusts them, not on the basis of opinion but on the basis of need. Now, needs change according to the situation of Men. There is quite a difference between natural Man living in the natural condition, and natural Man living in the conditions of society." (OC IV.483)*

*" . . . .choisit ses instrumens et les régle, non sur l'opinion, mais sur le besoin. Or les besoins changent selon la situation des hommes. Il y a bien de la différence entre l'homme naturel vivant dans l'état de nature, et l'homme naturel vivant dans l'état de societé."

Thus as Mankind and Nature are divided they are joined. Rousseau does not confuse the two; he fluctuates between them to show a larger picture, to bring something otherwise invisible into view. This process follows the architectonic structure of his thinking. It is a way of seeing motivated by the proposition that Mankind is inside Nature ($Q^{\text{ecological}}A^{\text{mankind} \in \text{nature}}$). This proposition, in turn, took shape at the intersection of Rousseau's theodicy and the natural-philosophical hypothesis that Nature stands outside Grace ($Q^{\text{fundamental}}A^{\text{nature} \notin \text{grace}}$).[186]

One of the most common questions two centuries of readers have asked of Rousseau is simply this: "Are civilization and social life at the same time natural and against nature?"[187] It is almost impossible not to reiterate this question now and to answer it with a resounding "yes." Rousseau offers a dialectical view of Nature and Mankind in which social evolution is driven by needs. Precisely because these needs are entangled in social relationships they change over time. Thus, the needs themselves can only be understood in relational terms; a methodological focus on individuals here is fruitless. Again, the keyword for such relational analysis is *dépendance*.

This powerful conjunction of claims, even if not explicitly entitled "evolutionary" by Rousseau, provides the reader with a refuge from, and an alternative to, both the sacred and secular creationism he advocates elsewhere by way of the *topos* of Will. It allows us, motivated by the two contradictory answers to the "fundamental question" — ($Q^{\text{fundamental}}A^{\text{nature} \in \text{grace}}$) and ($Q^{\text{fundamental}}A^{\text{nature} \notin \text{grace}}$) — and the initial tension between them, to consider an entirely different aspect of Rousseau's social theory of politics, in which *dépendance* itself is the principle of social motion.

The idea that dependence is the principle of social motion is too capacious and too generative to consider in a systematic way here. I note however that were we to pursue this line, it would lead toward a positive framework consistent with the many critical arguments in this book. This in turn would require an alternative approach not only to the topics we have drawn from the "main passage" but also to the social theory of politics more generally.

The critical framework that has organized all the material of this book will remain as the focus of this final part. After sixty-four sections many elements are on the table and several perspectives have been richly articulated. We may therefore now return to this key question and see it in a new light: What does it mean to say that "dependence-from-things has no moral valence [*la dépendance des choses n'ayant aucune moralité*]"?

I believe that it does not matter which of Rousseau's two answers to the "fundamental question" we take as a starting point. This question presupposes a categorical distinction between *dépendance-des-choses* and *dépendance-des-hommes*. All things considered, Rousseau does not provide a coherent justification for making such a distinction and, in the form he gives it, this distinction cannot be sustained.

What is the consequence of this criticism of Rousseau? It is simple in substance and radical in significance. It suggests that our current common ways of discovering and acting through the patterns of moral complexity—Rousseauean in form and perhaps in origin—do not and cannot advance the social theory of politics. In correspondence with the complexity of experience, which is to say the everyday and fundamental fact of dependence itself, the next steps toward an apt social theory of politics had better help us to identify and interrogate *dépendance-des-choses* in the fields of human relationship where civic life and its disorders take place. Indeed, *dépendance-des-choses* only appears as (perversely, you may say) a necessary part of human life as its very significant moral consequences come to the foreground.

These last few sections will show *why* this is the case; an account of *how* to develop the social theory of politics in this direction will have to wait for another occasion.[188] And while the argument here is meant to extend to and will be extended by contemporary frames of reference, it will again mainly be drawn out from the materials Rousseau himself has provided.

§66

THE MORAL VALENCE OF DEPENDENCE-FROM-THINGS

Suppose that dependence is the principle of social motion. Does that make it a principle of order? To answer this question, according to Rousseau, is to probe the foundations of morality.

We have seen that in Rousseau's view dependence-from-persons is disordered; he arrives at this view by measuring it against dependence-from-things. We have also seen that Rousseau believes dependence-from-persons has moral valence because it is disordered. Whatever sort of dependence is disordered, the "main passage" tells us, "ruins liberty . . . and engenders all the vices, and it is with this dependence that the master and the slave mutually deprave one another."* No wonder, then, that Rousseau is convinced—and for the most part we are convinced with him—that whatever sort of dependence leads this way must be understood as fundamental to moral and political life. What we need to keep before us, however, is that this claim is constructed or delimited by way of a contrast with dependence-from-things.

This point is extremely important and I want to highlight it now. <u>It means that the social theory of politics begins from beliefs about our relation to things. Society is defined by the exclusion of things, and this exclusion is justified by claims about a property of the things themselves. The decisive property is *ordre*.</u>

In the "main passage" Rousseau allows for two sources of order.

First: something is well-ordered when the Will that sets it in motion is unified or singular. I shall refer to this as W-O$^{\text{one will}}$.

Second: something is well-ordered when it follows the contours of laws that are inflexible in the sense of being clear, self-evident, and incontestable.[189] I shall refer to this as W-O$^{\text{perfect law}}$.

Those same things will be disordered/*désordonée* when either of the conditions W-O$^{\text{one will}}$ or W-O$^{\text{perfect law}}$ are not satisfied.

In light of contemporary understanding—which, by holding it anachronistically against Rousseau allows us to judge in turn the contemporary common sense that is aligned with him—we will see in this section and the next one that for the case of our dependence-from-things neither W-O$^{\text{one will}}$ nor W-O$^{\text{perfect law}}$ ever holds true in the sense that Rousseau has in mind. This means—by the same measures—that dependence-from-things must be disordered. Disorder is for us, because we are political beings embedded in society, morally consequential. Since disorder is morally consequential, dependence-from-things must be morally consequential as well. A sociology that does not respond to this fact cannot provide the basis for adequate thinking about politics.

Now consider more closely W-O$^{\text{one will}}$. This is Rousseau's claim that something is well ordered when the Will that sets it in motion is singular.[190] Given the architecture of Rousseau's social theory of politics, the central issue that appears with this claim concerns God's Will: How do we know that it is singular?

With one of his key assumptions—that "the Will is known to me by its acts,

---

* ". . . nuit à la liberté et engendre tous les vices, et c'est par elle que le maître et l'esclave se dépravent mutuellement."

not by its nature [*la volonté m'est connue par ses actes, non par sa nature*]" (OC IV.576; cf. §60 above) — Rousseau has identified the kind of evidence he believes is necessary to answer this question. It can thus be more narrowly drawn this way: What is there in the effects of God's Will that show it to be unitary?

Other considerations of the Will immediately stand in the way. If unbounded freedom is the primary quality of God's Will, then what could be said to manifest that quality more than inconsistent or unpredictable acts like miracles? Yet, even miracles, those of God's acts that are supposed to step outside of all law and order, do not necessarily indicate the *unity* of God's Will. The imputation of "freedom" at the source of diverse effects simply does not prove the unity of that source (cf. again §57).

Nor could the steady reiterated hum of natural facts prove this unity. Each and every rock or tree or sea may behave with perfect self-consistency and still have no relationship one to the others. No one except perhaps God Himself experiences everything as just *one* thing.[191]

Rousseau has told us explicitly that natural law could provide the paradigm for civic order because it is, from a human point of view, perfectly inflexible.[192] He also implicitly assumed that natural law indicates the unity of nature (§§55–57). We will come back to W-O[perfect law] later in this section, but here it is worth revisiting how certain beliefs about natural law fit into W-O[one will].

If natural law is an *act* of God, and God is always "true to himself [*constant à lui-même*]" (OC IV.591), then it may be that natural law, taken as expressing the unity of nature, is the best evidence for the unity of God's Will.[193] Rousseau's assertion — "the Will is known to me by its acts, not by its nature [*la volonté m'est connue par ses actes, non par sa nature*]" — seems to support this, first in the general way of identifying good evidence, and then with a pun on the word *actes* — referring to "everything done or that is done," to legally binding documents, and to "*authoritas consignata*" and "*tabulis & memoria publica*"[194] — that suggests that the best expression of the Will, even God's Will, may be as the outcome of authoritative deliberation, such as legislation or adjudication. Rousseau's sentence could therefore be read as saying that "the Will is known to me by the *laws* that it makes,"[195] with the one law mapping the unity of the Will.

An attempt of this sort to prove the unity of Will through natural law runs aground on Rousseau's own skepticism concerning such laws (cf. §§55 and 60). For when he cannot perceive the relationship between "general laws" and "matter" he does not merely question the utility of those laws. He asserts that

> If compelled to acknowledge some general laws whose essential relations with
> matter I do not perceive at all, in what way will I be advanced? These laws, in

no way real beings or substances, have therefore some other foundation which is unknown to me . . . they in no way suffice to explain the system of the world and the course of the universe. (OC IV.575)*

To say that laws of nature are not "real beings" or "substances" is of course to bring into question the status of natural law. If Rousseau's point is that natural laws are merely human conventions, such laws can be neither necessary features of the order of things nor commands from God. Thus they do not provide evidence for the unity of God's Will. It is implausible to think that Rousseau meant to reduce his theory to the tautological claim that civic order should be based on human conventions, but a tendency in that direction seems implied here. I will come back to this in a moment.

A more immediate problem arises if we return to the premise of W-O^one will. For why assume that in any given situation *only* God's Will is involved?

Now, it is true that as Rousseau lays down his "first article of faith" he refers to "one Will that moves the universe and animates nature [*une volonté qui meut l'univers et anime la nature*]."

This reiterates the question without advancing toward an answer. For, in the effort to persuade his reader, Rousseau does not offer God's Will as evidence. In a turn to the self—quite typical for him—for signs of the natural and the metaphysical, a gesture is made instead to his own experience of willing:

> How does a Will [*volonté*] produce a physical or bodily action? I don't know anything about this, but I experience [*éprouve*][196] in myself that it does produce the action. I want [*veux*][197] to act, and I act; I want [*veux*] to move my body, and my body moves.[198†]

Should we then take the status of the self as a reflection of divine Will, as natural lawyers like Burlamaqui took human reason to be identical with divine reason? That seems mistaken, too, since the absolute freedom of human Will is another foundation of Rousseau's system (cf. §§5, 7; cf. also §§58, 60).

The question this raises is not about God, but about Man. Where does human

---

* "S'il faut admettre des loix générales dont je n'aperçois point les rapports essentiels avec la matiére, de quoi serai-je avancé? Ces loix n'étant point des êtres réels, des substances, ont donc quelqu'autre fondement qui m'est inconnu. . . . elles ne suffisent point pour expliquer le sistême du monde et la marche de l'univers."

† "Comment une volonté produit-elle une action physique et corporelle? Je n'en sais rien, mais j'éprouve en moi qu'elle la produit. Je veux agir, et j'agis; je veux mouvoir mon corps, et mon corps se meut. . . ."

Will go when Rousseau considers the order of dependence-from-things? Why isn't it taken into account?

Eventually this concerns the assimilation of *things* and nature. Before that, however, the problem is more mundane.

Dependence-from-things is not a homogenous category. It divides easily into several types. At the end of Part III of this book I proposed that nonnatural dependence-from-things would be crucial to the analysis of Rousseau's social theory of politics. This is what most obviously disturbs his claims about *ordre* as well. For, when we encounter, and begin to depend from, *made* things, even the religious believer cannot deny that the form and motion of such things devolves from human Wills as much as from the singular Divine.

The effects of these two sorts of Wills are not symmetrically distributed in things. To see the importance of this we do well to keep in mind that Rousseau is not concerned with "things" in the abstract. He wants us to consider "things" as objects in a relationship in which we are the subjects. That relationship is one of dependence. And again, that relationship is not abstract. It must be measured by the specific effects it has on us. What counts for the real experience of dependence are particularities of things. Particulars are the contribution of humans.

This is why the asymmetry in the multiplication of Wills had better be taken seriously. The details of the objects of dependence are registries not just of some single divine act of Creation, but of the ongoing, "value-adding" and "value-consuming" creativities of multiple human Wills. God may have created trees and lead, but He did not issue the Dixon Ticonderoga Number 2 pencil you are obliged to use if you want your ballot in the local election to be counted. And why should Rousseau's declaration—"the Will is known to me by its acts"—be any less urgent for human beings than it is for God?

I think this is a point of surpassing importance. Almost no one scribbles with a pencil in awe of God's creation; the fact is that in their—utter, complete, awesome—generality, the marks of God's Will become trivial in comparison with earthly *poiesis*, notwithstanding that His Will is all-powerful and ours are—relative to God, but also relative to circumstantial social facts characterized by competing Wills—puny.

It is not my intention to compare Man favorably to God, or to cast Him out from the social theory of politics. Grant Him His place; grant, if you like, that the effects of God's Will have the greatest significance in human life. What remains is still devastating for Rousseau's argument concerning the moral valence of dependence.

Simply, the principles and tendencies that everywhere and everyday underpin the "order of things" and that bear most on our lives derive from multiple rather than single Wills. This is true even in a most minimal sense. It is enough that only one human Will and the one Divine Will are in play. From the perspective of the social theory of politics, this should *always* be the case. One side of the relationship called dependence-from-things must always be a human being. And for this reason if for no other the condition supposed to define order in terms of the unity of the Will, W-O^one will^, can never be met. And here even Rousseau himself would be forced to the inescapable conclusion that the disorder resulting from the contradiction of several Wills characterizes dependence-from-things just as it characterizes dependence-from-persons.[199]

I have made this point many times now. Yet each time it seems to drift away. *Things* still seem so different from *persons*. It is in part the continuing assimilation of *things* and *nature* that defies our efforts to see *things* another way. Within this irrepressible perspective Rousseau does allow for an alternative source of order. In the "main passage," he suggests that something is well ordered when it follows the contours of laws that are inflexible in the sense of being clear, self-evident, and incontestable (W-O^perfect law^). The model is nature. We turn to this now.

Even a cursory look at W-O^perfect law^ brings into sharp focus additional problems with Rousseau's view. From where we stand today, we can come at this two ways.

For the first approach let us enlist the aid of Charles Sanders Peirce, who more than a century after Rousseau and more than a century before our time proposed to consider "the common belief that every single fact in the universe is precisely determined by law."[200] Examining the "observational evidence for necessitarianism"—which is to say the perfectly lawful post-Newtonian materialist determinism held against Rousseau by his own contemporaries like La Mettrie, Diderot, de Sales, and especially d'Holbach—Peirce found that

> those observations which are generally adduced in favor of mechanical causation simply prove that there is an element of regularity in nature, and have no bearing whatever upon the question of whether such regularity is exact and universal or not. Nay, in regard to this *exactitude*, all observation is directly *opposed* to it; and the most that can be said is that a good deal of this observation can be explained away. Try to verify any law of nature, and you will find that the more precise your observations, the more certain they will be to show irregular departures from the law. We are accustomed to ascribe these, and I do not say wrongly, to errors of observation; yet we cannot usually account for such errors in any antecedently probable way. Trace their causes back far enough and you will be forced to admit they are always due to arbitrary determination, or chance.[201]

What was for Peirce in 1892 a moment of genial inspiration had a century later become the common sense of science itself. This is devastating for anyone who explicitly or implicitly maintains Rousseau's position today.

A second approach draws attention in a more subtle way to the reflexive-discursive human context within which anything called a "law" may emerge. In this perspective, it would only make sense for an individual, and only be possible for a society, to consider dependence-from-things ordered in Rousseau's sense if there were no contest about the laws governing the order of things.

Here a flood of theory and evidence utterly overwhelms any expectation that uncontested or uncontestable "laws of nature" are expressed in things and thus felt by us in the relation dependence-from-things. Organized science, at least since the end of the nineteenth century, is *founded* on the contestability of claims about the order of things. In the spirit of Hume's critique of induction, Ernst Mach, Henri Poincaré, and Pierre Duhem opened the way to a variety of conventionalisms, and uncertainty and undecidability became more or less the ruling dogma.[202] In a widely accepted vulgate—associated with Karl Popper—science is a relentless agonism of falsification.[203] As "laws of nature" are impossible to know with certainty, conventionalism multiplies contestation and raises competition—in the famous word of Thomas Kuhn—to the level of entire "paradigms" that may be "incommensurable."[204] Without sure empirical or theoretical foundations, the diverse or divergent justifications for multiple "paradigms" tend to equalize, making the entities they identify ever murkier, indistinct, and unfit to serve Rousseau's metonymical purpose of establishing the measure of dependence-from-persons on the back of dependence-from-things. Whatever "nature"—itself, in itself—may be, the meaning of the "book of nature" is an unending source of contest, contradiction, and, quite frankly, disorder. Moreover, it matters little whether or not this disorder exists under God's eyes in the world of things "itself." It is enough that its effects are felt as such in the stratum of human existence that is driven by cognitive engagement with those things and the reflexivity that makes that engagement into science, science into belief, and belief into action. Every time the order of nature has been ascertained, as a function of the constitutively human relationship of dependence-from-things it changes.

This fact is not just a form of mental confusion. It arises from other material facts. This is why the human significance of natural processes—under rubrics like "global warming" and "biotechnology"—is increasingly at the center of public debate today. It is also why such all-too-human debate has an impact on those decisively natural processes.

These materially effective changes in practices of human cognition are represented in the web of beliefs and practices that once supported but can no longer sustain Rousseau's thesis. This transformation of contemporary science, the inheritor of "natural philosophy," as much as or more than movements in theology over the past two hundred years, require us to cast off from the comfortable moorings of Rousseau's seductive idea. How can we cling to his conclusion that dependence-from-things is ordered if by our very own understanding of the nature of things those things do not satisfy the conditions he set for either $W\text{-}O^{one\ will}$ or $W\text{-}O^{perfect\ law}$?[205]

It is convenient to apply our contemporary insight (or perhaps blindness) and thus withhold agreement from Rousseau concerning the moral valence of dependence-from-things. But it may not be necessary. Rousseau himself seems to provide sufficient reason for just that. Indeed, the far-reaching survey in the book you are reading has shown what I reiterated earlier in this section: even Rousseau views with skepticism the claim that the laws of nature can be discovered at all. When he allows that possibility, he suspects that these laws will fall short, that they will not tell us everything we need or want to know about ourselves. Finally, the sort of reassuring certainty Rousseau seeks in "things" or "thingness" cannot be had because we are, inexorably, part of the Nature by which he proposes we should measure ourselves, and we are a measure always wanting.[206] How odd that the common but false view of Rousseau as first and foremost wedded to nature should from another angle provide a powerful reason to reject his social theory of politics altogether.

§67

NONNATURAL DEPENDENCE-FROM-THINGS

The issue now is how the architecture of this social theory of politics comes undone.

Rousseau claimed that politics could find new and stable ground were we to emulate dependence-from-things. Why? Because dependence-from-things is supposed to have no moral valence of its own. It is for this reason a corrective, a source of improvement. The standard that establishes the double relationship of *things* and dependence-from-things to moral life is *ordre*. What is without *ordre* wears away at moral life, what is with *ordre* sustains it. We already know that in Rousseau's system Will is the deepest source of *ordre*. But that is not what concerns us here. Look instead at this different level: are *things*, and thus is dependence-from-things, well ordered? and may therefore *things* and our relationship to them be excluded from the moral domain, from inquiry into society, and from engagement with politics? and by this exclusion, by their consequent austerity, one might say, may the example of *things* provide the essential guidance to help us make a civil life? These types of questions turned us in a general way to consider the status of *things*.

The issue here is shaped by indirection. It is not an enumeration of the objects of political science. The problem is rather what had better be *excluded* from inquiry. And what, by way of this exclusion, can serve as paradigm for the objects that remain within our scope and compass? In other words, *things* are for Rousseau not an object but an ideal, not the vessel but the navigation.

One may ask, are *things* so worthy? How general this question seems now. Nonetheless, in the preceding section it was treated in a specific way. It was narrowed again through the topic of *ordre*. It is *ordre* that reserves *things* from moral life and makes them a measure of it. This *ordre* derives from Will; in particular the attributes of unity and consistency are conveyed to the objects of the Will in the application of a single Will. Thus it seemed plausible to consider whether or not dependence-from-things fits into the architecture of Rousseau's social theory of politics by asking whether or not *things* meet Rousseau's criteria of unity and consistency. Even before this measure could be taken, however, there was something of an epistemological problem. It is not clear that we can know whether or not *things* are unitary or consistent. So I chose initially to follow again in §66, like Rousseau, the assimilation of *things* and *nature*, however misguided that may ultimately be. It is a modern philosophical twitch to associate *nature* and epistemology, and we did that, too. In other words, the question Can *things* perform in Rousseau's theory as Rousseau requires? was recast as if it were concerned only with the possible knowledge of natural laws that are supposed to pertain to *things*. This was a way of highlighting further difficulties in Rousseau's way of sorting out and attributing value to the two types of dependence. The result? Simply, there is no perfectly consistent or uncontested natural law and the standard Rousseau offered (W-O$^{\text{perfect law}}$) to justify his larger assertions fails. A concise but devastating argument by C.S. Peirce brought much of this to light. Peirce shows that the relentlessly fluctuating practical results of experimental science cannot be sufficient warrant for the claim that natural laws are universal and perfectly inflexible.

Thus, from the previous section, the conclusion is that nature is an imperfect tutor, for the craft of *things* and for the apprenticeship of mankind. This does not diminish the role of *things* in human life. It should only increase our efforts to understand what *things* mean for us. It compels, finally, a break between dependence-from-nature and dependence-from-things, specifically pointing toward nonnatural dependence-from-things.

To bring non-natural dependence-from-things under scrutiny will require a new tack. We do well to start over by asking Is epistemology really the issue that should concern us here?[207] For, perhaps without knowing a law, one still experiences the inflexibility it represents. Or perhaps the inflexibility is all that matters. Each and every time you put your hand in the flame you have the same painful experience. Drop that apple again, Mr. Newton, and we'll see where it goes . . .

What is the significance of such consistency? There can be no doubt that it bears on much of what is presented in the panorama of the *"île du genre humain"* offered to us by Rousseau (cf. §2 above). We think of this consistency as a defining characteristic of dependence (although in fact the failure of consistency is also central to the analytics of dependence; cf. Afterword below).

We have also seen at some length that consistency is deeply implicated in the question "How can we be happy?" (Cf. §§21, 22, 26, and 27 above). This intersection is telling. For, among the many aspects of experience condensed into the "formula for happiness" (recall this as *force* ≥ *besoins* = *bonheur* from §§19, 26, 37, and Part Two.A passim) is the fact that the object of need or desire may be either a thing or a person.

In other words, even Rousseau himself does not believe that the damaging effects of inconsistency are always captured in those categories by which he defines the problem of dependence (it might for example also be a matter of anxiety; cf. §§21, 22), even though he does see inconsistency as the pivotal feature of that problem, too. Unhappiness may as well correlate with inconsistency when the object of need or desire is a thing as when that object is a person. The far-flung pilgrim is, by Rousseau's lights, just as unhappy when he plants a crop that fails as when he is starved out by his neighbors.

Be that as it may. Everything hinges for Rousseau on the contrast case. It is one thing to say that our relations with things in many respects produce consistent effects. It is another thing to say, as the theory seems to require, that the effects of those relations with *things* are always the same. Absent the second much stronger condition, Rousseau's claim that dependence-from-things has no moral consequences, or that it is not relevant to political life, is by his own measures and reasoning no longer convincing.

Concerning consistency, is this difference between *sometimes* and *always* really important? I think so. So let me now trace out this significance.

Earlier in this book (§39 above) a digression brought to the foreground the tripartite distinction of dependent relations human beings have with nature, with things, and with other persons. Rousseau appealed to this framework within a limited consideration of types of education. It had, however, a wider effect. This gesture displaced the main distinction between dependence-from-things and dependence-from-persons. In this way Rousseau opened a line of inquiry that erodes his major argument. He did not pursue it.

I think this line merits further consideration. With a bit more persistence it is not difficult to see that the implied differentiation of "nature" and "things"—accepted in the digression but ignored in the "main passage"—both adds precision to and changes the significance of the primary distinction between two types of dependence. Indeed, taking seriously the three sorts of dependence—even in the narrow way Rousseau presents them—sharply undercuts Rousseau's claims about the moral valence of dependence-from-things.

The reason is that these two overlapping sets of claims are based on very different assumptions. Rousseau writes emphatically in the "main passage" that dependence-from-things "is part of nature [*est de la nature*]." This identity is obviously ruptured in the tripartite distinction (cf. also again §41).

To move the social theory of politics in this direction changes everything. It brings still further into question Rousseau's political project to restore order to society by way of laws so inflexible that "dependence-from-persons would thus again become dependence-from-things [*la dépendance des hommes redeviendroit alors celle des choses*]." Without the identity of "nature" and "things" this program loses its edge. Yet, as the division of "three educations" suggests, it is precisely this identity that Rousseau is unable to maintain.

Let me be blunt. From where we stand today the idea that *les choses* and *la nature* are the same in the ways Rousseau needs them to be the same is largely unconvincing. Although there are many ways to account for this I shall focus on the one derived from Rousseau himself.

Observe that much of our experience in the world is constituted by processes of social evolution of the sort Rousseau so aptly described. Moreover, these processes entail the development of material culture. This fact was meticulously catalogued in the *Encyclopédie* and subject to a kind of social-cultural analysis by Rousseau (further and famously articulated by Hegel, Marx, Benjamin, and literally dozens of subsequent other writers). Whatever similarities the doodads of culture may have with the rocks of nature, common sense as much as these deep thinkers makes clear that made objects and found objects do not play the same role in human life.

And yet Rousseau's social theory of politics is clearly based on the assumption that *les choses* and *la nature* feature in human life in essentially the same way.

The background belief that supports this assumption is creationism. That is, the concept of Will—a Will-centered theology and a Will-centered view of human agency at the core of Rousseau's social theory of politics—is the common point through which *les choses* and *la nature* are assimilated.

On its face this seems like a weird and perverse assumption. Think again. It is something that our contemporaries largely, although tacitly, share with Rousseau.[208]

What I have tried to show in this book, from various angles, is that this generalized creationism does not in any interesting or productive way contribute to an explanation of our social and political experience. Indeed, in some key respects it leads us profoundly astray. Rousseau's two approaches to classifying dependence are pertinent here precisely because in the contradiction between the two sets of terms we find resources with which to articulate an alternative, one that avoids the errors of generalized creationism and develops evolutionary-ecological possibilities only hinted at by Rousseau himself.

Specifically, the contradiction brings to light a whole class of relations unnamed by Rousseau. The sociology and the social theory of politics that developed for several centuries around Rousseau's insights and instigations paid little heed to this type of relationship and generally reduced it to forms of social interaction (whether interpersonal or collective).

The name most likely to come to mind at this point is Karl Marx. For what you are reading may be understood as a plan for a very unusual sort of sociological materialism. And it will seem that above and beyond all other thinkers, Marx was the patron of a tradition deeply antagonistic to the sociological worldview analyzed and rejected in this book. This, however, would also be a mistake. It vastly underestimates the extent to which even Marx, in some strange but fundamental sense (mentioned in §11 above), understood *things* as identical with the persons by whom they are made (his version of the "labor theory of value") and took relations between things to stand for relations among persons (the "fetishism of commodities").

By unwieldy extrapolation from Rousseau's vocabulary, I will call "nonnatural dependence-from-things" those relations in which human beings depend from things but the form of that dependence is directly attributable neither to a Nature wholly apart[209] nor to particular human beings or groups of human beings with whom one finds oneself entangled (the relation Marx called "capital," the reality underlying the appearance-world of the "commodity," would be a complex example of this).

Rather, the forms of "nonnatural dependence-from-things" derive from circulation in the broadest sense of that word, which is to say the processes through which things pass from hand to hand or otherwise move from one part of the human environment to another and are woven into and thus transform practices constituted among plural persons. This process is itself shaped by social evolution and therefore (for reasons mentioned in §§37, 42, 45, 46, 49.8, 49.29, 49.58, 65, etc.) implicated in the ongoing transformation of how human beings fit into nature and thus the transformation of nature "itself." At least from the perspectives discussed in this book and as framed by the commonsense terms available to us today, this process of circulation across space and time appears to be inherently complex (i.e., it cannot be reduced to one of its components or any "simple"). The composition of that complexity includes various moments or features. In one moment, "nonnatural dependence-from-things" brings forms to our relationships with the world that are conditioned by the practical characteristics of its objects. While this conditioning includes qualities (density, volume, color, etc.) that merge in those objects, a description that thematizes only these abstract qualities is insufficient. The practical characteristics of objects consist of the intermingling or push-and-pull of such qualities with human bodies within the gestures and movements of human communication, purposes, and projects. As concerns the *forms* of dependence, what matters is how objects come into our hands and the uses they allow us to make of them.

This pragmatic conditioning is the way practices are congealed in durable and transmissable physical forms. It, in turn, imposes another condition on the forms of "nonnatural dependence-from-things." This condition arises from the circumstances of interaction in which some or any thing becomes an object in the relationship of "nonnatural dependence-from-things." These circumstances include both the environment from which the object emerges and the environment in which the dependence-constituting engagement with the object occurs; these environments may range from distant in time and space to nearly identical.

I believe that the assignment or accretion of significations (not merely names) to objects, together with the emergence of a semiotic moment in which objects function as symbols within practices, are necessary corollaries in the processes of circulation mentioned here. While this crucial fact must be mentioned it is far too complicated to consider in any further detail in this book.

Having now sketched some conditions concerning the objects of "nonnatural dependence-from-things" I want to relate this to the question of consistency with which this section began.

Objects of "nonnatural dependence-from-things" are often remarkably consistent: pyramids still stand in the now dessicated valley of the Nile; the ancient Parthenon tops bustling Athens.

This consistency may not impress when measured in the "ideal eternal time" of God. Or the geological time of our planet. Or the evolutionary time of human existence. But these are not the appropriate measures for politics and moral life.

Human time-frames begin with breath and the beating heart. They include the stages of a life, the movements of a generation, the rise to global preeminence of a nation. By these and similar standards, nonnatural things can and often do have exactly the effective inflexibility that Rousseau has in mind. From this, however, Rousseau's logic would still urge us to conclude that such things are of no moral relevance.

Let me now again emphasize my point. <u>Setting aside for a moment Rousseau's perspective, we can see that the exact opposite is true.</u> "Nonnatural dependence-from-things" is persistently implicated in the web of *moeurs*, the play of *forces*, and the rise and (dis)satisfaction of *besoins*. It is therefore inevitably bound up with fundamental aspects of the political field in which the benefits and burdens of the *lien social* are distributed.

Recall that earlier I invoked social evolution to articulate "nonnatural dependence-from-things." The image of social evolution—following Rousseau and advancing far beyond him—cannot easily be disassociated from the ongoing transformation both of nature and of the place of humankind in nature. This conjunction is important because "nonnatural dependence-from-things" constitutes a marginal and typically indistinct zone between the human and the natural.[210] For just this reason it is an essential aspect of modern politics, a terrain on which some of the most significant gains and losses are made in political struggles. Think back to the tragic drama played out around Hurricane Katrina and the levees of New Orleans.

The larger the issue the more this holds true. It would be odd indeed to deploy the *topos* natural/social to promote the filling of potholes in center-city. By contrast, centuries of debate about slavery, freedom, and equality would have been unthinkable, unpronounceable, without that *topos*. This should weigh heavily on how we relate to Rousseau. For, the critical evolutionary-ecological perspective that I draw from him in order to criticize his own creationist views and those who share such views is most trenchant when it comes to exactly the topics—like equality—around which Rousseau first and most effectively oriented our political attention.

Nonetheless, all this looks bad for Rousseau's arguments. It is in fact even worse than it seems. We return our attention to the theological-sociological metonymy.

Consider once again the claim W-O[perfect law] with respect to the assumption of the incontestability of natural law rather than as measured by consistency.

Contest concerning natural law is contest over what is social and what is not.[211] The political relevance of such contest is not at all limited to determining a course of action after having learned that this or that is a *social fact*. Although it often seems that introducing a topic for debate is the point by which political contest is *initiated*, conditions deeply prejudicial to the outcome are typically set in place well before that. Agenda-setting is of course important but it is not what I have in mind here. The issue is the determination of a domain of discourse. It is usually at this level that decisive political contest goes into drawing the line between the natural and the social.

Rousseau's theoretical machinery leaves little space for this fact. Its excision from Rousseau's fundamental account of the *lien social* is striking. For, despite what Romantic readers may have inculcated in us, it is only a modernist conceit to think this only a modernist problematic. Indeed, in no thinker more than Rousseau should we expect this to be a central and finely articulated concern. He has no single fixed conception of nature (cf. §§42–45 above). Indeed, as we move away from these questions that bear on the largest architecture of his social theory of politics, we see that over and over again he problematizes and reasserts the boundary between the natural and the social. While his implicit and explicit intentions are often critical, here and there he proposes in a positive mode programs and institutions that depend on the "naturalization"—as reification, as sacralization—of social relationships. So, why doesn't he seem to understand that this is not where politics stops, but where it begins in earnest?

The difficulties involved in discerning the natural from the social can come before us in several ways. I have already mentioned (§66) some problems that may be said to be inherent in nature "itself." For example, as a totality nature is internally underdetermined; that is, its structure or structuration involves a large measure of chance or chaos. Then, too, another type of problem inheres in our relationship to nature (whatever it is). For example, nature may simply be beyond the capacity of human beings to comprehend. One way or another, this much is clear: the discourses of natural science have been and will continue to be heartily contested (cf. again §66). These various difficulties undoubtedly bear on Rousseau's social and political theory. I recall these things here but I want now to direct your attention to a somewhat different topic. It concerns a certain evasiveness in Rousseau's theory.

To see this we need to take one step back. Common sense reminds us that once the natural is distinguished from the social we associate a different class of values with each. However, what Rousseau steadfastly avoids bringing to the foreground is the process by which this distinction is made.[212] The discursive fact of the distinction and the process by which it is enacted are two very different matters. And as the differential association of values with natural or social objects orients human action in very different ways, a great deal is at stake in that process.

The example of famine is telling. Famines are generally conceived as natural disasters. However, researchers like Amartya Sen and Susan George have convincingly argued that in the modern world famines are the result of complex and long-run social choices and structures (no matter how much effects like hunger, malnutrition, or starvation are felt in hours, days, and weeks).[213] Famines are facts of human existence that derive from the social organization within which the effects of certain natural events—like a year of abnormally low precipitation—are felt and distributed among a given population. It matters for moral and political action, and it can be determinative for practical inequality and institutional arrangements in society, whether a famine is classed as an "act of God" or an "act of Man," a natural fact or a social one. It is a consequence of position and worldview that Americans could generally interpret the Asian tsunami of 2004 as a natural disaster and the following year's Hurricane Katrina as a manifestation of bad social policy.

Within this framework, it is a matter of high significance that only social facts are open to the language of *injustice*.[214]

No expert or commission can decide once and for all whether such occurrences are *really* natural facts or social ones. These matters make for hot dispute. So, consider for a moment the circular path along which such disputes develop.

Take famine again. For water, we depend on nature (meaning here the planetary circulation of hydrogen and oxygen in combination and at variable temperatures). A certain population organizes agriculture on the expectation of rain. That they eat bread, and bread is made from wheat, is an instance of "nonnatural dependence-from-things." In a year of drought, the absence of rain is not the proximate cause of hunger.[215] Lack of bread is the harm for these people. Shall others intervene to succor the breadless? Shall resources—water? wheat? flour? bread? money?—be diverted to relieve them? Which measures will we take? And how?

The answers to such questions are not self-evident. Nor can they be given by fiat. Answers emerge from disputes (which themselves are distributed in many different ways across the social fabric). Indeed, the time and manner in which each such question is answered will, more often than not, produce further dispute. These conflicts are political in the most banal sense: they involve a clash of interests and forces, and these clashes are conducted in speech. In such discursive conflict there are patterns. Keywords—properly speaking, rhetorical *topoi*—

are deployed to bring others over to one side or another. The distinction between the natural and the social is itself such a *topos*, although often proxies like "rain" and "bread" will be deployed. Once this gauntlet is thrown down, there will be pressure to interpret the relevant facts or events—for example, the malnutrition and starvation that are constitutive features of what we call famine—as social or as natural. Such assertions will be strategic; they will be motivated by interests of all sorts, some venal and some virtuous.

The assertions may be accepted or rejected; that is not the point here. What I want to underscore is that the *topoi* in which such a debate is conducted are invigorated by having been invoked and fought over. This is how their significance and utility evolve. This process occurs within the rhetorical setting.

What we have, then, is an overlap between two social processes that Rousseau wants to separate so as to ignore one of them. The rhetorical setting within which *topoi* evolve is, generally speaking, *made up of the same kind of social "stuff"* as the setting within which the categories will be applied and the consequences for action ascertained.[216] In slightly different but more familiar terms, this rhetorical setting is the moral and political life of citizens.

This fact bears on Rousseau's argument. There is, I believe, a kind of vicious, or blinding, circularity in the claim that dependence-from-things is morally irrelevant if what fits under that category is itself determined through politically charged contests. Rousseau can assert—as he did with great and lasting effect—that our dependence-from-things is not significant for what happens in that context because it is natural, but for the reasons just stated he cannot have the last word. There is no last word. It is just this open-endedness, this instability inherent in social life, that Rousseau seeks to evade. This, too, defeats his argument.

Perhaps we should not expect Rousseau to treat critically—and thus devalorize—the philosophical rhetoric he deploys to make his social and political arguments convincing. Yet, serious contemporary readers cannot avoid making those strategies explicit for themselves. The commonplace assumptions that held together arguments of the past feature in our reading in two ways. If dead, they will be as obvious as tombstones in a graveyard. If still living, they will be invisible presences, exerting forces that may no longer serve our ends or which, as invisible, have ceased to be subject to collective corrective checking.

In this respect, it is not enough to take Jean-Jacques as the judge of Rousseau's conception of *le lien social*. We must also assess his arguments in light of relevant ideas that were not his own. Since the eighteenth century, there have been significant developments not only in what we classify as natural or social, but also in *how we go about* classifying things as natural or social and how we fight over those classifications. The practical effects of these conceptual transformations are felt throughout modern societies, as the recently coined but now entirely familiar term "biotechnology" shows with startling immediacy. It represents hybrids of the natural and the social that only two generations ago would have been inconceivable.

Rousseau would like us to believe that because things produce consistent effects dependence-from-things is morally and politically inconsequential. The difficulties inherent in this way of thinking multiply if we go further to consider *the use* Rousseau wants to make of it. The use of this idea would be, of course, an effort to make *dépendance-des-hommes* become *dépendance-des-choses* through the imposition of perfectly inflexible law. As a metaphor this is attractive. But if this shift is to occur through social processes it cannot, as I have just suggested, be accomplished in a depoliticized and nonmoral manner. Every implication of our *dépendance-des-choses* in society has the opposite effect: it is transformed back into *dépendance-des-hommes*. Then consistency loses its sacred aura.

A perfectly doctrinaire evangelical Christian judge could tell you that he knows for sure what God's Nature is, and thus be ready to decide all the abortion cases before him with clockwork consistency; some could see this as just what Rousseau wants, a transformation of *dépendance-des-hommes* into *dépendance-des-choses* through the imposition of perfectly inflexible law; but absent the assurance of natural law others will understand it as precisely dependence-from-persons, and identify it as something typical of an utterly human and relentless patriarchy.

A master beats the slave every day at five o'clock sharp, but it's slavery nonetheless. It helps not a whit if the master is not guilty of pride, and beats the slave as a virtuous sacrifice to the love of order. And you can count on it.

§68

FROM WILL TO DEPENDENCE I
Ethical Sources of Order Revisited

Rousseau does not want to *apply* natural law to human relations; he knows that if such a law exists it always already applies. He seeks to model the laws made within society on certain attributes ascribed to natural law. In the preceding two sections (§§66 and 67) we considered the assumption that natural law is perfectly inflexible, as well as claims concerning the consistency of experience which that inflexibility is supposed to represent.

Rousseau also assumes that natural laws are perfectly general. As with inflexibility, generality is supposed to be an identifying feature of order. This presents important additional difficulties for Rousseau's project as a whole.

Suppose that a certain effect one experiences in the environment occurs with a high degree of regularity, or even that it has occurred in our experience without exception. Is there warrant in that fact to claim that it derives from a law that is perfectly general? What could prove that the order observed is not local, partial, or particular?

This sort of question was placed starkly on the agenda of modern thought by Rousseau's contemporary David Hume. We saw it reiterated in another way by Charles Sanders Peirce just above (§66). It remains vivid today. And it is relevant here because Rousseau believes that the paradigm he has chosen to support the social theory of politics is perfectly general. That is one of the main reasons why he insists that his proposal is the best way to "resolve all the contradictions of the social system." So, we do well to ask Rousseau, What if anything would be the source of the generality of law?

We have already seen from several angles that Rousseau's image of law as perfectly general is derivative. In his writings it emerges from a metaphorical transfer. The source is the archetypical image of God's Will as that which *orders* perfectly and completely because all powerful and infinitely good. Let us assume again for the sake of the argument here that the description of this source is accurate. A pivotal question for the social theory of politics remains: how can something resembling this divine generality be sustained in an account of civil *ordre*?

Our conversation around Rousseau in this book began as we considered the problems of happiness and evil in the society of mankind "abandoned to ourselves." We listened as Rousseau argued that these problems must be "resolved"—which is to say, analyzed and adjusted (§31)—in terms of the very basic human fact of dependence. Subsequently we saw that Rousseau traces the problem from the fabric of dependence to the more basic question of *ordre*, and then from the question of *ordre* to the foundational principle of Will. Thus, while Rousseau is a magnificent theorist of *société* and social evolution, perhaps the inventor of both, he is at heart, too, a creationist. This creationism has both a theological and a secular side (cf. §49.32–34 and §67). The Will/*la volonté* is not only the first principle of his metaphysics; Rousseau also asserts it, especially in the form of "the general Will/*la volonté générale*," as the "first principle of public economy and the fundamental rule of government" (OC III.247).

Rousseau ultimately believes that the *ordre* of dependence is grounded in Will. The source image for this belief is God's Will, which is unitary (cf. §66), and under certain conditions this attribute is transferred by analogy to human Will. However, it is an inherent feature of human Will — its plurality — that calls forth from this divine image a transformation of human Will from many into one. Given the complete extension of God's Will, as it models human Will, the attribute of unity becomes also the attribute of generality.

This resolution of the "contradictions of the social system" is required by the construction of the problem. It does not explain, and it certainly does not require, the construction of the problem in this way.

Moreover, Rousseau has not given an account of how something resembling divine generality can be sustained in an account of civil *ordre*. His writings, however, do suggest an approach we might take. I will sketch that now.

One may think — with that great reader of Rousseau, Tom Paine — that in a constitutional republic, and so as to "not appear to be defective even in earthly honors," we should "let a day be solemnly set apart for proclaiming the charter; let it be brought forth placed on the divine law, the word of God; let a crown be placed thereon, by which the world may know, that so far as we approve of monarchy.... THE LAW IS KING."[217] Perhaps just as absolutist kings presented themselves as gods, so too the law must be like a god.[218] And this might be simply an interpolation of Rousseau's anthropological insight (recall the discussion in §64) that "only if gods existed would it be possible to give laws to men [*il faudroit des Dieux pour donner des loix aux hommes*]," which is to say that before one can even imagine law, no less enact good ones, the symbolic form of God, which provides a certain conception of *ordre*, one which hinges on a perfect Will, a Will that only a God could have, must be in place. Then, in this complex and paradoxical version of secularization, law could only satisfy the demands Rousseau makes upon it, *it would only be law*, if revered like God (cf. §63).

Rousseau seems to dedicate himself in this direction when he remarks "as for me . . . I recognize no other sovereign than the law."[219]* This motto, or creed, is modest enough. Behind it, however, lies a more vigorous view. In an encomium committed to print in the famous entry on *"l'économie politique"* he wrote for the *Encyclopédie* Rousseau calls the law a "celestial voice that dictates to each citizen the precepts of public reason"† and waxes wildly this way, one erotema tripping after another:

* "... quant à moi ... je ne reconnois d'autre souverain que la loi. ..."

† "... voix céleste qui dicte à chaque citoyen les préceptes de la raison publique. ..."

By what inconceivable art could one have found the means to subjugate men so as to render them free? To employ in the service of the state the goods, the labor, and even the lives of all its members, without constraining or consulting them? To chain their Will with just what they avow? To realize their consent against their refusals, and to force them to punish themselves when they do other than what they wished? How comes it to pass that they obey and no one commands, that they serve and have no master; in fact much more free than under evident subjection, one loses from his liberty only that which can harm the liberty of another? These wonders are the work of the law. (OC III.248)*

Simply, Rousseau believes that the law is "the most sublime of all human institutions" and that, considered as a human possibility and practice in the abstract, the source of law is "a celestial inspiration that taught mankind to imitate here below the immutable decrees of the divinity" (OC III.248).†

It is difficult to imagine a clearer statement of the spirit that drives Rousseau's entire project.

And would it be so strange to propose this? That we should stand before the law as we would before a god? Wouldn't reverence, awe, *admiratio,* or even the more modest fact of having our attention focused on the law, tend to draw us all together? Direct us toward some common good?[220]

One may speculate further. Perhaps this reverence would, of itself, instill in law the inflexibility Rousseau seeks at the foundation of the social theory of politics. As a moral, social, and political fact reverence for the law would—in the way of a "self-fulfilling prophecy"—constitute law as the "real force [*force réelle*]" needed to back up "the general Will [*la volonté générale*]." For what the rule of law requires is that this *force* not be—except perhaps in the most punctual sense—held by the police or the army. Rather, it had better emerge as an ongoing long-term effect from the totality of how the people of a society live together. In

---

* "Par quel art inconcevable a-t-on pû trouver le moyen d'assujettir les hommes pour les rendre libres? d'employer au service de l'état les biens, les bras, et la vie même de tous ses membres, sans les contraindre et sans les consulter? d'enchaîner leur volonté de leur propre aveu? de faire valoir leur consentement contre leur refus, et de les forcer à se punir eux-mêmes, quand ils font ce qu'ils n'ont pas voulu? Comment se peut-il faire qu'ils obéissent et que personne ne commande, qu'ils servent et n'ayent point de maître; d'autant plus libres en effet que sous une apparente sujétion, nul ne perd de sa liberté que ce qui peut nuire à celle d'un autre? Ces prodiges sont l'ouvrage de la loi."

† "... une inspiration céleste, qui apprit à l'homme à imiter ici-bas les decrets immuables de la divinité"

the republican dream at least, the whole of the *cité* and its *citoyens* constitute the force and effect of the law. Indeed, when Rousseau writes in the "main passage" that

> if there is some way to remedy evil in society it is to substitute [*substituer*] Law for Man, and to arm [*armer*] the general Wills with a real force superior to the action of every particular Will.*

the meaning is not that one must first substitute/*substituer* and then arm/*armer*, but that to do the one is to do the other. Law itself—properly understood (cf. §5 *et passim*)—is the "real force [*force réelle*]" that is superior to individual interest. Perhaps the only way to constitute and ensure this is to inculcate a love of one's republic, and, specifically, to cultivate a *reverence* for the Law.[221]

Several pages back I observed that Rousseau asserts but does not adequately argue for the transfer of divine generality to conditions for civil *ordre*; from this observation I speculated about how, in Rousseau's way of thinking, the divine and the civic might come together in the practice of reverence for the law. As I carry this speculation one step further, however, we shall see that it still does not provide the foundation he seeks for the social theory of politics. Rather, it takes us farther away from the secular creationist architecture he proposes for that theory.

Although *reverence* may be an act of Will, the social consequences of reverence for the law are not ordered by or in accordance with the intentions guiding that act. If this reverence is what makes law an apt ruler for the virtuous republic, it cannot derive from a principle or metaphysical belief. It is an effect of social-symbolic practices. Such practices are in fact not analogous to divine Will or to the order of nature as Rousseau understands those things.

Rather, as *reverence* is woven into the relationship between natural order and civil order, it turns us away from the generality sought by Rousseau and back toward particularity. Here is what I mean.

Refer again to the "main passage." The paradigm case assumed God as the agent of *ordre* and the object of reverence. The political project, no matter how assiduously it applies the image of a "general Will [*volonté générale*]," assumes that each person, as sovereign agent and source of law, is not the object but the subject of this *reverence*. For the analogy to be convincing, the power of God must be inherent to Him; it cannot derive from our reverence for Him. Yet,

---

* "... s'il y a quelque moyen de remédier à ce mal dans la societé c'est de substituer la loi à l'homme, et d'armer les volontés générales d'une force réelle supérieure à l'action de toute volonté particuliére..."

within the social system and its political order, it is precisely by way of such reverence that the relevant "real force [*force réelle*]" is constituted. The issue concerns the source of sovereign power.

As Rousseau recognizes, there can never be a perfect match between the "Will of all [*volonté de tous*]" and the "general Will [*volonté générale*]."[222] The latter is what is supposed to mimic the Will of God and its *ordre* in nature. But when it comes to civic law, the practices of reverence for the law on which the attribute of generality actually depends are always situated in the realm of the plural "everyone [*tous*]." The effective fact of reverence can only be accounted for in sociological or symbolic-interactionist terms, not theological ones. And thus the analogy breaks down.

Worse still, that analogy is counterproductive. If there exists an accreted fact of the "Will of all [*volonté de tous*]," that fact is located in *société* in just the same way that the cumulative fact of contradictory self-interests is located there. Thus, however much we may strive to differentiate them, civic virtue (as generality)[223] and civic vice (as particularity) are brewed in the same pot, made of the same stuff, constitutive of the same field of interaction. Virtuous reverence for the law might serve many things, but grounded as it is in the social fact of plurality it could never provide a complete bulwark against the intrusion of particular interests. Thus, exactly what Rousseau sought to avoid—which is to say, *particularity*—by constructing his social theory of politics around an analogy to the divine paradigm returns to the scene insofar as the only source of the *generality* of human law is our reverence for it.

Thus, reverence for the law is an insufficient support for its claim to generality. This discussion again shows that because Rousseau's social theory of politics hinges, antithetically, on the *ordre* of *things* (§66) by virtue of the generality that *ordre* is supposed to derive from the strictures of Will, it is bound to fail. The point on which it fails is the distinction between the two sorts of dependence. The inevitable return to particularity just described ensures this failure as well.

FROM WILL TO DEPENDENCE II

Natural Sources of Order Revisited

Given the way that Rousseau has constructed the problem of social evil and unhappiness the failure of ethical sources of order like Will or reverence brings us to a devastating point. Within this construction, if the analogy between divine and civic *ordre* always turns us back to particularity, there can in his view be no adequate basis from which to resolve the contradictions of the social system. Human beings and our dependence from them cannot be ordered. Nonnatural things and our dependence from them cannot be ordered. And, if only because of the slippery boundaries between *la nature* and *les choses*, it is possible that even nature and our dependence from it cannot be ordered.

Now, as a matter of fact, even if the world and our experience of it are radically partial, something holds everything together. Thus, the conclusions required by Rousseau's theoretical framework are clearly false. To see why requires that we set aside the hinge proposition in Rousseau's resolution of *société* and, spurred by the failure of Rousseau's creationist approach, seek other ways to understand what constitutes an *ordre* and the facts of human dependence that condition order in the civic life of human beings.

As we have seen in this book, Rousseau himself offers an alternative to his own creationist views. This is the evolutionary-ecological approach to the social theory of politics that also appears in his writings. Within that frame, Rousseau identifies the location of the fundamental *ordre* of modern civic life, which is *société*, and its substance, which is *dépendance*; he nearly makes visible its motive force, which is *dépendance* again, and attempts to identify its composition, which is also *dépendance*.

Despite Rousseau's prescience and insight, however, he does not carry the evolutionary-ecological approach far enough. The exclusion of our relation to things from the composition of the dynamic order of dependence diminishes some of his most valuable discoveries.

I will now open a small window onto an aspect of contemporary thinking in this area. From evolutionary biology I borrow an example of radically partial order, or order-without-totality.[224] Once again, the primary purpose of this discussion is to advance the critical perspective on Rousseau's social theory of politics. If that theory requires an identification of order with totality it fails on its own terms; this example shows first that order and totality are not identical, and that alternative accounts of order explain real phenomena; the example also shows that those alternatives do not rescue Rousseau's theory. In this way we will be led into wider considerations of order-without-totality and its relation to dependence.

A complex and important but unavoidable ambivalence enters at this point and I think it would be misleading to try to suppress it. With just a few more steps my interpretation of Rousseau will draw to a close. These steps involve us further in a critique of a key element in the architecture of Rousseau's social theory of politics, which is to say his assumptions about natural order and the way that the whole theoretical edifice rests on a corresponding claim about the status of "things." To a certain extent these assumptions can be addressed most effectively by separating them from other familiar considerations. Not only will I now make this separation, but, so as to illustrate by contrast what I take to be the fundamental flaw in Rousseau's "resolution of the contradictions of the social system," I will present on this single point—the image of natural order—a positive perspective unknown in the eighteenth century. The example will be drawn from contemporary research on how animals form groups and operate within them. Schooling fish and flocking birds represent—within the domain explicitly circumscribed by Rousseau but by way of a discourse different from his—a type of order. As just mentioned, I refer to this as order-without-totality. The significance of order-without-totality here is that it does not require creationist modes of thought to make sense as explanation for phenomena. This is important because it shows that Rousseau's turn to creationism is unnecessary and that *his claim that a creationist foundation is necessary* is wrong. In other words, for the larger critical purpose of putting pressure on Rousseau and those who see things as he does I present a biological perspective in a positive way.

There is thus a two-phase movement in what I intend to convey, i.e., the positive argument is nested within the critical one. Because this complex exposition may confuse the issue, I want to state unequivocally that I do not believe that human beings are like fish in any way that is interesting or productive for the social theory of politics. The ambivalence I referred to a moment ago lies elsewhere. It emerges where my commitment to the specificity of human beings in general and to political theory in particular crosses with another seemingly contradictory belief: even as I deny the direct applicability of evolutionary biology to political questions, I nonetheless admit that the *type* of order manifest in animal behavior is relevant to and at least indirectly instructive for understanding how human beings, as *human beings* and not simply as *one animal among many*, form a fabric of connections and develop from that fabric political relationships. Simply, it is tempting to look for clues in every type of order-without-totality, and I want to admit to pursuing this temptation.

Still, temptations are beginnings not ends. Any appearance that biological examples may stand directly as a paradigm for the pursuit of political theory is mistaken and this is not my considered opinion. I admit no such paradigm and see only indirect, allusive, or metaphorical relevance for the remarkable and fascinating contemporary work being done in evolutionary biology and other disciplines in the natural sciences. I remain adamant that, from the human point of view, human beings are unique, and that in thinking about mankind "abandoned to ourselves" we require a distinctive mode of theory. With this strong qualification in mind we may now turn to the example.

There are many fish in the sea. Some move together. They form groups. They pursue common projects. Yet, schooling fish operate without any of the sorts of order Rousseau had in mind. Links are made between this fish and that one, between parts and parts, but nothing connects the parts to a whole. The fish do not think "we are a school." Perhaps only from the shark's point of view are they a school at all. For, what we, at some distance from the fish, refer to as their "school" is not stable enough in form or constituency to be called a "whole" in the sense required by the traditional concept of order (i.e., that the whole is in a mutually determining relationship with the parts with respect to the characteristic process of the entity, in this instance "swimming as a school"; cf. §53 above).

As a matter of order, which is to say as a relatively stable and predictably patterned dynamic set of relationships among a number of distinguishable entities, the school of fish has no unitary *whole*.

I emphasize all of this to strengthen the next point: despite having no unitary *whole*, the parts, the fish, organize themselves into some formation. It is an order, but it is an order-without-totality.

Perhaps to say even this much is an exaggeration. So let me restate the point from a slightly different angle: the school is an outcome of the actions of the fish. The resulting formation is both flexible and functional for the fish. It is an order related to action.

In the context of the frameworks discussed at length in this book, the next point is also crucial: although this order-without-totality derives from action it has nothing to do with a real or metaphorical Will.[225]

Again: I am not proposing a positive model; I do not recommend that we human beings go about our business the way that fish go about theirs. But it is likewise a mistake to suppose that these matters hold no interest for the historical and theoretical topics treated here. The fact and concept of a radically partial order-without-totality bears decisively on the core commitments of Rousseau's argument. It advances another powerful reason why that argument must fail *for us*. And it suggests one point of reference *not* for a direct analysis of human behavior but *for an alternative image of order* as we seek to reconstruct the social theory of politics.

We shall now see that what I want to bring to light by way of the example of the fish is not simple. Another aspect appears if we approach that example in a commonsense way. We may be powerfully inclined to suppose that in schooling one fish produces a message — "there's the food" or "there's the shark" — and communicates that message to the rest.

On this point common sense is misleading. This approach is on its face anthropomorphic; it makes the fish seem like people so as to prove that people are like fish; the reference to communication seems clearly symbiotic on creationist assumptions. We will see why these are problems if we ask what is missing from this approach, or what makes it insufficient for our purposes.

While all living beings produce communicative signals, I doubt that fish produce messages with recognizable semantic content.[226] The production and use of a meaningful representation like a plan — as opposed to a signal or a gesture — presupposes many specifically human things, including the faculty of imagination. I also doubt that animals have imagination in a sense even remotely similar to humans (a topic hotly debated from Aristotle to evolutionary theory). In any case I do not see how there could be sufficient evidence that they do; we are thus warranted in setting this possibility aside.

Its conjunction with imagination is what makes Will a projective faculty. Insofar as the Will is essentially a "mental organ for the future," without imagination there can be no Will.[227] Absent representation, imagination, and Will, it is certain that fish cannot have a collective self-representation like "we are a school" — as if analogous to the human dogma "we are a *nation*" — that brings members into line and provides a totality by reference to which they can attempt to order themselves. In other words, whether the totality is construed as a material fact or a representation, it is absent from this kind of order.

None of this negates the possibility that fish do form groups through more or less reliable mechanisms for sending and receiving signals. Rather, it shows that if we attempt to assimilate this possibility to familiar models of communication we are interpreting it in the wrong way. It shows that we need to ask different questions about exactly what information is being disseminated and how. This is the way to elucidate the issue of order-without-totality.

Again, a commonsense description of "schooling" in terms of communication would lead us to presuppose that a single message is shared by all members. Regardless of where that single message might originate—in a "leader" fish, or through some collective process—it is easy to think that it effectively functions as the plan or intention of the group. This again pushes us back to a sort of creationism, in which the content of a guiding message like "turn left" or "head for the food" constitutes the Will, or even more literally the *volonté*, that the school of fish may be said to follow. If that were correct, the formation of fish would constitute an order precisely because it is implicitly held together by a sort of command. Or, even without the image of command, it would imply a sort of secular creationism to sustain the idea that the formation as a whole derives from the distribution of information on the basis of which each fish makes, so to speak, an informed decision *to school* or *not to school*. According to a pattern familiar in the traditional discourses of order we would have to suppose that order[as condition] derives from order[as action] (cf. §§53, 55 ff.). In this case, a model of decision or a model of rational choice might seem appropriate.

Such a link between creationism and order would be, of course, consistent with what Rousseau had in mind. Indeed, if orders formed naturally by animals followed only this anthropomorphic—or theomorphic—schema they might well provide confirming evidence for the Rousseauean common sense concerning dependence, morality, and *le lien social*.[228]

My point here is that I think that just the opposite is the case. Indeed, the preceding comments are just a prelude to a radically different conception of order in nature. The evidence for natural order-without-totality—here in the example of the fish—has additional features that push hard against residually creationist modes of explanation and justification. Let me now explain this.

It is clear that among "animals that forage or travel in groups . . . few individuals have pertinent information, such as knowledge about the location of a food source, or of a migration route" and that "making movement decisions often depends on social interactions among group members."[229]

In an effort to understand this process, evolutionary biologists have investigated related questions first by way of formal mathematical modeling of animal behaviors and then through experiments that eventually included human beings (considered in ways that make us commensurable with other animals).[230]

For example, researchers from the Collective Animal Behavior lab at Princeton University constructed a simple model to "show how information can be transferred within groups both without signaling and when group members do not know which individuals, if any, have information." They found that "only a very small proportion of informed individuals is required to achieve great accuracy."

They also sought to understand how groups can come to a collective result "even though informed individuals do not know whether they are in a majority or minority, how the quality of their information compares with that of others, or even whether there are any other informed individuals." The research "provides new insights into the mechanisms of effective leadership and decision-making in biological systems."[231]

A closer look at this research suggests that the words "decision" and "leadership" apply here in only the loosest metaphorical sense. The pivotal observation is that schools, flocks, and herds may move and satisfy their needs even when no leaders emerge and most members of the group have no pertinent information. The conclusion is that two basic instincts may be sufficient to explain this kind of ordered collective behavior: the need to stay in a group, and the tendency of a small percentage (less than 5 percent) of individuals to act on their own information about where to go.

In cases like these, order cannot be in any express or imputed sense an act of plan or Will; nor is it an imposition of Law; nor is it constituted by any kind of "contract" or agreement that might be said to bridge between Will and Law. Far from being general and inflexible, this kind of order is locally effective because it operates from both stable patterns and maintains flexibility in an adaptive way.

One could characterize this type of order in many ways. Let us for the moment continue to take Rousseau's hypothesis about the social grounds of politics as the frame of reference.

Within this frame of reference, and given contemporary scientific evidence concerning order-without-totality, even in the limit case of nature, it becomes exceedingly difficult to continue to hold to Rousseau's claims concerning the moral and political significance of dependence. To see why cycles us back into the discussion of Will for one last time.

Rousseau can only state the problem of dependence as he does, and propose the solution he proposes, because he believes that order is and must be the manifestation of a unitary Will. Because he applies this belief to all types of dependence, nature must also be such a manifestation of God's Will. That is, even if at certain points in the constellation that makes up Rousseau's social theory of politics he steadfastly advances an alternative to creationism, as a functional matter what holds sway within the theory as a whole is the paradigm of the Will, of "intelligent design," or a generalized creationism that is as much secular as it is sacred.

I have shown that here and there Rousseau glimpses and asserts with remarkable insight and sophistication an alternative evolutionary-ecological conception of order. It is precisely by the measure of this alternative that flaws in the

architecture and substance of Rousseau's social theory of politics have been revealed in this book. In Rousseau's account and by his own reckoning, the theory
can only be coherent, and produce the desired consequence of "resolving all the
contradictions of the social system," if order is exactly what he believed it to be.

Yet, we know that order does not have to be of this sort. Indeed, Rousseau's sort
of order may not exist at all.

§70

FROM WILL TO DEPENDENCE III
The Ordinal Function of Order Revisited

There is yet another problem issued from the *nontotality* of natural orders. I
argued earlier (§66) that we cannot identify clearly and without contest which
things are natural and which are not and that even if we could make that distinction to follow Rousseau we would have to know with certainty when and how
nonnatural things are overwhelmingly governed by a law of nature, which is also
not within our reach.[232] Let us nevertheless leave all that aside and simplify matters to revisit one last time the ordinal function of order.

Suppose that we could have perfect knowledge of natural order. The problem
is that such knowledge could only offer up the meaning that Rousseau's theory
calls forth from it—*unshakable certainty over time*, for the life of mankind and
our creations—if it referred to a fixed and stable totality. Once natural orders,
including the natural order of mankind on our "island," in our world, are understood to *evolve*—*Eh bien!* Jean-Jacques, isn't this what *you* taught us? (cf. §§ 20,
37, 42, 45, 46, 58, *et passim*)—our knowledge of nature and its laws can only
predict (so to speak) with certainty events that have already occurred. In other
words, the only hope for the reassurance Rousseau seeks from a perfect knowledge of order hangs on this absurd or theological imaginary: that order exists only
in space. Even *perfect* knowledge of an order that exists in time would suffice for
only a day, and thus not at all.[233]

One may allow that a purely spatial conception of order provides satisfying
images for God's creations—from the infinite universe to the bounded eschatology of Mankind and the world.[234] But a spatial conception of order cannot

apply to historical existence, either natural or social. There is no complete circumstantial knowledge of history.[235] Whether the concordant principle comes from Heisenberg or hermeneutics, it is sure that no human being can step outside of history to see where history is headed. The relevant totality—if there should be one—from which to define the parts or moments is never visible from inside an evolutionary order. This is perhaps the most general point one may make about the perspective of mankind "abandoned to ourselves."[236]

At the same time—one may imagine here as one imagines for all sciences—I am also saying something that is barely contingent on the human perspective at all. Evolution—whatever it is, whether it involves slow processes of natural selection or unpredictable discontinuities that extend structures through the rupture of structures—is not teleological.[237] That is why it presents such a decisive challenge to the claims of "intelligent design" and creationism: these perspectives are constitutively teleological.

As a temporal entity measured in time by time, the problem posed by evolutionary orders for Rousseau and the common sense promulgated by him is not simply that they do not have "wholes" to which the parts are related. It is that the relevant totality—should there be one—could only appear in retrospect. The totality of an evolutionary order is what *it has been*.[238] One might even say that the totality of social evolution is mankind as we stand today, abandoned to ourselves. Nothing more, nothing less.

In any case, evolutionary order, order-without-totality, cannot provide a model of the sort Rousseau has in mind because morality and politics are themselves constitutively concerned with prospective action. The civic always wants more, it always gets less than it dreams.

A rather stunning paradox arises here from the fact that Rousseau's "first principle" is Will. No modern concept—not even "revolution"—has represented more intensely the possibility of a rupture from or within already existing order (see §7 above). However essentially teleological is the image of the Will, Will is the antiteleological model *par excellence*. Yet, what the creationist-Rousseau seeks in the well-ordered society is the construction of an impediment to human Will by means of Will itself. Because he tries to establish that impediment in terms of necessity or inflexibility, it cannot be modeled on evolution, with its unpredictability, indirection, and rupture. What is left to him is one—literally, One—Will against all the others.

The incomplete circumstantial knowledge that derives from location-in-time is not only a problem on the level of the vast historical transformation we call natural evolution. The same type of problem occurs in any situation, even the smallest and most local, in which we cannot have all the information we would like to have in order to act *for precisely the reason that we are in that situation.* This is usually an ordinal constraint of time:[239] for example, I can perfectly well know whether Intel share prices will go up next week by waiting until then to find out, but it does me no good to wait if what I want is to buy and sell them at a profit based on the change in price over the next week.

Thus, for one reason or another, a person may *of necessity* have incomplete knowledge of his or her own circumstances. As a characteristic of local orders, this is the rule, not the exception.

Rousseau is concerned with the effects of dependence from the point of view of the person, a perspectivism expressed in his insistence on not just "liberty" but "the exercise of liberty [*l'usage de liberté*]." As long as that person has incomplete knowledge of the way things work with respect to the local order of his or her particular situation, his or her relation with things will not be ordered. This, by Rousseau's own lights, means that his or her dependence-from-things will have moral consequences.

In preceding sections I have discussed the problem of radical partiality and the problem of incomplete circumstantial knowledge. Both militate against the distinction Rousseau makes between dependence-from-things and dependence-from-persons *because the distinction is drawn in terms of order.*

The remaining problems are simple and, for Rousseau, insurmountable. What if—as we have just seen (§69)—the "book of Nature" says nothing that relates "parts" to a "whole"? Or, even if the "book of Nature" does tell us something about the link between parts and some totality, perhaps no human being will be able to make sense of this relationship because of structural features that make *our* situations and *our* viewpoint *particular* (§68)?

Once forced, this way or that, back to the local level, the laws (should there be any) governing local orders, or the practical functioning of those orders, are almost never clear and self-evident to the persons who depend from them. This is the case regardless of whether we view them from inside or outside.

From every angle the result is relentlessly the same. As long as Rousseau's distinction is drawn in terms of order, and order is conceived in conformance with his perspective, we cannot conclude with him that dependence-from-things is not morally consequential. That is because dependence itself, in every sort of relationship human beings have with the world, is the fabric of society, the essentially heterogenous and infinitely differentiated substance of the order from which civic life emerges, endures, and into which it decays.

§71

---·•·---

FROM WILL TO DEPENDENCE IV

The Civic Implication of Order Revisited

In any event, design and creation by a Will, or as the outcome of several Wills, is not a necessary condition for order.

I cannot say whether this is good news or bad. And let me again be quite clear: in no way do I mean to recommend what counts as order for other animals as an attractive paradigm for the moral and political purposes of human beings.[240] The fact that such reduced and simplistic generators of order do at times seem to command human behavior—think of crowds[241]—suggests how important it can be to avoid, manage, or overcome exactly such natural tendencies. But neither does the model of the divinity, or mankind's fetish of the divine, point the way. Human beings are more like fish than like gods; we are part of nature and should stop pretending that we are not.

What matters is that human beings are different—from all of Creation? from any*thing* else?—because we can make ourselves different even as those differences are absorbed back into the nature from which they seek to escape. Rousseau—humanist, impassioned, loving and detesting his fellow inhabitants of the *"l'île du genre humain"*—perversely ignored the *differentia specifica* of the human by giving his first and defining attention to the peculiar perfection of *things*, those gods for us, as if we should or could only live up to and not surpass the trees and streams, the scribbles of words and music, the lever that lifts the world or the computer that levels it, the majestic imaginary of a dead empire or the mundane bowl of gruel. He should have known us better.

Before going on I want to make explicit something that you will probably have already noticed. It is that the critique of Rousseau is no longer the only or even the main issue. The issue is now also the characteristics of an order specific to civic life. The example of the fish (§69) leads toward a more general fact. Order is always and inherently incomplete, which is to say *partial* and complex rather than *total*, simple, and unitary.

This fact will not defer to Rousseau and this is where we must differ from him.

For, if *ordre* cannot successfully be patterned on Will, and there is no coherent creationist conception of *ordre*, Rousseau must conclude that disorder/*désordre* is inevitable, and *he is again wrong on this point.*

With this monumental error, Rousseau and those who have followed him in this regard make clear that we must take seriously the existence of another kind of order, one that is partial and complex. It must have another principle and motive force.

Here the ambivalence mentioned in the preceding section rears its head even higher. For, what my reading of Rousseau also suggests in this negative way is that the type of order-without-totality, connected with but not limited to nonnatural dependence-from-things (§67), is of great significance for the social theory of politics.

And it is at this point that the creationist paradigm of the Will at the center of modern political thinking must give way to a social theory of politics grounded on the fundamental fact of human dependence.

Order-without-totality has as its primary principle and motive force dependence itself. By this I mean that dependence is at once a description of the architecture of this type of order and a driving force that is internal to that architecture.

In this book I have attempted to develop a clearer image of how *dépendance* constitutes the composition and motive force of *société* by showing the failures of Rousseau's efforts in that very direction. An alternative approach to the topic of *ordre* has been articulated by way of Rousseau's own hypothesis of social evolution. This alternative has been given a form commensurable with Rousseau's thinking in the category of "nonnatural dependence-from-things" (§67). The major contribution to this alternative, however, has in this book issued from the way the alternative view itself has been reasserted time and time again as the antithesis of creationism. While still continuing the dialogue with Rousseau, I have also attempted to move some small steps forward toward a positive account of this alternative conception of *ordre*. Leading this way is the empirical existence of order-without-totality in nature. From this we may now turn to speculate further about the conditions of existence of such an order.

Probabilism and Peircean tychism have already revealed incorrigible flaws in Rousseau's project (§66). There is no need to replay that now. Nor will it add anything to once again hold against Rousseau the necessarily conventional and contestable character of knowledge. It is enough to reiterate that Will — as an act, a fact, or a symbolic form — is not a necessary constituent of *ordre*. And, absent reference to Will, there is nothing that requires *ordre* to refer to totality (§§53 and 62, and the Afterword). The real affinity of the concept of order is with the topic of *dependence*.

Rousseau promoted the topic of dependence and proposed a preliminary set of its types: first dependence-from-things and dependence-from-persons, and then dependence-from-nature. It has been convenient to add nonnatural dependence-from-things. I recite these here to emphasize a point. It is not my ultimate purpose to accept any of these categories. I have merely taken them as stations in a larger effort to show both that the field of dependence, while fundamental, is finally not susceptible to such categorical distinctions and that it is irreducibly heterogenous.

Everyone knows that in ways both familiar and strange human experience with nature is a foundation for Rousseau's entire enterprise. The so-called "state of nature" or other primitivist fantasies (§2 *et passim*) do not in my view play a significant role in this. Of central importance is the fact that Rousseau was convinced that natural systems provide an inflexible and general measure by which the *ordre* underlying human dependence takes shape and gains its significance.

Between natural philosophy and theology Rousseau was able to see nature in a dozen ways (§§41–45). I have argued that on balance, the view of nature he applies at the architectonic level of his social theory of politics is mistaken.

Rousseau is correct, however, in the assertion that *ordre*, even, or perhaps especially, the *ordre* characteristic of natural systems, can provide appropriate images with which to make precise the shape and significance of human dependence.

What actually carries over from natural *systems* would have surprised Rousseau and is surprising still for us. For we are called to reconsider what those *systems* actually *are*.

It is never Nature or the World or Man that confronts us; rather, there is always some particular tree or chimpanzee, the field behind your house or the path I take home, that person, that one, with just her gesture and voice. This sort of nominalism may seem trivial but it suggests something that is not.

In every respect relevant to the social theory of politics, such encounters between a human subject and his or her object may be entirely local. Whether or not they conform to a universal order, each tree, path, or person takes form within and gives rise to a relatively autonomous system. This means that for each set—from unimaginably large "Nature" to the "Tree," "Path," or "Person" apt for human senses—there must be many (although not an infinite number of) such systems.

It is this particularity that human beings "depend-from." To say the contrary— i.e., that x depends from universal y—is to entertain an entirely different sort of speculation, one that is, for inquiry into civic life, ultimately sterile.

My positive point here is that what we call Nature-as-a-whole—whatever is meant by that presumptive totality[242]—or the relation between "it" and each particular instance of "it" need not enter into consideration at all.[243] A person can and typically does live by attending to a more modest scale. Through living practices entities are still distinguishable and connections are still made or severed. Something holds everything together. My claim, inspired by Rousseau but extending exponentially beyond him, is that all this can be resolved in terms of dependence.

The critical thrust here is that by the way Rousseau states the categorical distinction between types of dependence and proffers conditions and beliefs to justify it, he invites the sterile sort of speculation just mentioned. Recourse to universals is only relevant as wishes or dreams are relevant. It sustains a powerful but misguided endeavor. In Rousseau's instance, that endeavor is ultimately creationist but not narrowly theological. Its wide band of concepts extends to what I have called secular creationism.

By contrast, experience with the world, common sense, and contemporary science bring before us something that is of high relevance for understanding dependence and its implications for civic life. It is the fact exemplified by the fish: at least some systems have no unitary *whole*. They are made up of nothing but parts. Composed only of parts, they are radically partial.[244] Such systems nonetheless have an order. That order perdures without totality; it is an order-without-totality.

Rousseau's construction of the social theory of politics forces this type of *ordre* upon our attention but cannot encompass it, no less explain it. Rousseau did not imagine this kind of order and did not take it into account. We had better do so.

Order-without-totality enters the story here because it is relevant to how dependence appears in and motivates civic life. This is important both for those who follow Rousseau and for those who do not. Because for Rousseau and for many others reference to natural systems provides a conceptual linchpin, I made reference (§69) to some such systems a key part of this discussion of order-without-totality. The implications are very much wider.

Different types of *ordre* have been discussed in this book. It may therefore seem as though order-without-totality is just one type on a par with the others. To counteract without necessarily denying this impression, I want to underscore here a point raised several times in passing. It is possible that absence of totality is a decisive characteristic for all types of *ordre*.

In other words, radical partiality may be — contrary to almost every traditional Western intuition — inherent in the idea of order itself. Consider that "the distinction between order and disorder tends to disappear when the domain of both is the universe." If this is correct, then the concept of order is not applicable to the whole; it is only applicable "to some proper part."[245] The pressure of this logic may be implicit in the fact that God is typically considered the source of order but is not said to have that attribute Himself.[246]

This inherent limit in the concept of order should bear heavily on any considerations of disorder. It makes clear that disorder is not absence and must be explained in another way. For instance, it may be rather "an excess of order" which "occurs when there are too many orders imposed upon a set of entities."[247] It is the evasion of locality and the assumption of totality that makes an excess appear as a lack. In civic life, then, disorder might be considered as derivative of the inescapable fact of human plurality, a fact which is itself constitutive of civic life.

As you will have seen, our love-hate relationship with Rousseau, now in its two-hundred-and-sixtieth-year and counting, corresponds to the fact that even if such observations contradict Rousseau's conclusions they are nonetheless consistent with his analysis. Indeed, the claim that order is inherently partial may allow us to elaborate his views more clearly than he did himself. The heterogeny of many Wills—this is how Kant would later call the problem he takes over from Rousseau—is not, is never, the interface of nothings; it is the unbearable proliferation of highly ordered entities, too highly ordered to compromise or meld into one. What better gloss on the aspirations manifest in Rousseau's social theory of politics than to say that if order is the "similarity between differences . . . disorder . . . is the difference among similarities"?[248] Disorder is indifference in a differentiated world.

Finally, there are issues of modality here. What Rousseau does is to make a complex claim about the source of evil in *société*. As a solution to evil, he does not propose a return to nature or enforcement of natural law. The order he attributes to nature plays a key but indirect part in an argument that is essentially negative, in which moral value in persons is demonstrated by contrast to its absence in things. In this final part of this book I have tested this argument in several ways somewhat more amenable to the contemporary mind. The outcome has been to insert, so to speak, order-without-totality into the place of classical and Will-oriented conceptions of order. To maximize the critical pressure of these experiments, I drew an example of order-without-totality from a natural context little susceptible to human influence. The result was that important flaws in Rousseau's argument showed themselves.

This example did not provide an alternative. I have already said that schooling fish cannot illustrate what may facilitate the civic life of human beings.

The general truth in Rousseau's theodicy—the one that issues in an evolutionary-ecological perspective he could not quite bring himself to embrace—is that the measure of Man is Man. Nothing human should be required to live up to the order of nature or the order of things.

Still, if we are in nature the pull to ask what of nature is in us is overwhelming. Here the door opens onto a vast terrain where Rousseau's gift to us could encounter and occasionally be corrected by contemporary theories of evolution, material culture, complexity, networks, hybrids, and so forth. Capacious thinkers like Jane Jacobs would present him with modern *civitas* as "organized complexity;" Friedrich Hayek would push upon him a new perspective concerning the social compositions of markets. Such dialogues could contribute to the great confrontation set forth in this book: between the still emerging evolutionary-ecological perspectives that I have traced back to Rousseau himself and the still predominant worldview of creationism—sacred, secular, and social—that also gains its modern impetus with him.[249]

Such encounters notwithstanding, readers of this book will no doubt wonder, Does an order-without-totality also emerge in the sphere of *société*? Does order of this sort play a part in the civic relationships which arise within that sphere?

These questions are for another study at another time. I will venture just one further observation here. It must be said that the topic is hardly new. Nor is it the first time we meet it in this book. Recall the pages spent (§32) looking at the way, under Condillac's pen, the word *système* served in the eighteenth century as a synonym for *ordre* and, under Rousseau's, it was closely joined to *société*. With those terms Condillac conceived and Rousseau, for a moment at least, advanced an image of order in the civic realm akin to the order-without-totality we considered in nature just a few pages back.

It was in the chapter of the *Traité des Systêmes* called "On the necessity of systems in politics" that Condillac (1749, XV) identified in a striking way the contingency at the heart of politics and noted that civic order breeds citizens skeptical of the perspective of totality. In civic life, the image of the whole through which the parts are related cannot be fixed. This image changes as the state is transformed by events.

Although this is not a recipe for chaos, it does point to a fundamental dilemma. How, Condillac asks, "is it possible to govern a State, if one does not bring all the parties under a general point of view, and if one does not bind them one to the other in such a way as to make them move in concert, and by one and the same spring?"

To our surprise, Condillac actually provides a primitive model—which he will reprise a quarter-century later in *Le Commerce et le gouvernement, considérés relativement l'un à l'autre* (1776)—in which contingency operates within an order constituted by a dynamic "reciprocal action of the parts" that passes through states of "equilibrium" (that is Condillac's word). Government can only "maintain perfect equilibrium" when it is "possible to find each citizen's interest within the interest of society. It must be that, in acting in accordance with different perspectives, and with each one making his own more or less local program, citizens necessarily conform to the perspective of a general system." This is not a call to virtue. The order is self-regulating because leading actors are constrained by the practical requirements of what allows citizens "to get along, one with the other." This is an image of a civic order-without-totality, an open-ended and generative system in which society evolves without teleology or plan.

Indeed, one may imagine this conception of civic order-without-totality as the true frame within which Rousseau gestures to a "fundamental pact": the pact is not the origin of society; nor is it a great and unitary "general Will" that imposes itself; it is rather a process, the *social contraction* by which society takes charge of itself, a way of life that "substitutes a moral and legitimate equality for whatever physical inequality may by nature occur among men" (OC III.367).[250]

This is a path Rousseau discovers but eventually shies away from. For better or for worse, what I have shown is that when Rousseau appeals to natural dependence-from-things as the basis for his solution to the problem of dependence, and thus as a solution to the problem of social disorder, he leads us away from order-without-totality. Rather than ameliorating our situation, I think this carries us further astray.

§72

CONCLUSION

The Human Remains

For more than a century, it has been easy to begin this kind of inquiry by supposing that God is, so to speak, dead. Had I adopted this posture it might have been possible to bypass many irksome features of Rousseau's thought. I declined this move for a number of reasons.

It should be obvious — but often is not — that one cannot argue with or against, or even seriously read, a thinker by ignoring what he says. Even with that in mind, the conclusions I reach in this book, encompassing a strong rejection of one theme in Rousseau and the incremental advancement of another, could have been imposed at the beginning. I could simply have cancelled out all theological elements and read, or pretended to read, Rousseau in purely secular terms. But I believe that kind of rationalized ignorance is a dead end; it is better, more promising, to pursue hermeneutic integrity in political theory, even for speculation, using magnificent past efforts as text and pretext for our more modest ones.

Another motive has pushed forward my engagement in this book with Rousseau and his theological positions. I hoped, arguing as I have, to bring to light a persistent but typically hidden theological moment in the architecture of common contemporary sociological understanding. This same secret also has its hand in political thinking.

I now want to restate something of what appears when we take seriously the discursive presence of God in both the architecture and the wider context of the social and political ideas of Rousseau and his followers. This is the symbolic world in which we live. Reference to Will—as it is very much present for us, and as it everywhere inflects our moral and political common sense—would lose much of its sense without eventual recourse to a conception of God.[251] I am referring now not just to applications of the concept of Will. Indeed, I am more interested in how Will functions as a *topos* of political theory, where the same thing is true.

If I say this, it may surprise you to read further that I am reticent to let the Will pass without more stringent critical investigation. However, that project, which I am convinced is an essential preliminary to a much-needed reconstruction of social and political theory, extends far beyond the limits of this book.[252] Thus, my argument here comes only to the point of showing how Rousseau's conception of dependence is grounded in *ordre* because *ordre*, he believes, is grounded in Will. I have laid out many details not only to illustrate these points but also to situate them in the past and in the present and in the future.

For, I also wanted you to see in brilliant detail the terrain on which we land when the edifice falls down. As Will is not the only source of order in Nature, and therefore not a unique paradigm for order in society, we may rightly conclude that Rousseau's account of *le lien social* in terms of dependence, while profoundly suggestive and in crucial respects correct, fails the project it is called by him to serve. This failure may even be symptomatic of the disease of a whole tradition of political thought that Rousseau is typically taken to represent. Certainly his account of dependence cannot support alternative versions of the main concepts—like power or responsibility—of a Will-centered theory of politics.

Where Rousseau's analytics of *dépendance* may ultimately contribute is in the entirely different evolutionary and ecological theory of society that is so vividly if incompletely concocted in his pages. But for that to be clear, it is exactly the shadow of the distinction between dependence-from-things and dependence-from-persons that must first be dispelled.

That would be a nice end to the story if it were not for one small point: it is quite clear that when one finds oneself dependent from a thing, the experience is not the same as when one finds oneself dependent from a person. Just as there *are* persons *and* things, there *is* some sort of profound difference between dependence-from-persons and dependence-from-things.[253] It would be hard, indeed, to disagree with Rousseau when he writes:

> and when a philosopher will tell me that trees feel and rocks think, no matter how he may entangle me with his subtle arguments, I can only see in him a sophist of bad faith, who likes better to give feeling to stones than to accord to Man a soul.[254]*

Do not, therefore, take me wrong. I do not deny the difference between persons and things. I only claim that this difference must be understood in some way we have not yet imagined, a way beyond creationisms secular and otherwise, and without the pathetic capitulations of physicalist or biological determinisms. Convincing as he was, convinced that to consider human beings fully meant leaving *things* out of the account, Rousseau made a profound and durable and destructive mistake. What this book has shown is that the social theory of politics must follow both routes, or rather must accept that persons and things inhabit the same world. Revived exploration of this, our real world, would inject a new significance into our relationship with things, made and found, natural and artificial, and, at the same time, compel us to accept the utter implication of these relationships in contacts, connections, and networks we entertain with others of our kind. This world only appears darkly in the all too familiar but now exhausted terms handed down to us from Rousseau. To see it more clearly we had better bid him farewell, and start in earnest down this long and largely uncharted road.

---

*"... et quand un philosophe viendra me dire que les arbres sentent et que les rochers pensent, il aura beau m'embarrasser dans ses arguments subtils, je ne puis voir en lui qu'un sophiste de mauvaise foi, qui aime mieux donner le sentiment aux pierres que d'accorder une âme à l'homme."

AFTERWORD

A Preliminary Typology of Complex Dependence

We have considered many aspects of Rousseau's complex theory of the social field from which political relationships emerge. Rousseau correctly identified "dependence" as the primary fabric of that social field and as the generative force of social evolution. We have seen, however, that his analysis of dependence is a variation on the theme I refer to as *secular creationism* and that it is insufficient for political theory in our time. The question remains: how should we understand the fundamental fact of human dependence so as to bring it to the center of political theory today?

It is not the purpose of *Abandoned to Ourselves* to provide an adequate answer to this question. In future publications I will address it in much greater detail. Nonetheless, at many points in this book I have alluded to my own research on this crucial topic. Thus, as a kind of herald for readers now inclined to think beyond Rousseau and toward the future of political theory I will make my own views a bit more explicit. What follows is a preliminary typology of complex dependence; it is an afterword but not an afterthought. Note that the exposition is organized around historical uses of the term "dependence" itself. Please do not be misled by this approach. This is not an exercise in etymology as analytic philosophy. I assume that these linguistic practices are entangled with and express other material facts about the human environment. The versions of dependence catalogued here are modes of possibility for and constraint on human action.

When we speak loosely, "dependence" first appears before us as a single quality. Speakers of English as well as French and a range of other languages have developed the habit of bringing a variety of life problems under this single classification. One of Rousseau's great virtues is to have demolished this appearance. His specific distinction between types may not hold, but he illustrates perfectly that dependence cannot be conceived in simple and unitary terms. To do so is to misunderstand the problems the invocation of the term is supposed to clarify.[1]

While I am convinced that Rousseau did not delve far enough into the structure of dependence, I actually want to say something quite a bit stronger than that. Rousseau also mistook the starting point for this crucial type of social and political inquiry. That mistake — brilliant, informative, insightful, provocative, convincing, durable — has been the guiding theme of this book. It is presented in the starkest terms in §§65–71.

This afterword offers a brief foray beyond Rousseau to suggest in a positive way what might be at stake in taking dependence as the primary motive force in a social theory of politics. What follows, then, is a very brief sketch of the structure of complex dependence, comprising its several aspects and some of the relations inherent among them. I want to insist that this complexity is both inevitable and a virtue; indeed, the living power of the term, its fruitfulness and utility, derives from the fact that many irreducible features of life are conveniently contained within the single word. This fact in turn lends to appeals to "dependence" — in social analysis and in everyday discourse — an astonishing range of possibilities for practical knowledge and effective action.

The literal meaning of the word dependence is "to hang from." A logical sense stems immediately from this. It may be described this way: there stand a and x side-by-side or in sequence of time; a depends on x if, were x to be removed, or had not occurred, a would be something other than a. In other words, dependence in this sense is meant to express a relation of *causality*. This logical dependence is assumed to be abstracted from the empirical context of both its object and its subject.[2] That tends to make it an ineffective category for thinking about society and politics.

However, much of what *causality* is supposed to describe is also captured by the more subtle notion of *influence*. Indeed, *influence* reflects more accurately real experience; in even the most awful sorts of dependence, it is rare that everything is at stake at once (as references to *causality* suggest). Moreover, the objective multiplicity of dependence makes it difficult to know which of its components counts most *right now* and thus actually determines *this* time-bound and irreducibly complex experience as dependence. By extrapolation, and against common intuitions, the first constitutive feature of complex dependence is its indeterminacy. Once again, to express with clarity and mnemonic precision the several modalities of a single yet polyvalent term I shall use an unwieldy notation. Thus, this first mode is *dependence*[indeterminacy].

Many modes of dependence — all of which appear clearly in the commonsense history of the word in various European languages[3] — can be loosely thought of as redescriptions of *influence*. Nonetheless, greater precision in social and political theory can be achieved with a more ample vocabulary.[4] These sometimes overlapping but distinguishable modes include dependence-as-*attachment* and as-*need*, dependence-as-*expectation* and as-*security*, dependence-as-*burden* and as-*subordination*. Let me briefly say something about each of these pairs.

Relationships of attachment and relationships of need are distinguishable, but they often spill over into each other. This ambiguity reflects a persistent element of continuity between them. We may refer more generally to this element as *affirmation*. Affirmation in the case of need is characterized by sustenance and replenishment; in the case of attachment it is characterized by recognition.[5] A tending toward affirmation or positivity is evidently and thoroughly interwoven with human experience.[6] We tend (for example) toward food and thousands of other things all the time. Satisfaction of the need for things puts us back in order, and affirms that order, whatever its source. It is not—obviously—only the mature and fully socialized personality that tends toward attachment to other people; the process of socialization from the first months of life follows to a great extent the contours of caregiver recognition; the program set forth in *Émile* is, Rousseau believes, based on this fact.[7] The central subjective feature of both dependence-as-attachment and dependence-as-need is the *desire for affirmation*.[8] This is *dependence*$^{desire\ for\ affirmation}$.

This way of treating dependence as desire for affirmation is sharpened by its relation to the next pair of the meanings of dependence: *expectation* and *security*. Dependence-as-expectation comes into play whenever people do something together. When there is a crisis, relatively straightforward expectations are brought to the foreground in a way that changes their relation to the other aspects of that situation and raises the question of security. In certain circumstances, the raised stakes of expectation as a problem of security may begin to resemble dependence of the strong logical sort. For example, under an extensive and deeply institutionalized division of labor, simple mistakes and misjudgments that in isolation seem trivial become increasingly intolerable. The accumulation of capital in technics, which undergirds the extension of divided labor, means that there is typically a lot at stake (due both to capital intensity and to augmented "productivity") for a lot of people when expectations are not met. Further, the failure to meet expectations at *any* point in the process is felt at the larger junctures of the system (example: coordination between firms) or where highly organized systems meet (markets are a typical example).

Managers of a system of production need a way to deal with mistakes. To do this, they design[9] sanctions that flow from the conditions of dependence-as-expectation and dependence-as-security, but which find their full effect in the context of *dependence*$^{desire\ for\ affirmation}$ (either as need or as attachment). Normal expectations as well as crisis expectations (such as security) are only fulfilled if there is no disruption or, in other words, mistakes are not made.[10] This is stated from the "system point of view," that is, from the manager's sanctioning point of view. We can say the same thing from the point of view of the "ordinary person" as positioned within the system of production: dependence means that "I must not make mistakes" and this becomes a categorical imperative. Self-government or self-command following this imperative opens possibilities for putting enormous pressure on people, for the more finely articulated the division of labor, the easier it becomes to pinpoint the locus of error and to sanction the agent at that point.[11] Countervailing pressures to hide within a complex system and evade responsibility also flow from this imperative. These pressures in turn compel the person to develop a world-version that does not jeopardize his or her attachments on the basis of those mistakes that leave expectations unfulfilled.[12] It is easier to accept this pressure than to reject or fight against it. This is not simply because people do not want to be blamed, but because they do not want to be left unrecognized or unaffirmed (a crude example: by having their wages cut) "as a result of their own mistakes."

The central feature of both dependence-as-expectation and dependence-as-security is *stability*. Stated subjectively, however, it is more precise to speak of the *fear of instability*. This is *dependence*[fear of instability].

Dependence-as-burden and dependence-as-subordination both underscore in no uncertain terms the relational character of dependence. It may have seemed, in what I have just said, that dependence can in some sense be confined as a quality of a single person; this appearance is false. It appears this way only because I am summarizing features of the experience of dependence from the position of the subject. The idea of dependence as a weight on or responsibility of that from which the dependent depends should help to make clear that no one person alone can be dependent; this is the fact toward which Rousseau gestures unintentionally when he refers to "natural independence" in order to disparage it. When it comes to dependence from other people, the sense of dependence as a relationship characterized by burden is easy to imagine (for example: "I wish Bob were not so dependent, I never get any time for myself"). When it comes to dependence as a relation between persons and things, it is immediately more difficult to see how the notions of weight or responsibility might apply. But then we can turn to dependence-as-subordination for help. For example: by projecting "I shall make my famous artichoke soup" I give an order to things, such as the artichokes themselves, certain other ingredients (which I shall not reveal here), pots and utensils, the stove, even water (which, as for a good beer, must be of a particular quality). Now, although it would be a stretch to say that the artichokes — these artichokes, here, today, fresh, with the calm and elastic odor of the field, willing to cast off their armor, to melt and mingle — are "responsible" to me, they do enter a relationship in which dependence is the placement of those magnificent green buds relative to me and relative to those other things and within the order I establish *via* my project. Before there is subordination there must be ordination, akin to the *ordre* we have considered in detail in this book. This relation does not necessarily commit us to any particular pattern of responsibility. Thus, the underpinning feature of both dependence-as-burden and dependence-as-subordination, with reference to both things and other persons, is *relation* of parts to parts. Sometimes one of these entities takes on the appearance or function of a "whole." This is *dependence*[relation] and it corresponds to a large extent with "order" (cf. §53 on classical notions of order and §§68–71 on alternative versions of order).

To summarize: these four general aspects of dependence—as an indeterminacy of effects, as desire for affirmation, as fear of instability, and as relation—provide a synthetic but still complex preliminary image of dependence. In some important threads of Rousseau's writings this single image or *topos* tends to displace the Will as the "gravity" of the *système social*. It is the one that a social theory of politics would do best to develop further today. Within the image of dependence a wide variety of human activities appear as overlapping and interconnected through the living experience of persons who every day must live, live together, and seek their happiness; within it the parts (or elements, or moments), whatever they may be, are perceived as dynamic forces that move social groupings one way or another.[13]

Notice that just now, referring to the elements of the *système social*, I added the qualification "whatever they may be." That is because, against our esteemed preceptor Rousseau, I want to emphasize the following point. All four aspects of complex dependence apply *no matter what the object of dependence may be*. Dependence-from-things places us in relations that constitute, through the growth of habit and its dispositions and proprieties, the temporality and consistency of experience which is the *système social*.[14] This is dependence[relation]. Dependence generates and erodes and regenerates the experience of *things* in processes underdetermined, overdetermined, and often aleatoric. And even when the "things-in-themselves" suggest an utter constancy, and the "dependence" of the earth on the sun is as close to perfect as God can imagine, the rising of the sun *we* attend *this* morning—which is not an "experience" for the earth or for God, but only for human beings—can have an entirely unpredictable significance. Indeed, "natural" facts insofar as they are the partners of human existence are never simple and sure beyond question. This is the extent of dependence[indeterminacy].

The uncertainty that blocks prediction does not follow merely from a lack of knowledge, although that, too, may be part of the complexity of dependence.

Rather, uncertainty is a feature of the matter at hand, of the living relation between a person and a thing. The anxious chance of being left dangling is, in greater or lesser degrees, always present as dependence[fear of instability], as is the tenacious motive for recognition which, because a mark of distinction, grounds both *ressentiment* and the "will-to-power." This is dependence[desire for affirmation].

My point is that the fabric of society in which politics grows, in which citizens strive and struggle, may be oriented by familiar topics like race, class, gender, religion, and the like, but underlying and composing them, interweaving them, is the infinite variety of distinct persons forming and deforming their particular situations of living with one another. We need a language for that, and it is *dependence*; we need a finer order of resolution to see it through, and that includes *modes of dependence* like dependence[indeterminacy], dependence[fear of instability], dependence[desire for affirmation], and dependence[relation].

NOTES

FOREWORD

1. When Rousseau writes the word *homme*, he sometimes means all of humankind and other times points to just the male of our species. Which uses are of which sort has been hotly debated. On the one hand it would falsify the texts considered here to adopt a gender-neutral term in translation. On the other hand, most of what I write in this book presupposes that we read *homme* in its general rather than its gendered sense. With these two caveats in mind I will use the English *Man* throughout. This issue is taken up briefly again in §18.
2. I borrow here from Pascal (1954, 1121) *Pensées* (120 [195]).
3. This trajectory, which did not primarily involve a rejection of biblical chronology or an account of natural history in itself, is tangential to the now familiar roster of precursors to Darwin that includes Linnaeus (1735), Buffon (1749–1804), Erasmus Darwin (1794–96), Lamarck (1809), Cuvier (1817), and Lyell (1830–33).
4. This synthetic perspective is hardly unprecedented; recently cf. Corning (2005).
5. E.g., OC III.156 and 475. This Hobbesian commonplace is restated in *Émile*: "For the first law of nature is the concern to preserve oneself" (OC IV.466).
6. One should mention that he is also unlike those evolutionists of the nineteenth century who stood against "social Darwinism" by admiring and elaborating on other aspects of Rousseau's own thought; Kropotkin's *Mutual Aid* (1902) is the most influential example in this regard, still respected a century later; cf. Stephen Jay Gould (1997).
7. Law, and particularly modernized impulses from Roman law, is an important channel through which this secularization is accomplished. For many reasons, both theological and sociological, it remains unclear exactly what "entirely humanized" could mean; nonetheless, I assert this here in the sense I find inherent in Rousseau's writings and which will be described in this book.

8. The word "radical" is used here in the sense developed by Israel (2002), who groups eighteenth-century intellectuals by their affinities with Spinoza.

PART ONE

1. "Classical" here means the canon as laid out in books like Aron (1967) and Alexander (1982); Alexander et al. (1997) and Calhoun (2007) attempt to establish a parallel lineage in the American context. Claims that sociology is a more ancient and global practice have long been common; cf. e.g., Hertzler (1936).

2. Gordon (1994, 51) correctly observes that "before the late seventeenth century, the word *société* did not refer to a durable and large-scale community. Instead, it referred to small associations and to the convivial life that took place within them. As late as 1694, . . . it was possible to define *société* without invoking in any way the concept of a general field of human existence." I agree with Gordon (1994, 52) that *société* is probably first generalized in Furetière (1690) but find that this fact passed more or less unnoticed until Rousseau developed, as I describe in this book, the significance of this generalization and his writings became the main means of its dissemination. Baker (1994, 118) asserts in passing that it was Pierre Nicole who "first analyzed the logic of society as a merely (and irremediably) human order"; I am not convinced. (However, see next note.)

3. Baker (1994, 96); his brilliant account relies heavily on the article *"Société"* in the *Encyclopédie* — cf. Diderot and d'Alembert (1751–72, XV, 252–58) — which dates from 1765. Although the author is unknown, it is clearly under the spell of Rousseau, whose relevant works had long since been published. We will touch again on the specific importance of Rousseau in this broader discursive shift in §35 below.

4. Cf. Husserl (1960) and transformation in Schutz (1973, 1982); see also Cefaï (1998). As these thinkers are associated with a certain conception of "interaction" and "intersubjectivity," it may be important to herald here that a major object of this book is to bring into question these very notions insofar as they do not adequately account for the *things* in which the *social* is also necessarily manifest.

5. Indeed, it is Rousseau himself who, in *Du Contract social* (OC III.391), identifies "liberty" and "equality" as the "two principal objects . . . of every system of legislation [deux objets principaux . . . de tout sistème de législation]."

6. One may cite as important precedents to Rousseau's political theodicy both Spinoza (1951) and Leibniz (1710, 1972). Cf., e.g., Colas (1997, 193–202 and 224–48). The term itself was coined by Leibniz sometime shortly before the publication of Leibniz (1710). The importance of the word of God in this philosophical tradition becomes decisively explicit with Augustine.

7. As concerns the general cultural refiguration of Augustine's topology, Rousseau was, of course, not alone. Cf., e.g., Becker (1932). Cf. Bouwsma (1975) for a broad statement concerning the general effects of Augustinianism on modernity.

8. Thus, when Baker (1994, 108) writes that "the eighteenth century resounds with the debate between those who favor one side . . . or the other" of stark oppositions like "so-

ciety" versus "religion" he gestures to exactly the discursive field that Rousseau, more than anyone else, brought into existence.

9. Pope (1733, last lines of Epistle I).

10. Pope (1736). The shift from Pope's "right" to Silhouette's *"bien"* is significant but will not distract us here. Rousseau read this translation of Pope at the latest in January 1742, when he thanks a friend for having lent him the book; see correspondence cited in Cranston (1983, 152). However, a poem by Rousseau, *"Le Verger de Madame de Warens,"* dedicated to Mme. Warens and published in 1739, includes Pope as one of his guiding lights, and thus suggests that Rousseau knew Pope's work earlier; OC II.1124–29.

11. It is Voltaire who, after Rousseau works out his approach to theodicy, makes of Leibniz's solution a risible commonplace in the figure (modeled on Leibniz) of Dr. Pangloss in his *Candide* (1759). Rousseau writes in *Les Confessions* (Book IX) that *Candide* was written as a riposte to him. Cf. Voltaire's chiding response to the *Discours sur l'origine et les fondemens de l'inégalité parmi les hommes* (in a letter dated 30 August 1755) which begins "I received, Sir, your new book against mankind, and I thank you for it. . . . One could not paint the horrors of human society in stronger colors. . . . No one has ever employed as much mental energy in the desire to turn us into beasts; reading your book gives one the desire to go about on all fours [*j'ai reçu, Monsieur, votre nouveau livre contre le genre humain, et je vous en remercie. . . . On ne peut peindre avec des couleurs plus fortes les horreurs de la société humaine. . . . On n'a jamais employé tant d'esprit à vouloir nous rendre bêtes; il prend envie de marcher à quatre pattes, quand on lit votre ouvrage*]." More on this just below.

12. From this point on, I shall abbreviate this title as *Discours sur . . . l'inégalité.*

13. "Lettre de J.-J. Rousseau à Monsieur Philopolis" was published in January 1756, following the publication of Bonnet's pseudonymous letter under the name "Philopolis" in the preceding October.

14. Letter to Voltaire "Sur la Providence," August 18, 1756; OC IV.1059–75. Much of this letter is a riff on Pope.

15. OC III.233. We know that Leibniz was of early interest to Rousseau, who cites him together with Pope (and others) in the 1739 poem to Mme. Warens (see note 10 above) and refers to him in Book VI of *Les Confessions* as one of the group of philosophical authors "in almost perpetual contradiction among themselves [*entre eux en contradiction presque perpétuelle*]." Cf. OC I.237.

16. Compare the convoluted discussion of nature at the beginning of the preparatory *"manuscrit Favre"* in OC IV.55 ff.

17. OC IV.1068. Rousseau's French at this point—*"au lieu de Tout est bien, il vaudroit peut être mieux dire: le Tout est bien, ou Tout est bien pour le tout"*—is a series of obvious word plays. Knots are created here for a translation back to English both by a desire to remain faithful to Pope and by the difference between "right" and *"bien."* I shall not try to untangle these. Generally on this problem, see Mark Twain's playful tale (1903).

18. These are, of course, words from the beginning of the American Declaration of In-

dependence of 1776; they express the persistence in common sense of issues to be discussed below (and may be pointed against Spinozism); cf., e.g., Becker (1932, especially chapter 2) and more generally on the Declaration, Becker (1922).

19. Defoe (1719); published in French in Defoe (1720).

20. Cf. Watt (1957) and (1996). From another angle, "with Gierke, we can see that *société* takes its modern meaning not in opposition to individualism, but as its essential expression. Society and the individual are not, in historical terms, fundamentally opposed. Instead, they appear together." Baker (1994, 112). This point is already familiar from Durkheim (1893) and, before that, Tocqueville (1835–40).

21. OC IV.454; cf. OC IV.546: "put all lessons for young people into actions rather than in discourse . . . they will not learn anything in books of what experience can teach them [mettez toutes les leçons des jeunes gens en actions plustôt qu'en discours . . . ils n'apprennent rien dans les livres de ce que l'expérience peut leur enseigner]." Generally speaking, books are lies; cf. OC III.133, OC IV.967.

22. Dickens calls *Robinson Crusoe* "the only instance of an universally popular book that could make no one laugh and could make no one cry." Cited in Bloom (1988, "Introduction," p. 2), the same *locus* as his own comment.

23. OC IV.454; Richard Twiss (1787, 6) reports that on visiting Paris in 1776 he found, beyond necessary furniture, nothing in Rousseau's fourth-floor apartment but "a spinet, and his library, which consisted only in Tasso's *Jerusalem*, in Italian, and *Robinson Crusoe*, in English."

24. Remember that, for Rousseau, knowledge is fundamentally based on comparison; e.g., "To think . . . that is to see some objects and compare them" (OC V.585). He has the *vicaire savoyard* go further to say that the constellation of Will/understanding/liberty (*volonté / entendement / liberté*) reduces to "the power/capacity [*le pouvoir*] to compare and to judge" (OC IV.586). That "comparison" is both epistemologically fundamental and of sociological significance is affirmed by Rousseau's reference to God as "incomparably" greater than us; cf. e.g., OC V.587.

25. OC IV.455. The profound and unchanging importance of this idea for Rousseau is suggested by the appearance of the same passage in the earlier "*manuscrit Favre*" of *Émile*; cf. OC IV.190. Note the resonance here with Condillac on one side and Adam Smith on the other.

26. Notice that with the figure of Robinson Crusoe, "state of nature" theorizing is exposed as what it really is: not nostalgia for a pre-social condition nor a condition of alterity, but rather a reductionist thought-experiment for contemporary Man and the resulting well-formed *topos*. Durkheim (1953) made a similar point in 1918 but developed it in a rather different direction.

27. The French word *moeurs* conveys a sense of common practices and the beliefs that guide them, and is not adequately rendered by the English word "mores," or by any other single term; elsewhere in this book it remains in the original and is discussed in some detail at §5 below.

28. The passing venture into Latin is in itself a noteworthy humanist gesture to Roman and romanist traditions.

29. The resonance here is with *La Divina Commedia* (*Inferno*, Canto XXXIV, verses 133–39)

Lo duca e io per quel cammino ascoso
intrammo a ritornar nel chiaro mondo;
e sanza cura aver d'alcun riposo,
salimmo sù, el primo e io secondo,
tanto ch'i' vidi de le cose belle
che porta 'l ciel, per un pertugio tondo.
E quindi uscimmo a riveder le stelle.

Note also that this canto begins with a *"vers latin."* Rousseau obviously knew Dante, and was infected with—in the words of Bernard Guyon (at OC II.1340)—*"italophilie ou italolâtrie."*

30. A similar figure, again (as at OC V.587, note 24 above)expressing Rousseau's perspectivism, appears in one of his most startling maxims: "The entire universe must be only a point for an oyster [*l'univers entier ne doit être qu'un point pour une huître*]" at OC IV.396.

31. Cf. similar usage in *Lettres morales II* (OC IV.1088). This gives an unexpected twist to Thomas Carlyle's comment (in *The Hero as Man of Letters: Johnson, Rousseau, Burns* [Lecture V, May 19, 1840]) that there is "something operatic" in Rousseau. In my view, nowhere is this figure of *theatrum mundi* more significant than in *Du Contract social*, where it underpins Rousseau's famous claim that whoever does not follow the *volonté générale* will be "forced to be free." The arguments in the present book do not depend upon this point, which I will develop in full in another work on Rousseau's notion of the *volonté générale* and a set of fundamental misconceptions about his book *Du Contract social* and its implications. On the figure in general, cf. Christian (1987); on one perfect instance, cf. Yates (1969).

32. An index is available at http://ghtc.ifi.unicamp.br/Sacrobosco/Sacrobosco-ed4.htm (accessed November 2, 2009); the widespread popularity of Sacrobosco's book shows as false the commonplace that before the sixteenth century everyone thought the world was flat.

33. This is the second discourse in volume one of Buffon (1749, 65).

34. Rousseau borrows from and even emulates his friend Buffon in many other ways, from the *Discours sur . . . l'inégalité* to the *Botanique*. Cf. Einaudi (1967, 47) who writes: "Buffon was another contemporary who raised the questions and doubts Rousseau felt had to be raised. . . . Buffon's *Histoire naturelle* had begun to appear in 1749, at the very moment when Rousseau was beginning to concern himself with the problem of original man. By 1753, when Rousseau was writing his *Discourse on Inequality*, the sixth volume of Buffon's work had been published, dealing with the natural history of man."

35. OC V.586. With these three related functions of geography, Rousseau stakes a substantially stronger claim than Montesquieu. The value of the third point, consistent with Rousseau's sporadic but pointed references to the theater, is suggested in *Émile* where he insists that "the mask is not the man [*le masque n'est pas l'homme*] (OC IV.525) and the student can be trained to see through the mask's illusion (OC IV.283). While in *Émile* he seems to consider single persons in a general way, the word *"l'homme"* in

the *Traité de sphére* gestures to mankind as a whole. We return to the methodological significance of this text in §9 below.

36. Near the end of his life Rousseau describes himself as "the most sociable and loving of humans proscribed by unanimous agreement" (OC I.995). The idea of solitude as "limited communication" is neatly developed by Todorov (2001/1985, 35–53).

37. OC IV.582. In a variant manuscript Rousseau actually makes a stronger claim, saying that "it is therefore true that man is the king of nature, at least on the ground he inhabits." Cf. OC IV.1534, note D. Recall what he says about Robinson Crusoe at OC III.354 cited at the beginning of §2 above.

38. Cf. Augustine (1965) *De civitate dei contra paganos* (XIV.28).

39. On this distinction, see OC III.361–62.

40. This is the subtitle of *Du Contract social*, written in tandem with *Émile*. It is worth keeping in mind that this phrase is borrowed from Jean-Jacques Burlamaqui's book of 1751, *Principes du droit politique*, which is, tellingly, a theory of public law.

41. In fact he had many tutors, from his beloved ancient authors to contemporaries like Montesquieu and Hume . . . but that is another story.

42. Defoe and Rousseau share this term, *solitaire*, cognate in English and French. Jaucourt writes in the entry *"solitaire"* for the *Encyclopédie* in 1765—in Diderot and d'Alembert (1751–72, XV, 324)—that "a *solitaire* is seen by the rest of mankind as an inanimate being."

43. Saltonstall (1636) is a good example, which, dividing "the art of navigation" into "Theorick" and "Praktick" parts, claims to be the first book on this crucial topic to have included in the "Praktick" what is clearly most important to it, i.e., "the way of working, ruling, guiding, governing, and constraining . . . a Gallant ship . . . to performe the expert navigators pleasure in the sea" (1636, 2). He identifies "the Theorick" as that which "will fully informe you of the compofition of the Spheare in general" (1636, 1), making clear his debt to the pedagogical tradition of Sacrobosco mentioned above. The proximate link is likely by way of the translation and elaboration by polymath Pedro Nunes (1537) in *Tratado da sphera com a Theorica do Sol e da Lua*, which was the first of the genre to include elements of navigation.

44. In Defoe (1719), Robinson Crusoe comes ashore with "books of navigation, . . . three very good Bibles, . . . some Portuguese books also; and among them two or three Popish prayer-books, and several other books . . ." (chapter IV), and finds comfort reading the Bible, for example, just after he first sees a footprint in the sand (chapter XI).

45. Rousseau consistently projects a negative light on makers of theoretical systems while using the word "system" himself to advance his own thinking; I touch on this again below.

46. The paraphrase is, of course, of the text just cited above.

47. In this perspective, Rousseau is what Wolin (1970) called an "epic" political theorist.

48. OC IV.466. The layering that often makes Rousseau's writing so effective operates here. The tutor occasionally uses the same terms to describe himself (e.g., "I advance drawn on by the force of things [*j'avance attiré par la force des choses*]") and his student (e.g., "with only the force of things one renders him flexible and tractable [*on le*

rend souple et docile par la seule force des choses]"), citing from OC IV.548, 321. This suggests again that Rousseau is—and because of his position as creator of a new social theory of politics must be—self-educated, and that *Émile* is not simply a manual for tutors and their students but a user's guide for humanity. In another stunning parallel, Rousseau sums up—in the first draft for *Émile*—his pupil's movement beyond sensations to the acquisition of ideas in nearly identical terms: "Here we are come again to ourselves. After having worked our way around the universe there is our child entered again into himself as an individual. There more than ever is the necessity that he attaches to things [*Nous voici revenus à nous-mêmes. Aprés avoir parcouru l'univers voila nôtre enfant rentré dans son individu. Le voila sentant plus que jamais la necessité qui l'attache aux choses]*" (OC IV.211). *Nota bene* that this return to the self is preceded by a journey that might well be described in a *Traité de Sphére* or *Cours de géographie*. The lines from later in *Émile* (OC IV.466) cited in the text are preceded this way: "we have profited from the overflow of our capacities relative to our needs so as to carry us outside ourselves, launching ourselves into the heavens, measuring the earth, gathering up the laws of nature; in a word, we have worked our way around the entire island [*nous avons profité de la surabondance de nos forces sur nos besoins, pour nous porter hors de nous: nous nous sommes élancés dans les cieux; nous avons mesuré la terre; nous avons recueilli les loix de la Nature; en un mot, nous avons parcouru l'isle entiere]*." It is in this light, too, that we should read the evocative and polysemic first line of the fourth book of *Émile*; "How rapidly we pass on this earth! [*Que nous passons rapidement sur cette terre!*]" (OC IV.489).

49. It is worth noting, although impossible to detail here, how this conjunction of extremes, where the totality and the irreducible part become complements, characterizes developments in political culture from Rousseau's time on. This second use of the figure of Crusoe is corollary to the unitary image of society upon which stands the famous rhetoric of *la volonté générale*. Imagine, too, the desperation when in the last years of his life Rousseau, feeling utterly abandoned by the whole of mankind, returns to the first use of the figure of Crusoe and opens *Les rêveries du promeneur solitaire* with the declaration "Here, finally, am I, alone on the earth, having no more any brother, any neighbor, any friend, any society than myself." Note, too, that here he, with unparalleled brilliance, reverts to a pre-Rousseauean sense of the word *société*.

50. For recent summary work on the multiple paths of reception of Rousseau's writings, see Hesse (2005).

51. Famously asserted by Mercier (1791); cf. Swenson (2000). Generally, see Mornet (1933), Furet (1978), Darnton (1982), Miller (1984), Darnton (1985), Chartier (1990), Gauchet (1995).

52. This list may be partially justified as follows. Hannah Arendt identifies the "rise of the social" with the coming to power of a Rousseau-inspired vision in the hands of Robespierre, cf. Arendt (1958) on the former, Arendt (1963) on the latter, expanding the common view borrowed for example by Tarde (1895) from Sighele that Rousseau was the *incubo* of Robespierre and responsible for the extension, through terror, of politics into society; Sighele (1895, 330–32). In other spheres the idea that "this sub-

lime genius who inspired the purest love of liberty had nonetheless furnished fatal pretexts for more than one sort of tyranny [*ce génie sublime qu'animait l'amour le plus pur de la liberté, a fourni néanmoins de funestes prétextes à plus d'un genre de tyrannie*]" had long since been expressed by Benjamin Constant in his famous "liberty of the ancients compared with that of the moderns" speech, in Constant (1820, IV, 238–74). The positive view of Rousseau "considered as one of the first authors of the Revolution" begins with Mercier (1791); on this see again note 51 above. How Rousseau appeared as the principal foil for the development of French political thought throughout the nineteenth century is traced in (though not the explicit theme of) Rosanvallon (2000). Tarde (1895, III) identifies himself with Comte against Rousseau; his distaste for the latter is made clear in Pickering (1993), although his ambivalence, like Constant's, is expressed at Tarde (1895, 120). Again, Durkheim's 1892 Latin dissertation on Montesquieu (identifying him as a founder of social science) was joined by long study of Rousseau—"who was one of his favorite authors" [Cuvillier, cited by Lukes (1973, 283)]—which bore fruit in his lectures on education from as early as 1889 and his lectures on *Du Contract social* from 1901–2; cf. Durkheim (1953) and Lukes (1973, chapters 6 & 14). Cf. Halbwach's introduction to *Du Contract social* in Rousseau (1943). Of high interest also is Fouillée (1890). Lévi-Strauss (1958, tome II, chapitre 2) famously identifies Rousseau as the founder of social science.

53. On Rousseau and the Scots, see, e.g., Hawthorn (1976, chapter 2) and Leigh (1986); Kettler (2005, 7) points to Rousseau's influence on Ferguson. On the Americans, cf. Kenyon (1955) and (1958), Rossiter (1964, especially chapter 4), or more generally Spurlin (1969). Before their quarrel, Hume wrote *of* Rousseau, "I think Rousseau in many things very much resembles Socrates: the Philosopher of Geneva seems only to have more Genius than he of Athens" (Mossner [2001, 512]) and he wrote *to* Rousseau, "I will use the Freedom of telling you bluntly . . . that. . . . you are the person whom I most revere, both for the Force of your Genius and the Greatness of your Mind" (Mossner [2001, 428–29]). Rousseau wrote in the same period that "M. Hume is more than anyone I know a true philosopher and the only historian who has ever written with impartiality" (CC XII.217, August 20, 1762). Errors in understanding Rousseau, combined with Hume's critique of "contract theory," have made it difficult to see their overlapping conception of society, but Forbes (1985, 105) correctly notes that "Hume's awareness of man's social interdependence is so striking a feature of his thought. . . . that it would be nearer the mark to say that for him society is the 'natural unit.'"

54. Cf., e.g., Cassirer (1945), Ritter (1965), Philonenko (1969), Althusser (1972), Colletti (1973), Lukács (1976), Riley (1982), Fulda and Horstmann (1991), Petersen (1992).

55. Cf. Ansell-Pearson (1991). Strong (1994) is an interesting reading of Rousseau that makes use of Nietzsche.

56. Obviously, I am not saying that these are the only sources of contemporary thought about society; I am saying that older sources—such as key religious texts—as well as newer ones have been powerfully and identifiably inflected by these modern traditions. This includes later American schools as well; see, e.g., Cooley (1902) and (1909), who is thoroughly wedded to a vocabulary descended directly from Rousseau but does not mention him by name.

56a. See the remarkable studies of Tanguy L'Aminot, e.g. 1992.

57. Bourdieu, in Bourdieu and Wacquant (1992, 209), identifies himself personally with Rousseau.

58. Cassirer's essay first appeared in 1932 as "Das Problem Jean Jacques Rousseau" in the *Archiv für Geschichte der Philosophie*, 41, 177–213, 479–513. It followed by one generation the flood of publication that marked the second centenary of Rousseau's birth in 1712. The text cited here is Peter Gay's translation in Cassirer (1932/1963).

59. E.g. Derathé (1970; first edition 1950), Burgelin (1952), and Starobinski (1971).

60. Cassirer (1932/1963, 128).

61. With regard to the first, part of what underpins the hegemony of the theme of democracy has been its ongoing redefinition. Among its central tendencies, the increasing emphasis on rights as the motor of democracy sits perhaps most uneasily with the doctrines of popular sovereignty or majority rule associated with Rousseau. The same is true, if in a more complicated way, for the priority of the "rule of law" that clearly marks Rousseau's texts. The emergence of a new antihistorical, antispeculative, and elite-oriented political science in the United States after 1945 — signal moments include Schumpeter (1950), Dahl (1961), Huntington (1968); consider also the historical analysis of the discipline in Gunnell (1993) and Gunnell (2004) — placed many of Rousseau's topics back on the table for dispute. Concerning the engagement of contemporary feminist scholarship with Rousseau, see, e.g., Okin (1979), Kofman (1982), Garbe (1992), Zerilli (1994), Fermon (1997), Habib (1998), Roulston (1998), Marso (1999), Lange (2002), and others. This recent wave should be read in light of earlier analyses of "the woman question" by Buffenoir (1891), Bazaillas (1914), and Ferval (1934). The original feminist critique of Rousseau is Wollstonecraft (1792).

62. The relation between these uses and what Rousseau actually wrote is not the point here.

63. "*Zwischen gleichen Rechten entscheidet die Gewalt.*" Marx (1867, *Kapitel* 8 "Der Arbeitstag," §1 "*Die Grenzen des Arbeitstags*"). N.b. that this appears in Chapter 10.1.344 of Marx (1976). No one has made a pithier statement of this common trope in political theory than Rousseau's great nineteenth-century follower.

64. Cf. Meyers (1995) and Meyers (2013c).

65. Giddens (1984) was an attempt to return an encompassing notion of constitution to sociological theory.

66. The general claim that dependence — together with the human capacity for speech and several other aspects of the human condition — is a primary fact that makes political life possible and is therefore an essential topic for political theory is developed in my trilogy *Democracy in America After 9/11*, especially in volume two, *The Position of the Citizen* (2012a, forthcoming).

67. I have shown this in Meyers (2008b) and will develop it at length in the sequel to this book. This point stands despite some complications deriving from the fact that the "*contract social*" and the "*pacte social*" are not the same; identifying these two has been an almost universal and profoundly consequential error of Rousseau's followers and interpreters. For a perspicuous parallel approach to this question, cf. Button (2008, 173 ff.).

68. The way the word *pactum* shifts from its sense in Roman law—as the broadest and often most informal sort of "agreement" (Thanks to Luigi Capogrossi Colognesi for conversations on this point)—to something more clearly juridical in the French of the eighteenth century is touched on in Meyers (2008b).

69. This is how, following Rousseau, Hegel developed his notion of *Sittlichkeit* in a more comprehensive direction. Cf., e.g., the *System of Ethical Life* from 1802/3 in Hegel (2002, 62), translated in Hegel (1979, 167): "The system of need has been conceived formally above as a system of universal physical dependence on one another." *Sittlichkeit* has been translated literally and obscurely as "ethical substance" or more suggestively as "ethical life." In my view, it amounts to a working out in the context of post-Kantian German romanticism of Rousseau's conception of *le lien social*. Hegel's account of the pervasive social relationship "discovered" by Rousseau is ultimately quite different from Rousseau's, especially with respect to the status of "dependence-from-things" discussed at length below. Cf. Meyers (1989, chapter 3). Moreover, it may be said that Hegel attempts to refute Rousseau's theodicy by arguing that even if his image of sociology is correct, and even with a further articulation of *le lien social* in terms of dependence, the development of *Geist* through philosophy subsumes all this again within God. Consider together the end of *The History of Philosophy* and the conclusion of *The Philosophy of History*: "Philosophy is thus the true theodicy, as contrasted with art and religion and the feelings which these call up—a reconciliation of spirit, namely of the spirit which has apprehended itself in its freedom and in the riches of its reality.... That the History of the World, with all the changing scenes which its annals present, is this process of development and the realization of Spirit— this is the true *Theodicoea*, the justification of God in History. Only *this* insight can reconcile Spirit with the History of the World—viz., that what has happened, and is happening every day, is not only not 'without God,' but is essentially His Work." Hegel (1896, III, 546).

70. Some gestures to the corresponding theory of action, which pivots around the notion of the "division of action," may be found in Meyers (2008a); the theory of divided action is developed further in chapter 5 of *The Position of the Citizen*, (2012a, forthcoming).

71. On the idea that dependence is a primary fact for political theory, see the summary statement in Meyers (2013a, forthcoming), and the provisional account of its marginalization in Meyers (1989); the concept, *topos*, and material history of dependence are treated in another book-length manuscript entitled *Dancing on a Landslide: Micropractical Foundations for a Political Theory of Power*.

72. Diderot on "*Indépendance*" (1765) in Diderot and d'Alembert (1751–72, VIII, 671). N.b. that *amour-propre* is a pivotal term for Rousseau that I shall discuss below.

73. Ibid.

74. This was a common operation throughout the hundred years preceding the publication of the *Encyclopédie*; cf. especially Ehrard (1994). Of course, there were no "scientists" in the centuries before Rousseau (the word is invented in English in 1834, and barely used in French in the English sense for a substantial part of the twentieth century). Well into the eighteenth century the word *science* in French (translation of

Latin *doctrina*) was applicable to every form of knowing (including, for example, theology and edicts from the king), and there is no singular substantive unpredicated *science* in the *Encyclopédie*; cf. Jaucourt's entry "*Sciences*," which suggests that in each area of inquiry a science is produced by reasoning about causes, itself a product of "*l'esprit philosophique.*" More tellingly, Jaucourt insists on a kind of dialectical interaction between *sciences* and *belles-lettres*, indicating that eloquence remains essential to inquiry in the mid-eighteenth century. More generally, see d'Alembert (1751, "*Discours préliminaire*"). This is of course the line spelled out most precisely by Giambattista Vico in his inaugural lecture of 1708, *De nostri temporis studiorum ratione*, translated in Vico (1709/1990), and peerlessly pursued in his masterwork Vico (1744/1984).

75. The new pantheon trumpeted, for example, by the *Encyclopédie*; cf. Jaucourt on "*Sciences*" (1765) in Diderot and d'Alembert (1751–72, XIV, 788); Diderot's friend d'Holbach will become the great publicist of this type of materialism with publication of the *Système de la nature* (1770) and *Système social* (1773), which begins with the line "Everything is bound together in the moral world as it is in the physical world [*tout est lié dans le monde moral comme dans le monde Physique*]."

76. The *locus classicus* of modern scholarship on the "great chain of being" is Lovejoy (1936). For a brief gloss on this point, cf. Israel (2002, 709–13); Israel makes a passing argument about Diderot's entry "*Spinosiste*" in the *Encyclopédie* which I do not quite understand. Pierre-François Moreau, in Garrett (1996, 418–19) gives a succinct account of the development of Diderot's thinking and his attempt—parallel to what I describe here—to use Spinoza away from theology.

77. Diderot on "*Indépendance*" (1765) in Diderot and d'Alembert (1751–72, VIII, 671).

78. Ibid. As ever a master of ironic play, Diderot here goes "over the top" by adding this astonishing commentary on the vocation and potential reception of the collaborative *Encyclopédie*: "There is however one type of independence to which one may aspire: it is that which philosophy provides. . . . An independence of this sort can never be dangerous. It has no impact whatsoever on the authority of government, on the obedience that is due to the laws, on the respect merited by religion; it does not tend to destroy every instance of subordination and turn the state upside-down, as is claimed in print by certain people who cry out 'anarchy!' from the moment one refuses to recognize the prideful tribunal that they themselves have raised up. . . . Happy in its obscurity, it will never succeed in crawling its way to the doors of the high and mighty. . . . If occasionally it has the misfortune to make more noise than it would like, that happens in the world of literature where some frightened or envious dwarves want to make it appear as a Titan laying siege to heaven. . . .'Til now, one has hardly ever seen philosophers who have incited revolts, overthrown the government, changed the form of states. . . . I see them everywhere surrounded by a crowd of enemies, . . . Just that is their destiny, and even the prince of Philosophers, the great and virtuous Socrates, taught them that they should consider themselves lucky if one does not prepare them a noose before exalting them with statues [*Il est pourtant une espece d'indépendance à laquelle il est permis d'aspirer: c'est celle que donne la Philosophie. . . . Une pareille indépendance ne peut pas être dangereuse. Elle ne touche point à l'autorité du gouverne-*

ment, à l'obéissance qui est dûe aux lois, au respect que mérite la religion: elle ne tend
pas à détruire toute subordination, & à bouleverser l'état, comme le publient certaines
gens qui crient à l'anarchie, dès qu'on refuse de reconnoître le tribunal orgueilleux qu'ils
se sont eux-mêmes élevé. . . . Content de son obscurité, il ne va point pour en sortir
ramper à la porte des grands, . . . Si quelquefois il a le malheur de faire plus de bruit
qu'il ne le voudroit, c'est dans le monde littéraire où quelques nains effrayés ou envieux
de sa grandeur, veulent le faire passer pour un Titan qui escalade le ciel, . . . L'on n'a
jusqu'ici guere vû de philosophes qui aient excité des revoltes, renversé le gouvernement,
changé la forme des états. . . . Je les vois par-tout entourés d'une foule d'ennemis, . . .
C'est-là leur destinée, & le prince même des Philosophes, le grand & vertueux Socrate,
leur apprend qu'ils doivent s'estimer heureux lorsqu'on ne leur dresse pas des échafauds
avant de leur élever des statues]."

79. The proper contemporary term for this is *individuation*, not independence.

80. See §2 above.

81. The only counter-examples are at OC III.394 (where citizens are said to be "independent" of one another against the background of an "excessive dependence on the
city"), OC III.399 (where a prince's aspiration to "independence" leads to tyranny),
OC III.407 (where again those who seek to become "independent" are striving to become "masters"), and OC III.462 (where Rousseau says that the pagans saw the early
Christians as "only looking for the moment to make themselves independents and
masters").

82. Again, in the *Discours sur . . . l'inégalité*; OC III.174.

83. OC III.375; cf. Montesquieu (1748, book XI, chapter 3) who asserts the same distinction.

84. The weight Rousseau places on the notion of *dépendance* in his account of the dynamics of society makes it a complement of what I shall refer to below as his theory of
"social evolution."

85. OC IV.286. The Anglophone reader should not confuse this with the famous references to chains (*fers*) at OC III.351 (cf. OC III.353, 429). With a high degree of consistency Rousseau differentiates *fers*—"irons" in the English sense of a sea captain who
says "throw him in irons!"—from *chaînes* and thus makes clear that the latter are not
always bad. The image of *chaînes* overlaps with the "ties"—*liens* in "*lien social*" or
Latin *ligare* in "*la religion civile*"—that are at the origin of *société*, writ large or small.
Cf. how the ambivalence of friendship reappears when Rousseau writes to Grimm in
a moment of despair (October 1757) of "the sweet chains of friendship"; from the *Correspondance complète de J.-J. Rousseau* IV.546, as cited in Cranston (1991, 86).

86. Together with a variety of supporting terms like *lien, rapport, engagement, convention,
contract*, etc.

87. Rousseau understood like no modern thinker before him (except in certain respects
Montesquieu) and few after that politics is embedded in society and that an adequate
sociology is a precondition for the study of politics. His view is clearly represented,
for example, in the organization of the first version of *Du Contract social*, in which
the first book discusses "first notions of the social body [*premières notions du corps
social*]."

88. E.g., Derathé (1970). Rousseau's view is more consistent with Durkheim's (1893) link between "organic solidarity" and individualisms. I will argue in my book on Rousseau's political theory that the significance of Rousseau's title—*Du Contract social*—has been almost entirely occluded by cultural developments in the nineteenth century. In any event, from this point on I shall refer to whatever role a juridical document, or the imaginary of a juridical document, might play in consolidation of *société* as *le pacte social*, which is in fact consistent with Rousseau's usage.

89. Shklar (1973, 277) is not incorrect to say "that is why the Will [the legislator] instills is far more important than the contract that first creates civil society." Indeed, as used here, the word "Will" captures the pragmatic force of *moeurs*. Nonetheless, it is somewhat misleading to suggest that what law constitutes in character is primarily "Will," just as it is misleading to call that education "virtue."

90. And even these words have been almost entirely misunderstood. In Hume (1987), see especially the essay "On the Social Contract," originally from 1741.

91. *Rousseau juge de Jean-Jacques* was his last work, published four years after his death in 1782. *"Fausses notions du lien social"* is the title of Chapter V in Book I of the so-called "Geneva Manuscript" of *Du Contract social*. The absurdity of a contract theory of society, at least in what is commonly held to be its strict Hobbesian form, is suggested at OC III.183. It is worth noting that *Rousseau juge de Jean-Jacques* contains some remarkable coded games that pick up on the trace clue provided in Rousseau's sly title of *Du Contract social*; I discuss these matters in Meyers (2008b), a preparatory study for a book on Rousseau's political theory.

92. We will see later that between *rapports* and *dépendance*, the latter is the more basic category. In the development sketched by Rousseau's philosophical anthropology, the appearance of proper *rapports* signals the advent of society; natural Man has *rapports* only with himself or identical others, whereas society brings us into relation with human plurality in its totality (OC IV.249). Important clues about the character of *rapports* include: from tears "is born the first *rapport* of Man with everything around him" (OC IV.286); even weakness is a type of *rapport* (OC IV.305); human beings living in society inevitably develop *rapports* with others (OC IV.329); *rapports* "determine historical facts [*déterminent les faits historiques*]" (OC IV.348); and our *rapports* with the things around us are essential (OC IV.370). The key to the word *"rapport"* is its etymology, indicating a circular process in which something is "brought back to" the person who "has" it. Cf. Montesquieu (1748, Book I) where law is considered as a kind of *rapport*. The reflexive constitution of society in Rousseau—we will soon see—starts from *dépendance*, develops through *rapports*, takes the form of *loix*, which ultimately reduces back to *moeurs*, *coutumes*, and *opinion*, which is to say the socially constructed fabric of *dépendance*.

93. Leibniz's letter to Des Bosses, Feb. 5 1712; the translation here is by Loemker from Leibniz (1969) and cited from Loemker (1973, vol. IV, p. 379).

94. When Durkheim (1924) recognized a radical break between theology and sociology—"we must choose between God and society"—he took himself to be following Kant. As Aron (1968, II.107) writes, "if there is one statement characteristic of Durkheim, this is surely it." Gauchet (1985) develops this point; Baker (1994, 96) makes the choice into a substitution. I suggest that its source, direct or indirect, is Rousseau.

95. OC IV.270 and, generally, Book I of *Émile*.

96. That is, press one to respond to a representation of some evil not present to our senses.

97. OC IV.692 ff., *Émile*, Book V, *passim*.

98. See especially §19 ff.

99. Given the specificity of these terms in French and the technical status they achieve in the following discussion I will use them in the original throughout.

100. I mean this in the contemporary sense of Hedström & Swedberg (1998).

101. Touraine (1973).

102. This paraphrase appears in Durkheim's Latin dissertation on Montesquieu (1953; originally 1892) and is translated back into French as *lien social*. It is, I believe, an essential point of contact with the Roman republican sense that "law is the bond that unites the civic association [*cum lex sit civilis societatis vinculum*]" (at Cicero *De Republica*, I.49), and more broadly with the sense of human interdependence as a fact of *civitas* that grows inexorably from our capacities; cf. "But it seems we must trace back to their ultimate sources the principles of fellowship and society that Nature has established among men. The first principle is that which is found in the connection subsisting between all the members of the human race; and that bond of connection is reason and speech, which by the processes of teaching and learning, of communicating, discussing, and reasoning associate men together and unite them in a sort of natural fraternity [*Sed, quae naturae principia sint communitatis et societatis humanae, repetendum videtur altius; est enim primum, quod cernitur in universi generis humani societate. Eius autem vinculum est ratio et oratio, quae docendo, discendo, communicando, disceptando, iudicando conciliat inter se homines coniugitque naturali quad am societate]* at Cicero (1913, Book I.XVI [50]); likewise as Cicero (*Pro Cluentio*, 53) writes of "the bond of this dignity that we enjoy in the republic, this is the foundation of our liberty, this is the source of justice [*hoc enim vinculum est huius dignitatis qua fruimur in re publica, hoc fundamentum libertatis, hic fons aequitatis*]." Cicero is not alone in using this language; cf. e.g. Livy (1912, Book 36) who points to common utility as the surest bond of alliance [*"una, communis utilitas, quae societatis maximum vinculum est"*].

103. OC V.114, from the *Lettre à d'Alembert*.

104. In these general terms, one may recall also that the very much different topic of the "freedom of the Will" was part of the theodicy question long before Rousseau.

105. Again, keep in mind that Rousseau intentionally uses this archaic French spelling; cf. "Note on Sources and Uses of Words" above.

106. I acknowledge that the relation of *état* to activity is somewhat more complicated.

107. From *ligo*, to bind. Cf. also OC III.460–69.

108. On this complex of issues, see, e.g., OC III.694–95. It is worth noting how this point is sustained by the equivalence given to the words *lien* and *noeud*. While the internal complexity of *lien* is manifest in its classification with other sorts of *rapports*, Rousseau states in a definitional way the organized complexity for which *noeud* (and by synonym, *lien*) is the proper name: it is defined in the *Fragmens pour un dictionnaire des termes d'usage en botanique* as a "joining point of stems and roots [*articulation des tiges et des racines*]" which is to say the conjunction of the "part of the plant by which it clings to the earth [*partie de la plante par laquelle elle tient à la terre*]"—its source

of security and nourishment—with the body that holds together "all its other parts [*toutes ses autres parties*]"; OC IV.1234, 1241, and 1244.

109. The term familiar to all readers of Rousseau that competes with *dépendance* to symbolize the necessarily problematic character of human relation is *inégalité*. The two discourses cross paths, and it may be said that *inégalité* is itself a kind of *ordre*; it is not, however, a primary account of order from which an account of social and political facts (like *inégalité*) might be developed. In any case, I shall be concerned here primarily with *dépendance*.

110. And not, for example, to Hume, the greatest of Rousseau's contemporaries to locate habit as foundational in human affairs.

111. Aristotle, *Nicomachean Ethics* at 1103a18: ἡ δ' ἠθικὴ ἐξ ἔθους περιγίνεται, ὅθεν καὶ τοὔνομα ἔσχηκε μικρὸν παρεγκλῖνον ἀπὸ τοῦ ἔθους.

112. Eckstein (1944, 265 *et passim*) makes this point about Rousseau and Spinoza. This conjunction is in some ways disguised by the different senses in which these two authors hold "naturalistic" views; I return to this point in Part Three below.

113. Schwab (1957) on Jaucourt's contribution to the *Encyclopédie*. N.b., too, that just before Rousseau began to write for the *Encyclopédie* Jaucourt published an edition of Leibniz's *Essais de Théodicée* (1747) of more than five hundred pages, half of which was taken up by a biography of Leibniz written anonymously years earlier by Jaucourt himself. We know that Rousseau was well acquainted with Leibniz by 1739 (cf. note 15 above) but it is likely that this interest was increased by Jaucourt and the Parisian circle.

114. Jaucourt in Diderot & d'Alembert (1751–72, "*moralité*" at X.702, "*morale*" at X.699 ff.). That *moeurs* can be the object of a science is already noteworthy. See note 74 above on Jaucourt's definitions of science, which suggest a stronger continuity between the "Enlightenment" and Dilthey's revived humanism than is ordinarily assumed. Of course, the basic distinction is from the rhetorical tradition, as Rousseau's near-contemporary Giambattista Vico shows clearly in his *De nostri temporis studiorum ratione* (1709/1990).

115. Definition from Lewis and Short (1991); Cicero's (1972, vol. IV) coinage is from *De Fato* (1, 1): "*quia pertinet ad mores, quos ηθη Graeci vocant, nos eam partem philosophiae de moribus appellare solemus. Sed decet augentem linguam Latinam nominare moralem.*"

116. The relation between the moral and the ethical becomes the issue relevant here after Kant's (1785/1964) austere new secular assertion of the moral; the distinction provides Hegel with a basis for arguing about ethics in a new sociological way in terms of *Sittlichkeit*; cf. Hegel (1979) and Hegel (1952, 394 ff.). Taylor's (1975, 376–78) crisp analysis of Hegel is helpful but remains too narrowly focused around the concept of obligation.

117. Jaucourt "*moralité*" in Diderot and d'Alembert (1751–72, X, 702); Diderot "*moeurs*" in Diderot & d'Alembert (1751–72, X, 611).

118. Elsewhere and under the heading of the "new model Will" I describe the transformation of the concept of "Will" as a characteristic feature of modernity; see §§7–8 below, as well as Meyers (1995) and Meyers (2013c, forthcoming).

119. My investigation of the history of the Will begins with Vernant's (1973) suggestion

that it *must* have a history because the ancient Greeks had no concept of the Will in its modern sense; cf. Meyers (1995). For an argument against Vernant, cf., e.g., Kenny (1979); for an intermediate position, cf. e.g., Williams (1993, chapter 2).

120. As if any doubt about the extension of *morale* remained, Jaucourt adds that "to justify all these truths, it would be necessary to enter into details that the limits of this work would not permit." Keep in mind that the "limits" here are the seventeen volumes of the *Encyclopédie!*

121. While I am convinced that this is the prevalent sense of *moeurs* in Rousseau's key writings, I acknowledge, with one caveat, that the guiding intention in the so-called "First Discourse" may have been to treat *moeurs* as equivalent to the English word "manners" (as it is translated in Fuseli [1767]). The caveat is that "manners" in the eighteenth century was already much closer to the proper sense of *moeurs* as I describe it here.

121a. Rhetoric is understood here in the sense of Meyers (2007) or Meyers & Streuver (2008).

122. The word here is *"disconvenance,"* which is the absence of *convenance*, the French equivalent of the fundamental rhetorical terms πρέπον or *decorum* in their broadest sense.

123. "Dialectic" here is, of course, to be understood in the ancient rather than the modern sense. On the modern genealogy of demonstration as a method of ethics, cf. Lachterman (1989).

124. This is a key rhetorical distinction that extends from Aristotle's ἐικός / ἀναγκαιον to Vico's *certo* / *vero* and beyond. In seventeenth-century French debates on poetics, the distinction probable/ἐικός/*certo* vs. necessary/ἀναγκαιον/*vero* is remade in terms of *vraisemblance* vs. *vérité*; I find this, for example, in Chapelain (1880) and (2007).

125. Implicating "the time and place in which one speaks, [and] that which one owes to oneself together with that which one owes to those who listen to us [*le tems, le lieu où l'on parle; ce qu'on se doit à soi-même, & ce qu'on doit à ceux qui nous écoutent*]"; from Jaucourt's entry *"invention"* (1765) for the *Encyclopédie*, in Diderot and d'Alembert (1751–72, VIII.849).

126. Assuming that "we only speak to invite those who listen to enter into our sentiments [*nous ne parlons que pour faire entrer dans nos sentimens ceux qui nous écoutent*]." Jaucourt, *"rhétorique"* (1765) in Diderot and d'Alembert (1751–72, XIV, 250).

127. The latter terms are introduced in Meyers (2008a) and developed in Meyers (2013a, chapter 5).

128. Cf. Jaucourt's *"rhétorique"* for the *Encyclopédie* (1765) in Diderot and d'Alembert (1751–72, XIV, 250), where he translates the key passage from Aristotle's *Rhetoric* (1355b25–26): "Let rhetoric then be a capacity [δύναμις] discovering [θεωρῆσαι] in each case the available means of persuasion."

129. Cf. §4 above.

130. Both quotes from OC IV.310–11, the "main passage" to be discussed below; see Appendix to Part One.

131. The theme we consider in this section and that surfaces in the following passage—that Rousseau is essentially concerned with νομος or *mos*, and not with the conception of law entirely inflected by nineteenth-century positivism through which his writings, and especially the claims of *Du Contract social*, have typically been read—requires a

much longer discussion than I can give it here. I will take this up again in a companion volume to the present book.

132. As I have shown in Meyers (2008b), by giving so much weight to the notion of "contract" Rousseau intended to bring to light the ambivalence of law in an age of its radical transformation.

133. The distinction between *l'État* and *le Souverain* as a way to distinguish passive from active modes of the reflexive experience of *la cité* is drawn from (OC III.361–62).

133a. On this key point cf. §20 below.

134. Plato *Gorgias* 484c.

135. OC V.115 (*Lettre à d'Alembert*).

136. It may be said that exactly what makes Rousseau's sociology coherent and consistent is his rejection of any sort of appeal to the strategy of *deus ex machina*; Plato makes fun of this approach to meaning in language at *Cratylus* (425d); Aristotle discusses the limitations on its use in drama at *Poetics* (1454b1).

137. While I mean "hermeneutic" in something close to Gadamer's usage, which is explicitly related to rhetorical traditions in *Wahrheit und Methode* (1975/1960), Francis Leiber's (1839) application of the term to law and politics is also suggestive; note that he adopts the same trope as Jaucourt to define his subject: "That branch of science which establishes the principles and rules of interpretation and construction, is called *hermeneutics* . . . and the actual application of them is *exegesis*. . . . Hermeneutics and exegesis stand in the relation to each other as theory and practice." Lieber (1839, 64). One could also use the word "cultural" at this point; cf., e.g., the recent pithy argument of Rosen (2006).

138. This is a pivot point of what I will refer to as the "main passage" below.

139. I leave open at this point which way the relationship runs—whether *moeurs, coutumes*, and *opinion* should be analyzed in terms of dependence or the other way around. The hinge here is the word "composed," which is closely related to *ordre*.

140. It is at this point that the mechanical metaphor of a "chain" of dependence fails to express Rousseau's conception and holistic images—like the one cited from Diderot above—become more apt. This perspective is consistent with Durkheim's reading of Rousseau.

141. ". . . to suffer is the first thing he must learn [*souffrir est la prémière chose qu'il doit apprendre*]." OC IV.300.

142. Cf. §4 above.

143. I grant that the word "natural" here may be confusing; as the issue of how nature fits into relationships constituted by human beings for themselves takes up many pages later in this book, I shall not tarry to resolve this here.

144. It reappears clearly in the *Déclaration des Droits de l'Homme et du Citoyen* of 1789, of which the first article asserts "Men are born and remain free, and equal in rights [*Les hommes naissent et demeurent libres, et égaux en droits*]." As Derathé (annotation to OC III.1433) points out, "The notion of Man's natural liberty is a theme Rousseau shares with most of the theorists of the Natural Law School." Pufendorf and others were perfectly aware of the Roman roots of this view, reflected for example in the *Digest of Justinian* (I.1.4) "*utpote cum jure naturali omnes liberi nascerentur.*"

145. On the specificity of injustice, cf. Shklar (1990); on the priority of injustice over jus-

tice, cf. Meyers (1989) and (1998). For a different but importantly related investigation, cf. Boltanski and Chiapello (1999). It is, but should not be, necessary to repeat
that the modern link between ethics and politics cannot be a "neo-aristotelianism," no
matter how much we may turn to and are indebted to that seminal thinker.

146. Arendt (1963, 78, 77); she refers in the second sentence to the retelling of the narrative
of Christ by Melville (in *Billy Budd*) and Dostoevski (in *The Grand Inquisitor*). This
view is, perhaps surprisingly, compatible with the Rousseau I try to evoke in this book.

147. Cf. Meyers (1998).

148. Cf. Arendt (1963, chapter 2).

149. Extending by analogy Freud's (1991/1914) definition.

150. OC III.371; this point reflects a more general perspective of political theory developed
in Meyers (2013a, forthcoming) and especially in Meyers (2013b, forthcoming).

151. To this must be added a crucial qualification: since the beginning of the nineteenth
century, almost no reader of Rousseau's book by that name has understood what that
phrase amounts to; cf. Meyers (2008b).

152. N.b. that what Rousseau says in the last paragraph of *Du Contract social*—"after
having posited the true principles of political right and attempted to found the State
on that basis [*après avoir posé les vrais principes du droit politique et tâché de fonder
l'État sur sa base*]"—is effectively a throw-away line that hardly describes the text
leading to that point.

153. OC III.187: "it is less important to consider the motives for establishing political
bodies" than to examine how they function, or fail to function, in context and over
time.

154. The former is the first title of the first version (the "*Manuscrit de Genève*") of the latter,
which initially had the subtitle "*Essai sur la forme de la république*"—already moving
away from any central concern with founding—and appeared finally as "*Principes du
droit politique*." Derathé (in an editorial note at OC III.1417) goes so far as to say that
"in the Geneva manuscript the problem of the origins of political societies is deliber-
ately left aside and Rousseau positions himself exclusively from the perspective of law."

155. Hobbes (1969, 4) from *Elements of Law*, part one, chapter 1, #8.

156. I refer here, of course, to each of the three major theoretical texts—*Discours sur l'origine et les fondemens de l'inégalité parmi les hommes* (throughout as *Discours sur . . .
l'inégalité*), *Émile, ou De l'éducation* (throughout as *Émile*), and *Du Contract social;
ou, Principes du droit politique* (throughout as *Du Contract social*).

157. Cf. for example Augustine *De civitate dei contra paganos* (X.3) on *diligere se ipsum*;
his usage mimics exactly the translation that had recently been made by Jerome from
Greek into the Latin vulgate of Romans 13:9 ("*diliges proximum tuum tamquam te
ipsum*") where *diligere* renders αγαπαω; the King James renders this comprehensive
commandment as "Thou shalt love thy neighbour as thyself."

158. The book by Abbadie, a Protestant, appeared in at least twenty-five French editions
before 1760, and, as he lived in London throughout the 1690s, was translated almost
immediately into English; a bold statement of the issue is made in part two, chapter
six (p. 129 of the English translation of 1695), where he writes "'Tis an advantage of
the French tongue that it can distinguish betwixt *l'amour propre* and *l'amour de nous*

memes; the former signifies *self-love* as 'tis vicious and corrupted, the latter denotes this love as 'tis lawful and natural." Masson (1914) identifies as additional proximate sources of this distinction Marie Huber, *Lettres sur la religion essentielle à l'homme, distinguée de ce qui n'en est que l'accessoire* (Amsterdam: J. Wetstein et W. Smith, 1738) and a text by Vauvenargues (1747) that Rousseau copied in his notebook called *"De l'amour de soi et de l'amour de nous-mêmes,"* which is number XXIV in the *Introduction à la connaissance de l'esprit humain, suivie de réflexions et de maximes.* While a discussion of this vocabulary in and around Rousseau's work is beyond the scope of this book, it may be worth mentioning that Rousseau only occasionally adopts the exact language of Abbadie; cf. the rare but telling *"l'amour de nous-mêmes"* (e.g. OC IV.599). It might be illuminating to discover why. In an annotation at OC III.1376, following Marcel Raymond (1957), Starobinski distinguishes "between the condemnation (Augustinian and above all Jansenist) of *l'amour-propre* and the apology for *l'amour-propre bien entendu* provided by the Philosophes (Diderot, Helvétius, d'Holbach)." However, both the qualification "rightly understood [*bien entendu*]" and the condemnation of *amour-propre* appear in the Protestant views of Abbadie as well, as they do in another important source for Rousseau, Burlamaqui, who makes the distinction (1747, II, iv, 183) by writing after *"l'amour de soi meme"* that *"j'entens un amour éclairé & raisonable."* In any case, the breadth of this hybrid notion is sufficient to encompass Diderot's critique of *indépendance* (see §4 above).

159. OC III.219–20, note XV.

160. This view of *amour de soi-même* is complicated but not contradicted by Rousseau's avowed dualism; the two topics converge in the *Lettre à Christophe de Beaumont* at OC IV.936.

161. OC IV.61; this is the first line of the first chapter of the first version of *Émile*.

162. *Perfectibilité* was in the mid-eighteenth century a neologism sufficiently recent to be bypassed by the *Encyclopédie*, and then included in the *Dictionnaire de Trévoux* (1771) and finally in the *Dictionnaire* of the *Académie française* in 1798. L'abbé de Saint-Pierre, a major source for Rousseau, uses prolifically the verb *perfectionner*, but the substantive *perfectibilité* only appears in the pages of Rousseau, La Mettrie, and Grimm. The research here is from Ehrard (1994, 753), who insists that there is a tight correspondence between the literal sense of the verb and the application of the substantive, and that therefore *perfectibilité* is a precursor to the word *progrès*, which did not yet exist; at least with respect to Rousseau I think Ehrard radically underestimates the latitude given to this term and thus its more abstract theoretical importance in Rousseau's thinking.

163. While the underlying idea here is one of the oldest in the sociological tradition— famously stated, e.g., by Merton (1936) and by Hayek, especially in his *Law, Legislation, and Liberty* (1973)—I adopt the vocabulary of fate into sociology in the spirit of Mills (1959, 182–83). It is developed further in Meyers (1989) and (1995), and again, with the notion of the "division of action" as applied in Meyers (2008a) and developed theoretically in Meyers (2013a, forthcoming).

164. On the *necessary* role of chance in social evolution, cf. the two penultimate paragraphs of *Discours sur . . . l'inégalité* (OC III.162).

165. In this section I use the English "Will" and the French *"volonté"* interchangeably because the differences are not relevant to the discussion at this point.

166. Cassirer (1932/1963, 96).

167. Kant cited in Hawthorn (1976, 28). Schneewind (1998, 487 ff.) effectively glosses what is known about Kant's relation to Rousseau in the context of a reading of the broader history of early modern ethics in the retrospective light of Kant's moral theory.

168. Dérathé (1948, 188).

169. Philonenko (1984, volume II, 270).

170. I identify this perspective as rhetorical in §5 above.

171. This distinction reflects a much longer and deeper divide between rhetoric—from which sociology properly understood is derived—and philosophy.

172. The former will not make sense unless one keeps clearly in mind the difference between *amour-propre* and *amour de soi-même*.

173. When Rousseau writes lines like *l'amour de soi-même* is "the source of our passions" (OC IV.491) it may seem as though the pair *l'amour de soi-même/perfectibilité* is analogous to passion/reason; in fact the former allows a more precise and more basic account of the "motors" of social evolution, and it is articulated in a different way from the latter. Where some, like Kant, thought that Will is the gravity of the human world, others, like d'Holbach (1770, 49) compared *amour de soi* with Newton's "force of inertia."

174. See the next section for more on this point.

175. I paraphrase from Foucault (1976).

176. The relationship between these patterns and eventual theories of evolution, both in traditions of social and political thought and in common sense, is a topic of high importance for understanding what remains alive in Rousseau's writings for a contemporary reader.

177. Cf. note 51 *supra* and more broadly l'Aminot (1992).

178. In the end, Émile becomes a citizen, not a tutor, and certainly not Rousseau.

179. From another angle, a critique of "natural religion" is implicit in the rhetorical form chosen by Rousseau—a *profession de foi*. Ehrard (1994, 419–44) makes clear that much of the competition between natural philosophy and theology in mid-eighteenth century operated through the distinction between faith/reason and was manifest in the different commitments of *loi naturelle* and *loi révélée*. These points become important later in this book.

180. On the historical identity of the concepts "polity" and "civil society," and the transformation of the latter to its distinctly modern sense around the end of the eighteenth century, see Colas (1997).

181. Of course there were older applications of the theories of contract and contracting to political situations; I am suggesting only that the context for such usage, which included transformations in the juridical concepts of contract and law themselves, was taking a new and different shape by Rousseau's time, and that this specific difference was exploited by Rousseau; cf. Meyers (2008b) for a preliminary summary of my research on this point.

182. This synthetic and paradigmatic statement connecting Freedom and the Will is from Kant's (1910, III, B476) *Kritik der reinen Vernunft: "das Vermögen, einen Zustand von selbst anzufangen . . . dem Menschen ein Vermögen beiwohnt, sich, unabhängig von der Nötigung durch sinnliche Antriebe, von selbst zu bestimmen."* On the New Model Will more generally, see fragments in Meyers (1989), Meyers (1995), Meyers (2008b), and Meyers (2013c). I plan, eventually, to publish a history of this crucial conceptual change in modernity.

183. With each occurrence of the word *contract* it is important to remember that for early eighteenth-century readers an inevitable ambiguity would appear between a strict, formalist, juridical sense (connoting *pactum*) and a broadly cultural sense (connoting *contrahere res*). The former is immediately compatible with the New Model Will, the latter is not; cf. Meyers (2008b).

184. N.b. the literal French sense of *informe* as "formlessness." Bataille (1929) hints at the significance of this notion for the logic of forms; for developments of this line of thought see Bois and Krauss (1997) and the especially perspicacious Rentzou (2002) and Rentzou (2010, 309 ff.).

185. There is deep irony in the trope of the "social contract" that it forced writers to make explicit the domain of nostalgia, the "state of nature," to be rejected and thus to make it increasingly attractive. With the growth of the New Model Will, another image of rupture without regret would come to the foreground in the generations after Rousseau under the sign of "industrial progress" and "modernization." This image was eventually figured—in ways too complex to mention here—as an antithesis to Will. It was represented as a blind "social structure," advancing with a logic of its own. On the one hand, it was exactly Rousseau's theodicy and his sociological conclusion that opened this possibility. On the other hand, the painful loss of control famously expressed by Marx (1852/1972, §1: "Mankind makes its own history, but not just as we want it, not under conditions we choose ourselves but rather under circumstances immediately found, given, and handed down to us; the tradition of all dead generations weighs on the brain of the living like a nightmare [*Die Menschen machen ihre eigene Geschichte, aber sie machen sie nicht aus freien Stücken, nicht unter selbstgewählten, sondern unter unmittelbar vorgefundenen, gegebenen und überlieferten Umständen]*"), a pain perversely amplified by the expectations of the New Model Will itself, and combined with the multiplication of human incapacities inherent in modernity (another of Rousseau's discoveries!), led by mid-nineteenth century to a new pastoral nostalgia. In what was then becoming the tradition of political sociology this took the symbolic form of *Gemeinschaft*, or "community." It was not coincidental that the defining opposite of this newly prominent term was *Gesellschaft*, or "society" in the sense that had been discovered by Rousseau a century before. Another similar parallel is also noteworthy: in the central contemporary sociological dichotomy agent/structure, exactly what is absent from the totality is Will—this was, of course, Rousseau's point about the social object identified by his theodicy and the reason he cast the solution to the problem of social evil in terms of Will.

186. OC III.378. It should be noted here that while the "transformation" just cited is often

taken as identical with the formation of the *"corps politique,"* these are two different (if ultimately related) processes.

187. See the last paragraph of Part One of the *Discours sur . . . l'inégalité,* which poses and complicates the methodological question in roughly these terms (at OC III.162–63). In a passage filled with ironic twists and turns, Rousseau sets up this relationship in another way, writing that "when one wants to refer to the land of chimeras, one mentions the education proposed by Plato. Had Lycurgus merely written his idea, I would find it very much more vain and fruitless. [But Lycurgus was a man of action, and so where] Plato only managed to refine Man's heart, Lycurgus 'denatured' Man, brought him out of nature," and "good social institutions are those that best know how to [do this]" (OC IV.250, 249). Likewise, his famous comment at the beginning of the *Discours sur . . . l'inégalité:* "Let us therefore begin by setting aside all the facts, for they do not in the least bear on the question" (OC III.132).

188. This is why Hegel believed that, when nothing remains to human action, we will have reached the "end of history."

189. There is another reason that is more directly topical in the rhetorical sense: the figure of "contract" was widely distributed in the transnational literary realm. The extent to which this topical distribution indicated a conceptual overlap or consensus has been greatly exaggerated by studies in political theory which ignore specific linguistic contexts.

190. On Rousseau against Hobbes, cf. for example Diderot on *"Hobbisme"* (1765) in Diderot and d'Alembert (1751–72, VIII, 240–41), who writes that "the philosophy of M. Rousseau of Geneva is nearly the inverse of that of Hobbes." Whether or not Hobbes's mechanistic assertions should be taken *au premier degré* is a question too large to be considered here.

191. The exact status of the section of *Émile* entitled the *"Profession de foi du vicaire savoyard"* — OC IV.558–635 (including the preamble) — is the object of long-standing controversy. For my purposes here, it is sufficient that Rousseau confirms that the voice of the Savoyard Vicar is his own in the *"Troisième promenade"* of *Les rêveries du promeneur solitaire,* at OC I.1018. This is likewise suggested by the treatment of the *"Profession"* in the first of the *Lettres écrites de la montagne,* at OC III.694 ff. I do not mean by this, however, that it is in some narrow sense a sufficient representations of Rousseau's theological commitments.

192. Cassirer (1932/1963, 99).

193. On the combination of theology, the new science, and humanist tendencies in constructivist ethics following Descartes, cf. Lachterman (1989).

194. Anti-Cartesian tropes appear with regularity, e.g., OC IV.570 ff., where the *"vicaire savoyard"* lurches forward this way: "I exist and I have senses by which I am affected. There is the first truth that strikes me, and to which I am forced to acquiesce [*J'existe et j'ai des sens par lesquels je suis affecté. Voilà la prémiére vérité qui me frape, et à laquelle je suis forcé d'acquiescer*]." Cf. note 208 below.

195. I assert this here without commitment to a particular version of the concept of the Will; while this problem is beyond the scope of this book, I return to it briefly toward the end.

196. Many casual readers of Rousseau would be surprised by the priority he occasionally

gives to reason; one remarkable example may be found in the first chapter of the *Traité de sphére*, OC V.585.

197. DeMan (1979, 229).

198. Nor is he in agreement with Diderot's account of the *volonté générale*, in which the conception of Will resonates strongly with what Kant would later develop. Cf. Diderot's entry "Droit naturel" in the *Encyclopédie*, in Diderot and d'Alembert (1751–72, V, 115). Jonathan Israel has stressed the difference between Diderot's and Rousseau's versions of the *Volonté générale*; see e.g. Israel (2010, 149–50).

199. There is a major exception to this which represents the great failure of Rousseau's sociological perspective and it will be considered in detail in the last part of this book.

200. Cf. the line from Kant at note 182 above. As suggested just below, Rousseau prompts the analogy with Descartes because he, like all his contemporaries, is thoroughly entangled in the terms propagated by Descartes; how he plays with these terms in the "*Profession de foi*" is suggested by the increased frequency (about 50 percent) of his already frequent use of the logical "*donc . . .*" as in the immortal phrase "*je pense, donc je suis*" from the *Discours de la méthode* (1637, quatrième partie); of course, there are also other sources for such usage.

201. Aristotle, *Nicomachean Ethics* (book III.ii, 1111b1–10); cultivation and the complexity of human interaction with language raise προαίρεσις above the field defined by the voluntary [ἑκουσίου] and the involuntary [ἀκουσίου] as spelled out in book III.i.

202. That is, this may be an *interrogatio* or ἐρῶτημα—the so-called "rhetorical question." Cf. Cicero (1954, IV.XV.22).

203. DeMan (1979, 229).

204. Ibid.

205. This is confirmed, again, by Rousseau's insistence on the "*usage de liberté.*"

206. It might place him again closer to Hegel (1896, III.402, 401), who while asserting that "the principle of freedom emerged in Rousseau" and thus furnished "the transition to the Kantian philosophy" nonetheless identifies "the practical" as "the sphere of the Will" in an entirely anti-Kantian way.

207. That is, to find the natural component of compassion, one must engage in the deeply abstract type of hypothetical reasoning exemplified in the *Discours sur . . . l'inégalité*; and while *pitié* is there discovered as a primary moving force in social evolution, it is precisely in the context of that evolution—long before the emergence of full-blown moral, social, and political relationships—that compassion becomes thoroughly and indistinguishably blended into "*seconde nature.*" Thus, just as the diagnostic of political circumstances is not conducted in terms of *pitié*, the solutions proposed do not appeal to it—*au contraire*.

208. OC IV.149. Cf. above at note 194 and the discussion of "natural independence" in §4.

209. One might conceive of this as refiguration of the inherent tension—present from the "beginning," articulated in the hypothetical "state of nature"—between *pitié* and *amour de soi-même*; with the development of *raison* in nascent social interactions, *amour de soi-même* ceases to be "*un sentiment absolu*" (OC IV.494) and is transformed into social *amour-propre*; in correspondence, *pitié* is required to take on new forms; the Will becomes the center of gravity in social action in ways that were irrelevant in the "state of nature," where other primary forces were more powerful and cir-

cumstances different. The most important circumstantial change is the exponential increase in the construction of needs through social interaction.

210. Cf., e.g., *Rousseau juge de Jean-Jacques* in OC I.657–992.

211. All unattributed quotes for the following paragraphs are from OC IV.966–67.

212. No recent writer has made more suggestive amplifications of this distinction than Hannah Arendt; cf., e.g., fragments collected in Arendt (2003).

213. Was this a tip of the hat to Leibniz? The *Nouveaux essais sur l'entendement humain* was not published until 1765 but may have circulated before that.

214. Book II of the *Rhetoric* is the model for a long tradition of *traités des passions* that analyze emotion in relation to action.

215. There is also an important sense in which confession is a method or practice of justification for claims that appeal to the reader's experience and do not stand on other authority; this seems to be behind Rousseau's (OC IV.966) turn when, midway through his point-by-point refutation of Beaumont, he invokes his *"méthode ordinaire . . . de donner l'histoire de mes idées"* (as mentioned just above).

216. Plato (1925), *Statesman* at 261c.

217. N.b. the first distinction in Justinian, the section *"De statu hominum"* (at Dig. 1.5.1, from Gaius 1 inst.): *"Omne ius quo utimur vel ad personas pertinet vel ad res vel ad actiones."*

218. I pick up again here the discussion from §2 above; all unattributed quotes in the next few pages are from OC V.586. There was a long tradition of *traités* of this type, from the thirteenth century Sacrobosco and increasingly into the eighteenth century, when they seem to have become a widespread form of educational manual for students of geography. An alternative approach to Rousseau's methodological fragments may be found in Goldschmidt (1974).

219. Cf. §2 above.

220. Cf. Starobinsky (1971, 383), citing Joubert (1938, II, 729).

221. This quote from Hegel (1979, 167), which translates the manuscript of the *System der Sittlichkeit* of 1802–3, might just as well have been written by Rousseau; cf., e.g., his note in the so-called *"Fragments politiques"* at OC III.528, as follows: "Man cannot suffice unto himself; as his needs are always being reborn, they impose upon him the necessity to search outside himself for the means of their satisfaction."

222. Hegel (1833, §189 ff.).

223. In this sense Rousseau's psychology may be considered proto-Meadian, as in Mead (1934), or a version of object-relations psychology, as in, e.g., Fairbairn (1952) and Klein (1975); on Fairbairn see Grotstein and Rinsely (2000). These parallels are not essential to the argument here.

224. Cf. Durkheim (1924), who identifies with Rousseau the view that society is prior to the individual and thus a source of individuation.

225. Cf. Husserl (1960), which may or may not allow for the transformation of "intersubjectivity" over time, and Schütz (1973) and (1982) for a transformation of the concept. Another, in my view, more fruitful direction is taken by Mead (1934). I hesitate concerning Husserl because, apart from its philosophical dress, one may see his account of intersubjectivity as an interpolation of the primary rhetorical concern with *sensus communis.*

226. "Emplotment" is Aristotle's μυθος as developed by Ricoeur (1983, chapter 2).

227. In other words, viewed retrospectively it has much in common with the sensibility expressed in Hegel's *Phänomenologie des Geistes*, which was aimed against the type of transcendental argument inherent in "state of nature" theorizing to which Kant gave formal expression.

228. On this line, Rousseau seems to herald part of the argument famously made by Weber (1958), originally written in 1904–5.

229. Rousseau depends heavily on poetic and rhetorical imagination (which, despite the modern tendency to assimilate them, are not the same for him). Famously, he introduces the *Discours sur . . . l'inégalité* saying "let us therefore begin by setting aside all the facts, for they do not in the least bear on the question" (OC III.132). *Émile* is inspired in the same way; the student with that name is, after all, a fictional character, and Rousseau makes explicit that he has conceived his book in dramaturgical terms; notice, for example, how Book V begins "we here are arrived at the final act of youth, but we are not yet at the dénouement" (OC IV.692).

230. From a different angle, we see here the way that *société* becomes for Rousseau an object of scientific, rather than humanistic, inquiry.

231. Cf. above at §§2 and 8. Comparison operates at the most basic level of Rousseau's epistemology and his social ontology; recall also that *liberté* is in crucial respects reducible to "the power to compare and to judge" (OC IV.586).

232. A famous (perhaps apocryphal) story about the uneventful life of Immanuel Kant tells of the day he perturbed his neighbors by failing to go for his daily walk at the regular hour: he was caught up in reading *Émile*.

233. Cassirer (1932/1963, 96).

234. Quote from G.D.H. Cole's introduction to Rousseau (1913, viii); the most vituperative statement on Rousseau and Romanticism is Babbit (1919).

235. I have argued elsewhere that rhetoric is the original social and political science.

236. Rose (1981, 1–2).

237. Matthew 7:12, King James translation.

238. Cf. Graves (1876), Hertzler (1934), Wattles (1996); also "The Golden Rule" at Wikipedia, accessed December 15, 2009.

239. The equivalence of things in market exchange attains ethical significance only within the framework of other types of human relationships.

240. Kant (1785/1964, 97 note).

241. Cf. Ricoeur (1990a) for an argument against this claim.

242. Kant (1785/1964, 88).

243. Kant (1785/1964, 96). Continuing the legalistic metaphor (at 106), an additional formulation of the "categorical imperative" concludes that "every rational being must so act as if he were through his maxim always a law-making member in the universal kingdom of ends."

244. This path of thought is also inspired by natural philosophy and the idea that laws govern the relationships among things, but that is not essential to my point here.

245. Cassirer (1945, 287) incisively distinguishes the complex problems posed by the concept of freedom for metaphysics and politics from the relative simplicity of the concept of freedom in Kantian ethical theory.

246. Bittner (1989) shows how difficult it is to work through the structure of the "categorical imperative."

247. Ingram and Parks (2002, 142).

248. Cf. Polanyi (1944, 56 ff.) and Polanyi (1947) are suggestive concerning the way that our relations to things, and relations among things themselves, are "disembedded" from society with the creation of supposedly self-regulating market institutions.

249. As it was likewise excluded in parallel developments in law; a paradigmatic trend is the displacement of the law of nuisance by the law of neglect; cf., e.g., McLaren (1983) and more generally Horwitz (1977).

250. Cf. §2 above. In a long and easily accessible bibliography of incisive publications, Lorraine Daston has elaborated an important perspective on the historical development "facts" and "objects," as well as the relation between them and scientific activity as a moral enterprise. This remedial endeavor has been long in the making. More narrowly, cf. Daston (2000) on the emergence of objects of scientific inquiry, with the caveat that the claims made in the chapter on "society" are not supported by my research.

251. These differentiations appear as a kind of fear of things across the *tableaux* of nineteenth-century legalism, which is, by the way, the interpretive framework retrospectively applied in most readings of "contract theory" in general and Rousseau in particular ... to disastrous effect.

252. Of course, this movement had already been set in motion in the philosophical domain by Descartes and Hobbes. It was becoming the ground for the liberal doctrine of rights that would seize the imagination of the world at the end of the eighteenth century. The modern conception of dignity — where worth is inherent and therefore a justification for liberty, and political participation follows from that fact — is in some respects the exact opposite of ancient conceptions — in which political participation is "the key to the accrual of *dignitas*" which is in turn associated with *libertas*; citing here Connolly (2007, 160) on Cicero. Cf. Wirszubski (1950, 15 ff.).

253. I do not think it is unfair to characterize, for example, the position of Progressives in late-nineteenth-century America in this way, and thus to suggest that without the object "society," and the participation of sociologists, the politics of this period would have appeared in an entirely different light; cf. Haskell (1977). Of course, the historical coincidence of politics and social science in the Progressive crucible of Chicago bears this out; cf. especially Feffer (1993).

254. Cf. Cassirer (1927/1963, 123 ff.), in which the developments leading up to Hobbes are examined as "The subject-object problem in the philosophy of the renaissance."

255. For Hobbes against Aristotle, see, e.g., *De Cive* (1983, I.1.2).

256. When this kind of language is taken up by Rousseau — e.g., in *Du Contract social* at OC III.399–400 — it is with the kind of sarcasm characteristic of an aggressively confident critique. Or, it is, as Starobinski noted, with the kind of strategic indifference that characterizes Rousseau's organicist metaphors as well: the totality of society is best understood as an "*être moral.*" As for Hobbes, *nota bene* that the totality is not *society*, as it will be in Rousseau; cf. §35 below. This observation is supported by the basic insight of Colas (1997), which demonstrates that prior to the late eighteenth century, gestures to "civil society" were in fact references to the *polis*, and to political relation-

ships, rather than to the post-Rousseau sociological conception of society. Hobbes's relation to this constellation of political traditions is much more complicated than he himself makes it seem; cf., e.g., Strauss (1936/1963, 30 ff.); Arendt (1993); Meyers and Struever (2008).

257. Much of the writing by Walter Benjamin from the late 1920s on provides extraordinary insight into the phenomenon of "consumerism"; cf. Benjamin (1972–89). Arendt (1958) makes explicit the possible function of Benjamin's approach within an account of the primary conditions for a theory of politics. Campbell (1987) attempts to link the origins of consumerism to a "romantic ethic" by analogy to Weber's account of the "Protestant ethic." There is of course a vast literature on these subjects.

258. As always, medicine constituted a gray zone between "human" and "natural" sciences that were supposed to be clearly distinguishable.

259. The most important attempts to close this gap in recent sociology are Bourdieu (1987) and Giddens (1984); my own as of yet unfinished efforts on this point appear first in Meyers (1989). In certain respects and with a different vocabulary late work by Michel Foucault also moves this way. Burke (1945, chapter 1) magnificently circumvents the whole problem.

260. Later variations on Marxian themes would shift this identification from producers to consumers; cf. Baudrillard (1968) and (1972).

261. A profoundly anti-Kantian twist is given to Marx's theme of the "fetishism of commodities" when Walter Benjamin writes of the seductive and spirited little doo-dads in the shop windows of Paris. On Benjamin's contribution to a sociology in which the relationship between persons and things is essential, see Meyers (1996), Meyers (1999), Meyers (2000), and Meyers and Struever (2008).

262. The treatment of this question in anthropology has followed a somewhat different course; the development of economics also requires a different narrative, but one that ultimately reenforces what I discuss here. Note, too, that while I provide a genealogy for the prevalent trend, I recognize important exceptions like Walter Benjamin (note 261 above) and some elements of the *Collège de sociologie* (see Hollier, 1995); consider especially this tantalizing statement by Mead (1934, 154 n. 7): "It is possible for inanimate objects, no less than for other human organisms, to form parts of the generalized and organized—the completely socialized—other for any given human individual. . . ." Moreover, in the last decade or so the situation I describe in this book has begun to change. "Science studies" has done much to bring this self-evidence under a critical light; a particularly incisive and influential approach may be found in Latour (1979), (1991), and (1999b) and Latour and Weibel (2005), all works that approach the central questions of this book from a different angle. Jane Bennett—in Bennett (2001) and subsequent papers—has done much to develop Latour's themes for American political theory. Literary studies always have (sometimes hidden sometimes prominent) rhetorical/anthropological content; the recent resurgence of attention to things and especially bodies is exemplified, and some extent influenced by, Scarry (1985). Finally, impressive work by Richard Sennett overlaps many of these countertrends and in some respects offers a vision of civic sociology far beyond them; Sennett's historically-grounded and synthetic approach encompasses human relation-

ships with things, ranging from the big "thing" of the *res publica* to the localized space of the human body; themes first developed in Sennett (1977) are brought to striking fruition in Sennett (1994).

263. Vico (1709/1990) and Hume (1739).

264. OC III.474–560; Vaughan (1915, I, 281 ff.) takes these notes to be draft material for the *Institutions Politiques*, while Derathé (at OC III.1515 ff.) is, I think without justification, more skeptical. On the chronology cf. Derathé (1970, 52 ff.).

265. OC IV.842–43, Rousseau's note; cf. OC III.470.

266. Long after I identified the significance of and link between these two passages I was delighted to learn that Derathé connects them as well; cf. his note at OC III.1533–34.

267. Cf. Meyers (1989, chapter 1); see also the Afterword of this book.

268. As at this point I do not record Rousseau's usage but rather theorize from it, and I intend that theory to be general, I freely apply the word "persons" where Rousseau has written "*hommes.*" Cf. also above at note 2 of the Preface and §18 below.

269. Cassirer (1932/1963, 62).

270. The identification of a true author, or the truth of the author, with his *corpus* is expressed in Rousseau's time by Mercier (1778), who, reflecting a complete reversal of terms from the preceding century, remarks that the word "author" [*auteur*] had lost its sublime meaning with the increase of publication, and specifies valuable writing with the term "writers" [*écrivains*], among whose ranks he includes "only those who publish works of imagination or Philosophy, and who fulfill the Public's expectations by successive productions every year." On the historical emergence of "the writer," cf. Viala (1985).

271. My translation from Benjamin (1972–89, II.i, 365).

272. As I have shown elsewhere, the minuscule difference between the older French word *contract* and its modernized cousin *contrat* stands for the ambivalent emergence of the modern political world; cf. Meyers (2008b).

PART TWO

1. On the use of the term "moral" throughout this book, cf. again §5 above.

2. The "main passage" is reproduced in its entirety above in the Appendix to Part One.

3. OC IV.250. Additional influences of Plato will appear when, below, we come to the central notion of "order."

4. It is worth noting that even some of the propositions most steadfastly associated with Plato (and his account of Socrates) — such as "the unexamined life is not worth living" — remain open to successful challenge; cf. e.g., the perspicuous Goldman (2004).

5. A hundred books, no less one, would not suffice to show exactly the broader historical context of Rousseau's ideas. Thus, I limit myself to exhibiting a certain overlap between Rousseau's version of happiness and Plato's. Rousseau was not alone in taking up this tradition, nor was he the only thinker to revise or reject it in various respects. Pierre Burgelin notes that "happiness is one of the themes with which the century passionately preoccupied itself" (cf. his note 1 at OC IV.1675). Readers who want a more precise mapping of how Rousseau assimilates, inflects, or rejects the views of *bonheur* presupposed and advocated by his Francophone contemporaries are advised to take

up the powerful and detailed Mauzi (1960); McMahon (2006) offers a paler but more recent overview in English.

6. OC IV.250. Note that this maxim immediately precedes Rousseau's introduction of Plato as a paradigm. Cf. also Plato, *Statesman*: 303.

7. As if to justify his own appropriations from *The Republic* in *Émile*, Rousseau immediately adds his positive assessment that "it is the most beautiful treatise on education ever created" (OC IV.250). For a variety of reasons too complicated to develop here, I find interesting and ultimately correct Rousseau's judgment that *The Republic* is not a work of political theory; I would add that if it is one, it is so by virtue of developing an anti-political position.

8. OC III.510. This ancient conceptual wheel was rediscovered with great flourish by economists who, rethinking the problem of the welfare of society as a whole in quantitative terms, had to confront the problem of interpersonal comparison. That they had anything to rethink is often traced to Bentham's utilitarianism but seems—through that path or along side it—really to derive from Rousseau's claims about general welfare and his obscure efforts at a theory of aggregation. Cf. the key text by Arrow (1951); for some responses to this problem, see Elster and Roemer (1991).

9. Ibid. The exact meaning of this pregnant sentence cannot be developed here; in my view, however, the word "interior" is not just anaphora but meant to advance the analogy between two "moral beings," the person and the polity, and is thus a gesture toward the rhetorical notion of *sensus communis*.

10. This would count as a second reversal; the one made more explicitly in *Laws* (716c) asserts pointedly that God, not Man, is the highest measure. I suspect there is a link between these two reversals (concerning how ordered totalities stand in relation to individual human beings) but I will not pursue it here. Cf. *Theaetetus* (152), *Cratylus* (385e); Protagoras' maxim (as reported by Plato) is actually πάντων χρημάτων μέτρον ἄνθρωπον ἔιναι, i.e., it is about χρημάτα, not πράγματα.

11. Cf. Aristotle's critique at *Politics* 1276b16, which seems aimed against the Socratic teaching of the unity of virtue; thanks to Harvey Goldman for reminding me that Plato's place in this debate is more subtle.

12. It is worth noting that strategies of spatialization are not limited to the representation of ideas; to give proper order to the developing passions in the child, we are told to "extend the space during which they develop [*étendez l'espace durant lequel elles se développent*]," suggesting that the composition of the body takes place in a space external to it, and that this makes manifest the social aspect of the temporal dimension in one's character as well (i.e., it prohibits the reduction of bodily temporality to organic processes of regeneration and decay).

13. The *topos* of microcosm/macrocosm originates with Plato—*Philebus* (29)—and continues to shape theories of human affairs through Leibniz; cf. Boas (1973.III, 126 ff.) in Wiener (1973). After this, and within the compass defined in these pages, it is displaced by the structurally and gesturally similar *topos* of individual/society; again, Rousseau is largely responsible for making *société* a secularized version of the macrocosm.

14. It is worth noting that the powerful synthetic efforts of recent sociologists—like Giddens's (1984) "structuration theory"—only seemed necessary with the coincidence

of the New Model Will and the monistic theory of the social field; this occurred well after Rousseau.

15. This again is the claim by Vernant (1973), notwithstanding, e.g., Kenny (1979).

16. I shall not discuss here the complex categorical matrix that emerges in *Du Contract social* as a framework for the relationship between society and polity. It is worth noting, however, that Rousseau makes a sort of homage to Machiavelli, writing that "the entire body [of magistrates] bears the name of Prince" and refers to the collective use of that name in Venice (OC III.396). Just a handful of paragraphs later, to clarify exactly the tension considered here, Rousseau goes beyond this position to distinguish between the Prince and the Government; cf. OC III.400 for the distinction, and OC III.399, where the problem is stated.

17. We know this because, in the next paragraph, he proposes an orderly arrangement: "In a perfect type of legislation, the particular will . . . must be nothing, the corporate will . . . very much subordinate, and as a consequence the general will [must] . . . always be dominant" (OC III.401).

18. OC IV.814. This kind of moral contradiction is discussed in Hirschman (1977).

19. Ibid. "*Sensible*" ["sensate"] describes the condition into which we are born, and thus our natural condition; cf. also OC IV.248.

20. Ibid. He poses the same question, almost verbatim, in the fragment "*Du bonheur public*" (OC III.510) and develops his answer again at length there, although with a different tone.

21. OC III.510; cf. OC IV.304, cited below. Cf. on this point Plato's *Gorgias* (495 ff.).

22. OC IV.303. Given that the two are ultimately connected, it is not surprising that Rousseau makes a similar point concerning "good government" in *Du Contract social*, book III, chapter 9: "As moral quantities lack precise measure, . . . when you ask which is absolutely the best government, you ask an unsolvable—because indeterminate—question" (OC III.419).

23. Cf. similar assertions, such as "the desire to command is not extinguished with the need that gave birth to it" (OC IV.289).

24. Cf. OC IV.288–89 *et passim*.

25. Cf., e.g., OC IV.289: "empire [here meaning the successful bossiness of a child over the adults around him] awakens and flatters *amour-propre*, and habit strengthens it."

26. In the *Discours . . . sur l'inégalité* these are the basic forces by which the evolution of society is driven. Elsewhere, Rousseau refers to *amour de soi* as a "primitive passsion, innate" (OC IV.491), but this may too much diminish the difference between it and the culturally constructed passions that follow, and it cannot refer to the *volonté*. Moreover, in *Émile*, *pitié* is a later development, even if it is born "according to the order of nature" (OC IV.505). My hesitation here is amplified by comments like "the passions, in turn, draw their origin from our needs" (OC III.143).

27. OC IV.284. This applies likewise to the "beginning" of the species; cf. OC III.158. N.b. that the image of latent, unawakened imagination occurs frequently in *Émile*. The related faculty of curiosity is another of those "*naturelle à l'homme*" which only come into play later in life; cf. OC IV.429.

28. Cf. for example OC III.152, where Rousseau says that passions and faculties remain latent ("*en puissance*") until one has "occasions to use them."

29. OC IV.407; but n.b. that human nature itself is transformed through social evolution, and this is not simply the accretion of habit on top of it.

30. Cf., e.g., where in *Rousseau juge de Jean-Jacques* (OC I.935) he writes: "But human nature does not run backward, and one never turns back toward the time of innocence and equality once one has moved far from it; this again is one of the principles on which [Rousseau himself] insisted most."

31. OC IV.289–90; *n.b.* the word "prejudice [*préjugé*]" here does not carry the negative connotation of contemporary English. It is literally a "prior judgment," roughly analogous with the German *Vorurteil*, and should be understood as the substance of *sensus communis*, and thus akin to *opinion*.

32. OC IV.290. Here is another overlap, since, obviously, *besoins* are justified.

33. OC IV.429; cf. in the *Discours sur . . . l'inégalité* (OC III.166) where the discovery of this principle—"love of well-being is the only motive of human actions"—plays a role in the development of self-consciousness and society; this does not mean that human beings always follow this principle (OC III.141). Thus, Starobinski may be too hasty in identifying this Platonic idea with Rousseau's conception of *amour de soi-même*.

34. There is less ambiguity with respect to *the idea of* (rather than *the fact of*) both *désirs* and *besoins*, which, in Rousseau's earlier view, arise in society and are, by imagination, "transported to the state of nature" (OC III.132).

35. Appendix to Part One, above; all lines without citation below are drawn from this "main passage."

36. Rousseau makes a pun here, as the verb also means "to train" or "to submit to a discipline."

37. Strictly speaking, this should be stated in the past tense, as the "state of nature" has long since ceased to be an option for mankind. This is complicated however by Rousseau's belief that social evolution is in fact a transformation of nature itself. We will return to these issues in Part Three, especially §§43–45 below.

38. *Émile* contains 1,359 occurrences.

39. E.g., OC IV.489.

40. Cited in Société Jean-Jacques Rousseau (1905, volume 1, 204–5).

41. However it may be that in Rousseau's "state of nature" the equality of men and women ends with the beginning of sexual intercourse, it must also be kept in mind that in fact heterosexually gendered sexual intercourse is entirely imbricated within and inflected by the characters and relationships of society; cf. the interesting discussion of this in Wingrove (2000, 63 ff.) and, on the relation between equality and sexual intercourse, Wingrove (2000, 157) and Pateman (1988, 96 ff.). Thus, when Rousseau adds here in a voice directly adopted from his Pascalian identification of nature as first habit and habit as second nature—cf. Pascal (1954, 1121) *Pensées* (120 [195])—that "we are, so to speak, born twice: once to exist, the other to live; once for the species and the other for the sex" (OC IV.489), he is guided by an evolutionary image that radically complicates the idea of nature and its relation to human beings in society. The discussion in Part Three below bears on all of this.

42. OC IV.692; from a strikingly similar line—"the fatherland shows itself as the common

mother of citizens [*la patrie se montre donc la mere commune des citoyens*]" (OC III.258)—Wingrove (2000, 155) brings to light the analogous equation of genders at the level of politics.

43. Description from Cranston (1997, 120).

44. Description from Damrosch (2005, 372).

45. Once we have analyzed the basic types of dependence and their moral weight, it would be worth sorting out how these various types are gendered, both in Rousseau's overall argument and in our experience. Such an inquiry, which is far beyond the scope of this book, would have to be preceded by additional theoretical work to discover the proper categories through which to undertake that "sorting out." Noteworthy efforts which initiated this kind of research include Okin (1979), Elshtain (1981), Pateman (1988, 96 ff.). This enterprise, at least with respect to Rousseau, is not as straightforward as it may at first seem. Of three classical "objects" of domination—women, slaves, and children—Rousseau makes central and visible theoretical use of the latter two. Whatever conclusions one were to eventually draw, one would have to take into account the complex question of the symbolic register within which references to "women" are made; cf. Zerilli (1994); the most sophisticated effort that I am aware of is by Wingrove (2000). An alternative research program asserts that to speak in terms of dependence is of itself to speak of women and the feminine. This argument has feminist and antifeminist versions. Even in its most cautious contemporary manifestations, I do not believe it illuminates the questions we have raised in this book; cf. Gilligan (1982), Tronto (1993), Meyers (1992), Meyers (1998). I underscore that part of the interest of Rousseau's account of dependence is that he, sensibly, believed no such thing, and that is why we may continue the discussion in the text without specific reference to gender.

46. This pragmatic and ultimately political account of happiness does not exclude the Platonic approach mentioned above. An approximation between the two models is made in *Émile* at OC IV.304.

47. He makes this perfectly clear by assessing how others have deployed this *topos*; cf. references to the Abbé de Saint-Pierre and Hobbes at OC IV.288.

48. Cf. §§5, 15, 16 above.

49. OC IV.249. N.b. that in the next section this provisional distinction between the psychological and the practical is not sustained. On Rousseau's use of mathematical language, cf. Françon (1949); it is noteworthy for several reasons that this article was reprinted in a thematic issue of the Lacanian journal *Cahiers pour l'analyse* (no. 8, 1972) on "*L'impensé de Jean-Jacques Rousseau.*"

50. Part of the difficulty in choosing the most appropriate path of interpretation derives from Rousseau's complex use of psychological notions that stem from rhetorical traditions, are inflected by his emerging sociology, and appear obscure for the modern reader accustomed to the disciplinary discourses of psychology of the nineteenth or twentieth century. Rousseau contributes to this confusion in a way that bears on the major topic of this book in passages—e.g., at OC IV.304, "[Man] is never less miserable than when he seems deprived of everything; for misery does not consist in having ones things taken away, but in the need that makes itself felt as a result"—where the

relation to *things* seems entirely psychological. While consistent with his conclusions concerning the moral status of *things*, it misrepresents Rousseau's psychological theory.

51. While Rousseau writes (OC IV.304) that "a sensate being whose faculties and desires were equal would be an absolutely happy being," elsewhere he allows for the possibility that one might be happy even if one's *forces* were greater than, and not simply equal to, one's *besoins*.

52. OC III.281–82 and 289. These passages are conspicuously absent from the final version.

53. OC IV.466. This picks up a thread first laid down in §3 above.

54. As far as I am aware, the only other scholar to have successfully thematized this simple ratio is David Gauthier, who applies a version of it in "The Politics of Redemption" in Gauthier (1990, 77–109) and again in Gauthier (2006, 27 ff.). However, by attempting to connect the ratio immediately to the topic of freedom, Gauthier underestimates what I take here to be the central and outstanding feature of Rousseau's innovation— the constitution of *société*—and the consequent significance of "social facts" in the way this ratio itself plays out. Gauthier also mistakes related matters, e.g., asserting (2006, 28) a third type of dependence—"on desires"— without properly understanding the foundations of the first two ("on things" and "on persons"). Although Gauthier claims that "the role of dependence on desires is clear in the *Social Contract*" and points to OC III.365, Rousseau does not use the word there; Gauthier's reading is only plausible if the identity of the ratio *forces/besoins* with *liberté* is assumed; as I have already shown, the relation is in fact much more complex; moreover, Rousseau explicitly states on the same page that "the philosophical sense of the word *liberté*"—which is what concerns Gauthier—"is not my subject here." For this and a variety of other reasons, I believe the version of this ratio I present in this book is more precisely integrated into the interpretation of Rousseau's thought and shows more clearly its significance for social and political theory. The larger arguments I intend to advance by reading Rousseau this way are quite different from Gauthier's; cf., e.g., Meyers (1989).

55. The discussion of the social field in this book is prerequisite to correct interpretation of Rousseau's infamous claim about "forcing . . . whoever refuses to obey the general will . . . to be free" (OC III.364), which ultimately resolves into the total *fait social* constituted by speech and action within the multiple overlapping temporalities of human existence.

56. Thus Rousseau avows with Saint Paul (Romans 13.1: *non est enim potestas nisi a Deo*) that "all power [*puissance*] comes from God" but sets this aside as irrelevant to his political sociology. Nonetheless, as the theological side of these questions inevitably enters in Rousseau's thinking, it will enter later in this book.

57. Although cf. §44 below.

58. OC III.364; cf. note 55 above. In general, see the "main passage" at OC IV.311. We shall have quite a bit more to say in Part Three below about what counts as nature and how much necessity this entails.

59. Cf., e.g., OC III.375.

60. Likewise, *puissance* is not violence; cf. the peculiar statement (at OC III.391) — *"quant à la puissance, elle soit au dessous de toute violence* [as concerning *puissance*, it is beneath all violence]" which seems to invert in a Clausewitzian way the familiar hierarchy between violence and other human capacities.

61. Cf. OC III.357 and 362. The schematic presentation of political bodies that includes *puissance* is carried over in close paraphrase in *Émile*: "This public person generally takes the name of 'political body,' which its members call 'state' when it is passive, 'sovereign' when it is active, '*puissance*' when comparing it to similar entities."

62. A survey of usage of the word *pouvoir* in *Du Contract social* and the *Discours sur . . . l'inégalité* reveals its primary affiliation with political agents, and with the notion of *souveraineté* in particular. This suggests that even where its use is more complex (e.g., in *Émile*) the word *pouvoir* should be read metonymically or metaphorically as a gesture to political experience. All these δυνάμεις are related within changing phases of action, which can be understood in terms of the structured composition and decomposition of action itself. That is, *pouvoir* appears in triadic relationships but typically involves an effort to align several *forces* into one (cf. OC III.375); there, we may read of *executifs* or *legislatifs pouvoirs*. Outside this composition — for example, where civil society is conceived as a body, its different members (*legislatifs* or *executifs*) have specific "organic" faculties which are *puissances* (cf. OC III.395). Absent conflict or purpose, even the *pouvoir souverain* reverts to *puissance*; this is possible because the *force* "the people" exerts over itself is not a relation of domination (cf. OC III.362–64).

63. For unexpected reasons, this is a point of convergence with such radically different and divergent thinkers as Hobbes and Hume.

64. This is, of course, the terminology of Durkheim. More precisely, *pouvoir* — and, indeed, practically all δυνάμεις relevant to the personal problem of *bonheur* and the political problem of *bon ordre* — may be said to always arise within the "division of action." Cf. Meyers (2013a, forthcoming) for a preliminary account of this sociological concept and Meyers (2008a) for an application thereof.

65. Combining OC III.372 and 375.

66. The title of part II, chapter IV, of *Du Contract social*; OC III.372.

67. Read this here as both "things that are good" and "property" in the sense of "goods" that belong to one.

68. General point at OC III.375; last quote from "main passage." Cf. OC IV.309, where Rousseau writes that "the first of all goods is liberty."

69. OC IV.308. It should be acknowledged here that the word *forces* is followed in this sentence by the adjective *naturelles*. Even a cursory examination of the page makes clear that this is reference neither to a "state of nature" nor to the pure being issued from natality; even in the second book of *Émile*, where the topic is formation of a child rather than an infant, Rousseau addresses an imagined *homme* threatened by quintessentially social dangers ("*esclavage, illusion, prestige*") which undermine power and liberty precisely in the aspiration toward domination. Here Rousseau's proto-Hegelian twist ("in order to guide them as it pleases you, you must conduct yourself as it pleases them") joins his deeply social-evolutionary view of what *forces* count as *naturelles*, as the development of new ones enter into our *seconde nature*.

70. On the triadic structure of the political, see a provisional account in Meyers (2013a, forthcoming) and my forthcoming work on power under the title *Dancing on a Landslide*.

71. The concept of the "division of action" is sketched in Meyers (2013a, forthcoming) and illustrated in Meyers (2008a).

72. This paraphrases loosely the last sentence of the "main passage."

73. That the "*pacte social*" and the "*contract social*" are not the same is a fact that none of Rousseau's interpreters have properly understood and which I demonstrate elsewhere; cf. Meyers (2008b).

74. *Order* in the verbal sense.

75. See the discussion of *moeurs* and *habitudes*, and especially the explication of this bit of text, in §5 above.

76. This is not to be confused with the much narrower phenomenon of interpersonal deliberation that has drawn so much attention in contemporary political theory; cf. Meyers (2013a, forthcoming, part three).

77. This is one reason why Rousseau insists that "civil religion" and its rituals are important in a well-ordered republic.

78. This trope refers back to Cicero's (1972, IX) magnificent oration *Pro Cluentio* (§146): "you must inevitably grant to me that it is a much more scandalous thing that the laws should be departed from in that state which is entirely held together by the laws; for this is the bond of this dignity which we enjoy in the republic, this is the foundation of our liberty, this is the source of justice. The mind, and spirit, and wisdom, and intentions of the city are all situated in the laws. As our bodies cannot, if deprived of the mind, so the state, if deprived of law, cannot use its separate parts, which are to it as its sinews, its blood, and its limbs. The ministers of the law are the magistrates; the interpreters of the law are the judges; lastly, we are all servants of the laws, for the very purpose of being able to be freemen." Rousseau riffs on the maxim "we are servants of the law so we can be free [*legum servi sumus ut liberi esse possimus*]" generally when he writes "One is free insofar as submitted to laws [*on est libre quoique soumis aux loix*]" (OC III.492) and specifically in an anecdote about the word *libertas* written in a prison in Genoa (OC III.440 note). The assimilation of *lois* and *moeurs* is likewise Ciceronian in a way that the generation immediately before Rousseau understood perfectly well: Montesquieu (1748, book XI, chapter 2) attributes the rule of law to Cicero; Vico (2000, 128) asserts Cicero's maxim and then inverts it to drive home the point as "we become subject by nature if we free ourselves from laws [*natura servi efficimur si legibus liberemur*]." Note that when Rousseau does *not* accept Cicero's authority, he is careful to excuse himself; e.g. OC III.452. Generally on Roman *libertas* cf. Wirszubski (1950, chapter 1.1).

79. Just how far *opinion* is understood by Rousseau as at once fundamental law and *force publique* is made clear in *Du Contract social* (OC III.458) when he writes that "public opinion is the species of law for which the Censor is the Minister, and that he can bring to bear in particular cases."

80. I mean this in a sense illuminated by Mead (1934 and 1938).

81. That is, characterized by reflexes; I do not mean here the complex set of reversals in-

volved in *reflexive* sociology of the sort undertaken by Bourdieu; cf. Bourdieu (1987), Bourdieu and Wacquant (1992), Calhoun et al. (1993).

82. For the battalion to move with devastating efficacy against an enemy position, every soldier's actions must be perfectly coordinated with the others; contingency and latitude are part of that coordination.

83. While this perspective is consistent with recent efforts in the theory of action—cf., e.g., the synthesis accomplished by Thévenot (2006)—it occasionally appears with great clarity in thinkers who precede Rousseau's theodicy (and thus are not impelled by their presuppositions to make Man the origin of all powers) and who precede the consolidation of the New Model Will (and thus do not need to locate human power in a single, God-like faculty); Machiavelli's dialectic of *virtú* and *fortuna* is an example.

84. Cf. Meyers (1989).

85. The common idea that Rousseau is not a systematic thinker—which he himself propagated—is a great myth that stands in the way of our understanding what he wrote.

86. One should, of course, keep in mind here the terminological proximity (but not identity) of the political and the social for Rousseau. Cf. Colas (1997) for a general discussion of the transformation of the related notion of "civil society."

87. The juxtaposition and difference is explicit at OC III.375.

88. That is, *dépendance des choses* is not supposed to have any moral weight.

89. This point overlaps to some extent with the distinction between the totality of society, which is essentially plural, and cannot even be conceived of as having one Will, and the *corps politique*, which is contingently and unfortunately plural, and thus the object of the dream of a *volonté générale*.

90. See again §5 above on the capaciousness of this concept in Rousseau's writings.

91. Following a vast tradition arising from Aristotle and developed recently in, e.g., Dumouchel (1995), cf. Meyers (2007) and Meyers and Struever (2008) on the significance of "rhetorical psychology."

92. An interesting twist occurs when Rousseau compares (at OC IV.249) the unity of "natural" and "civil" man, showing that different types of unity are possible, one absolute and one relative, and that the question of the unity of the "self" is prior to and distinct from the question of *bonheur*, and even prior to the hypothetical distinction between nature and culture. This undermines the arguments of those who place "authenticity" at the center of Rousseau's thought; it is consistent with my claim that Rousseau has, and must have, a theory of social evolution.

93. Again, the notion (at OC IV.251) that "by removing man's contradictions one would remove a large obstacle to his happiness" stands in the background.

94. Cf. *Du Contract social* at OC III.365. While beyond the scope of our discussion here, it should be said that Rousseau's evolutionary view problematizes any easy distinction between nature and culture/society/morality; at every moment in the development of society human nature is both new and the product of human activity. This was, of course, the conclusion Marx drew from Rousseau.

95. It is worth noting that when Hegel picks up the problem of dependence, in large mea-

sure adopting it from Rousseau, he distinguishes sharply among the relevant terms—*Kraft, Macht, Herrschaft*—in a manner that bears comparison with Rousseau. Cf. Meyers (1989, chapter 3).

96. Cf. §14 above.

97. There may be other limits on the application of the formula. I shall not consider them here.

98. OC IV.504. On "natural" *versus* "social" suffering, see §5 above.

99. Although Arendt (1963) finds Rousseau at the source of a distinctive modern politics of *pitié*, it may be worth noting that Bentham, by reducing (through the vocabulary of "pain" and "pleasure") suffering to its natural components, pushes this line even further; for him the ethical question to ask about all living creatures becomes "not, Can they *reason?* nor, Can they *talk?* but, Can they *suffer?*" Bentham (1789, chapter 17, §1, IV, note).

100. One might say, since *liberté* is reducible to the "capacity to compare and to judge [*pouvoir de comparer et de juger*]" (OC IV.586), as is the "understanding [*entendement*]" and the capacity to "think [*penser*]" (e.g. "To think . . . that is to see some objects and compare them [*Penser . . . c'est voir des objets et les comparer*]" OC V.585), and Rousseau's method is centered by operations of comparison, that the well-defined individual in society (a citizen) pursues the type of inquiry Rousseau himself pursues (civic inquiry).

101. Boas (1966) identified Rousseau as the origin of the modern idea of childhood; Ariès (1960) disagrees.

102. That "the child" and "childhood" are, for the Rousseau who abandoned his children, more emblems than representations should come as no surprise.

103. Thanks to Dr. E. Rentzou who reminded me of this figure; taken as a theoretical rather than a strictly grammatical gesture, it uses one word to open a bridge between two discourses, like a pun. Puttenham (1589/1970) also refers to syllepsis as "the double supply," echoing Erasmus (1513) *De duplici copia, verborum ac rerum*. Morgenstern (1996, 5 *et passim*) effectively thematizes the "ambiguity" to which I give this formal codification as an essential feature of Rousseau's attempt to "acknowledge . . . and deal with . . . the complexity of life."

104. This approach puts me fundamentally at odds with what I would refer to as philosophically motivated readings of Rousseau, which are oriented by an interest in arriving at one true reading and, as a matter of interpretation, seek conformance with a principle of "noncontradiction." An often brilliant and incisive critical study like Goldschmidt (1974) is ultimately misguided in this way. One could say the same about Cassirer's efforts from half a century earlier.

105. OC IV.252. This is consistent with what I have already said about the metonymical approach Rousseau borrows from Plato, his use of the *topos* macrocosm/microcosm, and remarkable statements like "*la femme est homme*" (cf. §18).

106. Sometimes, too, "child" is syllepsis–like the word "*homme*"—both denying and creating subtextual relationships between "girl" and "boy"; cf. OC IV.489, where we learn that a "child" cannot be a "child" forever.

107. Kant (1991, 54). Kant (1996, 94–95) seems also to have understood Rousseau's recognition of the limits of happiness as a political measure.

108. Cf. §7 above. That pleasure is hardly a Freudian invention. Rousseau was an avid reader of Augustine and knows inside out the magnetism of *libido dominandi*. Indeed, he sees it as essential to, and perhaps even beneficial for, political life; e.g., *Du Contract social* (book I, chapter 2) where he writes that "[i]n the political state the pleasure of commanding takes the place of that pleasure [the love a father has for his family] that the leader does not have for his peoples." Cf. W. Benjamin's reflections on the pointless manifestation of force in *Kritik der Gewalt* in (1972–89).

109. OC IV.307. Burgelin—at OC IV.1337, note 1—underscores the importance of the passage from OC IV.301 quoted in §20 above for the definition of happiness because it adds the element of memory, and thus temporality; cf. also OC IV.590–91. One might add that *"prévoyante"* is the adjective Rousseau uses to qualify the word *"mère"* on the first page of the book: should we say that he seeks the quality or the bearer of the quality?

110. We exclude for the moment the Platonic metonymy but will return to it later.

111. This is why I referred to it as a social and rhetorical psychology above; this merits comparison with developments in psychology that pass through George Herbert Mead (1934)—such as Feffer (1982) and (1999)—and more generally with lines of thought in Fairbairn (1952), Sullivan (1953), Winnicott (1992), and others. It seems to me that much of what Wolin (2001, 350–53) sees as Tocqueville's invention of a sociological account of individualism appears already in Rousseau. Meyers (2013b, forthcoming) attempts a synthetic account of the strategic integration of individualism into American politics.

112. This distinction is introduced at §12 above.

113. Including the gradual shift from any kind of legal formalism requiring (uncertain) interpretation to the everyday dependable judgments of *moeurs, coutumes,* and *opinion.*

114. OC IV.252. Swenson (2000, chapter 3 *et passim*) nicely articulates some of the ambiguities in the word *auteur.*

115. It is not relevant here whether this person remains perfect or virtuous, although one may admit that neither author (of nature or of the book) should hope for that.

116. Recall the priority of the learning capacity at OC IV.61.

117. Indeed, for social *evolution* this faculty is even more important than *amour de soi-même*, which by itself might lead only to functional, or even happy, repetition, but not to transformation over time. N.b., however, that *perfectibilité* is a necessary but not sufficient condition for social evolution; cf. OC III.162.

118. Fuseli (1767), an early reader outside polemics around Rousseau, recognized this; Lanson (1912) identified the unity of Rousseau's thought in the formulation "How, without returning to the state of nature, without renouncing the advantages of the state of society, could civil man recuperate the goods of natural man?" in Société Jean-Jacques Rousseau (1912, volume 8, 16).

119. Cf. §§40–41 below; Gauthier (2006) also points to a third category of dependence but mistakenly identifies it as "dependence on desire."

120. The reduction of historical time to the trope of "memory" is widespread, and often refers back to Halbwachs's sophisticated Durkheimian sociology; also a subtle reader of Rousseau, in Halbwachs (1994, 107 and chapter 3 *passim*) he relates what I have called the "formula for happiness" to memory and adds, in Rousseau and Halbwachs (1943), an extraordinary commentary to a wartime edition of *Du Contract social*. In Meyers (2000) I show how the experiential simultaneity of Vico's "three ages" and the ebb and flow of *corso* and *ricorso* are essential to his conception of politics and a source for Walter Benjamin's more explicit theory of *Jetztzeit*. Some of these issues are developed at length in Ricoeur (1983–85).

121. A topical inquiry into "dependence"—providing categories for a general theory thereof—may be found in Meyers (1989, chapter 1). For additional elements of this theory, cf. Meyers (2013a, forthcoming) and my forthcoming general theory of power in *Dancing on a Landslide*.

122. OC IV.308. It is worth mentioning that Rousseau also uses the commonplace of "the family" to signify "natural dependence."

123. OC IV.710. There is a somewhat convoluted way to read this as a claim that gender itself is an artifact of society, but it would lead too far astray to pursue it here.

124. I translate just one face of the obvious and persistent syllepsis here between individual and civic life.

125. OC IV.339. The special significance of this example derives from the fact that "the cry of nature" is "the first language of man, the most universal language, the most energetic, and the only one required before it became necessary to persuade assembled plural *hommes*." Yet, it seems that even this primitive language can be *dénaturé*. Cf. OC III.148.

126. The conditions supporting this fact are sketched in §20 above. I shall conclude at the end of this book that "natural education" is a misleading phrase: Rousseau's process of instruction makes explicit the dialectical relationship between Nature and Man, and in that sense is better described as *evolutionary*, or in certain respects *ecological* education.

127. This is a plausible definition of "*dépendance des hommes*": it is "from the instant that one man had need of assistance from another" (OC III.171) that natural independence fails.

128. The sentence continues: ". . . fearful, clawing, and his weak and effeminate way of living succeds in sapping both his *force* and his courage" (OC III.139). This underscores that *force* is both the opposite of weakness and a composite, the internal structure of which we shall not address in further detail here. It also suggests what becomes explicit later in *Émile*: there is a gender dimension in *forces*. There may be, likewise, a gender dimension in *bonheur*.

129. Vico (1744/1984, §§204–10); cf. discussion in Verene (1981, chapter 3) and, especially in Mooney (1985, 227–28) and Schaeffer (1990, 88–90) who link it to rhetorical-topical thinking. The necessity and difficulties of recuperating this kind of thinking are clear from Taylor (2004) and (2007), who attempts to theorize in terms of "social imaginaries"; with greater success in this modernization of rhetorical interests, cf. Burke (1945) and Burke (1950).

130. Cf. the expansion on this in the chapter called "De l'esclavage" in *Du Contract social* at OC III.355–58.

131. OC IV.305. It is not difficult to see how this line of thinking circles back to the moral assertion that it is possible to "render a being weak by rendering it sociable" (OC III.162). To point, as I do here, to the relative weight given to the *besoins* side of the formula is not to take sides in the debate concerning the relationship of Rousseau's thought to views commonly held by the collaborators in the *Encyclopédie*. In some places—e.g., the article on "Economie politique" he published in volume 5 (1755)—he advances their vision of a kind of sociability that derives from primary needs; in other places—e.g., in the *Discours sur ... l'inégalité*—he rejects it. Cf. Derathé on this point at OC III.LXXIV. This has implications for the "late state of nature" that I shall touch on below.

132. A theme, again, picked up by Kant (1991) in "What Is Enlightenment?"

133. This is complicated in an interesting but not decisive way by Rousseau's earlier view that in the "state of nature" Man "remains always a child"; OC III.160.

134. Plato's book is entitled Πολιτεια, which actually means "constitution" or "citizenship." It comes to us through Cicero's translation as *Republic*. Fletcher (2007) is an attractive statement of questions raised by this fact.

135. OC IV.250. References to Plato in the next paragraphs also come from this page.

136. Cf. above at §15. Spink in Société Jean-Jacques Rousseau (1905–, XXXV, 98) observes that by mid-eighteenth century there had emerged a new "network of associated ideas: public education, good *moeurs*, concern for the common good, citizen virtue, love of country" and that "for many political writers these terms are synonyms."

137. Cf. above at §21, where the key figure of syllepsis is introduced.

138. Cf. OC III.162, where this way of conceiving interpersonal dependence is confirmed. Compare also *Du Contract social* at OC III.381, where mutual dependence is rationally reconstituted for political purposes. This point will become important below.

139. Reminder: I use this odd preposition for reasons given at the end of §12 above.

140. It is from this point on that the discussion of *forces* in §20 should be understood as the background for the "formula for happiness."

141. For those dedicated to the idea that Rousseau is a "naturalist," here is a good point on which to pause. In many respects he is decisively a constructivist of the sort so ably discussed by Lachterman (1989). This may make him, as Cassirer said, a Kantian *avant la lettre*. But, as he also seems to believe that all natural forces could eventually be replaced by social ones, and that this process might be rationally directed, it also makes him a precursor of Marx. Cf. *Du Contract social* at OC III.381 ff.

142. Institutional arrangements may momentarily decrease the cost of mobilizing others on one's behalf, allowing particular people to benefit; the overall balance, however, will be, in Rousseau's view, negative. Increased needs will simply be shifted to a different part of social life. In a certain sense, this is the theme later developed by Marx in the concept of "capital"; in another sense, it is treated by Durkheim in terms of "suicide" or "anomie"—which one can imagine as an extended response to Rousseau's famous question in the *Discours sur ... l'inégalité*: "I ask if anyone has ever heard tell

that a savage at large had given the slightest thought to despise life and commit suicide?" (OC III.152). One could proliferate examples from the history and present practice of sociology.

143. N.b. that here I have provisionally entered the hypothetical game of the "state of nature" and thus simplify by admitting the figures of entirely individual *forces, besoins,* and Will. In fact—in part because, as Mead so exquisitely showed, individuation is a social process—these do not exist in any simple or immediate sense.

144. Only in a very loose sense is the motive force of anxiety captured by Rousseau's image of ferocious interpersonal comparison in the *Discours sur . . . l'inégalité,* or the odd solution proposed in the *Lettre à d'Alembert:* "make it so that each person sees and loves himself in the other, so that everyone is better united" (OC V.115). Likewise, Hegel's appeal to *Anerkennung* ("recognition") as a way to domesticate this dialectic of desire does not respond to the persistent anxiety that derives from the uncertainty-with-real-stakes component in dependence. Cf. Markell (2003, especially chapter 4) for an engaging discussion of "recognition."

145. In some circumstances, Rousseau seems to treat the accumulation and use of *forces* as a "zero-sum game." Cf. *Du Contract social* at OC III. 400.

146. This explains in part its affinity with an evolutionary worldview.

147. Materials are drawn from his own article *"Économie politique"* and Diderot's *"Droit naturel,"* both published in volume 5 (1755).

148. It is of high interest that in the final version the single *convention* is made plural; cf. Meyers (2008b).

149. Not surprisingly, in book V, encompassing the politics of gender and a summary of *Du Contract social,* the ratio goes up.

150. It may also be the case that no meaningful assessment can be made directly after this or that event. I do not address—because Rousseau does not address—the issue of who is in a position to assess his own or another's happiness. A related problem is discussed in Meyers (2006).

151. N.b. that I want to maintain here the difference between "uncertain" and the two related notions of "unforeseeable" and "unknown." I also ignore probabilistic quantifications of uncertainty like insurance, markets, or outright wagers (1) because these risk-distributing instruments quantify effectively only insofar as they ignore individuals (something that would lead anyone considering happiness into absurdity, or into a hyper-Rousseauean strategy like Bentham's [1789, chapter IV] "felicific calculus"), and (2) because such quantifications only bracket uncertainty, they do not make it disappear, and thus may shift attention away from or minimize stakes which prompt anxiety in the subject.

152. As Gadamer (1975/1960, 30) makes abundantly clear, even Kant understood that no transcendent "moral law," no matter how many deductive steps it might generate, could ever overcome the need for self-adjustment through *phronesis.* In rhetorical, anti-Kantian terms, this fact identifies *decorum* as a primary rule of action; a rare insight into the broad sociological significance of *decorum* may be found in Hariman (2001); this view is also developed in Meyers (2013a forthcoming).

153. This may be one of the few obsessions from which Rousseau escaped.

154. This process could be described in Aristotelian terms, but I do not believe this would accurately reflect the development of Rousseau's thinking.

155. On the problem of formalism in civic education, cf. Meyers (2003).

156. Although Rousseau does occasionally—as in *Du Contract social*, where he says there are too many historical types of government for him to analyze and must therefore offer only general guidelines—attach himself to the anti-rhetorical tradition of "method." On this latter, cf. again Meyers (2003).

157. Cf. Meyers (2013a, forthcoming, chapter 8).

158. On this point, one would have to consider the ambiguity of *Les Confessions* as a mode of theorizing; I generally ignore this topic in this book.

159. Because a quotation and a maxim are not the same, Walter Benjamin's (1972–89, II.i, 365) observation is again *a propos* here: "The desperate first discovered in quotation the power, not to preserve, but to purify, to tear from context, to destroy; this is the only thing in which the hope still resides that something from this time and place survives—precisely because one beat it out of it."

160. Recall Aristotle's opening comment in the *Rhetoric* (1354a): "rhetoric is the complement to dialectic [Η ρητορικη εστιν αντιστροφος τη διαλεκτικη]," not its antithesis.

161. This process is manifest in all authentic political theory; it is not unique to political theory.

162. I apologize for the fact that this may describe the present book.

163. On the centrality of security, cf. *Du Contract social* at OC III.419–20. See also the set of contrasts showing the importance of certainty in *Du Contract social* at OC III.375.

164. See above §22, where we mention that Rousseau assumes that even the dependent "subject" is an otherwise perfectly formed person who would not be anxious under conditions of certainty.

165. In light of the perspective that will come to the center of our attention below, it seems as though Rousseau believes there is no naturally occurring *akrasia*, or "weakness of the Will." This introduces some interesting complications. It is also a clue to the status of the Will in Rousseau's thinking: does the appearance in society of "weakness of the Will" suggest that the Will itself is somehow a social function, a constructed rather than a natural faculty? Whatever seems implied here would, however, have to be set against the "first principle" claim (OC IV.576) cited above in §7 and developed below.

166. That is one reason why I do not make much use of *Les Confessions* in this study.

167. A particularly interesting effort in this direction is Berman (1970).

168. The figure of dependence can also be brought to bear on the "formula for happiness" from the side of the person from whom others are dependent, or at least from whom they gain something without, at that moment, creating a directly reciprocal dependence. The formula for happiness is capacious enough to explain the special sort of pleasure obtained when one can apply one's force to satisfy the needs of others. In the sixth of his *Lettres morales* [OC IV.1116], Rousseau writes: "The exercise of beneficence, of course, pumps up one's pride with an idea of superiority; one recalls all of one's acts of this type as evidence that, beyond [the satisfaction of] one's own needs one still has the *force* to attend to the needs of others. By this sense of power, one takes

more pleasure in living and one lives more happily with oneself [*l'exercice de la bien-faisance flate naturellement l'amour propre par une idée de supériorité; on s'en rappelle tous les actes comme autant de témoignages qu'au de là de ses propres besoins on a de la force encore pour soulager ceux d'autrui. Cet air de puissance fait qu'on prend plus de plaisir à exister et qu'on habite plus volontiers avec soi*]."

169. Rousseau is contradictory on this point; however, in both versions of *Du Contract social* he writes clearly that "men cannot engender new *forces*, but only unite and direct those that exist" (OC III.289, 360).

170. The "formula for happiness" allows others into the picture in various ways: if your *forces* are sufficient to your *besoins*, you can use them to satisfy others; this gives you a feeling of power or benevolence, which satisfies you as well. Cf. again the sixth of the *Lettres morales* of 1757, which are earlier versions of material that later appeared in *Émile*; cf. specifically OC IV.1116. Cf. also De Man (1979) on this point. Likewise, surplus *forces* over what is needed to be happy become motors for the development of intelligence; OC IV.359. As his student enters into later childhood, Rousseau says "we have profited from the superabundance of our *forces* over our *besoins* so as to carry ourselves out of ourselves" (OC IV.466). At the same time, however, too much *force* can also be dangerous: "It was by a wise Providence that the faculties [natural Man] had *in potentia* only developed hand in hand with occasions to exercise them, so that they were neither a superfluous burden arrived before their moment nor lagging behind the call of needs and thus useless [*Ce fut par une Providence très sage, que les facultés qu[e l'homme naturel] avoit en puissance ne devoient se développer qu'avec les occasions de les exercer, afin qu'elles ne lui fussent ni superflues et a charge avant le tems, ni tardives, et inutiles au besoin*]" (OC III.152). Likewise, if a society is to be *bien ordonnée*, "concerning power, it should be below all violence and always exercised with respect to rank and the laws, and concerning wealth, that no citizen should be sufficiently opulent to be able to buy another, and none poor enough to be constrained to sell himself [[*il faut que*], *quant à la puissance, elle soit au dessous de toute violence et ne s'exerce jamais qu'en vertu du rang et des loix, et quant à la richesse, que nul citoyen ne soit assez opulent pour en pouvoir acheter un autre, et nul assez pauvre pour être contraint de se vendre*]" [(OC III.391–92). Cf. also OC III.367, 382.

171. I note a certain skepticism concerning the prospect of capturing the rationality alluded to here in the formal terms of "rational choice theory."

172. Contemporary versions of these two perspectives may be found in Roemer (1982) and Bowles and Gintis (1986).

173. This connection enters our discussion at §17 above and continues in §§19, 21, 23.

174. For example, Miller (1984) takes this for his title.

175. Miller (1984, 174), like many others, uses this phrase closely associated with Kant; cf. Kant (2004, 590). Kant in fact distinguishes between the *Ideal* and the *regulative Principien* through which the *Ideal* gains *praktische Kraft* at Kant (1787/1910–, III 384 [B597]). In my view, both "ideals" and "principles" are either heuristic or dialogical, but not "regulative."

176. Derathé concurs that this is the topic of *Émile* in his annotations at OC III.1450. Another account of liberty is developed in Viroli (1988).

177. OC III.365; Keohane (1978) discusses Rousseau's resistance to philosophy more generally; cf. also Meyers (2010).

178. Cf. OC IV.836–87.

179. I intend here a resonance with such practices as the rhetorical use of *exempla* (which is barely comparable with the use of thin fictional "examples" in contemporary analytic philosophy) or the symbolic interactionism developed by Kenneth Burke and his followers. The basic point is, of course, developed between C. S. Peirce and John Dewey.

180. It is worth noting here that *l'usage de liberté* is a common trope; Rousseau could easily have picked it up from the discussion of the Will in popular books like Crousaz (1720, I, viii, 220).

181. See §13 above.

182. Cf. Taylor (2007) for a recent inquiry into the entanglements of modernity and secularism.

183. Alternatives here might include justice, equality, conformance to a particular doctrine, etc.

184. This is, in my view, another reason why analysis of dependence is a prior condition for consideration of "authenticity." I will not address the question here whether recognition of one's own implication in dependence is prerequisite to recognition of relations of dependence anywhere in the environment.

185. See §15 above.

186. On the dynamic refiguration of dependence through the denial of dependence as one fundamental power strategy for politics, cf. Meyers (1989), Meyers (1998), Meyers (2013b, forthcoming), and my forthcoming work on power entitled *Dancing on a Landslide*.

187. Rousseau himself has often been described as longing for the "state of nature"; although by his own measure this might account for his personal unhappiness, this view remains incorrect.

188. Of course, after Rousseau this becomes a key commonplace of western modernity.

189. One could interpret this in terms of "collective consciousness" (as with Durkheim or Halbwachs), or as a circular process of externalization and internalization in the constitution of the social (as with Hegel or Mead).

190. Cf. Colas (1997, *passim*).

191. Spink in Société Jean-Jacques Rousseau (1905–, XXXV, 93 ff.) speculates that for this reason Rousseau's educational program is as incomplete as his political theory.

192. Cf. Meyers (2013a, forthcoming, part two).

193. He seems to cite here from Bodin (1576, I.I.vi).

194. He writes as if the πόλις/cité/city could exist again at OC III.365, 372, 383, 394, 429.

195. There is one reference to Sparta, one to Venice, three to the translation of Plato's book, and one that gestures toward the Aristotelian/Polybian classification of political regimes. In *Du Contract social*, the word *république* is somewhat more prominent but never serves the specific theoretical purpose I will now discuss.

196. See, for example, the terrifying last paragraph of Book II, Chapter 11 of *Du Contract social* at OC III.393.

197. This point bears on the concept of the "general Will" in ways I shall not develop here.

198. One context for this distinction is the so-called "quarrel between the Ancients and Moderns," the political terms of which will be squarely restated in 1819 by Constant (1820). While the latter pretends Rousseau's crime against modernity is precisely to have brought into the present the ancient conception of liberty, the reader will have understood that I do not agree; Rousseau's relationship to and use of the "ancients" is much more complex. The simple fact that Rousseau proposes to constitute the *pouvoir souverain* through the rule of law makes his approach, more or less by definition, incompatible with the Athenian model. Likewise, his appeal to the Roman model is more complicated than it seems at first. In any event, the issues here are not illuminated by the contemporary reductionist gloss of these issues as "negative" *versus* "positive" liberty in and following Berlin (1969).

199. These related but not identical uses of the verb *résoudre* are drawn from *Émile*, Book IV and Book V, respectively.

200. From the Latin *rĕsolvo*, which, carrying over the primary sense of the Greek ἀναλύω, means in a range of contexts "to untie" or "to loosen." The multiple senses of the early modern French *résoudre* and *resolution* listed here can be seen in Nicot (1606), Richelet (1680), Furetière (1690), Académie (1694), Richelet (1732). The Latin example cited is from Nicot's entry *"resolution."*

201. Cf. Crombie (1953).

202. Cf., e.g., Hintikka and Remes (1974).

203. Randall (1940, 197) argues that "Zabarella makes the Avveroistic distinction between the resolutive method suitable for natural science and the 'analytic' method of mathematics." It was, presumably, the intervening Platonistic reduction by Descartes that made Newton seem so novel when he explicitly asserted (in the *Optics*) "as in Mathematics, so in Natural Philosophy;" cited here from Hintikka and Remes (1974, 105).

204. I have in mind Lachterman's (1989) account.

205. Famously among Rousseau's contemporaries, Vico (1744/1984) begins the *Scienza nuova* with a vigorously anti-Cartesian discourse on "elements," "principles," and "method," and Hume (1739) gives his masterpiece the full title *Treatise of Human Nature, being an attempt to introduce the experimental method of reasoning into moral subjects.*

206. Cf. Meyers (2007).

207. Cf. Ong (1958) and the whole extraordinary program of Ong's thinking that derived from that work.

208. Cf., e.g., Cifoletti (1992), who argues for an even stronger historical link between rhetoric and mathematics.

209. Randall (1940, 188) points out that the terms *resolutio* and *compositio* come to the Paduan school and thus to Zabarella via the *Topics* of Cicero and Boethius.

210. Cf. my sketch of this development in Meyers (2003).

211. It does not matter that he was not a skillful mathematician, just as it does not matter that his knowledge of Greek and even Latin may have been insufficient for him to notice the etymological similarities between ἀναλύω and *rĕsolvo*.

212. This is Burgelin's view at OC IV.1417–18.
213. E.g., in the Second Reply to Objections against the *Meditations*, Descartes (1964, VII, 155).
214. Cassirer (1906, 134 ff.) identified the *methodo resolutiva* as central to Galileo's thinking and traced it back to Zabarella; this view was expanded by Randall (1940) and denied by Gilbert (1963); Randall responded in Kristeller and Mahoney (1976). Wisan in Butts and Pitt (1978, 48, note 5) reasserts Gilbert's position and goes further to say that the term does not really belong to Galileo, but one can easily find it, e.g., in the *Dialogus de Systemate Mundi* (*Dialogue on the Two Great World Systems*) at Galileo (1663, 61–62): "This is what is done for the most part in the demonstrative sciences: this comes about because when the conclusion is true, one may by making use of the *Methodo resolutiva* hit upon some proposition which is already demonstrated, or arrive at some axiomatic principle [*Sic enim proceditur in plerisq; scientiis demonstrativis, idq; propterea, quia si conclusio vera est, adhibita Methodo resolutiva facile deducimur ad aliquam propositionem iam demonstratam aut ad principium per se notum*]" (Drake translation).
215. Cf. Jardine's (1974, 249–50) summary specifically on these terms; cf. in addition to Ong (1958), e.g., Rossi (1960) and Yates (1966) on connections between Method and memory practices.
216. Randall (1940, 201 and 197).
217. Russell (1983, 131 ff. and notes 411); generally on Bacon, cf. the superb Jardine (1974, 59 ff. *et passim*).
218. As Roger Cotes referred to it in the introduction to the second edition of the *Principia* (1713).
219. Some places he calls resolution the "method of the mathematicians," uses the term in the *Principia mathematica* (1687, 14), and gives the subtitle "A Treatise of Arithmetical Composition and Resolution" to his *Universal Arithmetick* (1728); by contrast, the draft of the *Optics* (1706) uses "resolution" as a term of experiment where the published version settles on "analysis." Cf. Guerlac in Wiener (1973, 378–91), Guicciardini (2009, 315 ff.).
220. On Kant, cf. Hawthorn (1976, 28). Kant thought that Rousseau's social equivalent of gravity was Will, whereas materialists like d'Holbach (1770, 49), thinking with the same analogy, came to a different conclusion: "Conservation is the end towards which all the energies, the forces, the faculties of beings seem continually directed. The *physiciens* have named this tendency or direction *gravitation sur soi*; Newton calls it the force of inertia; the moralists have called it in Man *amour de soi*." I will argue later in this book that what Rousseau discovers by analogy to gravity is *dépendance*. Throwing around the "Newton prize" was a popular pastime: somewhere Rousseau calls Plato the Newton of *droit politique*. Cf. generally Larrère in Daston and Stolleis (2006, 249 ff.). Shank (2008) shows the contested cultural significance of Newton and, in turn, enlightenment.
221. In the many responses to critics of his *Discours sur les sciences et les arts* (1750) Rousseau underscores his admiration for science while distinguishing social consequences

of the use and abuse of *savant* knowledge. In the *Nouvelle Héloïse*, Rousseau has Saint-Preux "blame savants for making their science into a kind of social money in their efforts to succeed in society, instead of preserving its status as a pure search for truth"; cited by Launay (1989, 308).

222. Goldschmidt (1974), primarily a scholar of Plato, also focuses on Rousseau's attachment to Method; however, he sees this as foundational rather than pragmatic; Goldschmidt identifies Rousseau's method with "meditation," while I see in Rousseau rhetorical-sociological analysis; this leads to a wide divergence of our critical views. We may agree that Rousseau loved science and extolled reason but the opposite view—that Rousseau was nothing but an irrational Romantic sentimentalist—had long since been debunked by 1974.

223. For comments on this point, see Meyers (2003). Vico (1709/1990) may be seen as a kind of hinge between humanistic and scientific approaches to the study of Man, and may serve as a kind of yardstick by which to assess the better-known debates that emerged in the nineteenth century after the writings of J.S. Mill (1843) and Wilhelm Dilthey (1883).

224. There is debate about if and how they are Cartesians, but I find Miel's (1969) argument against that view convincing.

225. Arnauld and Nicole (1662, 303).

226. See Arnauld and Nicole (1662, 192).

227. E.g. Arnauld and Nicole use it to identify the "analytic" method (1662, Part IV, chapter I) at the same time that they disparage it (1662, 192 ff).

228. That is, it points to the creation of new knowledge rather than to the search for *topoi* which, drawn from the reserve of the *sensus communis*, might facilitate the negotiation of relationships; in *De Inventione* Cicero says that *inventio* is "the first and most important part of rhetoric" (II.LIX.178) and "is the discovery of true or verisimilar things that render one's cause worthy of consideration" (I.VII.9, translation altered from Hubbell); for Aristotle this could be a definition of rhetoric *tout court*.

229. Cf. §2 above.

230. Cf. Gadamer (1975/1960).

231. Voltaire, smelling a move to theology, objected that this *aporia* should lead to the hypothesis of a "language instinct"; other readers, like Nicolas Beauzée (cf. his entry "*Langue*" in the *Encyclopédie*) and Joseph de Maistre, took this either to admit God's creation or to imply the failure of Rousseau's sociology. Cf. note by Starobinski at OC III.1327–38. In fact, an evolutionary or historicized view like Rousseau's can afford equal primacy to society and language without falling into either of these conceptual traps.

232. A rare development of this idea is provided by Farrell (1993).

233. This is, of course, exactly the failure I hold against Rousseau in this book. I gesture to these three categories in terms from Arendt (1958) because in distinguishing them she also—sometimes inadvertently, sometimes with intent—weaves them together. I argue for their necessary interconnection elsewhere.

234. OC IV.558–635 (including the preamble), in *Émile*, book 4.

235. On the *vicaire's* voice as Rousseau's voice, see §7 above.

236. OC IV.569. It is with respect to theological matters that Rousseau emphatically adds that "it is not for a little girl to resolve these questions" at OC IV.728.

237. This sentence is intended for my extraordinary colleague Jonathan Israel.

238. I cannot stress enough how powerful this combination is, how in Rousseau and others it served to modernize rhetoric and keep it alive, and how invisible all this has become for today's readers.

239. On Rousseau and rhetoric, aside from the clues scattered in this book, cf. Meyers (2010). The question of a direct line between Vico and Rousseau remains tantalizing but unresolved. Since 1923, when Cassirer (1953, 150) asserted that Rousseau's *Essai sur l'origine des langues* is a gloss on Vico, various affinities between these two authors have been indicated—e.g., Nicolini (1949), Mora (1976, 389), Mooney (1985, 86), Gianturco (1990, xxxix–xli)—but rarely elaborated—e.g. Said (1975, 369–71). I am not the first to speculate that Rousseau may have encountered Vico's ideas in Venice in 1743; cf. Raymond and Gagnebin in OC I.1548, note 3, who refer to Masson (1913) and Claparède (1935).

240. I analyze this fact under the term *Sprachwelt*, taking the relativistic concept of space/time as paradigm, in Meyers (1996), Meyers (1999), Meyers (2000), and Meyers (2013a, forthcoming).

241. I think this view is essentially correct, although perhaps not as expressed by Rousseau in the *Essai sur l'origines des langues*.

242. I am convinced, too, that this quotidian metaphorical or transpositional practice between language and music is also essential to Rousseau's enormous creativity, which must be understood in terms of the ongoing, synthetic, refiguration of commonplaces and their (as Ricoeur would call it) *mythos*, "*mise-en-récit*," or emplotment. Even this way of creative thinking suggests a functional overlap between notes, commonplace books, drafts, sketches, etc., as well as letters of correspondence (of which Rousseau produced enough to fill fifty volumes). Said (1975) correctly identifies combination as essential to Rousseau's creativity.

243. Vincenzo Galilei (born 1520–died 1591); cf. OC V.926 and 1048, where Rousseau refers to this Galilei in entries on "*Musique*" and "*Son*" in the *Dictionnaire de Musique*.

244. Cf. dictionary entry "*Système*" at OC V.1082; see also Rousseau's entry in the *Encyclopédie* (15:779) under the same heading.

245. This is not to be confused with the various attempts to control some or all of these relationships through highly formalized methods of composition like dodecaphony or other serialized practices.

246. Cf. dictionary entry "*Dissonnance*" at OC V.771.

247. Cf. Lowinsky (1946) for a striking, and hotly debated, argument concerning a secret program of chromaticism in the Netherlands motet, a practice that separates the function of dissonance from the creation of musical movement; the close attachment to text and chromatic "painting" undertaken by composers like Gesualdo suggest something analogous in Italian practice; with Bach, by contrast, dissonance becomes essentially a generator for harmonic movement. Many musical traditions, e.g., the ragas of

northern India, rely on tightening and relaxing tensions; dissonance as practiced from the Baroque forward is an instance of this but nonetheless a distinct practice.

248. I am paraphrasing here from Ricoeur (1975a, 32) who writes this about metaphor in a discursive-topical treatment of that subject. He speculates further that this movement may be the generative feature of language itself.

249. Cf. dictionary entry *"Système"* at OC V.1095.

250. Cf. e.g. Hammerstein (1973) in Wiener (1973, III, 267–72) for an adequate if myopic reminder of this history; on totality as a secular aspiration in music, cf., e.g., Adorno (1973).

251. This terminology is introduced in §15 above and comes to the center in Part IV below.

252. Cf. Delmore Schwartz, "In the naked bed, in Plato's cave":

> So, so,
> O son of man, the ignorant night, the travail
> Of early morning, the mystery of the beginning
> Again and again,
> while history is unforgiven."

253. I am aware of no better account of why this glimpse is sublime than Burke's (1945) discussion of the paradox of "substance."

254. Cf. Vico (1989, 43, 235), where *elocutio* is identified as the "essential nucleus" of rhetoric, including "elegance, decorum, composition."

255. Indeed, one could take this farther: picking up once again the threads of his inquiry concerning God, Rousseau in book VI of *Les Confessions* writes this remarkable passage "Mama, on this occasion, was for me much more useful than all the theologians could even have been. She, who put everything into system, did not fail to put religion there as well" (OC I.228).

256. Cf. e.g. Struever (1970).

257. Berman (1970, 79) is in many respects correct in writing that the "genial self-certainty" of Montaigne "is strikingly absent in Rousseau." Thus, again and by contrast, his confidence on this point is important.

258. This is followed by a sort of throwaway line that utterly defies interpretation: *"et il est à présumer qu'il ne naîtra jamais."* Bloom (*Emile*, English translation, p. 458), quite plausibly, renders this as "and it is to be presumed that it never will be born." One wonders why then Rousseau several months before had published a book purporting to establish just such principles? Perhaps he refers to the fact that, whether by weakness (which I doubt) or by design (which, with Spinks, I think is likely; see note above), he had concurrently abandoned his *Institutions politiques*, and now believed that only he would have been up to the task. However, it may also be that the correct rendering of *présumer* here is not "assume" but rather "presumptious," and that the sentence in English should read: "and to think that it will never be born is outlandish," or "one would have to be quite presumptuous to believe that it will never be born." There are other problems that I will not enter into here.

259. As Derathé (1970, 54) correctly asserts, the "summary" that follows in *Émile* is not of *Du Contract social*, but of the larger and unfinished project of which this was supposed to be a part.

260. A patrimony forcefully denied, for example, by d'Holbach (1773, 9 & 190) who writes

that "politics, religion, and often philosophy have given us false ideas of man" and "do not for a minute listen to a cowering philosophy that invites us to flee society." That the job is still open, however, is sustained by the pertinent genealogy offered by Colas (1997). On the related "epic tradition" in political theory, cf. Wolin (1970).

261. The "how" question was answered ten years earlier, in the *Discours sur . . . l'inégalité*.

262. I will not consider the overall strangeness of the way his project is stated here.

263. For the framing of this claim see §28 above.

264. In the unparalleled collections of the *Bibliothèque nationale de France* the only book with the word "system" in the title dated before 1600 is a forgery about freemasonry that was actually published in 1794; nonetheless, a musical/poetic sense of the word, deriving from Latin usage, is clearly older.

265. Lohr (1988, 634) in Schmitt and Skinner (1988).

266. Blair in Porter et al. (2006, 381) underscores that Zabarella and Keckermann were not bound by Aristotelian traditionalism and Ong (1958, 299) points out that Keckermann largely amplified the impact of Ramus; the quote is from Ong (1958, 299). For more on Keckermann, cf. Hotson (2007, chapter 4).

267. Literally: "circulation of the blood through the oval hole in the human fetus."

268. This list is based on a rough survey of the library catalogues of Harvard and Princeton universities and the *Bibliothèque nationale de France*.

269. But consider, too, the tangential claim of Rorty (1979) concerning "philosophy and the mirror of nature."

270. The original version of the *Dictionnaire de l'Académie française* (1694) was based on Furetière (1690); the issue in contention here was probably materialism. Cf. Ost (2008).

271. It would nonetheless be anachronistic to call Condillac a "systematic philosopher"; cf., e.g., Rorty (1979).

272. D'Holbach (1770, 41).

273. D'Holbach (1770, 1).

274. Condillac (1749, 1).

275. OC III.29.

276. At OC I.404–5, we learn that his interest in political theory dated from his time in Venice in 1743; at OC I.351 we discover that one instant in the summer of 1749 Rousseau "saw another universe and became another man."

277. That Rousseau felt the impact of Condillac's more direct uses of the word *système* is obvious, e.g., in *Du Contract social*, book II, chapter XI.

278. These few sentences might as well have been written by the founders of the Chicago school of sociology.

279. All quotes in the following discussion are from Condillac (1749, 409–19). Cf. Aarsleff's (2001) illuminating introduction.

280. On the crucial difference between the *"contract social"* and the *"pacte social"* in Rousseau, cf. Meyers (2008b).

281. E.g., Rouvrai (1641, 17), who writes "men have a similar birth, they are all equal by nature [*les hommes ont une naissance semblable, ils sont tous naturellement esgaux*]."

282. Rousseau created several codes around 1743, the period in which he first came to think

carefully about politics; OC V.553 ff. On more elaborate use of coding in *Du Contract social*, cf. Meyers (2008b).

283. Aristotle, *Nicomachean Ethics* (1168b32) and Polybius *Histories* (II.38, 6).

284. This is exactly the point on which a second generation of Rousseaueans thought his project incomplete; Hegel is the prime instance.

285. See §18 above.

286. This last phrase could also be rendered "mutually deprave one another." As I do not think the difference amounts to much in this context, I emphasize the part of the act in relation to another that one does to oneself, a trope characteristic of Rousseau's most interesting insights.

287. This distinction ultimately sustains other key distinctions, such as between "moral" and "physical." I shall not consider this here.

288. Cf., e.g., in *Du Contract social*, book I, chapters VIII & IX, and book II, chapter XI.

289. There may be an implicit connection between this usage and the phrase *état civile*, which is common in Rousseau.

290. Cf. §32 above.

291. While there is a clear link here to ontology, it is partial and provisional; we shall soon see that what counts most for Rousseau and thus for our critique of his sociology is the tension between *actus* and *status* that inheres in the concept of *ordre*.

292. Although sometimes it seems to be. Consider, e.g., at (OC III.352) where he writes that the "social order is a sacred right, which serves for the basis of all the others."

293. In another line of inquiry, I establish the connection between the complex structure of dependence and the political problem of power. The theoretical strategy in Meyers (1989) is to displace the Will from the center of thinking about power and begin, instead, from dependence. Obviously, a conception of dependence defined with respect to the Will cannot be of much service in such an inquiry.

294. As Viroli (1988, 34) writes, for Rousseau, "the real opposition occurs, on the level of theory, between the concept of the natural order and social disorder in the human world."

PART THREE

1. Essential background for this point will be found in §5 above.

2. One might note here both overlap with and divergence from Elias (1983) and Habermas (1962); this *société* is neither the court nor the salon.

3. Cf. §32 above.

4. Of hundreds of discussions of this point, Burke (1945, 24–26) is noteworthy for its brevity and precision.

5. Baker (1994, 105).

6. Baker (1994, 95–96).

7. Gordon (1994, 51).

8. Gordon (1994, 52).

9. The background for this is spelled out in Colas (1997).

10. Baker (1994, 118).
11. Cf. Gordon (1994, 53–54); cited also by Baker (1994, 97).
12. Only in correcting the final manuscript for this book did I come across Baker (1994) and Gordon (1994) and have the delightful experience of having my argument supported in this way.
13. Following are the numbers that emerge from a very rough survey of French language books by decade taken from Google Books (during the very brief period that it was open enough for this kind of research). This shows the number of times the word *société* appears in some way or another across various and repeating instances of texts; unlike the study undertaken by Gordon, this approach does not tally every instance of the word in each case, and thus one problem with it is that there is no simple way to discount repetitions of the same text; the increasing trend would perhaps be more indicative if correlated to the growth in total publication of books, perhaps even more so if the results were given not in absolute numbers but in relative percentages; in other words, the increase in use of the word *société* to some extent must reflect the increase in the overall publication of books and not a change that is in a meaningful way relative to the discursive significance of that word. Nonetheless, the trend is suggestive and supports the thesis of Baker and Gordon, and thus my thesis as well. Finally, it is important to remember that the corpus of Google Books is increasing but in an uncertain and ad hoc way; therefore, these numbers reflect one specific moment in our knowledge of these books, as of June 1, 2011:

    1550–59 = 426
    1560–69 = 488
    1570–79 = 875
    1580–89 = 1,170
    1590–99 = 1,140
    1600–1609 = 1,780
    1610–19 = 3,130
    1620–29 = 2,070
    1630–39 = 2,690
    1640–49 = 8,950
    1650–59 = 6,590
    1660–69 = 11,600
    1670–79 = 7,450
    1680–89 = 14,800
    1690–99 = 13,900
    1700–1709 = 18,000
    1710–19 = 20,600
    1720–29 = 31,100
    1730–39 = 32,300
    1740–49 = 48,900
    1750–59 = 83,200
    1760–69 = 114,000
    1770–79 = 429,000
    1780–89 = 957,000

14. This sense is Ciceronian.

15. In my view, Marshall's (1890) textbook was the pivot point in this process. Although it can be traced to Montchrestien (1615) the phrase *économie politique* is established in political theory by Rousseau in Diderot and d'Alembert (1755, 5:337–349).

16. Condillac (1776) seems to develop a systems analysis of the economy under that single term. Clues for a view of this sort in Adam Smith were spurred on in Cournot, Walras, and others as mathematical treatment of economic topics converged with micro-analysis of markets. The classic exposé of the corresponding social facts—not counting Marx—is Polanyi (1944).

17. It should be obvious that I am not saying that Rousseau was the first person ever to write the word *société* without qualification; he is, as far as I can tell, the first to use it systematically in the sociological sense described here. Evidence from polemics Rousseau wrote to defend his work suggest that he was aware of innovating in this way: in the first of the *Lettres écrites de la montagne*, Rousseau mimics his attackers—"this word *society* presents a sense a bit vague [*ce mot de Société présente un sens un peu vague*]"—to then insist that they simply do not, or pretend not to, know what he means by this key term. The claim presented in this book concerning Rousseau's originality stands against a common idea that Montesquieu did the heavy lifting in the invention of social science, or that it was someone even before him, such as the Abbé Saint-Pierre (cf. Barnes (1948, 72)), or before him Pierre Nicole (cf. Baker [1994]), etc.

18. It may be fair to say that the phrase "civil society," which rarely occurs in Rousseau, does not have at mid-eighteenth century the modern specificity it would soon acquire. This, however, leaves open the question of whether "civil society" is to be identified in general with the πόλις/city. Cf. Colas (1997, 256–62, *et passim*), who takes this as a working hypothesis to discover the various historical versions of politics which flow from it. If this identity holds, given that "civil" is the opposite of "natural," and there is no society in the "state of nature," the phrase "civil society" is pleonastic. What I observe, to the contrary, is that *societas* by itself is of limited scope and specific application; to qualify it as *civilis* is to point specifically to that sort of association which arises in the πόλις/city; that is why Cicero needs to qualify the speculative idea of general human association as *societas generi humani* (*De natura deorum*, book I, part II, IV) or *in universi generis humani societate* (*De officiis*, I.50). Neither version of *societas* is identical with the Rousseauean "social" of the nineteenth century and after.

19. Consistent with my suspicion that Rousseau is ironic here, Spink in Société Jean-Jacques Rousseau (1905–, XXXV, 100) suggests that Rousseau, who did not have a low opinion of himself, saw clearly where his thinking about politics would lead and chose not to finish the *Institutions politiques* to avoid going to prison.

20. OC III.468; these articles would provide the basis, as the chapter "De la religion civile" of *Du Contract social* suggests, from which to eject anyone "*insociable*," which is to say anyone "incapable of sincerely loving the laws and justice, and incapable of sacrificing his life to his duty if the need arises."

21. Cf. OC III.254 on the activating moral value of "humanity concentrated among co-citizens."

22. OC III.706; on the analogous problems of secular cosmopolitanism, which has allowed the idea of Europe to overcome national identities, cf. chapter 3 of *Considérations sur le gouvernement de Pologne* at OC III.960.

23. Rousseau in a letter to Usteri, July 18, 1763. Cf. also book IV, chapter 8 of *Du Contract social*, around OC III.466.

24. This occurs in book I of *Du Contract social* between the end of chapter 1 and the beginning of chapter 2, around OC III.352. His next step is to confuse the issue of nature and convention, but that is another story.

25. While not relevant here, there are, of course, other options.

26. From this point for the next few pages, roman numerals in parentheses indicate chapters in Hobbes (1651).

27. Despite the narrative-structuring *topos* of "contract"—which emphasizes the distinction between (in our terms) nature/society—it may be said that the repeated distinction between "civil war" and "civil law" is more expressive of Hobbes's overall intentions.

28. Hobbes has a narrow and traditionalist use of the word "system"—as in σύστημα—as though he had not simply translated from the Greeks but was one himself. Rousseau has a much more complex usage; cf. §32 above.

29. Cf. Colas (1997, *passim* and particularly pp. 235–43 on Leibniz's critique of Hobbes).

30. That is, the developmental scheme illuminated by the counterfactual of the "state of nature" in the *Discours sur . . . l'inégalité*.

31. Which is to say, politics. Recall that all connections between law and society in Rousseau must be viewed through the multidimensional and ultimately νομος-like character of law discussed at §5 above.

32. Is the perverse origin of this insight Rousseau's personal experience of having been a Genevan and cast out, a family member and cast out, a courtier and denizen of the salons and cast out, a visitor to Hume's home and cast out, etc.? It seems that he needed the most capacious category of membership to feel in any sense at home with others.

33. Starobinski (1971, 52) develops this point.

34. Indeed, Rousseau is quite explicit in saying that social evolution transforms human nature itself, and not only in the supposedly metaphorical sense of adding the "*seconde nature*" of habit; cf. OC III.192.

35. Generally speaking, the primary quality of the social totality is—by analogy in somewhat different ways to Spinoza and Peirce—continuum.

36. I shall revisit the use of the word *contract* in great detail in a companion volume to *Abandoned to Ourselves* on Rousseau's political theory; suffice it to say here that in Richelet himself, as in earlier and in some later dictionaries, the primary sense of the word *contract* is indicated by kinship to *contrahere*—a general process of "coming together" or "drawing together"—and not by *pactum*, or "*ce que se passe devant notaires*" ["the which happens before a notary"]. It is further confirmation of my claim that, for the new edition of his dictionary in 1732, Richelet makes some alterations to the entry on *société* but maintains the same general definition; further down the page, he adds two unqualified senses of *société*, one which equates it simply with *amitié* and *liaison*, the other which refers to association for the "*avancement des siences*" like the Royal Society of London.

37. This definition was earlier limited to the word *peuple*; see below.
38. Cf. Cranston (1983, 213 ff.). Rousseau presumes that only a handful of *"beaux génies"* would be capable of judging his writings, including Montesquieu, Voltaire, and Buffon; cf. Michel Launay (1989, 186).
39. Comparison with Plato is in *L'économie politique* (OC III.273); the eulogy is from a letter to Pastor Perdriau, February 20, 1755, quoted in translation in Cranston (1991, 4). Hubert Humphrey's wife is said to have once reprimanded him: "you don't have to talk forever to be immortal."
40. On the early planning for the *Institutions politiques*, cf. *Confessions*, books 8 and 9 (OC I.394, 404). On the relation between these two thinkers, cf. Cranston (1983, 213 ff.), Derathé (1970, 52 ff.), Einaudi (1967, 34 ff.), and Shklar (1985, 33).
41. OC IV.836. There is an oddity in the French here, as Rousseau first spells the word *traitter* incorrectly with two "t"s and then correctly with one. The entry in Furetière (1690) for *retraitter* is the only place I have found the word spelled the incorrect way; it is not clear to me whether Rousseau meant something in particular by using two spellings for this word in the same sentence; given other research I have done on Rousseau's orthography I am reticent to attribute such oddities to typographic error.
42. OC III.281; this again seems like a gesture to Cicero, as in *De natura deorum* (book I, part II, IV) or *De officiis* (I.50).
43. This places him squarely against the romantic opposition of *Gemeinschaft* and *Gesellschaft* that develops a century later. Cf. Cladis (1992) on the parallels with Durkheim.
44. Hobbes (1651, book I, chapter XIII).
45. This point stands despite some complications deriving from the fact that the *"contract social"* and the *"pacte social"* are not the same; identifying these two has been an almost universal and profoundly consequential error of Rousseau's followers and interpreters.
46. OC III.394.
47. As is often the case in reading Rousseau, a fruitful comparison could be made here with Hume. Hume, too, understood that an irreducible moral plurality is intertwined with problems of justice. Unlike Rousseau, however, he (rather gleefully) abandoned the hope that anything would stop this plurality from generating moral and political problems. This is one reason for his rejection of so-called "contract theory." Hume also diverges from Rousseau in the ways he sees morality as shaped by particular types of relations to things. One example is the type of relation to things called "scarcity" that is, in his view, a condition for justice. More generally, in Hume's view politics hinges on that great sea of our relations to things, history.
48. The similar tone and phrasing of these two sentences should remind us of an intersection in the writing process of the two texts which were eventually published in the same year.
49. Appearance to the contrary, this act is not the origin of society but rather a way that society takes charge of itself; cf. Meyers (2008b).
50. All citations in this section, except where otherwise indicated, are from OC III. 281–83.

51. N.b. the use of the verb denoting the most natural human act: to be born. The significance of this sentence is amplified by the fact that Rousseau's largest but incomplete project was entitled *Institutions politiques*.

52. Again, whether or not Rousseau is explicitly paraphrasing Cicero, this is a modernized Ciceronian notion; cf. notes 18 and 42 above.

53. The profound anti-ecology of this general prospect has been spelled out by Merchant (1980) and Bookchin (1980).

54. OC III.282. This view is qualified in terms of relative limits on property ownership at the end of book I of the published version of *Du Contract social:* "In practice, laws are always useful for those who have property and harmful for those who have nothing: from this it follows that the social condition is only advantageous to mankind insofar as everyone has something and no one among them has too much" (OC III.367). Rousseau later adds that to ensure liberty, one must maintain equality, and that "by this word one must not suppose that the degrees of power and wealth are absolutely the same, but that, concerning power, it should be beneath all violence and always exercised with respect to rank and the laws, and concerning wealth, that no citizen should be sufficiently opulent to be able to buy another, and none poor enough to be constrained to sell himself" (OC III.391–92). Rousseau also frames this problem in terms of dependence in a passage at OC IV.524, as quoted in the text below.

55. As this is occurring in nascent society, Rousseau can claim that "Hobbes's error therefore is not to have established the state of war among independent men who have become sociable, but to have supposed that condition is natural to the species, and to have given as its cause the vices of which it is the effect" (OC III.288). Cf. also the fragment *"l'état de guerre"* in Vaughn's edition of Rousseau (1915, I, pp. 281–307).

56. Rousseau's reading of Bernard Mandeville makes itself felt when he adds that "these are the foundations of that universal benevolence, the necessity of which seems to extinguish the sentiment, and of which everyone would like to reap the fruit without being obliged to cultivate it." As Derathé correctly notes: "Rousseau could retain everything from Mandeville's analysis and still conclude in favor of virtue and against the seductions of luxury and riches" (OC III.1331, note 3). Rousseau goes so far as to leave in the text these words—"it is false that in the condition of independence reason, following the perspective of one's own interest, leads us to concur in the common good"—after having written and then scratched out a more balanced reference to the view so closely associated with Mandeville; (OC III.284 and editorial note a).

57. It may be considered an order of disorder; cf. Meyers (1989, chapter 6). This would be consistent with my conclusion, below, that Rousseau's image of society remains nested in and contingent on a particular theological viewpoint.

58. This is Derathé's observation at OC III.1412.

59. See above at §27.

60. As we shall see later, an evolutionary view of human beings always involves a fluid and dialectical conception of the relation between *nature* and *société*.

61. Or perhaps a falling away from *citoyen* to *homme*. . .

62. I have already mentioned (§34 above) the asymmetry of *ordre* and *état*; this complexity

is elaborated in Part IV below with respect to the pivotal ambiguity in the term *ordre*, indicated at §49.

63. OC III.283; see other discussions of this point elsewhere in this book.

64. Concerning the "love of order," Derathé (OC III.1412, note 6) points to the texts referred to by Pierre-Maurice Masson in his edition of the "*Profession de foi*." It is not necessary at this point to take a single position concerning whether this concept has Augustinian or, as Viroli (1988) argues, Ciceronian roots.

65. This is complicated to some extent by the differences between the verb *dépendre* and the noun *dépendance*.

66. From the Latin *dūco*, to lead, draw out, conduct, bring forward.

67. Cf. §21 (especially note 103, Part Two) where syllepsis as a theoretical figure in Rousseau's writing is introduced.

68. We assume here a short-term. This is belied in certain crucial respects by the very idea of social evolution and its ecological implications.

69. OC IV.306. The worst case, we may conjecture, would be predominantly symbolic systems like fashion.

70. OC IV.247. This is the sort of confusion which, in Hegel's analysis of an analogous problem, will lead to the dead end in the development of the "self" he calls "unhappy consciousness [*das unglückliche Bewußtsein*]." Cf. Hegel (1952, end of §I.IV, developed through subsection A ["*Herrschaft und Knechtschaft*"] into subsection B).

71. On *interrogatio* or ἐρώτημα—the so-called "rhetorical question"—cf. Cicero (1954, IV.XV.22).

72. Hume famously raised these kinds of questions both by challenging the image of the "state of nature" and by proving the necessary incompleteness of induction.

73. D'Holbach (1773, 190).

74. OC IV.245 and note.

75. In what follows I rely heavily on Ehrard's (1994) definitive study of the background debates joining philosophy and theology in the first half of the eighteenth century; this brilliant work of intellectual history was originally published in 1963; all translations are my own.

76. Morin (1735, 15), cited in Ehrard (1994, 59).

77. Diderot and d'Alembert (1751–72, XI.39). *Naturaliste* is probably by Diderot.

78. Vernière (1954) places Spinoza at the center of the action; Ehrard's brilliant book (1994) insists on the importance not only of Spinoza's influence but on the way his name became an obligatory *topos* of debate; more recently, Israel's (2002, especially chapters 13–17) impressive study has returned attention to Spinoza's pivotal role in the Enlightenment.

79. Spinoza, somewhat mysteriously, writes to Oldenburg in 1675—with the *Ethica* already complete—"the supposition of some, that I endeavor to prove in the Tractatus Theologico-Politicus the unity of God and Nature (meaning by the latter a certain mass or corporeal matter), is wholly erroneous." Letter LXXIII in Spinoza (1927, 342).

80. We see this most recently in the extraordinary reaction to Charles Taylor's *magnum opus* (2007).

81. OC IV.249. While—for reasons indicated in §18—I treat the word *hommes* as a reference to "mankind" as a whole, and have, since §33 above, thematized this interpretive approach by translating it with "persons," it would be important in other contexts to recall the ways in which gender becomes an essential (rather than tangential) feature of Rousseau's subject in book V of *Émile*. He writes, for example, that "dependence being a natural condition for women, girls feel themselves made for obedience," and that "it is in the order of nature that woman obeys man." In my view, this is contrary to his basic characterization of *l'état naturel*—in which there is no dependence—and contrary to the fundamental principle I want to draw from his social theory: domination can be built on dependence but is not identical with it. On this last point, see Meyers (1989, chapter 1).

82. Cited in Ehrard (1994, 792). Notice here the magnificent Voltairean irony: he addresses as a living subject, in the familiar voice, that of which he denies the existence.

83. As is the notion of the "secular" itself. I do not mean here the true but subsidiary point that key categories of modern science emerged from the *topoi* of theology. Concerning for example the omniscience, omnipresence, or omnipotence of God, cf. Funkenstein (1986) who develops in new detail a point previously well known. Cf. also again Ehrard (1994, 246–48).

84. Einstein and Born (2005, letter 52, December 4, 1926).

85. "Prejudice" is used here in the neutral rhetorical sense recently developed by Gadamer (1975/1960) and, unbeknownst to most of her readers, Arendt (2003). Perhaps it comes from Heidegger, but I doubt it.

86. Ehrard (1994, 790).

87. Ehrard (1994, 71) recites the view that, while older, had after Newton become a commonplace.

88. Mauzi (1960, 561).

89. Except where indicated this paragraph is drawn from Ehrard (1994, 790).

90. Ehrard (1994, 787).

91. I sincerely hope that some other scholar will pursue this enormous and useful task.

92. That, too, is a dialectical fact; cf. Daston and Park (1998).

93. Just as the analytic geometry associated with Descartes changed practices of abstraction and the conceptualization of space, the calculus refigured entirely perceived relationships between space and time, or motion. For an interesting take on the former, cf. Brodsky Lacour (1996); concerning the social history of clocks, cf., e.g., Cipolla (1967) and Landes (1998).

94. The origin of the world could more easily continue as a speculative question on which current experience had less bearing.

95. On Buffon and Diderot, cf. Ehrard (1994, 181–248); cf. also Israel (2002, 252) who insists on the "Spinozistic" element in early evolutionary thinking.

96. Cf. Ehrard (1994, 435–63).

97. Ehrard (1994, 81), referring to the entry *"cause"* in Diderot and d'Alembert (1751–72). See, more generally, Ehrard (1994, 419–35).

98. Ibid., citing Bayle's *Continuation des pensées diverses sur la Comète*, chapter CXI. This, of course, leaves out of consideration the possibility that *nature* itself is an ani-

mate being yet different from God. Bayle's *Dictionnaire historique et critique* (1702) was one of the best selling books of the first half of the eighteenth century; Israel (2002, 142–55) argues convincingly that "learned journals . . . were one of the most powerful agents of cultural and intellectual change during the Early Enlightenment era," a process in which Bayle again played a key role as editor of *Nouvelles de la République des Lettres*.

99. Ehrard (1994, 170–71), citing Maupertuis *Essaie de Cosmologie* (1750, 43–44).

100. Ibid., referring to Clark. Likewise other Newtonians, like Bentley and Whiston; cf. Israel (2002, 518–19).

101. Ehrard (1994, 147), citing Leibniz.

102. Ehrard (1994, 95); he points to the obvious ambiguity here — is the "or" [*sive*] a substitution of names or the alternation of substances? — to suggest how capacious such *topoi* are in debates.

103. On the role of this description in the development of the "new science," cf. Koyré (1957).

104. Rousseau himself is among those who facilely refer to *"l'athée Spinoza;"* cf., e.g., *Lettre à Christophe de Beaumont* (OC IV.931).

105. This encapsulating phrase is from Dijksterhuis (1986).

106. Ehrard (1994, 175).

107. Ehrard (1994, 177).

108. Ehrard (1994, 157).

109. Ehrard (1994, 247).

110. Ehrard (1994, 189), discussing the reception of Linnaeus. Such analogies, where *nature* appeared like God but not identical with the θεοσ, carried theological images and expectations far into the realm of a science that pretended to pure secularism. The central compromise of modern physics — the law of thermodynamics that energy can be neither created nor destroyed — mirrors the God-like *inépuisable* quality of the eighteenth-century view of *nature*. This, one may assume, had something to do with the existential terror many felt in the face of the concept of entropy.

111. Ehrard (1994, 104), who discusses at this point unpublished manuscripts by Boulainvilliers from 1715–20.

112. Ehrard (1994, 158–59).

113. These last words are from Israel (2002, 520), where Diderot is cited.

114. Ehrard (1994, 247). This common sense usage of *puissance* is consonant with Rousseau's application of the word to circumstances which are hybrid between action and nature — not like a falling rock or a smashing fist, but also not a feature of fully constituted society; a person preparing to enter *le pacte social* has *puissance* (OC III.361). Cf. §20 above.

115. Ehrard (1994, 214), who discusses at this point implications of Lémery's view on monsters.

116. That is, the basic hermeneutic premise of the *Geisteswissenschaften*, that one can never stand outside the "object" of inquiry and must therefore study it from "inside," is equally true for the study of *nature*. The "uncertainty" implied in this (in scare quotes here because the issue of what kind of certainty was attained through processes of

experimental objectification was never settled in the comprehensive sense discussed here) became again a central topic of debate in the age of Einstein, generally in the positions expressed by Duhem and Poincarré, and in the more limited and technical assertions of Heisenberg's famous principle.

117. And sometimes, with or without contradiction, several at once. As Ehrard (1994, 573) reminds us, throughout the first half of the eighteenth century, "it is not rare to find in the Pantheon of the sages Zeno seated fraternally next to Epicurus." Note that, by contrast, Rousseau occasionally contented himself, in perfect concordance with his contemporaries, to remove the study of *nature* from a humanistic frame, as when he writes at the beginning of the *Fragmens pour un dictionnaire des termes d'usage en botanique* (OC IV.1201) that the "the greatest misfortune of Botany was to have been, from its beginnings, regarded as a part of medicine," which is to say as something in the service of human beings rather than as something independent from us.

118. Cf. brief discussion at §§7 and 8 above; see also Meyers (1995), Meyers (2013a, forthcoming), and Meyers (2013c, forthcoming).

119. Cicero uses the word *voluntas* to translate the Stoic term βουλησιν.

120. It is not unfair to say that, if Rousseau can identify (at OC III.155) in the operation of *pitié* "a pure movement of nature, anterior to all reflection," then *la raison* and *la nature* must, in some sense, be distinct. Cf. summary statement at OC III.162.

121. Statements and restatements of this debate may be found everywhere, e.g. in Ehrard (1994, 331–96).

122. Cf. §6 above.

123. OC III.154. There is reason to think Rousseau changed his view, and perhaps had already done so when he composed the *Discours sur . . . l'inégalité*, where after it is introduced *pitié* is consistently qualified as *naturelle*, as if there could be some doubt. In any event, by the time of *Émile*, even *pitié* seems ready for mediation through an evolutionary view; when it finally appears well into book IV (OC IV.505), Rousseau writes "thus is born pity, the first relational sentiment that touches the human heart according to the order of nature." This is a very different view.

124. Although we need not consider Rousseau's affinity with Darwinian evolution in the strict sense, one should be attentive to statements—like this one from *Du Contract social*—which assert that "the passage from the state of nature to the civil state produces a very remarkable change in Man . . . from a limited and stupid animal is made an intelligent being and a Man" (OC III.364). At the same time, he attributes similarities between apes and humans to the natural imitation of the latter by the former; OC IV.340. Nonetheless, it is also worth noting, as Jean Starobinski does, that on the pivotal questions of the relation between human beings and apes Rousseau accepts—perhaps under the influence of Maupertuis's reading of Linnaeus—a "limited transformism" of species (i.e., that what God created has the capacity to transform into something else without the further intervention of God); cf. Starobinski at OC III.1369–70, note 3. Cf. Rousseau's comments on Linnaeus in the introduction of his *Dictionnaire des terms d'usage en botanique* at OC IV.1205–9. Damrosch (2005, 471) points out that Rousseau was constantly reading Linnaeus.

125. When in *Du Contract social* Rousseau seems to meander into speculation about *li-*

berté he simply writes that "the philosophical sense of the word liberty is not my subject here" (OC III.365). I suggest this self-consciousness is of general application.

126. This list recites the topics covered in great detail by Ehrard (1994, part two *"La nature humaine et ses lois,"* chapters 5–9, pp. 251–655).

127. One inspiration for this phrase and the perspective I bring at this point to Rousseau is Burke's (1945) essential synthesis of rhetoric and pragmatism in the analysis of the structure, function, and circulation of symbols as the organic and organizing principle of human motivations.

128. E.g., one must "distinguish among the desires of children those which come immediately from nature and those which come from opinion" (OC IV.290).

129. Although at one point he produces the tantalizing phrase "the art of nature [*c'est l'arte de la nature*]."

130. Cf. above at §6 on *amour de soi*.

131. See just below for a few words on this paradox.

132. Of Rousseau's famous comment — "it is necessary to choose between making a Man or a Citizen, for one cannot make one and the other at the same time" — Burgelin correctly remarks that while this "distinction is undoubtedly comforting and true in the first analysis . . . it is probably superficial"; cf. OC IV.248 and Burgelin's note at OC IV.1296–97. I would go further: to presume that this antithesis drives Rousseau's whole project in any immediate way is ridiculous.

133. OC IV.583; cf. also OC IV.524 on *"le tableau de tout l'ordre social."* The *tableau* is a favored image generally.

134. OC IV.612. See §57 below on this text in relation to miracles.

135. Κοσμος had this meaning of "harmony" before it was identified with either "the world" or "the universe" as a whole, or with *nature*; cf. Vlastos (1975, chapter 1). For a development of the notion of "cosmos" in a modern conception of order, see Hayek (1973, volume 1, chapter 2).

136. Cf. Barthes (1977), originally published in 1953.

137. On the dialectic of substance and the deployment of substantives as "God-terms," see Burke (1945).

138. Cf. Ricoeur (1983, volume one, part one) who insists on the link between narrative and *mythos*, derived from Aristotle's *Poetics*. In Ricoeur (1990b) his translators have settled on the word "emplotment" or the embedding-of-elements-into-a-plot to capture what he means by *mythos*.

139. For an intriguing representation, cf. Goodman (1978).

140. All preceding quotes from OC IV.483; I underscore the parallel structure, as Rousseau clearly intends.

141. OC IV.550–51. Of course, as always with Rousseau, things are more complicated. Reason itself is a development of society. But at least here this is compatible with the claim that *nature* and *société* can coexist, and consistent with the evolutionary perspective we will come to in subsequent sections.

142. I use here the categories of Walter Benjamin and Kenneth Burke; on the former see Meyers (2000); on the "representative anecdote" see Burke (1945, chapter 3).

143. Ehrard (1994, 790); cf. again §42 above.

144. Burke (1945, chapter 1) argues that this is a structural problem in the deepest sense.

145. And, as we shall see in the next section, the relative status of *nature* and *habitude* is a pivotal instance of the evolutionary transformation of human beings.

146. He does call on *"l'histoire"* to fill in the details; OC III.162–63.

147. *"La vie"* of *"le corps politique"* is declared at OC III.378; the other terms are borrowed from the titles of chapters X and XI in book III of *Du Contract social* (OC III.421, 424).

148. See §§7 and 19 above; the key arguments in §21, and as developed in subsequent sections, complicate but do not contradict this.

149. "Natality" in this theoretical sense is a key term in Arendt (1958), where it is developed as I intend it here.

150. This is exactly what Rousseau advises the *précepteur* concerning his pupil; OC IV.320.

151. My general paradigm for analyzing the performative effects of the choice and juxtaposition of genres derives from the research of Efthymia Rentzou; cf. Rentzou (2007 and 2010).

152. But see again note 132 on Burgelin in §43 above.

153. Spink in Société Jean-Jacques Rousseau (1905–, XXXV) observes both the novel use of the word *éducation* in the eighteenth century and its intrication with political theory; Ehrard (1994, 753–67) discusses the "birth of the myth of education." The influential distinction between formal and informal education, familiar today from e.g. Dewey (1916), derives in its modern form from Turgot (1749); this is clearly a driving force in Rousseau's program.

154. Meyers (2008b) does this in a preliminary way.

155. In our time the ever-clever Bernard Williams relocated this disjunction as an important philosophical topic; cf. Williams (1982, chapter 2), a project that continues in Williams (1993).

156. I will not have much to say about chance here; for a suggestive gesture toward chance in the development of natural faculties, cf. for example OC III.162. Glossing Rousseau with C. S. Peirce on "tychism" and evolution would be instructive.

157. The "main passage."

158. OC IV.458, interpolating advice given about how to treat the young Émile.

159. Diderot and d'Alembert (1751–72, III, 374).

160. This is hardly a new distinction; cf. Justinian, Dig.23.3.33 (Ulpianus 6 ad sab.): "*Si extraneus sit qui dotem promisit isque defectus sit facultatibus, imputabitur marito, cur eum non convenerit, maxime si ex necessitate, non ex voluntate dotem promiserat: nam si donavit, . . .*"

161. I generally follow Ehrard (1994) here, paraphrasing from his synopsis at p. 661, as informed by the detailed development of pp. 399–467, which weaves the role of the Jesuits into his narrative. The quote is from p. 452. On the Jansenists, Ehrard writes: "We have diverse indications that, in certain respects, the philosophy of the Enlightenment must be considered as prodigal daughter of Jansenist theology. First of all, it is not unusual that an ardent Jansenist is converted, without transition, to militant deism . . . a sociological study of the two movements would most likely discover many common elements in the social origins of both" (p. 662).

162. This point is suggested by Ehrard (1994, 189).
163. Rousseau (OC III.384, note) recognizes just this point by quoting gleefully a now famous passage from Machiavelli's *Discorsi*: "In fact, there has never been a commander who made extraordinary laws for a people that did not take recourse to God, because otherwise they would not have been accepted [*E veramente, mai non fù alcuno ordinatore di legge straordinarie in un popolo, che non ricorresse a Dio, perche altrimenti non sarebbero accettate*]."
164. Construed as in §6 above.
165. In the sense of Burke (1945).
166. That is, if you start from the wrong principles, you get the wrong result. Roman law explicitly exhibits this constructivist character; for example, in the Code of Justinian it seems that words from *necesse* and *necessitas* are typically connected in some way with the verb *facere*. Thanks to Bob Kaster (personal communication) who confirms for classical Latin in general that *necesse* and *necessitas* refer to "what's necessary because that's the way things are," with no implication as to why things are the way they are (whether the reasons are natural or made by human beings).
167. One way of developing this claim, with which I have some sympathy, may be found in Viroli (1988).
168. Just as for Hobbes laws/rights of nature persist after the construction of the state.
169. OC III.424. N.b. the difference between acting like God, or even pretending to act like God, and attempting to see things from what we imagine must be a God-like perspective. At the opening of the first version of *Émile* (OC IV.55) Rousseau tells us it is "one of the duties God prescribed for us . . . to raise ourselves occasionally to His perspectives."
170. On the basis of this and similar points, we shall ultimately reconsider the type of dependence ignored by Rousseau, the intermediate category of nonnatural-dependence-from-things, and suggest a place for it in post-Rousseauean sociology.
171. OC III.455 ff. I am inclined to read this as analogy to the deployment of miracles by God in the "*système du monde.*" See below at §57.
172. This is Kant's line in the *Grundlegung zur Metaphysik der Sitten*, where "admiration/attention before the law [*die Achtung vor dem Gesetzt*]" appears as a linchpin of moral obligation. The typical translation of *Achtung* as "respect" misses the sense of Kant's argument and may also ignore the historical status of *Achtung* in the tradition of *traité des passions* (stemming from book II of Aristotle's *Rhetoric*, although θαυμαστόν does not seem to be a keyword there, having joined Renaissance Latin more from the *Poetics* 25, 1460a11–18) as the first passion, *admiratio*. Cf. Gillet (1918) and Herrick (1947), who links development of the word to both of Aristotle's works.
173. Viroli (1988) stresses this perspective.
174. Tyler (1990) is a social psychological account of this fact. Among Rousseau's contemporaries, perhaps Hume was clearest on this point.
175. Shane (1986, 491–92).
176. Aristotle, *De memoria* 452a27.
177. Cf. Ehrard (1994, 691–717).
178. OC III.381. It is, I think, extremely interesting that he wrote God in the singular in the first version; cf. OC III.312–13.

179. Eckstein (1944) made this point prior to the recent revival of interest in Spinoza's explicit and implicit contributions to political theory; cf. e.g. a range from Negri (1991) to Israel (2002, 2006a, 2010).

180. That is, a perspective that would be difficult to imagine had Spinoza never seen the light of day.

181. That is why he writes easily to Voltaire that "all human developments [*progrès humains*] are pernicious to the species" (OC III.227), or that his task is "to expose the origin and steps forward of inequality [*d'exposer l'origine et le progrès de l'inégalité*]" (OC III.193). Obviously, it is impossible that Rousseau thinks inequality is "progressive" in our sense.

182. Cf. again the discussion at §16 above.

183. One may speculate that by giving priority to social evolution, Rousseau's version has ecological implications that Darwin's application of evolutionary thinking to "natural history" lacks.

184. It is striking to see how clearly Rousseau's friend Condillac understood the lesson that *besoins* drive social evolution and how he drew the obvious conclusion that the *besoins* of *société* over time are as natural as individual needs for food, etc.; cf. Condillac (1776, 8–9).

185. E.g., OC III.162, where he says "it remains for me to consider and bring together the different elements of chance that were able to develop human reason."

186. Ehrard (1994, 761).

187. Quotes from Ehrard (1994, 761,751).

188. Pascal *Pensées* (Brunschvicg) II, 93.

189. Inquiry of this sort is, of course, much older; cf. Aristotle *On Memory*, 452a26bff.

190. One might respond to George Kateb that the reason "it all" seems to come to nothing in *Émile et Sophie, ou les solitaires* is that Enlightenment may—as Rousseau said time and time again—turn out badly; *Émile* is not a utopia and social evolution is not in his, or our, control. He does not take this, however, as occasion to give up. With great historical imagination we might pretend that *Émile* is Rousseau's reply to Kant's "What is Enlightenment?"

191. OC III.162. Rousseau adds that because chance is involved, and many evolutionary paths are possible, the process has to be understood in probabilistic terms. This may be taken as precursory to Quetelet—cf. Stigler (1986, chapter 5), Desrosières (2000)—or as a reassertion of the first traditional commitment of rhetoric to εἰκὸς over ἀναγκαιον, the probable over the necessary; I prefer the latter reading; cf. Meyers (2007). Although it is sometimes mentioned in passing—cf., e.g., Daston (1995, 38, 40)—I do not believe that anyone has looked into the relation between the two.

192. He adds here in sly attack on the philosophers that "the reason why Diogenes never found man is that he sought amongst his contemporaries the man of a time past." N.b. that Voltaire often insulted Rousseau by calling him "Diogenes."

193. All quotes in this paragraph are from OC III.191–92, although reordered here.

194. This and the previous two quotes are from OC III.192.

195. Cf. OC III.162: "I admit that the events that I have to describe could have occurred in many ways."

196. Rousseau thinks he does the former, while pretty much everyone else does the latter; cf. OC IV.549.

197. I suspect that Shklar (1990) has written with some success about the fluid boundary between the "natural" and the "political" because she was a careful reader of both Rousseau and Hegel; cf. Shklar (1985 and 1976).

198. This is, of course, one of the most basic traditional distinctions between philosophy and rhetoric; Rousseau's writing, like all writing that is really about politics, owes more to the latter than to the former.

199. For why I will not hold to the distinction between *besoins* and *désires*, see again §16 above.

200. Whether the two are effectively matched is an entirely different questions; the emergence of *forces* from *besoins* is typically mediated through a variety of faculties, for example, imagination.

201. Marx seems to have drawn a similar conclusion from his reading of Rousseau.

202. Cf. here not only what might be called Saussure's "secular Spinozism" but especially the discussion of the mutability/immutability at Saussure (1960, part one.II); cf. also Vico (1744/1984 passim) on the fluctuating character of *sensus communis*; Rousseau's hesitation on the social status of language seems relevant here as well, cf. OC III. 151.

203. I mean to refer here to a specifically modern phenomenon, as ancient myths suggest that terms which we now translate as *nature* referred to something quite vocal and visible. Generally on the social processes of "naturalization" and their significance for politics, cf. Unger (1987a, 1987b).

204. This is the dialectical relationship developed in extraordinary detail by Hegel (1952).

205. Once again, this interesting use of the term "equilibrium"—resonant with Condillac? (cf. §45 above)—is Rousseau's (OC IV.304).

PART FOUR

1. At a minimum, *ordre* is an organization of *forces* and is thus distinguishable from them.

2. Intended in approximately the sense of Arendt (1958); cf. Meyers (2013a).

3. I use work of other scholars partly as source and partly as primer; I rarely rely on other people's research without reading their sources as well, a task now greatly facilitated by thousands of seventeenth- and eighteenth-century texts available in facsimile on Google Books.

4. That such large investments often entail contention should be obvious; cf. Israel's (2006b) strident attack on Kors et al.

5. Platonism is a rather different kind of problem.

6. Cf. e.g. Benjamin Ives Gilman, *"The museum docent"* in American Association of Museums (1915, 113–34).

7. However, the fact that all history *takes place* in the present further tightens this knot. It is also instructive that the famous Delphic inscription—"know thyself [γνῶθι σεαυτον]"—is so often cited in political theory in a temporalizing setting; cf. Rous-

seau in the *Discours sur . . . l'inégalité* (OC III.122). For more on these issues, cf. Meyers (2000) and Meyers (2002).

8. Although we differ on other points, Scott (1994) is rare in also discerning this structure.

9. Rousseau's corresponding epistemology is compatible with Natural Religion, since he believes "Will is known to me by its effects," which means we can know Grace through Nature.

10. I use the words "monist" and "dualist" here in their relatively narrow eighteenth-century philosophical sense, whereas later I will use them in a more general sense.

11. In the sense of the *Encyclopédie*, cited above at §41.

12. I say it "suggests" because another scenario is possible: God could at every moment be pulling the strings, just as some after Newton argued that gravity was a sign of God's constant intervention in the world.

13. Viewed another way, Rousseau's theory makes, at least in this respect, the so-called micro/macro link that seems so elusive for contemporary sociology.

14. N.b. that here we assume, as Rousseau does, the identity of dependence-from-Nature and dependence-from-things. This identity is exactly what we shall disavow in the next sections.

15. Strictly speaking, this would take us back to the assumption that $(Q^{fundamental}A^{nature \in grace})$, but it is important here to think of this in terms of the Will. Otherwise, the principle here would be gravity or a "naturalist" alternative appropriate to this setting.

16. Or, more precisely, the primary fact of *dépendance* that drives evolution.

17. Famously in Austin (1832).

18. Meyers (2008a) develops the concept of "monocracy" and points to its earlier usage by Thomas Jefferson.

19. On these and corollary fundamental principles, cf. Meyers (2013a).

20. I acknowledge that a view of creation as one and entire is possible, but then the distinction between mankind and nature moves to a different level, requiring a hierarchical order within creation and thus reasserting the monocratic tendency.

21. Although I will not develop them here, this point has profound implications for the significance of the phrase *contract social* where one holds what I referred to above as the "evolutionary perspective" on $(Q^{ecological})$; cf. also Meyers (2008b).

22. Heraclitean *avant-gardistes* like John Cage provide a counter-example.

23. N.b. that this is a reference to national laws, not to what today is called international law. Although the writings of Pufendorf and Barbeyrac appeared in English translation under the phrase "law of nations," the original Latin (*De jure naturae et gentium*) and French (*Le Droit de la nature et des gens*) did not use the word "nations." Likewise Vattel's *Le Droit des gens*. Rousseau mentions the former but not the latter.

24. Burlamaqui (1747), not to be confused with Burlamaqui's (1751) sequel from which *Du Contract social* borrowed its subtitle. Burlamaqui's extensive but now forgotten influence is reflected in the fifty-five editions in eight languages of his book; cf. Wright (1938).

25. Burlamaqui (1747, II, ii, 156).

26. Burlamaqui's influence on Rousseau was once well-known, as was his profound influ-

ence on the American Founders; cf. Harvey (1937). By the second half of the twentieth century, substantial disagreement emerged on this point, as registered for example in the argument—more emphatic than convincing—of Derathé (1970, 84–89). Even if Starobinski, following Gagnebin (1944) and Derathé (1970), is correct to say (OC III.1296) that "Rousseau was hardly influenced by the ideas of Burlamaqui," my point is simply that here they stand for the same common sense. Rosenblatt (1997, 3–7) shows a similar pattern concerning the related significance of Geneva for Rousseau.

27. Whether that is in the seconds or the centuries to come.

28. And "directly explicit" in the *Lettre à Christophe de Beaumont* and the *Lettres écrites de la montagne*. Burgelin argues with clarity and concision that "one can assert as indisputable that the Vicar is a mask of the author" and "this portion [of *Émile*] is one of the most thoroughly crafted in all the works of Rousseau"; cf. OC IV.CXXXIII–CXLVI.

29. The division into two parts is clear in the text and acknowledged by Rousseau elsewhere at OC IV.996.

30. This retrospective from the *"Troisième promenade"* of *Les Rêveries du promeneur solitaire*, at OC I.1018.

31. OC IV.960. This is likewise suggested by the treatment of the *"Profession"* in the first of the *Lettres écrites de la montagne*, OC III.694 ff., where Rousseau gestures to this and to a similar *"profession"* found in *La Nouvelle Héloïse*, adding that each of the two "can be explained with reference to the other, and from that agreement one may plausibly assume that if the author who published the books in which these two professions of faith are contained does not make either of them entirely his own, at least he favors them both to a large extent. Of these two professions of faith, it is the first that must be given precedence, as it is the more extended and the only one where the *corpus delecti* has been found." In the *Confessions* (book IX) he goes further to call these two "professions . . . exactly the same."

32. That some critics (e.g., Shklar 1985) insist that Rousseau was not a real "believer" is, aside from being false, beside the point; Gourevitch's (2001, 193–94) argument that the *Lettre à Voltaire* is "Rousseau's most authoritative discussion of religious issues" ignores the obvious fact that religious issues can be discussed for many purposes and inflected in many ways.

33. Willey (1961) gives some general considerations. The idea of "incomplete secularization" plays a part in books like Gauchet (1985), Funkenstein (1986), Riley (1986), and most recently Gillespie (2008). Some of the thorny questions concerning Rousseau's precise relation to Christianity are raised by Masters (1968, ii). A full, if narrowly conceived, account of Rousseau on religion may be found in Masson (1916/1970).

34. I do not take into account here extremely import occult elements that shaped this developing mixture in many ways because, while occasionally present in Rousseau's thought, they have been thoroughly mediated by these other factors. Otherwise, cf. excellent focused studies such as Yates (1964) and Grafton (1999).

35. Having mostly skirted the issues raised in this paragraph in Viroli (1988), Viroli (2010) attempts to link religion to republicanism.

36. This is the main argument of Viroli (1988). Cf. more recently, and from a very different angle, Wingrove (2000).

37. Cifoletti (1992).

38. Bouwsma's (1975) "ideal typical" account of a dialectic of stoicism and Augustinianism in the Renaissance lays out in an interesting way the uses of these two intellectual traditions in the centuries before Rousseau and, as Rousseau is in some key respects a later Renaissance rather than an Enlightenment figure, may be a useful way to conceive the contextual fabric of his writing. Dilthey (1914–, II) identified Lipsius as the source of neo-Stoicism; this point is developed by Oestreich (2008). Brooke in Riley (2001, chapter 5) applies Bouwsma's account to Rousseau. Charles Taylor proposes a somewhat different role for "neo-Stoicism" in the rise of Modernity; cf. Taylor (2007, 156–57 *et passim*).

39. E.g., Diderot, *Pensées philosophiques* XLII, cited in Ehrard (1994, 450).

40. Cf. Schmitt (1972) and Popkin (1979).

41. Cf., e.g., Shapin (1994).

42. Somewhat wider in scope, cf. Shapiro (2002) on the background in legal practices for the determination of scientific facts in the seventeenth century.

43. Brown (2000, 210–11); cf. also Wills (1999).

44. The topic was becoming important in the eighteenth century as, with the decreasing practical effects of kinship and rank, "strangers" began to ask themselves what they owed to one another. For an analytical development of this particular phrase, cf. Elster (1989).

45. Recall here Cassirer's claim that Kant drew from his reading of Rousseau a full-fledged *Gesetzes-Ethik*. While Cassirer may be right that such an ethic is already present in Rousseau, my point is that it is not *all* that is present in Rousseau; a much more comprehensive and balanced view of the elements in Rousseauean common sense is what I aim for here.

46. At this point, it does not matter whether or not Rousseau would have used the word *democracy* in this way. To acknowledge these strengths is not to ignore Rousseau's other astonishing weaknesses.

47. This is the little-remarked meaning of the word *condition* in the title of Hannah Arendt's (1958) most famous book; on the "political option" and its relation to "politics," cf. Meyers (2013a).

48. Shklar (1985, 114–15 ff.). In the preface to the second edition of her book, Shklar (1985, xiv) summarizes her view on this question, saying that "the Savoyard Vicar's faith was not Rousseau's." We have already seen—in the preceding section—that this is clearly wrong. In a sense, she may be right to say that the *"Profession"* was "what a young man approaching maturity ought to hear and accept," but Rousseau provides elsewhere much interpretive direction against her further claim that it was "only" that. Moreover, her apparent attention to rhetorical strategy here is made suspect by the peculiar combination of naïveté and non sequitur that clouds the following sentences, where she writes that "Rousseau's own opinions appear in the *Moral Letters*, written to a woman he loved"—actually the Sophie after whom he lusted relentlessly and whom

he, with great perversity, was trying (not) to seduce—as if that setting would be a guarantor of authenticity. When she adds that "many of its phrases reappear in the Vicar's 'Profession of Faith,' but God is not mentioned in that earlier and more genuine account of Rousseau's own state of mind," she reiterates the genesis of the *"Profession"* traced by Masson in his edition of Rousseau (1914) as if that somehow authorized her judgment of the *Lettres morales,* and as if the sentences lifted from the one into the other text could not serve several purposes. Of course "God is not mentioned in that earlier" document: Rousseau is the master there; in the final *lettre* he sends Sophie back off into the "solitude" of their duet promenades in the woods, the scene of their mutual masturbation; cf. Cranston (1991, 55–103). Masson's (1916/1970) monumental work runs perfectly contrary to Shklar's view.

49. Even if, as Masson (1916/1970, II.293–94) concludes, Rousseau manifests a Christianity peculiar to himself.

50. Shklar (1985, 114), citing Grimsley (1961, 242–43, 327–29).

51. While the thought extends far in time and space beyond Protestantism, it seems plausible to generalize in this way from Calvin's starting point in the *Institutio* (1536, book I, chapter 1): "That the knowledge of God, & of ourselves, are things conjoined." Religion, on the other hand, may have several motives.

52. Cranston (1991, xiv).

53. Wokler (1995, 82). While Wokler (1995, 120) tips his hat to Shklar (1985), he, against her, insists that the *"Profession de foi"* is where "Rousseau's conception of God receives its fullest and most eloquent expression" (1995, 82–83).

54. The context for this is laid out in detail in Ehrard (1994); the argument was made early by Lanson (1895) and elaborated in Masson (1916/1970, volume III).

55. Masson (1916/1970, II.243) speculates effectively from material evidence—traces on the pages of Rousseau's Latin copy of *De imitatio Christi* by Thomas à Kempis—concerning Rousseau's meditations on Christ.

56. The author was Jacob Vernet, cited in Cranston (1983, 327). Neither Shklar (1985, 123) nor the editor Osmont (at OC I.1747, note 3) seem to be aware that Rousseau may have had this book in mind when writing (in a footnote at OC I.973 to *Rousseau juge de Jean Jaques*) that *De l'utilité de la religion* would be "a great book to write."

57. Aside from polemics in which Rousseau defended himself—e.g., his *Lettre à Christophe de Beaumont, Archevêque de Paris*— and continuing attacks against him following the French revolution, the critical literature on this topic in the twentieth century begins with Lanson and especially with Masson's (1916/1970) monumental three-volume study, together with his edition of the *"Profession de foi"* (1915). Masters (1968, 54–55) provides a brief survey in English.

58. A charge that seems either trivial or obviously not true. See for example passages in the *Confessions* (OC I:143) where he discusses his own education. It is interesting to note that whereas in the first volume of Cranston's (1983, 324 ff.) biography, which ends with the trip to Geneva and return to its church, he inclines somewhat to Shklar's view, Cranston seems to have concluded after an additional nine years of reflection (cf. Cranston (1991, xiv, 1) that Rousseau was sincere in his religious attachment, be-

ginning the second volume with the assertion that "Rousseau saw himself as having become a true believer in the Reformed religion."

59. Cranston (1983, 52 ff.).

60. Cranston (1983, 324–30).

61. If the word "authentic" can have any real meaning outside the context of dogmatism.

62. Cf. his introductory note at OC IV.CLXXXVI.

63. Philonenko (1984, volume II) identifies several "big mistakes" to avoid in interpreting Rousseau. Considering his moment and several subsequent centuries of debate, it is important not to detach Rousseau from the Calvinist context of his reflections. Philonenko, however, misleads by asserting that one must not "misunderstand the essentially religious valence of the doctrine," for in the theological interests and arguments in Rousseau's writings the presence and formative quality of religious discourse is, literally, a discursive thing, not a doctrinal matter, and it is certainly not, as Philonenko would have it, a matter of "conscience" *per se.*

64. Voltaire (1734, 103); he adds that *"ils sont sans entousiasme,"* i.e., not susceptible to fanaticism; the latter point, while false, is not relevant here.

65. And, of course, Voltaire did eventually despise Rousseau himself. This gestures again to what Kant found ready-made in Rousseau, and — given, as Jean Ehrard (1994, 401) writes, that "around 1730 or 1740 French moral thought is as little Kantian as it is Christian" — to what extent he innovates.

66. OC III.955; this points back to the foundation of law first discussed above at §5.

67. OC IV.634; he means by *intolérans* "theologians" or, more generally, doctrinaire believers. While many of the motives and tendencies of "natural religion" appear in Rousseau's writing, I find it too imprecise to reduce his complex views to nothing more than an advocacy of that perspective. On the one hand, Rousseau supposes (OC I.1018) that what he had set down in the *"Profession de foi"* could "one day make a revolution among men if ever common sense and good faith were reborn [*peut faire un jour révolution parmi les hommes si jamais il y renait du bon sens et de la bonne foi*]"; on the other hand, as an advocate of patriotism and the state, he is suspicious of the cosmopolitanism inherent in Christianity. Cf. the remarkable letter of 24 June 1761 to Jacob Vernes, where he develops the point that "the devout Julie is a lesson for the philosophers, and Wolmar the atheist is one for the *intolérans*" at CC. IX.27, lettre 1436.

68. Calvin (1536, book IV, chapter 1 ff.); cf. discussion in Wolin (1960, 167ff).

69. Cf. Wolin (1960, 171): "In Calvin's view . . . wherever there was order, there was power. Hence, the kind of power that sustained a religious order might carry the adjective 'spiritual,' yet this did not transform it into a species of compulsion radically different from that present in the civil order."

70. I might add that this same shift makes Rousseau a crucial contributor to political economy: in addition to being the first to insist on that phrase before a wide public, he develops a conception of order-as-condition which (he hopes) can be maintained without political power. This is an extension of themes in Montesquieu and Hume that not one of the three would have admitted. It is later articulated in one way by the so-called Austrian School in economics. It is also tied together with the distinction be-

tween objective/subjective probability; cf. Hacking (1984, chapter 19), Stigler (1986), Daston (1995, chapter 4), Derosières (2000).

71. OC IV.30; this assessment appears in the *Mémoire à M. de Mably*, but, as Spink indicates in his editorial notes at OC IV.1264–65, is clearly cribbed from the *Spectacle de la nature* by l'abbé Pluche (1732).

72. OC III.29. While Rousseau did not generally admire philosophers—cf. Dent (1992, 191 ff.) and Meyers (2010, forthcoming) for two antithetical reasons—and there is some reason to take this as sarcasm, all things considered I do not do so. Note, however, that Descartes and Newton appear again in *Émile*, and again in a somewhat different light, cf. OC IV.575; in the third of the *Lettres écrites de la montagne* the progress of natural philosophy is exalted against the theologians, cf. OC III.736 ff.

73. Indeed, the very idea of "method" that binds together the enterprise of modern science is a self-recognition of this fact.

74. Dijksterhuis (1986, 405).

75. Cifoletti (1989).

76. OC III.29. The fourth name mentioned there is Bacon.

77. Cf. Lachterman (1989).

78. Dijksterhuis (1986). Rousseau suggests in various ways that there are limits to how much can be known, or at least on how much he knows.

79. A brief etymology is given in Rykwert (1998, 393, n. 7).

80. Duby (1982, 73).

81. This is a main Roman sense, originating the approach to dividing society into groups referred to by Rousseau; cf. Peck (1898, "*ordo*").

82. Duby (1982, 73). Cf. again Peck (1898, "*ordo*").

83. Of course, I use the word "dialectic" here in a modern sense, and not as it appears, as "complement," in Aristotle's *Rhetoric*. This and the preceding sentence may be said, however obscurely, to summarize the whole of political sociology. What all political and social theorists have missed is the way the discourse of Will, and by antithesis the discourse of dependence, only part of which we consider in this book, underpins the dialectic of *agent*, or *action*, and *structure*. Cf. Meyers (1989) on this point, as well as subsequent efforts to recast the object of inquiry in Meyers (1995), Meyers (2013a), etc. Even before rhetoric, it may have been Heraclitus who first proposed speech as the central operator in order; cf. the paraphrase and related fragments offered by Kirk and Raven (1957, 186 ff.).

84. Duby (1982, 73) is writing of Cicero at this point. For another excellent view of the proximate Ciceronian background for Rousseau in France, cf. Fumaroli (2002).

85. Duby (1982, 73). This is actually much more complicated than Duby makes it out to be, but it is not his purpose to develop this line of inquiry. This problem is revived in the sixteenth century as natural order comes, in the works of the new scientific methodists like Agricola and Ramus, to stand as the unique external model for the internal arrangement of parts in argumentation. For an interesting discussion of the implications of this in rhetoric, cf. Perelman (1969, §105), who shows how reflexive appeal to "order" problematizes naturalizing claims and illustrates the pragmatic link between "words" and "things."

86. This is clearly stated by Augustine (1965, book V, chapter 9) in his attack on Cicero. This tension between the Stoic and the Augustinian is refigured as a frame for understanding the Renaissance by Bouwsma (1975) in a way that has some relevance here.
87. Cf. *Rhetoric* 1403b. On how λέξις bridges between rhetoric, grammar, and poetics, and supports the idea that discourse is the basic unit of analysis for meaning (and, one might add, for effect), cf. Ricoeur (1975a, chapter 1).
88. The difference is itself often an effect of plurality.
89. E.g., *Rhetoric* 1366a2. This usage carries over into *Politics* (e.g., 1326a30), as well as to *Nicomachean Ethics*. It appears in what will become a paradigmatic way for the discursive field we consider here in Cicero.
90. Cicero *De officiis*, book I.XLff.: "*modestia sit scientia rerum earum, quae agentur aut dicentur, loco suo collocandarum. Ita videtur eadem vis ordinis et collocationis fore; nam et ordinem sic definiunt, compositionem rerum aptis et accommodatis locis*"; translation here is from the Loeb edition by Miller (1913).
91. Obviously, this applies only to monotheism. The Greek pantheon was a house of order and disorder, nearly of the sort that Rousseau seeks to avoid among mankind.
92. Although we have seen that the intervening order[as sequence] is also of high significance, to simplify matters here this will not be considered as distinct from the first two.
93. This analytic perspective is rhetorical in the sense outlined in Meyers (2007), Meyers and Struever (2008), and Meyers (2013a).
94. Dijksterhuis (1986:IV.§329–30), Ehrard (1994 *passim*); an illustrative example of "Boulainvilliers and the rise of French deism" is sketched by Israel (2002:565–74). Taylor (2007, 4 *et passim*) makes the analytic point that the emergence of modern science was not a necessary and certainly not a sufficient condition for "secularization."
95. A point reaffirmed with vigor by the Vicar in part two of the "*Profession de foi.*"
96. Ehrard (1994, 418).
97. Recall the definition given in the *Encyclopédie*, cited in §41 above.
98. Ehrard (1994, 418).
99. Cited in Ehrard (1994, 447).
100. For a recent example, cf. Gourevitch in Riley (2001, chapter 8).
101. Ehrard (1994, 451).
102. Diderot (1745); this is from the preface he added to his very loose translation of Lord Shaftesbury's *Inquiry Concerning Virtue*, originally published in 1699.
103. LeFranc de Pompignan (1751, 3), cited in Ehrard (1994, 456).
104. Ehrard (1994, 456).
105. I insist again that this is not the same as having an "instrumental" relation to religion.
106. CC, *lettre à M. De Franquières*, 25 March 1769. To this he adds the remarkable qualification "that the active being combines and modifies with a thorough-going force, but without having created it and without being able to destroy it"; i.e., he adopts the commonplace of Lucretian naturalism.
107. Quote from Rousseau cited in Viroli (1988, 20); Viroli's comment at (1988, 101). Burgelin elaborates the anthropological and theological consequences of Rousseau's opposition to d'Holbach in his long note 1 to OC IV.627, at OC IV.1587.

108. The attack on philosophy is widely distributed in his work; within the *"Profession de foi,"* cf. e.g., OC IV.577; the quote here is again from CC, *lettre à M. De Franquières*, 25 March 1769. Generally on this opposition, cf. Burgelin's note 2 concerning OC IV.632, at OC IV.1596.

109. This overarching theme is superbly spelled out in Ehrard (1994).

110. In my view, Rousseau's arguments both derive from and forcefully advance a number of streams in the genealogy of the specific type I call the New Model Will, which emerges in the convergence of complex and apparently unrelated aspects of historical experience. At this point I set some of these aside (e.g., political absolutism) despite their importance to the larger questions raised in this book. Cf. Meyers (1995) and (2012c). It can easily be shown (as I intend to in another work) that Riley's (1986) argument, while attractive in favoring an emphasis on theological accounts of the Will, presents an incoherent genealogy of "the civic" from "the theological."

111. This point is discussed in detail in the next section.

112. OC IV.576. In a draft version of this passage, Rousseau tried to show the contrary, failed, crossed it out, and asserted with the vigor visible here his "first principle."

113. Meyers (1989) argues that this hidden identity of agency and structure is the common core of all modern theories of power.

114. Although we must not ignore the human analogue (e.g., at OC III.247 *et passim*) and will bring it back into the discussion shortly.

115. OC IV.580. It may be said to favor the inquiry developed by Viroli (1988) that Rousseau, it seems, cannot even consider this sort of disorder without recourse to a social metaphor, *la foule*. It is worth noting in this passage as well the presence of language that will soon resonate in Kant's restatement of Rousseau's problematic.

116. OC IV.580; cf. OC I.392.

117. I employ this hyperliteral translation because the emphatic sense of the French word *faire* here is lost in more elegant alternatives.

118. *Ordonner*, in the verbal sense of "command."

119. OC IV.588; cf. also OC IV.429.

120. This is effectively the occasionalism that Malebranche developed out of debates following Descartes.

121. This is effectively the anti-occasionalist position laid down by Aquinas and highly developed by the end of the seventeenth century.

122. OC IV.245. Goodness and order are connected through "the goal of every sensate being [*la fin de tout être sensible*]" which is to be happy/*heureux*; OC IV.84.

123. Viewed retrospectively after Darwin, this raises again the basic tension between Rousseau's "creationist" and "evolutionary" views of nature.

124. I suggested this earlier and assert it more strongly now, as it is consistent with the theoretical architectonics discussed in §49 above.

125. OC IV.575. The sentence continues to connect animation with the social totality: *"puisqu'il est certain que nous qui sommes parties ne nous sentons nullement dans le tout."*]

126. We prepared for this in §§44 and 45 above.

127. Rousseau deploys precisely this kind of analogy elsewhere; cf., e.g., OC III.807, where he writes: "for it is not more permissible to slow the operation of natural laws by the social contract than it is permissible to slow the operation of positive laws by contracts between individuals, and it is only by these laws themselves that the liberty which gives force to the engagement exists [*car il n'est pas plus permis d'enfreindre les Loix naturelles par le Contract Social, qu'il n'est permis d'enfreindre les Loix positives par les Contracts des particuliers, et ce n'est que par ces Loix-mêmes qu'existe la liberté qui donne force à l'engagement*]."

128. This, again, shows how following the logic of ($Q^{fundamental}A^{nature \notin grace}$) leads to ($Q^{ecological}A^{mankind \in nature}$); see §49.

129. OC III.737. Ever ready to embarrass the contemporary reader, Rousseau adds a sarcastic reference to Psalms 78:19: "One would have to be a Jew to ask if God could lay out a meal in the desert [*il fallait être hébreu pour demander si Dieu pouvait dresser des tables dans le désert*]." This, and the next few citations, are taken from *Lettres écrites de la montagne*.

130. OC IV.1027–28; the corresponding passage in the final *Lettre* is somewhat toned down. N.b. that this standard of reasonableness applies across all domains, for example to law at OC III.743: "the authority of the laws can never extend so far as to force us to reason poorly."

131. OC III.736–37. In the word "immediate" we see that the identity of God and Nature is transferred to its antithesis: the miracle. I will not pursue this extremely interesting gesture here.

132. This was Samuel Clarke's position; gravity must be continuous intervention by God; cf. generally Clarke (1732).

133. OC IV.612. It is telling that Rousseau himself cites this passage in the *Lettres écrites de la montagne* at OC III.750.

134. Note to OC IV.612 at OC IV.1576. Burgelin contends that an "unknown hand" has changed the text; even if this is correct, I do not think that a transfer of the hesitation from the author to his reader undermines my point.

135. While these questions seem to refer to contradictions in two different domains— between Rousseau and himself and between two facts concerning *ordre*—for present purposes they are conjoined.

136. One could see this in light of Hegel's understanding of how living forms emerge over time, but also as consistent with C. S. Peirce's account of the inherent temporality of language itself.

137. Rousseau, like many others, uses the phrase *méchanisme du monde* and appeals to the *locus communis* of the watch; OC IV.578.

138. This translation is from the 1698 edtion of the "Geneva Psalter." Precisely the line that supports the image of God's Will against Nature is anomalous; it does not appear in the original or in any other translation. Macy (1992) considers why Rousseau might have inserted it; for our purposes here it is enough that it is there.

139. I have mentioned before in these notes that Bouwsma (1975) proposes a tension and complementarity expressed in "ideal typical" terms between Stoicism and Augustini-

anism as a key to understanding important intellectual developments of the Renaissance, and that there are aspects of his suggestive account that carry over into and illuminate Rousseau's context. Much of what I have said about Rousseau in this book could be construed as making him a later Renaissance rather than an Enlightenment figure, although he also resonates with post-Enlightenment and even post-Romantic ways of seeing the world.

140. Cf. Meyers (2013a, chapter 5).

141. All the following passages are from OC III.126–27.

142. Given Adam Smith's early reading of Rousseau, this may well be the source of the "invisible hand" trope so famously associated with him.

143. Cf. §§7–8 above and the next sections below.

144. For a summary statement of this problem, cf. Giddens (1984), Meyers (1989). One of the better discussions of Giddens is in Sewell (2005, chapter 4).

145. Hegel (1986, V–VI), contra Rousseau, reasserts this distinction when he differentiates the "doctrine of being" from the "doctrine of essence" in the *Logik*. Note that here the functional ambiguity in "order" — shifted toward action — is paralleled by a functional ambiguity in "law," which, while it stands likewise for the nexus of act and condition, is pushed by both the discourse of "natural law" and the discourse of "modern/bureaucratic law" toward the sense of *that which stands over the Will of the individual*.

146. Or vice versa, following Feuerbach.

147. N.b. that this does not decrease the extraordinary complexity of what it means *to say something*, but for present purposes that is a different matter.

148. This seventeenth-century phrase of Spinoza, taken over by Hegel in the nineteenth century, applies particularly to the innovative sense in which Kant conceived of the Will, which I refer to elsewhere as the "New Model Will." Cf. Spinoza's letter to Jarigh Jelles of June 2, 1674, number L in Spinoza (1927, 269); cf. also Hegel (1986, V, 121 [*Wissenschaft der Logik*, Erstes Buch, Erster Abschnitt, Zweites Kapitel, "b. Qualität"]) and Hegel (1986, XVIII, 288 [*Vorlesungen über die Geschichte der Philosophie*, Erster Teil, Erster Abschnitt, Erstes Kapitel, Paragraph über Parmenides]).

149. OC IV.589. Gourevitch (2001, 201 and note 26) claims that Rousseau believes "God is not omnipotent" and intentionally avoids that assertion (e.g., calling God only *"puissante"* and not *"toute-puissante"* in the catechism of "civil religion" at OC III.468); while this might be one way to reconcile the tension between order[as action] to order[as condition], the evidence he provides is far from convincing.

150. One of those problems is the matter considered at length by Hayek (1973). His distinction between two sorts of orders, for which he tries to find a pedigree in the terms *cosmos* and *taxis*, is not the same as the one that will be made here, nor is his purpose in making the distinction.

151. There are significant differences between the original in Pope (1733, Epistle I) and the translation of Pope by Silhouette (1736, 12–13) that need not detain us here. Cf. §1 note 10 of Part One above.

152. I qualify this in this way because together with this New Model Will an older view of

Will-as-judgment is present, as when, at OC III.142 for example, Rousseau refers to *"la puissance de vouloir"* and then adds, to clarify, *"ou plûtôt de [la puissance] de choisir,"* thereby specifying "the capacity to want" as "the capacity to want or rather to choose." I touch on the significance of this briefly below.

153. OC IV.311. Note that (a) the book to which he refers is *Du Contract social*; (b) the term *particulière* is ambiguous and may refer to either individuals or groups, neither of which has the *res publica* as their primary motive; and (c) the negated verb *être or-donée [sic]* here can mean both "improperly functioning within society" or "not in its proper place within society" or "not properly functioning by virtue of the system within which it stands." I think the last of these three options is closest to what Rousseau intends here. I do not think this point and the next ones are affected by the occasional pluralization of *volontés générales*.

154. As we saw above in §46, the alternative view, corollary to the "mutability of nature," identifies *dépendance* as that principle.

155. Cf. Richelet (1732). *N.b.* that Nicot (1606) gives the Latin *singularis* as synonym, but which points not to something unitary, but to the identity of "each" within a group, taken one by one; see Lewis and Short (1991).

156. Shklar (1985, 184).

157. Rousseau could not be more clear than he is at OC IV.636 in stating how natural philosophy leads to theology.

158. OC IV.996, from the resumé in the *Lettre à Beaumont*.

159. OC IV.614; Rousseau reiterates these views in the *Lettres écrites de la montagne*, OC III.749.

160. It may be worth noting that order[as action] at this point becomes, simply, action. The shift of order[as action] into order[as condition] also reflects the uncertain identification Rousseau makes of *dépendance-de-nature* with *dépendance-des-choses*; see again §§40, 49.28, and 49.58. We will return to this topic below.

161. N.b. that the word *concours* has at least three connotations: convergence (as in geometry), cooperation, and competition. Cf. the entries under this heading in Diderot and d'Alembert (1751–72, III, 826–28).

162. Cf. Liddell and Scott (1940) and Lewis and Short (1991), respectively.

163. Again, see Duby (1982, chapter 7). An interesting contrast may be drawn here to the "unity" of the "plot" discussed in Aristotle's *Poetics* (e.g., 1451a), where order is clearly a function of action in a way that moderns find so hard to grasp.

164. OC IV.593: *"la bonté de Dieu est l'amour de l'ordre; car c'est par l'ordre qu'il maintient ce qui existe, et lie chaque partie avec le tout."* There is an inadequate translation of this passage at Viroli (1988, 35), but he develops the point with some elegance at (1988, 53ff).

165. Willey (1961, 5).

166. From a different angle than Malebranche's occasionalism, followers of Newton like Clarke tried to subsume the latter under the former.

167. The parallel transformation in political rhetoric is pointed to by Perelman and Olbrechts-Tyteca (1969, §105), in which the order of nature becomes the external model for the internal arrangement of the parts of discourse.

168. Later social science will, of course, run into all sorts of confusion by taking these two

aspects of the same thing as antithetical. For just one synthetic account of this, cf. again Giddens (1984).

169. This "constructivist" sensibility—cf. Lachterman (1989)—may be found earlier in Hobbes, but also before the seventeenth century in the first contributors to modern algebra like Guillaume Gosselin.

170. Introduced at Burke (1945, 53–55).

171. The most thoroughgoing but ultimately unsatisfactory effort to elaborate this point may be found in Riley (1986).

172. OC IV.311; see note 153 above on the meaning of this sentence.

173. Viroli (1988, 34–35).

174. Viroli (1988, 57ff).

175. Viroli (1988, 21).

176. While I will assume that this is a plausible reading of Rousseau, it should be noted that Augustine writes in *De civitate dei contra paganos* (XV.22): "So that it seems to me that it is a brief but true definition of virtue to say, it is the order of love; and on this account, in the Canticles, the bride of Christ, the city of God, sings, 'Order love within me.' [*Vnde mihi uidetur, quod definitio breuis et uera uirtutis ordo est amoris; propter quod in sancto cantico canticorum cantat sponsa Christi, ciuitas Dei: Ordinate in me caritatem*]." Thus, the "brief and true definition of virtue" is not, as Viroli says, "the love of order," but "the order of love," which is a potentially related but nonetheless distinct matter. Marcus Dods translation in Augustine (1950, 511).

177. Cited by Burgelin at OC IV.1564, who notes also Diderot's attachment to a comparable but substantially different idea.

178. Kant (1785/1964).

179. Cf. Brown (2000), Dihle (1982), Arendt (1981).

180. The composition of this section follows Frederic Rzewski's strategy in the sixth of each set of six variations in *The People United Will Never Be Defeated*.

180a. Rousseau is the generally unacknowledged source for a modern line of Theorization of the social self that can be traced through writers as diverse as Tocqueville (1840), Durkheim (1912), and Mead (1934) up to recent theories of moral development that stem from Piaget (1932) and Kohlberg (1981).

181. On *amour de soi-même* and *perfectibilité* as driving forces in social evolution, see initially above at §6 and, generally, the *Discours sur . . . l'inégalité*, with a summary statement at OC III.162.

182. Peirce's tychism grapples with and accepts this fact.

183. Let's say that he is only matched by Hume, if we count Kant as the herald of the nineteenth century.

184. Quoted in a note by Rousseau at OC III.384.

185. When a page later a certain "genius" is attributed to the lawgiver, the modern reader will consider this another name for the "intelligence" described here; but for the eighteenth century these are not synonyms; the lawgiver has specific inspiration, capacities, and office; as I state above, "intelligence" here is not an attribute but rather a character.

186. This notation is developed beginning in §49.

187. Ehrard (1994, 751–52); his own approach to this question seems to be under the strong influence of Lucien Febvre, and thus of Marx.

188. One version may be found in Meyers (2013a).

189. Rousseau's complex deployments of the *topos* of *inflexibilité* are discussed at length above, beginning with §44.

190. We will see that W-O$^{one\ will}$ may be a special, and the most plausible, case of W-O$^{perfect\ law}$; if so, it would in any event go down with the failure of W-O$^{perfect\ law}$, which we will come to later in this Part.

191. This is a premise of the naturalism to which I gestured in §42. Nonetheless, monism is an argument, not an experience. I do not know how a Buddhist experiences the world.

192. Again, the relevant claim from the "main passage" is "if the laws of nations could have, like those of nature, an inflexibility that no human force could ever be able to overcome [*si les lois des nations pouvaient avoir, comme celles de la nature, une inflexibilité que jamais aucune force humaine ne pût vaincre*]."

193. Here again Rousseau riffs on typical pretensions of natural jurisprudence, e.g., Burlamaqui (1747, II, ii, viii, 163).

194. First two are from Richelet (1680), second two from Estienne (1549); n.b. that the word also evokes the biblical book of Acts, in which "signs and wonders" play a significant part in evangelical practice.

195. For this overlap, cf. also OC III.379. I will not consider here the dramaturgical connotation of the word.

196. The verb *éprouver* does not have a single satisfactory English equivalent: it can mean "feel" or "experience," but is also charged with the idea that the subject has been in some way tested as well; here it is used in opposition to a cognitive process, but it does not refer to immediate perception or emotion.

197. The common modal verb here is *vouloir*, which has the same root as the word *volonté*.

198. OC IV.576; cf. also OC IV.574: "You will thus ask me again how I know that there are spontaneous movements; I will tell you that I know it because I sense [*sens*] it. I want [*veux*] to move my arm and I move it, without this movement having any other immediate cause than my Will [*volonté*]."

199. This problematic is worked out in detail in Hegel (1952).

200. Peirce (1931–58, VI.36).

201. Peirce (1931–58, VI.46); complicating this as a critical perspective on Rousseau is the fact that he elsewhere recognizes the necessary operation of chance, cf., e.g., OC III.162.

202. The famous Heisenberg principle is only the peak of more than a century of rising probabilism and its formalization. The general sources and significance of this development extend far beyond the scope of this book.

203. Cf. Popper (1968a) and Popper (1968b) on falsificationism. Of course, in Rousseau's own time Hume made the argument against induction much more vigorously than Popper, and with a sense of humor to boot.

204. Kuhn (1970).

205. Bruno Latour has developed a different but related and provocative approach to the mix of humans and things; cf., e.g., the summary arguments in Latour (1991). Another parallel and still more encompassing approach can be found in Sennett (1994).

206. This suggests that only under a sort of anti-ecological assumption is the hermeneutic principle limited to the human sciences.

207. I ask this quite apart from reentering into the expression of such issues by Rousseau; in

that regard, I think that Derathé is correct to argue that science is a function of the evolution of society, in part because "Man must have a developed understanding to acquire it." For Rousseau, adds Derathé, the "law of nature is therefore not, as Locke believed, the law of the state of nature." See his note at OC III.1413 and Derathé (1970, 155 ff.).

208. I ignore here the transitional role played by Rousseau in the emergence of what I have dubbed the New Model Will.

209. That is, where $(Q^{ecological}A^{mankind \notin nature})$ because one holds $(Q^{fundamental}A^{nature \in grace})$.

210. It is on the cusp between the "human" and the "natural" that the inherent and emergent semiotic element in "nonnatural dependence-from-things" shows its essential importance.

211. Any libertarian or member of the Tea Party can tell you this.

212. This may be called a "metascientific" question before which the practices of Method stand silent. A consideration of the social processes by which materials become the object of the natural sciences is far beyond the scope of my argument. There are many other approaches to this topic, including instructive studies like Latour (1979), Latour (1999a), or the essays in Daston (2000). On the silences required by "Method" in political theory, cf. Meyers (2003).

213. Cf. George (1976) and Sen (1981); both have subsequently developed their initial arguments.

214. Shklar (1990); cf. Meyers (1989) for an account of this problem from another direction.

215. Nor, strictly speaking, need it be the final cause; in the modern world economy there is always enough food to feed everyone, the problems in fact concern ownership, distribution, spatial situation, and so forth.

216. On the circulation of *topoi* and the dialectic of speech acts and *sensus communis*, cf. Meyers (2013b).

217. Paine (1995, 34) from *Common Sense*, published in 1776.

218. For a synthesis of the enormous literature on absolutism, cf. Cosandey and Descimon (2002).

219. OC IV.1013 in fragments for *Lettre à Beaumont*.

220. Obviously, I mean here to invoke the tone of Kant, specifically in the sense noted above. As a matter of practical sociological fact one may note that the U.S. Constitution began to work this way for the nation by the late nineteenth century, or that The Universal Declaration of Human Rights has tended in an analogous cosmopolitan direction since 1948.

221. I repeat, however, that reverence for the Law and "love of order" are not the same; see §63 above.

222. On this famous point, cf. *L'Économie politique* at OC III.247–48 and *Du Contract social* at OC III.371, 438; cf. also the discussion in Durkheim (1953).

223. . . . or more precisely, a social potential for generality.

224. One might also approach this topic directly through mathematics; Mandlebrot's (1982) "fractal geometry of nature" considers natural orders that are only "parts," with larger structures reiterating the parts at various scales or levels of structure; these structures do not strictly speaking have or refer to "wholes." I doubt that this kind of order is significant for the topics we consider here.

225. I use the word "action" in a broad sense here; many claim that "action" must be re-

served to beings with Wills and therefore to human beings; by contrast, because I do not believe that action and Will (especially as that word is understood under the regime of the New Model Will) are necessarily related, I am confident in marking the opposite of the "creationist" view with the term "action." These matters are enormously complex and I shall not consider them further here.

226. This is not identical with the Aristotelian claim that the *differentia specifica* of Man is λόγος; nor is it a denial that humans at times and in certain respects act like fish or other animals. It is merely a claim within the argument presented in this book about what sorts of orders may serve as referents for the analysis of dependence, morality, and society. I accept the implication that if the concept of Will refers to anything, it is contingent on λόγος.

227. Quote from Arendt (1981, volume II, 13). This association of imagination and Will was conceived differently before the advent of the New Model Will; in *De Anima* Aristotle (427b35 ff.) suspects that some other animals have imagination but, lacking speech, cannot form beliefs; Vauvenargues (1747) gives a typical eighteenth-century perspective on the place of imagination within other faculties; cf. Bundy (1927) generally on pre-modern conceptions of imagination.

228. I leave open the question of whether *all* ways of conceiving order are anthropomorphic.

229. Couzin et al. (2005); this seems to be the key article on this topic; for many related papers, cf. the website of the Collective Animal Behavior lab at Princeton University: http://webscript.princeton.edu/~icouzin/website/lab-publications.

230. Dyer et al. (2009) seems to be the major paper on this from the group around Couzin.

231. All quotes in this paragraph are again from Couzin et al. (2005).

232. A rocket is subject to gravity but not governed by it, until its engine gives out, and the parachute fails, etc.

233. This is nearly tautological: perfect knowledge of the future states of an evolving order could only be had from a perspective that included its end; that perspective would have to be outside of the time defined by evolution itself. Christianity proposes one solution to this paradox.

234. I mean here by "space" the sense of the word which you, dear reader, are most likely to have in mind; I reserve to myself for another occasion a discussion of the concepts of space essential for political theory; cf. e.g. Meyers (2013a).

235. This is why theories that gesture to "the end of history" are, prima facie, nonhistorical and therefore without any descriptive or analytic value for politics or moral life (although they may carry great rhetorical weight).

236. Cf. Meyers (1999) and Meyers (2000).

237. On the deep radical implications of modern evolutionary understanding, cf. Simpson (1949), Gould (1977), Gould (2002), Lewontin (1984), Greenwood (1984), and many others. A recent transdisciplinary view is expressed by Corning (2005). The amount of drivel written on this subject is truly astonishing.

238. Of course, one may pretend that an order which has evolved is, now, a static entity; the ahistorical methods of economic analysis provide a good example of this. This returns to without resolving the problem mentioned just above.

239. A classical point neatly refigured for contemporary political science by Pierson (2004).

240. There seems to be a growth industry in this sort of nonsense; cf. e.g. Fisher (2009, chapter 10), who recommends ant-like behavior to his readers. The reduction of humans to "nothing but" animals is roundly rebuked by Simpson (1949, 284).

241. But cf. Meyers (2008a, chapter 1).

242. One might argue that general laws like gravity—which after Newton was, of course, the primary model of "perfectly inflexible" natural law that thinkers of the eighteenth century had in mind—only bear on the question of dependence as, or as characteristics of, local events. We do not need to consider this here.

243. Except, of course, in the discursive sense just mentioned: some people claim *this* aspect of experience is natural and others claim it is social. This is a different albeit ultimately related matter. Cf. §67 above.

244. Oddly enough, this may lead back toward a monist view of nature, but one that is both evolutionary and ecological: what mountain, avalanche, tree, coral reef, planet, etc. conceives of itself as "one thing?"

245. James K. Fiebleman, "Disorder," in Kuntz (1968, 10).

246. Cf. Burke (1945, "The container and the thing contained" *et passim*).

247. Paul Weiss, "Some Paradoxes Relating to Order," in Kuntz (1968, 16).

248. James K. Fiebleman, "Disorder," in Kuntz (1968, 11).

249. These and analogous issues appear pervasively in Western culture; one could say that Romanticism is the cult of order-without-totality, or that the majority of modern music enacts the temptation of order-without-totality.

250. Cf. Meyers (2008b).

251. But not all: even in Rousseau's writings, and certainly elsewhere, the Will has additional sources; the balance seems to tip in favor of the nontheological sources sometime after Kant. I should add, too, that we as readers and thinkers need not revel in nor even reveal our religious commitments to take this theological fact into account.

252. In fact, this book is one of the preliminary studies for that larger project, although the relation between the two cannot appear clearly until the genealogy of the Will is complete and becomes the basis for a thorough reconfiguration of the concept of power. Cf. Meyers (1989), Meyers (1995), and my long-stewing book on power, *Dancing on a Landslide*.

253. The force of such statements is discussed in Wittgenstein (1969).

254. OC IV.584–85; this seems to resonate with Proverbs 29:9.

AFTERWORD

1. From a political point of view, the most significant of these is the "problem of power." Cf. Meyers (1989), briefly restated in Meyers (2013a, "Principles"). All this will eventually be published in a book entitled *Dancing on a Landslide*.

2. This is, of course, the self-description of modern formal logic; one may view it with skepticism.

3. See Meyers (1989) and Meyers (2001).

4. An obvious point missed by many social scientists and stated with some eloquence by Hirschman (1984).

5. In Hegel's sense of *Anerkennung*; cf. Meyers (1989, chapter 8).

6. Of course, I am not making the anti-Freudian and obviously untenable point that *all* human beings *always* seek their own good.

7. Cf. e.g. Klaus and Kennell (1976, chapter 3), keeping in mind corrections by Eyre (1993).

8. Although I have avoided doing so in the discussion of Rousseau in this book (for reasons given in §16 above) it is of course common to distinguish between need and desire. One says that desire is social, need is natural. As should be abundantly clear from our interrogation of Rousseau, the familiar contraposition social/natural cannot be accepted at face value, if at all. Nonetheless, considering the structure of dependence at this finer order of resolution one may not want to simply collapse the two terms. Need and attachment refer to two facets of the more general term dependence. The desire for affirmation refers to the person's approach to the situation of dependence that cuts across both need and attachment. However "natural" need may be, it is always read through the "social" moment highlighted by the relational theory of the person, which in common language is desire. I find Mead (1934) particularly helpful on this point.

9. They finance entrepreneurial institutions like business schools to design sanctions for them.

10. Intentional disruptions, like strikes or sabotage, which are nonetheless "mistakes" from the "system-point-of-view," are not taken into consideration here.

11. With the same processes of technical change and division of labor having deskilled operatives or officeholders to the point that they can be replaced with relative ease; the organization of work leverages sanctions.

12. The naturalization of psychology mentioned above contributes to just such a world-version. As I have tried to show in Meyers (1989, chapter 5), the main ideological divide that serves this purpose is between the New Model Will and the unintended consequences of action. How this bears on the argument here is much too complicated to consider at this point.

13. I show elsewhere that this shift from the topic of Will to the topic of dependence is the best way to understand the rise of the New Model Will itself and to solve central sociological dilemmas like the "structure/agency problem." See, e.g., Meyers (1989) and Meyers (2006).

14. I continue to use Rousseau's terms, but in fact Hegel's development of the idea of a *System der Sittlichkeit* would perhaps be a clearer way to capture what is meant here.

WORKS CITED

Aarsleff, Hans. 2001. Introduction. In Condillac 2001.

Abbadie, Jacques. 1694. *Art de se connoitre soy-meme; ou, la recherche des sources de la morale*. Rotterdam: P. Vander Slaart.

———. 1695. *The Art of Knowing Ones-Self, or, A Diligent Search into the Springs of Morality. Wherein Is Sought, the Spring of Our Corruption, Self-Love Is Treated of, the Force of Its Indearments, the Extent of Its Affections, and Its Irregularities in General, and in Particular*. London: Printed by E.J. for R. Bentley at the Post-House in Russell Street, Covent-Garden.

Académie française. 1694. *Dictionnaire de l'Académie francoise, dédié au roy*. Paris: J. B. Coignard.

———. 1798. *Dictionnaire de l'Académie francoise*. 5th ed. Paris: J. J. Smits.

Adorno, Theodor W. 1973. *Philosophy of Modern Music*. New York: Seabury Press.

d'Alembert, Jean le Rond. *Discours préliminaire*. In Diderot and d'Alembert 1751–72.

Alexander, Jeffrey. 1982. *Theoretical Logic in Sociology*. Berkeley: University of California Press.

Alexander, Jeffrey, ed. 1997. *The Classical Tradition in Sociology: The American Tradition*. London: Sage Publications.

Althusser, Louis. 1972. *Politics and History: Montesquieu, Rousseau, Hegel and Marx*. London: NLB.

American Association of Museums. 1915. *Proceedings of the American Association of Museums; Records of the 10th Annual Meeting Held in Chicago, July 6–9, 1915*. Charleston, S.C.: The Association.

l'Aminot, Tanguy. 1992. Images de J.-J. Rousseau de 1912 à 1978. Oxford: Voltaire Foundation.

Anon. 1954. *Ad C. Herennium De Ratione Dicendi: (Rhetorica Ad Herennium)*. Loeb Classical Library. Cambridge, Mass.: Harvard University Press.

Anon. The Golden Rule. In *Wikipedia*. http://en.wikipedia.org/wiki/The_Golden_Rule_(ethics).

Ansell-Pearson, Keith. 1991. *Nietzsche Contra Rousseau: A Study of Nietzsche's Moral and Political Thought*. Cambridge: Cambridge University Press.

Arendt, Hannah. 1958. *The Human Condition*. Charles R. Walgreen Foundation lectures. Chicago: University of Chicago Press.

———. 1963. *On Revolution*. New York: Viking Press.

———. 1981. *The Life of the Mind*. One-volume edition. San Diego: Harcourt Brace Jovanovich.

———. 1993. *Qu'est-ce que la politique?* Paris: Seuil.

———. 2003. *Was ist Politik? Fragmente aus dem Nachlass*. Munich: Piper.

Ariès, Philippe. 1960. *L'Enfant et la vie familiale sous l'ancien régime*. Paris: Plon.

Aristotle. 1926–. *Aristotle in Twenty-Three Volumes*. Loeb Classical Library. Cambridge, Mass.: Harvard University Press.

Arnauld, Antoine, and Pierre Nicole. 1662. *La Logique, ou, l'art de penser: contenant, outre les règles communes, plusieurs observations nouvelles propres a former le jugement*. Paris: Chez Jean Guignart, Charles Savreux, Jean de Launay.

Aron, Raymond. 1967. *Les Étapes de la pensée sociologique*. Paris: Gallimard.

———. 1968. *Main Currents in Sociological Thought*. Garden City, N.Y.: Anchor Books.

Arrow, Kenneth Joseph. 1951. *Social Choice and Individual Values*. New York: Wiley.

Augustine. 1924. *De civitate dei contra paganos. Libri XXII*. London: Society for Promoting Christian Knowledge.

———. 1950. *The City of God*. New York: Modern Library.

———. 1965. *De civitate dei contra paganos. The City of God Against the Pagans*. Loeb Classical Library. Cambridge, Mass.: Harvard University Press.

Austin, John. 1832. *The Province of Jurisprudence Determined*. London: J. Murray.

———. 1869. *Lectures on Jurisprudence, or, The Philosophy of Positive Law*. 3rd ed. London: J. Murray.

Babbitt, Irving. 1919. *Rousseau and Romanticism*. New York: Houghton Mifflin.

Baker, Keith Michael. 1994. Enlightenment and the Institution of Society: Notes for a Conceptual History. In Melching 1994.

Balibar, Étienne. 1985. *Spinoza et la politique*. Paris: Presses universitaires de France.

Barber, Benjamin R. 1974. *The Death of Communal Liberty: A History of Freedom in a Swiss Mountain Canton*. Princeton, N.J.: Princeton University Press.

———. 1984. *Strong Democracy: Participatory Politics for a New Age*. Berkeley: University of California Press.

Barnes, Harry Elmer. 1948. *An Introduction to the History of Sociology*. Chicago: University of Chicago Press.

Barthes, Roland. 1977. *Writing Degree Zero*. New York: Macmillan.

Bataille, Georges. 1929. Informe. *Documents*. Paris: [s.n.]

Baudrillard, Jean. 1968. *Le Système des objets*. Paris: Gallimard.

———. 1972. *Pour une Critique de l'économie politique du signe*. Paris: Gallimard.

Bazaillas, Albert. 1914. *Rousseau et les femmes*. Paris: F. Alcan.

Becker, Carl Lotus. 1922. *The Declaration of Independence: A Study in the History of Political Ideas*. New York: Harcourt Brace.

———. 1932. *The Heavenly City of the Eighteenth Century Philosophers*. New Haven: Yale University Press.

Benjamin, Walter. 1972–1989. *Gesammelte Schriften.* 1st ed. Frankfurt am Main: Suhrkamp.

———. 1986. *Reflections: Essays, Aphorisms, Autobiographical Writings.* New York: Schocken Books.

Bennett, Jane. 2001. *The Enchantment of Modern Life: Attachments, Crossings, and Ethics.* Princeton, N.J.: Princeton University Press.

Bentham, Jeremy. 1789. *An Introduction to the Principles of Morals and Legislation: Printed in the Year 1780, and Now First Published.* London: Printed for T. Payne, and son, at the Mews Gate.

Berlin, Isaiah. 1969. *Four Essays on Liberty.* London: Oxford University Press.

Berman, Marshall. 1970. *The Politics of Authenticity; Radical Individualism and the Emergence of Modern Society.* New York: Atheneum.

Berrios, G. E. and M. Gili. 1995. Will and Its Disorders: A Conceptual History. *History of Psychiatry* 6 (21): 87–104.

Bittner, Rüdiger. 1989. *What Reason Demands.* Cambridge: Cambridge University Press.

Bloom, Harold, ed. 1988. *Daniel Defoe's Robinson Crusoe.* Modern critical interpretations. New York: Chelsea House.

Boas, George. 1966. *The Cult of Childhood.* London: Warburg Institute.

———.1973. *Macrocosm and Microcosm.* in Weiner (1973), vol. III, pp. 126 ff.

Bodin, Jean. 1576. *Les Six livres de la république.* Paris: Chez Iacques du Puys.

Bois, Yve Alain, and Rosalind E. Krauss. 1997. *Formless: A User's Guide.* New York: Zone Books.

Boltanski, Luc, and Eve Chiapello. 1999. *Le Nouvel esprit du capitalisme.* NRF essais. Paris: Gallimard.

Bookchin, Murray. 1980. *Toward an Ecological Society.* Montreal: Black Rose Books.

Bourdieu, Pierre. 1987. *Choses dites.* Le Sens commun. Paris: Minuit.

———. 1993. *La Misère du monde.* Paris: Seuil.

Bourdieu, Pierre, and Loïc J. D. Wacquant.1992. *An Invitation to Reflexive Sociology.* Chicago: University of Chicago Press.

Bouwsma, William James. 1975. The Two Faces of Humanism: Stoicism and Augustinianism in Renaissance Thought. in Oberman 1975, 3–60.

———. 1990. *A Usable Past.* Berkeley: University of California Press.

Bowles, Samuel, and Herbert Gintis. 1986. *Democracy and Capitalism: Property, Community, and the Contradictions of Modern Social Thought.* New York: Basic Books.

Brodsky Lacour, Claudia. 1996. *Lines of Thought: Discourse, Architectonics, and the Origin of Modern Philosophy.* Durham, N.C.: Duke University Press.

Brown, Peter Robert Lamont. 2000. *Augustine of Hippo.* Berkeley: University of California Press.

Brunner, Otto, Werner Conze, and Reinhart Koselleck, eds. 1972. *Geschichtliche Grundbegriffe: Historisches Lexikon zur politisch-sozialen Sprache in Deutschland.* Stuttgart: E. Klett.

Buffenoir, Hippolyte. 1891. *Jean-Jacques Rousseau et les femmes (XVIIIe–XIXe siècles).* Paris: Lemerre.

Buffon, Georges-Louis Leclerc. 1749. *Histoire naturelle générale et particulière, avec la description du Cabinet du roi.* 36 vols. Paris: Imprimerie royale.

Bundy, Murray Wright. 1927. *The Theory of Imagination in Classical and Mediaeval Thought.* Urbana: University of Illinois Press.

Burgelin, Pierre. 1952. *Le Philosophie de l'existence de J.-J. Rousseau.* Paris: Presses universitaires de France.

Burke, Kenneth. 1945. *A Grammar of Motives.* New York: Prentice-Hall.

———. 1950. *A Rhetoric of Motives.* New York: Prentice-Hall.

Burlamaqui, J. J. 1747. *Principes du droit naturel.* Geneva: Chez Barrillot & Fils.

———. 1751. *Principes du droit politique.* Amsterdam: Z. Chastelain.

Button, Mark E. 2008. *Contract, Culture, and Citizenship.* University Park: Pennsylvania State University Press.

Butts, Robert E., and Joseph C. Pitt. 1978. *New Perspectives on Galileo.* Boston: D. Reidel.

Calas, Nicolas. 1942. *Confound the Wise.* New York: Arrow Editions.

Calhoun, Craig, ed. 1993. *Bourdieu: Critical Perspectives.* Chicago: University of Chicago Press.

———. 2007. *Sociology in America: A History.* Chicago: University of Chicago Press.

Calvin, Jean. 1536. *Christianae Religionis Institutio . . . : Praefatio Ad Christianissimum Regem Franciae.* Basel: Thomas Platter and Balthasar Lasius.

Campbell, Colin. 1987. *The Romantic Ethic and the Spirit of Modern Consumerism.* New York: Blackwell.

Cassirer, Ernst. 1906. *Das Erkenntnisproblem in der Philosophie und Wissenschaft der neueren Zeit.* Berlin: B. Cassirer.

———. 1927. *Individuum und Kosmos in der Philosophie der Renaissance.* Darmstadt: Wissenschaftliche Buchgesellschaft.

———. 1932. Das Problem Jean Jacques Rousseau. *Archiv für Geschichte der Philosophie* 41: 177–213, 479–513.

———. 1945. *Rousseau, Kant, Goethe; Two Essays.* Princeton, N.J.: Princeton University Press.

———. 1953. *The Philosophy of Symbolic Forms.* New Haven: Yale University Press.

———. 1963. *The Question of Jean-Jacques Rousseau.* Bloomington: Indiana University Press.

———. 1977. *The Individual and the Cosmos in Renaissance Philosophy.* New York: Harper & Row.

Cefaï, Daniel. 1998. *Phénoménologie et sciences sociales: Alfred Schutz, naissance d'une anthropologie philosophique.* Geneva: Droz.

Chapelain, Jean. 1880. *Lettres de Jean Chapelain, de l'académie française.* Paris: Imprimerie nationale.

———. 2007. *Opuscules critiques.* Geneva: Droz.

Chartier, Roger. 1987. *Lectures et lecteurs dans la France d'Ancien Régime.* Paris: Seuil.

———. 1990. *Les Origines culturelles de la révolution française.* Paris: Seuil.

Christian, Lynda G. 1987. *Theatrum Mundi: The History of an Idea.* Harvard dissertations in comparative literature. New York: Garland.

Cicero, Marcus Tullius. 1913. *De Officiis.* Loeb Classical Library. London: W. Heinemann.

———. 1954. *The Speeches.* Loeb Classical Library. Cambridge, Mass.: Harvard University Press.

———. 1972. *Cicero in Twenty-Eight Volumes.* Loeb Classical Library. London: W. Heinemann.

———. 2003. *De Natura Deorum.* Cambridge Greek and Latin classics. Cambridge: Cambridge University Press.

Cifoletti, Giovanna Cleonice. 1989. Quaestio sive aequatio: la nozione di problema nelle Regulae. Working Papers of the European University Institute. Firenze: EUI.

———. 1992. Mathematics and Rhetoric: Peletier and Gosselin and the Making of the French Algebraic Tradition. Ph.D. dissertation, Princeton University.

Cipolla, Carlo M. 1967. *Clocks and Culture, 1300–1700.* London: Collins.

Cladis, Mark Sydney. 1992. *A Communitarian Defense of Liberalism: Emile Durkheim and Contemporary Social Theory.* Stanford: Stanford University Press.

———. 2007. *Public Vision, Private Lives.* New York: Columbia University Press.

Clarke, Samuel. 1732. *A Discourse Concerning the Being and Attributes of God, the Obligations of Natural Religion, and the Truth and Certainty of the Christian Revelation . . . Being Sixteen Sermons, . . . in . . . 1704, and 1705, at the Lecture Founded by the Honourable Robert Boyle, Esq; In Which Is Inserted A Discourse Concerning the Connexion of the Prophecies in the Old Testament. The eighth edition.* London: printed by W. Botham, for James and John Knapton.

Colas, Dominique. 1997. *Civil Society and Fanaticism: Conjoined Histories.* Stanford: Stanford University Press.

Colletti, Lucio. 1973. *From Rousseau to Lenin; Studies in Ideology and Society.* New York: Monthly Review Press.

Condillac, Étienne Bonnot de. 1749. *Traité des sistêmes: ou l'on en démêle les inconvéniens & les avantages.* La Haye : Neaulme.

———. 1776. *Le Commerce et le gouvernement, considérés relativement l'un à l'autre.* Amsterdam: Chez Jombert & Cellot.

———. 2001. Essay on the Origin of Human Knowledge. Cambridge: Cambridge University Press.

Connolly, Joy. 2007. *The State of Speech.* Princeton, N.J.: Princeton University Press.

Constant, Benjamin. 1820. *Collection complète des ouvrages publiée sur le gouvernement représentatif et la constitution actuelle, ou Cours de politique constitutionelle.* Paris: Pierre Blancher.

Cooley, Charles Horton. 1902. *Human Nature and the Social Order.* New York: C. Scribner's Sons.

———.1909. *Social Organization: A Study of the Larger Mind.* New York: C. Scribner's Sons.

Corning, Peter A. 2005. *Holistic Darwinism: Synergy, Cybernetics, and the Bioeconomics of Evolution.* Chicago: University of Chicago Press.

Cosandey, Fanny, and Robert Descimon. 2002. *L'absolutisme en France.* Paris: Seuil.

Couzin, Iain D., Jens Krause, Nigel R. Franks, and Simon A. Levin. 2005. Effective Leadership and Decision-making in Animal Groups on the Move. *Nature* 433, no. 7025: 513–16.

Cranston, Maurice William. 1983. *Jean-Jacques: The Early Life and Work of Jean-Jacques Rousseau, 1712–1754*. New York: Norton.

———. 1991. *The Noble Savage: Jean-Jacques Rousseau, 1754–1762*. Chicago: University of Chicago Press.

———. 1997. *The Solitary Self*. Chicago: University of Chicago Press.

Crombie, A. C. 1953. *Robert Grosseteste and the Origins of Experimental Science, 1100–1700*. Oxford: Clarendon Press.

Crousaz, Jean-Pierre de. 1720. *La Logique, ou système de reflexions, qui peuvent contribuer à la netteté & l'étendue de nos connoissances*. Amsterdam: Chez L'Honor & Chatelain.

Cuvier, Georges. 1817. *Le Regne animal distribué d'après son organisation, pour servir de base à l'histoire naturelle des animaux et d'introduction à l'anatomie comparée*. Paris: Chez Déterville, de l'imprimerie de A. Belin.

Dahl, Robert Alan. 1961. *Who Governs? Democracy and Power in an American City*. New Haven: Yale University Press.

Damrosch, Leopold. 2005. *Jean-Jacques Rousseau: Restless Genius*. Boston: Houghton Mifflin.

Dante Alighieri. 1955. *La divina commedia: Inferno*. Florence: La nuova italia editrice.

Darnton, Robert. 1982. *The Literary Underground of the Old Regime*. Cambridge, Mass.: Harvard University Press.

———. 1985. *The Great Cat Massacre and Other Episodes in French Cultural History*. New York: Vintage Books.

Darwin, Charles. 1859. *On the Origin of Species by Means of Natural Selection, or the Preservation of Favoured Races in the Struggle for Life*. London: John Murray.

Darwin, Erasmus. 1794. *Zoonomia; or, The Laws of Organic Life*. London: J. Johnson.

Daston, Lorraine. 1995. *Classical Probability in the Enlightenment*. Princeton, N.J.: Princeton University Press.

———. 2000. *Biographies of Scientific Objects*. Chicago: University of Chicago Press.

———. 2001. *Eine Kurze Geschichte der wissenschaftlichen Aufmerksamkeit*. Munich: Carl Friedrich von Siemens Stiftung.

———. 2007. *Things That Talk*. New York: Zone Books.

Daston, Lorraine, and Katharine Park. 1998. *Wonders and the Order of Nature, 1150–1750*. New York: Zone Books.

Daston, Lorraine, and Gianna Pomata, eds. 2003. *The Faces of Nature in Enlightenment Europe*. Berlin: BWV-Berliner Wissenschafts-Verlag.

Daston, Lorraine, and Michael Stolleis. 2006. *Natural Law and Laws of Nature in Early Modern Europe*. Burlington, Vt.: Ashgate Publishing.

Daston, Lorraine, and Fernando Vidal. 2004. *The Moral Authority of Nature*. Chicago: University of Chicago Press.

Davenport, John J. 2007. *Will as Commitment and Resolve*. New York: Fordham University Press.

De Man, Paul. 1979. *Allegories of Reading: Figural Language in Rousseau, Nietzsche, Rilke, and Proust*. New Haven: Yale University Press.

Defoe, Daniel. 1719. *The Life, and Strange Surprizing Adventures of Robinson Crusoe of York, Mariner: Who Lived Eight and Twenty Years All Alone in an Un-Inhabited Island* on the Coast of America, Near the Mouth of the Great River of Oroonoque; . . . Written by Himself. The fourth edition. To which is added a map. London: printed for W. Taylor.

———. 1720. *La Vie et les avantures surprenantes de Robinson Crusoe . . . traduit de l'anglois par Justus Van Effen et Thémiseul de Saint-Hyacinthe.* Amsterdam: Chez L'Honoré & Chatelain.

Dent, N. J. H. 1992. *A Rousseau Dictionary.* Cambridge: Blackwell Reference.

Derathé, Robert. 1948. *Le Rationalisme de J.-J. Rousseau.* Paris: Presses universitaires de France.

———. 1970. *Jean-Jacques Rousseau et la science politique de son temps.* 2nd ed. Bibliothèque d'histoire de la philosophie. Paris: J. Vrin. [1st ed. 1950]

Descartes, René. 1637. *Discours de la méthode pour bien conduire sa raison, & chercher la vérité dans les sciences. Plus la dioptriqve. Les meteores. Et la geometrie. Qui sont des essais de cete methode.* Leiden: De l' imprimerie de I. Maire.

———. 1964. *Oeuvres.* Paris: J. Vrin.

Desrosières, Alain. 2000. *La Politique des grands nombres.* Paris: La Découverte.

Dewey, John. 1916. *Democracy and Education: An Introduction to the Philosophy of Education.* New York: Macmillan.

Diderot, Denis. 1745. *Principes de la philosophie morale: ou, essai de M. S***. Sur le mérite et la vertu, avec réflexions.* Amsterdam [Paris]: Chez Zacharie Chatelain.

Diderot, Denis, *Moeurs.* In Diderot and d'Alembert (1751–72, X, 611).

———. *Chose.* In Diderot and d'Alembert (1751–72, III, 374).

———. *Indépendance.* In Diderot and d'Alembert (1751–72, VIII, 671).

———. *Hobbisme.* In Diderot and d'Alembert (1751–72, VIII, 240–41).

———. *Droit naturel.* In Diderot and d'Alembert (1751–72, V, 115–16).

———. *Spinosiste.* In Diderot and d'Alembert (1751–72, XV, 474).

Diderot, Denis, and Jean le Rond d'Alembert. 1751–72. *Encyclopédie, ou, dictionnaire raisonné des sciences, des arts et des metiers.* 28 vols. Paris and Neufchastel: Briasson et al. and Faulche.

Dihle, Albrecht. 1962. *Die goldene Regel.* Göttingen: Vandenhoeck & Ruprecht.

———. 1982. *The Theory of Will in Classical Antiquity.* Berkeley: University of California Press.

Dijksterhuis, E. J. 1986. *The Mechanization of the World Picture: Pythagoras to Newton.* Princeton, N.J: Princeton University Press.

Dilthey, Wilhelm. 1883. *Einleitung in die Geisteswissenschaften: Versuch einer Grundlegung für das Studien der Gesellschaft und der Geschichte; Erster Band.* Leipzig: Duncker & Humblot.

———. 1914– . *Gesammelte Schriften.* Leipzig: Teubner.

Donzelot, Jacques. 1984. *L'Invention du social: Essai sur le déclin des passions politiques.* L'Espace du politique. Paris: Fayard.

Duby, Georges. 1982. *The Three Orders: Feudal Society Imagined.* Chicago: University of Chicago Press.

Dumouchel, Paul. 1995. *Émotions: Essai sur le corps et le social.* Le Plessis-Robinson: Synthelabo.

Dunner, Joseph. 1955. *Baruch Spinoza and Western Democracy.* New York: Philosophical Library.

Durkheim, Emile. 1912. *Le Suicide: étude de sociologie (2. éd.).* Paris: Félix Alcan.

———. 1924. *Sociologie et philosophie.* Bibliothèque de philosophie contemporaine. Paris: Félix Alcan.

———. 1953. *Montesquieu et Rousseau, précurseurs de la sociologie.* Paris: M. Rivière.

Dyer, J.R.G., A. Johansson, D. Helbing, Iain D. Couzin, and Jens Krause. 2009. Leadership, Consensus Decision Making and Collective Behaviour in Humans. *Philosophical Transactions of the Royal Society B: Biological Sciences* 364, no. 1518: 781–89.

Earman, John. 1990. Bayes' Bayesianism. *Studies in History and Philosophy of Science Part A* 21 (3): 351–70.

Easton, David, John G. Gunnell, and Michael B. Stein, eds. 1994. *Regime and Discipline: Democracy and the Development of Political Science.* Ann Arbor: University of Michigan Press.

Eckstein, Walter. 1944. Rousseau and Spinoza: Their Political Theories and Their Conception of Ethical Freedom. *Journal of the History of Ideas* 5 (3): 259–91.

Ehrard, Jean. 1994. *L'Idée de nature en France dans la première moitié du XVIIIe siècle.* Paris: Albin Michel. [1st ed. 1961]

Einaudi, Mario. 1967. *The Early Rousseau.* Ithaca, N.Y.: Cornell University Press.

Einstein, Albert, and Max Born. 2005. *The Born–Einstein Letters: Friendship, Politics and Physics in Uncertain Times.* New York: Macmillan.

Elias, Norbert. 1939. *Über den Prozess der Zivilisation; Soziogenetische und psychogenetische Untersuchungen.* Basel: Haus zum Falken.

———. 1983. *The Court Society.* New York: Pantheon.

Elshtain, Jean Bethke. 1981. *Public Man, Private Woman: Women in Social and Political Thought.* Princeton, N.J.: Princeton University Press.

Elster, Jon. 1989. *The Cement of Society: A Study of Social Order.* Cambridge: Cambridge University Press.

Elster, Jon, and John Roemer. 1991. *Interpersonal Comparisons of Well-Being.* Cambridge: Cambridge University Press.

Erasmus, Desiderius. 1513. *De Duplici Copia Rerum Ac Verborum.* Strasbourg: [s.n.]

Estienne, Robert. 1549. *Dictionnaire francois latin, . . . corrigé et augmenté.* Paris: Robert Estienne, Imprimeur du roy.

Eyer, Diane E. 1993. *Mother-Infant Bonding: A Scientific Fiction.* New Haven: Yale University Press.

Fairbairn, W. Ronald D. 1952. *Psychoanalytic Studies of the Personality.* London: Tavistock Publications.

Farrell, Thomas B. 1993. *Norms of Rhetorical Culture.* New Haven: Yale University Press.

Feffer, Andrew. 1993. *The Chicago Pragmatists and American Progressivism.* Ithaca, N.Y.: Cornell University Press.

Feffer, Melvin. 1982. *The Structure of Freudian Thought: The Problem of Immutability and Discontinuity in Developmental Theory.* New York: International Universities Press.

———. 1999. *The Conflict of Equals: A Constructivist View of Personality Development.* Goteborg: Goteborg Studies in Educational Sciences.

Fermon, Nicole. 1997. *Domesticating Passions: Rousseau, Woman, and Nation.* Hanover, N.H.: University Press of New England [for] Wesleyan University Press.

Ferval, Claude. 1934. *Jean-Jacques Rousseau et les femmes.* Paris: A. Fayard.

Fisher, Len. 2009. *The Perfect Swarm: The Science of Complexity in Everyday Life.* New York: Basic Books.

Fletcher, Lancelot R. 2007. On the Title of Plato's Republic (POLITEIA). Accessed at www.freelance-academy.org May 29, 2011.

Forbes, Duncan. 1985. *Hume's Philosophical Politics.* Cambridge: Cambridge University Press.

Foucault, Michel. 1976. *Histoire de la sexualité, tome 1. La Volonté de savoir.* Paris: Gallimard.

Fouillée, Alfred. 1890. *L'Évolutionnisme des idées-forces.* Paris: F. Alcan.

———. 1893. *La Psychologie des idées-forces.* Paris: F. Alcan.

Françon, Marcel. 1949. Le Langage mathématique de J.-J. Rousseau. *Isis* 40 (4): 341–44.

Freud, Sigmund. 1991/1914. *Freud's "On Narcissism—an Introduction."* Contemporary Freud. New Haven: Yale University Press.

Fulda, Hans Friedrich and Rolf-Peter Horstmann, eds. 1991. *Rousseau, Die Revolution und der junge Hegel.* Stuttgart: Klett-Cotta.

Fumaroli, Marc. 2002. *L'Âge de l'éloquence.* Geneva: Librairie Droz.

Funkenstein, Amos. 1986. *Theology and the Scientific Imagination from the Middle Ages to the Seventeenth Century.* Princeton, N.J.: Princeton University Press.

Furet, Francois. 1978. *Penser la révolution française.* Paris: Gallimard.

Furetière, Antoine. 1690. *Dictionaire universel, contenant generalement tous les mots français tant vieux que modernes, & les termes de toutes les sciences et des arts.* The Hague: Arnout & Renier Leers.

Fuseli, Henry. 1767. *Remarks on the Writings and Conduct of J. J. Rousseau.* London: Printed for T. Cadel . . . ; J. Johnson and B. Davenport; and J. Payne.

Gadamer, Hans Georg. 1975/1960. *Wahrheit und Methode.* 4th ed. Tübingen: Mohr. [trans. 1975 as *Truth and Method.* New York: Seabury Press.]

Gagnebin, Bernard. 1944. *Burlamaqui et le droit naturel.* Geneva: Éditions de la Frégate.

Galilei, Galileo. 1635. *Systema Cosmicvm, Authore Galilæo Galilæi . . . : In Quo Qvatvor Dialogis, De Duobus Maximis Mundi Systematibus, Ptolemaico & Copernicano, Vtriusq; Rationibus Philosophicis Ac Naturalibus Indefinite Propositis Disseritur.* Avgvstæ Treboc[corum] [Strasburg]: impensis Elzeviriorvm, typis Davidis Havtti.

———. 1663. *Dialogus de Systemate Mundi.* London: Prostat voenalis apud Thomam Dicas.

———. 1890. *Le Opere di Galileo Galilei.* Firenze: G. Barbra.

Gaonkar, Dilip, and Keith Topper. Forthcoming.

Garbe, Christine. 1992. *Die "weibliche" List im "mannlichen" Text: Jean-Jacques Rousseau in der feministischen Kritik.* Stuttgart: Metzler.

Garrett, Don. 1996. *The Cambridge Companion to Spinoza.* New York: Cambridge University Press.

Gauchet, Marcel. 1985. *Le Désenchantement du monde: Une histoire politique de la religion.* Paris: Gallimard.

———. 1995. *La Révolution des pouvoirs: La Souveraineté, le peuple et la représentation, 1789–1799.* Paris: Gallimard.

Gauthier, David P. 1990. *Moral Dealing: Contract, Ethics, and Reason.* Ithaca, N.Y.: Cornell University Press.

———. 2006. *Rousseau: The Sentiment of Existence.* New York: Cambridge University Press.

George, Susan. 1976. *How the Other Half Dies: The Real Reasons for World Hunger*. Harmondsworth: Penguin.

Gianturco, Elio. 1990. Translator's Introduction. In Vico 1709/1990, xxi–xlvi.

Gibbons, Michael T. (ed.). 2012, forthcoming. *Encyclopedia of Political Thought*. Oxford: Wiley-Blackwell.

Giddens, Anthony. 1984. *The Constitution of Society: Outline of the Theory of Structuration*. Berkeley: University of California Press.

Gierke, Otto Friedrich von. 1883. *Natural Law and the Theory of Society, 1500 to 1800*. Cambridge: The University Press.

———. 1868. *Das deutsche Genossenschaftsrecht*. Berlin: Weidmann.

———. 1903. *Die historische Rechtsschule und die Germanisten*. Berlin: G. Schade.

———. 1915. *Die Grundbegriffe des Staatsrechts und die neuesten Staatsrechtstheorien*. Tübingen: Mohr.

Gilbert, Neal Ward. 1960. *Renaissance Concepts of Method*. New York: Columbia University Press.

———. 1963. Galileo and the School of Padua. *Journal of the History of Philosophy* 1 (2): 223–31.

Gillespie, Michael Allen. 2008. *The Theological Origins of Modernity*. Chicago: University of Chicago Press.

Gillet, J. E. 1918. A Note on the Tragic "Admiratio." *Modern Language Review* 13: 233–38.

Gilligan, Carol. 1982. *In a Different Voice: Psychological Theory and Women's Development*. Cambridge, Mass.: Harvard University Press.

Goffman, Erving. 1972. *Relations in Public: Microstudies of the Public Order*. New York: Harper & Row.

Goldman, Harvey S. 2004. Reexamining the "Examined Life" in Plato's Apology of Socrates. *The Philosophical Forum* 35: 1–33.

Goldschmidt, Victor. 1974. *Anthropologie et politique: Les principes du système de Rousseau*. Paris: J. Vrin.

Goodman, Nelson. 1978. *Ways of Worldmaking*. Indianapolis: Hackett Publishing.

Gordon, Daniel. 1994. *Citizens Without Sovereignty: Equality and Sociability in French Thought, 1670–1789*. Princeton, N.J.: Princeton University Press.

Gould, Stephen Jay. 1977. *Ever Since Darwin*. New York: Norton.

———. 1997. Kropotkin Was No Crackpot. www.marxists.org/subject/science/essays/kropotkin.htm.

———. 2002. *The Structure of Evolutionary Theory*. Cambridge, Mass.: Harvard University Press.

Gouldner, Alvin Ward. 1970. *The Coming Crisis of Western Sociology*. New York: Basic Books.

Gourevitch, Victor. 2001. *The Religious Thought*. In Riley 2001, 193–246.

Grafton, Anthony. 1999. *Cardano's Cosmos*. Cambridge, Mass.: Harvard University Press.

Graves, Kersey. 1876. *The World's Sixteen Crucified Saviors, or, Christianity Before Christ: Containing New, Startling, and Extraordinary Revelations in Religious History, Which Disclose the Oriental Origin of All the Doctrines, Principles, Precepts, and Miracles of the Christian New Testament, and Furnishing a Key for Unlocking Many of Its Sacred*

Mysteries, Besides Compromising the History of Sixteen Heathen Crucified Gods. 4th ed. Boston: Colby and Rich.

Greenwood, Davydd J. 1984. *The Taming of Evolution: The Persistence of Non-evolutionary Views in the Study of Humans.* Ithaca, N.Y.: Cornell University Press.

Grimsley, Ronald. 1961. *Jean-Jacques Rousseau; A Study in Self-Awareness.* Cardiff: University of Wales.

Gross, Neil. 2009. A Pragmatist Theory of Social Mechanisms. *American Sociological Review* 74 (3): 358–379.

Grotstein, James S. and Donald B. Rinsley. 2000. *Fairbairn and the Origins of Object Relations.* New York: Other Press.

Guicciardini, Niccolò. 2009. *Isaac Newton on Mathematical Certainty and Method.* Cambridge, Mass.: MIT Press.

Gunnell, John G. 1993. *The Descent of Political Theory: The Genealogy of an American Vocation.* Chicago: University of Chicago Press.

———. 2004. *Imagining the American Polity: Political Science and the Discourse of Democracy.* University Park: Pennsylvania State University Press.

Habermas, Jürgen. 1962. *Strukturwandel der Öffentlichkeit: Untersuchungen zu einer Kategorie der bürgerlichen Gesellschaft.* Neuwied: H. Luchterhand.

Habib, Claude. 1998. *Le Consentement amoureux: Rousseau, les femmes et la cité.* Paris: Hachette Littérature.

Hacking, Ian. 1984. *The Emergence of Probability: A Philosophical Study of Early Ideas About Probability, Induction and Statistical Inference.* New York: Cambridge University Press.

Halbwachs, Maurice. 1913. *La Théorie de l'homme moyen: Essai sur Quetelet et la statistique morale.* Paris: F. Alcan.

———. 1994. *Les Cadres sociaux de la mémoire.* Paris: Albin Michel.

Halmos, Paul R. 1974. *Naive Set Theory.* New York: Springer-Verlag.

Hammerstein, Reinhold. 1973. Music as a Divine Art. In Weiner ed. 1973.

Hariman, Robert. 2001. Decorum. In Sloane ed. 2001.

Harvey, Ray Forrest. 1937. *Jean Jacques Burlamaqui: A Liberal Tradition in American Constitutionalism.* Chapel Hill: University of North Carolina Press.

Haskell, Thomas L. 1977. *The Emergence of Professional Social Science: The American Social Science Association and the Nineteenth-Century Crisis of Authority.* Urbana: University of Illinois Press.

Hawthorn, Geoffrey. 1976. *Enlightenment and Despair: A History of Sociology.* Cambridge: Cambridge University Press.

Hayek, Friedrich A. von. 1973. *Law, Legislation and Liberty: A New Statement of the Liberal Principles of Justice and Political Economy.* Chicago: University of Chicago Press.

Hedström, Peter and Richard Swedberg, eds. 1998. *Social Mechanisms: An Analytical Approach to Social Theory.* Cambridge: Cambridge University Press.

Heeffer, Albrecht. 2008. The Emergence of Symbolic Algebra as a Shift in Predominant Models. *Foundations of Science* 13(2): 149–61.

Hegel, Georg Wilhelm Friedrich. 1833. *Grundlinien der Philosophie des Rechts, oder, Naturrecht und Staatswissenschaft im Grundrisse.* Berlin: Duncker und Humblot.

———. 1896. *Lectures on the History of Philosophy. Vol. 3.* Translated by Elizabeth S. Haldane and Frances H. Simson. London: Kegan Paul.

———. 1952. *Phänomenologie des Geistes.* 6th ed. Philosophische Bibliothek 114. Hamburg: Felix Meiner.

———. 1956. *The Philosophy of History.* Sibree Translation. New York: Dover.

———. 1979. *System of Ethical Life (1802/3) and First Philosophy of Spirit (part III of the System of Speculative Philosophy 1803/4).* Albany: State University of New York Press.

———. 1986. *Werke.* Frankfurt am Main: Suhrkamp.

———. 2002. *System der Sittlichkeit.* Hamburg: Meiner Verlag.

Herrick, Marvin T. 1947. Some Neglected Sources of *Admiratio. Modern Language Notes* 62 (4): 222–26.

Hertzler, Joyce Oramel. 1934. On Golden Rules. *International Journal of Ethics* 44 (4): 418–36.

———. 1936. *The Social Thought of the Ancient Civilizations.* New York: McGraw-Hill.

Hesse, Carla. 2005. Revolutionary Rousseaus: The Story of His Editions After 1789. In *Media and Political Culture in the Eighteenth Century,* 105–28. Marie-Christine Skuncke, ed. Stockholm: Kungl, Vitterhets.

Hintikka, Jaakko, and Unto Remes. 1974. *The Method of Analysis.* Boston: D. Reidel.

Hirschman, Albert O. 1977. *The Passions and the Interests.* Princeton, N.J.: Princeton University Press.

———. 1984. Against Parsimony: Three Easy Ways of Complicating Some Categories of Economic Discourse. *American Economic Review* 74, no. 2: 89–96.

Hobbes, Thomas. 1650. *De Corpore Politico. Or The Elements of Law, Moral & Politick. With Discourses Upon Several Heads; as of the Law of Nature. Oathes and Covenants. Severall Kind of Government. With the Changes and Revolutions of Them.* London: Printed for J. Martin, and J. Ridley.

———. 1651. *Leviathan, or The Matter, Forme, & Power of a Common-wealth Ecclesiasticall and Civill.* London: Printed for Andrew Crooke, at the Green Dragon in St. Pauls Church-yard.

———. 1969. *Elements of Law, Natural and Political.* 2nd ed. Routledge.

———. 1983. *De Cive: The Latin Version Entitled in the First Edition Elementorum philosophiae sectio tertia de cive, and in Later Editions Elementa philosophica de cive;* Howard Warrender, ed. Oxford: Clarendon Press.

d'Holbach, Paul Henri Thiry [Jean-Baptiste de Mirabaud]. 1770. *Système de la nature, ou Des Loix du monde physique & du monde moral.* London: [n.p.].

———. 1773. *Système social, ou Principes naturels de la morale et de la politique.* London: [n.p.].

Horwitz, Morton J. 1977. *The Transformation of American Law, 1780–1860.* Cambridge, Mass.: Harvard University Press.

Hotson, Howard. 2007. *Commonplace Learning.* Oxford: Oxford University Press.

Huber, Marie. 1738. *Lettres sur la religion essentielle à l'homme, distingué de ce qui n'en est que l'accessoire.* Amsterdam: J. Wetstein et W. Smith.

Hume, David. 1739. *A Treatise of Human Nature: Being an Attempt to Introduce the Experimental Method of Reasoning into Moral Subjects.* London: Printed for J. Noon.

———. 1987. *Essays, Moral, Political, and Literary, 3rd ed.* Indianapolis: Liberty Classics.

Huntington, Samuel P. 1968. *Political Order in Changing Societies.* New Haven: Yale University Press.

———. 1981. *American Politics: The Promise of Disharmony.* Cambridge, Mass.: Belknap Press of Harvard University Press.

Husserl, Edmund. 1954. *Die Krisis der europäischen Wissenschaften und die transzendentale Phänomenologie. Ein Einleitung in die phänomenologische Philosophie.* The Hague: M. Nijhoff.

———. 1960. *Cartesian Meditations: An Introduction to Phenomenology.* The Hague: M. Nijhoff.

———. 2008. *Die Lebenswelt: Auslegungen der vorgegebenen Welt und ihrer Konstitution: Texte aus dem Nachlass (1916–1937).* Dordrecht: Springer.

Ingram, David, and Jennifer A. Parks. 2002. *The Complete Idiot's Guide to Understanding Ethics.* Indianapolis: Alpha Books.

Israel, Jonathan I. 2002. *Radical Enlightenment: Philosophy and the Making of Modernity, 1650–1750.* Oxford: Oxford University Press.

———. 2006a. *Enlightenment Contested: Philosophy, Modernity, and the Emancipation of Man 1670–1752.* Oxford: Oxford University Press.

———. 2006b. Enlightenment! Which Enlightenment? *Journal of the History of Ideas* 67 (3): 423–45.

———. 2010. *A Revolution of the Mind.* Princeton, N.J.: Princeton University Press.

———. 2011. *Democratic Enlightenment: Philosophy, Revolution, and Human Rights, 1750–1790.* Oxford: Oxford University Press.

Jaeger, Werner Wilhelm. 1939. *Paideia: The Ideals of Greek Culture.* New York: Oxford University Press.

Jardine, Lisa. 1974. *Francis Bacon: Discovery and the Art of Discourse.* Cambridge: Cambridge University Press.

Jaucourt, Louis de. *Invention.* In Diderot and d'Alembert (1751–72, VIII, 849).

———. *Morale.* In Diderot and d'Alembert (1751–72, X, 699–702).

———. *Moralité.* In Diderot and d'Alembert (1751–72, X, 702–3).

———. *Rhétorique.* In Diderot and d'Alembert (1751–72, XIV, 250).

———. *Sciences.* In Diderot and d'Alembert (1751–72, XIV, 788–9).

———. *Solitaire.* In Diderot and d'Alembert (1751–72, XV, 324).

Joubert, Joseph. 1938. *Les Carnets de Joseph Joubert.* Paris: Gallimard.

Justinian. 1985. *The Digest of Justinian.* Latin text edited by Theodor Mommsen with the aid of Paul Krueger; English translation edited by Alan Watson. Philadelphia: University of Pennsylvania Press.

Kant, Immanuel. 1785/1964. *Grundlegung zur Metaphysik der Sitten.* Riga: J. F. Hartknoch. [Trans. as *Groundwork of the Metaphysic of Morals.* H. J. Paton. New York: Harper Torchbooks.]

———. 1787/1902–. *Gesammelte Schriften, III, Kritik der reinen Vernunft.* Hrsg. von der Königliche preussische Akademie der Wissenschaften. Berlin: Reimer.

———. 1991. *Kant: Political Writings.* 2nd ed. Cambridge: Cambridge University Press.

———. 1996. *The Metaphysics of Morals.* Cambridge: Cambridge University Press.

———. 2004. *Lectures on Logic.* Cambridge: Cambridge University Press.

Kelson, Hans. 1955. Foundations of Democracy. *Ethics* 66 (1), Part Two (June).

Kenny, Anthony. 1979. *Aristotle's Theory of the Will*. New Haven: Yale University Press.

Kenyon, Cecelia M. 1955. Men of Little Faith: The Anti-Federalists on the Nature of Representative Government. *William and Mary Quarterly* 12 (January): 3–43.

———. 1958. Alexander Hamilton: Rousseau of the Right. *Political Science Quarterly* 73 (June): 161–78.

Keohane, Nannerl O. 1978. "The Masterpiece of Policy in Our Century": Rousseau on the Morality of the Enlightenment. *Political Theory* 6 (4): 457–84.

———. 1980. *Philosophy and the State in France: The Renaissance to the Enlightenment*. Princeton, N.J.: Princeton University Press.

Kessler, Eckhard, C. B. Schmitt, and Quentin Skinner, eds. 1988. *The Cambridge History of Renaissance Philosophy*. Cambridge: Cambridge University Press.

Kettler, David. 2005. *Adam Ferguson: His Social and Political Thought*. New Brunswick, N.J.: Transaction Publishers.

Kirk, Geoffrey Stephen, and John Earle Raven. 1957. *The Presocratic Philosophers: A Critical History with a Selection of Texts*. Cambridge: Cambridge University Press.

Klaus, Marshall H., and John H. Kennell. 1976. *Maternal-Infant Bonding: The Impact of Early Separation or Loss on Family Development*. St. Louis: Mosby.

Klein, Melanie. 1975. *Envy and Gratitude and Other Works, 1946–1963*. New York: Delacorte Press.

Kofman, Sarah. 1982. *Le Respect des femmes: (Kant et Rousseau)*. Paris: Galilée.

Kohlberg, Lawrence. 1981. *The Philosophy of Moral Development: Moral Stages and the Idea of Justice*. San Francisco: Harper & Row.

Kors, Alan Charles, ed. 2003. *Encyclopedia of the Enlightenment*. New York: Oxford University Press.

Koyré, Alexandre. 1957. *From the Closed World to the Infinite Universe*. Baltimore: Johns Hopkins Press.

Kristeller, Paul Oskar, and Edward P. Mahoney. 1976. *Philosophy and Humanism*. New York: Columbia University Press.

Kropotkin, Peter Alekseevich. 1902. *Mutual Aid; a Factor of Evolution*. New York: McClure, Philips.

Krüger, Klaus. 2002. *Curiositas: Welterfahrung und ästhetische Neugierde in Mittelalter und früher Neuzeit*. Göttingen: Wallstein.

Kuhn, Thomas S. 1970. *The Structure of Scientific Revolutions*. 2nd edition. Chicago: University of Chicago Press.

Kuntz, Paul G. 1968. *The Concept of Order*. Seattle: Published for Grinnell College by the University of Washington Press.

Lachterman, David Rapport. 1989. *The Ethics of Geometry: A Genealogy of Modernity*. New York: Routledge.

Lamarck, Jean Baptiste Pierre Antoine de Monet de. 1809. *Philosophie zoologique, ou, Exposition des considérations relative a l'histoire naturelle des animaux*. Paris: Chez Dentu [et] L'Auteur.

Landes, David S. 1998. *Revolution in Time: Clocks and the Making of the Modern World*. 10th ed. New York: Barnes & Noble Books.

Lange, Lynda, ed. 2002. *Feminist Interpretations of Jean-Jacques Rousseau*. University Park: Pennsylvania State University Press.

Lanson, Gustave. 1895. *Histoire de la littérature française*. 2nd ed. Paris: Hachette.

———. 1912. L'Unité de la pensée de J.-J. Rousseau. In *Annales de la Société Jean-Jacques Rousseau*, 8. Geneva: Société Jean-Jacques Rousseau.

Latour, Bruno. 1979. *Laboratory Life: The Social Construction of Scientific Facts*. Beverly Hills: Sage Publications.

———. 1991. *Nous n'avons jamais été modernes: Essai d'anthropologie symétrique*. Paris: La Découverte.

———. 1999a. *Pandora's Hope: Essays on the Reality of Science Studies*. Cambridge, Mass.: Harvard University Press.

———. 1999b. *Politiques de la nature: comment faire entrer les sciences en démocratie*. Armillaire. Paris: La Découverte.

Latour, Bruno, and Peter Weibel. 2005. *Making Things Public*. Cambridge, Mass.: MIT Press.

Launay, Michel. 1989. *Jean-Jacques Rousseau, ecrivain politique (1712–1762)*. 2nd ed. Geneva: Slatkine.

Leibniz, Gottfried Wilhelm. 1710. *Essais de Théodicée sur la bonte de Dieu, la liberté de l'homme et l'origine du mal*. Amsterdam: [n.p.].

———. 1969. *Philosophical Papers and Letters; a Selection Translated and Edited, with an Intro. by Leroy E. Loemker*. Dordrecht: Reidel.

———. 1972. *The Political Writings of Leibniz*. Cambridge: Cambridge University Press.

Leigh, R. A. 1986. Rousseau and the Scottish Enlightenment. *Contributions to Political Economy* 5 (1): 1–21.

Lemert, Charles C. 2004. *Sociology After the Crisis*. 2nd ed. Boulder, Colo.: Paradigm.

Lévi-Strauss, Claude. 1958. *Anthropologie structurale*. Paris: Plon.

Lewis, Charlton Thomas, and Charles Short. 1991. *A Latin Dictionary Founded on Andrews' Edition of Freund's Latin Dictionary*. Rev., enl., and in great part rewritten. Oxford: Clarendon Press.

Lewontin, Richard C. 1984. *Not in Our Genes: Biology, Ideology, and Human Nature*. New York: Pantheon Books.

Liddell, Henry George, and Robert Scott. 1940. *A Greek-English Lexicon, revised and augmented throughout by Sir Henry Stuart Jones*. Oxford: Clarendon Press.

Lieber, Francis. 1839. *Legal and Political Hermeneutics*. Boston: Little, Brown.

Linné, Carl von. 1735. *Caroli Linnæi Systema Naturae, sive, regna tria Naturæ Systematice proposita per Classes, Ordines, Genera, & Species*. Lugduni Batavorum: Apud Theodorum Haak, ex typographia Joannis Wilhelmi de Groot.

Livy. 1912. *Titi Livi Ab vrbe condita libri præ fatio*. Cambridge: Cambridge University Press.

Loemker, Leroy. 1973. Theodicy. In Weiner 1973, IV: 378–84.

Lohr, Charles H. 1988. Metaphysics. In Schmitt and Skinner 1988, 537–638.

Lovejoy, Arthur O. 1936. *The Great Chain of Being: A Study of the History of an Idea*. Cambridge, Mass.: Harvard University Press.

Lowinsky, Edward E. 1946. *Secret Chromatic Art in the Netherlands Motet*. New York: Columbia University Press.

Lukács, Gyorgy. 1976. *The Young Hegel: Studies in the Relations Between Dialectics and Economics*. Cambridge, Mass.: MIT Press.

Lukes, Steven. 1973. *Emile Durkheim, His Life and Work: A Historical and Critical Study*. London: Allen Lane.

Lyell, Charles. 1830. *Principles of Geology Being an Attempt to Explain the Former Changes of the Earth's Surface by Reference to Causes Now in Operation*. London: J. Murray.

Macy, Jeffrey. 1992. God Helps Those Who Help Themselves: New Light on the Theological-Political Teaching in Rousseau's "Profession of Faith of the Savoyard Vicar." *Polity* 24, no. 4: 615–32.

Macpherson, C. B. 1964. *The Political Theory of Possessive Individualism: Hobbes to Locke*. Oxford: Clarendon Press.

Maine, Henry Sumner. 1861. *Ancient Law: Its Connection with the Early History of Society, and Its Relation to Modern Ideas*. London: J. Murray.

Malezieulx, Nicolas. 1679. *Nouveau traité de la sphere*. Paris: Arnold Seneuze.

Mandelbrot, Benoît B. 1982. *The Fractal Geometry of Nature*. London: Macmillan.

Markell, Patchen. 2003. *Bound by Recognition*. Princeton, N.J.: Princeton University Press.

Marshall, Alfred. 1890. *Principles of Economics*. London: Macmillan.

Marso, Lori Jo. 1999. *(Un)Manly Citizens: Jean-Jacques Rousseau's and Germaine De Staël's Subversive Women*. Baltimore: Johns Hopkins University Press.

Marx, Karl. 1852. Der achtzehnte Brumaire des Louis Napoleon. In *Marx-Engels Werke*, 8: 115–207. Berlin: Dietz Verlag.

———. 1867. *Das Kapital. Kritik der politischen Oekonomie*. Hamburg: O. Meissner.

———. 1976. Capital, Volume 1: New York: Penguin.

Masson, Pierre Maurice. 1914. *La "Profession de foi du vicaire savoyard" de Jean-Jacques Rousseau; édition critique d'après les manuscrits de Genève, Neuchâtel et Paris, avec une introduction et un commentaire historique*. Paris: Hachette.

———. 1916/1970. *La Religion de Jean-Jacques Rousseau*. Paris: Hachette. [Geneva: Slatkine]

Masters, Roger. 1968. *The Political Philosophy of Rousseau*. Princeton, N.J.: Princeton University Press.

Mauzi, Robert. 1960. *L'Idée du bonheur dans la littérature et la pensée françaises au XVIIIe siècle*. Paris: A. Colin.

McLaren, John P. S. 1983. Nuisance Law and the Industrial Revolution—Some Lessons from Social History. *Oxford Journal of Legal Studies* 3: 155.

McMahon, Darrin M. 2006. *Happiness: A History*. New York: Atlantic Monthly Press.

Mead, George Herbert. 1934. *Mind, Self and Society: From the Standpoint of a Social Behaviorist*. Chicago: University of Chicago Press.

———. 1938. *The Philosophy of the Act*. Chicago: University of Chicago Press.

Melching, Willem. 1994. *Main Trends in Cultural History: Ten Essays*. Amsterdam: Rodopi.

Merchant, Carolyn. 1980. *The Death of Nature: Women, Ecology, and the Scientific Revolution*. San Francisco: Harper & Row.

Mercier, Louis-Sebastien. 1778. *De la Littérature et des littérateurs: Suivi d'un nouvel examen de la tragédie francoise*. Paris: Yverdon.

———. 1791. *De J. J. Rousseau, consideré comme l'un des premiers auteurs de la revolution.* Paris: Buisson.

Merton, Robert K. 1936. The Unanticipated Consequences of Purposive Social Action. *American Sociological Review* 1 (6): 894–904.

Meyers, Peter Alexander. 1989. A *Theory of Power: Political, Not Metaphysical.* Ann Arbor: UMI.

———. 1992. I due percorsi dello sviluppo morale: una svolta nel cammino del femminismo? *Iride: filosofia e discussione pubblica* 8 (primavera): 164–79.

———. 1995. Theses on the Genealogy of the Will. Paper presented to the American Political Science Association. Chicago.

———. 1996. The Elements of Plurality. Manuscript. Paris.

———. 1996b. On the Geometry of Body-Space. *International Review of Sociology* 6 (3): 405–428.

———. 1998. The "Ethic of Care" and the Problem of Power. *Journal of Political Philosophy* 6 (2): 142–70.

———. 1999. The World of Speech and the Passage of Time. Manuscript. Paris.

———. 2000. Notes on Now: Benjamin's Vico and Vico's Benjamin. In Ratto, ed. 2000.

———. 2001. History of Dependence. Manuscript. Paris.

———. 2002. Le "Musée vivant" raconte sa propre histoire: une première lecture de l'*United States Holocaust Memorial Museum. Cités* 11:159–83.

———. 2003. Method and Civic Education. *Humanitas* 16 (2): 4–47.

———. 2006. Speaking Truth to Ourselves: Lukács, "False Consciousness" and a Dilemma of Identity Politics in Democracy. *International Review of Sociology* 16 (3): 549–89.

———. 2007. Rhetorical Inquiry and Political Science. Paper presented to the American Political Science Association. Chicago.

———. 2008a. *Civic War and the Corruption of the Citizen.* Chicago: University of Chicago Press.

———. 2008b. Rousseau and the Tradition of the "Social Contract." Paper presented to the School of Social Sciences, Institute for Advanced Study, Princeton.

———. 2010. Rousseau and Rhetoric. In Gaonkar and Topper forthcoming.

———. 2013a, forthcoming. *The Position of the Citizen.* Chicago: University of Chicago Press.

———. 2013b, forthcoming. *The Pathologies of the Citizen.* Chicago: University of Chicago Press.

———. 2013c, forthcoming. Will. In Gibbons 2012.

———. Forthcoming. *Dancing on a Landslide: Micropractical Foundations for a Political Theory of Power.*

Meyers, Peter Alexander, and Nancy S. Struever. 2008. Esquisse sur la modernisation de la rhétorique comme enquête politique. *Littérature* 149 (1): 4–23.

Miel, Jan. 1969. Pascal, Port-Royal, and Cartesian Linguistics. *Journal of the History of Ideas* 30 (2): 261–71.

Mill, John Stuart. 1843. A *System of Logic, Ratiocinative and Inductive: Being a Connected View of the Principles of Evidence, and Methods of Scientific Investigation.* London: John W. Parker, West Strand.

Miller, James. 1984. *Rousseau: Dreamer of Democracy.* New Haven: Yale University Press.

Mills, C. Wright. 1959. *The Sociological Imagination.* New York: Oxford University Press.

Mommsen, Theodor. 1876. *Römisches Staatsrecht.* 2nd ed. Leipzig: S. Hirzel.

———. 1887. *Le Droit public romain.* 2nd ed. Paris: E. Thorin.

———. 1892. *Zum römischen Bodenrecht.* Berlin: Weidmannsche Buchhandlung.

Montesquieu, Charles de Secondat. 1748. *De l'espirit des loix, ou du rapport que les loix doivent avoir avec la constitution de chaque gouvernement, les moeurs, le climat, la religion, le commerce, & c.* Geneva: Barrillot & fils.

Mooney, Michael. 1985. *Vico in the Tradition of Rhetoric.* Princeton, N.J.: Princeton University Press.

Mora, George. 1976. Vico, Piaget, and Genetic Epistemology. In Tagliacozzo and Verene 1976, 365–92.

Morgenstern, Mira. 1996. *Rousseau and the Politics of Ambiguity: Self, Culture, and Society.* University Park: Pennsylvania State University Press.

Morin, Jean. 1735. *Abrégé du mécanisme universel, en discours et questions physiques.* Chartres: J. Roux.

Mornet, Daniel. 1933. *Les Origines intellectuelles de la revolution française, 1715–1787.* Paris: A. Colin.

Mossner, Ernest Campbell. 2001. *The Life of David Hume.* Oxford: Oxford University Press.

Negri, Antonio. 1991. *The Savage Anomaly: The Power of Spinoza's Metaphysics and Politics.* Minneapolis: University of Minnesota Press.

Newton, Isaac. 1687. *Philosophia Naturalis Principia Mathematica.* London: Jussu Societatis Regiae ac Typis Josephi Streater; prostat apud plures Bibliopolas.

Nicolini, Fausto. 1949. *Vico e Rousseau.* Naples: Giannini.

Nicot, Jean. 1606. *Thresor de la langve francoise, tant ancienne qve moderne. Av qvel entre avtres choses sont les mots propres de marine, venerie, & fauconnerie, cy-deuant ramassez par aimar de ranconnet.* Paris: D. Dovcevr.

Nunes, Pedro. 1537. *Tratado de sphera com a Theorica do Sol & da Lua.*

Oestreich, Gerhard. 2008. *Neostoicism and the Early Modern State.* Cambridge: Cambridge University Press.

O'Neill, John. 1972. *Sociology as a Skin Trade: Essays Towards a Reflexive Sociology.* New York: Harper & Row.

Okin, Susan Moller. 1979. *Women in Western Political Thought.* Princeton, N.J.: Princeton University Press.

Ong, Walter J. 1958. *Ramus: Method, and the Decay of Dialogue; from the Art of Discourse to the Art of Reason.* Cambridge, Mass.: Harvard University Press.

Ost, François. *Furetière: La Démocratisation de la langue.* Paris: Michalon.

Paine, Thomas. 1995. *Collected Writings.* New York: Library of America.

Pascal, Blaise. 1954 *Œuvres Complètes.* Paris: Gallimard (Pléiade).

Pateman, Carole. 1988. *The Sexual Contract.* Stanford: Stanford University Press.

Peck, Harry Thurston. 1898. *Harper's Dictionary of Classical Literature and Antiquities.* New York: Harper & Brothers.

Peirce, Charles S. 1931. *Collected Papers of Charles Sanders Peirce.* Edited by Charles Hartshorne and Paul Weiss. Cambridge, Mass.: Harvard University Press.

Perelman, Chaïm, and Lucie Olbrechts-Tyteca. 1969. *The New Rhetoric*. Notre Dame. University of Notre Dame Press.

Petersen, Thomas. 1992. *Subjektivität und Politik: Hegels "Grundlinien der Philosophie des Rechtes" als Reformulierung des "Contrat Social" Rousseaus*. Frankfurt am Main: A. Hain.

Philonenko, Alexis. 1969. *L'Oeuvre de Kant: La Philosophie critique*. Paris: J. Vrin.

———. 1984. *Jean-Jacques Rousseau et la pensée du malheur*. Paris: J. Vrin.

Piaget, Jean. 1932. *Le Jugement moral chez l'enfant*. Paris: Presses universitaires de france.

Pickering, Mary. 1993. *Auguste Comte: An Intellectual Biography*. Cambridge: Cambridge University Press.

Pierson, Paul. 2004. *Politics in Time: History, Institutions, and Social Analysis*. Princeton, N.J.: Princeton University Press.

Plato. 1925. *The Statesman; Philebus; Ion*. Loeb Classical Library. Cambridge: Harvard University Press.

———. 1953. *Cratylus: Parmenides; Greater Hippias; Lesser Hippias*. Loeb Classical Library. Cambridge, Mass.: Harvard University Press.

———. 1982. *The Republic*. Loeb Classical Library. Cambridge: Harvard University Press.

Pluche, Noël Antoine. 1732. *Spectacle de la nature, ou Entretiens sur les particularités de l'Histoire naturelle qui ont paru les plus propres à rendre les jeunes gens curieux et à leur former l'esprit*. Paris: Chez la veuve Estienne & Jean Desaint.

Pocock, J. G. A. 1957. *The Ancient Constitution and the Feudal Law*. Cambridge: Cambridge University Press.

———. 1972. *Politics, Language, and Time: Essays on Political Thought and History*. New York: Atheneum.

———. 1975.*The Machiavellian Moment: Florentine Political Thought and the Atlantic Republican Tradition*. Princeton, N.J.: Princeton University Press.

Polanyi, Karl. 1944. *The Great Transformation*. New York: Farrar & Rinehart.

———. 1947. Our Obsolete Market Mentality. *Commentary*. 3:109–17.

Pope, Alexander. 1733. *An Essay on Man*. London: J. Wilford.

———. 1736. *Essai sur l'homme par M. Pope. Traduit de l'anglois en francois. Edition revue par le traducteur*. London: chez Pierre Dunoyer. Amsterdam: chez Jean Fredéric Bernard. [Trans. by Etienne de Silhouette.]

Popkin, Richard H. 1979. *The History of Scepticism from Erasmus to Spinoza*. Rev. and expanded ed. Berkeley: University of California Press.

Popkin, Richard H., and Charles B. Schmitt, eds. 1987. *Scepticism from the Renaissance to the Enlightenment*. Wiesbaden: In Kommission bei Otto Harrassowitz.

Popper, Karl Raimund. 1968a. *Conjectures and Refutations: The Growth of Scientific Knowledge*. New York: Harper & Row.

———. 1968b. *The Logic of Scientific Discovery*. 3rd ed. London: Hutchinson.

Porter, Roy, Katharine Park, and Lorraine Daston. 2006. *The Cambridge History of Science: Early Modern Science*. Cambridge: Cambridge University Press.

Puttenham, Richard. 1589/1970. *The Arte of English Poesie; Contriued into Three Bookes: The First of Poets and Poesie, the Second of Proportion, the Third of Ornament*. Kent, Ohio: Kent State University Press. [facsimile edition]

Randall, John Herman. 1940. The Development of Scientific Method in the School of Padua. *Journal of the History of Ideas* 1 (2): 177–206.

Ratto, Franco, ed. 2000. *Il mondo di Vico / Vico nel mondo*. Perugia: Guerra Edizioni.

Rentzou, Efthymia. 2002. Surréalisme et littérature: une comparaison entre le surréalisme grec et français. Ph.D. dissertation, Sorbonne.

———. 2007. Nikos Gatsos' Amorgos: Topography and the Poetics of Modernism. *Byzantine and Modern Greek Studies* 31: 191–212.

———. 2010. *Littérature malgré elle*. Paris: Association des Amis de Pleine Marge.

Richelet, Pierre. 1680. *Dictionnaire Francois: Contenant les mots et le choses, plusieurs nouvelles remarques sur la langue francoise*. Geneva: Chez Jean Herman Widerhold.

———. 1732. *Dictionnaire de la langue francoise, ancienne et moderne. Nouvelle édition augmentée d'un grand nombre d'articles*. Amsterdam: Aux dépens de la compagnie.

Ricoeur, Paul. 1975a. *La Métaphore vive*. Paris: Seuil.

———. 1975b. *Political and Social Essays*. Athens: Ohio University Press.

———. 1983–85. *Temps et récit*. Paris: Seuil.

———. 1990a. The Golden Rule: Exegetical and Theological Perplexities. *New Testament Studies* 36(3): 392–97.

———. 1990b. *Time and Narrative*. Chicago: University of Chicago Press.

Riley, Patrick. 1982. *Will and Political Legitimacy: A Critical Exposition of Social Contract Theory in Hobbes, Locke, Rousseau, Kant, and Hegel*. Cambridge, Mass.: Harvard University Press.

———. 1986. *The General Will Before Rousseau: The Transformation of the Divine into the Civic*. Princeton, N.J.: Princeton University Press.

Riley, Patrick, ed. 2001. *The Cambridge Companion to Rousseau*. Cambridge: Cambridge University Press.

Ritter, Joachim. 1965. *Hegel und die französische Revolution*. Frankfurt am Main: Suhrkamp.

Robespierre, Maximilien. 1939–. *Oeuvres complètes*. Nancy: Thomas.

Roemer, John E. 1982. *A General Theory of Exploitation and Class*. Cambridge, Mass.: Harvard University Press.

Rorty, Richard. 1979. *Philosophy and the Mirror of Nature*. Princeton, N.J.: Princeton University Press.

Rosanvallon, Pierre. 2000. *La Démocratie inachevée: Histoire de la souveraineté du peuple en France*. Paris: Gallimard.

Rose, Gillian. 1981. *Hegel Contra Sociology*. London: Athlone.

Rosen, Lawrence. 2006. *Law as Culture: An Invitation*. Princeton, N.J.: Princeton University Press.

Rosenblatt, Helena. 1997. *Rousseau and Geneva: From the First Discourse to the Social Contract, 1749–1762*. Cambridge: Cambridge University Press.

Rossi, Paolo. 1960. *Clavis universalis*. R. Ricciardi.

Rossiter, Clinton Lawrence. 1964. *Alexander Hamilton and the Constitution*. New York: Harcourt, Brace & World.

Roulston, Christine. 1998. *Virtue, Gender, and the Authentic Self in Eighteenth-Century Fiction: Richardson, Rousseau, and Laclos*. Gainesville: University Press of Florida.

Rousseau, Jean-Jacques. 1913. *The Social Contract and Discourses.* Edited by G. D. H. Cole. Everyman's Library no. 660. London: Dent.

———. 1915. *The Political Writings of Jean-Jacques Rosseau.* Cambridge: Cambridge University Press. [Vaughan edition]

Rousseau, Jean-Jacques. 1959–95. *Oeuvres complètes.* Paris: Gallimard.

———. 1965. *Correspondance Complète de Jean-Jacques Rousseau.* Publications de l'Institut et Musée. Geneva: Institut et Musée Voltaire.

Rousseau, Jean-Jacques, and Maurice Halbwachs. 1943. *Du Contrat social.* Paris: Aubier, Editions Montaigne.

Rouvrai, Jean Louis de. 1641. *Le Triomphe des républiques.* Berne: G. Sonnleitner.

Russell, Bertrand. 1983. *Cambridge Essays, 1888–99.* London: Allen and Unwin.

Rykwert, Joseph. 1998. *The Dancing Column.* Cambridge, Mass.: MIT Press.

Said, Edward W. 1975. *Beginnings: Intention and Method.* New York: Basic Books.

Saltonstall, Charles. 1636. *The Nauigator Shewing and Explaining All the Chiefe Principles and Parts Both Theoricke and Practicke, That Are Contayned in the Famous Art of Nauigation.* London: Printed [by Bernard Alsop and Thomas Fawcet] for Geo: Herlock, and to be sold at his shop in St. Magnus-corner.

Saussure, Ferdinand de. 1960. *Course in General Linguistics.* London: P. Owen.

Schaeffer, John D. 1990. *Sensus Communis: Vico, Rhetoric, and the Limits of Relativism.* Durham: Duke University Press.

Schmitt, Charles B. 1972. *Cicero Scepticus: A Study of the Influence of the Academica in the Renaissance.* The Hague: Martinus Nijhoff.

Schmitt, Charles B., and Quentin Skinner, eds. 1988. *The Cambridge History of Renaissance Philosophy.* Cambridge: Cambridge Univeristy Press.

Schneewind, J. B. 1998. *The Invention of Autonomy: A History of Modern Moral Philosophy.* Cambridge: Cambridge University Press.

Schumpeter, Joseph Alois. 1950. *Capitalism, Socialism, and Democracy.* 3rd ed. New York: Harper.

Schütz, Alfred. 1973. *The Structures of the Life-World.* Evanston, Ill.: Northwestern University Press.

———. 1982. *Life Forms and Meaning Structure.* London: Routledge & K. Paul.

Schwab, Richard N. 1957. The Extent of the Chevalier de Jaucourt's Contribution to Diderot's Encyclopédie. *Modern Language Notes* 72 (7): 507–8.

Schwartz, Delmore. 1967. *Selected Poems, 1938–1958: Summer Knowledge.* New York: New Directions Books.

Scott, John T. 1994. Politics as the Imitation of the Divine in Rousseau's "Social Contract." *Polity* 26 (3): 473–501.

Scott, John T., ed. 2006. *Jean-Jacques Rousseau: Human Nature and History.* New York: Routledge.

Seigel, Jerrold E. 2005. *The Idea of the Self: Thought and Experience in Western Europe Since the Seventeenth Century.* Cambridge: Cambridge University Press.

Sen, Amartya. 1981. *Poverty and Famines: An Essay on Entitlement and Deprivation.* Oxford: Clarendon Press.

Sennett, Richard. 1977. *The Fall of Public Man.* New York: Knopf.

———. 1994. *Flesh and Stone: The Body and the City in Western Civilization.* New York: W. W. Norton & Co.

Sewell, William. 2005. *Logics of History.* Chicago: University of Chicago Press.

Shane, Peter M. 1986. Legal Disagreement and Negotiation in a Government of Laws: The Case of Executive Privilege Claims Against Congress. *Minnesota Law Review* 71: 461.

Shank, John Bennett. 2008. *The Newton Wars and the Beginning of the French Enlightenment.* Chicago: University of Chicago Press.

Shapin, Steven. 1994. *A Social History of Truth.* Chicago: University of Chicago Press.

Shapiro, Barbara J. 2002. Testimony in Seventeenth-Century English Natural Philosophy: Legal Origins and Early Development. *Studies in History and Philosophy of Science Part A* 33 (2): 243–63.

Shklar, Judith N. 1973. General Will. In Wiener, ed. 1973.

———. 1976. *Freedom and Independence: A Study of the Political Ideas of Hegel's Phenomenology of Mind.* Cambridge: Cambridge University Press.

———. 1985. *Men and Citizens: A Study of Rousseau's Social Theory.* Cambridge: Cambridge University Press.

———. 1990. *The Faces of Injustice.* New Haven: Yale University Press.

Sighele, Scipio. 1895. *Mondo criminale Italiano.* Milano: L. Omodei Zorini.

Simpson, George Gaylord. 1949. *The Meaning of Evolution: A Study of the History of Life and of Its Significance for Man.* New Haven: Yale University Press.

Skinner, Quentin. 1978. *The Foundations of Modern Political Thought.* Cambridge: Cambridge University Press.

———. 2002. *Visions of Politics.* Cambridge: Cambridge University Press.

Sloane, Thomas O. 2001. *Encyclopedia of Rhetoric.* New York: Oxford University Press.

Société Jean-Jacques Rousseau. 1905–. *Annales de la Société Jean-Jacques Rousseau.* Geneva: A. Jullien.

Spinoza, Benedictus de. 1927. *The Correspondence of Spinoza,* translated and edited by A. Wolf. New York: Lincoln MacVeagh.

———. 1951. *A Theologico-Political Treatise and A Political Treatise.* New York: Dover.

———. 1988. *Ethica, Ordine Geometrico demonstrata/Éthique démontrée selon L'Ordre Géométrique.* Paris: Éditions du Seuil.

Spurlin, Paul Merrill. 1969. *Rousseau in America, 1760–1809.* University: University of Alabama Press.

Starobinski, Jean. 1971. *Jean-Jacques Rousseau: La transparence et l'obstacle.* Paris: Gallimard.

Stigler, Stephen M. 1986. *The History of Statistics.* Cambridge, Mass.: Belknap Press of Harvard University Press.

Strauss, Leo. 1936. *The Political Philosophy of Hobbes, Its Basis and Its Genesis.* Oxford: Clarendon Press.

Strong, Tracy B. 1994. *Jean Jacques Rousseau: The Politics of the Ordinary.* Thousand Oaks, Calif.: Sage Publications.

Struever, Nancy S. 1970. *The Language of History in the Renaissance: Rhetoric and His-*

torical Consciousness in Florentine Humanism. Princeton, N.J.: Princeton University Press.

Sullivan, Harry Stack. 1953. *The Interpersonal Theory of Psychiatry*. New York: Norton.

Swenson, James. 2000. *On Jean-Jacques Rousseau: Considered as One of the First Authors of the Revolution*. Stanford: Stanford University Press.

Tagliacozzo, Giorgio, and Donald Phillip Verene, eds. 1976. *Giambettistia Vico's Science of Humanity*. Baltimore: Johns Hopkins University Press.

Tarde, Gabriel. 1895. *La Logique sociale*. Paris: F. Alcan.

Taylor, Charles. 1975. *Hegel*. Cambridge: Cambridge University Press.

———. 1989. *Sources of the Self: The Making of the Modern Identity*. Cambridge, Mass.: Harvard University Press.

———. 2004. *Modern Social Imaginaries*. Durham, N.C.: Duke University Press.

———. 2007. *A Secular Age*. Cambridge, Mass.: Belknap Press of Harvard University Press.

Thévenot, Laurent. 2006. *L'Action au pluriel: Sociologie des régimes d'engagement*. Paris: Découverte.

Tocqueville, Alexis de. 1835–40. *De la démocratic en Amérique*. Paris: Librairie de C. Gosselin.

Todorov, Tzvetan. 1985. *Frêle bonheur: Essai sur Rousseau*. Paris: Hachette.

———. 2001. *Frail Happiness: An Essay on Rousseau*. University Park: Pennsylvania State University Press.

Tönnies, Ferdinand. 1887. *Gemeinschaft und Gesellschaft: Abhandlung des Communismus und des Socialismus als empirischer Culturformen*. Leipzig: Fues.

Touraine, Alain. 1973. *Production de la société*. Paris: Seuil.

Trévoux. 1771. *Dictionnaire universel françois et latin, vulgairement appelé Dictionnaire de Trévoux . . . avec des remarques d'érudition et de critique; le tout tiré des plus excellens auteurs, des meilleurs lexicographes . . . qui ont paru jusqu'ici en différentes langues*. Nouv. éd., corrigé et considérablement augmenté. Paris: Par la Compagnie des Libraires Associés.

Tronto, Joan C. 1993. *Moral Boundaries: A Political Argument for an Ethic of Care*. New York: Routledge.

Twain, Mark. 1903. *The Jumping Frog . . . in English, then in French, then clawed back into civilized language once more by patient unrenumerated toil*. New York: Harper & Brothers.

Twiss, Richard. 1787. *Chess: A Compilation of All the Anecdotes and Quotations That Could Be Found Relative to the Game of Chess; with an Account of All the Chess-Books Which Could Be Procured*. London: J.G.I. and I. Robinson.

Tyler, Tom R. 1990. *Why People Obey the Law*. New Haven: Yale University Press.

Unger, Roberto Mangabeira. 1976. *Law in Modern Society: Toward a Criticism of Social Theory*. New York: Free Press.

———. 1987a. *Social Theory, Its Situation and Its Task*. Cambridge: Cambridge University Press.

———. 1987b. *False Necessity: Anti-Necessitarian Social Theory in the Service of Radical Democracy*. Cambridge: Cambridge University Press.

494 *Works Cited*

Vauvenargues. 1747. *Introduction à la connaissance de l'esprit humain, suivie de réflexions et de maximes*. Paris: A. C. Briasson.

Verene, Donald Phillip. 1981. *Vico's Science of Imagination*. Ithaca, N.Y.: Cornell University Press.

Vernant, Jean-Pierre. 1973. *Mythe et tragédie en Grèce ancienne*. Paris: F. Maspero.

———. 1988. Intimations of the Will in Greek Tragedy. In *Myth and Tragedy in Ancient Greece*. New York: Zone Books.

Vernière, Paul. 1954. *Spinoza et la pensée française avant la révolution*. Paris. Presses universitaires de France.

Viala, Alain. 1985. *Naissance de l'écrivain*. Paris: Minuit.

Vico, Giambattista. 1709/1990. *De Nostri Temporis Studiorum Ratione Dissertatio*. Naples: Typis Felicis Mosca. [Trans. by Elia Gianturco as *On the Study Methods of Our Time*. Ithaca, N.Y.: Cornell University Press.]

———. 1744/1984. *Principi di Scienza Nuova di Giambattista Vico d'intorno Alla Comune Natura Delle Nazioni . . . 3. Impressione . . . Corretta, Schiarita, E . . . Accresciuta*. Naples: Stamperia Muziana. [Trans. by Thomas Goddard Bergin and Max Harold Fisch as *The New Science of Giambattista Vico*. Ithaca, N.Y.: Cornell University Press.]

———. 1965/1975. *Autobiografia*. Turin: G. Einaudi. [Trans. as *The Autobiography of Giambattista Vico*. Ithaca, N.Y.: Cornell University Press.]

———. 1989. *Institutiones Oratoriae*. Frontiera d'Europa. Naples: Istituto Suor Orsola Benincasa.

———. 2000. *Universal Right*. Amsterdam: Rodopi.

Viroli, Maurizio. 1988. *Jean-Jacques Rousseau and the "Well-Ordered Society."* Cambridge: Cambridge University Press.

———. 2010. *Machiavelli's God*. Princeton, N.J.: Princeton University Press.

Vlastos, Gregory. 1975. *Plato's Universe*. Seattle: University of Washington Press.

Voltaire. 1734. *Lettres écrites de Londres sur les Anglois et autres sujets. Par M. D. V**. Basle [London?: printed by W. Bowyer].

———. 1759. *Candide, Ou l'optimisme*. London [Netherlands?]: [n.p.].

Watt, Ian P. 1957. *The Rise of the Novel: Studies in Defoe, Richardson, and Fielding*. Berkeley: University of California Press.

———. 1996. *Myths of Modern Individualism: Faust, Don Quixote, Don Juan, Robinson Crusoe*. Cambridge: Cambridge University Press.

Wattles, Jeffrey. 1996. *The Golden Rule*. New York: Oxford University Press.

Weber, Max. 1922. *Wirtschaft und Gesellschaft*. Tübingen: J. C. B. Mohr. 1958.

———. 1958. *The Protestant Ethic and the Spirit of Capitalism*. New York: Scribner.

Wiener, Philip P., ed. 1973. *Dictionary of the History of Ideas: Studies of Selected Pivotal Ideas*. New York: Scribner.

Willey, Basil. 1961. *The Eighteenth Century Background: Studies on the Idea of Nature in the Thought of the Period*. New York: Columbia University Press.

Williams, Bernard Arthur Owen. 1981. *Moral Luck: Philosophical Papers, 1973–1980*. Cambridge: Cambridge University Press.

———. 1993. *Shame and Necessity*. Berkeley: University of California Press.

Wills, Garry. 1999. *Saint Augustine.* New York: Lipper/Viking.

Wingrove, Elizabeth Rose. 2000. *Rousseau's Republican Romance.* Princeton, N.J.: Princeton University Press.

Winnicott, D. W. 1992. *Through Paediatrics to Psycho-Analysis: Collected Papers.* New York: Brunner/Mazel.

Wirszubski, Chaim. 1950. *Libertas as a Political Idea at Rome During the Late Republic and Early Principate.* Cambridge: Cambridge University Press.

Wisner, David A. 1997. Ernst Cassirer, Historian of the Will. *Journal of the History of Ideas* 58 (1): 145–61.

Wittgenstein, Ludwig. 1969. *On Certainty.* Oxford: Blackwell.

Wokler, Robert. 1995. *Rousseau.* Oxford: Oxford University Press.

Wolin, Sheldon S. 1960. *Politics and Vision.* Boston: Little, Brown.

———. 1970. *Hobbes and the Epic Tradition of Political Theory.* Los Angeles: William Andrews Clark Memorial Library.

———. 2001. *Tocqueville Between Two Worlds: The Making of a Political and Theoretical Life.* Princeton, N.J.: Princeton University Press.

Wollstonecraft, Mary. 1792. *A Vindication of the Rights of Woman with Strictures on Political and Moral Subjects.* London: Printed for J. Johnson.

Worlidge, John. 1669. *Systema Agriculturæ, the Mystery of Husbandry Discovered: Wherein Is Treated of the Several New and Most Advantagious Ways of Tilling, Planting, Sowing, Manuring, Ordering, Improving All Sorts of Gardens, Orchards, Meadows, Pastures, Corn-Lands, Woods, & Coppices, and of All Sorts of Fruits, Corn, Grain, Pulse, New Hays, Cattel, Fowl, Beasts, Bees, Silk-Worms.* London: Printed by T. Johnson for Samuel Speed.

Wright, Benjamin F. 1938. Review of Harvey. *Yale Law Journal* 48 (1): 161–64.

Yack, Bernard. 1992. *The Longing for Total Revolution: Philosophic Sources of Social Discontent from Rousseau to Marx and Nietzsche.* Berkeley: University of California Press.

Yates, Frances Amelia. 1964. *Giordano Bruno and the Hermetic Tradition.* London: Routledge & K. Paul.

———. 1966. *The Art of Memory.* Chicago: University of Chicago Press.

———. 1969. *Theatre of the World.* London: Routledge & K. Paul.

Zabarella, Jacopo. 1582. *Iacobi Zabarellae Patavini In Dvos Aristotelis Libros Posteriores Analyticos Commentarii: Cum Antiqua Aristotelis in Latinum Conuersione.* Venetiis: Apud Paulum Meietum, bibliopolam Patauinum.

———. 1985. *Zabarellae De Methodis Libri Quatuor; Liber De Regressu.* Bologna: CLUEB.

Zerilli, Linda M. G. 1994. *Signifying Woman: Culture and Chaos in Rousseau, Burke, and Mill.* Ithaca, N.Y.: Cornell University Press.

INDEX